# FRANKLIN *and* LUCY

. . . . . . .

# FRANKLIN *and* LUCY

· · · · · · · · ·

## PRESIDENT ROOSEVELT, MRS. RUTHERFURD, AND THE OTHER REMARKABLE WOMEN IN HIS LIFE

· · · · · · · · ·

## JOSEPH E. PERSICO

RANDOM HOUSE
NEW YORK

Published in the United States by Random House, an imprint of
The Random House Publishing Group, a division of
Random House, Inc., New York.

RANDOM HOUSE and colophon are registered trademarks
of Random House, Inc.

Permission credits are located in the bibliography on page 416.

LIBARY OF CONGRESS CATALOGING-IN-PUBLICATION DATA
Persico, Joseph E.
Franklin and Lucy : President Roosevelt, Mrs. Rutherfurd,
and the other remarkable women in his life / Joseph E. Persico.
p.   cm.
Includes bibliographical references and index.
ISBN 978-1-4000-6442-7
1. Roosevelt, Franklin D. (Franklin Delano), 1882–1945—
Relations with women.   2. Roosevelt, Franklin D. (Franklin
Delano), 1882–1945—Friends and associates.   3. Roosevelt,
Franklin D. (Franklin Delano), 1882–1945—Marriage.
4. Rutherfurd, Lucy Mercer.   5. Roosevelt, Eleanor, 1884–1962.
6. Roosevelt, Eleanor, 1884–1962—Marriage.   7. Presidents—
United States—Biography.   8. Social secretaries—United States—
Biography.   9. Presidents' spouses—United States—Biography.
1. Title.
E807.P43 2008
973.917092—dc2     2007036851

Printed in the United States of America on acid-free paper

www.atrandom.com

2 4 6 8 9 7 5 3 1

FIRST EDITION

Book design by Simon M. Sullivan

TO ALL THE WOMEN
WHO INFLUENCED MY LIFE

# CONTENTS

· · · · · · ·

*Introduction* · · xi

*1.* SCARLET LETTERS · · 3

2. MASTER FRANKLIN · · 12

3. POOR LITTLE RICH GIRL · · 22

4. FROM RICHES TO RAGS · · 28

5. A HARVARD MAN · · 32

6. COURTSHIP · · 47

7. MR. AND MRS. FRANKLIN D. ROOSEVELT · · 60

8. "DEAREST MUMMY" · · 67

9. PATRICIAN POLITICIAN · · 73

10. THE SOCIAL SECRETARY · · 79

11. EVERY MAN WHO KNEW HER FELL IN LOVE · · 87

12. THE EXTRA WOMAN · · 94

13. INHIBITIONS SNAP LIKE COBWEBS · · 110

14. THE HOMECOMING · · 117

15. THE STORM · · 122

16. THE ADVANTAGE OF ADVERSITY · · 131

17. A BRILLIANT MARRIAGE · · 136

18. THE DIAGNOSIS · · 146

19. MISSY · · 157

20. SAFE HARBOR · · 167

21. ELEANOR AND FRIENDS · · 173

22. GOVERNOR ROOSEVELT · · 179

23. ELEANOR AND THE STATE TROOPER · · 189

24. ELEANOR AND HICK · · 200

25. "CLOSE TO BEING A WIFE" · · 215

26. FOUR MORE YEARS · · 227

27. EXIT HICKOK: ENTER SCHIFF · · 236

28. 1941: YEAR OF GAIN, YEAR OF LOSS · · 247

29. MISSY PROTECTED, LUCY INDULGED,
ELEANOR OUTRAGED · · 266

30. A DISTANT COUSIN, A CHERISHED DAUGHTER · · 280

31. ANNA'S DILEMMA · · 294

32. "MOTHER WAS NOT CAPABLE OF GIVING HIM THIS" · · 307

33. "WE MUST SPEAK IN RIDDLES" · · 320

34. THE DEATH OF A PRESIDENT · · 328

35. LETTERS LOST AND FOUND · · 348

36. "LUCY WAS FATHER'S EMOTION FOR LIFE" · · 354

37. FIRST LADY OF THE WORLD · · 357

38. A JUDGMENT · · 365

Acknowledgments · · 371

Notes · · 373

Bibliography · · 411

Index · · 417

# INTRODUCTION

· · · · · · ·

THIS IS MY SECOND BOOK on Franklin D. Roosevelt, the first having been *Roosevelt's Secret War*, a history of FDR and World War II espionage published in 2004. Both that book and the present work reflect a lifelong fascination, as a New Yorker growing up during the Roosevelt years, with this endlessly provocative figure.

The present theme, the women who figured prominently in Roosevelt's life, was prompted by my conviction that their influence was decisive. They formed and reveal him. However resistant this largely inscrutable man is to decipherment, he cannot begin to be understood without examining the shaping hand of his mother, wife, one true love, and other women who satisfied FDR's deep-seated need for adulation, admiration, approval, and respite from the crushing burdens of his office. They provided the oxygen to his soul. To study the man largely through his male associates, however key—Louis Howe, Harry Hopkins, Sam Rosenman, Henry Morgenthau, and his involvement with the leaders of the twentieth century—yields an incomplete picture. It is no coincidence that present with FDR at Warm Springs, Georgia, on the day he died were three close women companions.

When we see Roosevelt indulging or resisting his mother's domination, when we sense his bridling at his wife, Eleanor's, joyless hectoring, when we witness his politically perilous love of Lucy Mercer Rutherfurd, his dependence on Missy LeHand during the darkest years battling polio, the confidence he placed in an obscure, distant cousin, Daisy Suckley, a more intimate, more human FDR emerges than the larger-than-life figure who strides the pages of history. Obviously, the romantic episode that most awakens interest in FDR's life involved Mrs. Rutherfurd. Does this romance have significance beyond merely whetting public curiosity? The late Arthur Schlesinger Jr. concluded, "Historians have taken note of Thomas Jefferson and Maria Cosway, of the friends of men as different as Alexander Hamilton and Woodrow Wilson. [Lucy] was a part of Franklin Roosevelt's life and therefore the history of the times he dominated."

The common perception is, yes, FDR did have an affair with a beautiful young woman employed by his wife while he served as assistant secretary of the navy during World War I. And yes, that woman came back into his life toward the end, including her presence at Warm Springs on his last day. But a major discovery emerging from the research conducted for this book is the heretofore unrecognized scope, depth, and duration of this liaison. Letters and documents recently discovered by the heirs of Lucy Rutherfurd, never before published, and made available to me make the significance of that relationship unmistakable.

The story of FDR's women delves into Eleanor Roosevelt's often perplexing involvements with both men and women and how Franklin's conduct as a husband contributed to her behavior. The most extraordinary truth of their marriage is that the greatest man of his time, and arguably the greatest woman of her age, were wedded to each other. History offers nothing comparable. What still evokes puzzlement is what drew Franklin, the Adonis, and Eleanor, the Plain Jane, together in the first place. Through interviews and analysis of their early correspondence I have sought the plausible explanation of what attracted them when the future world leader was only a callow suitor and the eventually redoubtable Mrs. Roosevelt was still something of a lost lamb. Thus the book is as much Eleanor's as Franklin's story, refracted through the prism of relationships formative in both their lives.

The definitive Franklin D. Roosevelt will continue to fascinate and elude historian and layman alike. This first full-length portrait of the women who mattered in his life is intended to cast fresh beams of understanding into the character of this often exasperatingly opaque giant in American history.

JOSEPH E. PERSICO
*July 19, 2007*
*Albany, New York*

# FRANKLIN *and* LUCY

. . . . . . .

*Chapter 1*

# SCARLET LETTERS

· · · · · · ·

H E BELONGED IN UNIFORM. His country was at war. He was thirty-
six years old and bursting with vitality. Before going to work in the morning at the Navy Department he often played a round of golf. On
weekends, he rarely got in less than thirty-six holes. During the week he
worked out with Walter Camp, the football coach and fitness enthusiast.
Lathrop Brown, his Harvard roommate, was serving in the new tank
corps. Harry Hooker, his former law partner, was now Major Hooker, on
the staff of the 53rd Division American Expeditionary Forces. Another
law partner and Harvard pal, Langdon Marvin, was driving an ambulance
in France with the Red Cross. His four distant cousins, Archibald, Kermit, Theodore Jr., and Quentin, sons of Franklin's idol, former President
Theodore Roosevelt, had all enlisted. The exploits of TR's boys filled the
newspapers, arousing in Franklin competing emotions of pride and envy.
Even his nearsighted brother-in-law, Hall Roosevelt, had volunteered.

On the very day that war had been declared, April 6, 1917, the Roosevelt
clan gathered at the home of TR's married daughter, Alice Roosevelt Longworth. There the former commander-in-chief seized Franklin by the
shoulders, fixed him with his myopic gaze, and pleaded with him to resign
as assistant secretary of the navy. "You must get into uniform at once," TR
urged. "You must get in."

Franklin was all too willing. Patriotism was the main reason, but politics intruded as well. In 1898, when America had gone to war against
Spain over Cuba, TR had resigned from the very Navy post Franklin now
held. He had formed his own regiment, the Rough Riders. He had worn
the uniform, known war, and subsequently reached the political pinnacle. TR's trajectory was not lost on his ambitious young relative.
Franklin's chief, Navy Secretary Josephus Daniels, easily detected the

parallels. "Theodore left the position of assistant secretary to become a Rough Rider, later Governor of New York and then President, and both had served in the legislature of New York," Daniels noted. "Franklin actually thought fighting in the War was the necessary step toward reaching the White House." Franklin's mother, Sara, had recently written her son, "The papers say buttons and pictures of you are being prepared to run for Governor." But Franklin preferred to take TR's route, military service first.

Theodore Roosevelt, now fifty-nine, blind in one eye, partially deaf, his body racked by punishing expeditions into the disease-infested Brazilian jungle, was itching to answer his country's call again. He hoped to raise a volunteer division just as he had raised a regiment in the earlier war. He pleaded with Franklin to get him an appointment with President Woodrow Wilson. This request could prove ticklish. Ever since TR, as a third-party candidate, had been beaten by Wilson five years before in the 1912 presidential election, he had been lambasting the winner for everything from woolly-headedness to cowardice for not getting America into the European war sooner. Nevertheless, the day after the Roosevelt gathering at cousin Alice's house, Franklin did go to the secretary of war, Newton Baker, and persuade him to intervene with Wilson on TR's behalf. The president would later say of meeting with his old foe, "I was charmed by his personality . . . you can't resist the man." Evidently he was able to resist, since he told Baker afterward, "I really think the best way to treat Mr. Roosevelt is to take no notice of him." TR was baffled by Wilson's failure to seize upon his heartfelt offer. As he left the White House with Wilson's confidant, Colonel Edward M. House, he complained, "I don't understand. After all, I'm only asking to be allowed to die," to which House reportedly responded, "Oh, did you make that point quite clear to the President?"

Uncle Ted had not made it back into uniform himself, but his admonition still echoed in Franklin's ear: "I should be ashamed of my sons if they shirked war." After TR's White House visit, Franklin did submit his resignation as assistant secretary in order to enlist. But when the letter landed on Wilson's desk, the president rejected what he considered military romanticism. He told Secretary Daniels to inform his subordinate that he was no different from any draftee. "Neither you nor I nor Franklin Roosevelt has the right to select the place of service," he warned. "Tell the young man . . . to stay where he is." Unfazed, Roosevelt next went to Wilson personally, only to be turned down again. The rejection, nevertheless, did illuminate Roosevelt's rising star. Wilson's former Army chief of staff, General Leonard Wood, observed that "Franklin Roosevelt should under no circumstances think of leaving the Navy Department; that would amount to a public calamity." The real power in the U.S. Navy, Wood believed, was not Secretary Daniels, but his aggressive deputy.

As the country entered its fifteenth month of the war a still frustrated Franklin managed to wangle an assignment that lifted him, if not exactly to combatant status, at least to something more than a deskbound civilian. He urged Secretary Daniels to allow him to go to Europe "to look into our Naval administration in order to work more closely with the other services." The essentially pacifist Daniels felt no necessity himself to witness the bloodletting firsthand and eventually yielded to Franklin's ceaseless importuning, even allowing his assistant to write his own orders, essentially a blank check to pursue "such other purposes as may be deemed expedient upon your arrival." Franklin confided to his wife that he had been promised a commission as a Navy lieutenant commander upon his return. Before leaving, he sent President Wilson a letter saying he hoped the speculation about his running for governor of New York would end. He was not going to "give up war work for what is frankly very much a local political job in these times."

That summer of 1918, as the day of his departure approached, his behavior began taking on an air of mystery. He told Eleanor only that he must leave her alone with their five children, but could not disclose where he was going or for how long. She was not to see him off, since the mission was secret. "Don't tell a soul," he warned her, "not even Mama."

Franklin had one more goodbye to make before he left, one unknown to Eleanor, and one that moved him to mixed longing and pride. Meeting secretly, he and a beautiful woman made impassioned promises of letters to be exchanged, how this was to be safely carried out during his absence, and what needed to be resolved on his return, for Franklin Roosevelt was in love.

He sailed for Europe from the Washington Navy Yard on July 9, 1918, aboard the destroyer USS *Dyer*, rushed into service just eight days before and heading into the war zone without benefit of sea trials. Despite his position, he told his wife that he had requested no ceremonies. Once aboard ship, Franklin started a diary, the basis for a book he intended to write, an intention that showed through in the grandiloquence of his first entry: "The good old ocean is so absolutely normal just as it always has been, sometimes tumbling about and throwing spray, sometimes gently lolling about . . . but now though the ocean looks much unchanged the doubled number of lookouts shows that even here the hand of the Hun False God is reaching out to defy nature; ten miles ahead of this floating City of Souls a torpedo maybe waiting to start on its quick run."

The *Dyer* joined a troop convoy delivering another twenty thousand doughboys to the over one million already in France: "a wonderful sight," Franklin noted in the diary, "five monsters in the half light . . . it thrills to think that right there another division is on the way to the front." Every element of danger quickened his sense that at last he was in the war, as when the *Dyer* zigzagged to thwart marauding U-boats, "9 different course changes," in an hour; and when he learned that "only 15 or 16 of the crew" had ever been in the war zone; and when he was assigned his abandon ship station, whale boat number 2, should the worst happen.

He was gone just over ten weeks. Looking back, he counted the mission a brilliant success. He had met personally with all the Allied leaders, the fiery British prime minister, David Lloyd George, whom Franklin was delighted to find "is just like his pictures." Even more impressive to Roosevelt, with his weakness for royalty, was a private audience at Buckingham Palace with King George V. Franklin recorded in his diary that the king had given him forty minutes alone and seemed genuinely impressed that his American visitor had crossed the Atlantic on a warship. "His one regret," the king told him, "was that it had been impossible for him to do active Naval service during the war," reflecting Franklin's own disappointment. The king then confided that though he had blood relatives in Germany, particularly Kaiser Wilhelm, "in all my life I have never seen a German gentleman."

Franklin had next gone on to France, where he was again welcomed at the summit, meeting French president Raymond Poincairé and premier Georges Clemenceau. "I was in the presence of the greatest civilian in France," he wrote in his diary of Clemenceau. "He almost ran forward to meet me and shook hands as if he meant it." The sixty-six-year-old premier, known as "The Tiger," related to Roosevelt a thrilling account of his recent visit to the front where a French and German soldier were found "trying to bite each other to death when a shell had killed them both," their upright bodies still clinched. "And as he told me this," Franklin recalled, "he grabbed me by both shoulders and shook me with a grip of steel." Before the mission was over Franklin had met with Marshal Ferdinand Foch, commanding all Allied forces, the leader of the British army, Field Marshal Douglas Haig, General John "Black Jack" Pershing, commander of the American Expeditionary Forces, and Italy's prime minister, Vittorio Orlando—everyone who was anyone in the war.

At each stop he checked eagerly with the Army postal service and the American embassy's diplomatic pouch for letters from his wife, his mother, and his secret passion.

Though he savored his reception at the top, for Franklin, these moments paled alongside what had been the real objective of the trip. Before it was over, he could claim, with enough justification to satisfy his ego, that he had seen the face of war. His military escort, the American naval attaché in Paris, Captain R. H. Jackson, had interpreted his orders as making sure that Assistant Secretary Roosevelt came through this journey with his hide intact. As Franklin put it, Jackson's "plans called for easy trips and plenty of bombed houses thirty miles or so behind the front." He brushed Jackson aside and "from now on for four days I ran the trip," he wrote Eleanor.

Wearing vaguely military dress of his own invention—khaki pants tucked into leather puttees, a gray knee-length coat, a French army helmet, and a gas mask looped around his neck—he arrived at Verdun where the previous year the French and Germans had bled each other white with losses totaling 696,000 men. He was standing at an angle in a road snapping pictures of a devastated village, when an officer raced out and yanked him to safety just as "the long whining whistle of a shell was followed by the dull boom and a puff of smoke of the explosion at the Dead Man's Corner we had just left." He added in the diary, "It is indeed quite evident that we are on the battlefield."

He was briefly embarrassed at another village where a great bang of artillery sent him diving for cover. It turned out that a well-concealed American battery was firing into the German lines. The artillerymen howled with laughter as Franklin rose and dusted himself off. His equanimity quickly recovered, he strode over and greeted the doughboys with hearty handshakes. As they reloaded, they allowed him to pull the gun's lanyard, propelling a shell toward the German lines. Years later, retelling this experience he would say, "I will never know how many, if any, Huns I killed."

Roosevelt did eventually witness the end product of war. In Belleau Wood, site of America's first full-scale battle, he slogged through oozing mud, weaving his way around water-logged shell holes, and came upon "discarded overcoats, rain-stained love letters . . . and many little mounds, some wholly unmarked, some with a rifle stuck, bayonet down, in the earth, some with a helmet, and some too with a whittled cross with a tag of wood or wrapping paper hung over it and in a pencil scrawl an American name." The sight of these Marine graves especially moved Roosevelt since the Corps was under the Navy Department. He asked an officer to show him a list of the latest casualties among "my Marines," which revealed 760 killed and three times as many wounded. The sight of German dead moved him not at all. Near Rheims he came upon a stack of unburied enemy corpses and found the stench an offense to "our sensitive naval nostrils." Before leaving the war zone, Franklin authorized the Marines to wear the Corps insignia on their collars, though they were under Army command. He did so without consulting Washington. How else, he told friends, could he get anything done? When, during the mission, he met a Harvard acquaintance, Robert Dunn, who asked, "How's the job and Josephus?," referring to Franklin's chief, Franklin answered, "Gosh, you don't know, Bobby, what I have to bear under that man."

Back in Paris he stopped to visit his Roosevelt kin in a house near the Arc de Triomphe. There he found two of TR's sons, Archie and Ted Jr., recuperating from serious wounds. Another brother, Kermit, had volunteered for a machine gun unit. He "will at no very distant time share the fate of his brothers," TR had written. The younger Roosevelts spoke somberly but proudly of Quentin, the youngest brother. On July 14, Bastille Day, while Franklin was still aboard the *Dyer*, Quentin had flown his French Nieuport 28 behind German lines near Château-Thierry where a Fokker shot him out of the sky and to his death. TR put up a brave front, but a friend, Hermann Hagedorn, observed that after the death of his son in a war he had so vigorously supported, "the boy in him had died." The effect of these calamities on his cousins only sharpened Franklin's eagerness to get into uniform.

He ended his European adventure in a frenzy of activity, fearful that he might miss something. He began a marathon inspection of airfields and

Navy bases from the Spanish border to Brest. He slept on the floor of a barn, his sleep broken by an artillery bombardment and two air raids, followed by lunch the next day with King Albert of Belgium. Then it was up to Scotland's Firth of Forth to inspect the British Grand Fleet, a squadron of American battleships, and to ride in a Navy dirigible. He wrote Eleanor of his "frightfully busy week on the road each day from 6 am to midnight." Most gratifying, back in France, he was able to see a tactic of his own invention come to life. American cruisers carried fourteen-inch guns that could hurl a shell twenty-five miles. Why not place them on railroad flatcars, Franklin had urged, and have them blast deeply deployed German fortifications? He inspected, with ill-concealed pride, the first rail-borne guns headed for the front, with large white letters painted on the side reading "U.S.N."

His mission had followed his patented formula, work hard, play hard. Captain Edward McCauley, part of the mission, wrote his wife, "it didn't seem to matter to [Roosevelt] what he ate, where or when he slept or if he ever got a bath." To facilitate playing hard, Franklin had brought with him to Europe a friend, Livingston Davis, a pedigreed, but not necessarily proper, Bostonian, whom Roosevelt had made his special assistant. Eleanor Roosevelt found the rakish, hard-drinking, womanizing Davis a thoroughly bad influence on her husband, which was precisely his appeal to Franklin. Roosevelt called him "Livy," and Davis called Franklin "Rosy" or "Old Top." Livy had official duties, but it was at night that his true value to Franklin shone. After inspecting the battleships in Scotland, the two pals had gone into town drinking like the sailors serving under them. They spent the night singing raucously, and consuming copious draughts of "sublime scotch," as Livy put it. In London they went to a music hall to see a show called *The Good Humored Ladies,* then to the American Officers Club, followed by a pub crawl to their hotel. "Everybody got drunk," Livy recorded in his diary. He and Franklin finally turned in at 4:30 a.m. only to be "up at 7 to pack, all feeling pretty rocky." The punishing pace of work and play left Franklin with a fever for the last two weeks of the trip rising at one point to 102 degrees. Still he refused to slow down.

As the mission ended, there was no doubt in his mind that, in the old Civil War metaphor for battle, he had "seen the elephant." After the war, when Groton School raised a memorial to its sons who had served, Roosevelt was miffed that his name had been omitted and wrote that he should be included. "I saw service on the other side, was missed by torpedoes and shells and had actual command," he insisted. It was quintessential Roosevelt, not quite dishonest, but an improvement on the truth that he persuaded himself was fact.

On September 8 he boarded the world's largest ship, the *Leviathan*, a thousand-foot-long, smoke-belching behemoth confiscated from the Germans. He carried with him a leather valise he had packed with clothes, shaving kit, and medicines. In one corner he wedged a thick packet of letters bound with a velvet ribbon.

He anticipated a hero's welcome from a dutiful wife, a doting mother, and the woman he loved. It was not to be. It was as if his abused body had finally given him permission to collapse the moment he reached his bunk. A ship's doctor diagnosed him with double pneumonia and possibly influenza, the latter disease just then beginning its worldwide pandemic. As he lay prostrate in his stateroom, other victims of the flu, men who had survived the perils of the trenches and were now going home, were dying instead and being buried at sea.

Meanwhile at the Roosevelt estate, Hyde Park, Eleanor received an alarming phone call from Elliot Brown, a socially prominent builder, whom Franklin had lured into the Navy with a commander's commission. Brown was calling to warn Eleanor that when the ship docked in New York harbor, on September 19, she should be prepared to meet it with a doctor and an ambulance. By now, the flu epidemic was raging. Soon, over 1,350 New Yorkers would succumb to the disease in a single day. Draft calls were being postponed to hold down the contagion.

Livy Davis, who had arrived earlier on another vessel, the *Great Northern*, boarded the *Leviathan* and recorded in his diary, "Saw F.D. for the first time. Looked rotten." Eleanor, with Franklin's mother, took the train to New York where she enlisted a family physician, Dr. George H. Draper, to accompany her to the ship. There she tracked down her husband's stateroom and directed four Navy orderlies to lift Franklin onto a stretcher and trundle him down the gangway into the waiting ambulance.

The Roosevelts had a townhouse at 47 East 65th Street, a wedding gift from Franklin's mother and adjacent to her twin townhouse. The couple's home was currently rented, and so, to Eleanor's disappointment and his mother's satisfaction, the sailors carried Franklin to a guest bedroom on Sara's side. While her husband was put to bed, a distraught Eleanor tried to be helpful by unpacking his luggage. Her hand fell upon the packet of letters tied with the velvet ribbon, faintly scented, and addressed to Franklin in a familiar hand. An uneasy curiosity overcame her ingrained good breeding and she opened the first letter. What she read struck her like a body blow. Every succeeding letter hammered home what was unmistakable. Her husband was involved in a love affair. The letters were signed by the young woman she had for a time employed as her social secretary and made part of her family, Lucy Mercer. As she later described the moment, "The bottom dropped out of my particular world."

## Chapter 2

# MASTER FRANKLIN

· · · · · · ·

To UNDERSTAND WHY discovery of an affair could be so crushing a blow to one party and so cavalierly treated by the other—with love letters left carelessly about—requires tracing the road each had traveled to the liaison's discovery; one smooth, with almost every pebble removed, the other stony and rutted with pain and insecurity.

For Franklin, the gift of self-confidence and self-worth began at birth. His mother, Sara, was a Delano, a family, as she endlessly reminded people, that traced its lineage, depending on who was tracing, back to ever earlier ages. Some Delanos looked to Philippe de la Noye as the patriarch, who arrived in Plymouth on the *Fortune,* the next ship after the *Mayflower.* Family legend had it that Philippe came in pursuit of Priscilla Mullin, who instead gave her heart to John Alden, the swain in Longfellow's highly fanciful poem "The Courtship of Miles Standish." Still too nouveau for some Delanos, the progenitor was said to be Charles de Lannoy, a knight of the Golden Fleece who lived in the twelfth century. Other Delanos traced their roots to William the Conqueror and even to a patrician Roman family, the Actii, circa 600 B.C.

The Delanos were wealthy, the wealth somewhat tainted by its source. Sara's father, Warren Delano II, had gone to China in 1833 where he prospered in the tea and opium trade, the latter infinitely more profitable. His financial base secure, Warren returned to America thirteen year later and invested in more respectable enterprises—New York real estate, railroads, and other initially successful ventures. All went well until the Panic of 1857 when his investments plummeted. At the age of fifty, threatened with bankruptcy, he returned to China to rebuild his fortune, again in opium. The man was too self-aware to prettify what he was doing. He wrote home, "I do not pretend to justify . . . the opium trade in a moral and philanthropic point of view." Nevertheless, "as a merchant I insist it has been . . . fair, honorable and legitimate." Supplying the opium dens of Chinese addicts, in Delano's view, was little different than "the importation of wines and spirits into the United States." The argument was morally porous. The sale of opium had been forbidden by the Chinese emperor for over two hundred years, but circumvented in Delano's time by massive bribing of local officials. Within just six years, Warren returned home, his wealth restored.

Sara's father's Asian exploits created a colorful childhood for his daughter, the middle child of nine siblings. In Hong Kong the family had lived in a sumptuous villa, overlooking the harbor, the home staffed by platoons of Chinese servants whose language Warren Delano forbade his children to learn. After the second Chinese journey, Sara and the other children embarked on an odyssey of luxury living in a grand apartment in Paris, moving on to Germany where Sara spent two years in finishing school. She returned home at age sixteen to Algonac, the Delanos' forty-room mansion on the opposite bank of the Hudson River from Hyde Park, family seat of James Roosevelt. She had blossomed into a beauty, with cosmopolitan airs, fluent in German and French, yet still emotionally anchored to the Hudson Valley and her clannish family.

Sara was to know one grand passion in her life. Though wooed unsuccessfully by adoring suitors, she finally lost her heart at age twenty-two to a startlingly good-looking, magnetic nonconformist named Stanford White. White, twenty-three at the time, a brilliant future still before him, became a fixture at Algonac in the summer of 1876, to Warren Delano's annoyance. White was too brash, his talk, dress, and manner too flamboyant. The elder Delano called him the red-haired trial, a thoroughly unsuitable match for his daughter. The father employed the customary Victorian solution for unwanted liaisons. He packed Sara off to Europe for nine months to mend her wayward heart. The tactic was unavailing. Sara was next dispatched to her sister Dora and her husband, Will Forbes, living in Hong Kong and pursuing the family trade. Sara, still mooning over White, left within a month. In the end, however, she could not stand up to the iron will of a father who, she believed, could do no wrong. Warren Delano's instincts about White may have been harsh, but they were probably right. The red-haired trial went on to become the foremost architect of the Gilded Age, building homes for Delano neighbors, the Astors and Vanderbilts. En route, he had become, in the idiom of the day, "a cad and a bounder." His life ended violently in 1906. While chatting with friends on the roof of Madison Square Garden, he was shot by the half-mad Harry K. Thaw. Thaw's wife, the former Florodora girl Evelyn Nesbit, while a teenager had been seduced by White. Sara's romance with White had been derailed long before, but a relative later observed that "Stanford White was the only man Sara ever loved."

James Roosevelt, the man who would become Franklin's father, was fifty-two and four years a widower in 1880 when he too suffered disappointment in love. The object of his affection was a distantly related Roosevelt named Alice, age twenty-two, known to her family as "Bye" and whose younger brother, Theodore, would, twenty-one years later, become president of the United States. Bye, no beauty, was nevertheless a girl of extraordinary charm and spirit that made people forget a formidable handicap, a spine curved by Pott's disease, a rare form of tuberculosis. The condition was invisible to James Roosevelt. He proposed to a stunned Bye. He was her senior by twenty-seven years, a man she regarded as a favorite uncle. When she was a child, James had taken her tobogganing on his Hudson River estate along with his own little boy, also called James. The age gap did not deter the elder Roosevelt. Bye was a Roosevelt, he was a Roosevelt, and marriages within the family were common. James's first wife, Rebecca Howland, had been a cousin. As Franklin Roosevelt would one day describe these family matches, "In this way the stock kept vital and abreast of the times."

Bye was at a loss as to how to spare the kindly old man the pain of rejection. It fell to her mother, Mittie, herself six years younger than James, to summon all the tact she possessed to let him down gently. James took the setback goodheartedly, as if it were another of his business ventures, a long shot that had not paid off. He continued to visit the Roosevelt family's home on West 57th Street in New York, a still welcome guest. In April 1880, he was invited to a small dinner party to which Bye had brought along a dear friend. A rattled James found himself introduced to a tall, twenty-six-year-old beauty of imperious bearing. Masses of upswept auburn hair formed a radiant crown above her dark luminous eyes, a patrician nose, sculptured mouth, and swanlike neck. She wore a simple dinner dress, the close-fitting whaleboned contours accentuating a Junoesque figure. Bye had likely invited her friend to the dinner in order to deflect the recently rejected James's attentions from herself to someone else. If this were the objective, she had succeeded. After the guests departed, Bye's mother happily observed, "Why, he never took his eyes off her and kept talking to her all the time." Thus did James Roosevelt meet Sara Delano.

Various interpretations explain why, within a few months, Sara agreed to marry the much older James. It may be that, after the thwarted romance with the mercurial White, she saw in James Roosevelt the reassuring solidity she knew in her father. Another explanation has it that she initially fought marriage to the squire of Hyde Park and seemed intent on a melodramatic spinsterhood, but was pressured by her family to accept James. Her brother, also Warren Delano, was in a financial bind from which James Roosevelt could extricate him. Further, James and Sara's father were business associates in a venture to build a canal through Central America linking the Atlantic and Pacific. The elder Delano approved the match. James Roosevelt was certainly a far better prospect than the obstreperous White. Whatever the reasons, the winter-spring couple were married on October 7, 1880.

With her marriage, Sara merely traded the west bank of the Hudson for the east and a heritage that was, if not as illustrious as her own, highly respectable. The Roosevelts had been established in America some 235 years. In the mid-1640s a young Dutchman, Claes Martenszen, was rowed from a sailing ship to the tip of Manhattan island to New Amsterdam, a village then of some eight hundred people and far more pigs, dogs, ducks, and cows. He adopted the name of his native Dutch town and thus became Claes Roosevelt. His descendants would divide to form two branches, the Hyde Park Roosevelts and the Oyster Bay Roosevelts from which Theodore Roosevelt descended.

James, during his first marriage, to Rebecca, had purchased a Colonial-style clapboard house, near the village of Hyde Park, the property embracing 1,300 acres of virgin oak, hemlock, and pine that afforded breathtaking views of the Hudson Valley, then sloped down to the river. The couple added to the house until it would grow eventually to thirty-five rooms and nine baths. Formally, the home was Springwood, though the family appropriated the name of the town and invariably referred to it as Hyde Park. James had inherited his wealth from the West Indian sugar trade, shipping, real estate, coal, and railroads. He also took occasional fliers that alternately increased or diminished his fortune. His duties were hardly onerous, consisting largely of sitting on boards. His real passions were those of a country squire, exercising his horses while dressed in formal English riding attire, sailing the Hudson on his yacht in the summer, and on ice boats in the winter. The family kept a suite in the Hotel Renaissance on West 43rd Street in New York and James maintained a stable of horses nearby to facilitate the journey back and forth to Hyde Park.

The placid tenor of James's existence had known only one ripple of adventure. As a twenty-year-old, while vacationing with his family in Europe, he had made his way into the camp of Giuseppe Garibaldi, then fighting for Italy's unification and independence, and volunteered his services. As family legend had it, James wore the red shirt and plumed hat of the revolutionaries, drilled alongside peasant soldiers, but after a month, with poor rations, few weapons, and no promise of action, he decamped. His son would thrive on the tale of his father's fleeting service with Garibaldi, and the story never suffered from understatement as Franklin retold it year after year.

The novelist Edith Wharton captured the existence of the old-guard families among whom James had been reared—the Schuylers, Stuyvesants, Schermerhorns, Livingstons, Fishes, and Van Rensselaers in the Hudson Valley and New York City. "Our society was a little 'set,' " she recalled, "with its private catch-words, observances and amusements, and its indifference to anything outside of its charmed circle." Intellectuality, books, or art held little interest while conversation centered around horses, gardens, European travel, the best wines and places to dine. A principal occupation involved paying social calls, "leaving one's card, the upper left-hand corner turned down, with the servants." Patrician life in the country suggested a fiefdom in the Middle Ages. James and Sara would attend local weddings where a "picturesque custom . . . [was] having all the little village maidens, in their Sunday best and squeaky shoes," turn out to honor the bride and groom.

Sara, upon marrying, had become a stepmother to James's son, just a year older than herself. He was not simply James Roosevelt, but James Roosevelt Roosevelt, his father's way of further trumpeting the proud name and avoiding the "junior" form, which he disliked. The young man was always known in his circle as "Rosy," and his marriage a few years before had been one of the most brilliant in a generation. His bride was Helen Schermerhorn Astor, whose mother's Fifth Avenue ballroom accommodated precisely the four hundred people who mattered in New

York society. The marriage brought Rosy a then munificent $400,000 trust fund and his own Fifth Avenue mansion. Sara, upon her marriage, also became a stepgrandmother, since Rosy had a year-old child, again James, and known as "Taddy."

After their marriage, James and Sara had departed on a ten-month honeymoon to Europe. Sara's feelings matured, if not into wild passion, at least into dutiful love. Five months into the trip, she discovered that she was pregnant. Her labor began at 7:30 P.M. on January 29, 1882, a cold Sunday evening in Sara's upstairs bedroom at Hyde Park. By morning her pain had become excruciating and Sara's screams echoed throughout the huge house. At 7:00 A.M., an uneasy James, after spending the night at his wife's side, summoned the family physician, Dr. Edwin H. Parker. James also sent a telegram to his wife's mother pleading for her to come as quickly as possible. Mrs. Delano arrived that evening to hear her daughter's ceaseless, exhausted cries. Twenty-four hours had passed since labor began.

Dr. Parker attempted a desperate act to ease Sara's agony. He began administering increasing doses of chloroform. He went too far. Her screams were stilled but Sara sank into unconsciousness, her breath coming in shallow gasps, her skin turning blue. At last, nearing 9:00 P.M., the baby was born, lifeless and also blue. The doctor's slaps produced neither cries nor movement. He began blowing into the infant's mouth. Slowly, color came into his cheeks, and suddenly the infant emitted a healthy squall. The baby weighed ten pounds. As the doctor was leaving, a visibly relieved James asked him to drop off a telegram to his sister-in-law. Sara "has a bouncing baby boy," it read. "Poor child, she has had a very hard time." Sara had wanted to name the boy Warren after her father. But her brother's infant son, also christened Warren Delano, had recently died. Having another child given that name so soon was more than the bereaved parents could bear. And so Sara named her infant Franklin after her father's brother.

So arduous had been the delivery, so close had the mother and baby come to dying, that the doctor cautioned Sara to have no more children. One family tale has it that the warning was taken a step further and that intimacy between the Roosevelts thereafter ceased. However, Sara later claimed, "I knew my obligations as a wife and did my duty."

It is impossible to divine what the death of the mother and child might have wrought that night, not simply in the baronial mansion on the Hudson, but for the history of the world. Sara Roosevelt's influence over what her son was to become is beyond reckoning. Raising her child became the core of her existence. Fifty-one years later when he was president she wrote in a memoir entitled *My Boy Franklin*, "of his little blonde curls . . . they were shorn, oh, long before they should have been, but I still have one of them locked away—where I am afraid to disclose, lest he hear of it, rifle my bureau drawers in an attempt to find and destroy it." She dressed the boy in kilts, then Little Lord Fauntleroy suits until he was eight, provoking gibes from his earthier Oyster Bay cousins. Her reputation for doting on the child sparked family gossip that she breast-fed him until age six; Sara claimed to have done so for just a year. When Franklin came down with scarlet fever and the doctor banned Sara from his bedroom, she leaned a ladder against the house so that she could peer at him through his bedroom window.

Sara selected Franklin's playmates from the handful of suitable children along the Hudson. Archibald and Edmund Rogers, near Franklin's age, qualified and one of Sara's diary entries reads, "Franklin began going to the Rogers daily for two hours study with the boys and their governess." Further family gossip had it that Sara had to beg the neighbor children to play with Franklin since "otherwise he would bang his head against the wall in sheer frustration." Seeing her son through an adoring mother's prism, she wrote that Franklin, "for reasons I have never been able to fathom, always emerged the leader." As he said to her, "Mommie, if I didn't give the orders, nothing would happen." Sara's mother, who had raised nine children, made a commonsense observation regarding her undeniably attractive and precocious grandson. When, during a visit, Sara remarked to her mother, "Don't you think Franklin is a remarkably good little boy?" the older woman replied, "He can't help being good. He has no brothers and sisters to bother him."

One day when Franklin was four he came bounding into the living room to find a younger child standing awkwardly in the doorway, her finger in her mouth. With her were her parents, Elliott and Anna Roosevelt, houseguests from the Oyster Bay branch of the family. However genealogically remote, five generations by this time, the two clans clung together. Elliott and Anna had been engaged at a house party at Algonac given by Laura Delano, Sara's younger sister. Elliott Roosevelt was Franklin's godfather. The boy immediately took the child by the hand, led her to the nursery, where he dropped down on all fours and ordered her to climb onto his back. He then took her on a wild romp of "horsey." The little girl's full name was Anna Eleanor Roosevelt.

Sara Roosevelt was more than good breeding. She devoured literature, history, and poetry, Victor Hugo and Lamartine among her favorites. She read to her son constantly, stimulating his curiosity and intellectual growth. He eagerly awaited the mailman bringing the magazine *Scientific American*. One rainy afternoon, his mother found him curled up in a corner reading through the dictionary. His reading speed and powers of retention were to prove phenomenal throughout his life. What he read he remembered, and he had a gift for reaching back into his mental storehouse and extracting just the fact or phrase to illuminate his point.

Though suffocatingly pampered, Franklin did not grow up to be Little Lord Fauntleroy. Two forces mitigated against this outcome: the practical aspects of Sara's character and James Roosevelt's example. Having been reared in a large, lively family, led by an adventurous, strong-willed father, Sara expected vigor, courage, and enterprise in her boy, as did James. Father and son could be seen tramping the estate past the greenhouse, the icehouse, fields sown in grain, apple orchards, and vineyards with James issuing orders to his workers, who addressed the boy as "Master Franklin." When he displayed a keen-eyed interest in birds, his father gave him books on ornithology and taught him to shoot. Franklin learned to stuff and catalogue his prey according to breed and his preserved specimens were found throughout the house. Father and son fished and swam in the Hudson, and when the river froze over, they skated on it. Franklin began to ride from an early age and was particularly fond of James's trotter, Gloster, the first to do a mile in under 2:20 minutes. After Gloster was killed in a railroad accident, Franklin kept the tail and it hung on his bedroom wall even in the White House. From the beginning, a deep connection with his native soil was planted in the boy. As president, he would write a distant cousin and Hudson Valley neighbor, Margaret "Daisy" Suckley, "I miss our river . . . why is it our countryside and river seem so to be part of us?"

The family had a summer retreat on a Canadian island, Campobello, off the coast of Maine, where Franklin began his sailing apprenticeship aboard his father's fifty-one-foot yacht, the *Half Moon*. James eventually gave Franklin his own boat, the smaller *New Moon*. The sea became another of his abiding passions.

As workmen doffed their caps, as townsfolk bowed when the Roosevelts strolled through Hyde Park village, as the minister eagerly shook their hands as they left Sunday services at St. James Church, Franklin absorbed, by social osmosis, an awareness that to be a Roosevelt was to be someone above the ordinary. The sense of superiority was a birthright, assumed, and largely unselfconscious. The concomitant notion of noblesse oblige came with equal naturalness. His mother would take Franklin along in her carriage as she distributed food and clothing to the poor. But it was James who instilled the lasting social conscience in the boy. As a young man touring Europe, James had detoured from the country homes of titled friends to see for himself the continent's underbelly. He went into slums and sweatshops exploiting child labor. In London he watched a family descend by a crude ladder below the sewer and gas lines into the dank hovel they occupied among rats and vermin. He was moved to exhort, "Help the helpless! Help the poor, the widow, the orphan; help the sick, the fallen man or woman, for the sake of our common humanity. Help all who are suffering. . . . Work for humanity. Work for your Lord. . . . It was for that single cause that we have, all of us, one human heart."

James was that political rara avis, a Democrat among the landed gentry whose mansions lined the Hudson. President Grover Cleveland was an old friend. When Franklin was five, the family visited the Cleveland White House. On a mantel stood a Dutch clock with the sun and phases of the moon on the face given by the Roosevelts upon the president's marriage. Emerging from his office, a visibly weary Cleveland patted the boy on the head and said, "My little man, I am making a strange wish for you. It is that you may never be President of the United States."

In 1890, when Franklin was eight, his father suffered the first of recurring heart attacks and James gradually retreated into invalidism. The hunting, fishing, sailing, and swimming, even the walks with his son, ended. James's decline was to prove formative. His mother's constant admonitions made it clear that keeping her husband free of strife was paramount in the Roosevelt home. Consequently, the boy learned to turn a smiling face to the world and repress his feelings. If he displeased he might endanger his father's life. To spare James any worry, Franklin dealt with his own pain stoically. Once, a steel rod struck his head, gouging a deep, profusely bleeding gash. The boy pulled a cap over the wound to hide it from his father. At Campobello, he was hit in the mouth by a heavy stick. The blow knocked out one tooth, and broke another in half, exposing a raw nerve. In the pain-racked two hours it took to take the boy to a mainland dentist, as his mother put it, Franklin behaved without fuss. His determination to please, to avoid risking the loss of love, to find a manageable space between his mother's smothering attentions and her strictness, sharpened in Franklin an early blooming talent for evasion, obfuscation, even prevarication, traits he would carry into his political life.

A child overindulged is often regarded as a soft insufferable brat, spoiled by having every whim instantly gratified, thus leaving him unprepared for life's harsh realities. A child made the center of his universe can just as well grow to be utterly confident, tough, and demanding. The rarity of hearing the word "no" leads him to think that anything is possible and to expect success as his due. Young Franklin saw the world in this light. A darker side of this self-centeredness was his tendency to shift allegiances easily and opportunistically, another trait in him that would be carried into adulthood. At age seven, his playmate, Archibald Rogers, died of diphtheria. Franklin transferred his attentions to Archie's brother, Edmund, without missing an emotional beat.

If the child is father to the man, what did this idyllic childhood teach the man who was to be? Above all, he saw life as an adventure launched from a secure harbor, sailed aboard a vessel that always returns safely to port to a rousing welcome. As for the women en route, by the time he was old enough to leave home for school, Franklin had been conditioned by Sara to assume that a female presence in his life was there to serve and adore him. It was all he had ever known.

## Chapter 3

# POOR LITTLE RICH GIRL

. . . . . . .

F EW CHILDHOODS could have been less alike than that of Franklin Roosevelt and the woman whose heart he would one day win, then break. If Franklin was raised as the Little Prince, Eleanor Roosevelt's childhood combines elements of Little Nell, Griselda, and the Little Match Girl. She was born in an age when the worship of physical beauty was almost pagan. In her set, the first thing everyone wanted to know about newcomers, female or male, was were they attractive? Her genetic inheritance should have granted Eleanor the gift of beauty. Of her mother, Anna, the poet Robert Browning asked only that he be allowed to sit and gaze as her portrait was being painted. Eleanor's father, Elliott Roosevelt, was the third of four children and considered the hand-somest, most athletic, and most charming of all, including his older brother, Theodore, the future president.

Eleanor, Elliott and Anna's first child, was not born beautiful, as her mother regularly reminded her. One day when she was playing with her cousin Corinne Robinson, as their mothers had tea, Anna turned to her daughter and said, "Eleanor, I hardly know what's to happen to you. You're so plain that you really have nothing to do except be good." Alice remarked to another visitor, "She is such a funny child, so old fashioned we always call her Granny." During a trip to Europe the glamorous par-ents parked Eleanor at a convent "to have me out of the way," as she later recalled, with her mother warning, "You have no looks, so see to it that you have manners." Her Aunt Edith, the wife of Theodore Roosevelt, wrote to a relative about Eleanor, "Poor little soul, she is very plain. Her mouth and teeth seem to have no future." As a grown woman, Eleanor still recalled the sting of this thoughtlessness: "I often felt that I'd like to have the floor open so that I could sink into it." Though not loved by

Anna, Eleanor nevertheless adored her mother. She felt "grateful to be allowed to touch her dress or her jewels or anything that was part of the vision."

The demons that would haunt her father appeared early in Elliott Roosevelt's life, though his initial advantages could scarcely have been better: birth into a family of wealth and privilege, firm but loving parents, a family townhouse in Manhattan and a sprawling estate on Long Island's Oyster Bay, tutors and governesses, the looks, the charm, the grace. Yet, from age fourteen, fissures began to appear. Elliott wrote his father from St. Paul's school, "I had a bad rush of blood to my head, it hurt me so that I can't remember what happened." The mysterious spells continued. Whether brought on by a hopeless competition with an older brother with the seeds of greatness already planted in him or a congenital defect is unknowable. Elliott eventually dropped out of school, embarking on a soul-searching odyssey through the Himalayas. Still troubled on his return by his indefinable malaise, he sought escape in drink and drugs. Yet when sober his charm continued to enchant sufficiently for him to win the hand of a belle of the age. Anna Hall, of the Hudson River gentry, and Elliott were married in 1883 when he was twenty-three and she nineteen. The stunning couple had three children, Eleanor born in 1884, Elliott Jr. in 1889, and Hall in 1891. But the home was poisoned from the outset by arguments and recriminations, as Elliott staggered home at all hours, drunk, or returned not at all. On one occasion in New York, her father took an ecstatic Eleanor for a walk, one hand in hers, the other holding the leashes of their three fox terriers. They arrived at the Knickerbocker Club, where Elliott handed the leashes to Eleanor and told her he would be back in a few minutes. She waited for four hours, then saw her father carried out of the club. The doorman took her home.

The Roosevelt staff included a comely servant, Katy Mann, who became pregnant and pointed the finger at Elliott. Denying paternity, Elliott took off with his family for Paris. Brother Theodore was left to dispatch an agent to Brooklyn to see Katy and the child. Theodore subsequently wrote of the agent's mission, he "has seen the baby . . . he came back convinced from the likeness that Katy Mann's story is true." Katy Mann was paid off, reportedly with the $10,000 she had demanded, and the matter was hushed up. That Eleanor had a half-brother named Elliott Roosevelt Mann was to remain unknown to her for over forty years.

In Paris, Elliott and Anna sought to repair the marriage. But a city notorious for its temptations was no place for a soul irresistibly drawn to drink and debauchery. Elliott would disappear for days at a time. He took up openly with a married expatriate with two children, Mrs. Florence Sherman of Detroit. His profligacy alternated with fits of remorse, sobbing, melancholy, and descent into delirium tremens. Theodore Roosevelt now concluded that his brother was "a maniac morally as well as mentally . . . a flagrant man swine." He urged Anna to leave Elliott. To stay with him was "little short of criminal. . . . She ought not to have any more children with him and those she has should be brought up away from him." Facing financial ruin, Elliott agreed to be committed to an institution. To TR, at the time a Federal Public Service commissioner on the cusp of a brilliant political career, Elliott's behavior portended disaster. His conduct could not be hushed up this time. "Elliott Roosevelt Demented by Excesses" ran the headline in the *New York Herald*. "Wrecked by Liquor and Folly, He Is Now Confined in an Asylum for the Insane Near Paris." In January 1892, TR made the trip he dreaded and went to Paris. He found Elliott "completely, and utterly broken, submissive and repentant." The younger brother agreed to sign a financial arrangement placing his property, estimated at $175,000, in trust for his wife and children. Elliott then returned home. His enduring capacity to charm, however, is evident in the diary kept by his Paris mistress. Upon his departure, Mrs. Sherman wrote, "So ends the final and great emotion of my life. . . . How could they treat so noble and generous a man as they have. He is more noble a figure in my eyes than either his wife or his brother. She is more to be despised, in her virtuous pride, her absolute selfish position than the most miserable woman I know."

Back home, Elliott took the "Keeley Cure" for alcoholism in Dwight, Illinois. He then became something of a remittance man, living in tiny Abingdon, Virginia, ostensibly managing property owned by a brother-in-law. The local newspaper called him "The life of every party." Theodore wrote his sister Bye that Elliott, in his new home, had been found "reading stark naked, . . . upset a lamp and burned himself badly." When Elliott's neighbors urged Theodore to come and try to help his brother, "I declined with bland thanks," TR wrote Bye. "I explained to them it was absolutely useless."

Young Eleanor's father was largely out of her life, and the influence of her mother, for good or ill, was to be short-lived. Anna entered a hospital for an operation, contracted diphtheria, and died on December 7, 1892, a month after Eleanor had turned eight. Her father should have been Eleanor's consolation, but he was inconstant, swinging from loving to essentially abandoning the child. She was one day to say that he "dominated my life as long as he lived and was the love of my life for many years after he died." This obsession with her father is evident in Eleanor's reaction to her mother's death. The estranged Elliott had come home from Virginia upon receiving word of his wife's illness. Eleanor would recall of that day, "I can remember standing by a window when Cousin Susie told me that my mother was dead. Death meant nothing to me, and one fact wiped out everything else—my father was back and I would see him very soon." Before Anna died, she revealed, under ether, the horror of her existence with Elliott, muttering that her husband had made life miserable and that she had no reason to go on living.

A year after the death of her mother from diphtheria, the disease also claimed Eleanor's four-year-old brother Elliott Jr. It was the daughter more than the father who had to do the consoling. Eleanor, now nine, wrote Elliott senior in Abingdon, "Ellie is going to be safe in heaven and to be with mother who is waiting there." He had written sporadically to his daughter from his exile; but one day, the letters, the girl's emotional lifeline, ceased. His mind rotted by alcohol, Elliott tried to fling himself from a window. Even in that he failed. Soon thereafter he had a seizure, running up and down stairs like a man possessed. He collapsed and died the next day. He was thirty-four years old. "From that time on," Eleanor recalled, "I lived with him more closely, probably, than I had when he was alive."

Understanding what had destroyed this once promising man became a family quandary. Epilepsy? Inherently weak character? Drink? Even eighty-five years afterward, his grandson and namesake, Elliott Roosevelt, claimed, "It wasn't drink that killed him. He died of a tumor of the brain. My mother never said he died of drink. The truth of the matter was that the poor man was suffering from this horrible problem that existed from the time he was seventeen on. The drink was merely to stop the pain."

Eleanor, while not yet ten, had lost, within the space of nineteen months, her mother, younger brother, and father. A life out of Dickens was about to become even more Dickensian. She and her surviving brother, three-year-old Hall, had been sent, even before their father's death, to live with their widowed maternal grandmother, Mary Hall, who had a home in New York City and an estate at Tivoli on the Hudson. The country home was draped in perpetual cheerlessness, the shades pulled down leaving rooms dark and the doors between them always closed. Eleanor's younger cousin, Corinne Robinson, also a niece of Theodore Roosevelt, described the New York house: "My mother would ask me to go have supper with Eleanor. I never wanted to go. The grim atmosphere of that house! There was no place to play games. Unbroken gloom everywhere. We ate our supper in silence. It was not a house for children." Corinne found Madeleine, the woman entrusted with Eleanor's and Hall's care, "a terrifying character. It was the grimmest childhood I have ever known."

In Grandmother Hall and her daughter, called Aunt Pussie, Eleanor had been left, as a friend put it, "wholly at the mercy of singularly unloving female relatives who did their duty by her—and little more." The Halls were wealthy, yet Eleanor and Hall wore hand-me-downs, were fed indigestible meals, and harshly disciplined. Besides Pussie, Grandmother Hall also had two sons, Edward and Valentine, both hopeless drunks who had swiftly run through their fortunes. Valentine's drinking had so muddled his mind that one day, while Eleanor played in the garden, he took potshots at her from his bedroom window, fortunately too drunk to aim straight. Eleanor spent the years from age nine to fifteen in her grandmother's care. She grew to a gawky five feet ten inches. She did possess soft blue eyes, an abundance of wavy honey-colored hair, and the flawless, creamy complexion prized in that age. But the attractive features were diminished by a puckered mouth, protruding teeth, and a receding chin. Of Eleanor's teeth, Corinne lamented, "She could have had them all straightened out. Oh, it was terrible that she didn't have it done."

In her youth, Eleanor was harnessed into a back brace to correct a curvature of the spine, such as had deformed her Aunty Bye. Photographs from those years reveal an adolescent slouched apologetically, rarely smiling, eyes downcast as though if she could not see the camera, people could not see her. Corinne remembered the Eleanor of that period as "a person somewhat apart. She didn't seem to have any sense of humor."

Eleanor displayed behavior occasionally found in the children of alcoholics. These offspring may become distrustful of others, conditioned by parents who love them one moment and fail them the next. They may be insecure and thus uncertain how to comport themselves among people, covering their discomfort with nervous laughter. Eleanor exhibited classic symptoms. She also fibbed to create a fantasy world where her fears and failures might be banished. The actual world she inhabited was capable of sudden collapse in which people abandoned her, promises were broken, and love fleeting. She lived as though waiting to be betrayed.

The home of Eleanor's cousin Corinne in West Orange, New Jersey, was a place of joy and laughter and she was occasionally invited there, an experience akin to emerging from the dark into daylight. Still, she carried with her the deadening hand of Grandmother Hall. At a party thrown by the Robinsons, Corinne recalled that Eleanor "was dressed by her grandmother in a short white Nainsook with little blue bows on either shoulder, the hem above her knees, all hanging like a child's party dress. But she was fifteen!" Nainsook was a fabric ordinarily worn by children. Eleanor felt her liabilities keenly yet sought a relatively mature rationale to suppress her pain. She wrote at age fifteen, "It may seem strange but no matter how plain a woman may be if truth and loyalty are stamped upon her face all will be attracted to her and she will do good to all who come near her and those who know her well will always love her."

It was at a party in the Robinson home that Eleanor found herself in the company of her distant cousin Franklin, not seen since their childhood. She stood on the fringe, in her little girl's dress; her hair was not swept up in the current fashion, but hanging in braids, as her grandmother had insisted, watching suave, seventeen-year-old Franklin gaily mix with the more sparkling set. She was acutely aware of the handsome charmer but felt that she was invisible to him. After having danced with several of the girls, he finally came to Eleanor. She eagerly took his hand, extended out of duty or genuine interest, she could not tell.

*Chapter 4*

# FROM RICHES TO RAGS

· · · · · · ·

WHILE FRANKLIN WAS a princeling growing up at Hyde Park, a child was born in Washington, D.C., who, if anything, was his social superior and his equal in wealth. Her name was Lucy Page Mercer. She was born on April 26, 1891, and delivered by the capital's most fashionable gynecologist, Dr. Henry D. Fry. Her father was Carroll Mercer, whose roots ran deep in the American soil. His family had given Mercersburg, Maryland, its name. A maternal ancestor, Charles Carroll of Carrollton, was reckoned the second richest signer of the Declaration of Independence. The state anthem, "Maryland, My Maryland," resounded to the phrase "Remember Carroll's sacred trust." Both Carrolls and Mercers were represented in the Second Continental Congress and served in the Revolutionary War. With his impeccable pedigree, Carroll was a success in Washington and New York social circles, renowned for riding, shooting, gambling, and drinking. Unhappily for Carroll, his father managed to blow a considerable fortune, leaving the son, at twenty-three, with champagne tastes but no income to indulge them. He thus did what impoverished young gentlemen have long done, he entered the military. In 1880, Carroll used family connections to get himself commissioned a lieutenant in the Marine Corps.

Three years later, while serving with the Marine detachment aboard the USS *Richmond*, Carroll found himself temporarily stationed in Washington. Immediately caught up again in the city's social whirl, he met a married woman who was to become his fate. She was known at that time as Minna Norcorp, wife of Percy Norcorp, an English swell whose principal talent lay in squandering her fortune. The immediate attraction between "Minnie," as she was called, and Carroll was understandable. She would later describe a dashing figure, "a fraction of an inch over six feet in height, of fair complexion, with blond hair and gray-ish eyes." Carroll, in turn, was stunned by the statuesque, glossy-haired brunette, a dark-eyed beauty possessing the ample Lillie Langtry propor-tions then in vogue. A society arbiter described Minnie as "easily the most beautiful woman in Washington society . . . to be invited to one of her dinners was a distinction that qualified one for admission to any home."

Minnie too descended from a distinguished ancestry and substantial wealth. Her father, John Tunis of Norfolk, Virginia, unlike Carroll's fa-ther, had managed to hold on to his riches, which he had amassed by de-veloping land along the mid-Atlantic coast. When her father died, Minnie, then twenty, inherited a fortune and soon after married Nor-corp. While association with her provided entry into all the best Wash-ington homes, her own home was unraveling as Percy proved to be a spendthrift and inveterate philanderer. Minnie, at age twenty-three, al-ready possessed of an independent streak, took the society-be-damned risk of divorcing Norcorp after she met Carroll Mercer.

The love-struck marine managed to wangle a two-month leave of ab-sence doubtless to protract his acquaintance with Minnie. He was sub-sequently reassigned to the Marine battalion serving in the Isthmus of Panama. There he went on a tear once too often, too drunk to report for duty. According to the *Army and Navy Journal* of July 4, 1885, "2d Lieu-tenant Carroll Mercer . . . was tried by court martial in New York for drunkenness on the Panama expedition and has been sentenced to two years suspension on half pay." After thirteen months, he was reinstated and less than a year later made first lieutenant, his only promotion since he had joined the Corps seven years before.

Carroll and Minnie maintained an on-and-off again relationship in the years following her divorce, and in June 1888 she followed him to London where he was now serving aboard a steam and sail gunboat, the USS *Quinnebaug*, moored in the Thames River. They were married the following month in the Parish of St. Martin in the Fields in a Church of England ceremony by, as Minnie would always maintain, the queen's chaplain. Carroll was thirty and a vain Minnie, who was twenty-five, re-marked, "This is my birthday, my last one." She used her maiden name on the registration and described her status as single rather than di-vorced. She listed her late father's profession as "Gentleman." The young wife now followed her husband from London to Constantinople to Egypt, touring the Pyramids and the Sphinx. On March 31, 1889, their first child was born in Alexandria, Egypt. They named her Violetta after Carroll's mother. But the novelty of being a Marine wife soon palled for Minnie. She still had money and saw no need for Carroll to plod along as a junior officer going nowhere. She easily persuaded her pleasure-loving husband to resign his commission, which he did on June 30, 1890, and like her father, to pursue the life of a gentleman.

The Mercers moved into a luxurious Washington house on Rhode Island Avenue and plunged into the social round. They also kept a place outside Paris. Minnie's status as a woman with something of a past may have provided grist for the gossip mill, her smoking in public may have shocked, but her insouciance and stunning looks conquered all. If anything, she flaunted the divorce. Hers was a society where accomplishment counted for little, and good looks, breeding, and money counted for everything. And Minnie had all three.

Evidently, she did experience one deeper longing. Opposite her home, the Catholic Church was erecting St. Matthew's Cathedral. As the structure rose it touched something in her soul. Minnie converted to Catholicism. Her motives remain unclear. A relative, Elizabeth Cotten Henderson, recalled, "Cousin Minnie became a Roman Catholic for some highflown sentimental reason." Soon after, with the Mercers now occupying another grand home at 1744 P Street, Dr. Fry delivered Lucy. She and her sister were to be raised as Catholics. Their father, however, retaining his family's Episcopalian affiliation, attended St. John's on Lafayette Square.

Minnie continued as the queen of capital society, living in a style of glorious excess. She was whisked from party to party in a large brougham drawn by a pair of black horses in burnished harnesses, driven by a liveried coachman and with a footman wearing a cockade hat sitting on the box. The Mercers were charter members of the native-born Washington blue blood set. To insure their exclusivity, Minnie and Carroll founded the Cave Dwellers Club, for those born in the capital and at the pinnacle of its social pyramid. Carroll became a fixture on the club circuit. He also belonged to the exclusive Metropolitan, the Riding Club, and founded with his pals the Chevy Chase Club.

Minnie proved spectacular at despoiling her fortune, rivaled only by her husband. A handy excuse presented itself for the fast melting Mercer estate, the Panic of 1893, which triggered bank and business failures and a stock market crash. "Rubbish," cousin Elizabeth said. "They just spent it." As their pleasures dwindled and their debts mounted, the Mercers began quarreling. Minnie berated Carroll for precipitating their fall. Carroll responded by drinking more. Thus Lucy Mercer was raised in a rancorous household not unlike that of the young Eleanor Roosevelt.

When the Spanish-American War broke out in April 1898, Carroll spied an opportunity to escape the unhappy home and ease his fast approaching penury. This time he joined the Army. He regarded himself as one of Teddy Roosevelt's Rough Riders. Actually, he was commissioned a captain in the prosaic Commissary Corps, getting food to the troops and feed to the horses. He performed well enough to be promoted to major. When the war ended, Minnie wrote to President William McKinley and Secretary of War Elihu Root pleading that Carroll be kept on as a regular officer, even if he had to be reduced in rank. But the peacetime Army needed no more supply officers and, to Minnie's annoyance, Carroll was discharged on June 30, 1901.

He was now back with the family at still another fashionable but unaffordable Washington address, 1761 N Street, Northwest. The drinking went on, the quarreling intensified, and by 1903, all the money had run out. The Mercers separated. Gossip chroniclers now disparaged the once sought after Carroll. As one put it, he had "descended to obscurity and want, having dissipated [his] fortune and alienated his wife and nearly all his friends." Minnie, for the first time in her life, faced a repellent truth: she would have to go to work. She took her daughters to New York where she expected that her exquisite taste would enable her to become an "inside decorator" for the rich. Her position was still recognized in Dan's New York Social Blue Book, and the Social Register listed "Juniors Miss Violetta C. and Lucy P." But Carroll's existence rated only a laconic "Mr., absent." Tale bearers claimed that Minnie survived "by finding rich patrons upon whom she was said to bestow her favors." Further word had it that she had landed a particularly useful patron, Grant Barney Schley, a wealthy banker and broker. Thus, by her mid-teens Lucy Mercer was the product of a broken home, a penniless girl dependent upon a cunning mother with an instinct for survival. She did, however, enjoy one positive inheritance from her mother. Lucy was beautiful, not the smoldering beauty of her mother, but an understated allure and quiet charm that would one day entrance a giant of history.

*Chapter 5*

# A HARVARD MAN

· · · · · · ·

FRANKLIN WAS Sara Roosevelt's masterpiece and therefore to be treated as priceless. When he reached twelve, he should have been packed off to prep school along with his contemporaries, but his mother could not yet bear to be parted from him. Her decision was reinforced by her husband, James's, steadily failing health. With his father's decline, Franklin increasingly became the core of Sara's life. Finally, when he reached fourteen, Franklin's departure could be put off no longer. The boy had been enrolled since infancy at Groton, a relatively new school forty-five miles north of Boston founded by a forceful educator, the Reverend Endicott Peabody, who conceived his mission as preparing young gentlemen to rule the nation in the Christian spirit. In September 1896, James, Sara, and Franklin boarded a private railroad car to deposit Franklin at Groton. For weeks afterward, Sara broke down in tears every time she passed his empty bedroom. She began writing him daily.

Young Franklin was plunged into a settled world of 110 boys, their friendships, clubs, and cliques already fixed. Previously tutored at home, having only sporadic contact with boys his own age, so comfortable and admired among adults, Franklin now found himself isolated. The other boys taunted his manners as overly refined. He bowed deeply from the waist when bidding good night to the headmaster's wife when a simple nod would do. His otherness was accentuated by what his schoolmates saw as affected speech, a faintly English accent absorbed from governesses and during long sojourns abroad.

On arriving at Groton he was five feet three inches tall and weighed barely one hundred pounds. He was plagued, as he was to be all his life, by sickness, typhoid fever, throat infections, sinusitis, and cold after cold. His mother wrote to her brother, Warren, "I hope he will have no more [sicknesses] and doubt if any has been invented that he has not caught at Groton." He grew rapidly, but spindly as a reed, hardly the physique for displaying what mattered most among his fellow students, athletic prowess. He did not lack physical coordination and played golf and tennis well. He was an accomplished sailor who, at age sixteen, would sail a yawl from New York to Eastport, Maine, by himself. He, however, failed to impress in the sports that mattered at Groton, football, baseball, and crew. When, in his last year, he became manager of the baseball team, his mother trumpeted this as an athletic triumph, though Franklin knew better.

He did distinguish himself in one arena that pleased teachers but earned only his classmates' derision. Groton imposed discipline by a system of "black marks" for infractions of school regulations. Most boys collected three or four such marks a week, worked off by performing chores around the campus, raking leaves, mowing lawns, or shoveling snow. In his first year Franklin had not a single demerit. By the middle of his second year he finally earned a black mark for talking in class. "I am very glad I got it," he wrote his mother, "as I was thought to have no school spirit before." Further appreciated by his teachers and meaningless to his scribbling schoolmates, Franklin wrote a hand, in its beauty and uniformity, worthy of a professional calligrapher, a gift that would deteriorate only slightly as he rose in the world.

Some Roosevelt observers have suggested that his mother's dominance delayed Franklin's emotional maturation. Rexford Tugwell, one day to be a member of President Roosevelt's Brain Trust, saw a persistent pattern of lateness in Franklin's development. Of his adolescence Tugwell wrote, "When he approaches it slowly—more slowly than his intimates—he shares, yet does not share, their experiences. And since they are ahead of him, leading him, as they move into manhood, what he really thinks and feels needs to be concealed because his emotions would seem to be infantile to the intimates for whose approval he yearns. Those emotions seem unworthy even to him by the standards he has accepted. Outwardly he professes feelings and reactions he actually does not have. And those he does have he distrusts and would not under any compulsion express. It is my belief that Franklin was the victim of such circumstances and that his handling of the difficult problems at Groton became the model for behavior in later similar situations."

The first signs of Franklin's awakening to girls did not surface until he reached sixteen, and then, confirming Tugwell, most tepidly. Christmas of 1898 meant inviting a girl to a dance and party his mother was giving at Hyde Park. Franklin turned the matchmaking over to Sara. "I wish you would think of some decent partner for me," he wrote from Groton, "so that I can get somebody early, and not get paired off on some ice-cart." In the end, he showed no strong preference for anyone. "I was in a quandary as to whom to ask," he admitted, "and not caring at all, I drew lots."

How Dr. Endicott chose to deal with his charges' sexual stirrings was hardly calculated to produce wholesome attitudes, but rather fear, shame, and guilt. Each year the headmaster delivered a sermon based on the biblical prayer "Make me a clean heart, O God, and renew a right spirit within me." There followed a chilling description of the wages of gambling, drink, and, above all, impurity. Sex had no place outside the marriage bed, Endicott preached. Until that time, Grotonians were to sublimate their baser drives through physical exhaustion, cold showers, and prayer.

Franklin graduated from Groton in 1900. To assume from his shaky start that he had been a failure would be misleading, but neither was he a shining light. He was a sponge at absorbing history, wrote vividly, became a persuasive debater, sang lustily in the choir, and won a prize in Latin. Dr. Peabody judged him "of more than ordinary intelligence . . . but not brilliant." Francis Biddle, a fellow Grotonian and years later to be President Roosevelt's attorney general, remembered as a new boy that he looked upon Franklin, the upper classman, as "a magnificent but distant deity, whose splendor added to my shyness."

His enrollment at Harvard, in the fall of 1900 where his father, half-brother, Rosy, and Rosy's son, Taddy, and decades of Roosevelts had preceded him, was as natural as the change of seasons. He was now six feet one inch though he weighed only 146 pounds. He had grown handsome, but delicately so. His head was long and well shaped, the brow high with his hair parted near the middle, the mouth thin and sensitive, ever ready to break into an eager smile. The female ideal of the era was the Gibson Girl, hair upswept and offering a profile of delicate perfection. Franklin fit the description of the Gibson Man, a "firm jawed, clean shaven, well groomed, wholesome youth."

The new arrival was ambitious to please, ambitious to succeed, but not particularly ambitious to excel academically. In all his years at Har-

vard, his grades would rarely rise above the "gentlemanly C" that satisfied the well-born student. In his freshman year every one of his six
grades was a C. To grub over grades was poor form, the sweaty behavior
of scholarship boys from the outer darkness of public high schools.
Grades did not matter within Franklin's set since graduation would be
automatically followed by entry into the right law firm, brokerage house,
or bank. At Harvard his energies would be directed not toward what
pleased professors, but what counted with his peers—sports, parties,
and clubs. He made a manly stab at football and given his height tried
out for end on the freshman team. But burlier blocking backs brushed
him aside and he did not survive the final cut. He demonstrated his suit-
ability, however, for Brahmin social life and the better clubs through the
style he was able to afford. Private builders had erected sumptuous dor-
mitories along what came to be called Harvard's Gold Coast. Franklin
and a friend, Lathrop Brown, took a three-room suite in the Coast's
choice Westmorely Court. Sara had rented an apartment in Boston and
came over to decorate the boys' suite, sparing no expense. She wrote
apologetically to her brother, Warren, about having to leave Hyde Park,
"I want to be near Franklin."

In January of 1901 Sara's letters to her son began arriving on black-
bordered stationery. James Roosevelt had died the previous December.
In the summer of 1900, before Franklin entered Harvard, Mr. James, as
he was called, had suffered another heart attack, then another late in
November. A grief-stricken Franklin hurried to New York City where his
father had been taken to be near better medical care. James failed to respond. Sara, Franklin, and Rosy were at his side when he died. His father's will left Franklin a $120,000 trust fund, just shy of $3 million in
current value. There were, however, strings. Under terms of the will,
Sara was to control the trust and thus continue to control her son.

Sara believed that the outrageous behavior of her stepson, Taddy, had
hastened her husband's death. The youth was three years older than
Franklin but only one form ahead of him at Groton where he became a
society millstone to the younger Roosevelt. Taddy had immediately been
branded an odd duck, the target of cruel gibes by his classmates.
Franklin's embarrassment quickened when he followed Taddy to Harvard. He had once written his mother, "I know that Taddy has been on
to N.Y. several times without letting anyone know of it. . . . I think the
strictest measures sh'd be taken but of course Papa must not worry in

the least. . . . Some measures must be taken to prevent his having his full allowance next year, as even this year he has had just <u>twice</u> too much." Taddy's resources were indeed formidable. His father, Rosy, had wed Helen Astor, daughter of *the* Mrs. Astor. Thus Taddy stood in line for an immense inheritance.

In the fall of 1900, Franklin received a worried query from his mother. Did Franklin have any idea where Taddy might be? Where Taddy had disappeared was into New York's Tenderloin district and his favorite haunt, the Haymarket Dance Hall on West 30th Street, a notorious brothel. There he was welcomed, perhaps an upper-class ninny, but one with an open heart and an open purse. Here he met the love of his life, variously called Sadie Messinger, Mesinger or Meisinger, Hungarian-born, plump, pretty, and a whore. "Dutch Sadie," as she was called, was a familiar figure at the Haymarket where girls stood on a stage to be auctioned off to the highest bidder.

Days after Sara had asked Franklin where Taddy might be found, the missing heir, with his fiancée, was riding a brougham to City Hall where they were wed in a civil ceremony. The prominent name on the marriage certificate did not pass unnoticed and soon journalists nationwide were having a field day. One headline shouted, "BOY MILLIONAIRE WEDS: ASTOR SCION'S BRIDE WON IN DANCEHALL." Just two days after the news broke of his grandson's marriage to a prostitute, James Roosevelt had suffered the heart attack that would carry him off. Sara blamed Taddy. Mrs. Astor went into seclusion. Rosy sped back from a visit to England to attempt to have the marriage annulled. But by now Taddy had reached his majority and began receiving a $100,000 a year income.

The scandal was a serious blow to a Harvard freshman hoping to scale the social heights. Franklin wrote his mother, "The disgusting business about Taddy did not come as a very great surprise to me or anyone in Cambridge. I have heard the rumor ever since I have been here . . . the disgrace to the name has been the worst part of the affair one can never again consider [Taddy] a true Roosevelt. It will be well for him not only to go to parts unknown, but to stay there and begin life anew."

While hardly in a league with his son, Rosy's comportment was not spotless either. While living in London after his wife's death, Rosy had acquired a mistress, a woman light-years from Dutch Sadie. Elizabeth Riley was refined, soft-spoken, the daughter of a clergyman, who met Rosy while she was clerking at Harrod's department store. He eventually brought Elizabeth to America and married her, which his stepmother, Sara, bore with stoic resignation. "Life was full of problems," she said, "and of course those who had no principles were never much troubled." Upon first meeting Elizabeth, she would not take her hand. But as Elizabeth's ladylike qualities shone through, Sara accepted her, even inviting the couple to travel with her. Eleanor Roosevelt initially displayed a prudishness, writing a friend that she found it "so funny at times for such a respectable conventional family to be mixed up" with a woman like Elizabeth Riley. She too eventually came around to admit that the latest Mrs. Roosevelt was "a very unselfish, sweet woman."

As for Taddy and Sadie, the marriage failed, though he never divorced her. He eventually settled in Queens, living over a garage, where he worked as an auto mechanic. When he died, he left his fortune to the Salvation Army. Whatever demons had possessed this young man remained elusive. One member of the family offered her opinion: "He was a quite charming boy up to the age of twenty-one, perfectly capable of a normal life. [But] he was perfectly terrified that some people were going to marry him for his money. . . . Even when he was a small boy he had that fear." If so, Taddy's fear of gold diggers evidently extended only to women of his own class.

Though Franklin's first year at Harvard had been briefly marred by the Taddy scandal, he was about to recoup through a far more suitable family connection. During the 1900 elections, Eleanor's Uncle Ted was on the Republican ticket as the vice presidential candidate running with President William McKinley. Though Franklin's family were Democrats, a faded, buff-colored card found in the archives of the presidential library at Hyde Park reads: "This is to certify that Mr. F. D. Roosevelt is a member of the Harvard Republican Club." His best credential at Harvard had been his relationship to TR, the hero of San Juan Hill, the governor of the Empire State, and now a national figure. Franklin was not about to have his family's Democrat affiliation stand in the way of his capitalizing on the TR connection and he worked for the McKinley-Roosevelt ticket. "Last night there was a grand torchlight Republican parade of Harvard and the Massachusetts Institute of Technology," he wrote home. "We wore red caps and gowns and marched by classes into Boston and thru' all the principal streets, about 8 miles in all. The crowds to see it were huge all along the route and we were dead tired at the end."

In the custom of the day, Franklin did not resume social life until six months after his father's death. By now, his first serious amorous stirrings had begun. His mother chose not to notice the change. As she would later declare, "I don't believe I ever remember hearing talk about girls or a girl." On another occasion she wrote her brother, Warren, "I am trying to think of Franklin as a man, but [it is] not very easy."

Franklin now played the dashing campus blade decked out in white duck trousers, wildly striped shirts, and a straw boater worn at a rakish angle. Sara's ignorance of her son's private life is confirmed in the diary Franklin fitfully kept at Harvard. Numerous entries deal with girlfriends. After taking Dorothy Quincy to a dinner and dance, he wrote, "Everything was glorious. Got back at 6 a.m. Didn't go to bed." Other entries read, "Walk with Miss Carter in a.m. and she and I take 20 mile drive in p.m. and go to dance at Hotel Aspinwall in evening." "Supper with Minnie Lyman," "Dance for Miss Shattuck," "Rowed with Muriel," "Left N.Y. with Miss Tevis," "Supper with Miss Cobb." The diary records at least fifteen girls whose names rarely surface in his letters to his mother. He could be cruelly selective. Girls who failed to measure up were dismissed as "an awful pill," a "brat," "elephantine," or again, "an ice-cart."

He was a zealous suitor, full of fun, eager to please—and not taken seriously. His Oyster Bay cousin Corinne Robinson, close to young Eleanor Roosevelt, compared Franklin to the image on handkerchief boxes popular in her day. "On top of them were painted figures with a gentleman dancing a minuet with a handkerchief in his hand. . . . In our family we called a certain type 'handkerchief boxy' which meant a kind of dainty quality. . . . Franklin wasn't effeminate. I don't think you can say that. But he wasn't rugged. There was nothing that was, well, 'one of the boys.' He didn't have that quality." She would also say, "I loved Franklin in one way. I was awfully fond of him, but I just thought . . . he was just so superficial." Harsher still were the comments of TR's daughter Alice. A liaison between the two physically attractive distant cousins seemed natural given the family's penchant for intermarrying. But Alice found Franklin, under that "domineering tartar" of a mother, "a good little mother's boy . . . peevish . . . rather like a single child. . . . He didn't rough it." She even faulted Franklin because he sailed while Oyster Bay Roosevelts rowed. Franklin sometimes styled himself "F. D. Roosevelt," to which Alice and her set said behind his back that the initials stood for "feather duster." She further called him "Miss Nancy because he pranced and fluttered." Yet, like cousin Corinne, Alice's attitudes were inconsistent. She would also say, "Franklin was great fun. I used to see him when he was a boy. We had a very gay time together. Franklin was bursting with gaiety." Her contrary attitudes have to be examined through the prism of Roosevelt family rivalries. Among the two branches, mutual pride competed with resentment, and mutual admiration with envy.

Amid the flurry of his early ephemeral courting, one serious romance is alleged to have occurred when Franklin was nineteen, even talk of marriage. Her name was Frances Dana. Her grandfather was the poet Henry Wadsworth Longfellow and her father, Richard Henry Dana, the writer who had won instant fame with his success, *Two Years Before the Mast*. Photographs of Miss Dana reveal a lithe young woman with dark tresses piled atop her head and a winsome smile. Supposedly, the match ran aground on religion. Frances was Catholic, Franklin Protestant. The courtship is mentioned briefly in memoirs by two of FDR's sons, Elliott and James. But oddly, in Franklin's neat, concise diary entries, no word exists of Frances Dana.

The girl much mentioned in the diary and clearly a serious interest, likely his first, was Alice Sohier. Her father, William D. Sohier, was prominent and rich, a former Republican state legislator, a commissioner of roads, and an avid yachtsman. The Sohier family had four homes dotting New England, including a Boston townhouse. Miss Sohier's maternal line traced back to the Aldens, whose Priscilla was allegedly the object of Philippe de la Noye's affections. Geoffrey Ward, in his chronicle of Franklin's youth, has described a colorful introduction of Franklin into Alice's life. He and a pal, well known to the Sohier family, were fleeing a gang of upper classmen bent on hazing freshmen. The two youths took refuge in the Sohier home where Franklin promptly fell asleep on a sitting room sofa. He awoke to see a stunning young woman, just returned from shopping, eyeing him curiously. From that moment, Franklin launched a determined campaign to win the affections of Alice Sohier, not quite sixteen at the time, and whom he would remember "of all the debutantes," that season, "she was the loveliest." June 16, 1901, marks the first reference to Alice in Franklin's diary: "Drive with Sohiers to their camp." Over the next two years, entries regarding Alice surpass all others: "To see Sohiers in eve. Alice's knee nearly well," "Took the Sohiers out for good long sail," "See Alice off on Commonwealth for Europe," "Alice just getting over appendicitis." On one occasion in the Sohier home he casually announced that he might someday be president. A Sohier cousin scoffed, "Who else thinks so?"

The most mysterious diary entries regarding Alice are in a code of Franklin's own devising. Its existence was not spotted until some seventy years later when a keen-eyed researcher, Nona Ferndon, working with the diary at the FDR Library, noted tiny hieroglyphic-like symbols scattered among the plain text entries. The code was confoundingly clever. Initial attempts to break it stumped staffers at the Library of Congress, the National Archives, and the Roosevelt Library. The code was eventually deciphered by avid amateur cryptologists. Part of it involved substitution of numbers for letters. But what long baffled code breakers were seemingly random squiggles. These turned out to be parts of letters, the crossbar of a "t," the hump of an "m," the loop of a "p."

The first coded entry occurs on July 8, 1902, after Franklin had sailed the *Half Moon* into Beverly, north of Boston, where the Sohiers had a summer retreat. The plain language part of the entry reports that after a day of tennis, "all dined at Sohiers." It then shifts into the code, which deciphered reads, "and spend evening on lawn. Alice confides in her Dr." The next day's coded entry read, "Worried over Alice all night." His resort to secrecy in writing about a serious love interest is best explained by his desire to avoid confronting his possessive and intrusive mother. The gambit also revealed a trait that would endure throughout Franklin's life, his pleasure in the secret, the clandestine, the concealed, often solely for his own amusement.

The Sohier courtship deepened. Franklin, though only twenty, raised the prospect of marriage to Alice, now seventeen. As a Harvard man three years her senior, he seemed like a prize catch, good-looking, personable, well connected, and wealthy. The above cited coded entries, however, likely refer to a looming obstacle to their marriage. Alice Sohier was delicate and had been so since birth. In a peculiar diagnosis, her family physician concluded that her internal organs were too small for her body. The secret entries about a visit to the doctor and Franklin's subsequent concern over that visit may relate to a scare her suitor had thrown into the girl. As an only child with an invalid father and a suffocatingly protective mother, he had envied the happy tumult of TR's rambunctious brood during his visits to Oyster Bay. He confided to Alice that he wanted a flock of children, as many as six. A fragile girl with small organs might well heed her doctor's warning of the risks of pregnancy after pregnancy. In any case, a test of the youthful lovers' constancy was at hand.

On October 7, 1902, Alice's father sent his daughter off on a European tour. Franklin watched wistfully from Boston harbor as the ship set sail. Unfortunately for him, the tour was a triumph. In England, Alice was presented at court. The high-spirited, beautiful American heiress was fought over by gallant British officers. According to the granddaughter who would one day become Alice's confidante, "By now she was unimpressed by Franklin as a callow youth compared to the men she met in her travels abroad." And as far as Franklin's hopes to be father of a brood, "My grandmother said she did not choose to be a cow." Thus ended the romance. Alice Sohier was rarely mentioned again in the diary, and then relegated to "friend."

One aspect of the courtship, however, suggests a Franklin whom his mother would never have recognized. It was an age when the innocent feared a kiss could lead to pregnancy. Yet Franklin's attentions to Alice surpassed decorous kisses. During one of his visits to Beverly, Alice later confided to a relative, "In a day and age when well brought up young men were expected to keep their hands off the persons of young ladies of respectable families, Franklin had to be slapped—hard!" Boarding the train back to Boston, his cheek bore the stinging red mark of her outrage.

With the passage of time, Franklin managed to turn his failed suit of Alice Sohier on its head. Writing twenty-six years later, he persuaded himself that, "Once upon a time when I was in Cambridge, I had serious thoughts of marrying a Boston girl and settling down in Back Bay to spend the rest of my days. . . . By the Grace of God I took a trip at the time, meeting numbers of real Americans, i.e. those from the south and west. I was saved, but it was an awfully narrow escape." It was classic Roosevelt revisionism since it was Alice who caused the break. At age twenty-five she married an insurance executive and had two children. She apparently never had any regrets about the missed opportunity to be first lady. She remained a lifelong Republican and anti–New Dealer, deploring Roosevelt for being "so careless with the country's money."

As long as his actions did not reveal any serious attachments, young Franklin enjoyed teasing his mother about his budding savoir faire. In the summer of 1903, a year after the Sohier romance had failed, he sailed to Europe with a classmate, Charles Bradley. In a letter that August he described to Sara an elegant garden party he had attended. "As I knew the uncivilized English custom of never introducing people . . . I walked up to the best looking dame in the bunch & said 'howdy?' Things at once went like oil & I was soon having flirtations with three of the nobility at the same time. I had a walk with the hostesses' niece over the entire house which was really perfect in every way—I mean the house. . . . Then I inspected the gardens with another 'chawmer' & ended up by jollying the hostess herself all by her lonesome for ten minutes while a uniformed Lord stood by & never got in anything except an occasional 'aw' or an 'I sy.' "

An experience during this trip that he did not relate to his mother involved the young sports, each carrying a then substantial $1,000, meeting two attractive women seated at the next table in their Geneva hotel dining room. The women introduced themselves as "the baroness so and so and the countess so and so, aunt and niece." As Franklin later told the story, the foursome hit it off famously, traveling the tourist circuit around Lake Geneva, Bradley paired with the niece and Franklin with the older woman. After two days of promising companionship, the maître d'hôtel asked to see Franklin in his office. There he explained, "Monsieur, I am an old man. I have known your uncle and aunt for many years and I have known you since you were a child. You will forgive me if I speak frankly." He proceeded to explain that the lovely ladies were neither baroness nor countess, and "were not ladies at all, but the best known pair of international blackmailers in Europe." Their modus operandi was to maneuver well-heeled young gentlemen into compromising situations and then have them send home for money to hush up the indiscretion. Years later FDR confessed to Daisy Suckley that he had been genuinely frightened by this predicament, doubtless remembering Taddy's dishonor. He offered the two women a lame excuse about bad news from home, and then fled with Bradley on the next train to Paris, leaving no forwarding address.

If academics counted for little among Harvard's smart set, election to organizations, clubs, and athletics counted for everything. During Franklin's freshman year, Sara wrote her brother, "Franklin is trying to get on the *Crimson* and rowing. I think his exams will suffer." He made neither. He tried again at the end of his freshman year for the newspaper and was one of five candidates selected as a *Crimson* editor. Franklin quickly showed his mettle. He managed to get the special football edition of the *Crimson* onto the field at New Haven before the *Yale News,* a major coup in this circumscribed world. The *Crimson* became his life. While his interest in making the chic parties, and dating Boston belles, did not wane, he found in the *Crimson's* untidy newsroom something novel in his life: immersion in a pursuit that challenged and satisfied his intelligence.

The Republican victory in 1900 was to hand him another *Crimson* coup. The following spring, after TR had been sworn in as vice president, Franklin reported, "I telephoned to ask when I could see him. 'Don't come in,' he said, 'because I'll see you when I come out to lecture. I'm speaking for Professor Lowell, in Government One,' and he gave me the night and the hour. That was a beautiful piece of news and the neatest scoop in the world."

Vice President Roosevelt was returning from a summer trip to Europe when on the morning of September 18, 1901, as the ship passed the Nantucket Shoals, a man came out of the lightship and bellowed through a megaphone that President McKinley had died the previous Saturday. Franklin, now a Harvard sophomore, wrote in a letter home, "Terrible shock to all," with no mention of what the tragedy meant for the Roosevelt family's political fortunes. TR's daughter, Alice, made no bones about her reaction to the news: "My brother Ted and I danced a little war dance. Shameful! Then we put on long faces." Publicly still loyal to TR, Franklin had confided to Alice Sohier during their romance that since promising Republicans were thick on the ground, he would revert to the Democrat fold where his chances of standing out were better.

He continued his rise at the *Crimson.* In his junior year, a Boston newspaper headline read, "Franklin D. Roosevelt, President's Cousin, Elected Secretary of Harvard Crimson." The article went on to report that his election was "one of the high literary honors which Harvard University has to offer to its undergraduates. . . . The fact that he 'made' the *Crimson* and that he has since become one of the foremost men connected with it shows the kind of stuff he has in him, for it is an acknowledged fact that the candidates for the *Crimson* have a harder row to hoe than competitors in almost any other branch of Harvard undergraduate activity."

In 1913, long after Harvard, Franklin boasted to a *New York Telegraph* reporter that as a mere freshman, he had scored another scoop on the

*Crimson*. There had existed on the Harvard campus keen curiosity as to which party President Charles William Eliot would support in 1900. This interest was fanned by a feud between Eliot and Theodore Roosevelt. TR had branded Eliot, for his belief in international peace through amity, "a flabby timid type of character, which eats away at the fighting qualities of our race." Eliot, in turn, regarded TR as a chest-thumping jingoist. Thus far, Eliot's policy had been never to grant personal interviews to the student paper. Franklin claimed that he simply knocked on the stunned Eliot's door and said, "I came to ask you, Mr. President, whether you are going to vote for McKinley or [William Jennings] Bryan." Eliot was evidently so unprepared for this bold thrust that his defenses were down and he blurted out his choice. The October 29 issue of the *Crimson* carried a banner headline, "President Eliot Declares for McKinley." The story went on to report that "President Eliot gave the *Crimson* the following statement last night . . . I intend to vote for President McKinley, Governor Roosevelt, and Representative [Samuel] McCall." It was a triumph for a college newspaper, and the *Crimson* story reverberated nationwide.

The story appears to offer a revealing glimpse into the young Roosevelt, assured, resourceful, imaginative. Except that his account was untrue. What really happened would not surface for another thirty-one years. In a letter to a Michael E. Hennessy, dated October 22, 1931, New York's then governor, Franklin Roosevelt, confessed, "In some way I was a number of years ago given credit for getting a scoop from President Eliot in regard to the way he was going to vote in the Autumn of 1900. The real man who got that scoop was [Albert W.] DeRoode." His originally taking credit for the scoop and this admission were pure Roosevelt, a man to whom extrapolation and exaggeration came as naturally as breathing.

The confident, gregarious, ever smiling Franklin of later memory is hard to associate with rejection. But before he left Harvard, he was to know searing humiliation. The social structure at Cambridge was as fixed as the Indian caste system. In the fall of Franklin's sophomore year approximately 20 percent of his class were invited to join a club called the Institute of 1770. Franklin made it. Those nearest the top in the institute tallying automatically became members of a secret fraternity, Delta

Kappa Epsilon, known as "Dickey." Again Franklin made it. Now came the supreme test, which he faced with confidence. The Porcellian was *the* club at Harvard, a caste within a caste, self-contained and self-perpetuating. Qualifications were simple: social position, wealth, but only through inheritance, the right dress, right manners, and right prep school, with Groton fully qualifying. Merit, achievement, scholarship, counted for nothing. The purpose of being a member of the Porcellian was to be a member of the Porcellian. Franklin's father had been a member, as had TR. Franklin awaited the nod. Sixteen juniors and seniors gathered in the Porcellian clubhouse to debate whom to invite. Selection had to be unanimous. The members dropped either a white ball, signifying approval, or a black ball, signifying rejection, into a ballot box. Eight sophomores made it, but Franklin did not. What had gone wrong? Was it the too smooth, overrefined manners, the compulsion to ingratiate, the speech too conspicuously patrician even for a Harvard man, the Taddy scandal, or a single unsuspected enemy? Given the secretive nature of the Porcellian, he would never know.

He reconciled himself to membership in the Fly Club, still lofty, but rated third in the Harvard club pyramid. Ordinary Boston boys had no inkling that such games were played, nor would they have cared. But as one moved through the concentric circles of class, the pain of rejection grew more intense until, for those just outside the charmed circle the rebuff was devastating. Sixteen years later, Franklin, by then part of President Wilson's mission to the Versailles peace talks, was returning aboard the ocean liner *George Washington* with Aunt Bye's son, William Sheffield Cowles Jr., and confided that the rejection still rankled. As Cowles recalled the moment, "I was a lieutenant in the Marine Corps and an aide to Franklin. . . . We were walking up and down the deck and Franklin was talking a little about his life." By far the greatest disappointment, he told Cowles, was that he was not taken into the Porcellian Club at Harvard, "which to me was an extremely interesting and significant fact. At the time, he was assistant secretary of the Navy, he was an important man . . . to hear him say that that was the greatest disappointment in his life struck me as extremely odd." Far more pain lay in his future, tragedy that would dwarf this sophomoric defeat.

Franklin, because his grades were undistinguished and because he tasted occasional reversals, has been painted by some observers as a mediocrity at Harvard. Since grades were not paramount in his set, other standards must measure his success. He managed to graduate not in the usual four years, but in three. His editing of the *Crimson* meant that he was a big man on campus. He was elected to the select Signet Literary Society. He had majored in American political history and government and, while his grades fail to impress, his lifelong ability to summon from history's storehouse, with almost photographic fidelity, pertinent events, anecdotes, allegorical and literary allusions, and, most significant, to make decisions rooted in historical perspective, reveal an exceptional mind, grades or no.

He chose to stay on at Harvard as a graduate student for another year because he was not about to give up becoming editor-in-chief of the *Crimson*, which would have fallen to him in his fourth year. The position gave him the power to set the *Crimson*'s course and write its editorials. The topics he chose reflected a mind that as yet did not see beyond the Cambridge campus. He exhorted Harvard men to display greater school spirit, to cheer more lustily for the Harvard eleven, and urged more fire protection in the dorms. Still, in his universe, he had become a power to reckon with. He wound up attending two Harvard graduations, one for the bachelor's degree awarded him in June 1903, and the other in June 1904 when the rest of his class graduated. He always considered himself and was officially listed as a member of the class of '04. At the second commencement, along with his mother and numerous other family, he invited one more Roosevelt fast emerging in his life, his distant cousin Eleanor.

*Chapter 6*

# COURTSHIP

· · · · · · ·

A<small>T AGE FIFTEEN</small> a ray of sun was about to pierce the pervasive gloom of Eleanor Roosevelt's life. Grandmother Hall recognized that the girl could no longer remain under her roof with her drunkard sons. Thirty years before, Eleanor's Aunty Bye had studied under a remarkable teacher, Marie Souvestre, at a school outside Paris called Les Ruches. Mlle. Souvestre was a pedagogical force, the rare teacher whose strengths of mind and character could stamp themselves on her students for life. The Franco-Prussian War of 1870 had disrupted her school and also marked the period of greatest personal tragedy in Souvestre's life, the breakup of her lesbian affair with the co-mistress of Les Ruches. Souvestre thereafter reestablished herself in England and founded a new school, Allenswood, just outside London. Allenswood was small, with fewer than forty students, and served the daughters of rich Europeans and Americans. From the beginning its headmistress moved at the pinnacle of English intellectual life. She helped educate Lytton Strachey and his sister Dorothy, was an intimate of the Bloomsbury set, and Henry James urged his philosopher brother, William, to have his daughter educated at Allenswood. Eleanor arrived under this woman's tutelage in the fall of 1899 when Mlle. Souvestre was in her seventies. Eleanor's cousin Corinne, who followed her to Allenswood, described their headmistress: "She was not as tall as she should have been for her remarkable head. It was a beautiful face but it was a big face, a face for a person of real stature, a sculptured face, and her body was not tall enough for the beauty of the face."

Eleanor, coming from a world where conventionality and conformity ruled, was about to discover a fiercely independent thinker. While the war in South Africa against the Boers prompted frenzies of British chauvinism, Mlle. Souvestre sided with the underdog Afrikaners. She stood in the vanguard with those protesting the innocence of the Jewish captain Alfred Dreyfus, falsely accused of treason against the French army. She sided with oppressed workers against industrialist enemies of trade unions. She was an atheist. She refused to hide her lesbianism, though without proselytizing. For Eleanor, Marie Souvestre was like cold water thrown into the face of a sleepwalker. Her intellectual awakening was accompanied by an even more novel experience. Grandmother Hall had written ahead to Mlle. Souvestre of Eleanor's blighted childhood. The headmistress's piercing gaze that "penetrated right through to your backbone," intimidated her students, but softened when she looked upon the sad-faced Eleanor. As Eleanor saw herself at that time, "I was always afraid of something; of the dark, of displeasing people, of failure." Mlle. Souvestre invested in her emotionally, drew her out, and listened to her. She recognized what few had made the effort to see, that this gawky, insecure adolescent, while lacking the superficial sophistication of many of her young charges, possessed unusual qualities of heart and mind. The headmistress wrote Grandmother Hall that Eleanor was "the warmest heart I have ever encountered."

As the girl's fears subsided, she overcame the physical cowardice that had previously inhibited her. She went out for field hockey, the roughest sport at Allenswood, and made the first team. She later recalled, "I think that day was one of the proudest of my life." She excelled in every subject and recited poetry with true feeling. During school holidays it was Eleanor whom Mlle. Souvestre chose to take on travels through France and Italy. It was the headmistress who taught her the rewards of straying from well-worn tourist paths, and to seek out instead overlooked places where they came to know the local folk and their customs.

Cousin Corinne has captured Eleanor's transformation in three years from lost soul to a confident young woman. "When I arrived she was everything at the school," Corinne remembered. "She was beloved by everybody. Young girls had crushes and you bought violets or a book and left them in the room of the girl you were idolizing. Eleanor's room every Saturday would be full of flowers because she was so admired."

Long afterward, measuring the meaning of her years with Mlle. Souvestre, Eleanor wrote, "This was the first time in all my life . . . all my fears left me." She broke her "habit of lying," as she became comfortable with who she was rather than pretending to be what she was not. Of her headmistress's anti-bourgeois opinions, Eleanor remembered, "Mlle. Souvestre shocked me into thinking." She recalled that "Never again would I be the rigid little person I had been before. For three years I basked in her generous presence, and I think those years did much to form my character." Allenswood "started me on the way to self-confidence." She described her time there as "the happiest of my life."

The idyll, however, was about to end as her old life intruded. Her grandmother insisted that Eleanor, now eighteen, come home to make her debut in society. She arrived in New York in the summer of 1902 and was instantly pressed back into the mold she thought she had broken. She was, at least, spared returning to the Halls' grim Tivoli mansion where, as she later put it, "My grandmother was in the country trying to keep two of her sons from drinking themselves to death. Of course they did, but having strong constitutions, it took some time." She instead was taken in by Grandmother Hall's niece and her husband, Mr. and Mrs. Henry Parish Jr. Though the Parishes were kind to her, Eleanor felt rootless. She visited her Aunt Corinne Robinson, TR's younger sister, who later wrote of the occasion to her daughter, also Corinne, "Eleanor came to see me . . . [her] path is not all roses. She burst into tears and said, 'Auntie, I have no real home' in such a pathetic way that my heart simply ached for her."

Soon came the dread ritual that had necessitated her return home, her formal introduction into society. Her first hurdle was to be the New York Assembly Ball, set for December 11, 1902. It did not soothe Eleanor's anxiety when the gossip sheet, *Town Topics*, noted that she was the daughter of that brilliant beauty of the previous generation, the late Anna Roosevelt. The structure of the ball presented a daunting gauntlet of acceptance or rejection. Each girl had a dance card dangling from her wrist. A young man would ask if a particular dance was free and if so would write his name on the card. Eleanor faced the evening with foreboding. At five feet eleven inches, she not only towered over most of the girls, but the young men as well. Her Aunt Pussie had told her, "You're too plain ever to find yourself a beau, poor dear." She further lacked that essential social lubricant, the gift for small talk. For Eleanor, standing alone, palms clammy, while others swirled about the great ballroom, the event became a torment. Aunt Pussie's current swain, Forbes Morgan, a veteran of Uncle Ted's Rough Riders, finally asked her to dance, followed by blessed invitations from three more young men. But was it out of charity, courtesy, duty? Eleanor was unsure. Later, she was to describe the evening as "utter agony . . . by no stretch of the imagination could I fool myself into thinking I was a popular debutante." She fled the Assembly Ball as early as she dared. "I knew I was the first girl in my mother's family who was not a belle," she concluded; "I was deeply ashamed."

Mlle. Souvestre's wakening of the nobler side of her character saved her. Eleanor, fortunately, fell in with kindred souls, like Mary Harriman, daughter of the railroad builder E. H. Harriman and the sister of Averell Harriman, and other privileged women who were repelled by the filth, disease, poverty, overcrowding, and child labor they saw as soon as they stepped outside their own protected circle. Eleanor joined the Junior League, which created settlement houses to serve the poor, and the Consumer's League, which promoted intelligent spending of what little money the poor had. Refusing rides in her friends' carriages, she took the streetcar or the El downtown to a Rivington Street settlement house on the Lower East Side where she taught pasty-faced children ballroom dancing and calisthenics. "I went to a big hall on 14th Street where everyone sang Joe Hill," she recalled of the workers' anthem. "Of course my family didn't know what I was doing."

"You couldn't find two such different people as Mother and Father," Anna, the daughter of Franklin and Eleanor, was to write after both her parents were gone. The quandary as to why Franklin and Eleanor married has been examined exhaustively. Still the enigma persists. During the summer of 1902, while he was entranced by Alice Sohier, Franklin found himself sauntering down the coach aisle of the train from New York to Poughkeepsie when he spotted a familiar face. Eleanor, at that point recently back from England, was traveling to Tivoli to spend the summer with her grandmother. She was three years older than when Franklin had danced with her at the Robinsons' Christmas party. His greeting was effervescent, his smile blinding. She responded with rather more poise than he remembered from their earlier encounters. He sat down next to her and they began chatting easily. They were, however distant, kin; her father had been Franklin's godfather. Her uncle, the president, was Franklin's distant cousin. An hour passed quickly when Franklin suggested they go back to see his mother, who had taken a Pullman car despite the short sixty-five-mile ride. To Eleanor, Sara was "Cousin Sallie," friend of her late parents, and a formidable, even forbidding figure of regal bearing and arresting beauty. The effect this day was even more pronounced, with Sara, two years after her husband's death, still clad severely in black. Nevertheless, her greeting was warm, and she spoke to Eleanor as if to a favorite niece.

On November 17, 1902, five weeks after the chance meeting on the train, and while Alice Sohier was still abroad, Franklin and Eleanor were thrown together when his charming, extravagant half-brother, Rosy, invited several Roosevelts to his private box for the Madison Square Garden horse show. This was the typical occasion that had produced so many Roosevelt intermarriages, as one wag put it, because they never met anyone else. That night Eleanor made her first appearance in Franklin's diary, "Mary N & Eleanor Roos. At Sherry's horse show." They were soon meeting intermittently in New York City for lunch and tea.

Roosevelts from both branches, including Franklin and Eleanor, were together in all their glory on New Year's Eve 1902 at the White House, watching the triumphant TR, recently elected president in his own right, pump thousands of hands in the reception line. The next morning Franklin wrote in his diary, "At 11 with [Aunty Bye] to call at White House. Saw Cousin Edith. Large lunch at home. To afternoon tea with Alice who has Eleanor, Margaret. Dinner of 80 at Kean's. Dance at Post Club. Waites till 3. Supper with Miss Cobb."

Eleanor was still a peripheral remote cousin. However, a brief, coded diary entry appears six months later, on July 7, 1903, reading, "E is an angel." The brevity spoke volumes. Alice Sohier was now out of his life and, during those months, Franklin and Eleanor had been together repeatedly. He chose to say little of this budding relationship to his mother, hence the use again of the code. Sara, with no desire to see her son attached to anyone, nevertheless unintentionally threw the two together. She gave a three-day house party for Franklin at Hyde Park starting on July 20. Eleanor was among the guests and remained there with her maid all three days. She and Franklin played tennis, strolled happily in the rain, and when time came for Eleanor to leave, he saw her off on the train. Two weeks later, Sara had what she called her "young people" back, and this time Franklin demonstrated his skill as a sailor, taking his guests out for a night's cruise on the *Half Moon*, on the dark waters of the Hudson. Eleanor was aboard.

Toward the end of the month, Franklin, again sailing the *Half Moon*, followed Eleanor to a small port in Maine where she had gone to visit her Aunt Corinne and her daughter, Corinne. "I think he is crazy about her," young Corinne wrote in her diary. Eleanor displayed a rare coquettish streak when writing to Franklin of the two Corinnes. They "both undertook to talk to me seriously yesterday about you, because they thought I did not realize how serious you might be, and I led them on very wickedly."

The deepening relationship still begs the question, What lay behind this mutual attraction between the smooth, handsome youth and the old-maidish young woman? Franklin's feather-duster veneer misled even his closest acquaintances as to what lay beneath. He was bursting with curiosity, drawn to endless interests, and possessed, however vaguely at this point, of the social conscience implanted by his father. In Eleanor he found a different sort of young woman than those he was accustomed to, one who thought beyond fashion, parties, and appearance. Eleanor offered intellectual companionship, a novel experience for him with a girl. When they were together, there were, Eleanor noted, no "dreadful silences." She happily joined Franklin and his classmates as they argued the literary ideas of a favorite Harvard professor, Charles Townsend Copley, quietly offering her opinions. She was to say one day that she fell in love with Franklin because he read as much as she did. She also did something that would never have occurred to most girls he knew. She spurred him on, encouraged him to make more of himself, to fully realize the potential she saw in him. He was at the time editor-in-chief of the *Harvard Crimson*, a position, she told him, from which he could influence people's thinking. Her prodding at this stage pleased, flattered, even motivated him. It was a streak in her character that he would welcome less gratefully in years to come.

Eleanor brought him to the Rivington Street settlement house where he watched her teach her ragamuffins. Once while he was there, a stick-thin child fell sick. Eleanor asked Franklin to help her get the girl home. The stench, the squalor of her tenement, and the wretchedness of its denizens plunged him into an unimagined netherworld. He kept murmuring, "My God, I didn't know anybody lived like that." He was later to describe Eleanor's appeal to him. "She possessed what every member of the Roosevelt family seems always to have," he noted, "a deep and abiding interest in everything and everybody."

Eleanor possessed another attraction for him. In 1903 *the* Roosevelts were the Oyster Bay branch, and the Hyde Park Roosevelts a lesser tributary. Franklin was related to the president of the United States but only by a remote tie reaching back five generations. Eleanor, however, was the daughter of TR's only brother and the president's favorite niece. When the society press reported on Rosy's guests at the horse show, Eleanor's presence was noted but not Franklin's. Years before, his father had tried to forge another link between the families in his failed pursuit of TR's sister, Bye. Bye had once hoped to snag Rosy. And Rosy's daughter Helen had become engaged to Corinne Robinson's son Teddy. Should Franklin's courtship of Eleanor flower into another Roosevelt intermarriage, the connection could hardly hurt his political ambitions.

When marriage is the issue, whatever the affinities of pedigree, fortune, or position, in the end two souls and two bodies must meet, either compatibly or ill-fittingly. And here, particularly to later generations, the unlikeliness of Franklin and Eleanor as a couple, noted even by their own children, continues to perplex. Photographs of Franklin in his young manhood reveal a Golden Boy, over six feet tall, now filled out to 161 pounds, and stunningly handsome. He is invariably seen in poses that exude confidence and physical vitality. Eleanor, however, never rises above plain. That a young man of these gifts, an Adonis who could have easily won the hand of any number of more beautiful women, decided to choose Eleanor is either evidence of a then unsuspected depth in him or of the inexplicable choices of the human heart, or both.

A few other young men besides Franklin had also managed to see beyond the unimpressive exterior, the apologetic posture, the too prominent teeth, the large feet, the awkward dancing, to the rewarding human being beneath. Nicholas Biddle and Lyman Delano were taken with Eleanor. Howard Cary, a Franklin classmate, carried on a staid but insistent pursuit. But for Eleanor the magic was missing. As she later remembered Cary, he was "a charming man with a really lovely spirit, [who] wrote me occasionally about books, for we had a mutual interest in literature. His letters were charming, but formal and even stiff when they touched on anything but books." It was Franklin who set her heart racing.

Their son Elliott has caught the flavor of their courtship: "He must have taken enormous pleasure in bringing her out of her shell, to the best of his considerable ability to do such things with anyone. Franklin made parties fun for her for the first time." The girl who had clumped on the dance floor suddenly enjoyed going to balls. That this prize catch actually sought her out seemed like a dream come true. Here was someone to whom she could pour her heart out, who listened to her as though he truly cared. She gradually placed him on the same pedestal that her father occupied. She signed her letters to him "Little Nell," the endearment her father had called her. Franklin responded in kind, addressing her by the same name that held such happy childhood memories for her. Amazingly, she had a beau, and a dazzlingly attractive one.

Delano custom was to gather for Thanksgiving at a family seat in Fairhaven, Massachusetts, near Buzzards Bay, a solid house built by Sara's grandfather and managed by her brother Warren. Sara looked forward to any opportunity to display her fine-looking, impeccably mannered son to his admiring uncles, aunts, and cousins. During the holiday in 1903, after a songfest around the piano, Franklin asked his mother if he might have a word alone with her. They slipped into a room redolent of Delano history, the coat of arms of Philippe de la Noye, vases, cymbals, and other exotica from the China trade.

In what she was about to hear, no blow, even the death of her husband, would strike Sara harder. Franklin told her he was in love. He intended to marry Eleanor Roosevelt. He was not asking Sara, not seeking motherly advice, but telling her of a decision already made, thus shattering in an instant what she had believed to be an unbreakable bond of mutual trust and confidence between herself and her boy. Even two months before, when Eleanor visited the family's retreat on Campobello Island, Sara had not interpreted the visit as "boy brings girl home to meet the family." Eleanor was already family, but the relationship of daughter-in-law never occurred to Sara.

Their marriage would mean that Sara would no longer be the core of Franklin's life, the consolation easing her widowhood. She would be condemned to rambling alone through that huge house on the Hudson. The idea was absurd. Franklin was still at Harvard, yet to earn a penny on his own and thus far with no discernible profession in sight. And the girl was a child of nineteen. She was all well and good on paper, a member of the country's first family, possessing an independent income, a sweet thing so pathetically eager to please. Had anyone asked if Eleanor was a fine young woman, Sara would have answered, "Of course." Had she been asked if Eleanor would make a fine wife for her Franklin, she would have responded with equal vigor, "Of course not." Where was the spark, the vivacity, the patrician manner, and where was the beauty? This shrinking violet cannot have been the woman to turn Franklin's head, much less win his heart. She seized upon the only stratagem available on the spot. She made him promise not to say a word to anyone for now. An engagement unknown is more easily broken. Time would give her the opportunity to regain the upper hand. Give it a year, she begged him, to test the depth of their feelings. That night she wrote in her diary, "Franklin gave me quite a startling announcement." Sara's inability to grasp what actually went on inside her son's head was not her failure alone. It would mystify even his closest associates all of his life.

Just days before staggering his mother at Fairhaven, Franklin had gone to meet Eleanor at Groton, where she was visiting her beloved brother Hall, her only immediate kin and now a student there. In his diary, Franklin wrote of that day: "To Groton at 9 & get there just in time for church. Lunch with Aunt K's party [Mrs. Pierce Collier]." The entry then shifted into his code: "After lunch I have a never to be forgotten walk to the river with my darling." Never to be forgotten because it was the moment when he asked Eleanor to marry him. She accepted instantly. Franklin, with unaccustomed humility, told her, "I have only a few bright prospects now." She answered, "I have faith in you. I'm sure you will really amount to something someday."

Another piece fitting into the puzzle of Franklin's determination to marry so young was doubtless sexual frustration. In the current age of easy gratification for both sexes, it is difficult to re-create the pent-up desire, the repressed impulses at the time Franklin came of age. It was a period when "good girls" preserved their virginity, leaving "good boys" only the outlet of agonizing abstention, "bad girls," or the brothel. The fact that Franklin had contemplated marriage three times before ever reaching his majority strongly suggests not only his desire to loosen his mother's grip but to shed inhibition. Through marriage he could have it all, an unfettered outlet for his desires, a partial declaration of independence from Mama, and marriage to a girl he admired, recognized as an asset both in her character and her connections, and with whom he was sure he was in love.

As for Eleanor, she now had what had seemed forever denied to her,

someone to love, who loved her. She ended almost every day at the settlement house writing Franklin letters laying bare her heart. "I am so
happy. So _very_ happy in your love dearest, that all the world has changed
for me. If only I can bring to you all that you have brought to me all my
dearest wishes will be fulfilled." She quoted Elizabeth Barrett Browning's "A Woman's Shortcomings" to him:

> _Unless you can know, when upraised by his breath,_
> _That your beauty itself wants proving;_
> _Unless you can swear, "For life, for death!"_
> _Oh, fear to call it loving!_

She continued to sign her torrent of letters "Little Nell." We cannot
know the tenor of Franklin's replies because a time would come when
she would destroy all his letters to her from this period.

A week after springing the surprise on Sara, Franklin sought, while remaining adamant, to sound a conciliatory note. "Dearest Mama—I know
what pain I must have caused you and you know I wouldn't do it if I really could have helped it. . . . I know my mind, have known it for a long
time. . . . Result, I am the happiest man just now in the world; likewise
the luckiest—And for you, dear Mummy, you know that nothing can
ever change what we have always been and always will be to each
other—only now you have two children to love & to love you—and
Eleanor as you know will always be a daughter to you in every true way."

Eleanor, with desperate eagerness, had already written her prospec-
tive mother-in-law: "Dearest Cousin Sallie, I know just how you feel and
how hard it must be, but I do so want you to learn to love me a little. You
must know that I will always try to do what you wish for I have grown to
love you very dearly during the past summer. It is impossible for me to
tell you how I feel toward Franklin, I can only say that my one great wish
is always to prove worthy of him. . . . With much love dear Cousin Sallie, Always devotedly Eleanor."

As the determination of her son to marry remained unwavering, Sara
began to reconcile herself to reality. On December 4, she wrote Franklin
from her New York apartment at 10 West 43rd Street, "This morning I
called ER and we went together to the shops for nearly two hours and
had a nice talk. I have thought constantly of you and your hopes my dear

boy, and I feel that in gaining Eleanor's love you are very fortunate for I have always felt that she is a <u>true</u> loyal nature and even though I have not known her very well, I feel very sure of her. Already I am getting over the strangeness of it. . . . I can't bear to disappoint you even a little." Two days later she wrote again, "I am so glad to think of my precious son so perfectly happy. You know that I try not to think of myself. I know that in the future I shall be glad and I shall love Eleanor and adopt her fully when the right time comes."

Still, she was determined that the young lovers' secret not be compromised by their being seen together too often. She opposed their spending a whole weekend together in New York, and suggested that Franklin see Eleanor instead at Hyde Park, "it is a quiet place and no one can talk," she argued. "Were you in town both days you could not fail to be talked about and for every reason." Further, she wanted the secret concealed by a smokescreen of other social activity. "I would like you to accept any dinners or parties you will be asked to in the holidays in <u>New York,</u>" she wrote her son. Still desperate to keep the tie between herself and Franklin intact, she added, "Please don't think I am unsympathetic and that I do not understand for I do." Sara's objection to the couple's plan to spend a weekend in New York began to raise the old ghosts of Eleanor's insecurity, so recently overcome. She wrote Franklin, "Of course it will be a terrible disappointment to me not to have you on Sunday as I have been looking forward to it and every moment with you is very, very precious as we have so little of each other but I don't want you to stay if you feel it is your duty to go."

Sara invoked yet another strategy to place herself between her son and his intended. She told Franklin that she planned to rent a house in Boston again so that they could be near each other. Of course, she said she had no objection to having Eleanor come to visit "once or twice." But she did not expect the girl to be forever coming up to Boston or him running down to New York. The prospect of having his mother around his neck and rationing his time with Eleanor had scant appeal to Franklin. Mother and son agreed on a compromise. They would take a Caribbean voyage together aboard the Hamburg-American Line's *Prinzessin Victoria Luise* and bring along Franklin's roommate, Lathrop Brown, thus escaping the Boston winter, providing a companion for Franklin, and achieving the distancing from Eleanor that Sara wanted. His willingness to go off for six weeks on a pleasure cruise in the midst of his secret engagement to the love-struck Eleanor suggests that Franklin loved not as deeply, or at least differently, from his fiancée.

During his trip abroad the summer before with Charles Brady, Franklin had been a guest at the Lancashire estate of his parents' British friends, Sir Hugh and Lady Cholmley, parents of three unmarried daughters. Franklin quickly fixed on the youngest and prettiest and conducted a brief but ardent flirtation. Even while his courtship of Eleanor had been proceeding at a feverish pitch during the summer and fall of 1903, his diary records several outings with other girls: "canoe trip with M.E.N." (Mary Newbold), the twenty-mile drive and dance with "Miss Carter," a day at Alice Sohier's family camp. When the *Prinzessin Victoria Luise* put into Trinidad, the passengers were invited to a dance at the Queen's Park Hotel. Sara watched in horror as her son attached himself to an "older woman," a French femme fatale who seemed to have completely enchanted Franklin as they whispered into each other's ears and laughed gaily, while gliding across the dance floor. When the night ended, Sara upbraided her son. Couldn't he see the woman was a common adventuress? An amused Franklin teased her as a prude. His conduct on the cruise suggested a light heart, not one heartsick by separation from his beloved.

Despite momentary diversions, his intention to marry stayed on course. In the fall of 1904, Franklin had enrolled in Columbia University Law School, partly trying to find what to do with his life, but just as much to be near Eleanor, then living in New York with the Parishes. By November the pledge to keep the engagement secret for a year had been met and the young lovers were ready to proclaim their troth publicly. The plan was for Franklin to inform the Delano clan at the customary Thanksgiving dinner at Fairhaven. But he fell ill with jaundice and Sara, not wanting to leave him, canceled her visit as well. Instead, Franklin sent a letter announcing the engagement to be read at dinner by the head of the family, Uncle Warren. A public announcement followed in December. The newspapers were generous to the bride-to-be. *Town Topics* reported that the president's niece had "more claim to good looks than any of her Roosevelt cousins." Former suitors were genuinely disappointed. Howard Cary wrote Franklin, "You are mighty lucky. Your future wife is such as it is the privilege of few men to have." Nicholas Biddle also managed a grudging congratulation to the victor. But Franklin too left broken hearts. Mary Newbold's parents had thought something might have come of Franklin's attentions to their daughter. Alice Roosevelt claimed that as a result of her cousin's engagement, "One young Boston woman is known to have taken to her bed for several days out of sorrow and disappointment."

Sara, at bottom a practical woman, accepted her fate. She wrote her brother, Warren, "I am sure you will feel that my dear is very fortunate in his choice. I am very fond of Eleanor, and am happy in their happiness." She was sincere. The objective now must be to shape Eleanor into the wife Franklin deserved, a task Sara approached with relish.

## Chapter 7

# MR. AND MRS. FRANKLIN D. ROOSEVELT

·······

S HE WAS TO BE MARRIED, live her life through her husband, and ultimately bear children, thus fulfilling an upper-class woman's destiny in that age. At times, she could not stop the lingering insecurity from poking through the thin shell of her newfound happiness. Franklin to her was godlike, peerless. She broke down at one point and sobbed to another cousin, Ethel, TR's daughter, "I shall never be able to hold him. He is too attractive." Her treatment at the hands of her future mother-in-law did little to nourish her self-confidence. She was starved for the love and affection denied her since her father's death. She wrote Sara at one point, "I shall look forward to our next long evening together, when I shall want to be kissed all the time." And on another occasion, "I feel as though we would have such a long arrears of kisses and cuddly times to make up." At the same time, she feared being resented as an intruder standing between her fiancé and his adoring mother. When Franklin returned from his Caribbean voyage, Eleanor wrote of any future trips, "We three must take them together . . . and though I know three will never be the same to her still some day I hope that she will really love me and I would be very glad if I thought she was even the least bit reconciled to me."

Sara's wish was only to do right by those she habitually referred to as "her children." She was going to spare Eleanor making the mistakes of an inexperienced, unworldly girl. She began to instruct her in what to wear and when to wear it, whom to invite and whom not to, what to say and when, where to shop and where to dine. She corrected Eleanor in front of other people. Cousin Corinne concluded that it was not Eleanor's inadequacies, but that Aunt Sallie would behave the same toward any woman marrying her Franklin. "I've never seen such possession in my life," she observed. Should anyone suggest to Sara that her conduct might cause pain, she would have been puzzled. As she saw it, she was bearing up admirably under the sacrifice the marriage meant for her. As her grandson, Eleanor's son James, put it many years later, she "never quite forgave mother for marrying her boy, Franklin, right out of college at a time when granny was looking forward to enjoying a few years with Franklin all to herself."

The terra incognita for Eleanor, giggled at by equally innocent girlfriends, something that well-bred married women did not discuss with well-bred girls, was sex. When Eleanor once stumbled upon the word "whore" in the Bible and asked Grandmother Hall what it meant, the old woman replied, "It is not a word that little girls should use." Cousin Corinne recalled being kissed by a boy in the family's stable. "It frightened me to death," she remembered, "and I discussed with my intimate friends whether I would immediately have a baby." Eleanor's ideas of proper conduct between young men and women were drawn straight from Victorian primers on manners and morals. "You knew a man before you wrote or received a letter from him," she believed, "and to make the first move was unthinkable." Even the closing of a letter had to be carefully calibrated. "To have signed oneself in any other way than 'very sincerely yours,' would have been not only a breach of good manners but an admission of feeling which was entirely inadmissible. . . . And the idea that you would permit any man to kiss you before you were engaged to him never crossed my mind." Even gift giving had its protocol. "Flowers, books, cards were all possible," Eleanor had been taught, "but jewelry of any kind, absolutely not." Franklin, after he had become president, once reminisced about the social artificialities of his youth: "Gentle ladies were supposed to faint on proper occasions with very slight provocation and . . . young ladies received instruction in the art of fainting gracefully . . . ladies who had fainted were sometimes revived by burning feathers under their noses. A sofa pillow might be broken open for the purpose."

Cousin Alice Roosevelt, affecting worldliness, offered to guide Eleanor through the mysterious act. Eleanor's relationship with Alice, eight months her senior, would remain close but knotty throughout life. During a visit by young Eleanor to Oyster Bay, her Uncle Ted was teaching the girls to dive off a float, Alice going first. Eleanor, terrified of the water, stiffened, closed her eyes and dove in. She rose to the surface, gasping and choking only to have Alice shove her head under again.

At the time of Eleanor's engagement, Alice was the captivating daughter of a president, pursued by the press like a latter-day film star. She was good copy. Reporters seized upon her every brazen act and utterance. Seeing her chew gum in public, one society columnist wrote, "Miss Alice Roosevelt has set an example which will, I hope, be disdained by the soubrettish young women who copy the peculiar characteristics of the daughter of her strenuous sire. . . . At the theater she 'chanks' vigorously from curtain to curtain and at the closing day of the Morris Park races never paused in her violent mastication." When she was nineteen, she confided to her diary, "I smoked my first cigarette." She seemed to have been born with claws, witness diary entries dealing with unsuccessful parties or frustrated romances. A typical entry ended in large, fiercely scribbled block letters, "RETALIATE!" "REVENGE!" "RETALIATION!"

Alice's ambiguous attitude toward Eleanor was a compound of envy, grudging admiration, and sporadic affection. She, like Eleanor, had lost her mother as a child. When TR remarried, Alice's hungry ego was in competition with half-siblings for her father's attention. Her jealousy extended to Eleanor. TR, fond of his niece and aware of her tragic past, would embrace her with a warmth that Alice resented. Yet, whenever she came to New York, Alice made straight for Eleanor's home where they were inseparable. They lunched, shopped, paid social calls together, and were always partners in parlor games. In one month, Eleanor appeared in Alice's diary every day. When she drew up a list of twenty-seven young friends "With whom I should like to go into seclusion at a convent or a ranch," Eleanor topped the list. Eleanor, however, remained aghast at her cousin's brazenness. Alice had become "crazier than ever," she wrote to Franklin. "I saw her in Bobbie Goelet's auto quite alone with three other men." As Eleanor later described her feelings, "While I always admired her, I always was afraid of her."

As the wedding approached, Alice made a final attempt to acquaint Eleanor with the facts of life, gleaned largely by observing the habits of her pet rabbits and guinea pigs. As she described the anatomical details, Eleanor "suddenly leapt on me and tried to smother me with a pillow, saying I was being blasphemous." She left convinced that her cousin would go to the marriage bed, "not knowing anything about the subject at all." Cousin Corinne, after her own initiation, described what women of their class should expect. "To perform a duty was right, but to have zest for living—joy in living was not very nice," she wrote in her memoirs. The "purebred New England woman, when she finally married, knew her duty, lay on her bed, and murmured to herself, as the husband approached, 'for God, for country and for Yale.'"

The extent of Franklin's premarital experience is unknown. His pawing of Alice Sohier, his adventures in Switzerland with the phony noble-women and the older French woman in Trinidad suggest an intact libido. And doubtless some Harvard upper classmen found occasional release in Boston bawdy houses. But nowhere, including the coded entries in his diary or in the latter recollections of his college chums, is there a hint of what Franklin's early sexual experience might have been. He likely approached the marriage bed as innocently as Eleanor.

The wedding was set for March 17, 1905. The bride would then be twenty and the groom two months past his twenty-third birthday. Initially, Aunt Edith, the president's wife, had offered the White House for the wedding, much to Cousin Alice's displeasure. She wanted to be the first Roosevelt bride married there. The offer to Eleanor was left to languish. Still, she and Franklin hoped dearly that the president would take part in their wedding. It happened that TR was to be in New York to march in the Saint Patrick's Day parade and he agreed to give the father-less bride away, promising, "Only some unforeseen public need will keep me away." He could squeeze the wedding between the parade and two speeches on his New York schedule.

TR had just been sworn in as president two weeks before, and among those who had voted for the victor was Franklin. With characteristic logical sinuosity, he explained, "My father and grandfather were Democrats and I was brought up as a Democrat. I voted for the Republican candidate, Theodore Roosevelt, because I thought he was a better Democrat than the Democratic candidate." In early March, Franklin and Eleanor journeyed to Washington in a private railroad car loaded with Roosevelts for the inauguration. They were escorted to seats just behind TR's immediate family, and danced the night away at the inaugural ball.

On Saint Patrick's Day, Fifth Avenue became a human sea of shop-keepers, laborers, clerks, tourists, children perched on their father's shoulders all straining to catch sight of their wildly popular leader. Hibernians passed by decked out in shamrocks and green ties, shirts, and hats, many unsteady from the drink, followed by bands from the police, fire, and sanitation departments, students hoisting school banners, stiff-legged Civil War veterans, soldiers, sailors, and marines, thirty thousand strong, flags flapping. The crowd became delirious as the fabled Rough Riders hove into view, the president at their head standing in an open touring car, the outsized teeth flashing, waving his silk top hat. An urchin perched on a fence yelled out, "Hooray for Teddy. Ain't he the real thing!," winning a playful shake of the presidential fist. TR eventually peeled off and headed for numbers six and eight East 76th Street where his niece was to be married in the adjoining brownstones of Eleanor's relatives, Mrs. E. Livingston Ludlow and the Parishes with whom she had lived after returning from Allenswood.

Franklin was determined to display the Roosevelt family crest, of dubious provenance, during the wedding ceremony. He had personally designed stickpins for the ushers based on the crest of the Prince of Wales, three feathers above a cluster of roses. The bridesmaids wore a three-feathers motif on their heads. Franklin had designed for Eleanor a gold pin, her initials in diamonds crowned by the three feathers, a piece she would wear all her life. To perform the ceremony he enlisted his old Groton headmaster, the Reverend Endicott Peabody. Alice Roosevelt had accepted Eleanor's invitation to be maid of honor, assuming the role as her due. She found Franklin's faux royalty touches, however, an embarrassment.

As Eleanor approached the improvised altar on her uncle's arm, "The Wedding March" could barely be heard above "The Wearing of the Green," pouring from thousands of Irish throats on nearby Fifth Avenue. No sooner had the vows been exchanged than TR, flashing his picket-fence grin, boomed, "Well Franklin there's nothing like keeping the name in the family." He then marched off to the library where refreshments were being served. A trickle of guests came up to congratulate the newlyweds, but most headed straight for the president, leaving the bride and groom standing alone. Resignedly, they joined the rim of spectators pressing around the president while TR spun one amusing tale after another until he left with the same flourish with which he had arrived. He had confirmed a favorite jest of his children: "Father always wanted to be the bride at every wedding and the corpse at every funeral."

The wedding had drawn all of glittering New York society, Vanderbilts, Livingstons, Astors, Jays, Van Rensselaers, Belmonts, and Mortimers. But one family, who in earlier circumstances would have fit the guest list easily, would not be there. Living in genteel poverty in the semi-fashionable Holland House apartments on West 46th Street were

Minnie Mercer, working in the interior decorating trade, and her daughters, Violetta, now sixteen, and Lucy, fourteen.

A carriage rolled past the tree-shaded drive from the Albany Post Road to the Hyde Park mansion, its windows ablaze with candles. Franklin and Eleanor mounted the steps to be greeted by a stern figure as rooted in his childhood as his own mother, Elspeth McEachern, the estate's venerable caretaker. Inside, birds perched motionless in glass cases along the walls, specimens that Franklin had shot, classified, and stuffed as a boy. Other than staff, the newlyweds had the house to themselves since Sara had temporarily vacated it for them. She sent a note that warmed the ever unsure Eleanor's heart: "Dear you were a perfect bride and I am very proud of both my dear children." Eleanor could now believe that she had been accepted into the fold.

After the marriage, on June 7, when he had finished his law courses at Columbia for the semester, he and Eleanor embarked on a three-month honeymoon to England, France, and Italy aboard the British liner *Oceanic*. Eleanor's initial terror of the sea was quickly dispelled. Previously miserable on the water, she did not get seasick. A relieved Franklin wrote his mother, "Eleanor has been a <u>wonderful</u> sailor and hasn't missed a single meal or <u>lost</u> any either." The bride reveled in unaccustomed pampering. She wrote Sara, "Franklin has been a wonderful maid & I've never been so well looked after." The only time when she was torn from her present idyll was when, in the course of a ship's tour, the socially conscious bride went belowdecks, smelled the stench, and saw the gray-faced passengers jammed into steerage.

While in England, Eleanor detected a disturbing sign; perhaps her young husband's gaze was not reserved for her alone. They had gone to the Lancashire estate of Sir Hugh and Lady Cholmley where two years before Franklin had made a modest play for the youngest daughter, Aline. Watching Franklin's attentions to this English rose, Eleanor found the two alarmingly familiar with each other. She sought to mask her instant dislike for Aline and her sisters by writing Sara that the Cholmley girls were so artificial the way they caked themselves in makeup.

The honeymooners arrived at Cortina, Italy, in the Dolomite Mountains where Franklin could barely wait to don hiking boots and climb the steeply rising trails. While hardly Eleanor's preference, she had gamely gone along. However, when Franklin excitedly laid out the next day's program, an early rise and an assault on the four-thousand-foot peak Falovia, Eleanor, still exhausted, demurred. With disquieting speed, Franklin found another companion, Kitty Gandy, a fellow hotel guest. Gandy was single, a New York hat maker, slightly older, and ages more worldly than Eleanor. She had caught Franklin's eye on the first night. He had introduced himself and they slipped into easy conversation, as Franklin gallantly lit her cigarettes. The next morning, wearing an extravagant chapeau of her own creation, Kitty set out with Franklin to scale Falovia. They were gone three hours during which an increasingly wretched Eleanor haunted the hotel lobby. She found separation from Franklin physically painful, a condition he clearly did not share. She later confessed that her husband's forays without her left her "jealous beyond description." Franklin returned with Kitty too late for lunch, bubbling with excitement over the natural wonders they had witnessed, plunging ravines, profusions of wildflowers, and brilliantly hued rock formations. Eleanor's attempts to feign polite interest flagged as she sank into a deep funk. She failed to improve the situation when she refused to attend a dance that evening in the hotel dining room, which did not deter Franklin from going. Her mood was scarcely improved when she erupted in a case of shingles, commonly provoked by stress.

On August 11, upon their arrival in Paris, Franklin checked his mail only to discover that he had flunked two law courses at Columbia, Pleading and Practice, not a disaster he concluded, since he still viewed the vocation of law with well-contained enthusiasm. Besides, he could always make up the courses in the coming fall semester. And, for these newlyweds, finding a livelihood was not a pressing necessity. Franklin had his inheritance income, though doled out by his mother, and Eleanor brought into the marriage her own $8,000 annual income, worth in current value some $160,000.

A veil of privacy conceals people's most intimate behavior, as long as neither party chooses to lift the veil. Thus we cannot know how Eleanor's or Franklin's initiation into physical love proceeded. We do know the advice she gave to her daughter as Anna approached her own marriage: "Sex, my dear, is something a woman must learn to endure." Obviously the mechanics at least succeeded since, upon the couple's return home in September, Eleanor was pregnant.

*Chapter 8*

# "DEAREST MUMMY"

. . . . . . .

O<small>N</small> O<small>CTOBER</small> 11, 1905, Eleanor received a letter from her mother-in-law that lifted her to rapture. It was her twenty-first birthday and Sara had written, "I pray that my precious Franklin may make you very happy and thank him for giving me such a dear loving daughter. I thank you also darling for being what you are to me already. This is straight from my heart. . . . With dear love and kisses and one more to grow on. Your devoted Mama." The letter seemed to say that Eleanor could finally step off the emotional roller coaster that her marriage had become, tossed as she was between the unanticipated vagaries of her husband and his mother. After five months of marriage, she had been forced to face unpleasant truths. What she had been starved for, affection, warmth, above all intimacy with a soul mate, were not to be found in Franklin. As she was later to conclude, "It became part of his nature not to talk to anyone of intimate things." Faced with conflict, anger, unpleasantness, embarrassment, their reactions were diametrically opposite. Eleanor's response was to retreat into hurt silence, what she called her "Griselda" moods, referring to the medieval legend of the wife who bore her husband's every cruelty and indignity without protest. His reaction was to brush off any contretemps with a quip, a laugh, a diversion, and he could not understand why his wife let life's tempests knock her flat. She would write, "I think one of my most maddening habits, which must infuriate all those who know me, is this habit, when my feelings are hurt or when I am annoyed of simply shutting up like a clam, not telling anyone what is the matter and being much too obviously humble and meek, feeling like a martyr and acting like one." In a novel Franklin began to write but never finished, he described the "Richards," presumably stand-ins for the Roosevelts. "If there is anything in the theory that husband and wife should be as different as possible from each other," he wrote, "the Richards disproved it, for Mrs. Richards was in a thousand ways a female counterpart of her husband." Did he actually see his marriage in that light, or was he expressing an unfulfilled ideal?

Eleanor had learned during the honeymoon that Franklin's seemingly unruffled surface masked roiling undercurrents. After nights aboard ship, charming fellow passengers with his facile repartee and scarcely missing a dance, he would go to bed only to wake up, thrashing about, grinding his teeth, muttering incomprehensibly as his suppressed emotions boiled to the surface. On one occasion he rose from his bed, sleepwalking, rattling the door noisily as if trying to escape. During these early months Eleanor found herself torn in two directions. As her grandson Curtis Roosevelt later put it, "My grandmother early on showed some extremely neurotic tendencies to be both dependent and rejecting of that dependency." The hinge upon which this vacillation swung was her mother-in-law. Her letters to Sara grew increasingly intimate from "Dear Mama," to "Dearest Mummy." As a pliant product of the Victorian age, she accepted her subordinate position in the Roosevelt hierarchy while, at the same time, she could feel this imperious woman draining her of self-confidence and diminishing her status as a mature, married woman.

While Franklin was still studying at Columbia Law School, the newlyweds had been living in a small furnished apartment that Sara had found and paid for in the Hotel Webster on West 45th Street. On their return from their honeymoon, they learned that she had again smoothed the wrinkles from their lives, leasing for them a four-story brownstone at 125 East 36th Street, three blocks from her latest city address, 200 Madison Avenue. The couple stepped into a house completely furnished to Sara's taste and staffed with servants she had hired. However normal the impulse of a young wife to want to build her own nest, Eleanor's shaky self-esteem offered no resistance to Sara's taking over. Instead she wrote of her mother-in-law's largesse, "Thank you so much for everything you did for us. You are just the sweetest, dearest Mama to your children." When a household decision had to be made, buying new curtains, for example, "Eleanor went to Mama, because she didn't believe she was capable," as one member of the family put it. As for Franklin, he saw little to complain about. His mother had always arranged everything, including paying his bills. Still, Eleanor's ambivalence occasionally broke through. Franklin's Aunt Jennie Delano lived nearby, and "When Eleanor became desperate about her mother-in-law," Jennie's daughter, Laura Delano, remembered, "she would take refuge with my mother, and after two hours with her Aunt Jennie she would say, 'I'm straightened out now' and go back. . . . Aunt Sallie was a narrow person, my mother broad."

While living on 36th Street the Roosevelts became parents for the first time with the arrival in May 1906 of the comely blue-eyed Anna. As in all realms of domesticity, Eleanor felt overwhelmed. One morning she put the baby to nap in a crib outside a window. The child began a ceaseless screaming that went on for two hours. Eleanor had read in a maternity manual that "A modern mother does not pick up a baby when it cries." Finally, an outraged neighbor called and threatened to report her to the Society for the Prevention of Cruelty to Children. Franklin remained patient, tender, and solicitous toward his wife, brushing aside her fears of inadequacy with dismissive good cheer. She had fulfilled his keenest desire: she had made him a father. She was now, affectionately, his "Babs," the name he would employ throughout their married life.

During his third year at Columbia Law, Franklin took the New York State Bar examination and passed. He saw no need to complete his unfinished courses for a degree, since he could now practice. Lewis C. Ledyard, a partner in the prestigious Wall Street law firm of Carter, Ledyard and Milburn, was well known to Sara. Ledyard was also commodore of the New York Yacht Club, to which Franklin belonged. With Sara paving the way, Franklin was taken on by Ledyard's firm as a law clerk. He hung out his shingle with his usual breezy aplomb. "I beg to call your attention to my unexcelled faculties for carrying on every description of legal business," he wrote to friends. "Unpaid bills a specialty. Briefs on the liquor question furnished free to ladies. Race suicides cheerfully prosecuted. Small dogs chloroformed without charge. Babies raised under advice of expert grandmother etc etc etc." He took his duties scarcely more seriously. After four years, still a law clerk, his career had plateaued. He defended some Harvard friends on drunk and disorderly charges, won an acquittal for a defendant accused of second degree assault, and, even given his love of the sea, enjoyed his admiralty law cases only marginally more than the others. Franklin's colleagues regarded him as a lightweight, existing in a suspended state of buoyant adolescence.

Though he had failed to catch fire in the legal profession, he thoroughly enjoyed the New York social scene. Besides the Yacht Club, he was a member of the Harvard and Knickerbocker clubs where he played poker into the small hours. To Eleanor, a husband who came home at dawn with the taint of liquor on his breath aroused shuddering memories of her father's road to ruin. She would say nothing, but sulked, which her fun-loving husband found incomprehensible.

Franklin at this stage did display one sign of ambition. Only a year after he had gone with Carter, Ledyard and Milburn, while passing an idle afternoon musing with his fellow law clerks about their futures, one of them, Grenville Clark, recalled Franklin "saying with engaging frankness that he wasn't going to practice law forever, that he intended to run for office at the first opportunity, and that he wanted to be and thought he had a very real chance to be President. . . . I remember that he described very accurately the steps which he thought could lead to his goal. They were: first, a seat in the State Assembly, then appointment as assistant secretary of the Navy, and finally the governorship of New York." The parallel to Teddy Roosevelt's route was transparent, down to Franklin's summation: "Anyone who is governor of New York has a good chance to be President with any luck." Though his colleagues were unimpressed by his legal acumen, Franklin had set his course with such serene reasonableness that Clark did not recall that "any of us deprecated his ambition or even smiled at it as we might perhaps have done. It seemed proper and sincere."

Franklin had laid out his life path, while Eleanor's destiny remained chained to the home. She had a second child, James, born barely a year and a half since the first. When she felt well enough, she toyed briefly with going back to settlement work where she had felt happy and useful. As her daughter, Anna, would later recall, "Granny quickly managed to dissuade her, because she knew how to appeal to her, which was on the basis that working in that kind of place, mother would be prone to bring diseases home to her children. . . . And mother accepted that. She didn't do it."

When the family stayed at Hyde Park, Sara sat at the head of the table at dinnertime with Franklin at the other end, leaving Eleanor to find a place alongside. Two comfortable armchairs flanked the fireplace, one for Sara and one for Franklin. Eleanor planted herself anywhere she could find a chair or on the floor. Apart from the bedroom, she had no space wholly her own. The situation was about to become even more constricting. While Franklin and Eleanor were still living at 36th Street, they received a note late in 1907 together with a rough sketch of a five-story townhouse. "A Christmas present to Franklin and Eleanor from Mama," Sara had written, "number and street not yet decided." The house was finished in 1908 and the address became 47 East 65th Street adjoining a twin brownstone that Sara had built for herself at number 49. Eleanor had not been allowed into the home until it was completed. Its conception, construction, and interior decoration had been kept solely in Sara's and Franklin's hands.

In an oral history conducted years later, the Roosevelts' son Elliott provided a sharply etched portrait of life at 47–49 East 65th Street.

> Inside the house, on every floor—the first floor level: in the dining room areas there was a door through, that my grandmother could come through if my mother was giving a dinner party and see how my mother was setting up the table and she could criticize. Then on the second floor, where they had the parlors, on one side my grandmother would entertain for tea, and on the other side my mother would entertain for tea. She never hesitated to open the door between the two and come in and join the tea, and as a rule she would sit down behind the tea tray and serve the tea and move my mother out of the position of being hostess in her own home. On the third floor she had a doorway cut through so that she could move easily between the bedrooms on the other floors and see whether mother was housekeeping correctly. So this was a constant, nagging problem for mother in her own development of her own household abilities from the earliest years.

A few weeks after moving into the house, Franklin came home to find his wife sobbing. This was not her home, she said. Nothing in it bore her touch. A baffled Franklin shook his head, told her she was quite mad, and left the room.

Summers meant the annual journey to Campobello Island, a six-hour train ride to Boston, another two separate legs by rail to Eastport, Maine, then a boat to the island, with never fewer than fifty trunks, pieces of luggage, and barrels shipped ahead. Here too Sara was mistress of all she surveyed, since the Campobello house belonged to her. Yet on this island, Eleanor was to experience unexpected liberation. A fellow summer neighbor, Mrs. Hartman Kuhn, had grown fond of Eleanor from previous visits and had detected her chafing at Sara's well-intended tyranny.

In her will, Mrs. Kuhn gave Sara first refusal on the purchase of her thirty-room gabled and shingled home next door for the bargain price of $5,000, provided she gave it to the young Roosevelts. In 1909 after Mrs. Kuhn's death, Sara, her sharp business instincts trumping her compulsion to control, snapped up the property. For the first time in her life, Eleanor had a home of her own. She regarded the privet hedges that separated her from Sara as a bulwark against unwanted intrusion. Campobello might often be cold, shrouded in fog, and buffeted by howling winds, but Eleanor loved the island. She reveled in tramping its rocky, wave-lashed coast, reading by the fire as the wind rattled the windows, standing on the porch with megaphone in hand trilling in her flutey voice, "Chilll-drennn!" She had been a woman drowning in dependence until, at Campobello at least, she surfaced into her own.

But summer must end. The fall found her back at the twin brownstones and pregnant again. Her third child, Franklin Jr., was born on March 18, 1909. At eleven pounds, he was, she believed, her most beautiful baby. But from his birth something was wrong. The infant remained listless, his complexion sallow. At age seven months, Franklin Jr. was diagnosed with heart trouble and died a month later. The loss plunged Eleanor into despair. Though three times a mother, she still felt inadequate, holding her children awkwardly, utterly dependent on the servants for their care. Reflecting on the loss of the latest child, she reproached herself, saying, "I even felt that I had not cared about him." Franklin, who had borne the loss of a namesake son stoically, tried with scant success to comfort his wife. "I was even a little bitter against my poor young husband," Eleanor recalled, "who occasionally tried to make me see how idiotically I was behaving." Within a month after the baby's death, she was pregnant again. She would give birth to Elliott, her fourth child in just over four years, on September 23, 1910. As a grown man, Elliott revealed what he had learned from his sister, Anna, about their mother's knowledge of reproduction. "When Sis was a young woman," he wrote, "Mother confided to her that she had gone into marriage totally ignorant of any method of contraception whatever. Not a single female relative had ever told her that ways and means were available to forestall pregnancy." If Franklin did possess such knowledge, he was disinclined to urge it on Eleanor since a numerous brood was just what he wanted.

*Chapter 9*

# PATRICIAN POLITICIAN

· · · · · · ·

JUST SIX YEARS AFTER Franklin had made the offhand boast to his fellow law clerks, his timetable was astonishingly on track. On a Friday afternoon in 1910, as he was sitting idly at his desk at Carter, Ledyard and Milburn waiting for the hour that would free him for a leisurely weekend at Hyde Park, a Dutchess County neighbor, Ed Perkins, popped in. Perkins, a banker and the Democratic county chairman, represented the upstate reform wing of the party, which was looking for new faces to break the downstate grip of Tammany Hall politicos. He and other Hudson Valley Democrats had been keeping an eye on Franklin Roosevelt and saw in him a winning combination, an attractive young man with the most famous political name in America and a rich mother who could bankroll a campaign. Would Franklin, Perkins asked, like to be the Democratic candidate for the 26th State Senate District, including three counties along the Hudson River, Dutchess, Putnam, and Columbia? They could talk the matter over on the train to Poughkeepsie, he suggested.

En route, Perkins laid out the attractions, a nomination for the asking, and the beginning of a political career that need not end in Albany. Perkins underplayed to this wealthy novice that the district was largely rural, probably had as many cows as citizens, and that its farmers voted overwhelmingly Republican. One of Perkins's fellow reformists had put the odds of Roosevelt or any Democrat taking the seat from the Republican Party at five to one against. Franklin told Perkins that he would have to discuss the matter with his mother, without mentioning any need to consult his wife. A frowning Perkins commented that potential supporters "won't like to hear that you had to ask your mother." Franklin decided to snap up the offer without further question.

He leaped into the fray as a man who had suddenly discovered his reason for being. He crisscrossed the district, popping out of a new red Maxwell touring car at cow pastures, gripping the calloused hands of astonished dairy farmers; meeting trains at every whistle stop on the New York Central Railroad; haunting bars, churches, and clambakes. He came across as an affable young squire genuinely concerned about the welfare of his tenants, much as his father had done while riding over his Hyde Park estate. He polished surefire lines. Referring to the former president, he would introduce himself saying, "I'm not Teddy," to appreciative guffaws. Then he would tell of "a little shaver who said to me the other day that he knew I wasn't Teddy. I asked him why and he replied, 'Because you don't show your teeth.'" He liked to tell how he had bought a round for the house in a tavern only to find out he had strayed out of his district into Connecticut. Reporters proclaimed a rising star. "Roosevelt is tall and lithe," one wrote. "With his handsome face and his form of supple strength, he could make a fortune on the stage and set the matinee girls' hearts throbbing."

To Eleanor the campaign added vicarious excitement to a life of indifferent child rearing. She sent a steady stream of encouragement to Franklin begging him to inform her of every detail of the campaign. He would, she knew, justify her faith in him from their courtship days. That November, she stood with Sara, aunts, uncles, and cousins in her grandmother's village of Tivoli where Franklin, hoarse-voiced but still electric, delivered his final speech of the race. A stranger to self-doubt, Franklin won, as he fully expected he would. His original timetable had called for election to the Assembly, but the State Senate was even more prestigious. He not only won, but ran well ahead of the Democratic candidate for governor and became only the second member of his party to take the Senate seat in the 26th District since the Civil War. His mother, who previously had found politics vulgar, who cringed when his plebeian new associates called her son "Frank," wrote to him of her pride at having "my boy sitting in the State Senate, a really fine and dignified position."

Two years later, in 1912, with a reputation for standing up to Tammany Hall and taking the underdog's side in legislative clashes between the poor and the powerful, Franklin looked forward eagerly to running for a second term. That July he received a letter that began, "Beloved and Revered Future President." The writer invited him to come to his home for a swim and some political strategizing. His correspondent was Louis

Howe, a reporter for the *New York Herald* whom Franklin knew casually as something of a character around "the shelf," the state capitol press room.

Howe's past was as ragged as Franklin's was unruffled. His father was a bookish, dreamy loser who had been wiped out in a real estate speculation and who then scraped together just enough capital to buy a profitless weekly, the *Sun*, published in the fashionable upstate racing and spa resort of Saratoga Springs. Here, Louis grew up, a puny child from birth, with a head too big for his body, jutting ears, a bulbous nose, and chronic asthma. Dreams of a Yale education faded along with the family's fortunes and instead Louis joined his father at the *Sun* as co-editor and part owner. Their joint management failed and he was reduced to working as a $10 a week part-time reporter for the new owners, who soon fired him.

Though hardly the stuff of maidenly dreams, Louis had a lively appreciation of women and managed to woo and win Grace Hartley, a rich man's daughter, well above his station. Through a marriage scarred by chronic squabbling and lengthy separations, the couple managed to produce four children. In 1906, at the age of thirty-five, Louis finally found some stability for his family, landing the job with the *Herald* in the paper's Albany bureau.

Physically, Louis Howe was a sight. The child's disproportionate body had followed him into adulthood, along with the asthma, bronchitis, and a bad heart. He was barely five feet tall and never weighed over a scrawny hundred pounds. As his hairline retreated, his already high forehead seemed to stretch halfway to the back of his skull, and the fringe of hair around the protruding ears was sparse and lank. As a boy he had been thrown headlong from a bicycle, his face scraping along the gravel, embedding bits of stone and dirt that were to remain for life so that he always looked unwashed. Though just forty-one at the time Louis wrote Franklin, he looked far older, his face leathery and deeply ravined, his cheeks sunken and crosshatched with wrinkles, the eyes bulging over baggy pouches, the mouth a mere slit pulled down at the corners. His suits were unpressed and frayed, his ties food-stained, his white shirts yellowish with the collars sagging and soiled. Though constantly coughing, he chain-smoked a cloying brand called Sweet Caporals, and usually spoke with a cigarette bobbing from his lower lip, the ashes cascading down his jacket. He had adopted a matching persona, tough-talking, hard-bitten, with a croaking voice and abrupt manner, the very model of a Grub Street journalist as Dickens might have portrayed him.

As he worked the halls of the statehouse, cornering legislators, lobbyists, and officials, he became obsessed with one towering ambition. He himself could never hope to succeed in an arena where charm and magnetism were requisites; but he could apply his brains and ambition to making a president. A canny Franklin Roosevelt looked beyond the messy gnome and saw in Louis Howe the seeds of political genius and a kindred soul. The prince and the frog spoke the same language, idealism camouflaged under a jaunty, wisecracking facade. They shared the same brand of humor. Howe's favorite exclamation of "Mein Gawd" was met by Franklin's salutation, "Lieber Ludwig." Franklin made Louis his manager for the 1912 reelection campaign, though a bout of typhoid fever prevented Roosevelt from rising from his sickbed. However, with Louis in charge, Franklin won in a walk.

The rest of the family was hardly as taken with Howe as was his boss. Eleanor expressed herself as "very disapproving." To Sara, this strange creature was beyond the pale. Daughter Anna recalled, "I took my cue from an early age from my . . . grandparent and parent who couldn't stand Louis Howe. So I decided I couldn't stand Louis Howe. So for years all of us thought that Louis Howe was a kind of nuisance, you know. We would joke about him and make rude remarks about him."

In 1908, Theodore Roosevelt had made the first of two blunders that would haunt him all his life. The first was to respect the two-term tradition and let the Republican nomination, and ultimately the presidency, fall to William Howard Taft, TR's secretary of war. The second occurred when, disappointed with Taft's retreat from Roosevelt progressivism and hungering to recapture the power he had so ebulliently wielded, TR ran as the third-party Bull Moose candidate, splitting the Republican vote and handing the election to the Democrat, New Jersey's governor, Woodrow Wilson, a man whom TR despised. All of which turned out fortunately for Franklin Roosevelt. Before the election, in the summer of 1912, Franklin, as a state senator, had gone to the Democratic Party's national convention in Baltimore where Wilson was nominated. While making the rounds of endless parties, slapping backs, and cutting deals, Franklin found himself approached by a short, paunchy, older figure in a wrinkled white suit and string tie who addressed him in a rich Southern drawl. His fellow Democrat was Josephus Daniels, publisher of the Raleigh, North Carolina, *News and Observer,* who served as Wilson's press and public relations adviser. Daniels was instantly taken with the young man towering elegantly over him and remembered of that meeting, "I thought he was as handsome a figure of an attractive young man as I have ever seen. At that convention Franklin and I became friends—a case of love at first sight."

After Wilson was elected, a politician as ambitious as Franklin Roosevelt was unlikely to remain long in Albany as chairman of the State Senate's Agriculture Committee. Before the first month of his second term had passed, Franklin received a telegram inviting him to a conference in the president-elect's office in Trenton to discuss political appointments. He found the initial offers uninviting and bided his time. In the meantime Josephus Daniels became Wilson's surprise choice for secretary of the navy. Daniels had expected to be appointed postmaster general. The soon-to-be master of the world's third largest fleet was a pacifist and his wife found his appointment hilarious.

With his mother and Eleanor in tow, Franklin was in Washington for Wilson's March 4 inauguration. While milling about the jammed lobby of the Willard Hotel, he spotted Daniels and came over to congratulate him on his appointment as navy secretary. Daniels warmly shook the hand of the man who had so impressed him in Baltimore the summer before. He was direct; he asked Roosevelt, "How would you like to come to Washington as assistant secretary of the Navy?" To Franklin, enamored of the sea, ever aware of the trajectory that had propelled Theodore Roosevelt into the White House, Daniels's offer seemed heaven-sent. Echoing TR, he answered, "I'd like it bully well." The post would, he said, "please me better than anything in the world. All my life I have loved ships and have been a student of the Navy, and the assistant secretaryship is the one place I would love to hold." He resigned his seat in the State Senate with Tammany Hall happy to see the back of Franklin Roosevelt.

March 17, 1913, was the Roosevelts' eighth wedding anniversary, the first that Franklin spent away from Eleanor and the day he was sworn in as assistant secretary of the navy. Immediately afterward he went to his new office, found the imposing official stationery with four stars circling an anchor in the letterhead. "My own dear Babbie," he wrote, "I didn't know till I sat down at this desk that this is the 17th of happy memory. . . . My only regret is that you could not have been here with me, but I am thinking of you." He next wrote to his mother in his usual airy fashion, "I am baptized, confirmed, sworn and vaccinated—and somewhat at sea!" Sara wrote back how proud she was that he had assumed "a very big job," and advised him in so elevated a position, "Try not to write your signature too small."

Josephus Daniels wrote in his diary of his new assistant, "His distinguished cousin TR went from that place to the presidency. May history repeat itself."

## Chapter 10

# THE SOCIAL SECRETARY

· · · · · · ·

ELEANOR WAS GROWING ANXIOUS. As soon as Franklin had received his federal appointment in 1913, she sought help from Aunty Bye, the family's pillar of good sense, a seasoned Washington hand, and who, as a girl, had turned down Franklin's father's proposal of marriage. Aunty Bye, of the curved spine and stumpy stature, had stunned the family when, at nearly forty, she married a portly, older Navy commander, William Sheffield Cowles. She gave birth to a son, William Jr., at age forty-three. What this redoubtable woman said carried weight in family councils. Her niece Alice said of her, "If Aunty Bye had been a man, she would have been president." Eleanor's first question to her aunt was, "Will you tell me if there are any people I ought to call on at once. I don't know a soul in Washington & am afraid of all kinds of stupid mistakes." She must first master the ritual of afternoon calls, her aunt advised. Protocol demanded that the spouse of a newly arrived high-ranking government official call upon the wives of other prominent men in the government. Aunty Bye explained that if Eleanor was lucky, the woman called upon would be out, in which case she need only leave her card. If, however, the wife were in, Eleanor must visit for a respectable interlude. Some hostesses, having nothing better to do, stayed home, and took note of callers who merely left their card without inquiring if they were in, then crossed them off their invitation lists. Further, the new arrival was expected to set aside one day a week when she herself would be at home waiting to greet an unknowable number of callers.

Solving another pressing problem, Aunty Bye owned a four-story brick home at 1733 N Street, which she offered to rent to her favorite niece and nephew. The house was ideal, large enough for the three Roosevelt children, governess, nurse, chauffeur, and four live-in servants to cook, clean, and do laundry. For Franklin the address was only a brisk five-block walk down Connecticut Avenue to his office in the State, War, and Navy Building next to the White House. Adding to its attraction, 1733 N Street was a house with a history. While Aunty Bye's brother, TR, had been president, he used her home as a salon where he could meet privately with politicians, journalists, writers, and artists. His daughter Alice recalled, "We all used to go there for Sunday evening tea. . . . It was delightful! I don't know how many people he would meet there."

Eleanor was already familiar with the house from girlhood visits. Everything about it spoke of solidity, like the people who were to inhabit it. The furniture was made of sturdy maple, the windows hung with heavy drapes, and carved mantels adorned numerous tiled fireplaces. Large windows in the rear opened onto a garden bordered by a rose arbor. The Roosevelts moved in effortlessly as Franklin made the house his own, shipping from Hyde Park his nautical prints, ship models, books, stamp collection, and family photos.

Making the social calls proved more daunting than Eleanor had expected, threatening to swallow up her life. Nearly every afternoon she set out with a list of twenty to thirty calls to be made that day. If the wife was in, Eleanor would timidly introduce herself and try to limit the visit to six minutes of torturous small talk. She wrote a friend, "I've made 60 calls in Washington this week and been to a luncheon at the Marine barracks. . . . I've received one long afternoon next to Mrs. Daniels until my feet ached. . . . We've been out to dinner every night." After six weeks she had covered the president, vice president, the cabinet, Supreme Court justices, members of the New York congressional delegation, ambassadors, military attachés, and still she was not done. She reported to Aunty Bye, "I'm trying to keep up with my calls, but it's quite strenuous." As she later remembered those days, "Nearly all the women at that time were slaves of the Washington social system," and she felt grudging admiration for the handful with the courage to break free. One was her cousin Alice, married since 1906 to Nicholas Longworth, at this point a recently defeated congressman who would come back a year later and rise to great power. Her cousin was, as Eleanor put it, "quite frankly too much interested in the political questions of the day to waste her time calling on women who were, after all, not important to her scheme of life. . . . She wanted to know the interesting people but did not want to be bored doing uninteresting things." Eleanor recognized that she lacked her cousin's cheeky independence. "I was appalled" by it, she said, but "I was perfectly certain that I had nothing to offer of an individual nature and that my only chance of doing my duty as the wife of a public official was to do exactly as the majority of women were doing." She continued to reel under "tedious afternoon upon afternoon, loaded down by a carful of children, leaving calling cards at the home of other official families," followed by evenings of dining out or having guests in. Eleanor realized she was going under and desperately needed help.

The Mercers, mother and daughters, had left New York and were living back in Washington. Before their return, Minnie had managed one last step on the way to preparing the girls for polite society, a year at a finishing school abroad, though they were a bit old, with Violetta now twenty and Lucy eighteen. They returned to their mother and subsequently made the move to Washington. The Mercer marriage initially seemed mended. The gossip sheet *Town Topics* reported, "Mrs. Mercer has forgiven Carroll. . . . All goes merry as a marriage bell." In truth, no reconciliation had taken place nor ever would.

Minnie, still hard-pressed to support the family, took a job with an art gallery in Northwest Washington where she was to advise newcomers seeking refinement in the decoration of their homes. As in New York, she managed to live in genteel if hardly opulent circumstances, renting an apartment in the Decatur at 2131 Florida Avenue NW. She also enjoyed a desperately needed windfall. Another of Carroll's relatives undertook to see that the withering branch of the family survived, and a modest remittance arrived regularly and anonymously through an out-of-town law firm. Minnie, however, still could not support her daughters and herself in anything approaching style. No help could be expected from her husband. Stouter, grayer, his old spark faded, Carroll drifted from one Washington address to another, at times boarding with wealthy friends from palmier days, who, according to *Town Topics*, "stood between the wolf and the sadly changed gallant." Once a leader of the Riding Club, he now worked there as manager, but no longer a member. He was sick, plagued by Bright's disease and diabetes, aggravated by heavy drinking. His daughters visited Carroll from time to time, but Minnie never. Nor did she ever divorce him. Violetta, deemed the more practical of the sisters, went into the utilitarian career of nursing. Lucy sporadically helped her mother. A niece was one day to say of Lucy, "My aunt was not really trained to work." Nevertheless, at this point in the Mercer fortunes, Lucy had to find a job.

Eleanor Roosevelt badly needed help and once again Aunty Bye came to the rescue. Bye moved in Washington circles where the Mercers had once shone. The fights between Carroll and Minnie and their financial ruin had long been grist for the local gossip mill, thus Bye was fully aware of the family's straitened circumstances. Consequently, she knew exactly who Eleanor needed, the Mercers' daughter Lucy. Her parents had been founders of Washington's Cave Dweller aristocracy and the girl thus knew local society inside out. Her appearance was more than pleasing, she spoke beautifully, and had retained an innate dignity unaffected by her family's downfall. Lucy Mercer would possess perfect pitch in handling the social obligations of the wife of the assistant secretary of the navy.

To Minnie, the prospect of her daughter's employment as a social secretary to a prominent Washington family helped soothe her battered ego. The position was hardly that of a common domestic. A social secretary could be the nearest thing to the society hostess Minnie herself had once been. Furthermore, a Mercer need not feel subservient working for the assistant navy secretary's wife. Minnie and her daughters were still registered socialites and, in the Washington pedigree pecking order, a notch above the Roosevelts.

Late in the year, with a busy holiday season bearing down on her, Eleanor invited Lucy to interview for the job. Miss Mercer left the Decatur apartments on foot and walked past the grand home at 1761 N Street where her family had lived in loftier times, just a few doors from the Roosevelts' current address. The two women hit it off comfortably, speaking the same language and displaying the manners of their class. Eleanor made no secret of her desperation. As she later described the situation, "I tried at first to do without a secretary, but found that it took me such endless hours to arrange my calling list, and answer and send invitations." To Eleanor, the job applicant was obviously a lady to her fingertips. Lucy for her part found 1733 N Street homey chaos, the floors treacherous with toys, racquets, golf clubs, with umbrellas leaning in corners, jackets of all sizes hung from hall trees, and servants scurrying about. The children clearly had the run of the house and, as one visitor remembered, "the young Roosevelts had not been taught to blow their noses or just did not care to blow them." The two women quickly reached an arrangement: Lucy would come in three mornings and be paid $30 a week.

The duties of a social secretary were amorphous. As one woman who held the position for another prominent family described her day, along with managing her mistress's social calendar, she might expect to "air the dog and wash the baby." Lucy would arrive in the morning and because she had no desk, sit on the living room floor, engulfed by invitations, letters, bills, and any paperwork that demanded Eleanor's attention. Though new to the working world, she was in familiar waters and from the start handled her job with effortless competence, scheduling Eleanor's calls for that day, checking off those already made, accepting or declining invitations, and paying bills. To the Roosevelt children, she quickly became a familiar and welcome member of the household. Anna recalled, "When I was ten or eleven I remember feeling happy and admiring when I was greeted one morning at home by Miss Lucy Mercer. . . . I knew that I liked her warm and friendly manner and smile."

Franklin Roosevelt saw Lucy Mercer for the first time as she was arriving for work one morning and he was leaving home for his stroll down Connecticut Avenue to his office. He met a young woman not as tall as Eleanor, but five feet nine inches, who bore herself with the same regal assurance as his mother. Her hair was light brown, almost blond, thick and swept up in the Victorian style. Her milky complexion was set off by softly gazing blue eyes containing a hint of mystery. As a lifelong friend described Lucy, "I think she was the most beautiful woman I ever saw. It was a beauty the artist and photographer didn't catch. Her beauty was in her expression and in her graceful manner." On their first meeting, Lucy greeted her employer's husband with a smile that another friend described as unconsciously beguiling.

The man Lucy met was then thirty-one, dressed in a high-collared shirt, English-tailored suit, and handmade shoes. As a Washington newspaperman described the assistant secretary of the navy, "The face was particularly interesting. Breeding showed there, cleanly cut features, a small, sensitive mouth, tiny lines running from nostrils to the outline of his lips, broad forehead, close cropped brown hair, frank blue eyes, but above all the straight, upstanding set of the head placed on the man." An early Washington friend of Franklin's, Nigel Law, third secretary at the British embassy, described him as "the most attractive man whom it was my good fortune to meet during my four years in America." The only touch subtracting slightly from a picture of manly vigor was the pince-nez he wore to correct myopia. A pince-nez, however, had not slowed Uncle Ted's meteoric rise and President Wilson wore one too. Along with the startling good looks, the man radiated virility and on their first meeting turned his blinding smile on Miss Mercer. On their subsequent morning encounters, Franklin took to greeting his wife's secretary with, "Ah, the lovely Lucy."

Franklin was particularly pleased to have become the youngest assistant secretary of the navy in the nation's history, giving him a slight edge in the timetable he had set for himself alongside Uncle Ted's trajectory. He began his work with a boss who seemed his polar opposite. With his courtly manners and small-town mores, Daniels was a figure out of the departed nineteenth century while Franklin was a man of the emerging twentieth century. The short, soft, rotund secretary, who loathed physical exercise, was dwarfed by his aristocratically slender subordinate of whom the Yale football coach, Walter Camp, observed, "Mr. Roosevelt is a beautifully built man with the long muscles of the athlete."

The division of labor between superior and subordinate appeared, on the surface, to be clear-cut. The secretary was responsible for the operation of the fleet, while the assistant secretary was to handle supplies, purchasing, shore duty sailors, and civilian employees. Franklin saw the boundary as one to be breached rather than observed. From the outset, he lobbied for a more powerful Navy, one matching the Great White Fleet that Uncle Ted had sent around the world in 1907. All of which made him immensely popular with the admirals, who found the landlubber Daniels—who insisted on "left and right" over "port and starboard," "wall" over "bulkhead," and "floor" over "deck"—less credible as the leader of the American Navy. The teetotaling, populist secretary won little affection by banning alcohol from the officers' mess.

As puzzling as Daniels initially was to Navy professionals, they embraced Franklin from the start. To board a man-of-war, his white, four-starred flag of office waving from the mast, to stand on the open bridge while the winds of Chesapeake Bay lashed his face and tousled his hair, was the fulfillment of his boyhood dreams. Raised on sea stories told by his grandfather Warren Delano, he had once hoped to become a naval officer, but was blocked by parents who couldn't bear to lose him to long separations at sea. He nevertheless had become an accomplished sailor and few victories in life gave him greater pleasure than his experience aboard the destroyer USS *Flusser*. He had looked forward to sailing the vessel to Campobello Island, dropping anchor off its coast, and impressing his summer neighbors by coming ashore in the captain's launch. But first the *Flusser* had to pass through the narrow strait separating Maine from the island. Franklin told the skipper, Lieutenant William F. Halsey Jr., that he wanted to take the ship through the strait himself. Halsey was uneasy. A warship was not a sailboat. Any misstep threatening his vessel's safety could sink Halsey's career. Franklin insisted, claiming that he knew these waters well. Halsey was later to say, "As Mr. Roosevelt made his first turn, I saw him look aft and check the swing of our stern. My worries were over; he knew his business." Halsey would later become a favorite FDR admiral in World War II.

Friends had warned Daniels that Roosevelts expected to dominate and at times it seemed to the secretary that with Franklin as a subordinate, he was sitting atop a volcano. Twenty years older than his assistant, Daniels developed toward Franklin a father's mingled feelings of pride, affection, and occasional exasperation toward a gifted son who was at times too clever by half. It fazed Franklin not at all to let a major contract for constructing barracks on his own, and then after the project was completed to go to Daniels for permission. Nor did he, in private, show particular respect for his chief, doing dead-on impersonations of Daniels's fussy ways and drawling speech for his socialite friends, referring to him as "the funniest looking hillbilly I had ever seen." Daniels, as Franklin may have missed initially, was no hayseed. He was a country slicker with the self-confidence to hire a subordinate who might be smarter than he was.

When Franklin first began striding down the Navy Department corridors with an untidy runt trailing in his wake, the usually admiring secretaries stared in surprise. Franklin had brought Louis Howe to Washington as his "special assistant," to act as trouble-shooter and red tape slasher. In the assistant secretary's meetings with gold-braided, beribboned admirals, Howe sat in the back of the room puffing his Sweet Caporals, saying little and quietly calculating how these splendid figures could be made useful to Franklin Roosevelt. Repatching his marriage once again, Louis had brought Grace and his children to live in Washington. Eleanor excluded them from her social circle. Franklin nevertheless frequently dragged Louis to 1733 N Street to work at home, where the children regarded him as a smelly little intruder. This unlovely man still had an eye for an attractive woman and did not fail to notice the comeliness of Eleanor's new secretary, Miss Mercer.

No one encouraged Franklin more, in his impatient ambition, than Louis. When out of town, Franklin wrote, "Lieber Ludwig, Hier bin ich mit grosse gesundheit and very gnugen, which when translated means I feel like a whole flock of fighting cocks." Franklin had been in the Navy Department just over a year when he and Howe began plotting his next rung up the political ladder. A U.S. Senate election was to take place in New York in 1914. Based on Franklin's past experience in Albany with Tammany Hall, he and Howe could not imagine that the machine would put up a respectable candidate. Surely Franklin could beat their hack in a Democratic primary. Late in the game he decided to enter the contest. But Tammany trumped him. Instead of a stooge, the organization chose a distinguished former ambassador to Germany, James W. Gerard, who trounced Franklin, winning the support of two thirds of New York's counties. Franklin and Louis had learned a priceless lesson: impetuous, impatient candidates unbacked by a solid organization fare poorly even if the name is Roosevelt, as Uncle Ted had learned two years before when his Bull Moose bid succeeded only in putting Woodrow Wilson into the White House. The mistakes of the Senate race were never to be repeated.

At the Navy Department, Franklin, for the first time in his life, had become a salaried employee, earning $5,000 per annum. Every two weeks a Navy chief delivered his pay to him in cash. "I don't know where it went, it just went," he told an associate. "I couldn't keep an account with myself. And after about six months of this, certain complaints came from back home about paying the grocery bill. And so I began taking my salary by check and putting it in the bank." Eventually handling this checking account and paying the bills for the profligate Franklin was Lucy Mercer.

*Chapter 11*

# EVERY MAN WHO KNEW HER
# FELL IN LOVE

· · · · · · ·

$A$T THE TIME Eleanor engaged Lucy Mercer, late in 1913, she was in the early stages of yet another pregnancy. The following summer, the family, initially without Franklin, followed the ritual return to Campobello. When her time approached, Eleanor intended to summon the New York gynecologist, Dr. Albert H. Ely, who had delivered her four earlier children. Franklin was briefly up from Washington when Eleanor came banging on his door telling him that her labor had started. He shouted for the crew of the *Half Moon* to make ready and sailed to the mainland where he conscripted a country doctor, Eben Bennett, who delivered Franklin Jr. on August 17, the second son to bear that name. The four years between Elliott's and Franklin Jr.'s birth had been the longest that Eleanor had been free of the burdens of pregnancy. Abstinence, if adopted as her method of birth control, was not uncommon in a period when state law and the Roosevelts' Episcopal Church banned the use of contraceptives. Eleanor's revered Uncle Ted had described devices to thwart conception as "race suicide." Not surprisingly, it was TR's headstrong daughter Alice who made it her business to learn about contraception. A sister-in-law, Nan Wallingford, who already had three children, wrote Alice begging her for "one of those labor-saving devices" so that she might save her "tottering reason." When Franklin and Eleanor made occasional visits to Hyde Park, a newly added wing afforded them the privacy of separate bedrooms.

No evidence exists in the first years of Lucy Mercer's employment that Franklin saw the social secretary as anything more than a competent adornment to the Roosevelt domestic staff. His only written reference to her existence, and then in her subservient role, occurred in the spring of 1914. Eleanor was staying at Hyde Park, with the children. Franklin had just gone back to N Street and wrote her, "Arrived safely and came to the house and [the chauffeur] telephoned Miss Mercer who later came and cleaned up . . . dinner alone at 7:30."

During that summer, Franklin's mind was preoccupied with the global repercussions of two pistol shots that had rung out on June 28 on the other side of the world. Gavrilo Princip, an impoverished nineteen-year-old revolutionary committed to prying Bosnia's Slav provinces from Austria and delivering them to Serbia, had assassinated the Austrian Archduke Franz Ferdinand and his wife, beginning the world's slide into calamity. Within a month Austria declared war on Serbia. Germany pledged her support to Austria, and Russia mobilized to back Serbia, its Slavic cousin. When Russia refused to demobilize, Germany declared war on her. A web of treaties then drew France, Belgium, and Great Britain into the war allied with Russia against Germany and Austria. By August 6, the world's major powers were locked into what the British foreign minister, Sir Edward Grey, described as "the greatest catastrophe that has ever befallen the continent of Europe."

Franklin had just returned from Campobello aboard a Navy destroyer when he learned of the Austrian declaration of war on Serbia. He wrote Eleanor, "A complete smash up is inevitable and there are a great many problems for us to consider." Now, sixteen months into the job as assistant secretary, he chafed under what he considered Josephus Daniels's sluggish response to the upheaval. He next wrote Eleanor, "I am running the real work, though Josephus is here! He is bewildered by it all, very sweet but very sad." Eleanor responded loyally, "To understand the present gigantic conflict, one must have at least a glimmering of understanding of foreign nations and their histories," and added, "I can see you managing everything while J.D. wrings his hands in horror."

The majority of Americans saw the war as Europe's folly and their neutrality as an isle of sanity in a sea of madness. Not Franklin; he foresaw "the greatest war in human history" and wanted America at the side of the allies to defeat German militarism. "To my astonishment on reaching the Dept.," he again wrote Eleanor, "nobody seemed the least bit excited about the European crisis. Mr. Daniels feeling chiefly very sad that his faith in human nature and civilization, and similar, idealistic nonsense was receiving a rude shock. So I started in alone to get things ready and prepare plans for what ought to be done by the Navy. . . . These dear people like W.J.B. [Secretary of State William Jennings Bryan] have as much conception of what a general European war means as Elliott has of higher mathematics." He arranged, on his own hook, to advise President Wilson about how the Navy must prepare. Wilson's concern at this point, however, was fixed on the condition of Ellen, his wife of twenty-nine years, who was on her deathbed. Roosevelt's frustration mounted after Germany's U-boat 20 sank the Cunard liner *Lusitania* on May 7, 1915, with 124 Americans among the death toll of 1,198. Franklin practically gagged when Wilson, three days after the attack, still sought to steer America clear of the war by declaring in a speech in Philadelphia that "There is such a thing as a man being too proud to fight. There is such a thing as a nation being so right that it does not need to convince others by force that it is right."

For the next two years Franklin worked tirelessly, both openly and covertly, to prepare the Navy for a war he considered inevitable. He slipped information regarding U.S. preparedness to the pro-war TR, Wilson's arch-nemesis. Louis Howe fed tidbits to the press and Congress, hinting that the right man for the number one position in the Navy Department at such a time was the man currently stalled in the number two spot. Josephus Daniels, with saintly forbearance, neither criticized nor checked his nakedly ambitious, often condescending subordinate.

Lucy Mercer had begun moving beyond scheduler and bill payer, occasionally becoming part of the Roosevelts' social circle. In 1915 she began to appear in the "Dinner Record" Eleanor kept. In November of that year she was seated with the French ambassador, Jules Jusser, and Assistant Secretary of State William Phillips, both charmed by the poise and easy conversation of this attractive single woman. The next month Eleanor arranged a dinner party for Franklin's boss, Secretary Daniels, and Joseph Davies, years later to be FDR's ambassador to the Soviet Union. Again Lucy was the extra woman as she would be repeatedly given Eleanor's complete trust in her social graces.

Within eleven months of the birth of Franklin Jr., Eleanor was pregnant again, and gave birth to another son, christened John, on March 13, 1916. According to family accounts, that was enough for her. Her son Elliott has claimed that after John was born, "Mother had performed her austere duty in marriage, and five children were testimony to that. She wanted no more." Anna has said that her mother confided to her, "that was the end of any marital relationship." She had produced what Franklin wanted, as many children as Uncle Ted.

If Franklin had been shut off from conjugal relations at home, where, one wonders, would a virile thirty-four-year-old man seek relief? Long gone was the spindly "feather duster," the "Miss Nancy" of his Harvard years. A journalist, after interviewing Franklin in his Navy Department office, declared him an "engaging picture of American manhood." Aunty Bye called him "My debonair young cousin," and her husband, the admiral, told him, "the girls will spoil you soon enough, Franklin." One Washington hostess described him as the most desirable man she had ever known, and another marveled, "I had no idea that the Democratic Party ever recruited that type of person." His son Elliott would later offer this description: "Men and women alike were impressed by the sheer physical magnetism of Father. On meeting anyone, the first impression he gave was of abounding energy and virility. He would leap over a rail rather than open a gate, run rather than walk. The coach at the early-morning exercise classes which Father attended with a young group of other government officials said he was muscled like an athlete. Old ladies maneuvered to have him take them to dinner. Young women sensed the innate sexuality of the self-confident assistant secretary, who liked to work at his desk in shirt sleeves."

Franklin reciprocated the interest. "Nothing is more pleasing to the eye than a good-looking lady, nothing more refreshing to the spirit than the company of one," he told a friend. Twenty-seven years later, while president, he reminisced to his assistant, William Hassett, about a moment indelibly etched in his memory. As Hassett recorded the conversation, "Something set the President talking about a bronze statue he saw at the San Francisco exposition which he visited as assistant secretary of the Navy. It was set in the foreground of an elaborate and artistically devised peristyle and represented a young girl, beautiful in form and feature, petite and posed most impressively in a kneeling attitude, the hands of great delicacy, the curve of the neck and shoulders being exceedingly graceful. It was, the President said, a conception of youthful, feminine beauty and spirituality which had always lingered in his mind." Roosevelt would eventually acquire the statue.

When Franklin did escape his desk on weekends he played as hard as he worked. "I have been spending the whole day at Chevy Chase, 18 holes in the morning," he wrote an absent Eleanor, "lunch and 18 holes more." Despite his commitment to the work of the department, some associates still found a superficiality in the man. William Phillips recalled, "I knew him then as a brilliant, lovable, and somewhat happy-go-lucky friend. I doubt if it ever occurred to any of us that he had the makings of a great President."

Among Franklin's earliest work-hard–play-hard companions was the British diplomat Nigel Law. Law, eight years Franklin's junior, a product of Eton and Cambridge, had arrived in the capital in November 1914 aboard the *Lusitania* the year before the ship met its end. He was sharing bachelor quarters with other Britons on H Street when he and Franklin became friends. Law, as a bachelor, lived a style that well suited the extroverted American. His diary is peppered with "dined with Franklin," and "F dined with us." They frequented the Metropolitan Club, sailed on the Navy yacht *Sylph,* and spent time at a favorite watering hole, the Lock Tavern on the Potomac. They squeezed in hiking and swimming between twelve-hour workdays. Franklin would later describe the tenor of these times as "the saloon, the salon and the Salome." Josephus Daniels's son, Jonathan, who would one day write about Franklin, told a colleague, "I have my doubts about any of the guesses of psychiatrists that FDR was 'never very active sexually.' He certainly kept Eleanor steadily pregnant before 1915. . . . I'm suspicious of all such psychiatric judgments."

On a Monday morning in mid-August 1916, Franklin was annoyed to learn that his prized automobile had been wrecked by his chauffeur, Henry Golden. He told Louis Howe to find out what had happened. The married Golden had taken a fancy to another woman, Howe reported, and had secretly commandeered his employer's flashy car to impress his girlfriend. He was also drinking heavily, "with the usual highballs to prove oneself 'a good fellow,' " Howe noted. During a joy ride on Sunday night he had rolled the car over, breaking his leg and injuring other passengers. Howe's report included his customary tart touch. Golden's "anxiety as to whether his wife knew about the girl is a good sign. No man is beyond redemption if he don't want his wife to find out." Franklin paid

Golden's medical bills, then fired him. Eleanor was at Campobello when Franklin wrote her, "I think our nice Golden has been a weak, miserable wretch." He had already suspected the chauffeur of cheating him with inflated gas and repair bills. Eleanor wrote back commiserating over a loss that she knew upset Franklin, then added, "Isn't it horrid to be disappointed in someone. . . . it makes one so suspicious." The subtext in Eleanor's reply is the pessimism she attached to a fairly mundane matter. It was likely at that point that she had begun to have suspicions about a husband who was so attractive, so sought after by other women and so obviously pleased by their attentions.

The Lucy Mercer who had entered Franklin's orbit shared certain qualities with Eleanor. Both were tall, with abundant hair, translucent complexions, blue-eyed, bosomy, and well bred. There the similarities ended. Lucy was far more appealing. Her teeth did not protrude, her chin did not recede, as did Eleanor's, most noticeably in profile. Lucy's posture was regal while Eleanor's was stooped. She had a velvety, soothing voice, while Eleanor's was high-pitched, flutey, with every word, no matter how banal, seemingly freighted with meaning. When stressed her voice turned shrill. Lucy was poised while Eleanor was insecure. She was vivacious, Eleanor earnest. Elliott later recalled his mother as having "something of a schoolmarm's air about her." Lucy saw the humor in life. Eleanor usually failed to recognize humor. Within her means, Lucy was invariably chic. Eleanor was oblivious of fashion, choosing the sensible over the stylish. Eleanor was overwhelmed by five rambunctious children whom Lucy handled easily. But as Eleanor's daughter, Anna, remembered her mother, "She tried, you always felt that she was doing her darndest to do the right thing by her children. Including dutifully saying their evening prayers with them." As Eleanor herself later admitted, "It did not come naturally to understand little children or to enjoy them." She still bore the scars of her own blighted early years, remembering, "play had not been an important part of my own childhood."

Eleanor had to contend continuously with an interfering mother-in-law while Sara Roosevelt wrote of Lucy, "Miss Mercer . . . is so sweet and adores you, Eleanor." Lucy understood Franklin's need to be indulged at home, not hectored, to be recharged, not drained. She knew innately how to feed a man's ego, to make him feel significant, the king of his castle. In a contrasting example, Eleanor was having breakfast one morning with Franklin and their friends the Phillipses and she asked Franklin if he had received a certain letter. He admitted he had. Shouldn't he answer it? He agreed. Shouldn't he answer it right away? Wearily he left his guests to write a reply.

Lucy Mercer may have lacked the ravishing beauty of her mother. She was not overtly sensuous yet radiated an ethereal appeal. As a cousin put it, "Every man who ever knew her fell in love with her." Most perilous to the Roosevelt marriage, between trips to Hyde Park and Campobello, Eleanor was often absent while Lucy continued to report to N Street.

With the arrival of baby John in March 1916, five children and a houseful of servants began to strain the capacity of 1733 N Street. Franklin informed Aunt Bye, regrettably, that the Roosevelts must have more space. "I hate to feel you will no longer be at 1733," Bye wrote, "as it always gave me a homey sensation." In the fall of 1916 the family moved four blocks uptown to the roomier 2131 R Street. One of its attractions was again that husband and wife could have separate bedrooms. Lucy Mercer followed the Roosevelts to the new address.

The moment when the relationship between Franklin and Lucy shifted from employer and employee to two people "very much in love," as Lucy's cousin and confidante Elizabeth Cotten described them, remains uncertain. From the beginning, as their paths crossed in the early months of her employment, as Franklin turned his charm on to high voltage, as one observer put it, she came to "hero-worship" Franklin Roosevelt. The attraction had been immediate but in the case of a married man and a single, proper employee, was probably resisted initially by both parties. But by mid-1916 at least attraction had ripened into a love affair.

*Chapter 12*

# THE EXTRA WOMAN

· · · · · · ·

WASHINGTON IN THE SUMMER was near unendurable. The heat descended as soon as the sun rose and still baked the city as night fell. In the days before air conditioning, the capital was reportedly rated a tropical post entitling diplomats to a hardship supplement. Campobello, the Roosevelt family retreat, now became almost a matter of survival. In the summer of 1916, the escape became more crucial as a polio epidemic raged from Maine to Washington eventually striking 27,000 victims, mostly children. Eleanor had gone to Campobello without Franklin early in June, bombarded on her arrival by instructions from him for staving off the infection. Responding to one of his instructions to her to prevent polio, Eleanor wrote, "The flies have fairly well been exterminated." Under no circumstances, he ordered her, were the children to be brought back to Washington until the pestilence had lifted. Franklin promised he would join her in August when Washington was its most sweltering. "I will get that holiday in somehow," he wrote.

But just a week later he begged off, telling her he was overwhelmed with work, and adding, "I have had a bad three weeks." Franklin, who had loved Campobello from boyhood, was now dragging his feet while telling Eleanor to stay longer. Except for ten days squeezed in at the island in September, he found himself alone for the better part of three months that summer. Cousin Alice had her description of this state. "In those days the wives of families went to the country for the summer, or the seashore, or whatever they did. They didn't stay in Washington," she observed, "and I've always laughed and said that my friends among the politicians, they had their little summer wife and they had a happy two or three months and it was all rather respectable and pleasant." To a woman of so jaded a view of life, the likelihood that the husband of her oh so proper cousin Eleanor might have a "summer wife" was pleasing.

By early October 1916, Eleanor had returned to R Street. Years later, she was to write of that time, "I went back to Washington from a life centered entirely on my family. I became conscious, on returning to the seat of government in Washington that there was a sense of impending disaster hanging over all of us." No doubt she was referring to growing alarm that the country would be drawn into the European war. Nevertheless, a nagging fear about her own future may have abetted the gloomy tone. Soon after her return, she went upstairs to say prayers with the children and to kiss them good night, during which they witnessed a rare occurrence, their mother dissolving in tears. Franklin appeared and asked, "What's wrong, dear?" Their dinner guests would be arriving momentarily he warned her. She answered through her sobs, "I'm afraid I cannot face all those people, Franklin." Among her visitors might be those who knew what she vaguely suspected about her husband. "Do pull yourself together," he told her.

However Franklin may have spent his bachelor days that summer he remained keenly concerned with the upcoming presidential election on which not only Wilson's but his own future hinged. He and Louis Howe concluded this time around that Franklin's wisest move was to pass up any bid for elective office and work for Wilson's reelection. Franklin was much in demand, requested by Democratic party officials across the country to speak out against the presidential-looking but lackluster Republican candidate, Charles Evans Hughes, whom Teddy Roosevelt ridiculed as "the bearded lady." Wilson, campaigning on the slogan "He kept us out of war," managed a slim victory, winning the popular vote by only a 590,000 margin. Franklin, his own position secured for another four years, immediately resumed his call for greater naval preparedness, seeking, with limited success, in bringing along his pacifist chief. He did manage to win Daniels's support for a $500 million appropriation to build more warships and to enlist the crews to man them. In the meantime, Louis Howe was still quietly working the press, planting calls for Daniels's replacement by Roosevelt, judged a "virile-minded, hard-fisted American," according to the *Chicago Post*.

On January 3, 1917, Germany's Field Marshal Paul von Hindenburg, by now the country's de facto leader, allowed himself to be persuaded by his admirals that the Allies could be brought to their knees by unrestricted warfare against any vessel on the high seas, especially if done before the Americans could be drawn into the war. Four days later a German submarine sank the American freighter *Housatonic*. Franklin again confronted Daniels. If German warships were now going to attack any and all ships, Franklin argued, why not order our ships, in preemptive self-defense, to attack German submarines first? Daniels refused. Shortly thereafter U-boats sent three more American vessels to the bottom of the Atlantic, the *Algonquin, Illinois,* and *Vigilancia.* By now Franklin judged Daniels hopelessly out of touch. As soon as his chief was out of town, he arranged to see the president urging Wilson to put the fleet on a wartime footing. Wilson was not yet ready either.

On February 4, British cryptologists handed the president an intercepted and decoded cable written by the German foreign minister, Arthur Zimmermann. In it, Zimmermann proposed offering a deal to Mexico to ally herself with Germany. Should the United States enter the war, the Germans would support the Mexicans in reclaiming the lost territories of New Mexico, Texas, and Arizona. The intelligence was provocative and Wilson's pacifism began to erode. The accretion of German provocations finally impelled the president to ask for a declaration of war, which the Congress granted on April 6. Immediately afterward, Franklin had made his unavailing request to the president to be allowed to enlist and had asked Wilson to hear Uncle Ted's plan for raising a division. While deeply disappointed at Wilson's refusal, TR laid no blame upon Franklin. Instead, at one point in his ceaseless carping against Wilson, he wrote Sara apologetically that he could not accept her invitation to visit Hyde Park since it could harm Franklin as a member of the administration he opposed. According to his daughter Alice, TR had a "tribal affection" for both Roosevelt branches and "loved all his nieces and nephews." "I'm so fond of that boy," TR told Sara of her son, "I'd be shot for him."

On April 24, 1917, Eleanor arranged a small luncheon at which Lucy was again the extra woman. The following Sunday, she hosted a dinner largely for Navy officers also including Alice Roosevelt Longworth and her congressman husband. Again Lucy was at the table, a point noted by Alice as worth circulating within the Washington gossip mill. The consuming subject, however, was the war. During the months it was taking to mobilize, America did not seem to be in danger. And so that summer, Franklin urged Eleanor to make the customary trek to Campobello, again without him. Before she left he arranged a weekend cruise to escape the grueling days spent at the department. The Navy had at its disposal the *Sylph*, a gleaming white 124-foot vessel that held a special appeal for Franklin. The *Sylph* had been the yacht that TR used as president. He requisitioned the vessel for a sail to begin Saturday afternoon, June 16. He invited Eleanor, his Marine major cousin, H. L. Roosevelt, John McIlhenny, a golfing partner, and McIlhenny's wife and, apparently as a couple, Nigel Law and Lucy Mercer. Washington's social chroniclers had begun, indirectly, to link Law romantically with Lucy. *Town Topics* ran an item pairing a desirable Washington native and a handsome young diplomat, "closely akin to the loftiest of British nobility," and predicted an early engagement. Lucy and Law made for a natural match, a pose that Franklin found useful and in which Nigel played his role. He took it as a compliment to their friendship that Franklin, "a man I loved and admired," had confided to him his feeling for this woman.

The sea held few charms for Eleanor. On a previous occasion, she had accompanied Franklin aboard a ship on the Chesapeake Bay to observe target practice. The sea was choppy under a glowering sky. The vessel heaved amid the troughs and Eleanor began to turn green. A solicitous young officer took her frozen appearance for boredom and suggested she might want to climb the hundred-foot skeleton mast. "You will be able to see things much better from up there," he offered helpfully. When the *Sylph* pulled away that Saturday from the Navy Yard pier, it was without Eleanor. Yet, without explanation, she later appeared further down the coast. The prospect of another bout of sickness may have initially dissuaded her from coming. What is clear is that she underwent a change of heart, possibly after she learned of the passenger list. The *Sylph* slowed to a halt as it came abeam of the Indian Head naval facility where Eleanor had gone to intercept the vessel. The captain ordered a small boat ashore to pick her up and the *Sylph* again put out to sea.

The passengers spent two days sightseeing, visiting the birthplaces of George Washington and Robert E. Lee, swimming and hiking along the Virginia shore, picnicking on snowy tablecloths from a hamper of sandwiches, and drinking chilled white wine served by Navy stewards. Throughout the voyage, Franklin was expansive, in high spirits, parading his knowledge of nautical matters and the area's history. Meanwhile, an unspoken drama was being played out. In the absence of a single shred of hard evidence, lovers generate an aura that is felt and sensed by others, most acutely by the party betrayed. Lucy's supposed pairing with Nigel Law did not convince Eleanor. Within a week, she fired Lucy. The dismissal was cloaked genteelly and plausibly. Wartime, as she explained, meant curtailing the Roosevelts' entertaining. She no longer required a social secretary.

Franklin, however, proved resourceful. On June 29, five days after her dismissal, Lucy was at the Navy Yard where she found herself arrayed with women of every shape and walk of life while a drowsy, elderly doctor examined them with less cursory interest. Her vital statistics were recorded as age, twenty-five years and two months; height, five feet, nine inches; eyes blue, hair brown, complexion ruddy, her usually fair complexion likely still bearing the effects of the *Sylph* cruise. Whether through clerical error or vanity, Lucy's age was recorded as a year less than the truth. She was sworn in by Lieutenant Commander Downs L. Wilson as yeoman 3d class (F), for female, given serial number 1160, and promptly assigned to the Office of the Assistant Secretary of the Navy.

This always stylishly dressed young woman reported for duty doubtless dismayed by the unflattering uniform the Navy had devised for its "yeomanettes." It consisted of a shapeless belted jacket, a drab short skirt, and a hat that lay flat on the head like a pancake. Her first sight of the assistant secretary's office mirrored what she would have expected given the decor in Franklin's home, maps and nautical prints everywhere and numerous ship models poised above book-filled cabinets. The enlistment not only thwarted Eleanor's attempt to part the lovers, but provided critical income to Lucy, now deprived of her social secretary salary. Minnie had been forced to step down from the Decatur to the more modest Toronto apartments. Lucy's pay, $28.75 per month plus $1.25 a day for meals and miscellaneous, meant she could continue to pay the $35 monthly rent.

That summer Eleanor stalled her departure for Campobello. First, she said, she was waiting for three of her children to shake off whooping cough. Then she spent the next several days pressuring Franklin to join her. He was exhausting himself at the department, he said, as Daniels continued to resist his efforts to plunge full speed ahead in bringing the Navy to a war footing. Also, he said, he had a bad cold, was irritable, and not fit to leave town. They quarreled and finally on July 14 a sulking Eleanor left the steaming capital with only the children. The next day Franklin wrote remorsefully, "Dearest Babs, I had a vile day after you left, stayed at home, coughed, dozed, tried to read." He could not, he said, even muster the concentration to play solitaire. "I really can't stand that house all alone without you and you were a goosy girl to think or even pretend to think that I don't want you here all summer, because you know I do! But honestly you ought to have six weeks straight at Campo, just as I ought to, only you can and I can't! I know what a whole summer here does to people's nerves and at the end of this summer I will be like a bear with a sore head until I get a change or some cold weather. In fact as you know I am unreasonable and touchy now but shall try to improve." He wrote again the next day, "It seems years since you left and I miss you horribly and hate the thought of the empty house." The letters ring with sincerity and probably are honest, given the human capacity to embrace contrary sentiments simultaneously, including the fact that Eleanor's departure meant he was free once again.

That very day Franklin was staggered by a story appearing in *The New York Times* headlined, "How to Save in Big Homes." Shortly before her departure, Eleanor had signed a pledge card from the Patriotic Economy League and had granted an interview to a woman reporter who wanted to know how the Roosevelt home was economizing in wartime. As reported in the story, Eleanor had explained that there were seven in the family plus ten servants. The Roosevelts did not eat bacon, had only two courses for lunch, and three for dinner. "Mrs. Roosevelt does the buying, the cooks see that there is no food wasted, the laundress is sparing in her use of soap, each servant has a watchful eye for evidence of shortcomings on the part of others; and all are encouraged to make helpful suggestions in the use of leftovers." The reporter further quoted Eleanor boasting, "Since I have started following the home-card instructions prices have risen, but my bills are no larger."

Franklin fired off a letter to Campobello from which all contrition had vanished: "All I can say is that your latest newspaper campaign is a corker and I am proud to be the husband of the Originator, Discoverer and Inventor of the New Household Economy for Millionaires! Please have a photo taken showing the family, the ten cooperating servants, the scraps saved from the table and the handbook. . . . Honestly, you have leaped into public fame, all Washington is talking of the Roosevelt Plan, and I begin to get telegrams of congratulations and requests for further details from Pittsburgh, New Orleans, San Francisco." Eleanor wrote back, "I do think it was horrid of that woman to use my name in that way. . . . I'd like to crawl away for shame." Among her various chores, before her dismissal, Lucy had handled press inquiries for Eleanor with tight-lipped discretion. Franklin had to wonder if she would have fallen into this journalist's net.

On July 19, Eleanor, still at Campobello, received a thick envelope from Lucy. The curious aspect of this packet is that it has Lucy Mercer still carrying out secretarial tasks after presumably having been fired. She had evidently been at the Roosevelts' home and Franklin was still making use of her since the envelope contained letters Lucy had drafted for Eleanor to sign, prepared in response to people writing from all over the country curious about wartime economies for the rich. Clearly incensed, Eleanor wrote to Franklin, "Why did you make her waste all that time on answering those fool notes? I tore them all up. Please tear up any other results of my idiocy at once." She then added, "She tells me you [were] going off on Sunday and I hope you all had a pleasant trip." Then, either out of genuine dislike of the water or an attempt at nonchalance, she wrote, "but I'm glad I'm here and not on the Potomac."

Five days later, Franklin arranged another weekend cruise aboard the *Sylph*, this time inviting President Wilson's personal physician, Rear Admiral Cary Grayson, and Mrs. Grayson, Charles Munn, a Harvard chum, and his wife, and, again, Nigel and Lucy. In Hampton Roads they were piped aboard Admiral Tommy Rogers's flag, the battleship *Arkansas*, enjoyed a splendid lunch in the wardroom served by black mess boys in white, starched uniforms. They later stood on the bridge and watched the fleet pass in review for the assistant secretary down the York River. They listened, with hands clapping, feet tapping, as musicians aboard a nearby vessel broke into "Alexander's Ragtime Band." They donned bathing suits and swam along the riverbank with Lucy's modest swimsuit suggesting the splendid figure beneath. They had supper on deck under Japanese lanterns as sea breezes banished the day's lingering heat. That night they were rocked gently to sleep aboard the *Sylph* before returning to port the next day.

Lucy might have found her present situation untenable. She was twenty-six and still single, living in a society where young women were expected to be married by twenty-one. Her mother had been married twice while younger than Lucy was now. By Lucy's age, Eleanor had given birth to four children. Despite her genteel poverty, a woman of her beauty, charm, and breeding would have found little difficulty in making a suitable match during the years that she worked for the Roosevelts. Nigel Law, for one, would have made an ideal catch. But lovers are ruled by impulse, not reason. She was madly in love with Franklin Roosevelt and willing to sacrifice priceless years for him.

Forestalling tale bearers, Franklin was selectively open in describing to Eleanor his bachelor summer. He told her almost everything about the *Sylph* cruise. His guests may have made unlikely shipmates, he wrote, "but it worked out splendidly . . . a bully trip . . . and they all got on splendidly." Eleanor wrote back gamely, using her usual salutation, "Dearest Honey . . . I'm glad you are so gay, but you know I predicted it." A few days later, however, she was again cantankerous. On July 24 she wrote, "I wish you would come here but I want no one else! . . . I don't think you read my letters for you never answer a question, and nothing I ask for appears." She tried to arouse his guilt for not even getting up to Hyde Park to see his mother, adding, "I know she will feel badly about it." He did promise to come up to Campobello by the end of July, but within days he wrote, "I do miss you so <u>very</u> much, but I am getting busier and busier and fear my hoped for dash to Campobello next week for two days will not materialize."

He was to be plagued all his life with respiratory ills, colds, sinusitis, and early in August 1917 was felled by a serious throat infection. Sara, then visiting Lake Placid, was ready to speed to her son's sickbed, but Franklin managed to stall her and Eleanor beat her mother-in-law to Washington. Leaving the children with a governess and nurse at Campobello, she rushed back to find Franklin in the hospital with a raging fever. She was genuinely worried yet also saw the chance, through her nursing, to demonstrate his need for her. He mended quickly and was home in four days. By August 14, Eleanor was on her way back to Campobello, again alone. In her mounting uneasiness, she had been cultivating her mother-in-law, which seemed to be paying off. Sara wrote to Franklin of his wife, "You certainly were unlucky to get that horrid illness, but I think fortunate to have the most lovely person to rush to you as she did and stay." She then passed along a compliment from a friend who spoke "with <u>such</u> admiration and affection, she is clever enough to see how different E is from some of <u>her</u> friends."

Writing from the island, Eleanor laid down an ultimatum. She was tired of Franklin's lame excuses for not leaving Washington. "Remember that I <u>count</u> on seeing you on the 26th. My threat was no idle one." The threat implied that she would break off the vacation, come back to Washington, and end his suspect freedom if he did not come to Campobello. Elliott Roosevelt's memoir took her meaning a step further: "There was no mystery; she threatened to leave him."

Nevertheless, almost immediately Franklin was off on another weekend jaunt with Lucy. On Sunday, August 19, he finished eighteen holes of golf in the morning, grabbed a quick lunch, and then drove with her and Admiral and Mrs. Grayson to the farm of friends, the Horsey sisters, living near Harpers Ferry. He wrote Eleanor, "Walked over the farm, a very rich one run by the two sisters. Had supper with them and several neighbors. Left at nine and got home at midnight." He told her that Lucy was part of the party but this time there was no mention of Nigel Law. Toward the end of August he finally bent to Eleanor's ultimatum and came for a few days to Campobello.

In the fall of 1917, Nigel Law returned temporarily to England to recruit more staff for a British embassy eager to hurry America into the fighting in France. His friendship was soon replaced. Just as Roosevelt had imported Louis Howe as his political sidekick, he now recruited as his companion in play his Harvard classmate Livy Davis, the wealthy Boston Brahmin. Franklin's summons rescued the bluff, handsome, fun-loving Livy from prosperous boredom at his Boston banking house. He arrived in Washington in the fall of 1917 to become another Roosevelt special assistant, "My second pair of legs," as Franklin put it. Even before assuming his official post, Livy had earlier taken time off to accompany Franklin on an inspection trip of the U.S. Marines occupying Haiti and the Dominican Republic. The trip also included a stop in Cuba about which Livy had tipped off Franklin "I have heard tales of a very risqué theatre in Havana which if true should be too good to miss. . . . I will be host for the crowd." Once officially on board at the Navy Department, Livy was given undemanding tasks, overseeing the conduct of enlisted men, coordinating with state naval militias, and pursuing his proudest initiative, "Eyes for the Navy," a program through which yachtsmen, amateur astronomers, and operagoers were asked to donate binoculars and telescopes to the Navy. Livy described his use to Franklin as easing "in every way the burdens thrust upon his shoulders."

But Davis's principal purpose was to provide diversion from the hard-working, hard-driving side of Franklin's nature. They golfed together where Livy's role was to lose admiringly to Franklin. They played poker, went to stag parties, and renewed friendships with Harvard Gold Coast pals now living in Washington. This Good Time Charlie, married to the former Alice Gardiner, was not surprisingly a chronic philanderer. Among entries in the journal he kept while in Washington, he noted, "Dallied around on tennis courts with couple of beauts when Alice arrived"; "Took Postmaster General's two cutey daughters to dinner-dance. Danced until 2:30; Sat next to Mrs. Spear. Danced till 3; champagne flowing like water."

Eleanor loathed this libertine. To her, Livy Davis was "lazy, selfish, and self-seeking to an extraordinary degree, with the outward appearance of being quite different." Years later, after Franklin had been stricken with polio, Livy sought to cheer up his friend by reminding him that he now had time to do the writing he had often spoken of. He went on to suggest several subjects, including "The Ladies of Washington: or Thirty Days and Evenings as a Bachelor," and one for his own pen, "On the Trail of Roosevelt; or 29 Concussive Nights in a Different Place and Bed."

Franklin delighted in sidestepping naval bureaucrats and time servers. He had surrounded himself with men like Livy, old school chums he commissioned in naval intelligence, and the contractor Elliot Brown, who had such a free hand in building barracks and naval store-houses that Franklin would sign the requisitions with his eyes closed. His mind popped with ideas. His pet brainstorm was a scheme to lay what he called a barrage of mines across the North Sea between Scotland and Norway. In order for German submarines to enter into the Atlantic killing fields, they first would have to transit this strait. Franklin argued for this stratagem for months. But his idea was dismissed by American and British admirals as an amateur's meddling. Secretary Daniels, predictably, was no help. Franklin, undeterred, took the idea directly to President Wilson, winning his support, and continued promoting his brainstorm among the still resistant admirals.

The war enabled Eleanor to submerge her unease at home by enlisting her energies in a cause larger than her self-concerns. The leadership and organizing skills of her Allenswood and settlement house days, suppressed by the demands of motherhood and a controlling mother-in-law, began to resurface. Instead of pointless social calls, "I found myself spending three days a week in a canteen down at the railroad yards, one afternoon a week distributing free yarn for the Navy League, two days a week visiting the Naval hospital, and contributing whatever time I had left to the Navy Red Cross and the Navy Relief Society. I loved it. I simply ate it up." She would rise at five in the morning, don a baggy khaki Red Cross uniform, and head for Union Station, working in a sweltering tin-roofed shed making sandwiches and coffee to hand out to servicemen whose trains arrived in an endless stream. She wrote letters for wounded sailors at the Navy Hospital and consoled marines confined to the shell-shock ward in Saint Elizabeths Hospital for the mentally ill. One hectic morning she cut her hand almost to the bone on a bread-slicing machine. "There was no time to stop," she recalled, "so I wrapped something tight around it and proceeded during the day to wrap more and more handkerchiefs around it, until it finally stopped bleeding." She bore the scar for life. Her exit from the suffocating cocoon of domesticity restored my "executive ability . . . which had been more or less dormant up to this time, returning a certain confidence in myself and in my ability to meet emergencies and deal with them."

Cousin Alice asked Eleanor how she might help. She showed up at Union Station twice, then disappeared. Pouring coffee and handing out sandwiches had afflicted her with what she called "canteen elbow." Eleanor was dismayed but not surprised. "It is a pity so much energy should go to waste," she observed of her cousin. To Eleanor, Alice's life consisted only of "the long pursuit of pleasure and excitement." Alice's idea of helping the war effort involved recruiting Franklin in a mad spy caper. May Ladenburg was the beautiful daughter of the senior partner in a German-American banking firm, Ladenburg, Thalmann and Company. She was also an active Washington hostess and thus Alice knew well the layout of the Ladenburg home. Army intelligence suspected that May was extracting secrets from the financial wizard Bernard Baruch, soon to be head of the War Industries Board, and with whom she was having an affair. The secrets were supposedly passed along to May's uncle in Europe. This intelligence was then, presumably, helping German submarines sink Allied ships. When an intelligence officer approached Alice with a scheme, she leapt. "All I was being asked to do was to look over transoms and peep through keyholes," she recalled.

"Could anything be more delightful than that?" Franklin was enlisted to help set a trap by providing phony classified documents concerning ship movements to be carelessly left about May's house.

Using her knowledge of the Ladenburg home, Alice advised Army officers to place a listening device under a bed in a studio where May trysted with her lover. If the plan succeeded, May and Baruch might be heard discussing the contents of the fabricated documents. Adjoining the studio was a stable where Alice, Army agents, and according to one source, Franklin as well, monitored the sounds of love. The intelligence take was skimpy. Alice remembered, "We did hear her ask Bernie how many locomotives were being sent to Romania . . . in between the sounds of kissing. . . . Of course we were doing a *most* disgraceful thing in the name of looking after the affairs of our country, but it was sheer rapture." And far preferable to rising at dawn to hand out donuts to rumpled doughboys in a sooty railroad yard.

The espionage stunt confirmed Eleanor's belief that Alice was a bad influence on her husband. Once when they were all staying in the same hotel, she found Alice and Franklin huddled in a tête-à-tête in an alcove sipping mint liqueur and clearly enjoying a good gossip. Eleanor later confronted Franklin. "No one would know that you were her cousin," she complained. "I think it would be a good idea if you and Alice didn't see each other for some time." The warning fell on deaf ears.

In Eleanor's eyes, Alice's absent sense of duty was matched by her own mother-in-law's concept of patriotism. When Eleanor told Sara that her brother Hall was going to train for military aviation, the old woman was shocked. A man with a wife and small children should be hiring a substitute, she said. Eleanor had never heard of such a thing. Nonsense, Sara responded, "In the Civil War many gentlemen bought substitutes. It was the thing to do."

Lucy was now out of Eleanor's employ but not out of Franklin's sight and Eleanor let her jealousy show through. Among her myriad war projects were "wool Saturdays" at which volunteers came to the Roosevelts' home to pick up wool provided by the Navy League. The women then returned with sweaters, scarves, and socks they had knitted to keep sailors warm. Lucy had taken part as a volunteer, handing out the wool, a task she considered her contribution to the war effort. In September 1917, while at Campobello, Eleanor sent Lucy a check for the work as if to remind her that she was a former employee. Lucy sent the check back. Eleanor sent it again. Lucy returned it a second time with a note that she had no intention of cashing it. Eleanor wrote Franklin, "I knew she had done far more work than I could pay for. She is evidently quite cross with me." Franklin stepped in. He informed Eleanor, "You are entirely disconnected, and Lucy Mercer and Mrs. Mary Dunn are closing up loose ends." Wool Saturdays were over.

Franklin's affair, among rarefied Washington circles, was now sufficiently out in the open to dispel further speculation of any serious romance between Lucy and any other man. Edith and William Eustis were accomplices in the romance, a couple who bridged the Hudson River and Washington aristocracies. Edith was the daughter of Levi P. Morton, a New Yorker who had served as vice president under Benjamin Harrison, and was known as "Moneybags Morton." The Mortons had an estate, Ellerslie, at Rhinebeck eleven miles north of Hyde Park. Franklin, as a youth, had been a welcome and frequent guest at Ellerslie. Edith was the older, glamorous woman who fascinated him as a college boy and still did. She had managed to combine utter respectability with a streak of daring after her 1902 novel on Washington politics and society, *Marian Manning*, was published, its theme being infidelity. Her home in Washington was a formidable mansion at 1607 H Street, poised handily between Franklin's office and his home. She and Willie also maintained a country estate, Oatlands, near Leesburg, Virginia. By late 1917, Edith Eustis was providing a solution to the perennial lovers' dilemma, where to meet. Thus Franklin reentered the Eustis fold. He was a guest at dinners, and lunches, always seated next to Miss Mercer. When Eleanor was out of town or otherwise occupied, the two were weekend guests at Oatlands. For Lucy, her occasional seat at Roosevelt dinners and the hospitality of the Eustises had restored her to the social world the Mercers had known before their fall.

Occasionally, through the Eustises, Lucy met an older man, Winthrop Rutherfurd, Franklin's equal in patrician bearing and good looks, but reserved and lacking Roosevelt's effervescence and gift for sparkling repartee. Rutherfurd was Edith Eustis's brother-in-law and had been married to her sister, Alice. His reticence alongside the animated Franklin may have been explained by his recent bereavement. Alice Rutherfurd had died that summer of 1917 leaving him with six young children. It is not known if Lucy, so in love with Franklin, took particular notice of Rutherfurd at that time, but he clearly did of her, as subsequent events would prove.

Blinded by love, Franklin and Lucy were becoming reckless. Among Eleanor's fellow volunteers at the railroad canteen were three maiden sisters, Mary, Nellie, and Josephine Patten, known in Washington as the capital's swiftest gossips. The gibe in their circle was, "Don't telegraph, don't telephone, tell-a-Patten." The trusting Eleanor was particularly fond of the eldest sister, Mary, counted on her at the canteen, and was unaware of Patten's tale mongering about her husband and former social secretary. Sightings of Franklin and Lucy together began to occur. Aunty Bye's son, William Sheffield Cowles Jr., reported seeing them "often, I used to think too often." One day, Franklin received a call from an unmistakable voice, simultaneously cultivated and insinuating. "I saw you twenty miles out in the country," Alice Longworth said. "You didn't see me. Your hands were on the wheel, but your eyes were on the perfectly lovely lady." Franklin answered blithely, "Isn't she perfectly lovely."

Alice began inviting Franklin and Lucy, without Eleanor, to her brilliant dinner parties, where the dishes were Escoffier, the wines vintage, the talk witty, and the guests attractive, or at least powerful. When criticized for placing Eleanor in a humiliating light, Alice replied, "Franklin deserved a good time. He was married to Eleanor." Alice enjoyed amusing her guests with dead-on impersonations. One target was Helen, wife of William Howard Taft, the man her father had essentially made president and then turned against. She even did her Aunty Bye, one of the few individuals for whom she had unalloyed affection. But her favorite was Eleanor, whom she rendered in what she called "The Roosevelt voice . . . a way of making every word seem serious" and which "Eleanor had . . . really to an extreme." She was still doing the imitation fifty years later on television, long after Eleanor was dead. She enjoyed contrasting her glittering soirees with a night at the Franklin Roosevelts'. "They would have rather fine and solemn little Sunday evenings where one was usually regaled with crown roast, very indifferent wine, and a good deal of knitting. I remember going there once with my stepmother, who maintains that she could always tell when I was bored because I appeared to swell up. My eyes recede and my face becomes fat. My stepmother said she thought I was going to lose my eyes that evening. Both Eleanor and Franklin could be very boring together." Especially Eleanor, who with knitting needles clicking, "always wanted to discuss things like whether contentment was happiness and whether they conflicted with one another," Alice remembered, "things like that, which I didn't give a damn about."

A favorite tale that Alice marketed involved the Roosevelts taking their houseguests, Franklin's cousin Warren Delano Robbins and his wife, Irene, to a ball at the Chevy Chase Club where Lucy Mercer may have been present. Near midnight, Eleanor excused herself, though apparently she was not much missed since the other three came rolling back to R Street at 4:00 A.M., in Alice's phrase, "flushed with wine, women and song." There they found Eleanor sitting on the doormat in the vestibule. According to Alice, Eleanor rose, looking like "a string bean that had been raised in a cellar." An astonished Franklin asked, "Darling, what are you doing here?" Eleanor answered, "Oh, I forgot my key." Franklin pressed her, why didn't she wake the servants, or take a cab back to the ball? Why didn't she go to the neighbors for help, the Adolph Millers or the Mitchell Palmers just across the street? "Oh, no," Eleanor answered, "I've always been told never to bother people if you can possibly avoid it." And as for returning to the club, "I knew you were all having such a glorious time and I didn't want to spoil the fun." Mrs. Robbins, recalling that night, remembered thinking that she would not "have blamed Franklin if he had slapped Eleanor hard."

Not content with spreading tales that put her cousin in a ridiculous light, Alice could not resist rubbing Eleanor's face in the possibility of her husband's infidelity. The two met by chance in the Rotunda of the Capitol where Alice informed Eleanor of one of the recent occasions at which Franklin and Lucy had been at her home. Eleanor refused to be baited. "She inquired if you had told me," she later told Franklin, "and I said no and that I did not believe in knowing things which your husband did not wish you to know." The scene cast the cousins in *Gone with the Wind* roles with Alice as Scarlett and Eleanor as the long-suffering Melanie. Eleanor's reluctance to listen to Alice was understandable. Why risk confirmation of what, so far, was only dread suspicion?

Alice found Eleanor's nobility particularly insufferable because her own marriage was a shambles. Almost a year after Franklin had married Eleanor in 1905, Alice had married Nick Longworth, and had her wish to become the first president's daughter to marry in the White House since the marriage of Ulysses Grant's daughter, Nellie, thirty-two years before. Franklin was a guest, but only with his mother, since Eleanor, then six months pregnant, was not considered presentable in public according to the custom of the day. So maddening had Alice's behavior been that the parting shot of her stepmother, Edith Carow Roosevelt, after the ceremony was, "I want you to know that I'm glad to see you go. You've never been anything but trouble."

To the press, the wedding had been a glittering match, Alice the American princess, wed to Longworth, the well-bred scion of a prominent family from Cincinnati, a Harvard graduate and, unlike Franklin, a Porcellian with a gift for friendship that was to propel his rise in Congress, leading to the speakership of the House of Representatives. Though fifteen years Alice's senior, Longworth, from the outset, led Alice a merry chase. He was a gambler, his heavy drinking so risky to his political career that Alice once remarked, "He'd rather be tight than be President." Like many a successful politician, the same extrovert personality that fueled his political rise fed his carnal appetites. His philandering was notorious and publicly flaunted. The marriage went so out of control that Alice sought a divorce. When she raised the matter with her family, they informed her that in their circle divorce was simply unthinkable.

The impetuous Alice took a predictable vengeance. She began an affair with a married senator, William E. Borah, known on Capitol Hill as the "Stallion of Idaho." Alice in turn became known as "Aurora Borah Alice." At a party in her own home she caught her husband in a bathroom, in flagrante, with her dear friend, the newspaper heiress Cissy Patterson. On another occasion, again in Alice's home, Cissy sneaked off with the Idaho stallion. Finding hairpins in the library, Alice sent them to Cissy with a note, "I believe these are yours." Cissy wrote back, "And if you look up in the chandelier, you might find my panties." Given the tattered state of her own marriage, why should her saintly cousin Eleanor be allowed to think that her marriage was flawless? And so Alice continued to play the accomplice in the Lucy-Franklin affair. Cousin Corinne best caught the essence of Alice Roosevelt Longworth: "she lacked the power of loving."

*Chapter 13*

# INHIBITIONS SNAP LIKE COBWEBS

· · · · · · ·

W AS THE AFFAIR CONSUMMATED? The question appears fatuous in the contemporary world. The early 1900s, however, was another age. Respected Roosevelt scholars have found Franklin too straitlaced and Lucy too Catholic to bring their romance to its physical conclusion. Proof in so private a matter is elusive and as an old saying has it, "You can never tell unless you were in the room." Hugh Gregory Gallagher, who wrote an insightful history on Franklin's life after polio, reasoned that, as a young husband, "FDR did not seem to be at ease, even then with intimacy," and added that, "Even during the height of their liaison in 1918, there seem to have been no sexual relations." He concluded that they were at most sweethearts.

Still, if we grant that Franklin Roosevelt and Lucy Mercer were driven by the same impulses that rule other human beings, how would two people finding themselves in their situation likely have behaved? No power on earth surpasses that of sexual desire, the instinctual urgency that leads the sanest people to commit the most reckless acts. The overpowering force of sexual attraction will be denied only by rare souls who have never known it. Desire, when coupled with genuine love, creates a magnetism between two people that they are nearly helpless to resist. No purpose is served by saying that Franklin loved his wife and therefore was armored against infidelity. He did love Eleanor, but as a man loves a good woman after a dozen years of marriage, hardly with the consuming fire of a newfound passion. What had been sufficient to satisfy a callow bridegroom of twenty-two was not necessarily enough for a worldly figure of thirty-five. For the first time in his life, Franklin had been moved beyond love based on affection and mutual respect to the out-of-control ardor that conquers reason and convention. "In the face of great emotion, proprieties and their inhibitions," William James has written, "snap like cobwebs." "There's beggary in love that can be reckoned," Shakespeare wrote of Antony's abandonment of his fate to Cleopatra. Lucy had awakened in Franklin a depth of feeling that he had never before experienced, strong enough to lead him to abandon his innate caution. Her appeal to him became all the sharper by comparison with a wife for whom sex was a chore.

As for Lucy, this warmhearted young woman found herself in constant contact with an older man who was the fulfillment of her girlish ideals and whose breathtaking good looks exuded virility. She had witnessed the way he lit up a room or a boatful of guests by his very presence, by his humor and lively imagination. Further he was important, made visible in the deference paid him by his peers, even superiors. To Lucy, Franklin Roosevelt was godlike, and this prince among men gave her every reason to believe that he loved her. Those who contend that her Catholicism would have barred illicit love, that her religion would act as a chastity belt, are according Catholics an unlikely exemption from the passions that consume others.

The family histories of neither Franklin nor Lucy would have left them innocent of human fallibility. Lucy's mother was divorced from one husband, estranged from another, and was reportedly involved in affairs while living in New York. Her father led a dissolute life. The Roosevelts were even more instructive in displaying the upper-class capacity for waywardness. Eleanor's father's escapades were legion, including fathering an illegitimate son. Her brother Hall, whom she essentially supported during his alcohol-sodden years, kept a White Russian émigrée mistress whom Sara Roosevelt would never invite to Hyde Park, though he himself was always welcome. Cousin Alice Longworth and her congressman husband seemed to be engaged in a competition for outrageousness. On Franklin's side, his half-brother, Rosy, had conducted a long-term affair with Elizabeth Riley, the Harrod's shopgirl. As one family member put it, "Oh, no, they were not married, but they were everything else." Rosy did ultimately make Elizabeth an honest woman while his son and Franklin's half-nephew, Taddy, married a whore.

What do a thirty-five-year-old man who has sired six children and a twenty-six-year-old woman who is madly in love with him do when, by chance or design, they find themselves alone? That the well-bred Lucy allowed the kind of inevitable gossip to swirl around Washington society by being seen repeatedly in the company of a married man suggests that her infatuation with Franklin was so total that it overcame discretion. Further, the romance had developed to a point where sins of the flesh could eventually be absolved by the expectation of marriage ultimately to the man for whom she had risked everything.

One of the more curious "proofs" of the consummation of the affair has been offered by Franklin's son James Roosevelt in his family memoir, *My Parents*. Jimmy refers to "a rather well-kept secret that there came to light during this time a register from a motel in Virginia Beach showing that father and Lucy had checked in as man and wife and spent the night." If true, the matter of consummation is resolved. But the Virginia Beach motel story is full of holes. The first defect is in terminology. "Motel" had not yet come into usage at that time. However, Jimmy may merely have transposed an earlier term, "tourist cabin," to the more contemporary word. But even granting that explanation, there were not in those days in Virginia Beach accommodations resembling either term, only old-fashioned hotels, some quite grand—the Atlantic, the Shoreham, the Courtenay Terrace, the Arlington—mostly fronting on the ocean, any one of which could have served for a romantic idyll. Still, a 416-mile round-trip overnight drive between Washington and Virginia Beach along the primitive roads of 1917 seems daunting. The travel records of the assistant secretary of the navy during this period show no trips to that locale, and finally, it is unimaginable that Franklin Roosevelt would have signed his own name to a hotel register. What to make of a son's claim of a father's infidelity proved by a motel register that has never been produced? Jimmy Roosevelt at the time he wrote his book was a middle-aged man snared in unsuccessful get-rich-quick schemes. According to Verne Newton, former director of the Roosevelt Library in Hyde Park, "He needed the money. Writing books seemed a good way to get it. To sell he needed sensationalism." The weight of evidence destroys the Virginia Beach story, but does not resolve the question of consummation. For this, the most revealing source may be Lucy herself. After FDR's death, Betsey Cushing, Jimmy's first wife, while visiting Aiken, South Carolina, was invited to tea by Lucy, whose winter home was in the city. Cushing remembered that the ladylike Lucy wore white gloves for the occasion. As the meeting was related in a Roosevelt biography by Ted Morgan, "Lucy began to ask embarrassingly personal questions. She wanted to know whether any other woman had had the same physical claim on Franklin, whether there had ever been, after her departure from the scene, a rival for Franklin's love. Betsey found herself unable to respond to Lucy's inquiries, and was relieved when suddenly all the lights in the house went out. It must be Franklin, she thought, annoyed at the line of questioning."

The fuel that had powered Franklin's life thus far was political ambition, and he knew that exposure of the affair would deal his hopes a death blow. While running for president in 1884, New York's governor, Grover Cleveland, the friend of Franklin's father, woke one morning to a headline emblazoned in his hometown paper, *The Buffalo Telegraph*, "A Terrible Tale. A Dark History in a Public Man's History." The subhead read, "The pitiful story of Maria Halpin and Grover Cleveland's Son." Cleveland, as a young man, was accused of fathering a child with the attractive widow Halpin, well before beginning his political career. The *Telegraph*'s story was instantly echoed nationwide. As soon as the news broke, the candidate telegraphed his allies back in Buffalo, "Above all, tell the truth." A worldly-wise clergyman, Reverend Kingsley Twining, came publicly to his defense, pointing out that the young bachelor's indiscretion involved "no seduction, no adultery, no breach of promise, no obligation of marriage." The widow Halpin knew exactly what she was doing. Cleveland's honesty blunted the issue and he went on to win the presidency.

The very appearance of Woodrow Wilson, the long jaw, the thin line for a mouth, the cold, penetrating eyes, suggests a Calvinist minister castigating his congregation over weaknesses of the flesh. Nothing could be further from the man's true nature. Wilson was one of the most hopeless romantics ever to occupy the White House, and his conduct before arriving there was not monogamous. His first marriage, to Ellen Axson, was a love match. He wrote to her, "I am nothing if my heart be broken: and it would break if I could not have your love as absolutely as you have that of your own Woodrow."

In 1907, while president of Princeton, Wilson found himself vacationing in Bermuda where he met Mary Peck, then forty-five, once widowed, now unhappily married and assuaging her discontent through winters spent alone on the balmy island. Wilson was immediately smitten by this attractive, witty, sophisticated woman. In 1908, he was back in Bermuda for another two months and the two behaved as a couple,

taking long walks along the pink-tinged beaches, while he read her poetry from *The Oxford Book of Verse*. She was playful and would tease
him, a welcome lightness that the serious Mrs. Wilson could not provide, not unlike the contrast between Lucy and Eleanor. His biographer, Edwin A. Weinstein, states plainly, "Wilson fell in love with Mary
Peck in 1908."

Three years after their first meeting, the relationship had grown
deeper. Wilson wrote Mary that he thought of her "a thousand times."
Addressing him as "Best beloved," she responded, "the king can do no
wrong." In 1911, returning from Bermuda alone, he wrote his wife that
he would be held up in New York by quarantine and customs, and
would be late getting back to Princeton. He actually planned to call on
Mary first, writing to her before his arrival, that he must "see my dear,
dear friend."

Ellen Wilson died on August 6, 1914, of Bright's disease at age fifty-
four, seventeen months after becoming first lady. The passionate
Wilson was soon in love with Edith Bolling Galt, a handsome forty-
three-year-old widow descended from the Virginia aristocracy. The
most painful moment in the courtship occurred when the president
learned that his political enemies were trying to buy his love letters to
Mary Peck. He confessed the earlier affair during a furtive visit to
Edith, slipping from the White House to her home. His romance with
Mrs. Galt, prior to their marriage, became so widely known that Washington wags joked that when Edith heard the president propose, she
nearly fell out of bed.

Grover Cleveland's indiscretion did not harm him politically because
he behaved honestly, and honorably. Wilson's did not hurt him because
it was kept quiet. The discretion of the news media would in the future
protect presidential philanderers Warren Harding and John F. Kennedy,
but fail in the case of Bill Clinton. William Gladstone, four times the
British prime minister and a pillar of Victorian respectability, once confided to a friend, "I have known nine prime ministers, seven of whom
were adulterers." He added, "They had the good fortune not to violate
the 11th Commandment, 'Thou shall not get caught.' " Perhaps the wisest utterance on the difference between a man's private behavior and
public conduct was surprisingly made by the nineteenth-century femi-
nist Elizabeth Cady Stanton: "I have known men without one particle of

public spirit, or one throb of patriotism, oblivious to all the duties of a citizen, and yet kind and devoted to wife and children . . . men as chaste as [the goddess] Diana, who would not give a farthing to a little beggar. Again I have known statesmen, soldiers, scientists, men trusted with interests and empires devoted to the public good, whose patriotism no one doubted, yet reckless of their business and family affairs." As Alistair Cooke, a shrewd commentator of the American scene, put it during the Clinton presidential sex scandal, if an unblemished marital life was the standard, the public would be left with "having only monks and certifiable faithful husbands and wives running for the presidency."

What has happened in the past, what others have managed to get away with or not, what is wise and prudent is a useless guide to those in love. "Tell me where is fancy bred, or in the heart or in the head?" Shakespeare asks. Eleanor's cousin Corinne, aware of the affair, thought it had a "profound effect on Franklin. It is difficult to describe, but to me it seemed to release something in him. . . . Up to the time that Lucy Mercer came into Franklin's life he seemed to look at human relationships coolly, calmly and without depth. He viewed his family dispassionately and enjoyed them, but he had in my opinion a loveless quality as if he were incapable of emotion."

Whatever emotional liberation the affair provided had to be paid for by the intrusion of reality. Franklin understood the risks to his career, the potential pain he was causing to people whom he genuinely loved and who did not deserve to be hurt. The inner turmoil afflicting him broke to the surface in his increasingly testy relations with Eleanor as the shadow of suspicion, recrimination, and guilt darkened their home. The psychosomatic signs erupted in his frequent headaches, colds, and respiratory infections. "There are secrets," as Dostoyevsky wrote, "that a man is afraid to tell even to himself . . . and the more decent he is, the greater the number of such things on his mind." And Franklin, at heart, was a decent man. Thus far, no words had been exchanged with his closest ally, Louis Howe, about his romantic entanglement, but Franklin could not ignore the mixed expressions of disbelief and disappointment on the face of his dogged disciple. Was their shared dream of an ascent to the White House to be derailed by reckless passion?

The torment for Lucy was no less. She was flying in the face of her church's teachings, which had been her moral compass since childhood.

She had sacrificed crucial years when a young woman should be seeking the security of a good marriage. Her foreboding was assuaged by the hope that someday they might marry. But what if in the end Franklin would not leave his wife? Their lives had become a mélange of happiness and anxiety, pleasure and guilt, risk and deception. Yet, the price was paid and the affair went on.

*Chapter 14*

# THE HOMECOMING

· · · · · · ·

O N September 14, 1917, six men, gray-haired and most of them portly, bore a coffin from St. John's Episcopal Church to a waiting hearse from the Joseph Gawler's Sons funeral parlor. Carroll Mercer was dead at age fifty-nine, according to the death certificate, from "chronic nephritis and valvular disease of the heart." *The Washington Post* marked the passing of "one of the most widely known of the old residents of the District." *Town Topics* was less kind. "Poor Carroll Mercer was laid away with some semblance of his former state. . . . It was a dreary day in keeping with the mournful purpose." For the pallbearers, all loyal cronies from the Metropolitan Club, *Town Topics* drew a self-righteous moral: "At the church they may have reflected on what the primrose path had brought to their associate." Another comment was more blunt. Carroll Mercer, "a drunkard and unable to support his wife and two daughters, was to die a pauper." The old veteran was buried in Arlington National Cemetery. Apart from the pallbearers, the turnout at St. John's was sparse. Conspicuously absent were Minnie, legally still Carroll's wife, and his daughters, Violetta and Lucy. His obituary made no mention of their existence. Mercer's last hope to regain his former station had faded a few years before. A columnist had written that Carroll, "in all probability will inherit something from his Aunt Sallie, the Countess of Esterhazy, provided she does not lavish everything she possesses on her young admirers." Evidently, the seventy-two-year-old countess preferred her suitors over her nephew and Carroll never got a dime.

The impoverished Carroll's passing had no impact on the Mercer family's finances. Lucy's service as a yeomanette provided a modest income, made her feel part of the war effort against the kaiser, and most of all it kept her near Franklin. She brought to her duties her usual competence and cheerful outlook. She was soon promoted from yeomanette third class to second class, her performance rated 4.0, a perfect grade in the Navy. And suddenly it all ended. Four months after joining, she was discharged, by "Special Order of Secretary of the Navy," with no reason given. Such a separation by the secretary was unusual and ordinarily given only for medical reasons or family hardship. Carroll Mercer's death could hardly be cited in the latter category, since the man died penniless. The better explanation, however, was to be found in the ever widening knowledge of her affair with Franklin. Obviously, the upright secretary of the navy had undoubtedly caught wind of the rumors that swirled about in the circles in which Josephus Daniels and his wife traveled. The three Patten sisters and Alice Roosevelt Longworth were all audible town criers. Eleanor felt stymied that discharging Lucy had merely moved her from the Roosevelt home to her husband's office. The sensible solution, chosen by Daniels alone or with Eleanor's concurrence, was to remove Lucy from the Navy. She now had no income. In his family memoir, *The Untold Story*, Franklin's son Elliott states that though his father was financially strapped himself at the time, still dependent on his mother, he continued "supporting Lucy. . . . He would not have abandoned her to poverty."

Eleanor, feeling that she was losing her hold on her husband, now sought to further her alliance with the mother-in-law from whom she had long been trying to free herself. She began writing frequently to Sara, warm, gushing letters, addressed to "Dearest Mummy." Eleanor and Franklin were at Hyde Park the weekend of October 13, 1917, when something happened that shook the matriarch's confidence in the indestructibility of her way of life. The Delano family seat, Algonac, on the other side of the Hudson, had burned to the ground the previous March. The loss of this family fortress of her youth had jarred Sara, but the way her siblings rallied immediately to rebuild the home had confirmed her belief in the resilience and superiority of their kind. That Sunday evening, Sara, Franklin, and Eleanor sat in the Hyde Park library, the flames from the massive fireplace tempering the fall chill. Sara took the opportunity to extol the virtues of family solidarity, of permanence as displayed by the Delanos in resurrecting Algonac. She seemed to be looking for assurances that Hyde Park, even when she was gone, would never slip out of Roosevelt hands. Ordinarily, Franklin, who equaled her in love for his birthplace, would have agreed unhesitatingly. But Hyde Park was so costly to maintain, and at this point his own future had become uncertain, his marital state unforeseeable. As the discussion proceeded, he displayed his irritability, induced by the double life he was leading. He could guarantee his mother nothing, he said. Though saying little, Eleanor did not disagree. Hyde Park had never really been home to her. Nothing had been resolved by the time Sara saw them off on the late train to Washington.

She returned home and settled into her favorite room, the small cozy "snuggery," pondering what had happened that evening. It was dark, the sun had long since settled behind the Catskill Mountains. Still, she felt she must write before she turned in. The letter she addressed to "Dearest Franklin, Dearest Eleanor" is remarkable for its revelation of her class attitudes, her tribal allegiance, and an unexpected vulnerability in this doughty figure. Part of Franklin's argument had been that times were changing and people like the Roosevelts could not expect to remain in the saddle forever. "One can be as democratic as one likes," she wrote, "but if we love our own, and if we love our neighbor, we owe a great example [to others]." She was ready to throw up her hands if maintaining the conventions of her world counted for nothing. "I thought, after all, would it not be better to spend all one has . . . and not think of the future, for with the trend to 'shirtsleeves' and the ideas of . . . being all things to all men and striving to give up the old fashioned traditions of family life, simple home pleasures and refinements . . . of what use is it to keep up things, to hold on to duty and all I stood up for this evening." She met her son's late-blooming egalitarianism with incredulity. "I cannot believe that my precious Franklin really feels as he expressed himself." She closed citing her mystification at how misunderstood she was. "When I talk I find I usually arouse opposition, which seems odd, but it is perhaps my own fault, and tends to lower my opinion of myself."

As 1918 arrived, Sara could take comfort in one victory. Eleanor, it seemed, was finally coming around to see that what might appear to be a mother-in-law's intrusiveness was merely an older woman sharing her life's wisdom with those she loved. Eleanor was now writing to Sara almost every day, the tone growing ever warmer, more intimate, and grateful. "I miss you and so do the children," she wrote that winter. "As the years go on I realize how lucky we are to have you and I wish we could always be together. Very few mothers I know mean as much to their daughters as you do to me." She began signing her letters "Much love, always, dear Mummy." When Sara congratulated the couple on their thirteenth wedding anniversary, Eleanor wrote back, "As I have grown older, I have realized better all you do for us, and all you mean to me and the children especially and you will never know how grateful I am nor how much I love you dear." Sara had not changed, but her son had. Franklin's long hours away from home, his increasing irritation and impatience when he was there, the procrastination over coming to Campobello, the pitying looks Eleanor thought she saw in her friends, all contributed to her sense that she needed a powerful ally in preserving her marriage; and who better than the woman who ruled the Roosevelt roost.

Another ally, at least in distracting her from her nameless fears, was her work. It was in the summer of 1918 that Franklin had departed aboard the USS *Dyer* for his two-month inspection tour of the front in Europe, a period that proved something of an emancipation for Eleanor. She packed the children off to Hyde Park, lived with one servant, and went happily to the railroad canteen every day. She would arrive early handing out the sandwiches, coffee, and cigarettes, meeting as many as eight trains a day spilling over with soldiers, then stagger home at 2:00 A.M. and be back on the job again later that morning. "No place could have been hotter than the little corrugated-tin shack with the tin roof and the fire burning in the old army kitchen," she later remembered of that time. She felt the significance of what she was doing when the president's wife joined the volunteers and she noted that "Mrs. Wilson now has a uniform and comes to work fairly regularly." More gratifying still, "Yesterday late the President came down and walked down the tracks and all around and they tell me seemed much interested." But most inspiring, her organizational skill had been spotted and she was asked if she could go abroad "with a unit of five to start a canteen in England. It is quite a temptation." The offer was heady, but as the mother of five children, Eleanor found the option impractical. As she was later to describe her decision, "I had not acquired sufficient independence to go about obtaining permission to serve overseas." Nevertheless, she now could believe that her life had value apart from her position as the wife of a high government official and from the domination of her mother-in-law.

Just before he was to sail aboard the *Dyer*, Franklin experienced within just a few feet of his own home what he might expect in Europe. Late on a June night, he and Eleanor were parking their car on R Street when a deafening roar tore off the roof of the home of Attorney General A. Mitchell Palmer, who lived across from them. The Palmer family was unharmed but the assassin who had tried to kill the attorney general instead blew himself to pieces. Alice Roosevelt Longworth, upon learning from a policeman what had caused the explosion, rushed to her cousin's home and later described the scene: "A leg lay in the path to the house next to theirs, another leg farther up the street. A head was on the roof of yet another house. . . . When we left, a large number of pieces had been assembled on a piece of newspaper, and seemed no more than so much carrion." She found the experience "curiously without horror."

By July 9, Franklin was gone. He had made his farewell to Lucy to whom goodbyes were becoming part of her life. Her sister, Violetta, her ally in the efforts to placate their always needy, always demanding mother, had gone off to war. Violetta, a trained nurse, was now in France, attached to a mobile hospital with the First Division. At one point it seemed Lucy had lost her sister forever. Violetta had been felled by diphtheria and lay in a hospital corridor with numerous other victims. A doctor, moving down the row, came upon her and pulled a sheet over her face. But she revived and was eventually returned to duty. With Franklin gone, Lucy treasured a photo he had given her, not one in his present eminence, but as a Harvard undergraduate. The pose is a period classic. He is wearing a heavy knit white sweater, the turtleneck reaching to his chin, hair parted in the middle, his expression solemn. It was a picture she would keep to her dying day.

While he was away, letters from home indicated that all was going reasonably well. Eleanor wrote, "I hate not being with you." And she finally seemed to be getting along famously with his mother. She even chided him for not paying Sara more attention: "When you don't write Mama, send messages [through me] to her, otherwise I have to invent and it is painful." His mother wrote him of her pride in Eleanor's war work. Sara's sister Kassie had told her that "Eleanor is the willing work horse and they call her at all hours and all the time." What precisely he intended to do about his personal situation upon his return was eclipsed for the time being by the pride, the satisfaction, the excitement of his mission and by his penchant for compartmentalizing his life.

All had gone splendidly until on the voyage home he became deathly ill. And then, after he arrived, Eleanor found Lucy's letters.

*Chapter 15*

# THE STORM

· · · · · · ·

THIRTEEN YEARS BEFORE, Eleanor had sobbed to her cousin Ethel that she would never be able to hold Franklin, "He's too attractive." Now, like the dread knock on the condemned prisoner's cell, the moment seemed at hand. As she had said, the bottom had dropped out of her life with the discovery of Lucy's letters, and the deed had been done by a man who had vowed before God "to love and cherish her until death do us part." How hollow had been his promises, his protestations of missing her while packing her off to Campobello, his lies about needing to stay behind because of the demands of his work. Her trust not only had been betrayed, but mocked and defiled. Franklin had openly deceived her with an employee she had taken into her home, entrusted with her most private affairs, invited into her social circle, indeed made part of her family. How false that person's pose of friendship. And what kind of woman, presumably so proper, so well bred, would go behind her back to steal her husband? Eleanor also had to wonder who had been the lovers' accomplices in deceit, Nigel Law, Livy Davis, Cousin Alice, the Eustises, even her own servants? How ridiculous she must appear within the circle in which she moved. Washington was then not so large a town, her set within it even smaller, totaling a few hundred people. How many of those who had regarded her with sympathetic looks had known of Franklin's faithlessness?

What was collapsing in her external life could not compare with the disintegration within. She had always believed herself more unattractive than she was, a conviction confirmed early by her mother's cutting comments, a mean-spirited aunt's insults, and other detractors among her own family. Her father had promised her happiness, then snatched it away by his dissipation and death. Only lately had the confidence she had known under Mlle. Souvestre returned with her recognized contributions to the war effort. Now, in an instant, a packet of letters had swept away that fragile edifice, and raised instead her old certainty that she was neither loved nor valued. Because of her lack of interest in sex, other than to fulfill a woman's biological destiny, she had not grasped what an overpowering force it was. Now, faced with incontrovertible evidence that her husband had found satisfaction elsewhere, sexual failure was added to her catalogue of inadequacies. Had she, in her physical passivity, invited his straying?

After being carried from the *Leviathan* to the guest bedroom at his mother's townhouse on September 19, 1918, Franklin remained in New York until the end of the month when he felt strong enough to be moved to Hyde Park. In the immediate aftermath of reading Lucy's letters, Eleanor was too dumbstruck to confront him. The precise content of the letters can never be known because, as she confided years later to a curator at the Roosevelt Library, she had destroyed them. But, however genteelly Lucy might have expressed herself, her words left no doubt as to the seriousness of the affair. As Eleanor digested their awful import, she accepted what she must do. She approached Franklin as soon as he began to mend with the proof in hand of his infidelity.

Franklin's position was not unlike that of the Newland Archer character Edith Wharton drew in *The Age of Innocence*. She has Archer despising the casual promiscuity of a character called Lefferts while himself becoming involved with Ellen Olenska. "But to love Ellen Olenska, was not to become a man like Lefferts," she wrote. "Ellen Olenska was like no other woman, he was like no other man: their situation therefore, resembled no one else's; and they were answerable to no tribunal but that of their own judgment." Lucy was like no other woman, and Franklin was like no other man. What they had done and what they felt for each other therefore could not be compared to the lechery of a Livy Davis. Franklin suffered qualms of conscience, understood the risks to his marriage and career, but in the company of Lucy, they vanished. Since the day of his birth his parents had indulged his every wish—ponies, boats, trips abroad, a Gold Coast Harvard apartment, luxurious homes, denying him nothing. Why should he now be forbidden Lucy's love?

In the confrontation with Eleanor, Franklin admitted his feelings for

Lucy. In likely the most reckless move of his heretofore cautiously constructed life, he said he wanted to be free to marry her. Eleanor, years later, confided to her daughter, Anna, what happened next. "She told me that she questioned him, offered him a divorce and asked that he take time to think things over carefully before giving her a definite answer." Most importantly, she urged him to consider the effects of divorce on their children. He had not merely indulged another of his flirtations, which Eleanor had learned to accept, even joke about, but he was now prepared to throw everything away, family, public prominence, political aspirations, for a woman. At age thirty-six, he likely asked himself if he was ready to settle for thirty years in a marriage largely dutiful, if not exactly loveless? Eleanor's cousin Corinne had divined what Lucy meant to Franklin, quoting La Rochefoucauld, "There are good marriages, but they have not a bit of the *delicieux*," the delectable.

Eleanor accepted that she was beaten. How could she, unattractive in her own eyes, unexciting, duty-ridden, with a touch of the spinster about her, compete with a beautiful, younger woman who had stirred in her husband depths of passion that she had never aroused, never cared to, nor knew how to. Her Uncle Ted had once written to her Aunty Bye, two people she revered, concerning her own father, "it is criminal folly for a woman to forgive her husband's infidelity and go on living with him; it comes from weakness and wrong-headedness." Eleanor had advised a friend in a similar predicament to her own, "I beg you not to accept $1/2$ loaf of love." Years afterward, she would write of divorce, "Sometimes even when a marriage begins with every apparent prospect of success, people develop differently and find themselves over a period of years, unable to live together in harmony. When that happens, it seems to me there is nothing to do but resort to divorce. . . . For two people to live unhappily together seems to be bad for them and the children, if any." She had already accepted this painful inevitability when she confronted her husband in the fall of 1918.

Eventually, they would have to face his mother with the truth. Sara, as a young wife, had visited the Chicago World's Fair with her husband, James, and in their hotel lobby ran into Maggie Carey, a girlhood friend whom she had not seen for years and who was now divorced. Sara suggested they get together later that day. When she mentioned her plan to James, he objected vehemently. Under no circumstances was she to have anything to do with a divorced woman. Sara never saw Maggie

Carey again. After Cousin Alice's failed attempt to divorce the chronically faithless Nick Longworth, she noted, "I don't think one can have any idea how horrendous even the idea of divorce was in those days. I remember telling my family in 1912 I wanted one and, although they didn't quite lock me up, they exercised considerable pressure to get me to reconsider." Indeed, no one in either branch of the Roosevelt family had ever been divorced.

In a tense encounter in Sara's living room, its dark, massive furniture, thick carpets, and heavy drapery reflecting the solidity of Roosevelt life, Eleanor, resignedly, spoke of her willingness to give Franklin his freedom. He listened, still pale from his sickness. Sara was aghast. The idea that her son wanted to divorce Eleanor was the greatest shock she had suffered since thirteen years before when he had told her he intended to marry her. It is "all very well for you, Eleanor, to speak of being willing to give Franklin his freedom," she said. But imagine the wagging tongues and shaking heads at Oyster Bay. What would that pillar of rectitude, TR, think? Adultery could be concealed, even tolerated, but divorce was a calamity. If Franklin seriously meant to leave his wife and five children for another woman and bring disgrace upon his family, she could not stand in his way. Then the dowager empress of Hyde Park delivered her terms. If Franklin persisted, she would cut him off without a cent and forfeit his right to inherit the estate. He now confronted his choices, freedom at a high price or living on in the comfortable prison of convention. He enjoyed lavish living, and unthinkingly assumed it as his due. The annual income from Eleanor's trust, $8,000, and his own $5,000, could support a livable upper-middle-class life in that age. But not the life the Roosevelts led. Who would pay for the upkeep on their homes, the servants' salaries, write the checks for his memberships in the most exclusive clubs in New York and Washington, cover the children's tuition at the best private schools, and book the first-class cabins for travel abroad? Just the previous March when two of his children were ill, Franklin had written his mother, "You have saved my life or rather, the various doctors' lives, by making it possible for me to pay them promptly!" In the same letter he reminded Sara that a tax bill was due on his boat, the *Half Moon*, as well as payment of his life insurance premium.

Was Sara serious about cutting off the son whom she adored above all else on earth? She was a woman of granite will, and doubting her intentions was risky. He had to accept that he was kept by his mother on a golden leash.

On October 18, his health largely restored, Franklin and the family were back in Washington, warmly welcomed by a much relieved Livy Davis. Livy, long privy to the affair, soon learned of Franklin's present predicament. Within days they sought distractions back on the links, though Livy saw how tired Franklin was, managing to play only nine holes. During the crisis Franklin finally consulted Louis Howe about what he should do. For Howe, that Franklin was seriously considering leaving Eleanor for Lucy was as if a heavy bettor had seen his horse stumble midway in a high-stakes race. What of those White House dreams revealed as a college boy so long ago in the Sohiers' home, later repeated to his law firm colleagues, shared with Louis in the State Senate in Albany? Howe began trekking between his airless, messy office in the Navy Department to R Street, desperate to get his horse back on track. The previously unwelcome and untidy little man now became Eleanor's ally, while she held her breath, awaiting Franklin's decision. "It wasn't just Sara," Elliott Roosevelt has written, "it was Louis Howe going back and forth and just reasoning, convincing father that he had no political future if he did this." The grounds for divorce in New York State in Franklin's time were adultery, and the details of the affair, if revealed in court proceedings and pounced upon by the press, would spell his political death.

And if politics was out, what else would Franklin do? He was no businessman, no great shakes at the law. His most promising path and strongest ambition would be dead-ended. If he wanted to continue to rise in politics, Louis Howe warned, it would have to be with Eleanor at his side. Otherwise he could not run for dog catcher in Hyde Park village. If divorced, would he even be able to continue in his present job? Both he and Louis well understood Josephus Daniels's puritanical streak. How would a man who had rescinded the issuance of condoms for sailors going on shore leave, who believed that virginity and abstinence were the proper lot of healthy young men, react toward a subordinate enmeshed in an illicit affair? When his own brother-in-law, managing the *Raleigh News Observer* in Daniels's absence, a man who had twice loaned him money to rebuild the paper, told him that he wanted to divorce and marry another woman, Daniels told him to get out of town, which he did, moving to Texas.

Practicality and economics are the death of romance. Franklin now accepted what he had to do. But first, with his two-track mind well in command, he immersed himself in the department business he still relished. He prepared for Daniels an analysis and recommendations based on what he had found in Europe. The ever impressed Daniels sent Franklin's paper to President Wilson with a note praising the "clear, concise, and illuminating report [by] the clear-headed and able FDR." Finally Franklin knew that he must face Lucy. Where did they meet? That they did meet after Eleanor's discovery of the affair is known because many years later, Franklin's daughter, Anna, who had come to know a middle-aged Lucy, told an interviewer, "L.M. hinted to me there were a couple of such meetings to wind up loose ends." When they met, whatever their private anguish, the ego-driven Franklin could not resist sharing with Lucy the contents of his European diary, specifics of which she could still recall over a quarter of a century later. He showed her passages describing the high personages he had dealt with, the dangers he had endured, a rousing speech he had made before his old law partner Harry Hooker's regiment while sheltered in the woods near Amiens.

Before his departure to Europe, they had spoken of marriage. It could not be, he told her. Eleanor would not grant him a divorce. His deception was double-edged. He had first deceived Eleanor. Now he was deceiving Lucy with the claim that Eleanor stood in their way. Years later, Franklin's daughter, Anna, gave an interview to Joseph Lash, Eleanor's biographer, who asked her if "FDR may have used the story of ER's refusal to give him a divorce as a way of putting off Lucy." Anna agreed. As for Eleanor, though her heart had been broken and her self-esteem battered, Franklin's decision to stick with her came as a relief since, as Anna put it, "She loved the guy deeply."

When Franklin met with Lucy it is unlikely that he told her the principal demand Eleanor had extracted from him for staying in the marriage, that Lucy was to be effaced from his life; he was never to see her again. Eleanor had imposed on him a second condition: he was never again to share her bed. How much sacrifice this stipulation cost Eleanor, who once told her daughter that sex was an ordeal to be borne, cannot have been great. And according to family lore the latter condition had already been met to avoid further pregnancies.

A shattered Lucy fled to the home of her Henderson cousins, Mary and Elizabeth, in Salisbury, North Carolina. Elizabeth Henderson Cotten recalled of that time, "I know that a marriage would have taken place but as Lucy said to us, 'Eleanor was not willing to step aside.' " Lucy was not a "shrinking violet," Elizabeth further noted. "But she realized it was hopeless . . . [though] I am sure neither one of them ever loved anyone else." How much of Eleanor's understandable opprobrium did Lucy deserve for permitting the affair? She was a warmhearted, decent human being whose only sin had been to fall hopelessly in love.

The idea has been put forth that Lucy would never have married Franklin because she was a devout descendant of Maryland's Catholic founders. But her father's family were Episcopalians. Her mother had been divorced when she married Carroll Mercer. They had been wed in London in a Church of England ceremony, which, according to the Catholic rejection of divorce, meant she was not married at all. As Cousin Elizabeth put it, Minnie Mercer's Catholicism was a late-blooming affair that she had come by for sentimental not theological reasons. And Elizabeth further observed, "Nothing is easier in the Roman Catholic Church than annulment, especially among those occupying high places."

The discovery of the affair and Franklin's reaction offer a glimpse into the soul of this opaque man. His ambition ran deep. His passion for politics and public service ran deep; but his commitment to love, while real, was evidently less deep. In October, while recuperating at Hyde Park and in the throes of the divorce crisis, he still took time to pursue his dream of martial glory. He wrote his secretary, Charles McCarthy, "You are quite right in guessing that I am probably going to get into the fighting end of the game, but, if I do so I suppose it will be the Navy and not the Army." When well enough to return to Washington, he rode the crest of his admired report on Europe to gain another meeting with President Wilson set for October 13 to press again his case for getting into uniform. Earlier that day a story broke in the papers, doubtlessly planted by Louis Howe, that the assistant secretary of the navy intended to enlist as an ordinary seaman. Franklin managed to see a much preoccupied president at 11:00 P.M. that evening. Peace was in the air, Wilson informed him. He had in hand a proposal from the new German chancellor, Prince Max of Baden. The war could end within weeks, which it did. The slaughter was over, yet Roosevelt viewed the outpouring of cheering crowds into the Washington streets, impromptu parades, honking of horns, ringing of church bells, and shouts of "Hang the Kaiser!" with mixed feelings.

Aunty Bye's son, William Sheffield Cowles Jr., recalled Franklin telling him that "he had made a mistake taking the job of assistant secretary. If he had gone into the Navy at the beginning of the war with his knowledge of the sea and sailing, he would have been an executive officer on a destroyer." "I would have loved that," Franklin told Cowles.

Just before the Armistice, his scheme for 100,000 mines to block a major sea lane had finally been implemented but too late to affect the war's outcome. Not, however, in Franklin's recounting. "It may not be too far-fetched . . . to say," he later would claim, "that the North Sea mine barrage . . . had something to do with the German Naval mutiny and the ending of the World War." No matter how he inflated his experiences, the truth remained: he had been a civilian in wartime and the valor and political advantage of battlefield heroics had passed him by.

At some point, Eleanor destroyed the letters Franklin had sent her during their courtship. His tender affirmations of eternal and abiding love seemed to her a mockery. When this erasure of part of her past took place is uncertain, but likely not long after her faith in Franklin had been destroyed. During their courtship, their different characters had seemed healthily complementary, his confidence, magnetism, and extroversion coupled with her shyness, loyalty, and high principles. After his faithlessness had been revealed, the equation began to shift. His confidence began to appear to her as egotism, his extroversion as shallowness, his magnetism as a gift squandered on self-indulgence. James Roosevelt, writing many years later, marked the end of the affair as the beginning between his parents of "an armed truce that endured until the day he died." Franklin had promised to give up Lucy, but for Eleanor the doubts would never wholly vanish.

In the end, the three parties in the triangle behaved according to character, Eleanor self-sacrificing, Franklin self-preserving, Lucy lovelorn but resilient, as subsequent events would prove. While letters flew endlessly among Sara, Eleanor, and Franklin before discovery of the affair, none can be found for the months following. Perhaps communication had halted or more likely letters written were subsequently destroyed in an effort to erase Franklin's transgression. Nineteen years later, when Eleanor wrote her first autobiography, *This Is My Story*, it was to be an incomplete story. Recounting the year 1918, she wrote at length of Franklin's mission to Europe, of eighteen-hour shifts at the canteen, of her desperately ill husband being carried into his mother's house, even of her daughter, Anna, winning a German shepherd puppy in a lottery at the time. But of her heartbreak and the near destruction of her marriage that year, not a word. As she later said, "I have the memory of an elephant. I can forgive, but never forget."

If Sara had not threatened to cut off her son, if Franklin had divorced Eleanor and remarried, and if indeed his political career ended, how differently might the history of the twentieth century have read?

*Chapter 16*

# THE ADVANTAGE OF ADVERSITY

· · · · · · ·

IN THE FALL OF 1918 caretakers at Washington's Rock Creek Cemetery noticed a frequent visitor, always alone, who proceeded to a secluded holly grove. There she sat on a stone bench contemplating a statue of a beautiful, hooded woman, her visage a portrait of melancholy. The statue had been erected by the historian Henry Adams, grandson and great-grandson of presidents, in memory of his late wife, Marian, known as "Clover." The seated figure had been created by the country's foremost sculptor, Augustus Saint-Gaudens, and entitled *Peace of God*, though it became popularly known as *Grief.* Thirty-three years before, Clover Adams had killed herself, reportedly by swallowing photographic acid, after she learned that her husband had been involved in a love affair.

The current visitor was Eleanor Roosevelt, who drove the considerable distance from her R Street home to the cemetery several times a week. In the serenity of the grove, she found a kinship with the woman who had ended her life over a husband's betrayal. "As I looked at it I felt that all the sorrow humanity had ever had to endure was expressed in that face," she wrote of the statue. "Yet in that expression there was something almost triumphant."

Photos of Eleanor during this period reveal a woman unable to look directly at the camera, as if trying to conceal a private shame. In the months following the discovery of Franklin's affair, she had lost weight at an alarming rate. She had trouble keeping food down and reported after a dinner with Sara, "I might as well not have eaten it for I promptly parted with it all." The acids brought up by the vomiting began to damage her gums, causing her teeth to loosen, spread apart, and protrude even further.

President Wilson's inclusion of Franklin among officials attending the peace conference at Versailles in January 1919 and Secretary Daniels's permission to allow Eleanor to accompany her husband provided momentary relief from her shattered self-esteem. For a time, Franklin went out of his way to please her. He came directly home from the office after work, spent more time with the children, gave up Sunday morning golf and instead went to church with Eleanor, though her stomach rebelled even at the Communion wafer. She in turn tried to affect an unconvincing gaiety at parties they attended. Still, her resentment broke through. On the trip to France aboard the USS *George Washington*, attractive young women flirted openly with her husband, prompting Eleanor to write her mother-in-law, "Just wait till I get home and tell you what these respectable people let their daughters do. Your hair will curl as mine did." A comely English woman played up so shamelessly to Franklin that an angry Eleanor dragged him back to their stateroom at midnight. "We have nothing like some of their women or some of their men," she wrote Sara. From Paris she reported, "The scandals going on would make many a woman at home unhappy." On a cold gray dawn heavy with snow, Franklin departed Paris alone on an official trip to Belgium. "I hate . . . to have him go off without me," Eleanor confessed to her diary. She lived as a woman torn between the love she could not suppress and anger at the betrayer of that love.

Upon their return home in mid-February, the domestic climate failed to improve. Eleanor wrote in her diary, "I do not think I have ever felt so strangely as in the past year. . . . All my self-confidence is gone." Petty irritations erupted into long, bitter arguments, occasionally driving Franklin out of the house. In April 1919, she wrote in the diary, "Dined alone. . . . Franklin nervous and overwrought and I very stupid and trying, result a dreadful fracas." When he did hold out a conciliatory hand to her, according to their son James, "she did not take it." To escape the poisoned atmosphere, Franklin sought out male companionship, going off on one occasion with Livy Davis and the polar explorer Richard E. Byrd to Canada to hunt moose, play poker, and drink bourbon.

In July 1919, race clashes erupted in Washington between returning white and black doughboys. That summer, Eleanor had taken the children not to Campobello, but to Fairhaven, the Delano family's Massachusetts estate. After thirty-nine people had been killed in the capital's streets, she badgered Franklin, "No word from you, and I am getting anxious on account of the riots." Two days later she wrote, "I am worried to death. . . . I couldn't sleep at all last night thinking of all the things that might be the matter." When she returned to Washington, she began nagging him with phone calls at his office if he was not home on the dot. When her suspicions were aroused, she showed up at the department to make sure he came home.

Franklin's banishment from her bed appears to have been enforced. The fertile Eleanor, who had borne six children in ten years, never had another though she was only thirty-four at the time the affair was discovered. Where did that leave Franklin, still possessing the urges of a healthy thirty-six-year-old male? Renewed romantic liaisons? While the Lucy affair was fairly common knowledge within the Roosevelts' circle, no breath of scandal suggested his involvement with another woman at the time. Could he have found release among the demimonde of Washington or New York who served an upper-class clientele? Once again, the dark corners of private sexual behavior conceal the answer.

In the summer of 1919, Eleanor was about to undergo further trials. Her Grandmother Hall, who had dutifully if joylessly raised her after her father's death, died on August 14 at age seventy-six. It fell to Eleanor, as the most responsible member of that ill-starred family, to handle the funeral arrangements. Once again her innate competence as an organizer came to the fore. As she performed her duties, she pondered the narrowness of the dead woman's life, the opportunities lost, since Mary Hall had sacrificed considerable artistic gifts to family responsibilities. In one of her autobiographies, Eleanor wrote, "My grandmother's life had a considerable effect on me. . . . I was determined that I would never be dependent upon my children by allowing all my interests to center in them." Though burying her grandmother was a somber task, it did have one therapeutic effect. As she put it, "any work is almost the best way to pull oneself out of the depths." Even with the war over, she pressed on with her volunteer duties and organized teas for hundreds of guests of the Navy Department. In time disciplined activity became so ingrained in her that the original impetus, distraction from her aching heart, was supplanted by unshakable habit.

With her marriage saved, the temporary alliance between Eleanor and her mother-in-law again began to fray. She started to confront Sara head-on, disputing her over the children's upbringing, management of the servants, even handling of family finances. Sara remained as fixed in her certitude as ever, her outlook as inflexible as it was narrow. All of Eleanor's pretense of daughterly love for a surrogate mother began to unravel. She understood that in Sara she faced a woman whom she could never please and in whose presence she could never prevail. During her escape from Hyde Park to Fairhaven, she had written Franklin, "I feel as though someone has taken a ton of bricks off me and I suppose she feels just the same." That fall, she wrote in her diary, "Mama and I have a bad time. I should be ashamed of myself and I am not. She is too good and her judgment is better than mine, but I can bend more easily."

She began to display growing independence by taking charge of the domestic staff at R Street, who previously had cowed her. All were white, reflecting Sara's preference and New York society's convention that blacks could not be trusted to work inside the home. Now Eleanor fired the lot of them, cook, kitchen maid, house maid, and butler, all except an English nurse, and replaced them with what she called "my darkies," a decision that horrified Sara. At this point in her life, the woman who was one day to become a fighter against racial discrimination had not yet emerged. Upon meeting Mary McLeod Bethune, at the time the nation's most distinguished black educator, Eleanor found herself uncomfortable giving the woman a peck on the cheek.

Six months after the death of her grandmother, Eleanor received a telegram from Forbes Morgan, the man who years before had rescued her from neglect at the Assembly Ball and who was now the husband of her Aunt Pussie. It was Pussie who had despaired of Eleanor's marriage prospects, telling her she was too plain ever to find a beau. Pussie was a beautiful, charming, unstable creature, her emotions nakedly on display, her behavior described most kindly as arising from an "artistic temperament." Her marriage to the much younger Morgan, though producing three children, had been miserable and she frequently threatened suicide. Eleanor described her aunt as someone who "could not make life . . . an easy matter." Morgan's telegram informed Eleanor that her aunt had burned to death in the family's Ninth Street home in New York, along with two of her three children. Eleanor instantly took the train to New York to help Morgan through the tragedy. She arrived in a snowstorm on a bitterly cold day and trudged for miles through drifts to locate him. Looking back on those days, Eleanor wrote Franklin words that seemed to strike a note of hope between them. "It is a curious thing in human experience," she said, "people can be happy together and look back on their contacts very pleasantly, but such contacts will not make the same kind of bond that sorrow lived through together will create."

Finally she began to exhibit signs that her soul was healing. She clipped a poem from a newspaper entitled "Psyche" written by Virginia Moore:

> The soul that has believed
> And is deceived
> Thinks nothing for a while
> All thoughts are vile.
> And then because the sun
> Is mute persuasion
> And hope in Spring and Fall
> Most natural,
> The soul grows calm and mild
> A little child,
> Finding the pull of breath
> Better than death . . .
> The soul that had believed
> And was deceived
> Ends by believing more
> Than ever before.

It is tempting but futile to try to locate the single turning point that alters a life. Nevertheless, a trauma survived can open up a path that otherwise might have remained unseen. Looking back years later, Eleanor saw her time of trial as not utterly barren of value. "I think I learned then that practically no one in the world is entirely bad or entirely good. I had spent most of my life in an atmosphere where everyone was sure of what was right and what was wrong. . . . Out of these contacts with human beings during the war I became a more tolerant person far less sure of my own beliefs. . . . I had gained a certain assurance as to my ability to run things, and the knowledge that there is joy in accomplishing a good job. I knew more about the human heart, which had been somewhat veiled in mystery up to now." Spiritually this is where Eleanor found herself in 1920 as she and her husband neared the end of their sojourn in Washington.

## Chapter 17

# A BRILLIANT MARRIAGE

· · · · · · ·

MINNIE MERCER, who had once occupied herself with hosting the most glittering parties in Washington, now applied her energies to seeking a minuscule widow's pension from the U.S. government. On February 14, 1919, as the Roosevelts were returning from the Paris peace conference, she was at the U.S. Pension Office filing a claim based on Carroll's service in the Marine Corps and in the Army during the Spanish-American War. Minnie's lawyer, Henry E. Davis, a friend and fellow Cave Dweller, said in a deposition to pension officials, "she is now without resources of what kind so ever and wholly dependent as aforesaid." Carroll's last will had left all his earthly possessions "to my children Violetta C. and Lucy P. Mercer," with no mention of the woman still legally his wife. But since he possessed nothing, his daughters received nothing.

Minnie had already run through one windfall. When Carroll's aunt, the Countess d'Esterhazy, died about a month after her nephew, Davis had managed to obtain £1,000 for Minnie from the countess's estate. The fairly substantial sum was immediately swallowed up by Minnie's creditors. She attempted to go back to the well that summer, cabling the London firm of Oames, Edwards and Jones to contest the countess's will as having shortchanged her. The firm dismissed her claim out of hand, telling Minnie, "There is no possibility of you succeeding in an appeal against the decision." Instead, the lawyers billed her £10 for their services.

In March of 1920, she was back at the Pension Office with a sworn affidavit further establishing her destitution. She claimed incorrectly that she had received no support from her elder daughter, Violetta, "who was absent in France, being an Army nurse." By this time, however, Violetta was back from France and living in Washington with her husband, Dr. William B. Marbury, a descendant of an old and distinguished Maryland family. They had met on the Western Front during Violetta's nursing service and where Marbury had been a battlefield doctor. In her affidavit, Minnie stated that Lucy paid the $35 per month rent on the apartment in the Toronto "in addition to the living expenses." She herself only "helped with the housework, kept the house, did the mending and did the things that mother's do." The truth was that Lucy had, three days before her mother signed the affidavit, reversed her fortunes magnificently.

Immediately after the romance with Franklin, a heartsick Lucy had sought solace in the home of her Henderson cousins. Elizabeth was now married to Captain Lyman A. Cotten, a member of the General Board of the Navy, likely appointed through Franklin's intercession. The Cottens and Minnie were now neighbors. The couple's ten-year-old son, Lyman Jr., carried throughout life memories of "Cousin Minnie who used to take my brother and me to the movies and to tea at her apartment afterwards. I can not remember a single movie we ever saw, but I remember vividly the brilliant personality of Cousin Minnie. I thought her very daring for smoking cigarettes." As for Lucy, "she was very different from her mother. She was tall and stately and quiet in manner. Her features were regular, her skin exquisitely fine." Young Lyman found her smile the most beautiful and winning he had ever seen.

Before Lucy moved from the Toronto apartments on July 30, 1919, yeomanettes, present and former, staged a victory parade down Pennsylvania Avenue, inspected by Navy Secretary Josephus Daniels, and Assistant Secretary Franklin Roosevelt. Lucy was not among the marchers. Her life had taken its new turn. She, with Franklin, had occasionally been in the company of Winthrop Rutherfurd at the H Street mansion of Edith and Willie Eustis. "Winty," as he was known in his circle, was now in his late fifties, still trim, erect, and handsome. An aura of romantic mystery clung to the man described when young as "the handsomest bachelor in society." He had once won the heart of Consuelo Vanderbilt, "the most beautiful woman in the world," and the granddaughter of Commodore Cornelius Vanderbilt, who upon his death was the richest man in America. Consuelo's mother, Alva Vanderbilt Belmont, likely the most determined and manipulative social climber of the Gilded Age, was unmoved by the romance. Though wealthy and descended from one of America's most venerable families, with Peter Stuyvesant, the first governor of New York, and John Winthrop, the first governor of Massachusetts, among his ancestors, Rutherfurd was socially inadequate for Alva's ambitions. She had her sights for a son-in-law set on the ninth Duke of Marlborough, the master of Blenheim Palace, who was all too willing to wed an American heiress. Alva had reportedly thrown a tantrum upon learning of Consuelo's involvement with Rutherfurd, and claimed she would have a heart attack if the liaison did not end. Consuelo was eventually led to the altar in 1895 to become the Duchess of Marlborough. "Winty was outclassed," one society wit noted. "Six feet two in his golf stockings, he was no match for five feet six in a coronet."

Rutherfurd possessed immense wealth, an ancestral estate in New Jersey set amid a thousand acres, as well as homes in Washington, New York, and Paris. He rode to hounds with Theodore Roosevelt, and Eleanor's father, Elliott. He had not married until age forty, either waiting for the failed romance with Consuelo Vanderbilt to heal or, far more likely, as a sought-after bachelor who enjoyed his freedom. He was reputed to have had affairs with numerous married socialites, Ava Astor, wife of Colonel John Jacob Astor, among his rumored conquests. He was so attractive to women that Edith Wharton admitted that Rutherfurd was "the prototype of my first novels." When he married in 1902, he chose as his bride Alice, the youngest, tallest, and fairest of former Vice President Levi Morton's daughters. Edith Eustis, Franklin's accomplice in romance, was another Morton sister and hence Rutherfurd's sister-in-law. The Rutherfurds had six children, five sons and a daughter, at the time of Alice's death in June 1917, the youngest aged two. Shortly before she died she had converted to Catholicism and her husband had joined her in adopting the faith. Winty and Franklin had long known of each other, given their common Hudson Valley connections. Ellerslie, Levi Morton's estate, was close by Hyde Park. Though they represented different generations, Franklin and Winthrop were further acquainted through membership in several of the same elite clubs.

"It is a truth universally acknowledged that a single man in possession of a good fortune must be in want of a wife." Thus Jane Austen begins *Pride and Prejudice*. The widower Rutherfurd qualified on both counts. The nature of Lucy's personal involvement with Winty, beyond meeting him as a guest in the Eustis home, is clouded. Edith may have felt concern over the future of her motherless niece and nephews. Nurses, nannies, and tutors were not lacking, but knowing Rutherfurd's situation and Lucy's hardship, Edith possibly planted the idea that the children, the eldest still a teenager, needed supervision and that the young Mercer woman might be suitable. However it came about, sometime in early 1919, Lucy became part of the Rutherfurd family circle in an undefined role. Elizabeth Cotten later warned an author writing about her cousin, "Don't think that Lucy ever entered the Rutherfurd household as a sort of governess or foster mother! Such a position would have been out of the question. Under no circumstances suggest such a possibility." Which leaves uncertain what exactly Lucy's role was in the Rutherfurd home.

In February 1920, Eleanor had invited Frank Polk, the undersecretary of state, and his wife, Lilly, to tea. It was the first social initiative that she had taken since returning from the burial of Pussie and her aunt's two children. The invitation had been engineered by Mrs. Polk, as a favor to her friend Lucy Mercer. Lucy had asked Lilly to deliver a delicate message to Franklin. Her engagement was about to be announced in the newspapers, and Lucy did not want Franklin to learn of it so coldly. However, as the afternoon progressed Mrs. Polk found no opportunity to be alone with him. Instead, as she and her husband were putting on their coats to leave, she asked Eleanor casually but loudly enough for the two chatting husbands to overhear, whether Eleanor had heard that Lucy Mercer was engaged to marry Winty Rutherfurd. On hearing this, according to one family account, Franklin "started like a horse in fear of a hornet."

On February 11, 1920, Lucy stood alongside Rutherfurd, in the home of her sister, Violetta, to be married. Only immediate family were among the guests, and the wedding was hardly festive. The previous weeks had been an ordeal for Rutherfurd as he watched his eldest son, Lewis, aged sixteen, die of pneumonia. Minnie attended the marriage, dressed with subdued elegance, to watch her daughter marry a man only a year younger than herself. Also present were Rutherfurd's surviving children and Lucy's Henderson relatives. Lyman Cotten Jr., then eleven, was puzzled that his beautiful, gracious cousin was marrying an "old and ugly man." Jonathan Daniels, son of Secretary Daniels, who later chronicled the event, was even harsher. Lucy's new husband, in Daniels's judgment, "was a dull, dog-horse-and-golf man with few intellectual interests."

The age gap between the man Lucy had loved and the one she married was wide. Franklin Roosevelt had been two years old when Winthrop Rutherfurd graduated from Columbia College. What had motivated Lucy to marry a man twenty-nine years her senior? Rutherfurd's wealth and social position easily leap to mind. She had spent her adolescent and adult years as a firsthand witness to the anxieties and indignities of poverty. Even the oft rumored match with the elegant Nigel Law could not guarantee her security since the Englishman's fortune fell far below his social rank. Lucy was a healthy personality who had embraced true love when it came her way, yet practical enough to rebound when it failed. She was now twenty-nine, well past the ideal age for marriage in that era. Wedding a man possessed of wealth and position, who clearly adored her and whom she found attractive, if not her grand passion, would insure her future, recapturing everything her mother and father had squandered. Her mother, by contrast, was currently seeking a $30 per month pension from the government.

To suggest that Lucy married solely for money slights the character of a woman admired by almost everyone who knew her. From every account, she assumed the role of loving, supportive wife and stepmother much as Sara Roosevelt did whose marriage to James Roosevelt presented a similar age gap. As one of Rutherfurd's sons, Guy, described his feelings toward Lucy long years afterward, "She was never a stepmother. I never considered her anything but my mother. She was a fantastic woman, beautiful and very loving. We all got along very well." The other Rutherfurd children expressed similar closeness and affection. According to her cousin Elizabeth, Lucy "married Mr. Rutherfurd not for money but because she felt he needed her." In the end, the relevant point was not whether Lucy married for love or position, but that she found both.

While news of the marriage shook Franklin, it also freed him. A political career for a man divorced or immersed in a love affair was a dead issue. Lucy was lost to him anyway, and now any threat to his future that the liaison might have posed was essentially removed. He was a respectable husband and father. She was a respectably married woman. That was all the world need know. Eleanor was doubtless relieved too, as she wrote in a terse note to Sara, her erstwhile partner in preserving her marriage, "Did you know Lucy Mercer married Mr. Winty Rutherfurd two days ago?"

What happened to Franklin in the following months soon demonstrated the advantage of Lucy's removal from his orbit. As Woodrow Wilson neared the end of his second term, Franklin remained loyal to the beleaguered president, whom he found "more a man of thought than of action, but a most thoughtful man." At the July 1920 Democratic National Convention in San Francisco, he attempted to have Wilson nominated for a third term, futile in light of the president's plunging fortunes and political tradition. Wilson had promised peace and taken the country into war; his dream of leading the United States into the League of Nations had foundered; racial strife between white and black veterans had bloodied city streets. The delegates knew that the country craved a change from Wilsonian high-mindedness. Franklin's loyalty was commendable but further ill spent because never in American politics had a physically handicapped man, as a stroke had rendered Wilson, been elected president. At the convention, Frances Perkins recalled seeing Franklin vault over four rows of seats to reach the platform demanding to be heard before the speaker could gavel down further debate. "It was the most wonderful athletic feat," Perkins recalled, "very graceful and unstudied."

On the forty-sixth ballot, the delegates nominated Ohio's governor, James Cox, as their presidential candidate. Cox had made something of a mark during the recent war by demagogically supporting a ban on the teaching of German in schools to prevent the language from corrupting the minds of young Americans. When his floor manager phoned Cox to ask whom he wanted as his vice presidential running mate, he answered without hesitation, "Young Roosevelt." Franklin was indeed young, just thirty-eight, charismatic, exuding vigor, and eager to climb another rung up the political ladder. The fact was not lost on him that the vice presidency had propelled TR into the White House. He accepted the offer. Cox's choice was astute. Roosevelt came from a vote-rich state, carried the magic name, and his Tammany Hall antagonists eagerly supported any move to keep Roosevelt out of New York.

However confident, upbeat, and ever smiling as he crisscrossed the country delivering nonstop speeches until the patrician voice grew raspy, Franklin knew that the ticket was doomed. The Republican candidate, Senator Warren Harding, was offering Americans a return to "normalcy," a linguistic coinage of his own and exactly what the nation wanted. To Franklin and Louis Howe, the hopelessness of the race was not the point. They had balanced the pros and cons and concluded that the national exposure and political friendships to be forged throughout the country counted for far more. Cox's defeat would be his own, not Roosevelt's. For Franklin there would still be political tomorrows.

During the campaign, Thomas J. Lynch, who ran the Democrats' campaign schedule, had a conversation with Franklin that he never forgot. "He told me," Lynch recalled, "Tom, this is not my year. My year will be 1932." Pressed by Lynch as to why he was so certain, he merely repeated, "Oh yes, 1932 will be my year, Tom."

The 1920 campaign revealed the jealousies that ran just below the surface of familial loyalty between the Roosevelt clans. TR's son Theodore Jr. campaigned against Franklin. Ignoring issues, he privately expressed his true objection. "No one," he warned his kin, "should vote for Franklin Roosevelt. He doesn't wear the brand of our family." Franklin's college boy support of TR for president counted for nothing. Cousin Alice also found the growing prominence of another bearer of the name, and a Democrat to boot, intolerable. The right Roosevelt was her father, who, had he not died a year and a half before, would certainly, in her judgment, have been the next president. She voted against the Cox-Roosevelt ticket just as she would oppose Franklin in every election for the next twenty-four years. As expected, Cox went down to a thumping defeat with Harding taking nearly twice the popular vote.

For Franklin and Eleanor the campaign had offered an opportunity to muffle personal animosities beneath a nascent political partnership. Eleanor made the whistle stops with Franklin on the *Westboro,* the campaign train. While her husband unwound after a day's speechmaking, sipping whiskey and playing poker with his aides, Eleanor and Louis Howe sat together for hours watching the countryside slip past as he gave her a tutorial in practical politics. The teacher was delighted to discover an apt and eager student. Eleanor granted an interview to a reporter from the *Poughkeepsie Eagle News,* who gave his story the ideal twist for the times. She "is first of all a domestic woman," he wrote, "but she has one outside interest. That is politics."

Franklin appeared to have put Lucy behind him as he had promised, although unconfirmed sightings were occasionally reported. Frank Freidel, a Roosevelt biographer, wrote a colleague, "At the Roosevelt library among the press clippings for this period, I came upon a rotogravure picture of the vice presidential candidate and purportedly Mrs. Roosevelt at a baseball game. But it was not Mrs. Roosevelt, though a good-looking woman. I talked to Mrs. Roosevelt about this in the course of an interview, and she became quite agitated and changed the subject. I remember this only because of her curious agitation—such as had occurred otherwise only when she talked about her mother-in-law. Could it by some weird chance have been Lucy?"

Franklin's service in the Wilson administration would end on an embarrassing note, ironic in that it involved him in an excess of moral outrage. Reports had begun surfacing of homosexuality at the naval base at Newport. Franklin incorporated a unit into his office, "Section A," employing investigators who were "to go to the limit" to entrap suspects. The morals police managed to arrest sixteen men on charges of illicit sexual conduct, including the Reverend Samuel Nash Kent, Episcopalian chaplain of the Newport naval hospital, who was subsequently found innocent. Franklin righteously dismissed the idea that he had any knowledge of the sordid methods employed by Section A. However, a Republican-led Senate subcommittee began an investigation that produced a headline in *The New York Times* on July 23, 1920, reading "Lay Navy Scandal to F.D. Roosevelt" with a subhead, "Details are unprintable." Unabashed, Franklin pronounced the report "a premeditated, partisan hatchet job." He was fortunate in that the finale of this sorry episode occurred after the Wilson administration left office and public attention had shifted to raids on bootleggers, investigation into the 1919 World Series Black Sox Scandal, and married millionaires caught in flagrante with showgirls. In the end the Newport affair created scarcely a ripple, and Franklin's role faded.

With the inauguration of the Harding administration and the departure of the Wilsonites, Franklin found himself at loose ends. The adrenaline charge of tackling Navy Department problems was gone, and his boundless energy dissipated. He had lived well beyond his $5,000 annual government salary, his finances in such wretched shape that he told a friend, "I am honestly a fit candidate for a receiver." As the bills mounted, he was compelled to go back to his unfailing meal ticket, his mother. He wrote her, upon receiving a substantial check, "the question was not one of paying Dr. Mitchell for removing James's insides. The Dr. can wait. I know he is or must be rich." However, he had to pay "the gas man or the butcher lest the infants starve to death." Friends came to his rescue. He joined with Granville T. Emmet and Langdon D. Marvin to form a Wall Street law firm. With his contacts throughout government, social connections, and winning ways, he was expected to become the firm's rainmaker. Most useful, another friend, Van Lear Black, who owned *The Baltimore Sun* and controlled the Fidelity & Deposit Company of Maryland, dealing in "bonds and burglary insurance," made Franklin vice president in charge of the New York office at a hefty annual salary of $25,000.

His finances were for the moment secure, and freed from the demands of an exacting wartime post, the playboy in Franklin, lurking beneath the achiever, began to emerge. He drank and partied too much. He was visibly intoxicated at a Harvard class of 1904 reunion, and tested Eleanor's patience by raucous behavior at the wedding of Aunt Bye's son, Sheffield Cowles. Out of office, he also seemed more prone than ever to illness. Eleanor was relieved when the family left R Street for the 65th Street New York townhouse, hoping for a new beginning if she could just escape Sara's intrusions from the connecting house next door.

At this point, another woman entered his life. During the election the previous fall, Charles McCarthy, who had served as Franklin's secretary at the Navy Department and then as the vice presidential candidate's campaign manager, located a promising secretary bored with typing eight hours every day. Twenty-two-year-old Marguerite LeHand immediately made herself indispensable to the campaign staff, displaying an unflappability in juggling the candidate's chaotic schedule, answering the flood of correspondence, and displaying tact beyond her years. LeHand, tall, with a graceful carriage and always impeccably groomed, made a striking impression. While not a beauty in the Lucy Mercer mold, she had arresting blue eyes and dark brown hair prematurely streaked with gray pulled back into a bun. Her chin was strong, the effect softened by what the author Fulton Oursler described as "the lovely throaty voice and quick upturn of the face . . . lips parted in that strange secret smile composed of cunning influence, forever baffling." A future Roosevelt secretary, Grace Tully, who would later work with LeHand and who possessed her competence but not her appeal, described her colleague less generously as having "rather large features—a large nose and teeth a little protruding, but then everybody around Roosevelt had protruding teeth, including me."

LeHand had grown up in a working-class neighborhood in the Boston suburb of Somerville, the daughter of a hard-drinking Irish Catholic gardener who occasionally abandoned his wife and three children. Her mother made ends meet renting rooms to Harvard students. "Even as a high school girl she had a certain class to her," a neighbor recalled. "She had a dark suit on to go to high school. She stood out for having a better appearance and being smarter than most." She had gone straight from high school into office work, then as war approached, moved to Washington.

After the Democratic ticket was defeated, Franklin and Eleanor threw a party for the staff who had labored in the lost cause, Marguerite LeHand among the guests. Mail had continued to pile up while Franklin rode the *Westboro* and Eleanor suggested that he take on Miss LeHand temporarily to clean up the backlog. After the Roosevelts left Washington, LeHand moved into a relative's apartment in New York and found herself shuttling between the city and Hyde Park at all hours to meet Franklin's arbitrary demands. From the outset the chemistry worked. LeHand matched Franklin's style, combining competence with breezy good humor. She struck a balance of self-worth while knowing her station. As Franklin's distant relative and Hudson River neighbor, Margaret "Daisy" Suckley, came to know LeHand, she was amazed that someone with "no background at all" could possess such poise, good manners, and the appearance of breeding. Like Lucy Mercer, LeHand eventually endeared herself to the younger Roosevelt children, though they had trouble pronouncing her name. Thus Anna began calling her "Missy" and Missy she remained for life.

The temporary task completed, Franklin asked Missy to stay on full-time. At first, she balked, saying she found law work deadly, but Franklin assured her, "Oh, that's all right"—he also did "a lot of interesting things." His partner Langdon Marvin concurred. "Franklin gave most of his time to cleaning up his political matters and writing letters that had to do with it," Marvin recalled. "I don't remember that he was active in the law practice." Missy finally consented to take the job early in 1921, and Franklin knew he had found a jewel.

## Chapter 18

# THE DIAGNOSIS

. . . . . . .

FRANKLIN HANDLED HIS DESCENT from Washington somebody and political comer to defeated candidate and ordinary citizen with jaunty flippancy. He identified himself in a letter to an associate as "Franklin D. Roosevelt, Ex V.P., Canned (erroneously reported dead)." In his latest incarnation, he and his new secretary, Missy LeHand, began a fixed routine. Mornings they reported to Fidelity & Deposit, at 120 Broadway, then in the afternoon they switched to Franklin's law firm, Emmet, Marvin and Roosevelt, and she tagged after him to Hyde Park, whenever summoned. From the outset, her loyalty to him was total and unquestioning, her devotion resembling a calling more than a job. The sixteen-year gap in their ages seemed to vanish as they discovered in each other a similar sense of humor. Franklin signed himself "Father" on memos that passed between them. She was soon comfortable enough to address him as "FD," which she had picked up from his pal Livy Davis and which few others used. Unconsciously, she began to absorb Franklin's tastes, even speech mannerisms, describing agreeable experiences as "perfectly grand." After eight months on the job she felt confident enough to write him at Campobello asking for a raise from $30 to $40 a week.

On July 28, 1921, Franklin escaped the stuffy confines of Fidelity & Deposit for a long weekend to do something that satisfied both his love of the outdoors and his social conscience. He was now president of the Boy Scout Foundation of Greater New York and with other prominent city leaders boarded a yacht owned by his friend Baron Collier for a sail up the Hudson River to Lake Kanowahke on Bear Mountain where two thousand Boy Scouts were encamped. Franklin eagerly joined in long swims and hikes in the sweltering summer heat, completely at home with the boisterous teenagers. On August 5, he boarded another vessel, Van Lear Black's 140-foot oceangoing yacht, the *Sabalo*, bound for Campobello. Black, given his control of Fidelity & Deposit, was Franklin's boss, though the relationship remained one of kindred spirits. He was an avid party giver whether aboard the yacht or at his sprawling Maryland estate where bootleg liquor flowed freely. Black was also an unlikely businessman Democrat and allowed Franklin to bring his political partner, Louis Howe, onto the F&D payroll and aboard the *Sabalo*.

Missy was puzzled when two weeks went by and she had no response from her employer concerning the raise. Instead, she received a letter dated August 17, not from Franklin, but from his wife, apologizing for the tardy reply. "Mr. Roosevelt had a severe chill last Wednesday which resulted in a fever and much congestion," Eleanor wrote, "and I fear his return will be delayed." She also passed along Franklin's decision that "neither F&D nor Emmet, Marvin and Roosevelt would be willing to jump to $40, but he feels sure he can get you $35."

During the interval between these letters Franklin Roosevelt had undergone an event that would upend his life.

On August 8, Black's guests had boarded the *Sabalo*'s motor tender to go deep sea fishing. Franklin immediately took charge, organizing everything down to how to bait a hook. With the sea churning, he lost his footing and tumbled into the bone-chilling waters of the Bay of Fundy. As he later recalled the moment, "I'd never felt anything so cold as that water. . . . The water was so cold it seemed paralyzing." The next day, he and Howe went ashore at Campobello while Black sailed the *Sabalo* back to New York.

Ever since the Bear Mountain trip Franklin had felt fatigued. Then after the chilling exposure in the bay his legs began to ache. The cure, as was his habit, was to engage in more strenuous activity. Though still weary the next day, August 10, he took Anna and his two oldest boys, James and Elliott, for a sail on his new twenty-four-foot sloop, the *Vireo*. They spotted a pine needle fire on an island, brought the boat ashore, and spent the next several hours beating back the flames with their feet and tree branches. "We brought it under control," Franklin later recalled, but "our eyes were bleary with smoke, smarting with spark burns—exhausted." He next led the sooty, perspiring children on a two-mile jog across the island to cool off with a swim, first in a lake, then in the frigid waters of the bay. Finally, the children followed their father on a run back to the cottage, a day reminiscent of another Roosevelt, TR's, belief in the virtue of physical exhaustion.

But Franklin did not prove inexhaustible. Still in his wet bathing suit, he slumped into a wicker chair on the porch of the cottage and began rifling through accumulated mail and newspapers. "I didn't get the usual revitalization, the glow I'd expected," he remembered. "I sat for a while, too tired even to dress. I'd never felt quite that way before." As the afternoon faded, "he began to complain that he felt a chill," Eleanor recalled, "and decided he would not eat supper with us." Instead, he went to bed, swathed in blankets but still shivering. The morning after, groggy from a poor night's sleep, he staggered to the bathroom, his legs aching, pain spreading up his back and neck, even to his face. He managed to shave himself, which would prove to be the last act he would ever perform on his feet unaided.

Eleanor called in the local doctor, Eben Bennett, who found Franklin's temperature to be 102 degrees and diagnosed a bad cold. By Friday, he could not move his legs. On Sunday, Louis Howe took a boat to the Maine coast to locate a phone and began scouring New England for a doctor with deeper expertise than the Campobello general practitioner. In Bar Harbor he located a vacationing eighty-four-year-old physician from Philadelphia, Dr. W. W. Keen, once a distinguished surgeon, who agreed to come to Campobello on Sunday, August 14. After a few minutes' examination he diagnosed Franklin's creeping paralysis as a blood clot on the spinal cord that in time should dissolve. The next day, Dr. Keen sent Eleanor a rambling four-page letter advising her, "You will certainly break down if you do not have immediate relief. . . . As to the financial side, will you kindly send me at your convenience a thousand dollars."

Franklin was now in excruciating pain, even the weight of a bedsheet unbearable. His bowels and bladder had shut down. He became delirious. Writing later of this experience in a draft of an autobiography, Eleanor noted, "One night he was out of his head." The words were later deleted. Eleanor and Louis sought to revive his flaccid leg muscles by massaging them. But after two weeks, with Franklin's condition worsening, Howe called Uncle Fred Delano, Sara's brother, asking his help in finding a specialist conversant with Franklin's symptoms. Uncle Fred suggested Dr. Robert W. Lovett, a Boston surgeon and Harvard medical professor. Lovett came to Campobello on August 25 and his diagnosis was swift. Franklin Roosevelt had contracted infantile paralysis. Somehow he had breathed in, or transferred by hand to his mouth, viruses so small that microscopes of the period could not detect them. A likely source of the infection was Franklin's cavorting among the Boy Scouts.

Poliomyelitis is an inflammation of the nervous system that produces horrific pain. It strikes most fearfully at victims who are not strong, under stress, or fatigued. Franklin was basically healthy and not overtly stressed, though his susceptibility to illness was well documented by a catalogue of ailments including scarlet fever, lumbago, appendicitis, sinusitis, hives, typhoid fever, throat infections, pneumonia, and influenza. While possessing enormous vitality, he was not powerful in the strongman sense, but rather supple and long-limbed, his musculature slender rather than bulging. Clearly, his exertions had lowered his resistance to the disease and his overprotected childhood had robbed him of the immunities acquired by less fortunate children.

Polio in that era killed most of its victims. They routinely died of kidney and other infections, or pneumonia. No drug, no surgical procedure, no proven therapy could benefit its victims in the 1920s. If they did survive, the least fortunate would be warehoused in a handful of public rehabilitative hospitals. Those better off were usually shunted into a back room at home, their families embarrassed by having a cripple in their midst. Well-off victims might be cared for in private nursing homes. No matter the patient's economic status, the prevailing attitude was, out of sight, out of mind. However devastating Franklin's condition, his wealth spared him so stark a future.

Eleanor began what she would one day describe as "the most trying winter of my life." Franklin's condition brought the couple into an enforced intimacy unlike anything they had previously known. In the weeks before Eleanor could find trained help, she administered enemas to empty her husband's clogged bowels and a glass catheter to pump the urine from his blocked urinary tract. She bathed him, brushed his teeth, shaved and fed him. With the scrawny Louis's help, she wrestled the large, inert, pain-racked body, turning Franklin from one side, then another as he silently bore the indignity of being lifted on and off a bed pan. At night, Eleanor slept on a couch at the foot of his bed, getting up to answer his every need.

Still in the dark as to what actually was going on, Missy wrote Franklin on August 22, "I never would have bothered you about the question of salary if I had known you were ill." Within days, much to her gratification, she was summoned to Campobello. She found her employer stubbornly upbeat. Bedridden scarcely two weeks, he began dictating letters to her, resuming their usual bantering style, though he could not sign the correspondence because his hands were partly paralyzed. Howe had mastered through the years a convincing Roosevelt signature and signed the letters himself. He also immediately embarked on a campaign to keep Franklin's political future alive while keeping his condition secret. Just eleven days after polio struck, Howe managed to have Franklin made a member of a fund-raising committee for Vassar College and soon after that, saw him appointed to the New York State Democratic Committee.

The first news account that the former vice presidential candidate was unwell appeared on August 27, a story in which Howe persuaded the reporter to mention that the patient was on his way to recovery. The gravity of Franklin's condition was confided only to a few family members. Eleanor wrote a favorite aunt, Annie Delano Hitch, admitting Franklin's condition. Aunt Annie replied, "It is perfectly marvelous how you have kept the secret and we will be very careful." Rumors, however, had circulated, and Mrs. Hitch added, "I was asked by several persons interested in the Boy Scouts affair at Bear Mountain if Mr. Roosevelt was seriously ill and it was easy to answer that he had taken a bad chill and was laid up with a fever and we hoped he would soon be his old self again."

Franklin could not believe, or chose not to believe, that he would not recover. Yet the prognosis was grim. Moderate exercise and a favorable environment could help, but only minimally. As Hugh Gallagher, the definitive writer on Roosevelt's illness and a polio patient himself, put it, "The extent of recovery would be determined by the degree of permanent damage caused by the polio virus to the . . . central nervous system. Recovery was not increased or improved by extraordinary amounts of exercise."

The Apollo who had won the admiration of men and the desire of women, who confidently breezed through his world, played golf within two strokes of his club's record, who could ride until he tired a horse, who vaulted obstacles at a bound, had been reduced in an instant to helplessness, dependent for his most elemental needs on the ministrations of others. As months passed and the paralysis retreated to a point from which it would not withdraw further, his physical destiny was sealed: control of his upper torso, but paralysis of his legs. What demons haunted him as, morning after morning, he faced his waking nightmare can barely be imagined by anyone whole in body. Yet he presented a face of irrepressible optimism to the world. His mother, who had been abroad during the initial onset of the disease, arrived at Campobello three weeks later, consumed with trepidation when she learned what had befallen her Franklin, but amazed by the mood she encountered. "The atmosphere of the house is all happiness," she wrote her brother Fred, with "Eleanor in the lead." She intended to follow their "glorious example," she added. Displaying the self-discipline ingrained over a lifetime, she succeeded. "I am sure, out of sight, she wept many hours," Eleanor observed, "but with all of us she was very cheerful." The same was true of Eleanor.

Doctors familiar with the consequences knew all too well the torments of mind and body that a polio patient would confront. The family physician and friend, George Draper, an associate of Dr. Lovett's, wrote to a colleague about the Roosevelt case speculating as to how the patient might react "when we sit him up [and] he will be faced with the frightfully depressing knowledge that he can't hold himself erect." Blows to the man's psyche could be as traumatizing as anything physical, Dr. Draper feared. "He has such courage, such ambition, and yet at the same time, such an extraordinarily sensitive emotional mechanism that it will take all the skill which we can muster to lead him successfully to a recognition of what he really faces without crushing him."

The partnership between Eleanor and her mother-in-law in the face of disaster soon ran aground on misplaced assumptions. Sara expected that Franklin would now retire from public life and that the logical place for him to live out his days was in the tranquillity of Hyde Park where he could become a country squire, however incapacitated, as had his invalid father. Eleanor assumed that Sara must know her son well enough to recognize that such a retreat from active life amounted to spiritual death. She and Louis Howe set out to forestall that fate. She contacted Franklin's friends urging them to write cheerful letters. One of the first to respond was Livy Davis. It was in this letter that he urged "Dear Old Rosy" to use his convalescence "to do a little of the writing of which you have spoken so often" and included among eight suggested topics, one chronicling their twenty-nine days and evenings as Washington summer bachelors. Eleanor tore articles from magazines and newspapers that she knew would continue to nourish her husband's obsession with politics. She and Howe drew him into debates over the prospects of Democratic figures and the party's fortunes. She invited old political partners to come visit Franklin. Thus his future became something of a battleground for his soul between two women, one convinced that the other was pushing a sick man beyond his limits, the other convinced that her rival was blind to the man's emotional need to engage life as fully as possible. The tension at times became palpable and Franklin found himself caught in the middle. He employed his time-tested strategy with his mother, passive resistance, humoring her while going his own way.

Within a year he was as well as he would ever be, though he would never accept that verdict. He was now being moved between Hyde Park and the 65th Street townhouse and spent hour upon hour pulling himself along the floor of his homes, sweat dripping off his brow, shaking with exhaustion. In the city his room was on an upper floor and being able to go up and down stairs became vital to his sense of security. He was well aware of the hideous deaths of his mother's sister, Laura, when an alcohol lamp fell on her, and of Eleanor's Aunt Pussie and her children trapped by fire. He found an awkward but serviceable method for mounting stairs. Swinging himself around onto the bottom step, he would place his hands on the step above, lean back, and lift his body to the next step by sheer arm strength. He began showing off the biceps his exertions produced. He practiced using crutches until his armpits were sore, dragging his dead legs behind him. He performed these efforts in full view of anybody present, family, friend, or visitor. Whether dragging himself along the floor or up the stairs he kept up a nonstop chatter, telling stories, making wisecracks, laughing and poking fun at himself, attempting to put people at ease so that the man shone through, not simply his disability. When Josephus Daniels visited Franklin, the former navy secretary was visibly shaken to see his once vital, dashing assistant paralyzed. Roosevelt motioned Daniels to come closer and then gave him a playful punch in the stomach, warning that he could still "knock you out."

"I couldn't help but feel a wrench in my heart," his daughter, Anna, fifteen at the time, recalled of his days on crutches. "I would see him walk out our Hyde Park driveway, oh so slowly, and see the beads of perspiration on his forehead after he'd gone a short distance." She further remembered how "He apparently knew it would be a shock to realize that the useless muscles in his legs would cause atrophy. . . . So father removed the sadness by showing his legs. . . . He would shout with glee over a little movement of a muscle that had been dormant." Gradually she grew comfortable sitting on a chair next to his bed, chatting and recovering the earlier ease that had existed between an adoring daughter and a father's favorite child.

When not on crutches, he moved about in a wheelchair. He was fitted with ten pounds of cumbersome metal braces extending from his heels to his waist that he could not put on by himself. He learned to use his arms to lift one lifeless leg out of his wheelchair, snap the brace in place, repeat the procedure with the other leg, push himself up by his arms, make himself rigid, lean forward and rise uncertainly to a standing position where, without someone to support him, he would come crashing down like a plank. Without the braces and crutches, his condition was little different from a legless amputee. Ralph Waldo Emerson's observation seemed cruelly apt to describe Franklin Roosevelt at this time, "A man is a God in ruins."

He eventually returned to work. Missy LeHand had greeted his imminent return writing, "Everyone is much excited about your coming back and much pleased." She signed off, "By the way, I wish I could say, 'Your Majesty.' " Employees of Fidelity & Deposit became accustomed to seeing a chauffeur pull up at 120 Broadway where Franklin would swivel himself from the back seat, connect his braces, and begin to enter the building on crutches. On the morning he slipped and slammed to the marble floor, he gave a dazzling smile to people who stopped and said, "Do you mind giving a hand to help me up?"

He suffered setbacks. Just after his fortieth birthday, his hamstrings contracted and drew him into a fetal coil that the doctors feared would be permanent. The legs had literally to be pried open, an agonizing procedure, and then locked into place by a cast running from hip to ankle until the legs were straight again. These reversals fed his mother's argument that he belonged at home, not dragging himself around Manhattan, but to no avail.

He would try almost anything in his certainty that somewhere, somehow he could find a cure. A former governor of Oklahoma, Charles Haskell, after visiting Hyde Park wrote Franklin, "Now please don't laugh," and begged him to see a New York city doctor who practiced the osteopathic "Abraham's Treatment," which "cannot hurt you, if it don't do you a bit of good." Franklin wrote back saying, "The Abraham's Treatment sounds most interesting," and promised to ask his doctor about it, though he feared "my own particular ailment is such a definite one that my present method of treatment is the only one possible." He closed assuring Haskell, "It is merely a question of time before I am able to get about again without the use of crutches as at present." All the rage in the 1920s, Dr. Emile Coué preached self-hypnosis, urging people to repeat "Every day in every way I'm getting better and better." Franklin consulted Coué. Former Treasury Secretary William G. McAdoo suggested gland treatments to him. Over the years he would stake his hopes on hot baths, cold baths, saltwater, fresh water, working with gravity, working against gravity, parallel bars, overhead bars, electric current, and ultraviolet light, none of which could overcome his central condition, which one doctor described as "flail legs," limbs attached to but uncontrolled by his body. Eleanor put the best possible face on her husband's condition, writing at one point that he "was entirely well again and lived a normal life in every way restricted only by his inability to walk."

Young Anna had been touched by the courage and hope displayed by her mother and father in facing the ordeal that she described as "two years which deepened my respect and understanding of both my parents." The new relationship came as something of a relief to her after having watched a once happy home become one of inexplicable coldness, broken only by bickering and acrimony ever since something she did not understand had happened in 1918. The explanation for this bitterness was to come from an older cousin, Susan Parish, with whom Eleanor had lived upon her return to America from Mlle. Souvestre's school in 1900. In 1923 during Tennis Week at Newport, Anna was taken aside by "gossipy old Cousin Suzie," who revealed that "Father had had a romance with 'another woman' during World War I in Washington, that many people talked about it at the time and that it was all very hard on mother. . . . My recollection is one of feeling highly annoyed at the old lady for telling me because even though I was an unsophisticated seventeen, I could feel her relish in the telling." Anna found, "I couldn't talk to my mother about it. I didn't know who to talk to."

Some months after Cousin Susie's gleeful revelation, Anna arrived home to find her mother sitting on a couch waiting up for her. Her daughter "was an adolescent girl and I still thought of her as a child," Eleanor recalled of this period. In fact, Anna had grown into a lean, long-legged, blond beauty, possessing the lithe movements of a thoroughbred and much admired by young men. As Anna remembered that evening, "Out of the blue," her mother told her that she was now old enough "to know of a difficult period which she and Father had gone through." Eleanor, tense but controlled, then spilled out the full story, Franklin's 1918 return from Europe, the discovery of Lucy's letters, the offer of a divorce, her husband's pledge never again to see the woman whom Anna vaguely but fondly remembered from her childhood in Washington. She further told her daughter that, though the marriage had been salvaged, physical relations between husband and wife had ceased. Eleanor's studied control during the confession finally broke down and she burst into tears. Her unburdening was rare. As she once described herself, "I have always had a bad tendency to shut up like a clam, particularly when things are going badly." As Anna listened to the confession, "I remember my first reaction was that I was mad at father for hurting mother," a feeling sharpened by her knowledge of "my mother's traumatic childhood with so little love and security and of my father's very secure and much loved childhood." She also sided with her mother, "because I was a woman, you see. You can realize as a woman . . . this could happen to me." Her mother's trust pleased Anna. "I had been accepted on a par as an adult," she believed, "capable of understanding adult problems, accepted by the one person of my own sex whom I admired most."

While Franklin was undergoing his trial of body and soul, Lucy, now Mrs. Winthrop Rutherfurd, had become a society matron and the mother of a daughter, Barbara, born three years after the discovery of the affair, and eleven months after Franklin had been afflicted with polio. Livy Davis was one of the few outside the family privy to the affair and along with his enduring friendship with Franklin, he occasionally saw Lucy. Inevitably, in spite of Louis Howe's best efforts, the nature of Roosevelt's illness became known publicly; but it was through Livy that Lucy personally was kept abreast of Franklin's life.

Franklin had another link to Lucy through Daisy Suckley. The closeness between FDR and Daisy was revealed by Geoffrey Ward, in his 1995 book, *Closest Companion: The Unknown Story of the Intimate Friendship Between Franklin Roosevelt and Margaret Suckley*. Daisy had been born and raised at Wilderstein, ten miles north of Hyde Park, a steeply peaked mansion with gables, turrets, and a port cochere, a setting straight out of a Victorian melodrama. She descended from the Beekmans, a prominent family whose lands once stretched across both banks of the Hudson and a clan to whom Franklin claimed a distant connection. Daisy, nine years Franklin's junior, was remotely related both to him as an eighth cousin and to Eleanor as a seventh cousin and he always introduced her as "Cousin Daisy." She had come into Franklin's life after polio struck through his mother's determination to make sure her son never lacked for companionship. Daisy would make the short drive down from Wilderstein to Hyde Park to visit with Franklin, the two chatting away while he exhausted himself trying to learn to walk by sliding along bars set parallel to the lawn. A year after Franklin's onset of polio, she, like Livy, had gone to Aiken and informed Lucy of Franklin's current life. "I remember her as tall and calm and pretty sad," Daisy recalled of their first meeting.

*Chapter 19*

# MISSY

. . . . . . .

BY 1923, two years after the onset of polio, Franklin began to take greater control over his life. That year, as the approaching New York winter began to seep into his bones, he longed to be where he could swim, fish, and exercise in gentle waters under the warmth of the sun. He persuaded Eleanor to come with him to Florida where he had rented a small houseboat, the *Weona II*. She managed a few days, but lolling on a boat deck offended her sense that time spent should produce something of value. "I had never considered holidays in winter or escape from cold weather an essential part of living," she explained of the visit, "and I looked upon it now as a necessity and not a pleasure."

Eleanor's impatience with easy living was prompted by her growing independence. Recognizing the imperfection of her marriage, she gradually came to see that she need not be simply the subordinate half of a couple. Louis Howe had been invaluable to her in finding herself. On those cross-country train trips during the vice presidential campaign, he had fired her interest in politics and nourished her self-confidence. He became close enough that the once scorned hanger-on was invited to spend weekdays living on the third floor at the Roosevelts' 65th Street townhouse, a room that a grumbling Anna was pressured to give up while she was consigned to a top floor cubbyhole. Louis proved an exasperating guest, pacing all night, chain-smoking, his frail body so racked by coughing that he could scarcely complete a sentence. He littered his clothes and the room with ashes, and the sweetish incense he burned failed to overcome the stink of stale tobacco. Yet Franklin felt adrift without Louis close by, while Eleanor overlooked his failings and developed genuine affection for him. "I remember going into mother's room and I would find Louis sitting in mother's deep, comfy chair and mother at his feet," Anna recalled. "I would be violently jealous."

Howe's purpose in involving Eleanor in politics was two-pronged. First, he knew that she burned with as yet unfocused idealism and unrealized potential. Even more important to him was the advancement of Franklin's career, which, in the man's diminished state, depended more than ever on his having a politically sophisticated and involved wife. Eleanor had already begun, even before Franklin was struck down, to engage in nonpartisan activities. In 1920 she met a woman, Narcissa Vanderlip, who talked her into running the legislative agenda for the League of Women Voters. Vanderlip put Eleanor in touch with a brilliant lawyer, Elizabeth Read, to guide her through the legislative thicket. Read marked Eleanor's introduction to a new class of women, accomplished, professional, driven by public service, to whom men did not figure in their emotional lives. Read had a long-standing lesbian relationship with Esther Lape, an English professor and journalist with whom she lived in Greenwich Village and who also became Eleanor's friend.

In June 1922, almost a year after Franklin was stricken, Eleanor finally yielded to Howe's constant importuning that she involve herself in party politics, which led to another female pairing. Nancy Cook, at thirty-eight, was a pretty, curly-haired, liberal ball-of-fire who headed the Women's Division of the New York State Democratic Committee. Cook understood the public relations value of a famous name and phoned Eleanor, whom she had never met, asking her to speak at a fund-raising luncheon in New York City that summer. Though frightened and uncertain, Eleanor, at Howe's insistence, accepted. Louis, an amateur thespian, served as her drama coach. Before an audience she became nervous and her voice would jump an octave, followed by a disconcerting giggle. "Nothing to laugh at," Louis would scold her. Thereafter, whenever she spoke, he sat in the back of the room, lifting his hand to quell this distracting tic.

Eleanor invited Nancy Cook to Hyde Park for a weekend and found her a witty, irreverent companion, an unlikely soul mate for the straitlaced patrician. Eleanor described Cook as "an attractive woman who had distinct artistic ability and could do almost anything with her hands." They became close enough that Eleanor bought twin tweed knickerbocker suits that they occasionally wore together. Nancy Cook had a partner too, Marion Dickerman, seven years younger, with whom she had lived for thirteen years and who taught at a swank girls school in New York City called Todhunter. The long-standing Cook-Dickerman relationship soon expanded to include Eleanor. These burgeoning friendships, which drew Eleanor into ever more causes, explained her near zero interest in spending time on Franklin's houseboat. Further, though his polio had given Eleanor a second chance to become the most important figure in his life, in time the ingredients of character that had grated on each other before his illness began to resurface. Franklin still disliked Eleanor's heavy touch, her hectoring, her inability to amuse him. While solicitous in tending to him, she also failed to match his optimism about his ultimate recovery, which he interpreted as a lack of support.

Early in May, Franklin persuaded an old school friend, John S. Lawrence, to go in with him to purchase a run-down seventy-one-foot houseboat berthed on Florida's Fort Lauderdale River. They bought the vessel for $3,750 and, combining their last names, christened her the *Larooco*, pronounced La-row-co. Lawrence may have come into the deal as a kindness to his afflicted friend since he would use the boat only once. Franklin hired a crew, Charles Morris as captain, and his wife to cook and clean for $125 a month along with an engine room mechanic. In the view of Franklin's grandson, Curtis Roosevelt, his grandfather bought the *Larooco* "to get the hell out of the house" and escape the three-cornered strife between Sara, Eleanor, and himself.

Eleanor had no more interest in the *Larooco* than she had had in the *Weona II*, but someone else was all too willing to join Franklin. Missy LeHand followed him to Florida where he proudly showed her the boat's layout. The stern provided an ideal perch for fishing. Forward were the crew's quarters, the engine room, and galley. A passageway ran through the foremost part of the boat with a large stateroom and a bath for Franklin on one side and two small staterooms with double bunks on the other side. The stateroom opposite his cabin, Franklin pointed out, would be Missy's and she would share his bathroom. His room had originally contained a brass double bed, but Franklin had it removed and replaced with two single beds. Above the sleeping quarters was a spacious glass-encased living room and above that a sundeck under an awning. However worn, the *Larooco* was a comfortable floating home.

On February 2, 1924, only eight days after they had settled in, Missy received a telegram reporting that her ne'er-do-well, but well-loved, father had died. She immediately took a train to Massachusetts. During her absence a restless Franklin made a stab at what often stirred him with time heavy on his hands. He began writing on yellow legal pads "A History of the United States," which, like most of his literary efforts, was never finished.

Missy was back in two weeks and the arrangement of companionable souls resumed. She happily entered into Franklin's sophomoric humor, referring to Washington's birthday as "Birthington's Washday" or the parlor game of "Ma and Pa Cheesy," behavior unthinkable with Eleanor. Franklin invited a steady stream of friends aboard the *Larooco* where Missy played the gracious hostess, charming them with her easy conversation and contagious laughter. When she was not handling his correspondence she fished with Franklin off the fantail and sunbathed with him on the upper deck. She slipped into the warm waters, helping him perform exercises that by now had become his addiction. Tall, erect, and amply proportioned, she cut an attractive figure in a bathing suit. Franklin's greatest compliment to the role she occupied in his life was his dropping the mask of chronic good cheer when they were by themselves. As one therapy or therapist after another failed, Missy alone witnessed his bitter disappointment. She once confided to Frances Perkins, later to be FDR's labor secretary, "There were days on the *Larooco* when it was noon before he could pull himself out of depression."

Toward the end of March that first year aboard the houseboat, Franklin eagerly awaited an unfailing tonic to his spirits, a visit from Livy Davis. Livy arrived as cheerily outrageous as ever. The next day Franklin wrote in a ship's log he kept, "L.D. went to the R.R. bridge to fish and came back minus trousers—to the disgust of Missy and Mrs. Morris. Earlier he had exercised on the top deck a la nature. Why do people who must take off their clothes go anywhere where the other sex is present? Capt. Morris remarked quietly that some men get shot for less." Finally Livy went too far. Franklin's March 20 entry described a storm rocking the vessel and he wrote, "Hell to pay. Davis got the awning off but had to disrobe to do it as it was raining." Livy left on April 5, banned from future visits to the *Larooco*. Franklin and Missy were again alone until April 13 when the crew began to put up the vessel for the following season.

. . .

Jonathan Daniels, son of Franklin's old chief at the Navy Department, was studying law in New York in the early 1920s. Young Daniels remembered a time when a "great lady asked me to bring my roommates to Sunday supper with her crippled husband. One of them, on his way to fortune as a stockbroker, declined. He just didn't have time, he said, for a has-been. The has-been was Franklin D. Roosevelt."

After leaving the *Larooco* the presumably politically finished Roosevelt began an arduous climb back into the arena. Louis Howe had kept Franklin's name alive as a player in the Democratic Party. Though apparently with no hope of running for office himself, therefore posing no threat to other politicians, Franklin still bore a resounding name, was a Protestant patrician in a party heavy with working-class Catholics, had been the party's vice presidential nominee, and consequently his support could benefit Democratic candidates. When the proud Alfred E. Smith, New York's governor and an aspirant for the presidency in 1924, asked why he needed Roosevelt, an aide replied, "Because you're a bowery Mick and . . . he'll take the curse off of you." Smith thereafter invited Franklin to nominate him at the Democratic convention that June in Chicago.

With his rich, aristocratic voice and rolling cadence still intact, delivering the speech would be the least of Franklin's worries. Getting to the podium and standing upright before thousands while he spoke was the challenge. He had continued his exertions and experiments to defeat the odds against recovering from polio. He had a metal contraption erected over his bed to lift and lower his legs for exercise. His mother bought him an expensive electric tricycle, which he used once, then abandoned as unworkable. He had a strap with a loop hung over his bed so that he could pull himself onto a wheelchair. He began practicing for what could be the longest journey in his political life. He had devised a method of movement that might pass for walking. He would first swing his left hip out in a semicircle, then bring the left crutch forward to support his lifeless leg. He would then thrust the right hip forward and repeat the process on his right side, in effect propelling his body ahead without the use of his legs.

At noon, on June 26, the day he was to address the convention, he stood some fifteen feet from the podium, a crutch under his right armpit, his left arm gripping his son James's upper arm so tightly that it left bruises on the sixteen-year-old's flesh. In the gallery, with the other Roosevelt children and her now inseparable friends, Nancy Cook and Marion Dickerman, sat Eleanor, knitting furiously, eyes fixed on her work as if fearing to witness a looming disaster.

As Senator Thomas J. Walsh of Montana introduced Franklin the crowd applauded enthusiastically. Then the hall went eerily silent as all eyes fixed on the man whose voice had been publicly stilled for three years. James slipped a second crutch under his father's left arm and slowly let go as if balancing an egg on its end. With agonizing slowness, Franklin began inching toward the podium, his eyes riveted on the floor, sweat dripping off his chin. James moved two paces behind the father he had seen fall again and again during practice runs. If Franklin fell this time, a helpless cripple before twenty thousand members of his party, his public life was finished. He finally reached the podium, threw back his shoulders, flashed the signature Roosevelt grin, and began speaking with a strong, carrying voice, proclaiming Al Smith "the happy warrior of the political battlefield." When he finished, he gripped the podium with one hand, then dared lift the other in a wave, the smile never ceasing. The convention erupted in thunderous applause that reverberated in waves throughout the auditorium. Roosevelt's triumph, however, was not matched by Smith, who lost the nomination to John Davis, a former West Virginia congressman.

That political season offered the Hyde Park Roosevelts the sweet taste of revenge. Theodore Roosevelt Jr. had assailed Franklin during the latter's vice presidential campaign, attacking him as an unprincipled opportunist. Now, four years later, TR's son and namesake was running for the office his father had once held, governor of New York. This time, an unexpectedly feisty Eleanor traveled the state by car towing a giant teapot to remind voters of the Teapot Dome scandal during the Republican Harding administration. TR Jr. lost. Alice Longworth, who had delighted in her half-brother's lambasting of Franklin in 1920, said of Eleanor's teapot, "It was a base thing to do."

As fall approached, Franklin received a letter from a New York banker and friend, George Foster Peabody, dangling before him the prospect of full recovery. Peabody was part-owner of a resort hotel called the Meriwether in the Georgia hamlet of Bullochville. The banker had mentioned the place to Franklin before without arousing a spark of interest. Now he was telling him of a young polio victim, Louis Joseph, who had abandoned his wheelchair and could walk with canes after bathing in the warm thermal springs at the Meriwether. On October 3, Franklin, with hope rekindled by Peabody's latest inducement, accompanied by Eleanor, Missy, and a chauffeur-valet, journeyed to Bullochville, a town of 550 people eighty miles southwest of Atlanta. The Meriwether turned out to be a dilapidated Southern gothic monstrosity that Peabody had tricked out in a fresh coat of yellow and green paint for the Roosevelts' arrival, though Franklin saw immediately that the property was "in awful condition." The hotel was flanked by fourteen equally tumbledown cottages. Bullochville's heyday as a popular resort was at least a half century in the past.

The next day Franklin slid into a thermal pool fed by mineral-rich springs that pumped water at a rate of 1,800 gallons per minute at an unfailing temperature of 88 degrees. He was thrilled. The buoyancy allowed him to "walk around in water four feet deep without braces or crutches almost as well as if I had nothing the matter with my legs." For the first time since that fateful August three years before he began to feel slight movement in his toes. The Roosevelts stayed for two weeks during which time Peabody saw that they were feted constantly. As Franklin wrote his mother, "every organization has invited me to some kind of party." While the visitors were there, the canny Peabody persuaded the town fathers to change stodgy Bullochville to Warm Springs.

Franklin was ecstatic, but Eleanor's dislike for the Deep South was instantaneous. From the moment they had left the railroad station and were driven along dusty roads into town, she was appalled by the wretched state of blacks living in shanties, dressed in patched overalls and faded dresses, their condition seemingly unchanged since the era of slavery. She was offended by the supremacist racial attitudes among even the poorest whites. The suffocating heat and overly lush Spanish moss, even the drawling speech grated on her nerves. She soon left. But Missy stayed on. How could Eleanor leave her husband alone with a single woman? her friends wondered. The truth was that she no longer subsumed her life in Franklin's. She had written a magazine article in which she confessed, "if anyone were to ask me what I want out of life I would say the opportunity for doing something useful, for in no other way, I am convinced can true happiness be attained." Rather than a cause for jealousy, Missy's presence at Warm Springs provided Eleanor with a guilt-free ticket out of this abhorred place allowing her to get on with her own life. Nor was Franklin upset by his wife's departure; "she and I both feel it is important for her not to be away at the end of the campaign," he wrote his mother, referring to the 1924 election.

In 1925, from February through March, Franklin and Missy were again aboard the *Larooco*. Afterward they went to Warm Springs for another month and a half. Eleanor remained in New York, to which Franklin returned only briefly. While his physical progress was largely illusory, he continued to surprise visitors to his home by his indomitability. Eleanor's cousin Corinne described an occasion, "so gay and so delightful and so enchanting . . . that it will always be a red-letter evening in my life." She had joined Franklin, Aunty Bye, now in a wheelchair herself, and Emory Gardiner, a master at Groton School, immobilized by a severe heart condition. "You felt such gallantry in all of them," she remembered, "you know, such humor, such complete elimination of any problem about bodies."

Late that summer Franklin resumed the search for the grail of recovery. He and Missy went off this time to Marion, Massachusetts. He had heard reports of an unorthodox but effective polio treatment devised by a neurologist, Dr. William McDonald. He rented a cottage on Water Street, just down from the doctor, and commenced McDonald's therapy. The treatment proved painful and ineffective yet Franklin persuaded himself that he was improving and stayed in Marion with Missy until December 5, which meant that he had been away from his wife for the better part of the year. For all practical purposes, he was living with another woman.

March 17, 1926, marked the Roosevelts' twentieth wedding anniversary, and Eleanor agreed to spend it with Franklin on the *Larooco*. But first she had to enter a New York hospital to be treated for a minor gynecological problem. She left for Florida brooding because Franklin had sent no letters, no flowers, and made no phone calls during her hospitalization. When she arrived aboard the *Larooco*, Missy stayed away and Eleanor allowed herself to remain for ten days. As soon as she left, Missy rejoined Franklin for a few days aboard the boat before they moved on again to Warm Springs.

That Missy had come to love him was beyond question. Asked by a friend, as the years in Franklin's employ slipped by, if she were not concerned about getting married, she responded, "Absolutely not. How could anyone measure up to FD?"

These were, as Winston Churchill would one day describe a bleak stretch in his own life, Franklin Roosevelt's wilderness years. Whether during periods of stubborn optimism or patches of despair, it was Missy at his side, while the increasingly occupied Eleanor made speeches for the League of Women Voters, attended lunches with college deans, and read magazines to tired workers in the evening at the Women's Trade Union League. She wrote Franklin chatty, wifely letters almost daily to "Dearest Honey," telling how dreadfully the family missed him. But it was Missy who stayed with Franklin. When she was separated from him, her letters were those not of an employee, not of a companion, but of a pining lover. On a rare vacation by herself in Norway, she found a flower in a glacier, pressed it, and sent it to him with a note that read, "I'm going to be so good when I get back and never get cross or anything. Isn't that wonderful?" Visitors saw her on the *Larooco*'s deck sitting on Franklin's lap. How far that behavior could be extrapolated romantically depended on the observer. "Anna and I often sat on his lap during horseplay parties aboard that boat," James Roosevelt later wrote. "Father, I think, thought of Missy as another of his children," though a distinction might be drawn between a child sitting on a man's lap and his secretary doing so. Son Elliott believed the relationship was sexual. And even James recognized that Missy "filled a need and made him feel a man again, which mother did not do." When an interviewer asked Anna point-blank "whether father was having an affair with Missy" she answered, "Who could tell?"

What did they do during those months alone? The question is not only one of morality but of capability. Could this gravely handicapped man have performed sexually? Central was the extent of his paralysis. Polio had destroyed feeling and movement in his legs, but elsewhere his body was unaffected. That fact was to be authoritatively established years later when he had himself examined by three eminent physicians, who found him capable of handling any high office. Further, they found "no symptoms of impotentia coeundi." In plain English, he could sustain an erection. Dorothy Schiff, publisher of the *New York Post* and a friend of Franklin's, once asked a doctor during a Warm Springs visit, "Is the

President potent?" According to Schiff he answered, "It's only his legs that are paralyzed." Admittedly, for this once athletic, graceful man to have to perform sexual contortions would have been as much emotionally as physically daunting. Some Roosevelt watchers conclude that with a puritanical mother and a sexually repressed wife, extramarital sexual involvement would have been beyond Franklin's emotional range. He appears, however, to have rebutted this argument convincingly in the arms of Lucy Mercer. The likelihood that a man who had once been so physical and was working so hard to regain his physicality might extend these efforts to the performance of sex seems not at all improbable. As for his highly visible impairment inhibiting sexual behavior, Franklin had already shown that he did not shrink from having his condition known. As Eleanor put it, "He lived his life exactly as he wished." He was in the company of a woman who adored him to the extent that Eleanor poked fun at Missy's slavish devotion to her husband. She may have been a practicing Catholic, but Missy loved this married man unconditionally and more than likely Missy would have done what Franklin wanted.

By 1927, after three annual cruises, the *Larooco* began losing its allure for Franklin. "He learned that, while frivolity and aimlessness were enjoyable in small doses," his son James noted, "he could not take the life of a dilettante as a steady diet." The decision to sell was hastened when a hurricane battered the vessel, driving it four miles inland from the Fort Lauderdale River. With salvage impractical, Franklin and John Lawrence sold the boat for scrap. The end of the *Larooco* devastated Missy. The idyll where she had Franklin all to herself had been torn from its moorings much as the boat had been. From now on, their life together would shift to places where she must share him with others and with his new passion, Warm Springs.

*Chapter 20*

# SAFE HARBOR

. . . . . . .

By now, Franklin had become enamored of Warm Springs. He reveled in the liberating effects of the baths on his body. He loved the pure, clean scent rising from the surrounding stands of pine, the warm colors of the peach orchards, the unspoiled vistas from Pine Mountain Ridge. He wanted to be free to reach these places. With a surprising grasp of mechanics, he designed a car to be operated by manual controls. He bought a battered Model T Ford for $50 and found a local mechanic, Tom Bradshaw, who believed he could turn Franklin's sketches into a functioning vehicle. It worked. The driver's legs might dangle uselessly from the seat, but Franklin could steer, brake, and accelerate using only his hands. He had been released from the prison that had confined him for the past six years. He soon became a familiar figure, waving and smiling, as the Ford rattled along Meriwether County's back roads. His favorite destination was Dowdell's Knob, a rocky overhang seven miles south of Warm Springs atop Pine Mountain. The Knob's 1,400-foot elevation offered a panoramic view of the farmlands below. He began immersing himself in local history and loved driving his guests to the Knob all the while recounting how Creek Indians, wounded in battle, had long ago discovered the healing powers of the local waters.

He enjoyed his newfound neighbors, even preferred them in some ways to the elegant company he had kept most of his life. He told Marion Dickerman that Northeasterners were less friendly. "Few people dropped in to see him or showed any particular interest," Dickerman recalled of a conversation with Franklin. "When he was in the South, many people dropped by with a few flowers, with a chicken, with some wood for the fireplace. I think it was this difference in attitude that helped to enhance his affection for Warm Springs." Louis Haughey, who eventually came to work at Warm Springs, recalled of FDR, "I am a dyed-in-the-wool Republican, but I just lost my heart to him personally. I've seen him go to a tenant farm, a man totally illiterate and pale with embarrassment and fright, and in a few minutes he'd be leaning on the side of the President's car waving his arms and talking animatedly."

From the time it became known publicly that Franklin Roosevelt was taking the baths at Warm Springs, other polio patients began arriving, first in a trickle, then in a stream, looking to him as their savior. As he later described the experience, "There I was, large as life, living proof that Warm Springs . . . had cured me of 57 different varieties of ailments. . . . Every human being, male or female, between Florida and Alaska who has a stomach ache, a cold in the nose or a gouty toe, it would seem writes to old Dr. Roosevelt with the firm belief that I can point out to them, from personal experience, how to get cured."

His affliction had driven him from mainstream life to a periphery that the handicapped must inhabit. But here, as the spa attracted other polio patients, he found himself in the rare position of being among the majority. On his arrival he could start wearing his braces outside his pants where they were so much easier to take on and off, without prompting awkward stares. His fellow sufferers understood the accommodations to a life of pain and impairment. His confidence that one day he could stand on his own two feet never waned. He engaged a physical therapist named Helena Mahoney who wanted to know how much he expected to accomplish. "I'll walk without crutches," he told her. "I'll walk into a room without scaring everybody half to death. I'll stand easily in front of people so that they'll forget I'm a cripple."

His profound contentment with Warm Springs hatched a dream that it could be made into a resort for the able-bodied and a rehabilitation center for polio patients. He was warned against such folly by a new influence in his life, a legal dynamo, compact as a fireplug, named Basil O'Connor. Franklin had ended association with his previous law firm and had established Roosevelt and O'Connor in which essentially O'Connor did the work while Franklin was to attract the clients. O'Connor sought to dampen Franklin's uncritical enthusiasm for his Warm Springs retreat, pointing out that well people might not be comfortable vacationing among crutches and wheelchairs. Franklin nevertheless pressed on.

In the spring of 1926 he bought the Meriwether Inn, its surrounding cottages, its pools, and 1,200 acres of land, for $195,000, sinking almost two thirds of his personal fortune into an untried venture. His record as a businessman was dismal. Caught up in the speculative frenzy of the 1920s, he loaned his name to half-cocked schemes, put up money and usually lost it in helium-filled dirigibles, lobsters, timber, vending machines, even devalued German marks, and a venture to generate electricity by harnessing the tides. Eleanor and his mother shuddered. He made this massive diversion of the estate while his wife was trying to pay tuition bills for their five children in pricey private schools. He brought Sara to Warm Springs hoping she too would be seduced by its charms. After she left he wrote urging her to invest. "You needn't worry about my losing a fortune in it, for every step is being planned either to pay for itself or to make a profit on." The hard-nosed Sara committed herself only to buying one cottage for rental income, no doubt to humor her son. So sure was he of the venture's success that he also persuaded the practical Missy to invest in a rental property. By now he had built a larger cottage for himself. A visitor, Barbara Muller, the sister of one of Missy's high school friends, described the arrangement: "There was a big living room and three bedrooms, but they were very small. He had done a lot of the designing himself. One bedroom was Missy's. Missy and I would have to go through his bedroom to get to the bath," Muller remembered. "We didn't think anything of it."

Just as aboard the *Larooco*, Franklin invited friends down to visit, hoping some might invest in his enterprise. Again, Missy served as hostess at cocktail parties, helping Franklin prepare drinks with bootleg whiskey in the era of Prohibition. He continued to prize her aplomb. When, during a party, she answered a knock at the door to find the local Baptist preacher standing there, she maneuvered him toward a smiling Franklin's outstretched hand. While the man of the cloth was thus distracted, she whisked a tray of drinks into the kitchen and out of sight. As soon as the preacher was gone, Franklin doubled up with laughter.

He had always been fond of his older half-brother, Rosy, and grieved at his sudden death from pneumonia on May 7, 1927, at age seventy-three. Rosy's departure, however, meant a substantial bequest to Franklin and helped ease the heavy burden of acquiring Warm Springs. He needed every penny. Not only had he bought acreage making him almost the largest landholder in the county, but he intended to invest in farm machinery, hire local labor, and make Warm Springs work. Eventually he did raise chickens, plant corn, and harvest fruit. But as far as profits, his farming never earned a penny.

In June 1927, in the seeming contentment of Warm Springs, the third year of her stay, Missy, at age twenty-nine, was inexplicably stricken, collapsing in the cottage she shared with Franklin. She passed through alternating bouts of delirium and depression. She suffered from dysentery, and Franklin wrote his mother, she "is rather low and miserable." The doctor Franklin entrusted her care to, LeRoy Hubbard, was not a professional in emotional disorders but rather a specialist in muscle rehabilitation whom Franklin had lured to Warm Springs. Hubbard arranged a room for Missy in the rehabilitation center he had established from which he removed any object she might use to harm herself.

Franklin hired a full-time nurse from Atlanta and asked one of Missy's brothers to come down from Massachusetts to look after her. Bernard LeHand arrived to find his sister improving, allowing Franklin to leave Missy in Warm Springs while he returned to New York. Bernard wrote Franklin on July 10, "She, of course, has not regained her strength," but she could read, and "remembers everything—in detail except for the first eleven day period at the hospital during which time she is hazy on happenings except perfectly conscious of her deliriums. Since the 28th of June she has been normal." Still the brother was apprehensive. "She would like her fountain pen. A pencil does not appeal to her, although a pen is really considered a dangerous 'weapon.' " Bernard harbored no doubts about Missy's centrality in Franklin's life. "I am confident you will decide to take her to Hyde Park for August," he ended.

What had happened to this poised, assured, even-tempered woman? Barbara Muller, present at the time, was direct: "It was a nervous breakdown." Grace Tully, who would later work with Missy, was even more to the point. Missy had suffered a "crack-up." The likely explanation as to why she fell apart lies in a continuing relationship between Franklin and Lucy Mercer Rutherfurd.

Until recently it has been assumed that Franklin Roosevelt had little or no personal connection with Lucy between the time of the affair's discovery in 1918 and her reentry into his life in 1941 after he had become president and she was a middle-aged woman. Jonathan Daniels once wrote a Roosevelt biographer, Bernard Asbell, "I can't find any contact between Roosevelt and Mrs. Rutherfurd between 1920 and the early 1940's," which Asbell concluded, "would entirely corroborate that the relationship did come to an end." Absence of contact for some twenty-one years would suggest that what had happened between Franklin and

Lucy, rather than a grand passion, had been a fleeting affair now put be-hind them.

Then, in 2005, letters from Franklin to Lucy written between 1926 and 1928 were discovered by her granddaughters, Lucy and Alice Knowles, revealing that they had remained in frequent contact. Franklin's letters are chatty, neighborly for the most part, but include a curious specificity as to his movements. The first letter recovered, dated May 22, 1926, be-gins with his telling Lucy that he is buying Warm Springs on the install-ment plan, and that it offers considerable promise in the treatment of polio. He then reports that "Between now and the 16th I am in New York." He asks if that summer she will be in Allamuchy, the Rutherfurd New Jersey estate, fifty-one miles from New York. A letter written on September 15, 1927, tells her of heavy rains that have swept away houses and bridges in his native Dutchess County, then informs her that about October 20 he will return to Warm Springs "for a month or six weeks." He hopes that her sick children are recovering and regrets that she says nothing about herself, hoping it means she has been "well—really well." A letter later that year to Lucy, then in the Rutherfurds' summer home in Aiken, South Carolina, advises her "I am just off for Warm Springs for four days." He writes her on May 18, 1928, that he has just ended a wearying traveling schedule for the Fidelity & Deposit Company and adds that he will be attending another convention in Houston on June 19, then "I am stopping off at Warm Springs on the way home." He also asks what date she is moving back to Allamuchy. The context suggests that these were not the sole letters Franklin sent Lucy during the 1920s, but rather only those discovered from an ongoing correspondence. His ex-actness in describing where he will be and when, their occasional near-ness to each other, and Eleanor's absence during those periods, would seem to confirm rumors that had occasionally drifted out of the South that Franklin and Lucy not only corresponded but saw each other dur-ing this period.

Besides the recently discovered correspondence, two letters in the Roosevelt Library confirm that Lucy also was writing to Franklin. After Franklin's daughter, Anna, gave birth to her first son, Curtis, in March 1927, Lucy wrote, "Dear Franklin, I hear you are a grandfather. And though I do not know exactly what one's feelings are on that question, still I am sure in this case it is a subject of congratulation." She went on to refer to a property Franklin was interested in, told him she has had a visit from Livy Davis, and announced that she would be off to Europe that summer with her husband and children. Upon her departure for Europe aboard the SS *Belgenland* she wrote Franklin on July 2, 1927, referring to the Rutherfurds as "a traveling circus." She encouraged him, despite his condition, to try such a trip himself, telling of an acquaintance "who cannot walk [and] went abroad last year. They had a special chair made that would fit easily in the French trains. I am not sure it was collapsible. It simplified things a good deal. I could find out about it more definitely if you ever wanted to know." She was aware of his sidetracked but still burning political ambition and teased him, ending the letter, "I hope you have a happy summer and that I shan't go home to find you President, or Secretary of State." She signed the letter "Ever Yrs, Sincerely, LMR," then added a postscript telling him where she could be reached: "If there is anything I can do for you on the continent or in England let me know care Morgan and Co. Paris."

Marriages that end in divorce often leave a bitterness not only between the parties but toward the institution itself, while a romance ended only when fate intervenes or death separates the pair leaves a residue of warm feelings and positive memories. Such appears to have been the case between Franklin and Lucy nearly ten years after their affair had been discovered. Eleanor never had any knowledge that her husband was still in communication with the woman he had pledged never to see again, thus in a sense continuing the betrayal.

One woman, knowing of his continuing contact with Lucy, likely found it too much to bear. Missy LeHand, so emotionally invested in Franklin, whose whole being was intertwined with his, upon discovering that he stayed in touch with and possibly saw Lucy Mercer, had cause to plunge into the breakdown that reduced her to delirium and depression. Other explanations may exist, but no medical evidence was ever found for her collapse. Her devotion to Franklin was such, however, that no matter the pain that further association with him might cause, she returned to work by November 1927 to her and Franklin's mutual relief. The closeness between them stands out in a striking set of dates. Of the 208 weeks between 1924 and 1928, Franklin was away from home 116 weeks. During these absences, Eleanor was with him for four weeks and his mother for two. The rest of the time, 110 weeks, day and night, he was essentially alone with Missy LeHand.

*Chapter 21*

# ELEANOR AND FRIENDS

· · · · · · ·

IF ELEANOR COULD NOT FIND the love, intimacy, and understanding she desired from marriage, where could she fulfill these longings? Her homes, both at 65th Street and Hyde Park, were not tranquil harbors. After more than twenty years of marriage, she still had to contend with Sara suddenly materializing on her side of the twin townhouses. Eleanor further accepted that the Hudson River estate "was my husband's home, and my children had a sense that it was their home." But it was not hers. Now in her forties, she was still treated by her mother-in-law as the wife who had not yet measured up.

With a dining room full of guests, Sara told Eleanor, "If you just ran a comb through your hair, dear, you'd look so much nicer." Aunty Bye's son, Sheffield Cowles, remembered Sara telling her daughter-in-law, "Before us why can't you dress decently?" After a long evening listening to Sara and two of her sisters pontificate, Eleanor vented her anger in a letter to Franklin. "They all in their serene assurances and absolute judgments on people and affairs going on in the world make me want to squirm and turn Bolshevik." She had begun to exhibit her independence in the Washington home, hiring the black servants against Sara's preference. But that had occurred on her territory. In their face-to-face collisions on Sara's home ground Eleanor's response to the constant carping was usually a head-bowed, "Yes, Mama." A few years later she was to write an article entitled, "Rules for Success in Marriage," in which she appeared to be lecturing herself. "I have known many promising marriages to be wrecked because the young people began their life together in the home of their parents."

Not only did she feel that she possessed no home of her own, she did not believe that she controlled her own children. Sara might have been a source of constant stress to Eleanor, but to her five grandchildren, "Granny" was sheer delight, a "grand dame," as Anna put it, "and she could be one of the sweetest people." A grandson described her as "the source of all the good things in life when we were little kids, if you knew how to handle her." When Eleanor said no, the grandchildren turned to Granny, who invariably said yes. It was as if their grandmother was the Supreme Court to whom they could appeal unfavorable decisions handed down by the lower court, their parents. If Sara hated Louis Howe, the children were to hate Louis Howe. "By the time I was about sixteen," Anna recalled, "I could be used as a football by Granny in trying to influence mother." It was Sara "who persuaded me not to go to college," Anna later admitted. "Mother and Father never took a stand, she fed me to the gills with the danger of being an old maid."

Sara's intent was all too clear to Eleanor. "What she wanted was to hang onto Franklin and his children. . . . As it turned out Franklin's children were more my mother-in-law's children than they were mine." Anna found her mother at least partly to blame by her supine surrender to Sara. "If mother had the self-assurance to stand up to Granny," she believed, "what happened would never have happened." It was not that simple. "Franklin could banter with his mother, I saw him being cheeky as hell to Granny," Anna also recalled. "He would tease her. . . . Father loved his arguments with Granny. And when he got tired, he just wheeled himself out." Eleanor's seeming lack of spine had its rationale. Given the unbreakable bond between her husband and his mother, given that the comfortable life she and Franklin led depended upon Sara's largesse, Eleanor found herself trapped. The person she so deeply resented was the same person Franklin loved and upon whom the couple's way of life hinged. Hence, the "Yes, Mamas" went on. Anna came to believe, "From the polio time on, Granny became a very destructive force in the family."

In time, Anna found the tensions between her parents and grandmother wearying, and in 1926, at age twenty, she agreed to marry a stockbroker, Curtis Dall, ten years her senior, not out of love, but as she said, "I wanted to get out from the ambivalence I found between Granny and mother and father." Sara planned a wedding present for the couple, a luxury apartment, and Anna was not to breathe a word of it to her mother. When Eleanor found out she was outraged. "I am so angry at her offering anything to a child of mine without speaking to me if she thought I would object and for telling her not to tell me that it is all I can do to be decent. . . . I've reached a state of constant self-control that sometimes I'm afraid of what will happen if it ever breaks." Learning of Eleanor's anger, Sara wrote her a letter that passed for contrition. "I did not think I <u>could</u> be nasty or mean," she wrote. "I love you dear too much to ever want to hurt you. Well, I just must bear it."

On the eve of Anna's wedding, Eleanor faced what she regarded as a dread duty. She approached her daughter in the bathroom and asked if there was anything she wanted to know. Anna stifled her laughter at her mother's visible discomfort. It was on this occasion that Eleanor, likely untouched as a woman for over eight years, delivered her view that sex was something a woman must learn to endure. Much later, when Anna had become a mother herself, her son Curtis brashly asked about his grandmother's sexual attitudes. She replied that her mother told her she found the mechanics sweaty and unappealing, and that after the Lucy Mercer affair, her husband had never as much as entered her bedroom. Though she had become active in the birth control movement, supporting Margaret Sanger, her son Elliott remembered, "We kidded mother . . . she still had not the least understanding of the practice and techniques."

Eleanor's friendship with the lesbian couple Nancy Cook and Marion Dickerman continued to ripen. In the fall of 1925 she and the two women were enjoying a picnic at a favorite site along the Val-Kill, "stream of falls" in Dutch, two miles east of Hyde Park and owned by the Roosevelts. When Franklin heard the women lament that the picnic would be the last of the season, he offered a solution. He suggested they "build a shack" and hollow out some earth "so as to form an old fashioned swimming hole," and thus have a year-round retreat. He drew up the lease, gave them a life tenancy, engaged an architect, Henry Toombs, appointed himself the general contractor, and charged the women $12,000 to build the structure. He favored a stone version of the Dutch Colonial style popular in the Hudson Valley. Hence they would call the house "Stone Cottage."

On New Year's Day 1926 the three women found themselves sitting on nail kegs amid wood shavings, enjoying their first meal in their hideaway. Franklin's support had been both selfless and self-serving. He knew the stress his wife lived under at Hyde Park and knew she deserved time under a roof of her own. He also knew that, with Missy LeHand, he had created a life apart from Eleanor. Building Stone Cottage for her and her friends assuaged him of whatever guilt he might have felt for neglecting his wife.

She, Nancy, and Marion bought Todhunter School in New York, the progressive academy for girls from well-to-do families. Marion became the principal and Eleanor assistant principal and a teacher. "I gave courses in American history, and in English and American literature," Eleanor recalled. "We visited the New York City courts," and she took students to see tenements as she had done as a settlement house volunteer before Sara put a stop to it. "All this made the government of the city something real and alive, rather than just words in a textbook," she said. So committed was she that her son James remembered, "She got involved in things like Todhunter and lost touch with her children."

Her association with forward-looking feminists began to uproot the last remnants of her Victorian prejudices. Just five years before, she had resisted attending a party for the financier Bernard Baruch, knowing many Jews would be present, and complaining, "I'd rather be hung than seen." She went anyway, but afterward said that she found "the Jew party appalling. I never wish to hear money, jewels, and . . . sables mentioned again." While Franklin had served in the New York State Senate, she opposed giving women the vote and the Equal Rights Amendment. Before visiting Warm Springs, she had shown little sensitivity to the plight of blacks. But, with her eyes opened by socially conscious companions, she found herself increasingly comfortable with people whose color, ethnicity, religion, and culture she would once have found beyond the pale. Eleanor supported the admission of Jews to Todhunter. She became more tolerant of the less well bred. Marion Dickerman recalled a lunch where "a certain gentleman was sitting on her right and fingerbowls were placed in front of us, then ice cream was passed and he put his ice cream in the fingerbowl. When it came to her she put her ice cream in the fingerbowl."

The three women began imagining a purpose for Stone Cottage larger than merely a place to unwind. In Dutchess County were skilled craftsmen with time on their hands during the winter months and rural youths who could benefit by learning a trade. They decided to start a business in the cottage to be called Val-Kill Industries, manufacturers of fine furniture in the Early American tradition. The versatile Nancy Cook had just the skills required. During the Great War she and Marion had served at the Endell Street military hospital in London, where Nan quickly mastered the craft of making artificial limbs. Franklin was an enthusiastic supporter of the new enterprise. Once underway, Eleanor opened her home on East 65th Street as a showroom. Val-Kill Industries began selling furniture in cherry, mahogany, and walnut to Vassar College, Sloane's, Altman's, and Marshall Field's department stores and Schrafft's restaurant. They found captive customers, building furniture for the Todhunter School, Warm Springs, and through sales to relatives. Val-Kill Industries soon outgrew its first home and a two-story cinder block factory was built two hundred feet from Stone Cottage.

Spurred on by the physically active Nan and Marion, Eleanor began to shed her timidity. On her honeymoon in Switzerland, she had feared scaling the peaks and watched as Franklin marched off with a glamorous hat maker. Now she hiked mountains with long, confident strides, outpacing everyone else. She, who long had been terrified of the water, became a graceful swimmer and took up horseback riding. After a shaky start in which she ran into a stone gatepost at the entrance to Hyde Park, she became a competent driver. She began to feel stronger and healthier. The headaches and colds she chronically suffered seemed to vanish.

One autumn afternoon, Eleanor, Nan, and Marion showed up at Oldgate, Aunty Bye's country home in Farmington, Connecticut, a serene setting with carpetlike lawns sloping down to the Farmington River. The Cowles family was jarred from its summer reverie by the sight unfolding before them, the three visitors stepping from their car in identical brown jodhpurs. At another family get-together, Rosy's daughter, Helen, was wakened in the middle of the night by shrieking laughter in the next-door bedroom where Eleanor and her friends were staying and was aghast to see her deadly earnest aunt engaged in a pillow fight. Visitors to Stone Cottage were curious to find the linens embroidered with the intertwined initials, "EMN." When Eleanor was separated from Nan and Marion, she felt their absence so keenly that on one occasion she wrote, "I feel I'd like to go off with you and forget the rest of the world existed."

Franklin and Louis Howe took to calling Eleanor's friends "she-males." Alice Longworth, getting word of her cousin's current set, acidly referred to them as "female impersonators." These intimate friendships were to mark the beginning of a persistent debate over the nature of Eleanor's relations with women. On the train during the trip she had made to join her husband in Florida for their twentieth wedding anniversary, she read *The Constant Nymph*, by Margaret Kennedy, the story of a fifteen-year-old girl in love with a man who marries someone else, leaving her bereft. The book contained a sentence, "No sort of love ought to be despised . . . it is the first source of civility." That night, Eleanor copied the words in her journal. Yet, when another lesbian friend, Esther Lape, gave her André Gide's *Les Faux-Monnayeurs*, with its depiction of explicit homosexual behavior in a boys school, "She was absolutely shocked by it," Lape recalled. Esther saw the book as a sensitively told love story. But of Eleanor's reaction she remembered, "She read it in terms of a forbidden subject. She couldn't even bring herself to consider homosexuality. . . . She nearly took my head off. Such a blast. Generally her reaction was not so final, but in this case it was."

One evening soon after Stone Cottage had been finished, Eleanor, Nan, and Marion were relaxing in the living room. The mood was subdued, the only sound the crackling of logs burning in the fireplace. Eleanor broke the silence and began speaking quietly. The other two women had long been puzzled by the obvious strain between Eleanor and her husband. Franklin appeared to be the soul of geniality toward the rest of the world, and Eleanor at least, in their company, was warm and affectionate. But between the Roosevelts the coolness was inescapable. They were about to find out why. As Eleanor spoke, the story of Franklin and Lucy's affair began to spill out, its discovery through the love letters and the hard bargain Eleanor had exacted if the marriage was to continue. It was the rare moment when the secret had been confessed outside the family. "Her whole background was a Victorian concept of fidelity and she had been hurt, cruelly hurt, in a way that clung I think as long as she lived," Marion remembered of the revelation. "She said she had forgiven but could not forget. I never had a feeling that she had completely forgiven because she seemed to feel that he had taken from her an ideal and concept of life together that could never be completely restored. I remember afterward getting the social register out and looking up Mrs. Rutherfurd." Esther Lape reported that Eleanor once told her she had not loved Franklin since the affair. Her confidence to Lape may have been her wounded pride speaking louder than her heart. Her daughter, Anna, remained convinced that her mother would forever love her father.

Chapter 22

# GOVERNOR ROOSEVELT

· · · · · · ·

Among the letters discovered by the descendants of Lucy Mercer Rutherfurd in 2005 was a curious and revealing document, a slim blue bound printing of a lecture delivered on May 18, 1926, at the Milton Academy in Massachusetts for the Alumni Memorial War Foundation and entitled *Whither Bound?* The lecturer was Franklin Roosevelt. He had inscribed a blank page at the end of the booklet, "I dedicate this little work, my first, to you." The lecture was one of his few writings to be published and curiously was not dedicated to his wife, his mentor, Louis Howe, or anyone else close to him, but to the woman he had promised to eliminate from his life yet still loved. The small publication was to remain in Lucy's possession until the day she died.

By the time she received this work Lucy had been married for six years, was the mother of a four-year-old daughter, stepmother to five other children, and mistress of two large estates, plus a house in Washington, a townhouse in Manhattan on Madison Avenue, and a home in Paris. Her pinched life with her mother at the Toronto apartments seemed now as remote as the moon. Allamuchy, the principal estate, was set amid eight thousand acres in New Jersey, and included five farms, most of the land in the Rutherfurd family since the 1780s. The mansion was immediately surrounded by a thousand-acre park, with woods, winding streams, velvet lawns, a rose garden, a private lake, and a golf course. The house had been built in 1904, in the English Tudor style, its red-brick walls encircling thirty-three rooms and seventeen baths, its magnificence suggesting a stately home in Buckinghamshire more than a property in rural New Jersey. Overflow from the lake powered a generator that provided the mansion with electricity when surrounding country folk were still using kerosene lamps. Above the doorway of the house was engraved the motto found in the family coat of arms, *Nec Sorte Nec Fato*, roughly "Neither chance nor fate," which suggested that good fortune had been earned not handed to the Rutherfurds.

Everything material, even spiritual, was at Lucy's fingertips. Father George Smith, a family friend, lived at Allamuchy and said Mass on Sunday mornings in a fieldstone chapel accommodating sixty communicants that Winty had built for his first wife. Butlers, maids, cooks, nurses, and chauffeurs anticipated every need. Five gardeners, against whose dominance Lucy gently rebelled, tended the flower beds. Violetta's daughter, also named Lucy, remembered her aunt saying to one gardener, "Oh Jim, just leave me a little patch of ground to weed, please," which she would tend always wearing French kid gloves and under a huge hat to protect her flawless complexion. On one occasion, riding with Violetta, Lucy asked the chauffeur to stop by a woman selling flowers along a country road. She got out and bought every bloom. Asked why she had done so given the profusion of flowers at Allamuchy, she answered that this woman, barely scratching out a living, could at least go home early for one day.

After his marriage to Lucy, Winthrop Rutherfurd had built his second estate, Ridgely Hall, in Aiken, South Carolina, horse country where polo was popular and to which the rich escaped from northern winters. While lacking the palatial grandeur of Allamuchy, Ridgely Hall was a handsome Georgian mansion with a mansard roof and parapet. It contained fourteen bedrooms, an equal number of baths, and was conveniently located across the road from the Palmetto Golf Club where Winty served as chairman of the greens committee. So exclusive was Palmetto that when President-elect William Howard Taft sought to play there, he was refused. Members felt they did not really know Mr. Taft.

Rutherfurd's style was as English as his homes. His passion, if such a word might be used to describe so reserved a figure, was breeding smooth fox terriers. He would happily pay $1,500 for a dog with a strong bloodline in an era when that sum represented a year's pay for a working man. He also dabbled in cattle breeding and expected his farms to be profitable. Violetta's daughter, a frequent guest to Allamuchy, recalled her uncle's dealings with his farm manager, Edward Danks. "Mr. Danks would come to report to my uncle. My uncle would be in the downstairs library sitting behind his desk. He would say, 'All right, Danks, what's the problem today?' He was always 'Danks' and never asked to sit down." A visitor described Allamuchy's master as "the epitome of a snob, very, very English." The Rutherfurds always dressed for dinner, black tie for father and sons, even with no guests present. Since Winty cared little for company, he and Lucy seldom entertained and rarely went out evenings.

However austere with others, the man was passionate about his wife. "He worshipped the ground she walked on," her niece Lucy recalled. Mrs. Eulalie Salley, a self-made real estate success—"We do everything but brush your teeth"—and a suffragist pioneer who had dropped leaflets on Aiken from a plane, became a valued friend of Lucy's and a frequent witness to the Rutherfurd ménage. "He was desperately in love with her. He kissed her every time he saw her," Salley observed. Lucy reciprocated as a devoted and dutiful wife to her husband, sensitive to his every expectation. But as Salley said of her, there was not much "demonstration of love, just total sympatique."

Lucy and Violetta had remained close since girlhood, like survivors of hard-fought campaigns against the poverty their parents had inflicted upon themselves. Violetta and her daughter spent summers at Allamuchy where they occupied a comfortable old stone house and to which they brought their own servants. Minnie Mercer, now supported by her daughters, was also an occasional guest at the Rutherfurd homes, though Lucy rarely visited her mother. Minnie's imperious conduct as a guest was not easily borne. On one occasion, Lucy, whose voice rarely rose above a well-modulated purr, was drawn into such an argument with her mother that a hapless Winty tried to referee. Minnie turned on him and snapped, "Why, you're almost as old as I am." She became for a time persona non grata.

While Winthrop Rutherfurd was leading the squire's life that Sara Roosevelt had wanted for her own son, Franklin was about to commence a resurrection that no one watching this sweat-soaked, gasping man drag himself upstairs in 1921 could have imagined. For the previous seven years, Sara had essentially won the battle over the existence her son should lead. He had lived as a gentleman of leisure, entertaining his friends, pursuing his interests in stamp collecting, fishing, model boats, ornithology, and spending as much time as he wished on the *Larooco* or at Warm Springs. His law practice and association with Fidelity & Deposit could best be described as undemanding.

In 1928, less than a year after Missy had recovered and been restored to her ambiguous but pivotal role in Franklin's life, her emotional under-pinning was threatened once more. Franklin had made a political toe dip when he nominated Al Smith in the latter's unsuccessful bid to become the Democratic Party's candidate for president in 1924. Two years later he was invited to deliver the keynote address at the New York State Democratic convention where Robert Wagner was nominated for the U.S. Senate and Al Smith chosen for a fourth term as governor. Missy had been much relieved when Franklin was approached to run for the Senate seat and demurred, saying that he had not yet recovered suffi-ciently, and more facetiously, "I am temperamentally unfitted to be a member of the uninteresting body known as the United States Senate." In 1928, he yielded to Smith's plea that he again nominate him for pres-ident at the Democratic National Convention in Houston.

On June 27, as Roosevelt approached the podium, delegates could not escape noticing the change in Roosevelt's vigor over his previous ap-pearance. He had learned to conceal his impairment with dissembling skill, creating the impression that a man who could not stand unaided was merely "lame." On this day, he moved forward holding on to the arm of his eighteen-year-old son, Elliott, and using a cane in his right hand. Behind the podium, the delegates saw a broad-shouldered, deep-chested man whose ebullience fairly exploded as he hailed Smith as a leader who possessed "the quality of soul which makes a man beloved by little children, dumb animals . . . [who] will avoid the bottomless morass of crass materialism that has engulfed so many great civilizations in the past." And once again he proclaimed Smith the "Happy Warrior." But as for his own political ambition, Missy thankfully noted, Franklin still seemed to exhibit none. He appeared content to make Warm Springs the focus of his life, having by now created the Warm Springs Founda-tion, raising money often from his own pocket to meet a simple stan-dard: that no polio victim, however poor, should ever be turned away.

Missy's serenity was tested on September 30, a cool, sunny afternoon at Warm Springs. The day started out splendidly as they drove off for a picnic on Dowdell's Knob. The outing was deliberately intended to avoid phone calls from Al Smith, who had not been content simply to have Roosevelt nominate him in June, but now had in mind a strategic role for Franklin. Roosevelt had to run for governor of New York, Smith pleaded. The political math demonstrated that without the state's forty-five electoral votes, Smith did not have a prayer of being elected. And the key to taking New York was to have a rejuvenated, magnetic, famously named candidate at the top of the state ticket. Franklin and Louis Howe had already decided against taking the bait. Partly their wariness reflected Franklin's conviction that with just a little more time he would be back on his feet. Furthermore, Howe believed that, as in 1920, the Democratic presidential candidate was destined to lose and Franklin should not be trapped aboard a sinking ship. The Republican, Herbert Hoover, would surely be elected in these prosperous times and probably be reelected in 1932. The smart move, Howe calculated, was for Franklin to win the governor's office in 1932 as a warm-up for a presidential bid in 1936 when by then he might be able to walk with only a cane. In the meantime, Roosevelt should keep using his disability as an excuse to Smith as to why he could not run for governor. "If they are looking for a goat," Louis telegraphed Franklin at Warm Springs, "why don't [Senator Robert] Wagner sacrifice himself?"

After the picnic, Franklin and Missy went to a school in Manchester, Georgia, five miles from Warm Springs where he was carried up three flights of stairs to deliver a speech supporting Smith. After his speech, Franklin did allow himself to be taken to a phone in a Manchester drugstore to await a call from a desperate Smith. To Missy's relief, the connection failed. As they drove back to Warm Springs she broke a brittle silence asking, "You're still not going to take it, are you?" No, he answered, he was not. "Don't you dare let them talk you into it," she warned.

When they arrived back in Warm Springs, Smith was calling again on a phone in the lobby of the Meriwether Inn, his rasping, big-city accent employing blandishments that badly misjudged Roosevelt's character. Once he was elected, Smith promised, an able candidate for lieutenant governor could do all the heavy lifting. Franklin need only show up for his inauguration, sign bills, and otherwise spend nine months of the year at Warm Springs. "Don't hand me that baloney," Roosevelt replied. This argument failing, the anguished Smith said, "Frank, I told you I wasn't going to put this on a personal basis, but I've got to." His victory or defeat, he pleaded, lay in Franklin's hands. Missy sat close enough to detect growing hesitancy in Franklin's refusals. "Don't you dare," she whispered. "Don't you dare."

But he did, and on October 2, Roosevelt was chosen to run for governor in a delegate stampede at New York's Democratic nominating convention. The siren song of ambition and what the party's hot pursuit said about his acceptability physically and politically were forces too compelling to resist. Within days of his acceptance of the nomination, Missy had another nervous collapse. She played no part in Franklin's gubernatorial campaign. It was as if, when she lost her grip on him, she lost her grip on herself.

With this, his first campaign since contracting polio, Roosevelt faced a dreaded question. Would his disability become an election issue? The then Republican *New York Post* had a harsh answer. "There is something pathetic and pitiless in the 'drafting' of Franklin D. Roosevelt by Alfred E. Smith," the *Post* editorialized. "The governor made this most loyal of friends agree to serve his ambition at a price that is beyond all reason." Defending Roosevelt's capacity to serve as governor, Smith shot back, "We do not elect him for his ability to do a double back flip or hand spring. The work of the governorship is brain work. Ninety-five per cent of it is accomplished sitting at a desk." In a memorable line, he concluded, "The governor did not have to be an acrobat." On November 6, Franklin Roosevelt was elected by a hairbreadth 25,564 votes while, ironically, Smith, who had sought to use Roosevelt, was soundly trounced by Herbert Hoover. The Catholic Smith, referring to the rosary, observed dryly that it was too soon before anyone "said the beads in the White House."

Missy was not the only woman in Franklin's life uninvolved in his election. Eleanor had campaigned, but only for Smith. Discussing the matter with a friend, she remarked, "Governor Smith's election means something, but whether Franklin spends two years in Albany or not matters comparatively very little." After her husband had won, a *New York Post* reporter asked for her reaction, to which she answered, "If the rest of the ticket didn't get in, what does it matter." When pressed that she must feel some excitement over her husband's elevation as governor of the country's most populous state, she answered, "I don't care. What difference does it make to me." She said that she would give him a half a week in Albany, then, on Sunday night she would take the train to New York to make her classes at Todhunter on Monday morning. Whatever time was left she intended to devote to the Val-Kill furniture business. Marion Dickerman read Eleanor's abdication unambiguously. It was "as if to emphasize that she considered her 'first lady' duties to be less important than others she performed in her own right as Eleanor Roosevelt."

On New Year's Day 1929, the Roosevelts took up residence in the governor's mansion in Albany, a mélange of Second Empire and Queen Anne styles with a tower, mansard roof, dormers, and wraparound porches, derided by architecture critics as gingerbread. Franklin's election to high office, however, brought his income low since he had to leave the Fidelity & Deposit payroll. Again his mother came to the rescue, happy to make up the difference, as she put it, "now that Franklin is grown up and is the governor." The assignment of the mansion's nine bedrooms on the second floor, each with private bath, was Eleanor's to make. Franklin was given the master bedroom. For herself, Eleanor chose a smaller bedroom around the corner from her husband. She assigned Missy a larger bedroom than her own with an adjoining doorway to Franklin's room and with a window in the door covered only by a curtain. The bedroom arrangements might well raise eyebrows, as it did for Elliott Roosevelt. But his brother Jimmy, in his memoir, countered, "Elliott makes a lot of Missy being seen entering or leaving father's room in her nightclothes, but was she supposed to dress to the teeth every time she was summoned at midnight? . . . None of us thought anything of it."

The easy camaraderie between Franklin and Missy quickly resumed. Upon receiving a semiliterate letter from a surgical hardware manufacturer asking questions about his condition, Franklin scribbled mock answers in pencil in the margins and passed them along for Missy's amusement. The writer asked, "Can you walk without a cain or some assistants? (I cannot walk without a cain because I am not abel.) Does both your shoes fit you even? (They fit me even unless by accident I put on an odd shoe.) Are you inclined also to have a weakness in the ankle? (I have my little weaknesses like anybody else.) Are you sure of your step? (We all have to watch our step with so many prohibition agents around.) Have you any pain below the hips? If so, tell me where. (My principal pain is in the neck when I get letters like this.)"

His first year in the governor's office included a triumphal return to Harvard. He was invited to be chief marshal for the college's tercentenary celebration. Most satisfying to him, he received a Phi Beta Kappa key, albeit honorary.

Eleanor's time-consuming outside interests reopened the way for Missy to resume her place at Franklin's side, the duties of hostess often falling into her all too willing hands. She and Franklin decided which furniture was to be brought to Albany from the other Roosevelt homes to achieve Franklin's comfortable clutter. They chose to demolish three greenhouses that Al Smith had built and replace them with a swimming pool into which she unenthusiastically followed Franklin. "I don't like exercise," she admitted, "but for years I hated to say no." The observant Dickerman found further that Missy's "wholehearted loyalty to [Franklin] is beyond any sense of dedication I have ever known." In Marion's view, Missy was better than anyone at decoding this essentially undecipherable man. "Her judgments sometimes I felt were almost intuitively reached and were invariably sound. . . . She often planned relaxations for the governor," Dickerman remembered. "On an evening when she knew a condemned man was going to the electric chair, she would ask Sam Rosenman and Grace Tully to come in and play bridge so that nothing serious would be discussed." Her concern over Franklin's sensitivity appears not to have been warranted. Years later, on the day that six captured Nazi saboteurs were electrocuted, President Roosevelt affably reminisced over drinks with Rosenman, his confidant and speechwriter, while he spun stories of similar death watches they had held at the statehouse in Albany.

What now existed in the governor's mansion was something of a ménage à trois, although which was "the other woman" was not easily discernible. Eleanor's solicitude toward Missy seemed genuine, as she urged her to take care of her fragile health, cut down on her smoking, and get more rest. They shopped together and took long walks along the banks of the Hudson River. One visitor reported seeing Eleanor kiss Missy good night and thinking, "How could she?" Missy, for her part, never exploited her position or misjudged her place. In a Christmas note to "Dear F.D.," she wrote, "just being with you is a joy I can't express," and added, for both Roosevelts, "you are the ones who have my love and only real devotion—without which I would have little reason for taking up space." It was a triangle of mutual advantage. Franklin gave Missy her reason for being. Missy provided the adoring female companionship that Franklin required. And his dependence on Missy freed Eleanor to pursue the life she wanted.

Ten years had elapsed from the time Franklin left public service in 1921 until he reentered the arena as New York's governor. How someone so severely disabled accomplished this leap has engendered endless speculation over the effect of polio on the man Roosevelt became. Did the disease shape the character, or did the character shape his response to adversity? The most appealing legend is Eleanor's view of his infirmity as a blessing in disguise. He had come through the ordeal, she believed, a more serious, more empathetic human being. The struggle against polio "gave him strength and courage he had not had before. He had to think out the fundamentals of living and learn the greatest of all lessons, infinite patience and never ending persistence." One day she was taking questions after a lecture in Akron, Ohio, when someone in the audience caught her off guard, asking, "Do you think your husband's illness has affected his mentality?" Pausing, Eleanor calmly answered, "I am glad that question was asked. The answer is 'Yes.' Anyone who has gone through great suffering is bound to have a greater sympathy and understanding of the problems of mankind." Her response won a standing ovation. Frances Perkins also endorsed the character-building interpretation of his affliction. "Franklin Roosevelt," she wrote in her memoirs, "underwent a spiritual transformation during the years of his illness. I noticed when he came back that the years of pain and suffering had purged the slightly arrogant attitude he had displayed on occasion before he was stricken. The man emerged completely warmhearted, with humility of spirit and deeper philosophy." His grandson Curtis concluded, "I think polio shaped his character in the sense that it provided the one thing we all need, deep frustration, that keen sense that you cannot do everything you want to do. The only thing that mattered to FDR really was his political ambition and to have it thrown in his face that it looked impossible must have entered into his soul." Franklin had always been self-disciplined even before his illness. Now, having had so much of his previous life torn from him, his capacity to shut out unpleasantness grew stronger. "The only thing that stands out in my mind of evidence of how he suffered when he finally knew that he would never walk again," Eleanor remembered, "was the fact that I never heard him mention golf from the day he was taken ill until the end of his life." Previously, the game had been his passion. "He could pull a curtain down," Eleanor noted.

The most underappreciated dimension of Roosevelt's life, according to Hugh Gallagher, as a fellow polio patient, was in his overcoming the handicap. "The man was a paraplegic, yet this important fact is given very little attention," Gallagher has observed. "FDR's disease and seven years of convalescence are treated as an episode . . . and never mentioned again." To Gallagher this dismissal ignored the centrality of the blow that robbed the man of his physical completeness. Gallagher points out that having a handicap, especially one so visible, "affects every relationship, alters the attitude of others and challenges one's self-esteem. I have never met any person for whom the paralysis was not vital," he reported, "if not the most vital-shaping event of his life." Franklin Roosevelt was no different. His merely appearing at a routine political event entailed an ordeal. His daughter, Anna, described him mounting a fire escape, wearing the heavy braces, in order to reach a platform for a speech in Brooklyn during the gubernatorial campaign. "I guess that will always stick in my mind. . . . He had to swing way out, first one leg and then the other leg. . . . When I looked and saw the sweat was just pouring off his face and his shirt was wet, I realized the effort."

The effect of polio on his life has been so little appreciated because it was so well concealed. Displaying again his mechanical bent, he had outfitted an ordinary kitchen chair that could slip easily through any doorway with wheels that looked more normal than those on an actual wheelchair. Through ceaseless practice he had learned to shift back and forth from the wheelchair to an ordinary chair so quickly that the move was scarcely noticeable. He could walk, however awkwardly, over short distances by clutching someone's arm while in his other hand he held a cane.

Fortunately, he had reentered the glare of the political spotlight in a more chivalrous age. During the gubernatorial campaign, when newsreel cameras were turned on as he was lifted from his car, Roosevelt admonished the cameramen firmly but with a grin, "No movies of me getting out of the machine, boys." If a photographer tried to catch the candidate in a wheelchair, he might find his camera accidentally knocked to the ground or his view suddenly blocked by another reporter. The press simply did not write of Roosevelt's incapacity. Concealing his true condition became something of a conspiracy of civility that lasted throughout his life. Consequently, upon his death, millions of Americans were shocked to learn that their leader over the previous twelve years, through depression and war, had been a cripple.

*Chapter 23*

# ELEANOR AND THE STATE TROOPER

· · · · · · ·

Soon after becoming governor, Franklin Roosevelt spotted a familiar-looking trooper among the state police he had inherited from Al Smith's security detail. The man turned out to be Earl Miller, a World War I Navy veteran who had been assigned security duties in Washington when Roosevelt was assistant secretary. Corporal Miller was tall, broad-shouldered, with the square-jawed good looks and clear-eyed gaze of a silent movie hero, a man not easily forgotten. His athletic prowess was limitless, a marksman, horseback rider, and champion swimmer, who excelled at any sport requiring speed, strength, and coordination. When Franklin first knew Earl, he had just won the Atlantic Middleweight Boxing Championship. Born in Schenectady, New York, in 1897, Miller said of his youth, "I was without a home at 14 & an acrobat in a circus which helped support two sick parents." He also performed as a stuntman, contortionist, and trick rider before enlisting in the Navy. Miller, a talker given to the dramatic, claimed that knowledge of the Roosevelt-Mercer affair had seeped down even to the Navy's enlisted ranks.

As the state's first lady, Eleanor was expected to travel in a chauffeured limousine. She balked. She wanted to keep driving her own blue Buick. Franklin reluctantly agreed, but said that she had to have a bodyguard. Corporal Miller was chosen and promoted to sergeant on the spot. Few women could resist Miller's appeal, who, along with his physical attributes, had an engaging, unaffected manner in dealing with anyone from fellow troopers to the state's patrician first lady. Eleanor was impressed early on by Earl's take-charge approach in handling her obstreperous drunkard uncle, Valentine Hall. As Earl remembered the man, "I had to go on to Tivoli and put him under wraps two or three times. She told me I was the only one who could do anything with him." His gift for male camaraderie attracted the Roosevelt sons as well. Elliott wrote of a canal inspection trip taken with his parents during which, "To while away the monotony as we dawdled along in the [boat] *The Inspector*, I played cards with some of Father's party, notably with a muscular young roughneck who had been a circus acrobat among other things. . . . I was down twenty-five dollars to Earl Miller before we got to Buffalo." As Elliott put it, "Miller may have been only a bodyguard . . . but with his brash, barrack-room manner he soon made himself more than that within our susceptible family."

Eleanor saw in Earl an appealing amalgam, a man's man and a woman's man who displayed an unexpected sensitivity. Miller detected in Eleanor a woman who still needed to shed lingering inhibitions. In her determination to continue conquering her early fear of water, she had long wanted to master diving. Earl began teaching her in the pool at the governor's mansion. Her progress was slow, measured in countless belly flops. Earl would not let her give up, and eventually she learned to dive competently. He taught her to fire a pistol, at first a terrifying experience, but one that in time she came to enjoy. He loaned her his chestnut mare, Dot, and gave her riding lessons. She gave up riding only after Dot died. "I never again could find a horse in whom I had the slightest confidence," she claimed, suggesting that her confidence was as much in Miller as in the horse. Perhaps most incongruous, he taught Eleanor Roosevelt to shoot craps.

He began referring to her as "The Lady" or "Dear Lady." She began to include him on hikes, and camping trips with her friends, Nan and Marion. They stayed in rustic Adirondack Mountain cabins where Eleanor would read poetry aloud by the light of the fire. When Earl accompanied her to Val-Kill, a room always awaited him. When she rented a Manhattan pied-à-terre at 20 East 11th Street in Greenwich Village from Esther Lape and Elizabeth Read, Earl always had a room there, too. At Christmastime, friends gathered around the piano at the governor's mansion while Earl played and led the singing. He willingly took on thankless chores. "I did all the Christmas shopping for the people in the Executive Department," he recalled. Eleanor "was at a loss what to get people and was very pleased with that." As she drew him closer into her private life, her mother-in-law remarked tartly, "He used to be 'Sergeant' and eat in the kitchen, but now he is 'Earl' and eats with the family." Eleanor came to trust Miller's judgment and took him along on official inspections to prisons and mental hospitals where the immobile Franklin sent her to serve as his eyes, ears, and legs.

Miller found The Lady easily duped in practical matters. During the summer of Franklin's first term as governor, the Roosevelts had gone on vacation, leaving only three staffers in the mansion. Earl began checking the household bills, especially the butcher's. "They must have eaten a ton of filet mignons," he remembered. "I don't know whether they ate them or whether they were being charged and splitting." He checked gas consumption for the automobiles assigned to the governor and found 1,100 gallons had supposedly been burned during the family's absence. "I made out a detailed report," he said, "and it knocked The Lady right out of her chair." He found Eleanor "not easy to protect. I would say, 'people aren't all good.'" "The trouble with you, Earl," she responded, "is you're too much of a cop. You don't trust anybody."

Newspaper photos of her upset him. "Her expression was as if she hated photographers," he remembered of her pained poses. She had always been the severest critic of her appearance, telling a friend, "My dear, if you haven't any chin and your front teeth stick out, it's going to show on a camera plate." Earl began coaching her, "Now, listen, try to smile for just one picture." To get her to do so, he said, "I used to stand behind the photographers and make funny faces." When Eleanor saw the improvement she began a lifelong habit of smiling directly into the camera. "She credits me with that," Earl claimed.

Miller had a deserved reputation at the state troopers' barracks as a ladies' man, particularly in his conquest of younger women. "When they saw Eleanor's picture," he remembered the troopers saying, "We don't envy you having to live with that old crab." When he accompanied Eleanor to a speaking engagement in Elizabethtown, he heard a woman whisper, "I wish someone would teach her how to dress." Another commented, "She certainly knows how to pick handsome troopers to drive her around. . . . I could have strangled them," Earl recalled. Marion Dickerman detected an unlikely communion of souls between Earl and Eleanor. She, an orphan, was, according to Dickerman, "concerned about his early life which had not been too happy. . . . Earl became very fond of her and I think she of him."

The bond between Eleanor Roosevelt and Earl Miller is best understood when viewed through the prism of class. To Eleanor's grandson

Curtis, "The fact that Earl was not of her class was attractive to her," perhaps an unconscious expression of her social worker impulse, or more likely the appeal of raw vitality to the overly refined. For his part, the once homeless, hungry urchin was bound to be impressed by his growing importance to the wife of the state's governor and a Roosevelt to boot. Upon becoming part of her circle, he soon had a misconception corrected. It usually comes as a surprise to the working class that the upper classes, possessing that apparent solution to all problems, money, can still be discontented, lonely, and insecure. Yet, Earl found that he could influence Eleanor, saw her follow his advice, even take his orders. He could speak to her as if no gulf existed between them, even from a position of superiority in his spheres of expertise. As he came to understand her patrician uncertainty alongside his proletarian assurance, his sympathy and affection for her grew.

The closeness between them was not universally appreciated. To Nan and Marion, Earl Miller was too pleased with himself, too vain, too preening. "He used to annoy me the way he talked to her," Dickerman remembered. "I didn't like his tone of voice when he told her what to do, or when he didn't like what was being served at table." He behaved much too familiarly for their taste, a feeling prompted no doubt as much by jealousy as by his lack of decorum. He freely put his arm around Eleanor's waist or shoulders. The two held hands and sat poolside, fingers touching each other's knees. Anna remembered once seeing her mother rub Earl's back at Val-Kill. Esther Lape told of going upstairs unannounced one evening to the apartment Eleanor had rented from her and ringing the bell. Eleanor, obviously having taken special care of her appearance, opened the door, smiling brightly. "Oh," she said, the smile vanishing, "I was expecting Earl, but do come in." Clearly, these lesbian women could not take to an Earl Miller, who represented a rival for Eleanor's attentions and affection. She, however, appeared oblivious of their disapproval. And so, knowing what the man meant to Eleanor, her friends tolerated him. Marion understood that "Earl gave Eleanor a sense of confidence in herself." Her son Jimmy admitted that Earl "gave her a great deal of what her husband and we, her sons, failed to give her. Above all he made her feel that she was a woman."

Earl taught the resistant Eleanor how to have fun, how to let her hair down. On a visit to Chazy Lake in upstate New York, Eleanor joined with Earl, Nancy Cook, Malvina Thompson, her secretary, and two unlikely new friends whom Earl had recruited, the dance team of Mayris "Tiny" Chaney and Eddie Fox. There, Earl directed a home movie in which he, in bathing trunks, a painted mustache and goatee, a patch over one eye and a bandanna around his head, played the pirate Captain Kidd. Eleanor was cast as a damsel in distress and the others performed supporting roles. As the film unfolds, Earl is fastening a gag over Eleanor's mouth and then ties her to a rock. For the finale, two state troopers were enlisted to play her rescuers canoeing across Chazy Lake to set the damsel free. The movie was entitled *Kidnapping the First Lady*. To her Oyster Bay cousins and Todhunter students, the Eleanor Roosevelt whom Earl helped liberate would have been unrecognizable.

The nature of the closeness between the two raises the inevitable questions, Was it a romance? Was it sexual? An association that brings a man and a woman together in her homes, in remote cabins, and marked by unconcealed affection must inevitably provoke such speculation. Upon their first meeting in 1929, Earl was thirty-two and ruggedly handsome. Eleanor was forty-four, about to become a grandmother and no beauty. "Mother was self-conscious about Miller's youth," Jimmy Roosevelt noted, "but he did not seem to be bothered by the difference in years." In his memoir Jimmy claimed, "I believe there may have been one real romance in mother's life outside of marriage. Mother may have had an affair with Earl Miller. . . . Victorian as mother may have been, she was a woman, too, who suffered from her separation from father." Jimmy believed that well-intentioned efforts by biographers "to protect her reputation," by dismissing the possibility of an affair, shortchanged her by implying that "because of her hang-ups she was never able to be a complete woman." If Franklin had noticed the closeness between his wife and her bodyguard, Jimmy said, "he did not seem to mind." Blanche Wiesen Cook, in her biography of Eleanor, concluded obliquely, "It is obvious that ER and Earl Miller had a romantic life enhancing friendship."

Joseph Lash, on the other hand, another Eleanor biographer, who enjoyed a closeness to her that sparked its own gossip about their intimacy, was among those Jimmy found to be overprotective of his mother's reputation. Lash granted Miller's value to Eleanor in that Earl helped her overcome lingering fears and inhibitions. But to go to bed with him? Lash concluded, "He interested her physically. It pleased her to have the handsome state trooper squire her about, even to 'manhandle' her as one of Eleanor's friends put it disdainfully." He granted that Eleanor loved Earl Miller, but just as she loved Louis Howe, Nan Cook, Marion Dickerman, Esther Lape, and Elizabeth Read, people who entered and stayed in her heart. But in reducing the question to its essence, did she or didn't she, Lash concluded, "she was unable to let herself go."

Whispers within her circle, however, had it that the relationship between Eleanor and Earl was reaching a drastic culmination. The strongest case was offered by Marion Dickerman almost forty years later. Another Roosevelt historian, Kenneth S. Davis, interviewed the elderly Marion in the 1970s, who claimed that Eleanor had written her that she was going to leave Franklin and go off with Earl. The rumor also intrigued Joe Lash, who went to the source, Earl Miller, for confirmation. In the course of cultivating Miller for his Eleanor biography the two men would go on long drives carrying on teasing dialogues. On one such trip, Lash fired point-blank, "Wouldn't Mrs. R. have married you?" "I never asked her or would have done so," Earl answered. Lash persisted, "But might she have asked you?" Earl's answer was indirect but likely definitive as to speculation about sex between him and The Lady. "You don't sleep with someone you call Mrs. Roosevelt," he told Lash. He went on to describe what did appeal to him: "my taste was for young and pretty things." The likeliest scenario is that Earl served as something of a rascally favorite nephew who had won over a rather stuffy aunt, the two coming to care for each other and close enough in age to become pals. If one requires hard fact to form conclusions about how romantic the relationship might have been, the evidence is meager. No letters, no diaries, no memoirs revealing a love affair between them have ever surfaced.

While the reliability of Earl Miller's statements generally ring true, he seems to have embellished an account of an amour with Missy LeHand. In Earl's telling, Eleanor was deeply upset by "the affair between Missy and F." He had noted how demonstrative LeHand was with FDR and how her affection occasioned rumors around the state capital. "When Mrs. R. told me about the situation, I said I would break it up," he claimed. He would do so by turning his charms on Missy. According to Earl, his strategy succeeded and he maintained that he carried on an affair with her for two years. "Missy had me put on night duty so that I could come to her room. My main purpose in playing up to Missy was because I knew The Lady was being hurt. Missy knew I was playing around with one of the girls in the Executive Office. Missy found out and was quite upset and cried in bed for three days." The only witness to the claim that Miller had courted LeHand to spare Eleanor's feelings was Miller himself. The story appears far-fetched. Nowhere does Eleanor seem anything but solicitous of Missy, and grateful for the woman's attentions to her husband, which freed her to pursue her own interests. If anything, Eleanor seemed bent on keeping Missy healthy, happy, and in the Roosevelts' embrace. In 1931, when Missy again fell ill, Eleanor took her along on a speaking engagement to Maine followed by a brief convalescence in fashionable Newport. She wrote Franklin that Missy "smoked less today and I thought seems more ready to sleep tonight. She is eating fairly well." That Earl and Missy, two unattached, attractive people on the Roosevelt staff, flirted with each other, may even have gone out together, is not surprising. But even this is dismissed by Elliott Roosevelt, who claimed that Earl "simply made passes."

According to Miller, his alleged involvement with Missy failed to quell the rumors that he was romantically entangled with the state's first lady. "I was never successful in killing the gossip," he averred. And so, he said, he settled on a desperate act of loyalty to Eleanor. "That's why I got married in 1932 with plenty of publicity. I got married with someone I wasn't in love with." He already had one failed marriage behind him. The bride he chose this time was seventeen-year-old Ruth Bellinger, a cousin of his first wife. The marriage took place on September 8, 1932, in Val-Kill cottage with the Roosevelts present and son Elliott as Earl's best man and his sister, Anna, as matron of honor. "As a present," Earl said, "the newlyweds were given a piece of land at Hyde Park."

Earl's second marriage would last just over a year. Ruth's parents had it annulled on grounds that their daughter was underage when married and did not have their consent. Earl's account to Lash of sacrificing himself in a loveless marriage was made thirty-five years after the fact when he was living alone in Hollywood, Florida, old, lonely, plagued with crippling pain and skin cancer. By then he had three broken marriages behind him, his low spirits nourished by romanticized memories of The Lady who went on to become a world figure and whom he had known simply as a woman.

Miller revered both Roosevelts. "As I sat in the back of the Packard and saw the back of FDR's head," he once remarked, "I thought it was my dad." While reverential, he read the Roosevelt psyche with a cop's earthy shrewdness: "after you get to know the guy," he noted, "you knew he was an actor to the nth degree. Department heads came in fighting like hell. He would start off asking about their families, then told them one of his anecdotes. Had them laughing. They would all leave smiling and he hadn't committed himself to a damn thing. After they'd go, he would say, 'How'd I do, Sergeant?' You couldn't help but love the guy." Earl saw a finer character in Eleanor than in her husband. "I think she would have made a better President than he if she had someone to control her liberality," he concluded. "She had a keener insight into what people of the country needed. Unless FDR saw a return in the voting booth, he would not go for something." He later regarded his life as having been consumed by the Roosevelts. As he wrote a friend, "They were my weakness. I had relinquished long friendships if they spoke derogating them and I'm sure many of them don't know why to this day."

Early in 1932, a part of Franklin's past was wrenched from him. That January, Livy Davis committed suicide at the age of forty-nine. The loyal, fun-loving pal of the "29 Concussive Nights in a Different Place" who had golfed with him, cavorted with him throughout Europe during the war, who came to the *Larooco* to lift Franklin's spirits, had shot himself in the head with a .32 caliber revolver in a woodshed near his home in Brookline, Massachusetts. He left no note and had given no hint as to what had exhausted his interest in living. "Livy's death certainly was a great shock," Franklin wrote a mutual friend, "and I shall miss him dreadfully. I cannot understand it." The role of aging bon vivant had likely offered little nourishment to the man's spirit. Livy's death not only ended a treasured friendship for Franklin, but broke a link to Lucy Mercer, as Livy had continued visiting her through the years.

Franklin had squeaked through to his 1928 gubernatorial victory as a Democratic candidate running in an era of unprecedented Republican prosperity. Two years later he was swept back into the governor's office on a tide of disillusionment with the GOP. He had been governor only ten months when the stock market crashed on October 29, 1929, Black Tuesday, driving the Dow Jones Industrial Average down the equivalent of almost two thousand points in one day by today's measure. The Great Depression was about to beggar the country and Republican candidates began to pay politically. In just two years as governor Franklin had forged an impressive record on public utility regulation benefiting the consumer over power company magnates, promoted hospital and road construction, and made early use of radio in talks that presaged his "fireside chats" as president. But it was in confronting the economic debacle that he displayed his boldest imagination. He decried the control over the country wielded by a handful of corporations. "If Thomas Jefferson were alive," he charged in a Jefferson Day speech on April 26, 1930, "he would be the first to question this concentration of economic power." While one American worker in three was jobless, Roosevelt gave New Yorkers hope, creating TERA, the Temporary Emergency Relief Administration. Essentially for the first time, the destitute could look to their government rather than depending on charity for food, clothing, and shelter. Roosevelt began recruiting the best minds from universities to shape strategies to combat the Depression, the roots of his later presidential Brain Trust. He favored repeal of the misbegotten, crime-breeding experiment of Prohibition. He was catapulted to national attention as people detected in the Roosevelt brand of leadership a hopeful antidote to hard times. On November 4, 1930, he was wheeled into campaign headquarters at the Biltmore Hotel to hear the election returns. When the counting was over, his winning margin had swelled to thirty times what it had been just two years before; he had scored the largest majority for a Democrat in the state's history. Eleanor's routine was again unruffled by her husband's victory. She wrote him a penciled note, "Much love & a world of congratulations. It is a triumph in so many ways, dear & so well earned. Bless you & good luck these next two years.—ER." She put the note on his pillow, then rushed off to make her classes at the Todhunter School.

The marriage continued to present crosscurrents. Earlier, in 1931, when Franklin learned that his mother had contracted pneumonia in Europe, he sailed off to be with her. Eleanor wrote of his departure, "I hate so to see you go. . . . We are really very dependent on each other though we do see so little of each other! Dear love to you. . . . I miss you & hate to feel you so far away. . . . Ever devotedly, ER." When in Warm Springs, which he visited as often as his official duties permitted, he continued the stream of "Dearest Babs" letters. Anna wrote her mother early in the second term, "Father's letter to me was mostly trying to persuade you to go to Warm Springs for a week with him. He feels you are tired, and ought to 'slow up.' If you think it would give you any rest at all

to go to Warm Springs—do go. Pa seems to want you there so badly too."
The correspondence between husband and wife reflected the climate of
the Roosevelts' marriage at the time. They followed separate lives, yet it
was as if an invisible undergirding still held them together, often undis-
cernible to outsiders, without which both structures would collapse.

As governor of the then leading state, one who had shown daring and
imagination in attacking hard times, Franklin Roosevelt was automatically
propelled to national prominence for the presidency in 1932, except that
no nation had ever elected a paralytic as its leader. Doubts had to be banished with equal boldness. Earl Miller had already devised one tactic two
years before. To those aware of the severity of Franklin Roosevelt's paralysis, the news photograph of FDR on horseback came as a shock. There
was the governor in November 1930 at Warm Springs, smiling, accompanied by Eleanor and Miller also on horses. The picture had been arranged
by Earl to shatter any doubts over Roosevelt's physical capacities. "I had
him atop a horse and invited the *Atlantic Journal* reporter and photographer in. They spread it in the rotogravure brown section full page." As Earl
described the occasion, "We rode four miles that day, at a walk of course,
but [the reporters] didn't follow and know he didn't trot or canter."

As the election neared, FDR invited a neurologist, orthopedist, and
diagnostician to evaluate his health. "We have today examined Franklin
D. Roosevelt," the panel reported. "We find that his organs and func-
tions are sound in all respects. There is no anemia. The chest is exceptionally well developed, and the spinal column is perfectly normal; all of
its segments are in alignment, and free from disease. He has neither
pain nor ache at any time. Ten years ago, Governor Roosevelt suffered an
attack of acute infantile paralysis, the entire effect of which was ex-
pended on the muscles of his lower extremities. There has been progressive recovery of power in the legs since that date; this restoration
continues and will continue." These were the same doctors who also
found him with "no symptoms of impotentia coeundi." He was sexually
viable. "We believe," they concluded, "that his powers of endurance are
such as to allow him to meet all demands of private or public life."

The Depression deepened, the bread lines lengthened, men in frayed
suits peddled apples on street corners and "Hooverville" shantytowns
made of wooden crates and cardboard sprang up across the country.

Herbert Hoover had not caused the Depression but he was afflicted by a paralysis of imagination in confronting it. By contrast, Franklin Roosevelt continued to demonstrate that he burst with ideas and radiated hope. On July 1, 1932, after a bruising fight, he won his party's nomination for president at the Democratic national convention in Chicago. Missy by now was resigned to his ambitions. "There's a star guiding this fellow," she told Rexford Tugwell, the Columbia University professor advising Franklin. "She had a kind of mystic feeling about him," Tugwell recalled.

Eleanor felt even greater dread at the prospect of Franklin becoming president than when he ran for governor. Immune to notions of glamour, she had a clear-eyed, unromanticized vision of life in the White House gathered through her visits during Uncle Ted's presidency. Her education had been completed during Franklin's service in the Wilson administration. On the eve of her husband's nomination, she wrote a letter to Nancy Cook, then attending the Chicago convention, that Nancy shared with Marion Dickerman and Louis Howe. Dickerman recalled the tone of Eleanor's letter as "hysterical." She hated the idea of becoming first lady, of being "a prisoner in the White House, forced onto a treadmill of formal receptions, openings, dedications, teas, official dinners." Dickerman was convinced, "She won't do it. She'll run away with Earl Miller. . . . She'll flee with Earl who loves and respects her as Franklin never did. Nor her sons. She'll file for divorce." Upon seeing Eleanor's letter, a horrified Howe tore it to pieces and threw it in a wastebasket, warning the two women, "You are not to breathe a word of this to anyone, understand? Not to anyone!" Years later, Eleanor was brutally honest about her feelings at this time. "From a personal standpoint," she admitted, "I did not want my husband to be President. I realized, however, that it was impossible to keep a man out of public service if that was what he wanted and was undoubtedly well equipped for. It was pure selfishness on my part, and I never mentioned my feeling on the subject to him." Leaving for Washington risked rupturing cherished bonds between herself and Earl, Nan, Marion, Esther, and Elizabeth and leaving behind the work she loved, Val-Kill Industries, the Todhunter School, and the ever-growing number of her causes.

The move also threatened to separate her from a new presence in her life, someone who had become increasingly essential to her happiness, an Associated Press reporter named Lorena Hickok.

*Chapter 24*

# ELEANOR AND HICK

· · · · · · ·

O<small>N THE EVE</small> of the presidential election of 1932, nearly a third of American workers had no job and no recourse but dwindling savings or charity. When the Soviet Union advertised for six thousand skilled Americans to work in Russia, 100,000 people applied. Over five thousand banks had failed. The Dow Jones Industrial Average had plummeted 90 percent from its heady 1929 highs. Families were being thrown out of their homes through bank foreclosures at the rate of one thousand a day. Young Joseph Alsop, the future columnist and a Roosevelt kinsman, recalled driving along Manhattan's East River and seeing people, "mostly respectable-looking older men and women, climbing precariously about on the enormous dumps in the hope of finding bits of edible garbage! That was the state of the nation." At this dark hour Franklin Roosevelt was voted into office by the greatest electoral tide up to that point in American history. He beat Herbert Hoover by over seven million votes, won forty-two of the forty-eight states, and took 472 electoral college votes to Hoover's 59.

On election night, with the race decided, Jimmy Roosevelt helped his father into bed, unsnapping his cumbersome braces and leaning them in a corner. As Jimmy kissed him good night, the president-elect, who rarely presented any face to the world but one of complete self-assurance, said, "All my life I have only been afraid of one thing—fire. Tonight I am afraid of something else." Jimmy waited for his answer. "I'm afraid I may not have the strength to do this job."

Courage, too often, is envisioned in its physical dimension, standing up to enemy fire, trekking an uncharted wasteland, saving someone from a burning building. To awake every morning knowing that half of one's body will fail again and yet press on, demands courage of another order.

Franklin Roosevelt had not simply displayed the will to rise above pain and paralysis but to bear these crosses while gaining the summit in American life. Some critics overlooked his indomitability and saw only a shallow opportunist. Walter Lippmann, the much respected columnist, dismissed FDR as "a slippery, unprincipled, amiable lightweight," and "a pleasant man without any important qualifications for the office." But ninety-one-year-old retired Supreme Court justice Oliver Wendell Holmes, upon meeting Roosevelt, delivered a verdict likely closer to the mark. "A second class intellect," he said after a conversation with FDR, "but a first class temperament."

On March 4, 1933, a black, unmarked government automobile pulled up before a townhouse at 2238 Q Street near Washington's fashionable Georgetown neighborhood. A tall, stately woman stepped from the door-way, pulled a fur collar around her neck against the cold, and entered the car. The townhouse was the residence of Dr. and Mrs. William Marbury, and the woman leaving it was Violetta Marbury's sister, Lucy Mercer Rutherfurd. Lucy and Violetta still remained close, though by now the elder sister lived comfortably while the younger lived grandly. Lucy had left her winter retreat, Ridgely Hall in Aiken, in order to be in the capital on a day that had as much personal resonance for her as it held political significance for the nation. The car had been dispatched from the White House at the orders of the man about to be inaugurated as president. Eleanor knew nothing of the arrangement. The driver handed Lucy an envelope with a ticket and edged the automobile through streets clogged with 400,000 spectators who had come to witness the swearing in.

On arriving at the East Portico of the Capitol Lucy found a spot at a discreet distance amid the crush of people. The portico balcony was wreathed with garlands, and above it there hung a massive Great Seal of the United States. Four rows of dignitaries lined the balcony, many of the men in silk top hats. In the front row stood a woman, looking un-comfortable, taller than anyone around her, the wife who, fifteen years before, had survived Lucy's threat to her marriage. On the other side was Sara Delano Roosevelt, the mother who had doomed any hopes Lucy might have had that Franklin would marry her. The man Lucy studied in the distance was far removed from the slender gallant she had loved so long ago. His upper body had become massive from ceaseless exercise to compensate for his withered legs. He had a chest expansion, as he boasted, greater than that of the heavyweight champion, Jack Dempsey. He weighed 182 pounds. And had polio not withered his legs, he would stand six feet two inches tall and weigh nearly 225 pounds. Though he had to be supported, Franklin, nevertheless, stood as erect as a parade ground cadet, with his son Jimmy placed strategically nearby. Franklin rested his hand on the Roosevelt family's 1686 Bible, as the bearded, stolid Supreme Court chief justice, Charles Evans Hughes, swore in the new president.

"I am certain that my fellow Americans expect that on my induction into the presidency, I will address them with candor," Franklin began his inaugural address. His voice carried to the back of the crowd. It possessed "fine shadings and nuances . . . infinite variety," Sam Rosenman noted, his ear as a speechwriter acutely tuned to FDR's cadences. "He knew how to give [his voice] strength, sarcasm, humor, volume, charm, persuasiveness. . . . He read his lines like a finished actor." The crowd responded with hushed expectation as Franklin intoned, "So, first of all, let me assert my firm belief that the only thing we have to fear is fear itself—nameless, unreasoning, unjustified terror which paralyzes needed efforts to convert retreat into advance." The origins of the "fear itself" phrase have long been debated. One suggested source is the education philosopher John Dewey, who had said four years before, "it is even possible to get rid of fears of specific things and still retain a kind of underlying fear of fear itself." A homier explanation has it that a Roosevelt associate spotted the words on a placard in a barbershop window. With the ceremony ended, Lucy reentered the limousine and returned to Violetta's home. Her husband, Winthrop, and practically everyone in her set were rock-solid Republicans, contemptuous of Franklin Roosevelt, but she had voted for him.

In the days leading up to the ceremony, Eleanor had to be ordered by Franklin to come with him aboard his special railroad car as part of the official entourage. Her intention had been to drive herself to Washington in her Buick with two dogs and the reporter Lorena Hickok, known to her friends as "Hick." Eleanor's attitude toward moving into the White House was much the same as it had been about moving into the statehouse, an infringement on her personal freedom and an existence in an even more confining gilded cage. "I was happy for my husband, of course," she later granted, "because I knew in many ways it would make up for the blow that fate had dealt him when he was stricken with infantile paralysis." On the morning before the inauguration, Eleanor had returned to a haunt familiar from her melancholy after her discovery of the Lucy Mercer affair. At 7:45 A.M., the ground still damp with dew, she arrived with Hick at the secluded holly grove in Rock Creek Cemetery where they stood contemplating the Saint-Gaudens statue of *Grief*. Hick, in her later book on Eleanor, described the moment: "After a long pause, she spoke, 'In the old days when we lived here, I was very much younger and not so wise. Sometimes I'd be very unhappy and sorry for myself. When I was feeling that way and couldn't manage it, I'd come out here alone. And I'd always come away somehow feeling better. And stronger.' "

During the inauguration, Eleanor wore a sapphire ring with diamond chips surrounding the stone. The ring had been given to Hick years before by Madame Ernestine Schumann-Heink after the journalist had written a glowing review of the opera star. Subsequently she gave it to Eleanor. On Hick's fortieth birthday, Eleanor wrote her from the White House, "Your ring is a great comfort. I look at it and think she does love me or I wouldn't be wearing it." The afternoon after the inauguration, the servants witnessed their new mistress in a puzzling scene. As Eleanor later described the moment, she had granted an interview to Hick to be conducted in her new sitting room: "I do remember that we were interrupted so often that we finally retired to the bathroom to finish the interview." All likely true, except that to one White House maid, Lillian Parks, who later recorded her memories in a book, entitled *The Roosevelts: A Family in Turmoil*, "It was hardly the kind of thing one would do with an ordinary reporter. Or even with an adult friend."

Earl Miller, once so integral to Eleanor's life, had been left behind in Albany. He nevertheless was well taken care of by the outgoing governor, given an elevated post for a state police sergeant. He was appointed personnel director for the New York State Department of Corrections. Franklin had brought another bodyguard with him to Washington, Gus Gennerich, a legendary New York City detective who had once captured a mob of gangsters single-handed in a shootout. The tough-talking, gum-chewing, Runyonesque Gennerich had particularly impressed the Roosevelt sons through his acquaintance with New York's best speakeasies, knowledge admired by their father as well. Why Gus and not Earl? Miller by now had become wholly associated with Eleanor's camp while

Gus had become the president's sidekick, FDR's stand-in for the common man. Eleanor did not fight for Earl's inclusion as she departed for Washington. She now had in Lorena Hickok a far more significant companion.

The intensity of Eleanor Roosevelt's involvement with Hickok would not come fully to light for another forty-five years. In June 1978, a former *New York Times* reporter, Doris Faber, journeyed to the Roosevelt Library at Hyde Park to research a biography of Eleanor Roosevelt for teenage readers. Just weeks before, the library had opened to the public some two thousand of the approximately 3,500 letters between Eleanor and Hick. The trove had been given to the library by Lorena, with the proviso that the contents not be made public until ten years after her death, which occurred in 1968. As one of the first persons to see the letters, Faber found herself so shocked that she asked to see the library's director, William Emerson, privately. She later claimed that she urged him to embargo the letters "at least for several decades," which would spare her an "acute personal dilemma: what use could I or should I make of this sensational material I had stumbled upon?" Emerson was similarly conflicted and agreed to take a second look at the material with his staff. A week later he called Faber, then vacationing with her husband on Cape Cod, to tell her that after consulting with the National Archives as well, a decision had been reached to leave the Hickok-Roosevelt collection open.

One letter written the day after FDR's inauguration began: "Hick my dearest, I cannot go to bed without a word to you. I felt a little as though part of me was leaving tonight, you have grown so much to be a part of my life." She wrote further, "Oh! I want to put my arms around you, I ache to hold you close," and wrote in another letter, "My pictures are nearly all up & I have you in my sitting room where I can look at you most of my waking hours! I can't kiss you so I kiss your picture good night & good morning. Don't laugh!" Hickok wrote back trying to put a brave face on their separation but with a tinge of remorse showing through. Whereupon Eleanor replied, "I miss you so much & I love you so much & please never apologize." A week after the inauguration, Eleanor wrote, "I couldn't bear to think of you crying yourself to sleep. Oh! I wanted to put my arms around you in reality instead of spirit. I went & kissed your photograph instead & tears were in my eyes. Please keep most of your heart in Washington as long as I'm here for most of mine is with you." During a phone call to Hick, Eleanor realized that her son Jimmy was within earshot and wrote afterward, "I couldn't say je t'aime et je t'adore as I longed to." In a later letter to Eleanor while she was alone in a hotel in Bemidji, Minnesota, Hickok wrote, "I remember your eyes, with a kind of teasing smile in them and the feeling of that soft spot just northeast of the corner of your mouth against my lips. I wonder what we'll do when we meet—what we'll say."

The woman who prompted this intimacy had been born Alice Lorena Hickok in the hamlet of East Troy, Wisconsin. Her upbringing had been hell. Her father drifted from job to job in the dairy country. "The first contact with a human that I recall vividly was with my father," she later wrote. "I had started biting my fingernails. One day he thrust the tips of my fingers into my mouth, and made me bite on them, holding my jaws together with his big, strong hands, until the tears rolled down my cheeks." He beat her black-and-blue with a butter stave. He horse-whipped her dog to a pulp for chasing cars. Her mother was a hapless witness to her husband's brutality, and Lorena "kept wondering, all through the childhood years why my mother, who was a grownup too, and just as big as my father, let him do those things." Her mother was dead by the time she was thirteen and Lorena left the father for whom she felt only a "bitter hatred." She worked for her keep as an unpaid ser-vant in boardinghouses. She slaved in a kitchen for a dozen threshers from sunup until sundown, an experience she described as "an agonizing routine of boiling, baking, frying through bushels of grimy potato peel-ings, through sliding avalanches of greasy dishes," a description that sug-gested her one possible avenue of escape from this purgatory, a gift for observation and expression. Between fourteen and sixteen, she held nine jobs and managed to squeeze in a high school education, emerging as a class leader and a top student. She ultimately worked her way through two years at Lawrence College in Appleton, Wisconsin, before being taken on as a cub reporter at the *Battle Creek Journal*. She proved a reporting meteor, cracking the women's page barrier that held back most female journalists, and by age thirty-five had risen to bureau chief of the Associated Press in New York City where she was handed the choicest assignments, tracking political scandals and sensational mur-ders, including the kidnapping and death of the infant son of the aviator Charles Lindbergh.

During Franklin's race for governor, while hunting for stories at the

Democratic National Committee headquarters, she met stocky, ma-
tronly, full-faced Malvina Thompson, at the time married to a shop
teacher in the New York public school system. The Bronx-born Thompson, known as "Tommy," worked at the headquarters part-time as secretary to Eleanor Roosevelt, who came there not for her husband's
gubernatorial campaign but for Al Smith's presidential bid. Thompson
thought that Hick ought to know her boss. The first meeting of what
would become a pivotal association in both their lives was unremark-
able. Hickok asked a few pro forma questions, all the while inventorying
a woman whose principal interest to her was that this woman with the
awkward posture, buck teeth, a hairnet drooping over her forehead, an
overly long skirt, a blouse of bile green, and clearly oblivious of her person, was the niece of former President Theodore Roosevelt.

What Eleanor saw was a strapping five-foot-eight-inch woman, fighting to control a weight that often topped two hundred pounds. Her dark
hair was gathered sensibly, if not fashionably, at the back of her head.
Her face was broad with a twinkling merriment in her eyes and in her
smile. Among fellow reporters she was one-of-the-boys, riding the bus
and playing poker with Minnesota football players during her Midwest
days, hanging out at New York speakeasies favored by the press, knock-
ing back bootleg bourbon, smoking cigars, and swapping risqué stories
with the bawdiest of them. She was good company, witty, irreverent, and
bighearted toward anyone with a hard-luck story. She expressed her con-
victions on politics, sports, music, and people with passion, earthy language, and good humor. On the job she wore makeup, earrings, flowered
scarves, and painted her fingernails. She favored flat-heeled oxfords,
however, because stylish footwear was hard on a woman who traipsed all
over the country getting her stories. In her free time she preferred pants,
and in the country wore plaid flannel shirts and boots. Men liked her,
but did not fall in love with her. As one colleague put it, "Hick had a tendency to fall in love with women." While working on *The Minneapolis
Tribune*, she had met Ella Morse, a part-time society page reporter. Ellie,
as she was known, was Hick's antithesis, petite, fair-haired, utterly feminine, and from a wealthy family. They lived together for eight years,
until Ellie, without warning, eloped with a former boyfriend, devastating
her "Hick Doodles" and explaining in part why Hickok abandoned the
Midwest for New York.

After Franklin Roosevelt had been elected governor, Hick interviewed

Eleanor again, this time in the elegance of her East 65th Street drawing room. On this occasion New York's first lady wore a lacy, attractive hostess gown and served tea from a silver pot. Hick became aware of a more attractive Eleanor, noticing the woman's radiant blue eyes, aristocratically slender hands, and tapered fingers. The AP story she wrote after this encounter ended, "The new mistress of the Executive Mansion in Albany is a very great lady." Her editor found the sentence too subjective and cut it.

Two years later, during the 1932 presidential campaign, Hick was assigned to cover Eleanor, which threw the two women into constant contact. The relationship soon outgrew reporter-to-source. They began having dinner together, going to the theater, speaking on the phone every morning. They were with each other on the evening of February 15, 1933, when Eleanor was staggered by news out of Miami that an unemployed bricklayer and political crackpot, Giuseppe Zangara, had taken a shot at the president-elect, missed, and struck instead Anton Cermak, the mayor of Chicago. Franklin called to tell his wife that he was all right and that the mayor's wound was not serious, an unwarranted assumption since Cermak soon died. Franklin assured her at the moment, however, that she need not interrupt her schedule, which allowed Eleanor to catch a train for a conference at Cornell University. Hick went with her. As Doris Faber wrote, "Nobody can ever say what had occurred privately before the Cornell visit or what occurred during it. But it is likely that the friendship between the two women changed in the course of their sojourn there—under the stress of the attempted assassination of Franklin Roosevelt."

After FDR's inauguration, Hick returned to her job in New York. Both she and Eleanor found the separation painful, and an almost daily flurry of letters continued. While Franklin was summoning the Congress into special session to explain how he planned to shut down the banks temporarily, a "bank holiday" he called it, to stem ruinous withdrawals, while working with his Brain Trust to draft legislation that would become the New Deal, and while fine-tuning his first White House fireside chat, Eleanor was in her sitting room writing to Hick. The separation that left both women unhappy was soon solved. Hick resigned from the AP in the summer of 1933 and moved to Washington. There, she presented her dilemma to Eleanor. She had not yet been able to sublet her New York apartment and she could not afford renting even in the depressed Washington market. Eleanor had a simple solution: Hick could move into the White House. She was given a tiny bedroom in the northwest corner of the second floor family quarters next to Louis Howe's room. "Money was not the only reason why I stayed at the White House," Hick would later admit. "Although I never told Mrs. Roosevelt, I couldn't bear the idea of being in Washington and hardly ever seeing her." As for the president and first lady, they were to occupy separate bedrooms with Eleanor's substantial study and sitting room between them.

Hick had given up the profession she loved for the woman she loved even more, and at a cost to her sense of self-worth. She found it humiliating to be identified in photographs as Eleanor's secretary, even her bodyguard. Still she could not make the break. Louis Howe, a former newsman himself, questioned Hick's decision to abandon journalism. He had warned her earlier that "a reporter should never get too close to a news source." Now Hick was witness to the biggest story in the country with no place to report it. Years later, Eleanor's granddaughter and namesake, Eleanor Seagraves, who came to know Hick, concluded that she had "let herself slip into a role where she lost her old identity and became dependent on my grandmother." In order to stay in Washington, Hick took a job as executive secretary at the Democratic National Committee's Women's Division, a position apparently arranged by Eleanor and with Howe's intercession. She would later move on to another job that Eleanor arranged, one better suited to her reportorial talents. She became chief investigator for the Federal Emergency Relief Administration, the New Deal umbrella welfare organization.

Hick became the source of near obsessive gossip backstairs at the White House. The maid Lillian Parks, a polio victim herself who used a crutch, remembered, "When the Roosevelts first arrived in 1933, there was a short honeymoon stage around the White House when Hick was an open guest, welcomed by the President, joining the family for dinner. But eventually, so the sub rosa story went, he got the drift and feared the situation could give the White House a bad reputation. The President was heard raising his voice to Eleanor, telling her, 'I want that woman kept out of this house.' That woman meant too much to Eleanor, and instead of keeping her out of the house, she simply kept her out of FDR's sight." Franklin recognized that Hick was smart, accomplished, and on balance good for Eleanor. But she violated all of his ideas of femininity and might have worn better with him had she been a man.

The staff was put off by Hick's bulldozer stride and bluff manner. Another maid remarked, "Put a seam down the middle of her skirt and I swear, old Hicky will be wearing a man's suit." Lillian Parks was quick to grasp that "Eleanor's live-in friend was especially important, because Mabel Webster [another servant] started doing Hicky's mending and washing her underwear. Hick, incidentally, was the only person around the White House who mended silk stockings. Even the maids threw theirs away rather than appear with mended runs." Still, Hick "wasn't a bad looking woman," Parks concluded, "and had she kept her weight down and tried to look and act feminine, she could have been most attractive."

The maid was amused, she said, "when I hear people say that the kisses exchanged between Lorena Hickok and Eleanor Roosevelt . . . have no meaning, that Eleanor kissed everyone." She never saw the two "in a compromising situation," she admitted, "that is, I never saw them in bed together. But I was at the White House on many occasions when Hicky, as we all called her behind her back, slept in the First Lady's bedroom suite, on the daybed in her sitting room. Supposedly, the reason was that there were so many guests."

The first lady "used to try to get me to call her 'Eleanor,' but I couldn't do it," Hick recalled. "My dear, I protested one day, I can't go around bawling 'Eleanor' to the wife of the President of the United States." Hick was well aware of the eyebrows that her continued presence with Eleanor could raise. When her duties required her to escort Democratic women to the White House, "I had an understanding with the doormen and the ushers that when I arrived with one of my delegations there must be no indication that I ever entered the White House except on occasions such as these. They would greet me formally, along with the rest, take our names, and escort us to the Red Room, announcing us to the other guests assembled and waiting for Mrs. Roosevelt to come down. Mrs. Roosevelt would play the game, too, greeting me with, 'Why, how nice to see you!' as though she hadn't seen me for a month, although we had actually had breakfast together that morning! One day one of the ushers murmured as he assisted me out of my coat: 'In residence today? Or just a visitor?'"

The endearments in the letters, the absorption of Hick into Eleanor's personal life, the reporter's abandonment of a brilliant career in order to be near Eleanor inevitably raise the question of the nature of this tie.

During her first term at Mlle. Souvestre's Allenswood School, Eleanor had developed a crush on a girl she later identified only as "Jane." Jane was beautiful, exciting, and hotheaded. "There were perhaps eight other girls in our class," Eleanor recalled, "but as far as I was concerned there was no one but Jane." The fiery beauty was expelled for hurling an ink-stand at her German teacher, which both shocked and thrilled the "quiet and docile Eleanor," as she described herself. She was heartbroken and begged Mlle. Souvestre to change her mind, without success. It was Eleanor whom the lesbian headmistress took on her summer sojourns. The trips, however, with Mlle. Souvestre suggest a teacher's interest in a promising but lonely student, with nothing erotic ever hinted at in the association. And the Jane episode was no different than countless crushes that occur in single sex schools.

Eleanor had been brought up in a Victorian world and the social his-torian Carroll Smith-Rosenberg explored that era in a landmark paper entitled, "The Female World of Love and Ritual: Relations Between Women in Nineteenth-Century America." The author found that intense emotions between women were "casually accepted in American society." She studied thousands of letters and diaries of women and men from thirty-five families and found, "Girls routinely slept together, kissed and hugged each other," which did not interfere with their becoming wives and mothers. Some of the correspondents whose words she quoted sug-gest relationships paralleling those of Eleanor and Hick. "Assure me that I am your dearest," a girl named Jeannie wrote to a companion, Sara, in 1864. "I am not jealous but I long to hear you say it once more & it seems already a long time since your voice fell on my ear. So just fill a quarter of a page with caresses & expressions of endearment." Both women sub-sequently married. A girl named Molly wrote to a friend, Helena, in 1873, "I'm going to hang onto your skirts. . . . You can't get away from [my] love," and then added, "I really was in love with you. It was a pas-sion such as I had never known until I saw you. I don't think it was the noblest way to love you." Again, both women eventually married. Smith-Rosenberg offered a plausible rationale for these intense relationships. In that era, "Contacts between men and women frequently partook of a formality and stiffness quite alien to twentieth century America." Thus women sought freer emotional expression with other women.

Henry James's 1886 novel, *The Bostonians*, dealt with what in the nineteenth century was called a "Boston marriage," a bond between two women more intimate than friendship, but not necessarily sexual. Did the phrase fit Eleanor and Hick as well? While parallels exist, there are also sharp differences. The latter women lived their adult lives in the twentieth century with no Victorian barriers separating the sexes. And Lorena Hickok was certainly no Victorian, but an assertive homosexual. Eleanor's vision of the relationship may best be found in what she told her biographer Joe Lash, "Every woman wants to be first to someone in her life, and that desire is the explanation for many strange things women do." Hick provided Eleanor with just such unconditional adoration, and more. It was she who persuaded Eleanor to hold press conferences, thus helping her establish her own identity, and to write articles that ultimately grew into the popular syndicated column, "My Day." Eleanor recognized her debt. "You've made me so much more of a person just to be worthy of you," she told Hick. Lorena fed another of Eleanor's impulses. As Curtis Roosevelt put it, "My grandmother needed to be needed."

If a woman had written to a man, "I love you beyond words and long for you," which Eleanor wrote to Hick, few would deny that their relations went beyond friendship. In the manuscript of her book that she deposited at the FDR Library, Doris Faber, Hickok's biographer, wrote, "It hardly seems likely that those letters at Hyde Park could be the expression of a purely platonic relationship, especially because, among Hick's miscellaneous papers, there were also effusive affectionate letters from two later associations."

Blanche Wiesen Cook in her biography of Eleanor apparently supports an erotic relationship. "The fact is that ER and Hick were not involved in a schoolgirl 'smash.' . . . They were neither saints or adolescents nor were they mermaids or virgins." Indeed, at the beginning of their involvement, Eleanor was forty-eight, and Hick nearing forty. Cook goes on, "They were two adult women, in the prime of their lives, committed to working out a relationship under very difficult circumstances. . . . They gave each other pleasure and comfort, trust and love." Also arguing for a love affair, Rodger Streitmatter, who studied thousands of letters between the two women in compiling his book *Empty Without You*, concluded that they "shared a relationship that was not only intense and intimate, but also passionate and physical." The ever spiteful Alice Roosevelt Longworth rarely missed an opportunity to describe her cousin as a lesbian.

Joe Lash, taking the opposite tack, has written that Eleanor's letters to others "used expressions of endearment that were as passionate as those to be found in the Hickok correspondence, and that were equally subject to misinterpretation as suggestive of a physical relationship." Lash's wife, Trude, also Eleanor's friend, concluded that she "had so many emotions stored up inside, that when Hick came along it was like a volcanic explosion. But does that mean that Eleanor acted on her words, that she had a lesbian relationship with Hick? I do not think so." Eleanor's daughter, Anna, asked by Lash about the nature of her mother's and Hick's involvement, answered, "Sometimes people noting the women she had surrounded herself with would suggest there was something homosexual in the relationship. But I don't think any such thing would ever have occurred to Mother in her innocence. That was just totally out of her ken. But for her, sex was something you had to bear." Eleanor's son Elliott has said simply that his mother was beyond arousal. "Her sensibilities were not tuned to sexual attraction of any kind," he believed, "whether it existed between a man and a woman or between members of the same sex."

Children are not the most reliable sources as to their parents' sexuality, however, and the woman who told her daughter that sex was an ordeal was not necessarily the same woman a decade later, whose horizons had broadened so surprisingly. Her growing moral liberalism was evident in her attitude toward Anna's own trials of the heart. Her daughter had not married Curtis Dall out of love but to escape the tension between her mother, father, and grandmother. Divorced in 1934, she had fallen in love with John Boetigger, a strapping, handsome reporter with an appealing manner and a rich voice that she found "calm and reassuring." Prior to the couple's marriage in 1935, according to Doris Faber, Eleanor "abetted this new affair by arranging a tryst now and then, unbeknownst to Franklin." Anna was not the only one to benefit from her mother's late-blooming broadmindedness. Her homes were occasionally made available for liaisons to Lash, Earl Miller, and to her other children between their frequent marriages and divorces.

A case can be made that Eleanor and Hick planned a future together. Regretting their frequent separations, Eleanor wrote Hick, "We'll have years of happy times so bad times will be forgotten." On another occasion after visiting an elderly friend, she wrote, "It is sad to be helpless & poor and old, isn't it? I hope you & I together have enough to make it gracious and attractive." After examining new pieces of furniture from the Val-Kill factory, Eleanor wrote, "One corner cupboard I long to have for our camp or cottage or house, which is it to be? I've always thought of it in the country, but I don't think we ever decided." However, in less fanciful moments, she accepted, "I know I've got to stick. I know I'll never make an open break & I never tell F.D.R how I feel. . . . Darling I do take happiness in many ways & I'm never likely to fight with F. I always 'shut up.' "

The furtive nature of some of the correspondence appears to contradict a purely platonic friendship. "My dear, if you meet me may I forget there are reporters present or must I behave?" Eleanor wrote Hick. "I shall want to hug you to death." Proposing an outing away from the White House, she wrote, "I think one night anyway we'll stay away. Otherwise we might have to be polite a while in the evening unless the guests all dine out which is quite unlikely." After the two women had spent time together at Warm Springs in January 1934, Eleanor's letter included an enigmatic underlined word. "Dearest, it was a lovely weekend. . . . Each time we have together that way—brings us closer, doesn't it." Eleanor once wrote of her marriage, "though I was only 19, it seemed an entirely natural thing and I never even thought that we were both young and inexperienced. . . . I know now that it was years later before I understood what being in love or what loving really meant." The sentiment does not necessarily refer to Lorena Hickok. It could just as easily apply to anyone Eleanor valued in her life and to whom she wrote affectionately. In a likely accurate key to Eleanor's attachments, Susan Ware has written of her in *Letter to the World: Seven Women Who Shaped the American Century*, "In her lifelong quest for love, she drew no artificial boundaries between men and women." What had life taught her? In her pure-hearted love for an essentially nonreciprocating husband, she had found pain. In the love of others, particularly her female friends, she found understanding and reciprocity.

The verdict of the press when the Eleanor-Lorena letters became public was near unanimous: "clear implications of lesbianism," *The Washington Post* reported. A "lesbian love affair," *Newsweek* magazine concluded. *The New York Times* believed that the letters supported a "homosexual affair," and the *Los Angeles Times* found the likelihood of a same-sex involvement "incontrovertible."

The evidence indeed seems overwhelming that Eleanor Roosevelt and Lorena Hickok engaged in a passionate attachment. Yet judgments of sexual orientation are inevitably subjective as they pass through individual, societal, and cultural filters. Contradictory interpretations of Eleanor's behavior throw the idea of sexual identity into a confusion that is only easily solved by resort to simplistic stereotypes. In arriving at a final judgment it is helpful to consider the word "lesbian" in its two uses, a noun—"She is a lesbian"—or as an adjective—"The two women engaged in a lesbian act." In the first case, sexual attraction is centered wholly on other women. In the latter, one may engage in acts describable as lesbian without precluding heterosexual attraction and behavior. The line may be fine, but it is discernible and useful. Using this distinction we can argue that Hick fit the first definition and Eleanor the second. At the very least, Eleanor experienced what might best be defined as an intense, late-life schoolgirl crush, while Hick had fallen in love.

Thousands of letters passed between the two women over the course of thirty years, many running over a dozen longhand pages, sometimes two letters sent in a single day. In 1936 Hick began retrieving letters she had written to Eleanor. She made typed summaries of 129 of them and burned hundreds more that she had written, most dating from the first half of 1933 when the relationship was at its peak. Esther Lape recalled an evening spent at Lorena's home after both women had grown old, during which "Hick brought ER's most expansive letters and slowly burned them as if it were an eastern rite." The best evidence of what Eleanor Roosevelt and Lorena Hickok had been to each other likely went up in those flames.

Chapter 25

# "CLOSE TO BEING A WIFE"

. . . . . . .

THERE WAS NEVER A COMPLETE BREAK between Franklin and Lucy. Given distance and long separations, the signal might become faint at times, but never ceased entirely. During the first hectic months of his presidency, when it seemed FDR would have time for nothing but matters of state, he made time for her. He was unleashing a hail of legislation that history would record as "The First 100 Days" of the New Deal. His financial reforms following the bank holiday enabled three quarters of the banks to reopen. TERA, the agency that Governor Roosevelt created to bring Depression relief to New Yorkers, became FERA, the Federal Emergency Relief Administration, doing the same for all America. Over 300,000 formerly unemployed youths were carrying out flood control, reforestation, and building parks and beaches. Bonus Marchers who had been driven from the capital under Hoover came back under Roosevelt and were given food, shelter, and a meeting with the president during which he led the ex-doughboys in singing the haunting wartime favorite, "There's a Long, Long Trail A-Winding." For the first time in over a dozen years, as Prohibition ended, a grown-up American could order a glass of beer without breaking the law. And FDR had found his medium for shaking a benumbed country out of its torpor, simultaneously educating and inspiring Americans through his fireside chats. "People edged their chairs to the radio," the novelist John Dos Passos remembered of the experience. "There is a man leaning across his desk, speaking clearly and cordially so that you and me will completely understand."

In the midst of trying to save the country, he had to contend with a mother who still regarded him as her obedient little boy. "When Father first became President," his son Elliott recalled, "Sara would call to tell

Franklin, 'I'm sending so-and-so down . . .' who were her social friends, and said they wanted to see Father. She'd call down and make an appointment, and Father would say, 'I can't see them. I've got a cabinet meeting.' It made no difference, she'd have them down there at the time that she said, and Father would have to change the other appointment."

Even as the Oval Office witnessed an endless parade of congressional leaders, cabinet secretaries, businessmen, labor officials, governors, and mayors, one ordinary citizen could break through. FDR always took phone calls from a Mrs. Paul Johnson (sometimes identified as Johnston). She called a half dozen times during the First 100 Days and made ten more calls over the next feverish months. White House switchboard operators had instructions to put Mrs. Johnson through, though telephone logs reveal that no other calls were accepted except from prominent figures or family members. Mrs. Paul Johnson, it would subsequently be revealed by Secret Service agents, was Lucy Mercer Rutherfurd. Most of Lucy's calls were placed from Augusta, Georgia, fifteen miles from her estate in Aiken, South Carolina, or from New York City where the Rutherfurds had a townhouse. None was placed from her homes in Aiken or Allamuchy. During these early months of his presidency, Lucy prevailed upon Franklin to help assuage a tragedy that had struck her family. Her sister, Violetta's, teenage son, Billy Marbury, had died of leukemia, and the family hoped to have the boy buried in Arlington National Cemetery with his late grandfather Carroll Mercer. Franklin arranged for the burial.

Since Lucy was now a married woman and her contact with Franklin indirect, she was unable to provide much of what his nature demanded from a woman: adulation, submission to his wishes and whims, and unfailing support for whatever he was doing. Eleanor, in contrast, lectured him, pressured, and pushed like a lobbyist for worthy causes who had entrée into the Oval Office. Her ability to get under Franklin's skin grew out of her relentless social conscience. Years later, when capable of greater self-understanding, she would write in the last of her three autobiographies, "I still lived under the compulsion of my early training. Duty was perhaps the motivating force in my life, often excluding what might have been joy or pleasure. I looked at everything from the point of view of what I ought to do, rarely from the standpoint of what I wanted to do. In fact, there were times when I think I almost forgot that there was such a thing as wanting anything." Her goading moral conscience is reflected in something her son Franklin Jr. never forgot. He had been taken by his mother on an inspection of a women's mental hospital where he watched deranged patients bang their heads against padded cell walls and defecate on the floors. "It was pretty rough," he recalled, but "Mother thought it would be good for my education."

Her daughter, Anna, has caught vividly how her mother's earnestness annoyed her father. Missy was mixing cocktails for FDR and his guests in his study in the White House living quarters when Eleanor entered. "Mother always came in at the end so she would only have to have one cocktail," Anna remembered, "that was her concession. She would wolf it—she never took it slowly. She came in and sat down across the desk from Father. And she had a sheaf of papers this high and she said, 'Now, Franklin, I want to talk to you about this.' I just remember, like lightning, that I thought, 'Oh God, he's going to blow.' And sure enough, he blew his top. He took every single speck of that whole pile of papers, threw them across the desk at me and said, 'Sis, you handle these tomorrow morning.' . . . She got up. She was the most controlled person in the world. And she just stood there a half second and said, 'I'm sorry.' Then she took her glass and walked toward somebody else and started talking. And he picked up his glass and started a story. And that was the end of it. Intuitively I understood that here was a man plagued with God knows how many problems and right now he had twenty minutes to have two cocktails. . . . He wanted to tell stories and relax and enjoy himself—period. I don't think Mother had the slightest realization."

The servants were eyewitnesses to occasionally frayed tempers. Lillian Parks remembered the president one afternoon having a cocktail with Missy when suddenly Eleanor popped in and asked if she might bring in her female friends. According to Parks, "The boss gave her a loud and clear, 'No you may not.'" When Eleanor left, FDR exploded, "I can't stand those 'she-males.'" Jimmy Roosevelt has told how his mother, without saying a word, "would leave things by [FDR's] bedside that she wanted him to absorb." So common had this practice become that Franklin kept an "Eleanor basket" in his room. Her notes began with her habitual "Dearest Honey," and were signed, "Much love." But their content could have been written by any federal official.

Politics, as it has endlessly been observed, is the art of the possible. Eleanor's affliction was that she saw compromise as surrender of principle. How does one say "Yes, but" to what is right? She befriended a psychiatrist who discussed with her the moral ambiguity of much human behavior. She responded asking him why people could not simply do the proper thing. FDR, in contrast, was a congenital compromiser. "It is common sense to take a method and try it," he once said. "If it fails, admit it frankly and try another. But above all, try something."

While she could get on his nerves and his political waffling could frustrate her, their styles clashed more than their objectives. They recognized each other's strengths, wanted the same things for the country, if perhaps at different speeds, and never lost sight of their mutual usefulness. When FDR wanted a frank appraisal of a New Deal initiative—the operation of the Civilian Conservation Corps, for example, he sent Eleanor to visit a CCC camp. He might resent her nagging and humorless zeal. But as Jimmy concluded, "he would forcefully resist her views and then end up doing exactly what she wanted. . . . He would not admit to her that he had done so." And Franklin was proud when foreign officials said they hoped for the opportunity to talk to Mrs. Roosevelt before they headed home. The appreciation was mutual. "It was he who taught me to observe," Eleanor admitted. "Just sitting with him in the observation car at the end of the train, I learned how to watch the tracks and see their condition, how to look at the countryside and note whether there was soil erosion and what condition the forests and fields were in as we went through the outskirts of a town or village. I soon learned to look at the clothes on the wash line and at the cars and to notice whether houses needed painting." The speed of his mind amazed her. When the novel *Gone with the Wind* was sweeping the country, she tried to get a resistant Franklin to read it. She left the book by his bedside and the following morning when she asked about it, he told her that he had read it through. Disbelieving, she started grilling him, whereupon he astonished her with his detailed grasp of the characters and plot.

Yet, for all the shared admiration, the White House staff detected early on an emotional gulf between the president and the first lady. While tediously dusting his miniature pig collection or each tiny sail and gangplank on the president's ship models, while making sure not to disturb the arrangement of his magnifying glass, albums, scissors, stickers, and stamp catalogue, while Eleanor sat in her room chatting with Lorena Hickok, the servants absorbed everything. Commenting on the first lady's perpetual motion, Lillian Parks remembered, "Even if Eleanor was home she did not see her husband for stretches at a time, except for 'Good Morning' as they passed in the hall." The president created an almost instant bonhomie with key associates, coining nicknames for them. New Deal lawyer Thomas Corcoran became "Tommy the Cork," Treasury Secretary Henry Morgenthau Jr. was "Henry the Morgue," and the ever ailing Harry Hopkins, FDR's closest confidant and most versatile aide, "Harry the Hop." Eleanor could be openly affectionate with her friends. But no warmth or intimacy was observed between the president and first lady. When Franklin did seek to embrace Eleanor, the servants reported, "she would recoil and back away." As she told Hick, "one can be personally indifferent and yet do one's duty."

Hopkins, whom FDR had initially brought from New York to head FERA, told a colleague, "Watch them, because they do all their communication with each other in public." "I accepted their relationship as a partnership," Jimmy Roosevelt concluded, "not a love match." His mother, he remembered, "just did the dutiful things. She tried to get the family together for dinners on Thanksgiving and Christmas, for example." J. B. West, the White House usher, remembered that he "never saw Eleanor and Franklin Roosevelt in the same room alone together. They had the most separate relationship I have ever seen between man and wife."

While she tended to her family conscientiously if not joyously, Eleanor leapt into her personal crusades. West carried an unforgettable memory of his introduction to the first lady. "She smiled, showing more teeth than I had ever seen." He recalled, "Eleanor Roosevelt never walked anywhere. She always raced down the halls of the White House from one appointment to another, skirts flapping around her legs. And then she would sail out the front door at full speed, jump into her waiting car, and call out to the driver: 'Where am I going?' . . . and on her way back, she gathered up people to bring home for lunch." Eleanor's disregard for form put off the White House's guardians of decorum. Howell G. Crim, the usher preceding West, remembered the day, "I was sitting in my office with the door open, and there she came padding down the back stairs—barefoot. She had on a yellow bathing suit! She came up to me with some letters and said she was on her way to a swim, and wouldn't I please mail these." When his predecessor told the story to West, "Mr. Crim was still aghast."

What Franklin's character needed, Missy LeHand provided, which led to occasional friction, however politely conducted, between her and Eleanor. The White House staff paid Eleanor the deference due a first lady and found her cheerful and kind. In her whirlwind crusading they also sensed a woman of budding greatness. But as Lillian Parks observed, Missy LeHand "was sunshine and laughter and all the maids loved her." In the beginning, she presented a mystery to the staff. But before long they gauged Missy's significance in the president's life. As Parks put it, "when Missy gave an order we responded as if it had come from the First Lady. . . . We really had two mistresses in the White House." The servants concluded "that Missy was the substitute wife, and we honored her for it." By the standards of the 1930s, Missy was reasonably well rewarded for her twenty-four-hour-a-day devotion. Her salary, in the midst of the Depression, was $3,100 a year.

The servants noted how comfortably Missy meshed with the president. He was not a particularly early riser and usually stayed in bed flipping through newspapers with a rapidity that created a breeze while breakfasting on his customary orange juice, toast, soft-boiled eggs, and bacon. On the floor above him, Missy would follow the same routine in the quarters Eleanor had assigned her, a living room, bedroom, and bath that lacked the proximity to Franklin of her Albany days, but was comfortable enough. While the third floor room was sparsely furnished, two small tables, a little desk, a phone, a bookcase, the walls revealed the borrowed nature of Missy's personal life. They were hung with photographs of Franklin, Eleanor, and the Roosevelt children. Barbara Curtis, who had come into the Roosevelt orbit through her hometown friendship with Missy, noted, "Without making a point of it she had absorbed certain upper class speech mannerisms over time." When the president was wheeled into the Oval Office on the main floor, Missy would be waiting, steno pad poised on her knee, surrounded by the homey clutter Franklin quickly imposed on any space he occupied. Portraits of his mother and Eleanor eyed each other from opposite sides of the room. Immediately behind his desk he had hung a painting of the USS *Dyer*, the destroyer that had carried him to the war zone in 1918. On his desk stood a can filled with Camel cigarettes, forty or more of which would be smoked before the day ended.

The staff had originally been perplexed by what appeared to be a four-way domestic arrangement. "What goes?" one servant asked. "FDR was spending his evenings with Missy LeHand, while Eleanor Roosevelt was spending evenings with Lorena Hickok." "Missy was somehow involved with everything FDR did for fun," Lillian Parks recalled. "Eleanor never showed any interest in FDR's stamp collection. Missy was an excited assistant collector, working on his collection with him and reminding him of where he had stashed some missing stamp." She tore items out of newspapers and magazines that she knew would amuse him, particularly cartoons in which he was the butt. Others, including Eleanor, might balk at getting into the manually controlled Ford that the president drove with hair-raising recklessness. Missy never declined. As in Albany, the servants became accustomed to seeing Missy in and out of the president's suite at all hours clad only in a nightgown and robe. According to Lillian, the familiarity went further. "A man has no secrets from his valet," she wrote in her White House memoir. "The valets knew there was nothing incomplete about FDR's love life." His only concern was that, "he just didn't want anything heavy pushing on his legs." These bald assertions of intimacy may have been prompted by a publisher's financial inducements to a White House domestic to tell all, since elsewhere Lillian was to claim that between Franklin and Missy, "there was no question of anything improper." Lillian wrote her memoir nearly a quarter of a century after the events occurred and the reader is left with a choice as to which version of FDR's love life she remembered best.

Sensing Missy's importance, the news media had become curious early on about the ever present LeHand. *Newsweek* magazine published an effusive piece on her five months after Roosevelt entered office. "She knows when he is bored before he realizes it himself," the article noted. "She can tell when he is really listening to an interlocutor and when he is merely being polite—which no one else can—and she sometimes even senses when he is beginning to disapprove of something that he still thinks he likes." The reporter described how Missy's position cramped her social life. "Even the most ardent swain is chilled at the thought that to invite her to a movie he must call the White House which is her home." Doris Fleeson, a journalist who profiled Missy for *The Saturday Evening Post*, wrote, "No invitation is accepted by Missy if it means leaving the President alone. . . . Missy is attuned to his moods, knows how to keep him company both with conversation and with silence." Eleanor was not particularly pleased to read of LeHand's indispensable role in her husband's life.

Fulton Oursler, a prolific reporter, lecturer, biographer, playwright, and later author of the wildly successful life of Christ, *The Greatest Story Ever Told,* was a popular guest at the White House. During a 1935 visit Oursler described the rapport between Missy and her chief. At late afternoon cocktails in FDR's study, Missy offered to mix the drinks, but Franklin turned her down, enjoying the ritual himself. He called for a servant to bring him gin, orange juice, and a cocktail shaker. "Then he served the cocktails, which were excellent. But Missy refused them," Oursler remembered. "She insisted on Scotch and soda. There was a little tiff between them because she declined the cocktail and he at once offered to make her a Martini. She insisted that she would have the Scotch and soda and nothing else. Looking at her then I thought how lovely she was in the same light blue evening dress which she wore when she had visited our home at Sandalwood." Missy joked that she did have another dress but that it was at the cleaner's. The repartee between Franklin and Missy suggested to White House visitors the spoofing couples in 1930s movie comedies, Clark Gable and Claudette Colbert, or William Powell and Myrna Loy. For all the spirited interplay between FDR and Missy, Oursler could not help thinking, "how odd was the whole arrangement. The President admitted that he did not know where Mrs. Roosevelt was that night. . . . His only companion was Marguerite LeHand. And what did Marguerite think of that I wondered. She was young, and attractive, and should have been off somewhere cool and gay on a happy weekend. Yet month after month and year after year she gave up date after date. . . . Here she sat with her knitting, keeping company with a very lonely man."

"Missy had great tact," FDR's distant cousin Daisy Suckley observed of the working-class girl from Somerville, Massachusetts. "She knew when to escort people in, how to seat a table, and how to keep a conversation going with charm and ease." If he was going to be alone at lunch, she came and ate with him, Daisy noted. If he sat sorting through his mail he wanted her at his side. "I noticed Missy LeHand time after time to have an engagement in the evening," Marion Dickerman remembered, and, "if he was alone she would cancel her date and bring people in to play bridge." Missy and Franklin were always partners. When he saw a solitary evening looming he would send Missy a note, "Can I dine with you or will you dine with me? 7:30."

Missy had FDR's power of attorney to write checks and pay bills.

Grace Tully, the able secretary who had been hired to assist Missy, recalled the two huddled over his checkbook, when "I have seen him work for hours to track down a five-cent discrepancy," she noted. Needing an address from which to vote, Missy listed Hyde Park. Eleanor happily unloaded tedious domestic chores onto Missy's lap. She wrote her a note about a large doctor's bill, "for Franklin Junior's treatment for piles," adding, "I know F.D.R. will have a fit!" Missy passed the memo on to Franklin, who wrote, "Pay it. Have had the fit."

However easy her own relationship with the president, Missy did not countenance familiarity from others on the staff. "There was never another laugh like Franklin Roosevelt's," Fulton Oursler had observed. "I can hear it now clearly and directly—as joyous, hearty, rolling, thunderous laughter as ever was heard on this sorrowful globe." Barbara Curtis's husband, Egbert, who helped manage Warm Springs, once questioned Missy about FDR's distinctive laughter, particularly the man's hilarity over his own stories. "That's his political laugh," she explained. But when Curtis used the same phrase in front of others, "She got madder than hell. I wasn't supposed to say that." She only reluctantly returned to Somerville for the holidays. "Christmas is still a bad bit to go home to," she wrote Eleanor, "but while the girls are there and the house I think I should."

Late in 1936, FDR sailed to Latin America aboard the heavy cruiser *Indianapolis* to demonstrate his commitment to his Good Neighbor Policy, the first U.S. president to set foot in that part of the world while in office. As he drove through cheering throngs in Rio de Janeiro, FDR's host, Brazil's strongman president, Getulio Vargas, turned and said sheepishly that perhaps President Roosevelt had heard "I am a dictator." Roosevelt replied, with a mischievous grin, "Perhaps you have heard that I am one too." As the presidential party prepared to return home, FDR was stunned by the sudden death at age fifty of his chief bodyguard, Gus Gennerich, for whom his affection was genuine and who served as the president's one-man cross section of American public opinion. When the *Indianapolis* arrived in Charleston harbor in South Carolina, the president was handed a letter from Missy addressed to "Dear Effdee"; ". . . you know how upset we all are about Gus," she began. Her concern, however, was more for Franklin's feelings than for the loss of Gennerich as she added, "I hope it has not spoiled your trip. I can hardly bear to have that happen." She had not seen him for over three weeks and closed, "it will be good to get my eyes on you again. This place is horrible when you are away."

Where did such devotion leave Eleanor? Upon moving to the White House, she had had to give up teaching at the Todhunter School. She had immediately sought something else to turn her restless hand to, and offered to look after Franklin's correspondence. He gave the idea a dismissive wave. Missy, he said, would think Eleanor was poaching. "I know she resented Missy's place in Father's life," Jimmy Roosevelt noted, but added that his mother behaved the same toward any woman who might displace her. "I think she did like [Missy] a great deal," daughter Anna believed. But "she was apprehensive of anyone whom she felt got too close." At times, Anna too felt supplanted by Missy. When she would enter a car with her father, she would note annoyedly that Missy had already taken the seat next to him. However, "I think you have to put Missy in a different category," Anna concluded, "because she was the office wife—quote, unquote. And she was there—she lived in the White House."

Yet Missy took pains to express her devotion to the whole family, and not simply to "Effdee." One Christmas she wrote, "Dearest Eleanor, I have had such a happy year and I hope you know how much I appreciate being with you—not because of the W.H. but because I'm _with you._" She closed, "I love you so much. I can never tell you how very much." Privately Eleanor could be cutting when describing to friends Missy's self-sacrifice for FDR. The woman's imperturbable good nature grated as well on Roosevelt's son Franklin Jr. "Are you always so agreeable," he shot at Missy. "Don't you ever get mad and flare up." Head bowed, tears welled in her eyes.

The differing styles of Eleanor and Missy put the first lady at a disadvantage, particularly given FDR's appreciation of femininity. Missy's room may have been plainly furnished but her closet held the latest fashions, many of her dresses in Franklin's favorite blue. To the staff, she could be the most glamorous woman in the room. Eleanor had come to the White House largely fashion-inert, though upon becoming first lady she engaged a leading New York couturier, and to her astonishment, the fashion industry, in 1934, voted her among "the ten best dressed women of the year." "Missy made sure to wear high heels that clicked along pleasantly instead of the low heels and sensible oxfords the First Lady wore," Lillian Parks observed. Heels, however, would have done little for

Eleanor's already five-foot-eleven-inch frame, while Missy, at five foot seven inches, benefited. Missy enjoyed dining elegantly and Eleanor ate simply. For FDR's cherished cocktail hour, Missy had the staff lay out caviar, smoked turkey, smoked clams, and imported cheeses, delicacies that Eleanor barely touched and considered extravagant. The difference in Franklin's treatment of the two women was obvious. While the staff rarely witnessed tenderness between Franklin and Eleanor, visitors saw unconcealed warmth between him and Missy. As Florence Kerr, a women's relief official in the New Deal, saw it, "he certainly was affectionate with her and said nice things to her, but he never did to Eleanor." Kerr was not unaware of the roots of the coolness between husband and wife. Harry Hopkins had confided to her the Franklin and Lucy affair. Asked long years afterward if Hopkins condemned FDR's infidelity, she answered that Hopkins found the president "so severely handicapped and so much of life was shut away that any pleasure he could have, he was more than entitled to."

Both women would stand up to Franklin, but with far different results. Sam Rosenman found Missy the "frankest of the President's associates, never hesitating to tell him unpleasant truths or to express an unfavorable opinion about his work." Eleanor challenged him too, but in a harping manner that got Franklin's back up, while Missy's humoring amused him. When Missy told FDR what a palmist had read in her hand—"You must also have confidence in yourself. You must learn to speak up"—Roosevelt burst out laughing. Eleanor tried to inflict people on him whom he did not want to see. Missy was the gatekeeper protecting him from bores, special pleaders, and visitors of no use. Missy's praises were effusive. Eleanor's were qualified, reminding him of how he could do even more. "She was, all in all, fairly indispensable," Rosenman concluded of Missy. "There is no doubt," Raymond Moley, a member of the Brain Trust, noted, "Missy was as close to being a wife as he ever had—or could have."

It was not that Eleanor failed to understand her husband but that she was a compulsive uplifter, driving him just as she did her other associates and herself. She read her husband's relationship with Missy in this curious ménage with startling clarity. She knew that, for Missy, Franklin was life itself, and once remarked, "If I should outlive FDR, Missy would be the one I should worry about." Franklin "might have been happier with a wife who was completely uncritical," she admitted; yet she understood the synergy among the three of them. "Franklin loved Missy," she confided to a friend. "He couldn't have lived without me, but neither could he have lived without Missy." She concluded, in the end, however, of Missy LeHand, "If he had met her earlier, it would have been different."

*Chapter 26*

# FOUR MORE YEARS

· · · · · · ·

O N MARCH 4, 1937, just as four years before, an unmarked government automobile pulled up before 2238 Q Street in Washington. A Secret Service agent jumped out carrying an umbrella against a pouring
rain. As he approached the door to the home, three people emerged. The
president had arranged invitations to his second inaugural not only for
Mrs. Rutherfurd but for her sister, Violetta Marbury, and Violetta's
daughter, Lucy.

By now, the arrival of official cars at Q Street had become common-
place. Whenever Lucy visited, her niece remembered her mother saying, " 'Go look out the window. President Roosevelt is coming to pick up
Aunt Lucy!' I would look out and sure enough the president had come to
pick her up. A car just pulled up, no fuss. He was sitting in the back and
a Secret Service man came to the door and escorted my aunt. We were
on a pretty busy street, but people didn't pay any attention," yet the
strong, mobile face, chin lifted upward, was one of the most recogniz-
able on earth. Lucy would slip hurriedly into the back seat as the chauffeur drove off, a backup car trailing behind. For an hour or so, the driver
would leave the city's streets and begin weaving leisurely through the
leafy roads lacing Rock Creek Park. Lucy's niece had been cautioned to
say nothing about these outings.

In the four years since Lucy had been escorted to the first Roosevelt
inaugural, her life had continued its untrammeled way. She looked after
her daughter, Barbara, a girl now fourteen and described by a friend as
"wearing glasses, with features that promised to be much better looking
later on," a stepdaughter, and the four young men, strapping six footers
who excelled at golf, tennis, and scull racing. She treated them all with
an attentiveness and care that had long since erased any distinction be-

tween stepmother and birth mother. The health of her husband, Winthrop, now seventy-four, had begun to fail, and Winty required full-time nursing. A society painter and White Russian émigrée, Elizabeth Shoumatoff, had become Lucy's close friend in the course of doing portraits of the Rutherfurd family, and observed that the woman was "constantly preoccupied with her husband's health." Throughout their winter-spring marriage Lucy had accommodated her husband's every wish. She found boxing a brutal sport, but Winty enjoyed it, particularly since his six-foot-six-inch son John, a Princeton student, was a Golden Gloves champion. When the Rutherfurds stayed at their Manhattan apartment, Lucy went with her husband to the fights, a rare, demure female in the raucous crowd.

Her still demanding mother occasionally ruffled the even tenor of the Rutherfurds' life. During the mid-1930s, Lucy Blundon, Lucy's namesake and niece, recalled the world of grandmother Minnie. "She stayed in Washington in her apartment with a maid. She was always perfectly dressed, always outfitted. I never saw her in a nightgown or negligee. She was absolutely regal, ramrod straight, just gorgeous. She had dark hair, she may have dyed it. . . . She never did anything, [but] she was an interesting woman. I just adored her, though as she grew older she got a little cranky." A family division of labor met the needs of the seventy-two-year-old former doyenne of Washington society. "My mother did all of the calling, seeing her, taking care of her and my aunt footed the bill," niece Lucy remembered. One activity that Minnie did pursue tirelessly was to badger the government for more support beyond her pension as a veteran's widow. In 1933, she wrote to the Pension Office describing her poor health and inquiring about government-paid medical care. "No provision has been made for medical treatment for the widows of veterans," Minnie was informed. Two years later she was back with the same request and again rejected. Her second appeal had been written from the comfort of her daughter Lucy's estate in Aiken.

In a conversation with Fulton Oursler, FDR, perhaps unconsciously, revealed that he still fantasized about what might have been between himself and Lucy. On May 12, 1935, the president had invited Oursler to a quiet supper at the White House. FDR was in an expansive mood and began spinning a story that he said he had been thinking about for years.

Oursler remembered the president describing his protagonist as a rich man who is "tired, fed up with his surroundings and habits. Perhaps his wife, to whom he has been married for twenty years, now definitely bores him. Perhaps, too, the sameness of his middle-aged routine has begun to wear him down. Furthermore, he is disheartened at the hollowness of all the superficial friendship surrounding him." The man wants to disappear and begin a secret life in some small town where he can escape his past. The problem was how to vanish yet bring his wealth with him. The president told Oursler that he believed the dilemma was insoluble. His guest was immediately intrigued by the possibilities for a magazine series. After the conversation, Oursler began lining up authors of detective fiction, each of whom was to write an account of how the man might pull off the scheme. The series was to be entitled "The President's Mystery Story." Roosevelt, a lover of the genre, went along with Oursler and happily accepted $9,000 from the magazine, which he donated to the Warm Springs Foundation.

Echoes of Franklin's 1918 romantic dilemma are unmistakable in his premise. His press secretary, Stephen Early, however, strongly recommended that the millionaire's boredom with his marriage be dropped since "it might be construed by some readers as the President's personal feelings." Franklin too had been married at this point for twenty years. Subsequently Oursler learned that the first lady also had a story. Eleanor's idea was for a novel about a disillusioned wife. The suggested title was "All Passion Spent."

By now, Eleanor had become a success in her own right. Beginning in FDR's first presidential term she had written for a new magazine, *Babies, Just Babies,* which paid her $500 per issue, but which folded in six months. *Woman's Home Companion* next contracted with her to write a monthly question-and-answer column for which she was paid $1,000 per issue. Between 1935 and 1936, she earned nearly $66,000 from radio broadcasts alone. Her lecture bureau booked her on the circuit for $1,000 a speech. She sold serialization rights to her first autobiography, *This Is My Story,* to *The Ladies' Home Journal* for $75,000, equal to the president's annual salary. Her biggest breakthrough came in 1935 when United Features signed her for a daily syndicated column that ultimately became "My Day," an enterprise praised for its homey wisdom or ridiculed as simplistic pap. Still it was widely read. Within four years, sixty-two newspapers reaching four million readers carried "My Day." Eleanor wrote to the publishers of *The Ladies' Home Journal*, "I can't tell you how happy this makes me, to receive all this attention for something I've done by myself and not because of Franklin." She donated most of her income to charity.

So all-consuming had her other activities become that she and her business partners, Nan Cook and Marion Dickerman, accepted that they could no longer carry on Val-Kill Industries. In 1936 they sold the company to its employees. Eleanor converted the factory into a home for herself. Her busyness, however, did not tell the whole story of the enterprise's collapse. Eleanor's closeness to Hick in the preceding years had stirred resentment in Cook and Dickerman, who felt pushed aside.

Her perpetual motion, the columns, broadcasts, and speeches, written on the fly aboard trains, planes, cars, and ships, exhausted those around her. Anna Roosevelt, speaking of Eleanor's secretary, Malvina Thompson, described the personal cost of working for her mother. "Tommy," she recalled, "never for years and years had a life of her own. I used to just cringe sometimes when I'd hear Mother at eleven-thirty at night say to Tommy, 'I've still got a number of columns to do. Come on, you've got to take a column.' And this weary, weary woman who had just finished working and didn't have Mother's stamina would sit down at a typewriter and Mother would dictate to her. I think both [parents] unwittingly and unknowingly never realized that these people lived their lives through them and had nothing of their own."

Eleanor's biographer Joe Lash has described the delicate balance holding the Roosevelt marriage together in the 1930s. "She was not in love with him," Lash wrote. "Yes, she was prepared to render him a labor of love by serving his work . . . if he would be thoughtful, considerate, and treat her as a partner and confidante." As Eleanor put it in a letter to Hick, "I realize F.D.R. is a great man, & he is nice to me but as a person, I'm a stranger & don't want to be anything else." She viewed her role in the 1936 reelection campaign as superfluous. "Everyone's cocksure & I can do nothing about it. They are talking landslide." FDR made no claim to have ended the Depression. The hardships still besetting the country would have mocked such a boast. Yet, his contagious self-assurance had persuaded ordinary Americans that the country was on the mend and that this man could save them.

His image of invulnerability literally came close to crashing down on an August night as he prepared to accept his party's renomination at the Democratic convention in Philadelphia. Spotlights followed FDR lurching toward the microphones at Franklin Field, his left arm clutching son Jimmy, his right hand holding the cane. He spotted a familiar bearded white-haired figure. He switched the cane to his left hand in an effort to reach out and shake the hand of the poet Edwin Markham. The shift upset his balance and the lock on his left leg brace popped open. He swayed helplessly and began to fall. Only the reflexive reaction of a bodyguard saved him. Jimmy, also attempting to catch his father, knocked the speech out of FDR's hand and the pages went fluttering to the floor. As Jimmy hastily knelt to retrieve them, the president, still smiling and waving to the crowd, spoke through clenched teeth, "To hell with the speech," he ordered, "fix the brace. If it can't be fixed, there won't be any speech." He heard the blessed click of the brace snapping back into place and went on to give a rousing denunciation of the "economic royalists" who had controlled America before he took office.

He also had a fresh warning for the country. He had watched with growing alarm the truculence and anti-Semitism from Nazi Germany. FDR by now judged Adolf Hitler a pathological liar bent on aggression, particularly after the dictator had seized the Rhineland the previous March 7 in violation of the Treaty of Versailles. Roosevelt warned the convention that "the world cannot trust a fully rearmed Germany to stay at peace." He was engaged in a high-wire act, trying to awaken the country to potential danger without being seen as a warmonger. To achieve balance, he harked back, in a massively attended outdoor speech later that month in Chautauqua, New York, to his memories of 1918. "I have seen war," he began, his tone ominous. "I have seen war on land and sea. I have seen blood running from the wounded. I have seen men coughing out their gassed lungs. I have seen the dead in the mud. I have seen cities destroyed. I have seen two hundred limping, exhausted men come out of line—the survivors of a regiment of one thousand that went forward forty-eight hours before. I have seen children starving. I have seen the agony of mothers and wives. I hate war."

He understood the threat that Hitler posed to peace and democracy, yet the Depression was still unbeaten and he had to keep Congress primarily focused on his domestic agenda. The New Deal had not put the country fully back to work, but in four years the number of jobless had dropped by nearly a third. American business had moved from the red to the black, from losses of $2 billion in 1932 to $5 billion in profits in 1936. The Social Security Act meant that at the end of a working life the pensionless majority would have something to fall back on. Workers were now entitled to a minimum wage and maximum working hours. Some 24 million people began receiving unemployment benefits. The Works Progress Administration, attacked at first as a leaf-raking boondoggle, had built schools, hospitals, bridges, parks and thousands of miles of highways. Investors bamboozled in the Roaring Twenties now had the Securities and Exchange Commission to protect them from dishonest practices. The Tennessee Valley Authority had moved tens of thousands from the gloom of kerosene lamps to electric lighting. With Roosevelt at the helm, Depression-stricken Americans no longer felt alone in facing their tribulations.

After Eleanor delivered a speech in Kansas City, "A rather grand, gaunt looking detective" approached and told her, "I was lost in 1933, didn't believe in the country or anything. I'm 53, I've worked for the public all my life and never been late to work once and I've been a Republican, didn't vote for Mr. R in '32 but in two years he had me. He gave me back all I thought I'd lost and this year I worked for him." Eleanor's cousin Corinne continued in the Oyster Bay tradition a staunch Republican, a member of the Connecticut state legislature, and would second the nomination of Kansas Governor Alf Landon to be Roosevelt's opponent this political season. Yet she was to say of Franklin, "you went in feeling allergic to him politically as I did, and at the end of an hour you were completely charmed. You felt here was somebody who really was thinking about the problems. . . . For the time being you felt it was the most exciting thing you'd ever heard! At least I did. I probably was gullible." Alice Roosevelt Longworth, however, remained implacable in her antipathy toward Franklin. Amid the flurry of alphabetical agencies FDR had launched to put the country back on its feet—AAA, SEC, NRA, SSA—Alice added her own creation, the SAA, which stands for "Smart Aleck Administration."

A few months before the 1936 election, Franklin lost his guiding star of the previous quarter century. Louis Howe's coughing spasms had begun to worsen, echoing along the White House corridors. Clad only in pajamas, he would drag his pain-racked body from his room, his ghastly presence alarming Eleanor. In August 1935, Howe had entered Bethesda Naval Hospital where he remarked to a visitor, "Franklin is on his own now." At times he became delirious, seizing a phone and barking incoherent orders in the president's name to puzzled Washington officials. Eleanor visited him often, a closeness that her daughter, Anna, found ironic. "Here was mother for years and years hating Louis," she recalled, "and here was mother swinging over. When she swung, she swung." So mutually trusting and admiring had the friendship become that Louis had once told Eleanor, "if you want to be President in 1940, tell me now so I can start getting things ready." She appreciated the compliment but laughed it off. The country, she told him, was not ready for a woman president.

On April 18, 1936, FDR delivered a speech before the press corps's annual evening of humor and satire, the Gridiron Dinner. Eleanor had also been making a speech that night. She was barely back in the White House when the president's physician, Admiral Ross McIntire, called to tell her that Louis was dead. She later wrote Hick of her quirky mentor. "He was like a piteous, querulous child, but even when I complained, I loved him & no one will ever be more loyal & devoted than he was."

During the previous months in which Howe's illness had driven him from the political stage, FDR's cool pragmatism emerged. "I had a feeling with Father," Anna told an interviewer, "that as soon as he felt that Louis was not capable of producing or moving intellectually and politically as fast as he needed, he began to block him out. He was going on— had things to do." Still, at the end, Franklin recognized his profound debt to Howe, arranging an almost unheard of homage for someone whose role had been behind the scenes and rarely official. FDR decreed a state funeral for Louis Howe to be held in the East Room of the White House and ordered flags in government buildings lowered to half-mast. He and Eleanor boarded a special train to bring Louis to his final resting place in Fall River, Massachusetts. The president composed the epitaph to be chiseled into Howe's headstone, "Devoted friend, adviser, and associate of the President."

That fall FDR went on to score the greatest presidential triumph in history up to that time, winning 61 percent of the popular vote to 37 percent for his opponent, the decent, bespectacled, mild-mannered but hapless Alf Landon. FDR took forty-six out of forty-eight states and swept the electoral college by 523 votes to 8. It is arguable that without Howe's steadfastness through Franklin's darkest hours, without the man's political genius, FDR might never have been elected president even once.

· · ·

By the time of his reelection, FDR had been crippled for fifteen years. His condition had stabilized and he was not in pain. But to ignore his paralysis as a determinant in his life is myopic. He could not get out of bed by himself in the morning. To do so he was utterly dependent on his valet, Irvin McDuffie, a garrulous black barber from Warm Springs whom FDR took a liking to and brought to Washington. Every morning McDuffie stretched the president out in his bed, snapping his metal leg braces into place, the straps of which ran up to Franklin's waist. He next worked the man's inert feet into shoes attached to the braces. Rocking the heavy torso from side to side, McDuffie then wrestled FDR's pants over the shoes and over the cumbersome braces. The shoes, socks, and exposed part of the braces were all painted black to make them less conspicuous. Finally, McDuffie pulled the president up to a sitting position from which FDR could swing himself onto his wheelchair. Curtis Roosevelt recalled of living in the White House with his paralyzed grandfather, "A pencil drops on the floor, somebody has to pick it up. He wants a glass of water, somebody has to bring it. He needs a book, someone has to pull it from a shelf." The most demeaning moment Curtis remembered was when the valet had to bring a bottle to the president's desk so that FDR could urinate.

During campaigns, at each whistle stop his senior military aide, General Edwin "Pa" Watson, or Sam Rosenman, would knock on FDR's compartment door and announce, "Mr. President we'll be in Buffalo in ten minutes." The valet would then come in, take the president's pants off, attach the metal braces, and put on the trousers again. During this ritual FDR kept up an incessant chatter, his customary device for distracting observers from what he was going through. He would then lurch down the aisle on the arm of an aide, emerge at the end of the car clutching the rail, turn his familiar smile onto the crowd, and make his speech. He then returned to his compartment, had the valet undress him again, until they reached the next stop where the procedure was repeated. The journalist and radio broadcaster Olive Clapper once rode a White House elevator with FDR and witnessed the man with his public mask off. "As I stood above him," she recalled, "he looked so crumpled, broken and invalided I could hardly restrain the tears. For the first time

I realized that here was a man who fought a gallant battle with himself every day."

On an occasion when Roosevelt was discussing the bank crisis with Governor Herbert Lehman, Eleanor recalled her husband's frustration. "I can remember [Lehman] walking up and down in our library and hall and I remember thinking . . . because Franklin couldn't walk, of course, this constant pacing was irritating to him. And yet he couldn't say anything to Herbert." Few ever heard him complain. A rare outburst occurred when Senator George Norris of Nebraska came to see him and the conversation turned to FDR's possibly running for an unprecedented third term. "You sit in your chair in your office, but if something goes wrong or you get irritated or tired, you can get up and walk around, or you can go into another room," he told Norris. "But I can't, I'm tied down to this chair day after day, week after week and month after month. And I can't stand it any longer. I can't go on with it any longer."

That inauguration day, after he had been sworn in, Roosevelt turned to face a sea of umbrellas and began speaking of the trials that vast numbers of his countrymen still faced. "I see millions of families," he said, "trying to live on incomes so meager that the pall of family disaster hangs over them day by day. I see millions whose daily lives in city and on farm continue under conditions labeled indecent by a so-called polite society half a century ago. I see millions denied education, recreation, and the opportunity to better their lot and the lot of their children. I see millions lacking the means to buy the products of farm and factory and by their poverty denying work and productiveness to many other millions. I see one third of a nation ill-housed, ill-clad, ill-nourished. It is not in despair that I paint you that picture. I paint it for you in hope—because the nation, seeing and understanding the injustice in it, proposes to paint it out."

After the ringing applause died away, Lucy Rutherfurd would leave the sodden lawn in front of the Capitol and resume the grand life at Allamuchy and Ridgely Hall. She would continue to accommodate her husband in almost all his preferences. Yet, while Winty remained an arch-Republican who echoed his wealthy friends' barb that Roosevelt was "a traitor to his class," she again had voted for Franklin.

*Chapter 27*

# EXIT HICKOK: ENTER SCHIFF

· · · · · · ·

W ELL BEFORE FRANKLIN'S REELECTION the affinity between Eleanor and Lorena Hickok had begun to travel a familiar trajectory, from warm to hot, to temperate, to tepid, to cool. On February 1, 1935, Eleanor had written a letter doubtless puzzling to Hick. "Of course you should have had a husband & children," she wrote, "& it would have made you happy if you loved him & in any case it would have satisfied certain cravings & given you someone on whom to lavish the love & devotion you have to keep down all the time." The letter was odd in that it chose to ignore or never grasped Hick's obvious sexual orientation, the second explanation highly unlikely. The "cravings that she had to keep down" apparently referred to the socially condemned homosexuality of that era. The letter went on to hint that Eleanor understood how Hick was struggling not to become a burden to the woman in whom she had invested so much emotional capital. "Dear one," Eleanor wrote, "I do love you & appreciate the fight you make not to make me unhappy, but there is no use trying to hide things from me because I know just how you feel."

That same February, Earl Miller, now divorced from his second wife, Ruth, came to visit Eleanor in Washington with his latest romance, a woman named Jane. Hick, at this point no longer living in the White House, announced that she too was coming to see Eleanor. The crossed wires produced a disaster. After the visit, Eleanor wrote Hick reminding her, "You told me you would entertain yourself in Washington before I had time to tell you whether I was busy or not." Upon Hick's arrival at the White House, Eleanor had been making a radio broadcast and her letter further reminded Hick that "You went right by me at the studio without speaking to me." She pointed out that she had already told Hick that she planned to take Earl and his friend to a play and had invited

Hick to come along. "You barely spoke to Earl and Jane at the play who were my guests & certainly did nothing rude to you. . . . When I asked you to go in so you could sit by me you deliberately changed & sat as far away as possible." As for the coming weekend when Hick would again be with her, she warned, "At least let's try to be cheerful & polite & not make everyone around uncomfortable!"

As in every romance where one loves too much and the other too little, Hick's pouts, her sullenness, her demands became tiresome to Eleanor. She included Hick on a trip to Yosemite Park, where the ugly underside of passion erupted. Tourists and park rangers thronged admiringly around the first lady, ignoring her frumpy companion as if Hick did not exist. She yelled and stomped about like a wounded animal. Afterward she was mortified by her behavior. "Oh I'm bad," she wrote Eleanor, "but I love you so, at times life becomes just one long, dreary ache for you."

The situation took another downward slide when Eleanor began sending money to the ever hard-up Hick, an act almost invariably poisonous to friendship. The sums, $50, $100, $200, were disguised as birthday or Christmas presents, but Eleanor knew that Hick simply needed cash. As Christmas 1937 approached, she wrote, "Hick darling, I think it may be a help for you to have the enclosed <u>now</u>. . . . & please don't spend money on <u>things</u> for me, love means so much more & heaven knows you give me that 365 days of the year."

In a 1937 letter, Eleanor wrote regretting Hick's sexual orientation. "I think you will remember that I once told you," she said, "I wished you had been happy with a man or that it might still be. I rather think that the lack of that relationship does create 'emotional instability' but people do seem to weather it in time." Later, Eleanor circuitously but undeniably let Hick know that their former meaning to each other no longer held. "Over the years the type of love felt on either side may change," she wrote, "but if the fundamental love is there I believe in the end the relationship adjusts to something deep and satisfying to both people. I love other people the same way or differently but each one has their place & one cannot compare them."

The scales had tipped against Hick. She was the one who had lifted herself from poverty and obscurity to reach the pinnacle of her profession, which initially much impressed Eleanor, who herself was then seen principally as Mrs. Franklin Roosevelt, a reflection of someone else. At that time, her love for the brash, confident, successful journalist satisfied her emotional neediness. But four years of the Roosevelt presidency had propelled Eleanor to national, even international, stature, as famous and controversial, as loved or deplored, as self-sufficient and even more independent-minded than her husband. Hick, in contrast, now occupied a shrunken space hemmed in on one side by her resentment and jealousy of rival claimants on Eleanor's attention and on the other side by her having given up a once brilliant career for increasingly unrequited love. Eleanor lacked the calculating self-protectedness of FDR, and the hurt she knew she was inflicting on Hick pained her as well. "I went to sleep saying a little prayer," she wrote her. "God give me depth enough not to hurt Hick again. . . . I know you have a feeling which for one reason or another I may not return in kind, but I feel I love you just the same."

Painfully, Hick began to accept her fate. She had entertained the idea of writing a book about her experiences as an investigator for the Emergency Relief Administration and found that her letters to Eleanor comprised a handy record of those years. One dreary Sunday afternoon at the White House, camped out in Louis Howe's old bedroom, she began to attack the piles of correspondence that had passed between the two women. "I am now about halfway through," she wrote Eleanor, then staying at Hyde Park. Today "I stumbled into a lot of the early letters, written while I was still with the [Associated Press]. Dear, whatever may have happened since—whatever may happen in the future—I was certainly happy those days, much happier, I believe, than most people ever are in all their lives. You gave me that, and I'm deeply grateful. . . . I don't suppose anyone can ever stay so happy as I was that first year or so, though. Do you?"

Dorothy Schiff was thirty-three years old when she entered Franklin Roosevelt's life and, by her own description, "I was considered very sexy in those days." She liked to quote Serge Obolensky, hotelier and society figure, who "said I had the 'finest gams' in New York." She was in fact a striking woman, if not conventionally beautiful. Slender, fine-boned, with agate blue eyes, she carried herself gracefully, and her size ten figure was made for the chic, simple clothes she favored. Dorothy Schiff was rich, Jewish, and initially Republican. Her grandfather was the banking magnate and philanthropist Jacob Henry Schiff. Her education matched her class, Manhattan's Brearley School and Bryn Mawr College. She wore her Republicanism lightly, while her chief interest had been hobnobbing with the rich and glamorous in the international set.

Her association with FDR began after Schiff's life had undergone a sea change. She divorced her socialite husband, a broker, Richard B. W. Hall, and in 1931 married a liberal writer and activist Democrat, George Backer, who introduced her to the wit and sophistication of the Algonquin Round Table. Dorothy Schiff thereupon became a Democrat and a supporter of Roosevelt's New Deal. Her husband managed grandstand tickets for the 1933 inauguration where she shivered in the cold waiting for FDR to speak. "I heard that glorious voice for the first time," she remembered. "I was thrilled and inspired as those words rang around the world, 'Let me assert my belief that the only thing we have to fear . . .'" By 1936, now deeply enmeshed in liberal causes, particularly child welfare, she attended the Democratic National Convention in Philadelphia that renominated FDR. Shortly afterward she was among a group of Democratic women invited to meet Roosevelt at Hyde Park. The outwardly cool, seemingly self-possessed Schiff was also at the time seeing a psychiatrist to whom she confessed her terror at meeting the president of the United States. Arriving with the other women at Hyde Park she spotted FDR seated out front of his home in his manually controlled Ford. The president's daughter, Anna, took Schiff by the hand and introduced her by her married name, "This is Dorothy Backer whom we've been telling you about." The president greeted her with a dazzling smile suggesting that meeting this stranger was the high point of his day. "Dorothy," he said, "I'm so glad you're with us. I knew your father on the board of the Boy Scouts." Her greatest fear was realized. "Something happened to me that I have never experienced before or since," she remembered. "My tongue literally clove to the roof of my mouth." After the introduction, Schiff went with Anna and others to the Val-Kill cottage pool for a swim.

Though she was left speechless on meeting FDR, something about her evidently impressed him. She had dressed and finished lunch when she was informed that the president was now poolside and asking for her. She hesitantly approached him and he said, "Sit next to me." She sat down, "barely aware of his leg braces," she remembered. Words, beyond a mutter, again failed her. "I was still too petrified," she remembered. FDR kept her at his side while well-wishers lined up for the next hour to greet him. To her the president "had this tremendous glowing self-confidence that helped me," and in a phrase she would frequently repeat, she found Franklin Roosevelt "the sun-god."

Thereafter, invitations to Hyde Park came frequently. Often Schiff found herself alone at Saturday lunches with Franklin and his mother. "Granny sat at one end of the table and the President at the other with me on his right," she recalled. "It was very much her house and she was very much the hostess. . . . She was in love with her son and watched him closely." However socially prominent, Dorothy Schiff was not blind to anti-Semitism, and was delighted to have somehow overcome that prejudice with Sara. "She was aware of the Jewish thing, never failing to ask, 'How are your aunt Mrs. Lehman and your aunt Mrs. Warburg?' Her kind of person assumed all Jews of German descent were related. So I would let it go and say, 'Fine, thank you.' Certain Jews were acceptable, the 'Our Crowd' type!" Mrs. Herbert Lehman was not related to her at all and Mrs. Paul Warburg was Schiff's great-aunt. Sara conferred her greatest compliment on Schiff: she was "a lady." Dorothy found the old woman "not too discreet and frivolous." On one occasion Sara asked her son about the man who epitomized unfettered capitalism. "Franklin, why don't you like Mr. [J. P.] Morgan," she chided him. "I always thought he was such a nice man."

Sara's principal objective, Schiff detected, was to have her son come to Hyde Park "as often and for as long as possible and I was the draw." As for the president, Schiff thought he "was a snob—horrible word, and I wish I could think of a better one—and he liked women who were well-bred and brought up. Ladies is the word, I guess. I was a rich kid of the right kind—not the robber baron type—and had been to the right schools. As to being Jewish, C. P. Snow wrote that once you reach a certain financial level, people don't think of you as anything but very rich."

During her visits, Schiff stayed with Nancy Cook at the Val-Kill house. There, Dorothy became accustomed to an experience that left her feeling faintly foolish, the president of the United States honking his horn for her to come out like a teenager picking up his date. "He loved driving recklessly along his miles of wood roads," she remembered, "particularly pleased at giving his secret service agent the slip." The blue Ford V-8, purchased after Edsel Ford had made a generous gift to the Warm Springs Foundation, was now Franklin's favorite. Of her rides with the president, Schiff recalled, "whenever I would be slid across the front seat away from him, a strong right arm would pull me back." Rounding one particularly sharp curve he told her, "This is where Sam Rosenman always crosses himself." Her husband, George Backer, showed no displeasure at her spending so much time with another man. "George was overwhelmed by the President," she said. He "saw it all in a sort of droit de seigneur way, his wife being tapped by the lord of the manor. He was proud of it and it gave him tremendous prestige with his friends."

She was amused after lunch during her Hyde Park weekends to see the nation's leader all by himself happily bent over a table steaming stamps off envelopes for his collection. Dorothy knew that she had been accepted into FDR's most intimate circle by his lack of self-consciousness about displaying his disability before her while at home. He usually took off the braces and she watched Secret Service agents make a seat for him, by crossing their hands, lugging him about like a sack of wheat, and depositing him in his wheelchair. "He would ask me to walk alongside the chair, and at first I couldn't look and would turn my face away," Schiff recalled. "Sometimes he would ask me to push him about in it, and this was sort of a shocker for me. I had pushed my children occasionally, but here was this great, strong radiant sun-god, the answer to the prayers of millions, seeming the child I had pushed in the park. It was . . . well, confusing for me. Embarrassing too."

Schiff was particularly impressed by FDR's "ability to ask the right questions, come up with the jokes and stories to make a point and transfer his enjoyment to others." In time she grasped that while FDR talked almost endlessly, he asked "Not a word about myself. . . . He wasn't interested in me. He was interested in himself, and having what he thought was this well-dressed young woman whom he could ramble on to. He was amused by my clothes which were sort of New York designer in those days. . . . And he was fascinated by . . . John Frederick hats." The other people he saw, in her judgment, "were not attractive. There was just no competition." She described Eleanor as a dowdy dresser who had "a peculiar figure with stomach sticking out."

During FDR's musings she came to learn his heroes, Woodrow Wilson and TR. She further discovered surprising quirks. She had returned from a trip to Holland and showed Roosevelt postcards she had brought back from the Rijksmuseum, including Rembrandt's surgically graphic *The Anatomy Lesson*. FDR reacted viscerally. "I hate that," he told her.

He disliked rhododendrons because they reminded him of funerals. She found that he shrank from sickness, ugliness, any unpleasantness, and was capable of occasional prudery. He had been rehearsing a speech in front of her and came upon the word "adult," which he accented on the first syllable. One of his staff reminded him that the preferred pronunciation accented the second syllable, a-DULT. "I can't say it that way," he objected. "It sounds too much like adultery."

She was disappointed by an unexpected facetious streak, even in his dealings with serious issues. With tensions mounting in Europe, she was disturbed by the president's insouciant treatment of his key appointment to Britain. "I remember when he appointed Joe Kennedy as ambassador to the Court of St. James," she recalled, "he said he thought it was the greatest joke in the world to put an Irishman there. That bothered me."

At the time of Schiff's visits FDR was risking a constitutional crisis through his 1937 plan to outflank a Supreme Court that repeatedly frustrated him by striking down New Deal legislation, including the National Recovery Administration and the Agricultural Adjustment Act to raise crop prices for desperate farmers. He told her, with what she considered unseemly levity, about his plan to drive obstructionist justices off the bench. He had proposed in February that those over seventy, of whom there were four, retire at full pay, or see their votes potentially canceled out by FDR's appointment of assistant justices with full voting power. Roosevelt's opponents cried "dictator" and accused FDR of "packing the court." To Schiff, "He thought it was a great joke to put the old men, the nine old men," out to pasture.

He may have handled the serious issues lightly with Schiff, but not with Eleanor. The virulence of the Supreme Court fight "has got under his skin," Eleanor wrote her daughter, Anna. "I thought stupidly his little outburst . . . was amusing and human and used it in my column. Pa was furious with me . . . he would certainly say nothing more to me on any subject!" She closed the letter to her daughter saying, "Will I be glad when we leave the W.H. and I can be on my own!" FDR's frustration was not soon to be allayed. For once his political antennae failed him and his bill to expand the Supreme Court never made it to a vote.

Dorothy Schiff learned that a price had to be paid for her proximity to the great man. At the same time that he had been fomenting a constitutional crisis over the court issue, he was maneuvering her into buying a plot of land she did not need or want. On September 12, 1937, a gorgeous

fall day with the red, gold, yellow, and green leaves beginning to be reflected onto the waters of the Hudson, Schiff and her husband, George,
were invited for a cruise aboard the presidential yacht, *Sequoia*. She was
sitting with him and other guests when she received word that the president wanted to see her below deck, alone. He asked her to sit down and
explained that he intended to buy a farm property near Hyde Park and
he wanted her to take half of it, some forty-five acres. He took a yellow
legal pad and began sketching a map of what he had in mind. Her portion, he explained, would cost her only $9,000. "I didn't say anything,"
she remembered of the moment, "because it was the last thing I wanted
to do, [already] having a large house in Oyster Bay." She asked what she
was supposed to do with Hudson Valley property and FDR replied airily,
"Why, you would build a house on it. I'll talk to Toombs. He'll design it
for you." Henry Toombs had designed Val-Kill for Eleanor and her
friends and was FDR's favorite architect.

Two months later, on November 28, Schiff was surprised to receive a
"Dear Dorothy" letter from the White House in which FDR informed
her that the property line for her parcel had been surveyed. She read it
and did nothing. Two days before Christmas, the president wrote again
asking, "If you would be good enough to send your check for $9,000."
She stalled, her interest in the deal still nil. She then received a visit
from an uneasy Sam Rosenman. The president was waiting for his
money, Rosenman informed her. "Well Sam," she said, "I really didn't
take it that seriously." "But he did," he answered. "He's very serious. . . .
When the President asks you to do something," he advised her, "you do
it." She finally surrendered. FDR engaged Toombs for her, who soon was
showing Schiff preliminary sketches for a cottage. "In his spoiled child
way he didn't get mad or anything," Schiff concluded of FDR, "he just
expected people to do what he told them."

While nudging Schiff to start building, FDR was moving ahead himself in pursuit of a long-held dream, a place where he could retire after
his presidency and write his memoirs. His share of the parcel lay on high
ground above Val-Kill offering a sweeping panorama of the Hudson Valley. He insisted that Toombs shape the house to his physical condition,
everything on one floor, wide doorways with no sills for easy wheelchair
access. He wanted a stove low enough so that he could reach the burn-
ers and make simple dishes himself such as the scrambled eggs he loved.
His mother was puzzled by this latest passion. First Eleanor at Val-Kill,

now Franklin at the place he began calling "Top Cottage." Why were her nearest deserting her? She exacted a promise from Franklin that he would never spend a night in the cottage, and construction began.

Late in 1938, Dorothy Schiff was favored with an invitation, more accurately a summons, to Warm Springs. "You don't say no to the President of the United States," she now accepted. She left in the midst of a dinner for New York mayor Fiorello La Guardia in order to catch a train south. Her husband was delighted with the invitation, though FDR had not included George. She had expected to be staying at Roosevelt's cottage, dubbed by the press "The Little White House." FDR had overseen its construction on the north slope of Pine Mountain affording a sweeping vista of the wooded ravine below. The house had cost him $8,738, and when it was completed, he threw a housewarming party inviting Warm Springs neighbors and rural folk from miles around. Schiff, to her uneasy surprise, learned that she would not be staying in the Little White House but with Toombs. "I didn't really recover until I saw the President in the morning," she admitted. "The minute I set eyes on him I was all right; he was the sun-god again . . . this marvelous, unneurotic and confident man, and he really was that for me."

Though she had become used to seeing Franklin with his disability unconcealed at Hyde Park, she was in for another jolt at Warm Springs. "It threw me a bit to see him in the pool with all those other cripples," she remembered, swimming in his old-fashioned two-piece bathing suit. "Later, his doctor took me for a drive and explained that it was better that way, that together they didn't feel so inferior physically."

On a Saturday afternoon sometime later, back at Hyde Park, Dorothy was picked up by a beaming FDR, who took her in his Ford along a twisting road to the recently completed Top Cottage. The dwelling they came upon reflected the Dutch roots of his beloved Hudson Valley, steeply peaked roofs and fieldstone construction, the stones from the walls of nearby farms. She had brought along as a housewarming gift two Delft ceramic cows. "We got there and we went in," Schiff recalled. "He got into the wheelchair and told me he wanted to show me the bedroom. Secret Service were standing, their backs to us, at the French windows. . . . And I said, nervously, it's very nice." She was worried about "what the President really wanted," and that Eleanor might show up. She retreated to the living room, the president following. "A lot of my friends think I should run for a third term," he said matter-of-factly. "What do you think?" The question, she believed, was out of her league and she answered, "What do you want to do?" She watched him for a time, at the window, lost in thought, gazing across the Hudson River to the Catskill Mountains. "I don't know," he said. "But my friends think I should."

At that moment, Eleanor, who was thought to be in Vermont, did suddenly appear. Franklin greeted her brusquely, Schiff thought. "Why darling, where did you pop up from?" he asked. She was carrying a picnic hamper with cold chicken and wine, and said, "Franklin, I thought maybe you and Dorothy wanted sustenance." Eleanor's arrival sent Schiff mixed signals. She thought the hospitable gesture might indicate Eleanor's approval of her time spent with Franklin. It could also mean she was "confirming her claim on him. I still think she was in love with him in spite of everything."

Top Cottage became only the second home ever designed personally by a president since Thomas Jefferson's Monticello. The hideaway had nine rooms, including three bedrooms and a forty-foot living room with an eighteen-foot cathedral ceiling. The retreat satisfied FDR's quest for simplicity and remoteness. There was no telephone and no formal landscaping, only the wild growth planted by nature. Schiff did eventually build on the land she had reluctantly bought and called her place the Red House. The president came to inspect it, found favor, and took credit for the architecture. He asked what style she considered her new home to be. "Franklin the First," she replied.

It was at Top Cottage on a Sunday afternoon in June 1939 that the Roosevelts served hot dogs at a picnic for the king and queen of England. Just before the arrival of George VI and Elizabeth, Eleanor had written in her "My Day" column, "Oh dear, so many people are worried that the dignity of our country will be imperiled." To FDR's pleasure, the king asked for a second "delightful hot-dog sandwich." Should the humble frank fail to satisfy the royal palate, the Roosevelts had a backup menu of Virginia ham and smoked turkey and strawberry shortcake.

Dorothy Schiff through her frequent visits to Hyde Park eventually learned of the Lucy Mercer romance. One evening while staying at Val-Kill with Nancy Cook and Marion Dickerman she was told how the affair had been discovered, Franklin's plea for a divorce, Eleanor's urging that he consider the effect on their children, and Sara's clinching financial argument that the couple stay together. Of her hostess, Schiff recalled, Nan had "goosed her and then let her alone."

Dorothy Schiff's ultimate opinion of Franklin Roosevelt was ambivalent, even contradictory. She wanted to paint herself as desirable in his eyes, at one point claiming that "he probably saw me as a 'sex object.'" After her divorce from George Backer, her next husband, Theodore Thackeray, the *New York Post* editor, told her that the press believed she had been the president's mistress. "At first I was flattered," she said. She wanted to know, however, what evidence Thackeray had, and he answered, "Well, you're always up there and in that house with him." He then taunted her, asking if that was what she wanted to be remembered as, a president's mistress, and she shot back, "Of course not. I'm better than that." Asked point-blank by Jeffrey Potter, her biographer, if she had loved FDR, she answered, "Of course not. Everybody I knew was so impressed with my relationship with him, I thought I either ought to love him or be in love with him. . . . I liked him very much. He was interesting to me, in many ways and boring a lot of the time. I had known more intellectual and exciting people." She further claimed, "Before long I began to wonder if he was really of first magnitude and if it wasn't merely the sun-god quality." When Potter's biography of her was published in 1976, she complained, "The book was cleverly edited to make it appear that I had an affair with FDR." She had her lawyer, Morris Abram, issue a statement declaring, "She did not ever have and has never claimed to have had an affair with the late President Franklin D. Roosevelt." While dismissing a physical relationship, at another point she noted that FDR "was fairly bold and everything about his body—except for his legs—was so strong."

The Schiff friendship says more about FDR's character than about Schiff's vacillation. Her involvement with him illuminated his egotism, his pleasure in manipulating people, and the man's seductive charm over women despite his physical limitations. She was one among several whose affections he juggled simultaneously, including at this point, besides Schiff, Missy LeHand, Lucy Mercer Rutherfurd, Eleanor, however reluctantly, and others who entered his magnetic field. Schiff's fascination with FDR further displayed the superiority of women in their attitudes toward men in that they consider the whole man, his intelligence, power, humor, and charm as producing attractiveness, not simply physical appeal, an approach that cannot always be said of male attitudes toward women.

*Chapter 28*

# 1941: YEAR OF GAIN, YEAR OF LOSS

· · · · · · ·

THE 1940 PRESIDENTIAL ELECTION was to illuminate two facets of the labyrinthine Roosevelt character, his capacity to perform both as a manipulative pol and as a visionary statesman. With the outbreak of war in 1939, the concern he had expressed in his second inaugural address four years before about Nazi Germany's menace to peace had proven all too prescient. When France fell on June 20, 1940, after only a six-week battle, with Poland, Belgium, Denmark, the Netherlands, and Norway all under the Nazi heel, Roosevelt recognized that Hitler's appetite was still not sated and that as long as it was not, the world was unsafe. Who should lead America through these parlous times? Roosevelt had hinted that at the end of his second term he intended to leave public life and withdraw to Top Cottage. Missy expected that she would go off with him into this sunset and have the first real home of her own. He daydreamed with Harry Hopkins about buying a Florida key and opening a fishing resort. Though accustomed to living high, FDR had little concern about his financial future. He told Jerome Frank, his Securities and Exchange Commission chief, "Jerry, after this crisis is over, do you think either of us will have trouble earning money?" Arguing most formidably against a third term, his leaving the White House would respect a tradition as old as the republic. Only nine presidents had run even for a second term, while twenty-one ran but once.

On June 28, 1940, in Philadelphia, the Republicans nominated a Wall Street utilities lawyer and political neophyte as their presidential candidate. Though untried, Wendell Willkie possessed enormous political potential. The rumpled, six-foot, 220-pound bear of a man, a shock of unruly hair framing a leonine head, exuded unaffected charm backed by brains. Further, Willkie was a liberal Republican who would not frighten

Americans, still reeling from the Depression, by attempting to dismantle the New Deal, which they believed had saved them. Willkie would be, by FDR's own admission, "the most formidable candidate . . . that the Republicans could have named."

With the Democratic nominating convention just over two weeks away, FDR had yet to show his hand. Like a master puppeteer, he remained out of sight and any strings he pulled went unseen. On July 16, at the convention in Chicago Stadium, the chairman, Senator Alben Barkley of Kentucky, rose to announce that he had a message from Roosevelt. He "never had any wish or purpose to remain in the office of President . . . after next January," Barkley reported, and FDR "wanted to make it clear that all the delegates to this convention are free to vote for any candidate." The statement was colossally disingenuous. No sooner had Barkley finished when a sepulchral voice boomed repeatedly from a microphone concealed in the basement reverberating throughout the hall, "We want Roosevelt! We want Roosevelt!" FDR swept to renomination virtually uncontested.

His playacting that he was prepared to give up the role he had been born to perform was Roosevelt at his wiliest. But once embarked on the campaign, he revealed himself at his most fearless as well. Most Americans wanted no part of another European war, believing that the country had been bamboozled into entering the first one. Isolationist sentiment was strong and respectable. Yet, facing an unprecedented third term campaign, Roosevelt dared propose a peacetime draft, to the dismay of his political advisers, who begged him to put off the move at least until after election day. "Any old-time politician would have said [it] could never take place," Sam Rosenman believed. In FDR's priorities, however, the risk of an unprepared America outweighed any threat to his future, and his towering self-confidence persuaded him that he was taking no risk at all. A lukewarm Congress passed the draft. To counteract any impression that he sought war, Roosevelt pledged in a fervent speech at the Boston Garden during the last days of the campaign, "I have said this before, but I shall say it again and again. Your boys are not going to be sent into any foreign wars." Afterward, he told his speechwriter, the playwright Robert Sherwood, "If we're attacked, it's no longer a foreign war."

On election day FDR shattered a century-and-a-half tradition, winning a third term and defeating Willkie by a comfortable five million votes and an electoral college rout of 449 to 82. On January 20, 1941, the newly adopted inaugural date, just as the Supreme Court's chief justice, Charles Evans Hughes, was about to administer the oath of office, Roosevelt whispered under his breath, "I don't know how you feel about this, but I'm getting sick of it."

Among the items Lucy Rutherfurd left upon her death was a coin with FDR in profile on one side and the date on the reverse. It had been given to her as she was driven to the Capitol for the third time to watch Franklin sworn in as president. Lucy's husband, Winthrop, seventy-nine years old now, his health continuing its downward slide, suffered a stroke in the spring of 1941 and another, more devastating, that June. The beau ideal of another age was now a shipwreck, confined to a wheelchair, a lap robe over his bony knees, his right arm all but useless. Lucy brought Winty to Washington where she sought out Franklin's help. FDR arranged for a specialist from Walter Reed Hospital to look after the ailing scion. His impairment had rendered Rutherfurd more cantankerous and fiercely jealous than ever. His wife at fifty was still striking. Montague Blundon, who married Lucy's niece, recalled attending a wedding where the Rutherfurds were present and at which his father nudged him asking, "Who is that magnificent woman?" When painters were redoing a room in one of the Rutherfurd homes, Rutherfurd pounded his cane on the floor and ordered them to keep their eyes on their work and not on his wife. He once fired a footman who dared to swim out to a raft where his daughter was sunning herself.

J. B. West, the White House usher, described in his memoir one of FDR's stratagems for being with Lucy. Accompanied by his Scotch terrier, Fala, and protected by Secret Service agents, the president would ride through the Virginia countryside. There he ordered the driver to turn down a dirt lane, remarking casually, "There seems to be a lady waiting along the road. Let us ask her if she needs a ride." After she had entered the car, the driver was directed to follow a circuitous route to deliver the woman to her destination. After this experience had been repeated several times, the agents began to wonder who the woman was. One of West's assistant ushers asked if he might go along in the backup car to see if he might recognize her. Spotting the usher, the president said cheerily, "I see it's your turn to find out what's going on." FDR's latest bodyguard, Mike Reilly, another loyal, burly, fast-talking Irishman, described a bolder tactic. FDR would simply have his car pull up alongside an auto parked on the Georgetown Road where Lucy would get out of her car and sit beside him. Reilly remembered the mysterious lady as "charming and beautiful." He further recalled of these outings, "The President would return to the White House much relaxed and happy."

In the long ago, when Franklin had been assistant secretary of the navy, he and Lucy had met at Edith Eustis's home in Washington and Oatlands, her country estate near Leesburg, Virginia. Now that he was president, Edith would call him at the White House to say that she had a visitor who was eager to see him. To rendezvous in the country was daring enough; but for the married Lucy, whom Franklin had promised Eleanor never to see again, visiting the White House would require audacity of another order. Nevertheless, FDR was willing to risk it. Though considered relatively robust for a paralyzed man, it is likely that intimations of his own mortality, of opportunities fleeting, emboldened him. He made arrangements for Lucy to come to the White House on June 5, 1941, a visit that Missy LeHand would have had to know about and likely had been told to schedule, for a "Mrs. Paul Johnson." The pseudonym had been resurrected from Lucy's phone calls during the early months of FDR's presidency.

By now, Missy's subordination of self to Franklin was not an act of discipline but her very being. Opportunities to break free had come along. She was a popular guest at Joseph P. Kennedy's palatial estate, Marwood in Maryland, where the former ambassador to Great Britain and father of the future president gathered his Irish Catholic pals, including Missy. There she met attractive and accomplished men. They in turn were drawn to this utterly feminine woman, whose appeal was heightened by her unrivaled access to the president of the United States. At one point, the bachelor prime minister of Canada, Richard Bennett, paid court to her when he came to Washington. William Bullitt became another suitor, desirable from every standpoint, handsome, wealthy, and well born into an old Philadelphia Mainline family. FDR had appointed Bullitt as America's first ambassador to the Soviet Union and subsequently as envoy to France. The man was brash, bullet-headed, dashing, taking a keen pleasure in women and with two marriages already behind him, the second to the beautiful Louise Bryant Reed, widow of the communist writer and romantic John Reed. Bullitt pursued Missy with expensive jewelry and flowers. "He used to call her all the time from Russia," Barbara Curtis recalled, "and when he'd come to

Washington, he'd take her out." The romance advanced far enough for Missy to travel once to Moscow to see Bullitt. After the fall of France, Bullitt was back in Washington and scheming to be appointed to Sumner Welles's job as undersecretary of state. Thus, Bullitt had ample reason to court Missy in a perhaps fortuitous convergence of romance and opportunity. Bullitt's strategy failed, and so did the Missy romance. Some within the Roosevelt circle, among them Henry Morgenthau III, son of the treasury secretary, believed, "Bullitt used her as a way of getting access to FDR. . . . He was a great operator, and he led Missy to believe he would marry her when he never intended to." Barbara Curtis claimed that Bullitt "wanted to marry her, but her attraction to Roosevelt was simply too overpowering." FDR's son Jimmy thought that his father had initially encouraged the match, "feeling I think she had devoted a lot of her life to him and was entitled to a life of her own." He may also have done so in the sure knowledge that Missy would never leave him.

Nothing had really changed in the past twenty years. The young Missy had asked how anyone could measure up to her "FD." But she was now forty-three, a woman with youth fled, past child-bearing age, and continually reminded, as with the imminent visit of Lucy Mercer Rutherfurd, that she was just one woman in the admiring constellation orbiting around Roosevelt. "I don't think she ever felt that she was his great heart's desire," FDR's son Elliott has said. "She was too honest with herself for that."

Another woman had recently been drawn into FDR's circle and affections. As he had said long ago he found nothing more refreshing to the spirit than the company of "a good looking lady." And now, added to that inclination was Roosevelt's weakness for royalty, which explained the entrance into his life of Princess Martha of Norway. With Germany's defeat of the country on June 10, 1940, King Haakon and his son, Prince Olav, Martha's husband, fled to England to establish a government-in-exile. Martha, however, fearing for the safety of her three children, Prince Harold and the princesses Ragnhild and Astrid, sought a haven for them further from danger. The president offered Martha asylum in the United States. The princess and her husband had first visited America the year before to dedicate the Norwegian exhibit at the 1939 World's Fair. During that visit, FDR and his mother invited the royal couple to Hyde Park. Martha's attractiveness to him was not lost on Missy or the rest of the White House staff. The thirty-seven-year-old princess fulfilled all the president's expectations of femininity, statuesque, shapely, fine-boned, with aquiline features and utterly regal. As the reporter Bess Furman described Martha, she looked "exactly as a princess should." Martha also had the lightly worn charm, the easy conversation, and flirtatious eye that enchanted FDR.

After her country's defeat, the princess fled Europe, arriving in New York in September 1940 aboard a transport, the *American Legion*, following a harrowing Atlantic voyage from the Arctic port of Petsamo, Finland. She, the children, lady-in-waiting, court chamberlain, and servants were whisked off to Hyde Park. FDR directed Marion Dickerman to find a home near the estate for the royal exiles, which she halfheartedly attempted to do and failed. Dickerman considered Martha imperious and demanding, remarking, "She never forgot she was the crown princess." The president next brought Martha and her entourage to the White House where she was given the Rose Room suite. She soon became part of FDR's after-hours clique, joining him for cocktails at the end of the day, and taking long drives with him through the countryside. She performed exactly as required, gazing into his eyes adoringly, hanging on his every word. The White House servants found her cloying, as Lillian Parks commented, "putting on a little girl act," as Martha uttered the nickname FDR told her to use, "Dear godfather." Another servant remarked, "It looks like the boss has found a new Missy." Commenting on her father's relationship with Martha, Anna Roosevelt observed, "He loved her and being admired by her." The princess finally left the White House after an estate was found for her, Pook's Hill, near Bethesda, Maryland. "We might go out and have tea with her," Anna remembered. "And he loved this . . . or he would go out alone. I wouldn't go along." She described how "Father and Mother had a completely different way of looking at flirtatiousness. Father became friendly with . . . Princess Martha, he'd reach out and give a pat to her fanny and laugh like hell and was probably telling a funny story at the same time, whereas to Mother this was terrible."

Eleanor had endured for a quarter of a century what she described as the "lovely ladies who worshipped at his shrine." "There was always a Martha for relaxation and for the non-ending pleasure of having an admiring audience for every breath," she told Joe Lash. So natural was the attraction between the man and so many women that while questions may be raised about FDR's sexual capacity from a wheelchair, there is scant reason to believe he would have been a faithful husband if spared polio. As his grandson Curtis Roosevelt phrased it, "My grandmother was addicted to doing the right thing. FDR was not addicted to doing the right thing." Eleanor could live with his dalliances however irritating because she had a life of her own. Missy had no such refuge. FDR was her life. She confided to Dorothy Schiff that she often suffered "nightmares of the President being assassinated."

Every year, Harry Somerville, manager of the Willard Hotel, hosted a dinner for FDR's top staff. In 1941, Somerville decided to hold the event on June 4 and shift it from the Willard to the White House so that the president could attend. Eleanor was away at Hyde Park, and Missy again served as hostess. The servants rolled in a piano and Marvin McIntyre, FDR's appointments secretary, began playing Roosevelt favorites, including "Home on the Range," while guests gathered around and began singing. The president was at his effusive best, though Missy seemed subdued. She had been plagued of late with insomnia and was taking opiates to help her sleep. The woman famed for her composure under the severest stresses had also been bursting into inexplicable fits of temper.

Grace Tully recalled what happened the evening of the Somerville party: "Near the end of the dinner, Missy rose from her chair to tell me she felt ill and very tired. I urged her to excuse herself and go upstairs to bed." But the woman who for twenty years had exhausted herself anticipating FDR's every need refused to break protocol and leave before the president. Roosevelt was finally wheeled off to his bedroom at 9:30 P.M. Within minutes, the guests were jolted by a scream. Missy began swaying and fell to the floor. The president's physician, Admiral McIntire, and Commander George Fox, FDR's physical therapist, who had treated President Wilson after his stroke, carried her to her third floor room where McIntire sedated her. The admiral, a nose and throat specialist, made a spot diagnosis that Missy was exhausted by overwork and needed only to rest. Her slightly slurred speech was explainable by her fatigue.

Lillian Parks remembered the next morning, "when I arrived at the third floor sewing room, across from Missy's suite, a distraught nurse was outside her door. . . . I asked what was wrong, and she told me what had happened and that Missy was refusing to stay in bed. 'She's gotten up and I can't get her back to bed.'. . . . I went in and said sternly, 'Come on, Miss LeHand. Come into bed.' She meekly climbed in, and I stood by her so she wouldn't get up again. Missy held onto me and lay stroking my arm. She was distraught, moaning that her work was piling up. F.D. would be counting on her and she would not be there for him." In a few minutes Admiral McIntire arrived with a second doctor and "stood watching us from the doorway. . . . He too told me what had happened. Then I left to start my own work, across the hall. My mother, Maggie, who had been retired for two years, received a call from Eleanor Roosevelt. 'Missy loved you,' she said, 'would you come back and sit with her at night? She is so lonely.' Mama did not come home at all but stayed at the White House with Missy. Mama came away saying, 'It's sad to love a man so much.' "

The president was informed of what had befallen Missy the night before. The White House log of his movements showed, "11:30 am: To Marguerite LeHand apartment." He came to see Missy again, at 3:55 P.M., at which time the log reported, "Returned from office to study accompanied by Mrs. Paul Johnson." Though under a pseudonym, this was the first recorded visit to the White House by Lucy Mercer Rutherfurd. Eleanor, at the time, was away. When Lucy entered the president's private study, she found a room not unlike the one she had known as a Navy yeomanette twenty-four years before when she visited the office of the assistant secretary: the ever-present ship models and naval prints dominated, the floor a disarray of yellowing sheaves of paper tied with string, book-filled cabinets, and the omnipresent family photos. Looking south, a magnolia planted by Andrew Jackson grew, and across the Ellipse, the Washington Monument could be glimpsed. The idea may well have struck Lucy that, had fate dealt her a different hand, this might now be her home. She stayed an hour and twenty minutes with Franklin, and the president's log then reported: "17:40 to Marguerite LeHand's apartment," the third visit that day.

It is too facile to conclude that because Missy knew Lucy was coming to the White House the next day that this knowledge precipitated what would ultimately be diagnosed as a stroke. Even without Lucy, the preconditions were there for a cerebral episode: a woman who burned herself out working under endless pressure, who smoked up to three packs of cigarettes a day, and who likely had a genetic predisposition to vascular disease. Yet, a clear pattern emerges in Missy's major illnesses. Her two earlier nervous breakdowns and now the stroke occurred in conjunction with shifts in FDR's life interfering with her hold on him— his abandonment of the *Larooco* for Warm Springs, his returning to public life to run for governor of New York, and now the obvious reentry into his life of Lucy Mercer Rutherfurd. Curtis Roosevelt concluded, "I think it's not entirely speculative to tie Missy's eventual breakdowns to her frustration with the fact that she was in love with somebody who was probably not in love with her."

The stroke that felled Missy the evening of June 4 was minor. A clot had likely formed in a chamber of her heart and been carried to her brain where it blocked the flow of oxygen. Seventeen days later, she suffered a massive second stroke, paralyzing her right arm and leg, and largely destroying her power of speech. A Navy ambulance was called to take her off to Doctors Hospital on I Street. She failed to improve and when the hospital staff had done all that could be done, the president arranged to have her sent to the one place where she might find peace, Warm Springs. One day Missy LeHand had been at the epicenter of power, seated at the right hand of the president of the United States. Powerful figures chatted with her at her desk outside FDR's office, hoping to glean the mood of the man they were about to see. In an instant that existence ceased, like a candle blown out, never to be relit.

Three weeks after Lucy's first visit, her eldest stepson, Winthrop Jr., now thirty-seven, was at the White House, reportedly to seek FDR's advice about entering the military, as war loomed from both the Pacific and Atlantic. Whatever crises crowded his agenda, Franklin would find time for her family, as if every encounter somehow kept a part of Lucy close to him.

Ten months before Rutherfurd Jr.'s visit, the president, disregarding neutrality, gave a beleaguered Britain fifty old destroyers, which he did before Congress had a chance to say no. Some six months later, with Prime Minister Winston Churchill warning him that Britain's treasury was empty and "we shall no longer be able to pay cash for shipping and other supplies," the fertile Roosevelt imagination hatched another scheme to help Britain survive. The United States would send Churchill weapons and war matériel without charge. After the war, the British could return them or pay for them, a fanciful likelihood. On March 11, Congress endorsed Roosevelt's initiative, and enacted Lend-Lease.

By August 1, Lucy was back at the White House, still as Mrs. Johnson. She arrived at 8:40 P.M., had dinner alone with the president, and stayed until almost midnight. She was back again the next afternoon at 3:00 P.M. and stayed until 5:30 P.M. On all three occasions Eleanor was out of town. Lucy made another visit on October 22 and by now the ushers had established a routine for handling "Mrs. Johnson's" visits. A government sedan would pick her up, usually at her sister, Violetta's, house, and deliver her to the White House. There, an usher would be waiting to escort her immediately to the president on the second floor living quarters where a butler served tea and then left them alone. She and Franklin would remain undisturbed until he rang for the usher to escort her back to the waiting automobile. On one visit she wore a black ribbon around her neck and the president immediately caught the significance; it was the same fashion touch she had worn in the midst of their early romance.

A week after the October visit, while Eleanor was in Chicago, Lucy's nineteen-year-old daughter, Barbara, was escorted into the president's office. She was pretty, quiet in manner, tutored at home by French governesses and had been raised like a flower in her mother's well-tended garden. A girlhood friend from Aiken, Rosamund Durban McDuffie, described Barbara as "extremely reserved," speaking with a refined mid-Atlantic inflection. "I would invite her to things with me but there were no reciprocal invitations," Rosamund remembered. "I felt it was just a private, close family. As my mother explained it, if you want, invite her and don't expect anything else." As for sports and parties that drew other Aiken youth together, "she didn't participate in any of those." Rosamund recalled of Barbara's mother, "Mrs. Rutherfurd always looked gorgeous. I found her delightful."

Franklin was clearly taken with Barbara and his impressions were reported in a letter to Lucy discovered among family papers nearly sixty-five years later. "The littlest Babs," he calls the girl, and says she is all he had dreamed. He reports that they had lunch together, and he makes a point of noting that Barbara was neither worried nor nervous, as if they had known each other for years. The president adds in his bold longhand that Barbara would be coming to see him again soon and he makes a veiled reference to their having a conspiracy between themselves about her mother. The letter, just as those he had written Lucy in the 1920s, included an itinerary of the specific dates for a visit to Hyde Park, then back to the White House, and when he will be making a ten-day trip out of Charleston, South Carolina, to the Bahamas. He closed with a veiled hint of long-ago intimacy, "I do remember the times—so well—a toujours et toujours." He signed the letter simply, "F." The White House visit by Barbara, while the first occasion FDR had met with the girl personally, had not been their first contact. Two years before, for her debut, he had sent her an aquamarine stone from a Roosevelt family necklace, which she had set in a ring. On another occasion, FDR invited Barbara to join him for dinner with Harry Hopkins, now living at the White House, while Eleanor was on the West Coast. The White House was not the only place Franklin met with Rutherfurds. Barbara told the writer Jonathan Daniels about "happy visits with her mother to various places where Roosevelt was staying. He treated her as a well loved child."

Some observers of FDR, in defiance of the laws of biology, were bent on making the relationship closer. Jonathan Daniels, in a letter to Roosevelt biographer Frank Freidel, raised the possibility of Barbara being FDR's offspring. "When I talked to that child several years ago," he wrote, "she rather gave the impression that she thought so too." However, at the time Barbara would have been conceived, Franklin Roosevelt was in the early throes of infantile paralysis and near death. And in a letter to another FDR biographer, Bernard Asbell, Daniels admitted that he had searched out but "I could not see any resemblance between [Barbara] and the President." He further reported that he spoke with Raymond Corry, a former director of the museum at the Roosevelt Library, who indignantly insisted that the rumors had it all wrong. Barbara Rutherfurd was FDR's "goddaughter," not his daughter. In the end, Daniels concluded that rumors about FDR's fathering Barbara were "preposterous."

For FDR, 1941 would prove to be a year of personal gains and losses, of fragile peace and sudden war. Lucy was back in the fold, however intermittently. Missy appeared to have been removed permanently. His mother, Sara, now in her eighties, remained a commanding presence in his life. The curvaceous "Sallie" of her youth had thickened through the middle, her lustrous hair had turned white, accenting the black and white fashions she favored. Her face, grown broader through the years, resembled more than ever the great handsome head of her son. His flashing smile, now known throughout the world, had also been her bequest to him. Whenever he returned to Hyde Park, she would be waiting at the door, her posture still queenly, her eyes brimming with adoration. "I know I am getting old and will have to die someday," she told a friend, "but I hope it won't be while Franklin is in office. When I die, he will feel so bad, and if it is while he is in office, it will upset him for his duties, and I don't want to be the cause of that." She still seemed to regard him not so much as a world figure, but as the schoolboy son, always at the top of his class, doing his parents proud. When a sister was stranded in Europe at the outbreak of war in 1939, she could not understand why Franklin did not simply send one of his warships to fetch her. At a lunch at Hyde Park, a visitor turned to Eleanor and asked, "Mrs. Roosevelt, what is the President going to do about the budget?" Before she could answer, Sara broke in, "Budget? . . . Franklin knows nothing about the budget. I always manage the budget." And indeed, through the trust she still held Franklin's purse strings.

By now, Eleanor's reaction to Sara's absolute pronouncements wearied rather than upset her. Her mother-in-law was a cross to be borne with dutiful resignation, but it was too late for affection. In recent years writers on the Roosevelts have sought to moderate the impression of Sara as overbearing. As distinguished a historian as David McCullough has found her "considerably more appealing and admirable than is generally understood," the unflattering portrayal, he notes, being based "on the view point of her daughter-in-law, Eleanor." Sara was indeed a woman of great charm, intelligence, and a royal air to most who knew her. But Eleanor's attitude is understandable. Sara had been a near impossible mother-in-law, and as a grandmother, her overindulgence of the children created constant family friction. When Franklin Jr., while a student at Groton, wrecked a small, cheap car, his parents decided he would have to grow up before he could have another. Young Franklin simply turned to Granny, who promptly bought him a new, bigger, more expensive car. His parents complained but, as Eleanor resignedly recalled, "She never heard anything she did not want to hear." Curtis Roosevelt has told of his mother, Anna, while living in Seattle, getting a letter from Eleanor about a forthcoming Christmas visit from Sara. "She wrote my mother, how long are you going to be able to put up with her, one week, two weeks?" Sara had become "a legitimate object of hostility," in Curtis's interpretation, adding, "I use that term because it has a very specific meaning from a psychological viewpoint, meaning when you have fingered somebody who it is legitimate to be hostile to."

Back in September, Eleanor had felt duty-bound to return to Hyde Park. Her mother-in-law had suffered a stroke the previous June, was steadily failing, and Eleanor wanted to make sure she was being well cared for. One morning at breakfast, noting the old woman's ashen pallor and labored breathing, she phoned Franklin at the White House and urged him to come at once. He boarded an overnight train while Eleanor assured Sara that her son would soon be with her. The old woman's eyes lit up and she announced, "I will be downstairs on the porch to meet him."

At 9:30 A.M. on September 6, a Saturday, Franklin made the familiar drive to the house, but Sara was not there to greet him. She would never rise from her bed again. On September 7, this redoubtable woman died, two weeks before her eighty-seventh birthday. Franklin was at her bedside, holding her hand. In a finale that even the purplest novelist would not have dared, within minutes of her death, one of the great oaks at Hyde Park came crashing down. An awed FDR had himself wheeled out to see where the felled giant had been torn from the earth. Elliott Roosevelt remembered, after his grandmother died, that Franklin had gone through her possessions: "Father came across some carefully labeled packages containing his baby clothes and dozens of mementos of his childhood. He wept when he found them."

After Sara's death, Eleanor wrote her daughter a painfully honest letter. For public consumption, she had said in her "My Day" column immediately after Sara died that she had gazed upon the woman's face, "with all the lines smoothed out and the stark beauty of contour," and saw "the rich, full, confident life" Sara had lived. "She had seen her only son inaugurated as President three times and still felt that her husband was the most wonderful man she had ever known." The phrase "Grande Dame," Eleanor concluded, "was truly applicable to her." This observation was the fair-minded, insightful Eleanor. But an inner Eleanor could not subdue the accumulated hurt of decades. "I couldn't feel any emotion or any real grief or sense of loss," she told Anna, "and that seemed terrible after 36 years of close association." Dutiful to the last, she attended to all the funeral arrangements.

Eleanor's ordeal was not yet ended. On the very day that Sara died, she learned that her beloved brother, Hall Roosevelt, had collapsed, a misfortune but hardly a surprise. Though brilliant, a Phi Beta Kappa at Harvard, and for a time successful in business and government posts, Hall had become, in the footsteps of his father, a hopeless alcoholic driven to outrageous behavior. Earlier, his sister had found him a small place to live near the main house at Hyde Park. He further enjoyed the selfless attentions of his mistress, Zena Raset, a White Russian emigrée. Hall, however difficult, was family and Sara occasionally invited him to Sunday dinner. Zena Raset never set foot in her home. As a friend observed, "it's always the woman who pays." Hall Roosevelt died at age fifty of cirrhosis of the liver.

While unmoved by her mother-in-law's death, Eleanor was grief-stricken by Hall's end. She had spent the final days of his life sitting at his bedside in a hospital, sleeping in her clothes. As she watched him gasping for breath, struggling to speak, she thought, "This was the little boy I played with and scolded, he could have been so much and this is what he is." She found losing Hall "like losing a child." The adjacent deaths of a mother and a brother prompted long dormant warmth between Franklin and Eleanor. "She showed him more affection when his mother died," Jimmy Roosevelt recalled. When she went to FDR with the news that " 'Hall has died,' Father struggled to her side and put his arm around her."

Within four days of his mother's death, FDR was back at the White House, his face drawn, his voice somber; on the right arm of his seer-sucker jacket he wore a black band. Though still in mourning, Roosevelt could not resist an opportunity to host royals. He had nothing but disdain for the defeatist, pro-German attitudes of the Duke of Windsor, who had abdicated as Britain's King Edward VIII to marry the American divorcée Wallis Simpson. Yet with all his other appointments canceled because Eleanor's brother had died the day before, FDR nevertheless made time to entertain the duke and his duchess at lunch, then took them on a personal tour of the White House upstairs living quarters. Privately FDR still referred to the former monarch as "Little Windsor," and held no serious conversation with him. Yet he would have the duke to the White House or Hyde Park eight more times during his presidency. At nine that evening he was wheeled before a microphone in the East Room for a fireside chat, arousing the American people with a not wholly accurate accusation that a German submarine had attacked a U.S. Navy destroyer, the USS *Greer*, without justification.

Not long after Sara's death, Eleanor had another reminder of her mother-in-law's domination removed from her life. Franklin sold to Hunter College the twin townhouses on East 65th Street. The address held a sharp, stabbing memory, since it was in a bedroom on Sara's side that Eleanor had discovered the packet of letters from Lucy to Franklin. The place further recalled her husband's earliest desperate search for treatment that might halt the crippling effects of polio. On moving day she and Franklin moved through the home for the last time, circling packing crates and barrels. The house had been Sara's wedding gift to the young bride, and Eleanor associated it with the woman's intrusiveness and possessiveness. "Many human emotions have been recorded by many people within the walls of these rooms," she later wrote, "and if walls could talk, an interesting book might be written."

Difficult as a mother-in-law, pampering as a grandmother, Sara Delano Roosevelt had nevertheless been a magnificent mother. Franklin, after her death, claimed, "What vitality I have is not inherited from the Roosevelts. . . . Mine, such as it is, comes from the Delanos." She had further conditioned him to having women surround him to whom he was the sun and they were his planets. The journalist and political commentator Dorothy Thompson captured the gift the mother had given her son. In the midst of his burdens, Thompson wrote, "she kept a place apart, full of memories and traditions of a quieter age, to which he flew for refuge." She concluded, "No one will ever be able to estimate the place of this woman in American history." Though she had almost died doing so, Sara had given the world Franklin Roosevelt. All else could be forgiven.

Events that fall of 1941 were to illustrate how the president relieved the crushing burdens he bore through pleasurable distractions. On the weekend of October 24–25, days after the hard-line general Hideki Tojo became Japan's prime minister, boosting the odds of war, FDR invited Princess Martha to Hyde Park. Eleven days later, on November 5, military code breakers delivered to the White House a message intercepted from the Japanese foreign office to Japan's embassy in Washington classified "of utmost secrecy." It warned ominously that an agreement had to be signed by November 25 (later updated to the 29th), when "things are automatically going to happen." The day following Japan's threatening message Martha was again with FDR for dinner, this time at the White House, and stayed until almost midnight. She was there for lunch on November 15, after which the president had an Army projectionist run the new Walt Disney movie, *Dumbo*, for the two of them.

Two visits from Lucy were sandwiched in between the princess's visits. Lucy had been to the White House with Barbara in tow four days after the disturbing Japanese cipher, and stayed on by herself for a quiet dinner with the president. She was back again the next night, after a hectic day during which FDR had been tied up preparing an order that major dams, bridges, harbors, and power stations be protected against sabotage. As on all the previous occasions, whether involving the princess or Lucy, Eleanor was out of town usually conducting business on FDR's behalf.

Roosevelt's ability to switch gears effortlessly astonished Sam Rosenman. After a daring speech earlier in the year before the Pan American Union calling for the United States to provide every assistance to Britain short of war, FDR returned to the White House to find the songwriter Irving Berlin waiting to see him. Brushing aside the gravity of the day, he sat the composer down at a piano and requested his first hit, "Alexander's Ragtime Band," followed by an impromptu concert of other Berlin favorites. "The President was able to relax completely, or the job would have killed him," Rosenman noted. The playwright and occasional speechwriter Robert Sherwood found, "Although crippled physically and prey to various infections, [FDR] was spiritually the healthiest man I have ever known. He was gloriously happily free from the various forms of psychic maladjustment."

Princess Martha's visits involved no subterfuge. But the spiritual refreshment that Lucy's visits provided FDR could only be enjoyed through the complicity of others. A handicapped man living in the White House, surrounded by assistants, and tended round-the-clock by servants, could have few secrets. Secret Service agents tracked his every move. His phone calls to arrange the time and place for "Mrs. Johnson" to be picked up for country rides or White House visits had to be put through by staff operators. Secretaries had to carve out time in his schedule to see her. Government drivers had to pick her up. Valets led her to the president's private quarters. Some of Lucy's visits were so closely timed that, in one instance, Eleanor was leaving the White House for New York at 4:30 in the afternoon while Lucy arrived at 5:30. On another occasion, Eleanor popped in after returning from out of town, then left again at 4:35 P.M., while Lucy arrived in time for tea with FDR an hour later. The closeness of the comings and goings suggested the banging doors in a French bedroom farce. The grace and elegance of the mysterious visitor, however, seemed to immunize her from criticism by FDR's staff. On one early visit by Lucy a valet told Lillian Parks, "Oh my, I have just delivered a lovely lady to the President's room." A Secret Service agent in on the arrangements described Lucy as "ladylike to her toes."

The conspiracy of silence was designed to protect two people. The American public must not know that their president was frequently in the company of an attractive married woman cloaked under a false identity who saw the president only when the first lady was absent. The other person protected was Eleanor. Those who served her understood, through the president's contrivances, that the presence of this woman in his life would pain and humiliate her. And so the furtive arrangements went on and Eleanor was never to be the wiser as long as Franklin lived.

Franklin and Lucy met, they spoke on the phone in French, and they wrote each other. One letter from her, undated, but written in the months before Pearl Harbor, began with the disclaimer, "This kind of letter is best unwritten and unmailed, and poor darling, to give you one more thing to read on or think about is practically criminal." She wrote in a stream of consciousness as thoughts popped into her head and in a bold, confident hand not unlike Franklin's. As FDR faced the mounting likelihood of war, she said, "Day by day the news becomes increasingly ominous and complex." She condemned the apathy she found in the country, "Living as we do here, in a community of pleasure seekers, who cannot see further than the glasses in their hands." She passed along thumbnail appraisals of people possibly useful to Franklin. Writing of Bethlehem Steel's Eugene Grace, she offered to check into his loyalty to the administration. "I can easily find out. He has always seemed to be clever. Nonetheless, I wouldn't trust him around the corner. I imagine he has the arrogance of the self-made man." She informed Franklin that the ablest man she knew was George Mead of the Mead Corporation. "I always feel he could be a help to you in some capacity as an ironer-outer of sorts. . . . You might get Harry Hopkins to bring him to lunch with you sometime." She sought Franklin's counsel on family matters. "I should like to ask your advice about my youngest step-son [Guy Rutherfurd] who is studying law at the University of Virginia. . . . He wonders if it would be more interesting and better training for him to take a job in Washington perhaps with a political slant to it, or go immediately into estate work where his cousin . . . has offered him a job."

The last passage of the letter was redolent of nostalgia and vanished dreams. She mentioned that she had a bad cold, adding playfully, "caught on the telephone." The woman who had lived for the past twenty years in unimaginable luxury suggested that a return to "a horse and buggy era . . . won't break my heart. . . . A small house would be a joy and one could grow vegetables as well as flowers or instead of . . ." Here her thought trailed off unfinished. She had recently seen a newspaper photograph of Franklin that alarmed her by his appearance, "what my colored man here would call 'tired, tired, till yet.' " Finally, she confronted the price his stature had exacted from them in personal happiness. "I know one should be proud, very proud of your greatness, instead of wishing for the soft life, of joy—and the world shut out." But she found "the fate of all that is good is in your (undecipherable) capable hands." She closed, "As Ever, LMR."

The letter offers a rare opportunity to hear the woman's voice, how she thought, how she expressed herself, her judgments of people and events. It makes clear her political sophistication, the almost familial tone their relationship had taken, and the love that endured despite separations and competing obligations. One of Lucy's grown-up stepchildren once asked her outright, "I have heard that Franklin Roosevelt was in love with you. Was that true?" She made no denial but tactfully left the question unanswered.

At the time she resumed contact with Franklin at the White House, Lucy was fifty, still attractive; he was fifty-nine and permanently disabled. They were often alone together for hours. Doris Kearns Goodwin, in her Pulitzer Prize–winning story of Eleanor and Franklin, *No Ordinary Time*, discreetly suggests that while FDR and Lucy "did not share the same bed, it is reasonable to imagine that there was a pleasing sexuality in their friendship." However that observation may translate, it is clear that love can take many forms. If the relationship was simply the shared companionship of old friends, why all the machinations to conceal it? There clearly remained between Franklin and Lucy a continuing physical attraction, however expressed. After the president died, Betsey Cushing Roosevelt, Jimmy's first wife, visited Aiken and claimed that Lucy told her "although she loved Winthrop Rutherfurd and owed him much, Franklin Roosevelt had nonetheless been the love of her life."

Toward the end of November 1941, with tensions in the Pacific mounting, the president risked a brief getaway to Warm Springs to celebrate a belated Thanksgiving with fellow polio victims. As though there was nothing else on his mind, he regaled his guests over turkey and pumpkin pie with stories of Thanksgivings past. Missy was also there where Franklin had sent her, and her presence hung like a cloud over the holiday. FDR, a man who shrank from sickness, had again to confront the broken figure who had once been so close to him. He had taken Grace Tully along on the trip to act as something of a buffer. As he was wheeled into Missy's cottage, she lurched toward him, one leg in a brace, and leaning on a crutch. She could manage a few tortured words. Egbert Curtis, now managing Warm Springs, described the stiffness of the scene. "You had to have at least two people so you could talk across Missy to the other person. . . . She could only participate by listening, maybe by small signs of her face. And you know, people who have had strokes are very prone to cry easily." Soon, the larger world intruded. Secretary of War Henry Stimson phoned urging the president to get back to Washington at once. A Japanese attack, somewhere, appeared imminent.

*Chapter 29*

# MISSY PROTECTED, LUCY INDULGED, ELEANOR OUTRAGED

· · · · · · ·

IT WAS A DAY DESTINED to be the darkest in America since Abraham Lincoln had watched the Union disintegrate eighty years before. The morning started off serenely. Pealing bells from St. John's Church on Lafayette Square across from the White House summoned worshippers to Sunday services. The sky shone bright blue, the temperature a bracing 43 degrees, drawing hardy golfers out to Burning Tree and other Washington links. FDR had on his schedule only a perfunctory visit from the Chinese ambassador, Hu Shih. The rest of the day he intended to devote to his passion since age eight, his stamp collection. The hobby had flourished since he had become president. Mail from all over the world poured into the State Department, and every Saturday, a messenger delivered a batch of the most interesting issues to the White House. The president polished off the Hu Shih visit in his private study in classic Roosevelt style, monopolizing a half hour conversation so that the ambassador listened, then left, given little time to say anything.

With Hu Shih gone, FDR summoned Harry Hopkins, his alter ego, now living next to the Lincoln Study, to join him for lunch. They ate off trays, the president's set in a removable rack attached to his homemade wheelchair. Both stabbed desultorily at the food prepared by the White House chef, Henrietta Nesbitt, described by Jimmy Roosevelt as "the worst cook I have ever encountered." After lunch, Hopkins stretched out on a couch, while the president leafed through his stamp album, munching an apple, their conversation bantering and inconsequential. At 1:47, a ringing phone shattered the silence. The White House operator apologized for intruding but explained that the secretary of the navy, Frank Knox, insisted on speaking to the president. "Put him on," FDR said, adopting his reflexive genial manner. "Mr. President," Knox said, his voice choking, "it looks as if the Japanese have bombed Pearl Harbor!" "No!" Roosevelt gasped.

Soon, grim-faced generals, admirals, and staff aides began streaming into the study to update the president on the dimensions of the catastrophe. Roosevelt summoned congressional leaders and cabinet officers for an 8:30 briefing that evening. On their arrival, they began filling seats set in a semicircle around FDR's desk. The president looked ashen but composed. Eleanor had long since observed of her husband that "His reaction to any great event was always to be calm. If it was something bad, he just became almost like an iceberg, and there was never the slightest emotion that was allowed to show." FDR began reciting the inventory of destruction. "It looks as if out of eight battleships, three have been sunk and possibly a fourth," he said. "I have no word on Navy casualties, which will undoubtedly be very heavy." The chairman of the Senate Foreign Relations Committee, Tom Connally, banged his fist on the president's desk. How could it have happened that the ships "were caught like lame ducks?" Connally demanded. "I don't know, Tom," FDR answered. "I just don't know."

Near ten o'clock that evening, a harried Grace Tully took a phone call. From the garbled mutterings at the other end she was able to make out that it was Missy calling from Warm Springs. Tully hesitantly handed the preoccupied president a note. "Missy telephoned and wanted to talk with you," it read. "She is thinking about you and much disturbed about the news. She would like you to call her tonight. I told her you would if the conference broke up at a reasonable hour—otherwise you would call her in the morning." He did not call her that night nor the next morning. Over two weeks later, on Christmas Day, Eleanor asked Franklin if he had talked to Missy. No, he had not, he answered irritably and did not plan to do so. Her grandson Curtis remembered Eleanor telling the tale years later. "She was still shocked."

Days later, one of Missy's relatives wrote the president, "She started crying New Year's Eve about 11:30 and we couldn't stop her, and then she had a heart spell and kept calling 'F.D. come, please come. Oh, F.D.' It really was the saddest thing I ever hope to see. . . . She was especially expecting you to call on Christmas day, and when we sat down to dinner, her eyes filled with tears." Whether or not Roosevelt responded to this letter is unknown. What is known is that during the holiday season, the

Warm Springs medical director, Dr. C. E. "Ed" Irwin, was wakened after midnight and asked to come immediately to Missy's cottage. He dressed hurriedly and did not return until dawn. "I don't know what I'm going to do about Missy," he told his wife, Mabel. "I think she tried to kill herself tonight."

LeHand was brought back to the White House on March 18, 1942, to her old suite on the third floor, tended by round-the-clock nurses. The doctors hoped the familiar surroundings might trigger her recovery. A speech therapist was engaged to help this once articulate woman learn words by constant repetition as if she were a baby. Her progress was dismal. Franklin visited Missy's room, steeling himself by putting on his most winning smile, wheeling his chair in and unraveling a string of amusing anecdotes from the day's events. Nothing remotely resembling conversation took place as Missy struggled to get out an occasional syllable. Then tears would well up in her eyes and her face took on an expression of hopeless melancholy. FDR found the visits emotionally draining and after a few minutes he would wheel himself out with a forced, "See ya tomorrow." "He didn't like weepy women," his grandson Curtis observed. "He was turned off by people who could no longer fit into his game." Grace Tully, who had replaced Missy, loyally sought to pique her friend's interest by showing her secret White House cables. "I wanted her to feel that she was keeping up with things," Tully explained, "I don't know how much she took in." Though she could not get the words out, her mind still hungered for expression. She spent hours dashing off letters to old friends, her thoughts twisted by the damaged circuitry of her brain. "The letters told of this one being in love with her, and that one wanting to marry her," a life existing only in her fantasies, the president's daughter, Anna, observed.

Given FDR's seeming detachment toward someone once so central to his existence, the temptation is to dismiss him as cold, calculating, and exploitive. A pattern does emerge suggesting a shallowness in his emotional attachments as when he considered marriage to several young women over a short period when he was a student at Harvard, followed later by his expedient handling of the Lucy affair when it threatened his fortune and his political future, and now by his pro forma attentions to the stricken Missy. Colleagues, so used to seeing Missy inseparably at his side, judged him harshly. "It seemed only that he resented her for being sick and leaving him in the lurch," Eliot Janeway, a New Deal economic adviser, concluded. "He had ceased to be a person; he was simply the President. If something was good for him as President, it was good." Harold Ickes, the secretary of the interior, studied an unruffled FDR at a cabinet meeting and subsequently wrote in his diary, "I felt a clear conviction that I had lost my affection for him . . . despite his very pleasant and friendly personality, he is as cold as ice inside." FDR might miss a Harry Hopkins or a Missy, Ickes concluded, but not "for a long period. When Louis Howe died, so far as appearances, the President was not noticeably affected, although no one has ever had a more devoted friend than Louis Howe." It was not that Roosevelt trampled unfeelingly over people. Rather, a man who had undergone a staggering physical blow himself might well reason, it happened to me; I got on with my life. So must others. His psychological shield, blotting out unpleasantness, had served him well and he could not abandon it, even for Missy LeHand. FDR was no ordinary mortal but a leader whose thinking and decisions affected the destiny of a nation. Since Missy's stroke, he had been confronted with the debacle of Pearl Harbor, Germany's declaration of war on the United States, and the consequent necessity for him to marshal the strength of the country to fight this two-front war, as defeat followed defeat in the early months of 1942.

In arriving at a final judgment of Roosevelt's treatment of Missy, the truest measure is not necessarily what he felt, or could not feel, but what he did. Missy's salary over the years had risen to $5,000 annually. But now, with her income stopped and facing heavy medical expenses, this severely incapacitated woman was left with only meager savings. FDR's gross estate was by now just under $2 million, and apart from his personal extravagances, Warm Springs most notably, he was something of a penny-pincher. Yet he called in Basil O'Connor, his onetime law partner and now president of the Warm Springs Foundation, for lunch and stunned him with what he had in mind. He was already meeting all of Missy's current expenses, but what if he should die? He told O'Connor that he intended to change his will to leave half of his estate to Missy to make sure she never lacked for care. Eleanor was to get the other half. He told his son Jimmy, "Some may try to make something of that. They shouldn't, but they will. If it embarrasses Mother, I'm sorry. . . . [Missy] served me so well for so long and asked so little in return." LeHand's share was to be carved out of what would otherwise have gone to his five children. O'Connor argued that such a will amounted to disinheritance.

Roosevelt took a pragmatic view. Missy could no longer look after herself; his children should be able to do so. Furthermore, he arranged the will so that upon Missy's death, her portion would revert to them.

He met Missy's material needs, but he could not meet this crippled, rudderless woman's emotional hungers. Her return to the seat of power failed in its therapeutic objective. She only became more acutely aware of her uselessness. "There was nothing for her to do," Grace Tully observed. "She was getting depressed." The White House maid, Lillian Parks, claimed that while Missy was there she had tried to set herself on fire. FDR, Eleanor, and the doctors decided that it was best to return her to Somerville to live with a sister, Ann Rochon. Missy meekly submitted. Before she left, Franklin stopped by to say goodbye, then returned for cocktails and dinner with Princess Martha and Harry Hopkins. At 7:00 P.M. Missy was bundled into a waiting car and left the White House never to return.

FDR had depended vitally on Missy for nearly twenty years, taking almost for granted her capabilities, companionship, humor, above all the unstinting love that consumed her life in meeting his wishes. Now she was gone, leaving a void. In a remarkable turnabout, he looked to Eleanor, after their long emotional estrangement, to fill that empty place. According to Jimmy, his father wanted her "to be his wife again in all respects. . . . He had always said she was the most remarkable woman he had ever known, the smartest, the most intuitive, the most interesting." Couldn't Eleanor cut back on her peregrinations, spend more time with him, become his hostess? Franklin pleaded. To Eleanor what he was proposing was the wish so long denied that by now it had grown stale and without savor. Too many memories had to be erased, too many hurts forgiven, too much of the freedom and self-confidence she had won in remaking herself would have to be surrendered for her to be again what he wanted.

They went on as before. The author Louis Adamic deftly captured the woman she had become after a dinner at the White House. "Upper class by birth, she's a good deal like a peasant woman. Big, strong, down to earth," Adamic wrote. "Awkward at first glance, but if one studies her, really graceful, agile. . . . She is endowed with immense energy and drive. Those large hands of hers, with that old-fashioned ring. They mean business. . . . She's out for results—not to enhance her own standing or her own ego, but because she believes the results she's after are the right ones."

Even before Pearl Harbor, three of FDR's four sons were already in uniform, James in the Marine Corps, Franklin Jr. in the Navy serving aboard destroyers, Elliott a pilot in the Army Air Corps, while John enlisted in the Navy soon after the war began. Lucy now started to use her influence over Franklin to get for her stepsons, all eager to serve, the branch they wanted. At her request, Franklin agreed to see the youngest, Guy Rutherfurd, a fellow student and shooting partner of Franklin Jr.'s at the University of Virginia Law School. The intervention worked. Young Rutherfurd received a Navy commission. "Dear Mr. President," he wrote in the summer of 1942, "At your suggestion I stayed in Charlottesville long enough to get my law degree and then get through the New York Bar exams. I was so glad to see [that] Franklin . . . also passed the exams." The president helped the Princeton boxer, John Rutherfurd, obtain a Navy commission too, telling him to be patient about getting into the fighting. "My Johnny is furious," he wrote young Rutherfurd, "because he applied for duty on an aircraft carrier and instead was made a supply officer!" Another Rutherfurd brother, Hugo, bridled at shore duty, and through Lucy's intercession was able to call on the president. Soon afterward, Admiral McIntire, the White House physician, received a call from FDR to arrange sea duty for Rutherfurd. Lucy's eldest stepson, Winthrop Jr., who had already visited the president before the war, had three subsequent meetings at the White House. While it is unknown if any son of Winthrop Rutherfurd Sr. ever voted for a Democratic candidate, FDR never failed to come through for them.

Lucy's daughter, Barbara, continued in the president's affections. She received a telegram at Allamuchy from FDR telling her, "It is today even more essential that you stop in Washington to visit your godfather." Barbara had been eager to contribute to the war effort, and during the visit mentioned that she had volunteered for the Red Cross. The president picked up the phone and put through a call summoning the organization's director to the White House. "I want you to meet somebody who works for you," he said. On his arrival, the director asked what her job was and Barbara answered, "I'm a file clerk."

In March 1942, Lucy wrote Franklin seeking help for a boy named Gerald, the grandson of an English friend, Camilla Lippincott. Gerald at the time was a student in the United States. He "will be 15 in August and is anxious to join the British Navy for which he must pass his examinations at 16," Lucy told FDR. "If you could do anything to get him a place on any plane about that time, it would be wonderful." She closed, "I know you haven't time for long letters, so this must be brief . . . but it brings you—as always—my love." Gerald's best recommendation, which Lucy did not fail to mention, was that he, like FDR, was a Grotonian.

The most curious wartime adventure between Lucy and the president followed her visit to the White House on October 20, 1942. Three days after Lucy's visit the president summoned the FBI director, J. Edgar Hoover. The dour Hoover and the effervescent Roosevelt made an unlikely partnership, but both shared something akin to paranoia over fifth columnists infiltrating the country. FDR greeted "Edgar" with outstretched arms and a dazzling smile that seemed to say he had been waiting all day just to see him. Hoover reveled in his rapport with FDR and liked to boast, "I was very close to Franklin Delano Roosevelt personally and officially." This day, the president told Hoover that he had intelligence from a reliable source that something suspicious was going on in New Jersey. His information, he said, had come to him from a friend in New York City who had it from an eyewitness, thus he was instinctively employing the age-old espionage gambit, the cutout. As FDR explained, the witness was driving in New Jersey from Andover to Sparta and had turned down a dirt road for a better view of Lake Perona. The car was stopped by an "Italian-appearing individual," who told the driver in a heavy accent to turn around and get back to the main road. Before leaving, however, the informant made other observations. Standing by a parked car was a "very German looking" man who kept staring. Some sort of suspicious construction was also underway and a German-American Bund camp, called Nordlund, had operated near this site before the war. As Hoover left, the president handed him a penciled map that he had drawn himself of the area in question.

Hoover, ever eager to please FDR, immediately dispatched a senior FBI agent to New Jersey to investigate. As the agent dug into the case, the story began to unfold. The eyewitness, driven by her chauffeur and accompanied by her invalid husband and his nurse, a stepson, and daughter, had indeed gone down the dirt road to catch a better glimpse of the lake situated on farmland owned by a John Perona, whose family was described by neighbors as all "loyal Americans." The suspicious construction was a culvert being built to drain a field. The Italian-appearing individual was a gardener who could barely speak English and who had tried to warn the party to turn back because the construction blocked the road. The Nordlund Bund camp had been empty for years. The source of FDR's intelligence, the agent informed Hoover, was a Mrs. Winthrop Rutherfurd, who lived on an estate in Allamuchy township.

Hoover reported the findings, not directly to FDR, but tactfully to the president's aide, General Pa Watson. He made clear that his agent had gathered the evidence through third parties. "No contact," he told Watson, "was made with Mrs. Rutherfurd because her name was not given to me by the President and I gathered that it was not desired that it become known who may have been the original informant in this matter." Watson passed Hoover's report along to the president. FDR showed it to Lucy on her next visit and she complained of inaccuracies. Since no reason now existed to pretend to Hoover that the Perona informant was anyone but Lucy, FDR insisted that she be interviewed personally to get the facts straight. Hoover again dispatched his agent, but not a word Mrs. Rutherfurd said materially altered the truth. Nothing remotely resembling sabotage had gone on at the site in question. Hoover, however, who maintained dossiers on Washington's prominent and powerful, now had proof that the president still saw his long-ago love. While the files of FBI investigations are customarily meticulously kept, no document exists at the FBI regarding Franklin and Lucy's spy caper, the record possibly destroyed at Franklin's request or filed in Hoover's personal "Do Not File" file. The misleading designation meant that such information was not to be placed in the FBI's regular archives, but to be kept in the director's office for his personal use.

In the midst of war, the stuff of daily life, love affairs, friendships, and rivalries, went on. After taking a job as executive director of the Women's Division of the Democratic National Committee, Lorena Hickok moved back into the White House in 1941. A year later, she was still there. Tommy Thompson, Eleanor's secretary, told Esther Lape, "The ushers call her the enduring guest. . . . She can't pay rent and her income tax and her dentist bill, so she has cut out paying rent." By now, Thompson had reason to regret the long-ago role she had played in bringing Hickok into Eleanor's life. She was intent on protecting the first lady from indiscretions by someone whom she regarded as a sentimental blabbermouth. "One night when Hickok was rather mellow and ranting on about how she adored Mrs. Roosevelt etc.," Tommy told Lape, "she said that if anything happened to her I was delegated to destroy all the letters which Mrs. R. had written her. . . . I did not add that I had already made up my mind on that score."

Eleanor was too softhearted to deliver a coup de grâce to a relationship that had once mattered so much in her life, but had now grown tedious. Whenever she could make time, she invited Hick to her study to have breakfast with her. Though still lovelorn, Hick recognized that Eleanor had traveled well beyond her. "I'd never have believed it possible to develop after 50 as you have in the last six years," she noted on one occasion, and added with resignation, "my trouble, I suspect has always been that I've been so much more interested in the <u>person</u> than in the <u>personage</u>." Eleanor, the "person," had loved Lorena Hickok, but the "personage" lacked time to satisfy Hickok's cloying needs. She was relieved when a new visitor began showing up for Hick at the White House gate. The woman was Marion Janet Harron, a judge in the U.S. Tax Court, ten years younger than Hick and her latest passion.

Hick's lost love had indeed become a world figure. Eleanor's schedule was now so full that her own children had to make appointments to see her. "Let a good cause raise its head," her son James remarked, "and Mother came running." She had become a subject of such intense interest that eventually she would produce three autobiographies. The dedication of the first, *This Is My Story*, was revealing. She had lost her father by age nine. The dark side that drove him to drink, dissipation, and an early death had hardly left him time to be a fit parent. Yet, the book was dedicated "To the memory of my father who fired a child's imagination and to the few people who have meant the same inspiration throughout my life." While she described in the book her sick husband's return aboard the *Leviathan* from the European war zone in 1918, the shattering discovery of the Lucy Mercer affair went unmentioned.

On October 21, 1942, Eleanor left on an inspection tour to obtain for the president an eyewitness account of Britain at war. Clementine

Churchill, the prime minister's wife, served as her guide. Eleanor was particularly eager to see how clothing donated by Americans through Bundles for Britain was being distributed among bombed-out families. The operation was run from the fourth floor of a shabby London building. Exhausted after a long day, Clementine begged off while Eleanor sprinted up the four flights of stairs. An English reporter asked if she ever relaxed or even slept. "Why do you ask?" Eleanor said. "Because," he answered, "I wish you would . . . I'm tired!" On another occasion, while she was off on a 26,000-mile visit to troops in the Pacific, Franklin entertained the ex-empress Zita of Austria-Hungary at Hyde Park. Won't his wife be exhausted? Zita asked the president. "No," Roosevelt answered, "but she will tire everybody else."

In Eleanor Roosevelt's relationships, intensity might wane, but never loyalty. Her friendship with Earl Miller survived some fifteen years after their first meeting. With the jealous Hick moved to a back burner it became easier for Earl and Eleanor to get along as before. Earl had gone into the Navy, commissioned a lieutenant commander, and succeeded the former heavyweight boxing champion Gene Tunney as director of physical training at the Naval Air Station in Pensacola, Florida. He was then reassigned to New York where he spent much of his free time at Eleanor's apartment on East 11th Street in Greenwich Village. She kept a piano there that the old state trooper had given her. When the Broadway producer John Golden offered her a new one, she declined. "I'd rather have Earl's in the future for purely sentimental reasons," she answered. Whenever Earl came to Washington, he was Eleanor's guest at the White House. On one occasion when the president's mother was still alive and visiting at the same time, she recognized the raffishly handsome naval officer and updated an earlier opinion of him. "First it was Corporal Miller," she observed to J. B. West, the White House usher, "then it was Sergeant Miller. Then it was Commander Miller. Now, it's Earl, dear," she said, imitating Eleanor's trilling voice.

Eleanor continued to provide a sympathetic shoulder for Earl to lean on as his turbulent love life continued. After the failure of his second marriage, he began courting Roberta Jonay, a young actress and dancer, "the only girl I ever really wanted to marry." Earl's friendship with the nation's first lady failed to enhance his prospects as a future son-in-law. Roberta's parent was a "stage mother if there ever was one," Earl wrote Joe Lash. The woman confronted the couple, "hysterically upbraiding

Roberta, pointing out that she had exerted all her efforts into training" her daughter for the stage. Still desperate to appease the woman, Earl went to Eleanor for help with Roberta's career. She managed to get the girl a part in a White House entertainment. Thereafter, "the offers came in aplenty, her first engagement $1000 wk. at the Shoreham," Earl claimed. But instead of winning over the mother, Roberta's success simply whetted her ambitions for her daughter. Finally, Earl accepted defeat. On June 23, 1941, he married a woman named Simone von Haven, as he later said, "on the rebound."

Earl Miller was rarely content to let the bare facts of a story suffice, and in this respect was rather like FDR. He had, while Roosevelt was New York's governor, accompanied Eleanor on prison inspections. In a letter to friends, written some twenty years after the president's death, he claimed that FDR, while New York's governor, had also sent him on similar missions with Lucy Mercer Rutherfurd, whom he found "a very fine person and was always regarded as kissable by all the Rs, and that's the way all the children greeted her." Thereafter the letter gave a jumbled account of his association with Lucy. "I was not surprised when I accompanied her on many tours through Ga. countryside to check living and factory conditions. . . . I even took her on one of my inspections of prisons after that boy died in a 'sweat-box' in Fla. for not saying, 'Sir' to his White Trash Guard. Got a conviction & abolishment of the boxes in both Ga. & Fla. And she wrote when I got back with the Gov. to Albany and was proud that she was part of it." No record of such inspections appears in either the President Roosevelt or Governor Roosevelt papers.

During the Roosevelt years in Albany, rumors had circulated about a liaison between Eleanor and her state trooper bodyguard. With FDR now president, the Army's Counter Intelligence Corps produced a more shocking and presumably official report of an alleged hotel tryst between Eleanor and another friend, Joe Lash, a man twenty-five years her junior. Joseph P. Lash, who would eventually become one of Eleanor's most insightful biographers and who personified the ultra-liberal politics of young intellectuals in the 1930s, was the son of Russian Jewish immigrants who ran a small grocery store on the edge of Harlem. Graduating from Columbia University in the depths of the Depression, Lash, a literature and philosophy major, found himself essentially unemployable. Capitalism had failed, many of Lash's generation believed, and the idealistic young intellectual turned to left-wing social movements. He veered

Sara Delano Roosevelt, mother of Franklin, who first fell in love with the brilliant, roguish architect Stanford White, a suitor her father found unsuitable. Sara subsequently married a Hudson Valley squire and widower twenty-seven years her senior, James Roosevelt. FDR LIBRARY

Franklin, age eleven, with his mother, Sara, the most formidable force in his life. He once noted, "What vitality I have . . . comes from the Delanos" instead of the Roosevelts. FDR LIBRARY

Franklin, age seventeen, with the Groton football team. While reasonably skilled at tennis and golf, the then spindly Roosevelt had scant success on the gridiron. Lucy Mercer Rutherfurd kept a similar photograph of FDR all her life. FDR LIBRARY

Alice Sohier at seventeen. Franklin wrote of her in code in his diary and proposed marriage. He wanted many children, however, and she chose not to be a "breed cow." She subsequently became anti–New Deal and blamed President Roosevelt for being "so careless with the country's money." EMILY T. SHAW

Franklin as a member of the Harvard class of 1904. His grades rarely rose above the "gentlemanly C." But he achieved campus prominence as editor of the school newspaper, *The Crimson*. FDR LIBRARY

Elliott Roosevelt, father of Eleanor. He squandered a future of promise in drink and dissipation and was dead by thirty-four. Still he remained an adored and idealized figure in Eleanor's imagination throughout her life. FDR LIBRARY

Eleanor and Franklin soon after their 1905 marriage. During their honeymoon, the timorous bride discovered that her husband had a flirtatious streak that other women reciprocated. FDR LIBRARY

Franklin Roosevelt, age thirty-one, serving in the Woodrow Wilson administration as the nation's youngest assistant secretary of the navy, a career step that paralleled his distant cousin Theodore Roosevelt's ascent to the White House. FDR LIBRARY

Franklin with his superior, Navy Secretary Josephus Daniels, who adored his young assistant but whose pacifist tendencies led Roosevelt to complain to a friend, "You don't know . . . what I have to bear under that man." FDR LIBRARY

Minnie Mercer was a stunning
beauty of the Gilded Age and a
doyenne of Washington society
until she and her husband,
Carroll, managed to squander
their wealth and find themselves
in a state of genteel poverty. Their
daughter Lucy would win the enduring love of Franklin Roosevelt.
NORTH CAROLINA COLLECTION,
UNIVERSITY OF NORTH CAROLINA LIBRARY

Lucy, about age fifteen. Though
the Mercer family was now in
straitened circumstances, a titled
aunt supported Lucy and her older
sister, Violetta, for a year at a
fashionable girls' school in Austria.
MR. AND MRS. MONTAGUE BLUNDON

Violetta Mercer Marbury, Lucy's
beloved elder sister, a frontline nurse
in World War I. Lucy usually stayed at
Violetta's Washington home when she
visited the president at the White
House. MR. AND MRS. MONTAGUE BLUNDON

Lucy Mercer shortly before she became Eleanor Roosevelt's social secretary in 1913. Her family needed the money and Eleanor, overwhelmed by a houseful of children and the protocol demands of the wife of a high-level official, was desperate for help. KNOWLES FAMILY

Alice Roosevelt Longworth, daughter of President Theodore Roosevelt, possessor of a mischievous charm and a waspish tongue, was Eleanor's first cousin, a lifelong rival, and an accomplice in furthering the romance of Franklin and Lucy. LIBRARY OF CONGRESS

Lucy Mercer at the time of her romance with FDR. Her poise and blueblood background led an initially trusting Eleanor to bring her social secretary into the Roosevelts' circle as a member of the family.

FDR LIBRARY

Franklin during a two-month mission to the front during World War I. Eager to get into uniform, he was refused by President Wilson. His return home turned disastrous when his wife, unpacking his luggage, found letters from Lucy to him. FDR LIBRARY

An emaciated and emotionally shattered Eleanor at a fleet review with her husband four months after discovering his infidelity. FDR LIBRARY

Winthrop Rutherfurd (seated at right), whom Edith Wharton described as "the prototype of my first novels," seen here as a member of the Rockaway Polo Club. Lucy Mercer married him a year and a half after her romance with Franklin was discovered. Rutherfurd was twenty-nine years her senior.

KNOWLES FAMILY

Lucy Mercer after her marriage to Winthrop Rutherfurd. She subsequently had a daughter, Barbara, and became the stepmother to five children, all of whom regarded her simply as their loving mother. RUTHERFURD FAMILY

Lucy, by now a society matron with homes in Washington, Paris, New York, New Jersey, and South Carolina, seen in the 1920s with husband Winthrop. LEITH RUTHERFURD TALAMO

Allamuchy, the principal estate of the Rutherfurds in rural New Jersey, a mansion boasting thirty-three rooms, seventeen bathrooms, a private lake, a golf course, and kennels for Winthrop's prizewinning smooth fox terriers. MR. AND MRS. MONTAGUE BLUNDON

A 1937 painting of Lucy by the émigré Russian artist Elizabeth Shoumatoff, who was to become a trusted friend to whom Mrs. Rutherfurd confided her romance with FDR. FDR LIBRARY

FDR (left in white shirt) as president of the Boy Scout Foundation of Greater New York at Camp Kanohwahke on Bear Mountain. The likelihood is that an energetic Franklin contracted polio while cavorting with the scouts. FDR LIBRARY

The last known photograph of Franklin Roosevelt when he was able to walk, at the Boy Scout encampment shortly before polio struck. FDR LIBRARY

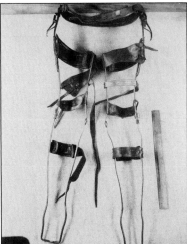

The braces Roosevelt was compelled to wear throughout his life. He could not stand or walk unaided. FDR LIBRARY

Missy LeHand, who would essentially live with FDR during his years aboard a Florida houseboat and in Warm Springs, Georgia, while he struggled to recover from polio. As his closest White House intimate, she was described as "as close to being a wife as he ever had." FDR LIBRARY

Eleanor with her state trooper bodyguard, Earl Miller. Rumors about the intimacy of their relationship would swirl around Mrs. Roosevelt for years. FDR LIBRARY

The extroverted Earl Miller managed to draw the inhibited Eleanor out of her shell. The two are seen here in a home movie, *The Kidnapping of the First Lady,* in which he plays a pirate and she is the damsel in distress. FDR LIBRARY

The usually staid Eleanor Roosevelt in a pose many acquaintances would have found astonishing, carrying out pistol practice, coached by Earl Miller. FDR LIBRARY

Miller ingratiated himself with the entire Roosevelt family. FDR's son Elliott was the best man and his daughter, Anna, the maid of honor at Miller's marriage to Ruth Bellinger. FDR, then New York's governor, also attended.
FDR LIBRARY

Miller wanted to demonstrate to the press that FDR was fit to serve as president, so he posed Governor Roosevelt on horseback at Warm Springs in 1930. Eleanor, on horseback, is on the right. FDR LIBRARY

The rumpled, irreverent newspaperman Louis Howe told a young state legislator, Franklin Roosevelt, that he could become president. Howe became FDR's political guru and urged him to stick with his wife to preserve his future during FDR's 1918 marital crisis. FDR LIBRARY

Eleanor with reporter Lorena Hickok. When letters between them surfaced after the former first lady's death, the press reported a "lesbian love affair" and claimed that the evidence of a same-sex involvement was "incontrovertible." WILDERSTEIN PRESERVATION

Lucy Mercer Rutherfurd in her fifties, at about the time she came back into President Roosevelt's life, visiting him at the White House, Hyde Park, and Warm Springs. KNOWLES FAMILY

The president with Princess Martha of Norway, described as looking "exactly as a princess should." FDR's daughter, Anna, said of Martha that her father "loved her and being admired by her." WILDERSTEIN PRESERVATION

Margaret "Daisy" Suckley, FDR's little-known confidante, seen here in a photo that FDR took of her in his study. The moment likely expressed FDR's sense of humor by portraying the proper Miss Suckley in a faintly vampish pose. WILDERSTEIN PRESERVATION

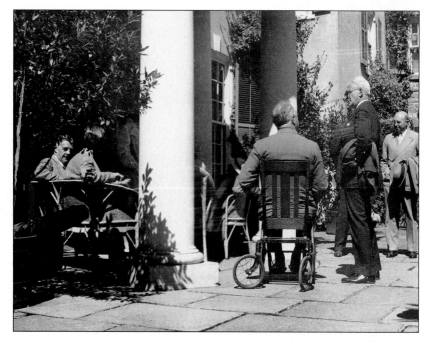

FDR in one of only two known photos of him in his wheelchair. So well respected by the press was his wish not to be seen as impaired that many Americans never realized their president was crippled. WILDERSTEIN PRESERVATION

While initially opposed to FDR's politics, Madame Shoumatoff was charmed by the president after Lucy Mercer Rutherfurd arranged for her to paint him twice, first in 1937 and then in 1945, on the day he died. FDR LIBRARY

While Madame Shoumatoff was painting FDR at Warm Springs, he insisted that her assistant, Nicholas Robbins, take this photo of Lucy. Robbins later claimed that he also took the only photograph of Franklin and Lucy together, but he never produced it. FDR LIBRARY

The last photograph of FDR, taken by Nicholas Robbins at Warm Springs while Roosevelt tested various poses for Madame Shoumatoff's painting. The difference between the president's deathly appearance and the subsequent painting demonstrated her technique, once described as "discreet glorification." FDR LIBRARY

The now iconic portrait that Madame Shoumatoff was painting at Warm Springs when FDR died. She kept it in a warehouse for years but finally gave it to the Little White House Museum in Warm Springs, where it remains on display. FDR LIBRARY

to within a hairbreadth of becoming a communist while secretary of the American Student Union, an organization that included a communist wing. But the Nazi-Soviet pact of 1939 was more than many on the American left could stomach, including Lash, who abandoned the idea of joining the party, instead becoming a noncommunist voice within student politics. His decision, however, did not spare him from being summoned before the House Un-American Activities Committee to answer charges that the American Student Union was communist-dominated.

On the train to Washington, he met Eleanor Roosevelt, who told him she planned to attend the HUAC hearing herself to demonstrate her support for progressive student activism. Lash's willingness to stand up to congressional red baiters appealed to Eleanor and a union of souls was born. In February 1940, Eleanor persuaded FDR to meet with Lash and leaders of an umbrella organization, the American Youth Congress, which included the Young Communist League. He met with them in the basement of the White House where Lash listened while the executive secretary of the YCL, Gilbert Green, lambasted FDR as a warmonger and capitalist tool. As Lash described the moment, "FDR just sat there with his cigarette-holder pointing to the ceiling and the harsher the speeches got, the more his smile gleamed."

Later in life Lash pondered what had drawn the well-born Eleanor to this son of poor immigrant Jews. "What deep needs within her nature I answered I could never quite fathom," except a "moral affinity," he concluded. He did detect in her a craving "to have people who were close, who in a sense were hers and upon whom she could lavish help, attention, tenderness . . . without such friends she feared she would dry up and die." As they grew close Lash saw what most others missed: "At times there is a haunting beauty about her expression in profile." The judgment paralleled a harsher yet well-intended compliment by the author Howard Fast, who upon meeting Eleanor found her "Tall, absolutely beautiful in her ugliness." An interviewer came away concluding, "In repose she is homely; but when she talks, she is like a magnet." Her daughter, Anna, well understood the strengths and limitations of her mother's appearance. "Put a hand over her mouth on a picture and it is a lovely face, eyebrows, eyes, and such a lovely figure," she once observed.

Lash was romantically involved with Trude Pratt, married but separated from her husband. The obstacles the couple faced had led Eleanor to confide the Mercer affair to Lash. It reminded her of "what I went through the year I was Trude's age," she told Lash. "There was a war then too & the bottom dropped out of my own particular world. . . . I really grew up that year. . . . I guess the most important thing I learned was that you can live thro' anything." Trude "must be all yours," Eleanor warned, "otherwise you will never be happy." Joe must never "accept 1/2 loaf of love," she said, reflecting the aridity of her own marriage after Franklin's betrayal.

With the war's outbreak, Lash had attempted to obtain a commission in naval intelligence using Eleanor as a reference. His radical past, however, still shadowed him and he was rejected. In April 1942 he was drafted and eventually stationed at the Army's school for weather observers at Chanute Field, south of Chicago. Though in uniform and serving his country, Lash's every move was dogged and his mail opened by the Counter Intelligence Corps. By now, the first lady had become widely detested by the political right, whose adherents considered her an intrusive, moralizing, left-wing busybody, and what was about to happen served their predilections perfectly. In March 1943, during a speaking tour, Eleanor, traveling with Tommy Thompson, had taken a room in the Hotel Blackstone in Chicago. She invited Lash to come up from Chanute Field for a visit, reserving and paying for an adjoining room. That night they played gin rummy until Lash fell asleep. The room was bugged by the CIC, and agents thereafter filed a report to Washington that "indicated quite clearly that Mrs. Roosevelt and Lash engaged in sexual intercourse during their stay in the hotel room." The report became part of a hundred-page dossier consisting of other surveillance reports and photocopies of seemingly incriminating letters that Eleanor had sent to Lash. "I'm so happy to have been with you," one read, "you forget how much you love certain movements of the hands or the glance in the person's eyes or how nice it is to sit in the same room & look at their back." The letter was reminiscent of Eleanor's intimate expressions to Lorena Hickok and equally subject to damaging interpretation.

What had actually happened? The week after the bugging at the Blackstone, Lash had checked into the Lincoln Hotel in Urbana near Chanute Field with Trude Pratt. Monitoring him again, the CIC agents reported this time, "Subject and Mrs. Pratt appeared to be greatly endeared to each other and engaged in sexual intercourse a number of times." By design or incompetence, the two eavesdropping instances became transposed in the CIC's final report, and the Lash-Pratt affair became a Lash-Roosevelt tryst.

Upon being tipped off by a hotel employee that her room had been bugged, an outraged Eleanor went to Harry Hopkins, who asked the Army chief of staff, General George C. Marshall, to investigate. Marshall was appalled and, at FDR's insistence, ordered the surveillance files destroyed and the CIC's domestic spying operation disbanded. But not every copy of the report on Eleanor was lost. George Burton, J. Edgar Hoover's liaison with the Army, managed to obtain a copy and slipped it to his chief. While the relationship between Hoover and FDR was warm and mutually useful, the FBI director despised Eleanor. Earlier, when she learned that Hoover had been looking into the loyalty of Tommy Thompson, she sent him a scathing letter charging, "This type of investigation seems to me to smack too much of the Gestapo's methods." Soon word was out among Washington insiders that the first lady had stood up to the feared FBI director, armed with his potentially damaging dossiers. "Oh gosh," Treasury Secretary Henry Morgenthau told his staff, "Hoover has apologized to Mrs. Roosevelt and to General Watson . . . and to everybody else." One thing the thin-skinned Hoover could not forgive was ridicule. He kept his copy of the discredited CIC report on Eleanor and Lash in his "Do Not File" file where it remained until his death.

The remote likelihood of a sexual liaison between Eleanor and Lash was best expressed by Lash himself. While he was her political and spiritual offspring, he did not find the much older woman physically appealing and spoke of "the inability of men to desire her sexually."

## Chapter 30

# A DISTANT COUSIN,
# A CHERISHED DAUGHTER

· · · · · · ·

Missy LeHand was not long gone before Dorothy Schiff was on the scene offering to be helpful to FDR. She had become a Hyde Park neighbor after Franklin wheedled her into building the nearby Red House. "He wanted the house to be built, and to have me in it," she said, "but it was all for him." On every possible weekend, FDR still sought a soul-restoring escape from the White House to Hyde Park, traveling by private railroad car. On a Saturday in early October 1941, he invited Schiff to join him at the estate. They sat in the "snuggery," his mother's favorite room, just barely accessible for a man in a wheelchair, crammed with furniture, books, and family photos. Though by now Schiff was publisher of the *New York Post*, the president began describing something more that she might do for the country and to broaden her influence beyond the city. "He explained that there is much to be done in the education of farm women," Schiff remembered of the conversation. Wartime wages were spiraling upward along with the cost of farm products, and these women did not understand "that control of prices and products is absolutely necessary during the present crisis to prevent dangerous inflation," he told her. He urged that, "I should go work for the 4-H Clubs, farm stuff." To this thoroughgoing cosmopolitan, FDR's suggestion had all the appeal of a forkful of manure. "Mr. President," Schiff answered, "there is another job I would much rather have. While I could never replace Missy, there are parts of her job I think I could do," though she admitted that she did not type well and could not take shorthand. "Shhh," the president interrupted, a finger to his lips and looking aghast. "You'd better not let Grace Tully hear you say that." Tully, while lacking Missy LeHand's polish, attractiveness, and intimacy with Franklin, had nevertheless quickly acquired the Roosevelt stamp of approval. Like Missy, she was Irish Catholic and working-class, the daughter of a Staten Island grocer and local Democratic leader. While serving as secretary to a cardinal, Tully had been spotted and hired by Eleanor and became, with her genial, breezy competence, first Missy's assistant, then her successor. As Dorothy Schiff was making her pitch, Tully was working in the next room, and an agitated FDR quickly changed the subject.

Schiff already had a sense that she was slipping in the president's standing and began "kidding him about a new girl he was supposed to be keen about, Princess Martha of Norway." FDR brushed aside the insinuation. The Norwegian king, Haakon, was an old friend of TR's, he explained, and had asked FDR to look after his daughter-in-law. As for Schiff working for him, "He didn't want me in his hair that much of the time," she concluded. "He thought it was ludicrous. . . . He was scared to death of my suggestion. Of course, I felt terribly rejected."


Years before, the president had proudly taken Schiff to see Top Cottage. Missy LeHand had dreamed of living there before illness felled her, and now another woman, Franklin's distant cousin, Daisy Suckley, thought the retreat might hold her future. Daisy, who had turned fifty in 1941, was no raving beauty but not unattractive, small, petite, with prominent cheekbones, and a well-shaped mouth. She was said to have rejected several proposals of marriage in her youth, choosing instead to remain within her close-knit family. She wore her hair pulled back in a severe bun, and dressed in good-quality, long-lasting, no-nonsense clothes. She had been described as a little brown wren and played, in her own words, "my part of prim spinster." Daisy was an ideal companion for Franklin, a full-fledged member of that loosely associated society, the Hudson Valley squirearchy. She shared with him the almost mystical rootedness to the valley, and he had written to her once of "our river" and "our countryside" pondering the source of this fierce attachment to their locale. "Perhaps it is the common Beekman ancestry," he concluded. Franklin further appreciated that Daisy made no emotional demands on him. She once said, "We Suckleys are so suppressed by our inborn reserve and shyness that we find it hard to let out what is deepest and strongest in us!" Daisy displayed the prejudices of her class. She was judgmental and quick to brand people as "common" or "coarse," especially Jews. Yet she was large-minded enough to recognize true character whatever its origins. She had regarded with astonishment the poise and tact of Missy LeHand after she had come to know this daughter of a scapegrace gardener.

With a peer like Franklin, Daisy was comfortable, displaying a sharp mind and wicked wit. She was always au courant concerning the latest gossip circulating among the gentry, a subject Franklin relished and that made Eleanor uncomfortable. It was to Daisy that Franklin confided how at the age of twenty-one he and Charles Bradley had been lured by the phony baroness and countess into a potentially compromising situation exposing them to blackmail. It was the sort of tale that the unworldly Daisy enjoyed vicariously, her dashing cousin in a youthful peccadillo of the sort she could scarcely imagine.

By the time Franklin became president, he and Daisy had exchanged letters totaling in the hundreds, hers signed, "your affectionate cousin." The tenor of their correspondence indicated both her understanding of him and his need for someone to whom he could unburden himself. She pasted in her notebook a copy of a letter he had written to Supreme Court Justice Felix Frankfurter that she believed explained "why he is able to 'get through' when many physically stronger men collapse under heavy responsibility." The answer was Franklin's "sense of humor." The letter dealt with the quadricentennial anniversary of the death of Copernicus, the Polish astronomer. "Strictly between ourselves," he wrote Frankfurter, "I have little sympathy with Copernicus. He looked through the right end of the telescope, thus magnifying his problem. I use the wrong end of the telescope and it makes things much easier to bear."

Daisy confided to her diary her impressions of the abdicated former king of England, Edward VIII, now the Duke of Windsor and governor of the Bahamas, whom she met during a ten-day pleasure cruise with the president aboard the USS *Tuscaloosa* out of Pensacola in 1940. FDR had invited the duke and his wife, the former Wallis Simpson, aboard the warship after they had come to Florida for dental work. Daisy observed of the sleek, tanned, and elegantly attired former monarch that, "Windsor is completely insignificant looking but charming and quick. You can't help liking him and feeling sorry because he is an exile from home and country." During this exile, his former subjects were living on scant rations and suffering the horrors of the Blitz, while the Windsors basked under the sun on a government estate. Daisy went on, "His wife, a completely unscrupulous woman, as is proved by her past life, does, however, seem to keep his devotion and make him happy." After Daisy returned home from the cruise, Franklin gleefully wrote her about how he had fooled the reporters with an imaginary itinerary he had concocted for the voyage. "We have all been laughing at the complete ignorance and gullibility of the press!" he wrote her. "They fell for the visit to the Andaman Islands (Indian Ocean), Celebes (North Pacific) and South Hebrides (Antarctic) and believe it or not, the Cherubic Isles from Edward Lear's Book of Nonsense!"

A year later, the president was again aboard a warship, this time for one of the decisive moments of the war. On August 9, 1941, two ships drew alongside each other in Newfoundland's Placentia Bay, the U.S. Navy's heavy cruiser *Augusta,* and the Royal Navy's massive new battleship, the *Prince of Wales*. A short, rotund figure wearing a seafarer's cap and smoking a large cigar boarded the *Augusta* as the ship's band played "God Save the King." Except for a fleeting moment at Gray's Inn in 1918, Franklin Roosevelt and Winston Churchill were about to talk for the first time. At that point, before Pearl Harbor, Britain was still fighting alone and reeling from losses at sea, with nearly 1,500 ships sunk by the middle of that year. After several days of intensely personal talks in the *Augusta*'s wardroom, Churchill departed, not with America's entrance into the war, which he had hoped for. He did have, however, Roosevelt's pledge that American warships would protect British convoys and patrol three hundred miles into the Atlantic to seek out and attack German submarines. Thus FDR had all but declared war on Germany on the high seas. It was to Daisy Suckley that Roosevelt confided his private impressions of Churchill: "He is a tremendously vital person and in many ways is an English Mayor La Guardia. Don't say I said so," he warned. "I like him and lunching alone broke ice both ways."

Daisy witnessed the rare occasion when the fears roiling beneath FDR's outward unflappability broke through. While a guest at the White House she wrote in her diary, "The P. had an awful nightmare last night. I woke out of a sound sleep to hear him calling out for help in blood curdling sounds!" The next morning at breakfast the president told her, "I thought a man was coming through the transom and was going to kill me." Suckley ended the entry, "I wondered why the SS [Secret Service agent] didn't rush in, but he says they are quite accustomed to such nightmares."

She rode in presidential motorcades, usually seated in the fourth or fifth car, looking after the latest in a series of Scotch terriers she had given to FDR. The most renowned had been christened by Franklin "Murray the Outlaw of Falahill," shortened to Fala, a dog who would make front-page news. The president sought to rebuff Republican charges that he had accidentally left Fala behind in the Aleutian Islands and then sent a destroyer back to pick up his pet. In a convention speech before the Teamsters Union, adopting a tone of mock outrage, he began: "These Republican leaders have not been content with attacks on me, or my wife, or on my sons. No, not content with that, they now include my little dog, Fala. Well, of course, I don't resent attacks, and my family doesn't resent attacks, but Fala does resent them. You know, Fala is Scotch and being a Scottie, his Scotch soul was furious."

Daisy had known early of Franklin's dream to build a hideaway of his own but not the extent of Missy LeHand's involvement before her stroke. Missy had helped plan Top Cottage, its layout, furnishings, and decoration. Until 1940, both she and Daisy had marked time waiting for FDR to serve out his second term and retire, each believing that she would accompany him to his hilltop refuge. During the planning stage, Daisy had taken to referring to the site as "our hill." Franklin encouraged her, writing on one occasion that the cottage should have "very thick walls to protect us." Franklin dashed both their hopes by running for a third term. Neither ever knew of the other's expectation.

Daisy's longing for a special place in Franklin's life was buoyed when he confided another dream to her, to build a presidential library at Hyde Park. Prior to FDR, preservation of presidential papers had been a catch-as-catch-can affair. Franklin had begun thinking of his historic legacy almost immediately after being sworn in for his second term in 1937 and he had made a sketch of the library soon afterward, again adopting his favored Dutch Colonial fieldstone style. He had Daisy put on the federal payroll as an "archivist," and she happily began cataloguing his papers. When he turned the completed library over to the government on Independence Day in 1940, the national archivist, Robert D. W. Connor, proclaimed, "Franklin D. Roosevelt is the nation's answer to the historian's prayer." Daisy treasured a letter, signed by the National Archives personnel director, informing her, "Dear Miss Suckley, you are hereby notified that you have received a within-grade promotion in salary from $2000 to

$2100 per annum." She was perfectly cast in the role, competent, serious, and bookish. The job also provided FDR with a credible explanation as to why this woman was so often seen at his side.

To Daisy, Eleanor remained "Mrs. Roosevelt," though they were more closely related than she was to Franklin. "His wife is a wonderful person," Daisy wrote in her diary, "but she lacks the ability to give him the things his mother gave him. . . . She has so many people around—the splendid people to do good and improve the world, the 'uplifters' the P. calls them—that he cannot relax and really rest." *The Eleanor Roosevelt Encyclopedia* describes Daisy as "chaste, but distinctly flirtatious . . . yet no one—including the President's wife and mother—seems ever to have suspected it." Eleanor saw Daisy merely as another of Franklin's handmaidens, close to him but no threat. Franklin's comfort level with Daisy is clear in that, of thousands of photos of him at the Hyde Park library, only two published shots show him in a wheelchair, both taken by Suckley, and at Top Cottage.

While it is tempting to dismiss the likelihood of romance between the impaired Franklin and a woman as seemingly repressed as Daisy Suckley, there exists evidence to the contrary. Among the hundreds of letters they exchanged during the 1930s, Franklin would refer to "M.M." for "My Margaret" and "C.P." for a "Certain Person." Gaps in chronology suggest that he asked her to destroy some of their correspondence, but he wrote in one surviving letter that he had to "bite my tongue" to keep from talking about her. Away on a trip to Boulder Dam, he wrote, "There is no reason I should not tell you I miss you <u>very</u> much." During a cruise to Panama he wrote, "I have longed to have you with me."

There exists among the Suckley files at Wilderstein, Daisy's estate, an unlikely photograph in which the proper maiden lady is sitting on a bearskin rug on the floor of Franklin's study, her legs tucked under her and Fala at her side. FDR took the picture on her fiftieth birthday. It is hardly a vampish Theda Bara pose, but Daisy looks pleased with herself and wears a faintly mysterious smile. Did Daisy and Franklin enjoy the same "pleasing sexuality" that Doris Kearns Goodwin found between him and Lucy? In 1933, Daisy wrote in her diary, "The President is a MAN—<u>mentally, physically & spiritually</u>. What more can I say."

· · ·

"You should really paint the President," Lucy Mercer Rutherfurd suggested to her visitor, as they sipped tea at her Aiken home on an afternoon early in 1943. "He has such a remarkable face. There is no painting of him that gives his true expression. I think you could do a wonderful portrait, and he would be such an interesting person to paint." Her guest was Elizabeth Shoumatoff, who spoke with a thick accent, betraying her Russian origins. Her path to a career in art had been circuitous and something of a comedown. She was born Elizabeth Avinoff, the daughter of a wealthy general in the czar's army. In 1917, she traveled to America with her husband, Leo, who was on a mission for the provisional government of Alexander Kerensky that had succeeded the deposed czarist regime. Before the year was out the Bolsheviks, under Vladimir Ilyich Lenin, seized power and the Shoumatoffs concluded that a communist dictatorship would prove inhospitable to the once privileged classes. They remained in America where, eleven years later, Elizabeth suffered a devastating loss. Leo, who had been a success in business, drowned off Long Island's Jones Beach. The widow now found it necessary to earn a living for herself and her children. She had a gift for flattering likenesses that soon won her a following among wealthy patrons. Her grandson, Nicholas Shoumatoff, shorthanded her technique as DG, for "discreet glorification."

Shoumatoff was soon sought out by rich winter residents of Aiken. While staying at an inn in the town, "an extremely tall, good-looking girl came to see me," the painter later recalled. "She said that she was very anxious to have a portrait of her mother. She spoke of her so affectionately that I was surprised later to discover that Lucy Rutherfurd was her stepmother." Thus Shoumatoff had come to paint several members of the Rutherfurd family. She found that Winthrop Rutherfurd, "in spite of his advanced years was one of the handsomest men I have ever painted." She detected in her subject a vague resemblance to Franklin Roosevelt.

Over years of painting various Rutherfurds, Elizabeth grew close to Lucy. "She impressed you not so much by her striking appearance but by the shining quality of her features, particularly in her smile," she commented. She also observed that Lucy "had no extraordinary intellect, but she possessed the most idealistic, almost naive mind, with a really unselfish understanding heart." As for her friend's style of life amidst great wealth, Shoumatoff was struck by its simplicity and by Lucy's total immersion in pleasing her ailing husband. She noted that this exquisite woman dressed in clothes that made her look older, which Shoumatoff interpreted was deliberate to narrow the twenty-nine-year gap between Lucy and Winty.

On that day when Lucy asked if she would like to paint Roosevelt, the artist could not imagine how the president of the United States could be approached to sit for her. She was stunned when Lucy called her at her hotel the next day to tell her that everything had been arranged. The president would allow her two sittings to begin in two weeks. Since coming to Aiken she had heard stories that Lucy "had been romantically involved with Roosevelt many years ago," but "I did not think, at that time, that she actually talked with him or saw him."

On the appointed date, she showed up at the White House gate clutching a portfolio containing drawing boards, pencils, brushes, and in her purse a silver box of paints and a tiny four-inch palette. A White House aide "led me into the inner sanctum" where FDR's welcoming embrace seemed "to stretch across the entire room," she remembered. The president, dressed rather drably she thought in gray suit and blue tie, began chatting easily as she laid out her Winsor & Newton paints of primary colors only. FDR kept rattling on as if they had known each other forever. He told her of a portrait of himself that a Mexican artist had once done posing him by a fireplace with the flames framing his head. The artist had called the work *Fireside Chat*. FDR told Shoumatoff that he called it *Roosevelt in Hell*. He was pleased to note, as he gallantly lit her cigarettes, that Madame Shoumatoff, like himself, smoked through a holder. He showed intense curiosity about her early life in Russia, which led him to express feigned exasperation over the number of European nobility now living off of him. The Grand Duchess Charlotte of Luxembourg, he said, had seized on his invitation to take refuge in Washington, arriving penniless with a husband and seven unsuspected children and expecting to be maintained in the grand manner. The Norwegians, including his favorite Princess Martha, he said, were almost as bad, thinking he was subtly trying to democratize them by showing scant regard for court etiquette. Queen Wilhelmina of Holland, whom he found utterly devoid of humor, interpreted his irrepressible teasing as deliberate offense. The royals were most disturbed, he said, because they failed to understand that Americans were not dying in this war to restore their pomp, privilege, and empires, but rather to achieve self-determination for all people. While Shoumatoff painted, checking perspective in a small jade mirror, he confided to her that he was aware of his reputation for inscrutability. "Some people think that a lot of things I do are unbalanced," he said, "and they probably do [seem] so if one thinks only in terms of the present. But I'm thinking of twenty-five years from now."

The painting could not be finished in the allotted two sittings. Yet when Grace Tully informed Shoumatoff that the president's schedule was full and she could have no more time, FDR overrode his secretary, telling her to cut one of his lunches short and give the artist another half hour.

John Singer Sargent, likely America's greatest portraitist, once described a portrait as a work in which the mouth was always somehow wrong. The finished Shoumatoff painting was judged by FDR's congenitally blunt aide, Bill Hassett, as "too pretty," and he found the artist much too assertive. Lucy Mercer did not agree with either verdict. She thought the painting splendid and Madame Shoumatoff sympathetic, discreet, a true lady. The final arbiter was pleased with her, too. FDR told the artist that he wanted color copies of the painting to give to his friends. She was soon back in the White House with the framed portrait and the copies. FDR, she remembered, "was all praise." In years to come, she objected to a widespread impression that Lucy had commissioned FDR's portrait. "While it was Lucy's idea," she corrected, "I did it on my own and presented it as a gift to the President." After the White House experience, Shoumatoff found her resistance melting under Roosevelt's spell. She began to see Roosevelt much as Lucy did. Clearly, her warm reception by FDR was explained, like his welcoming of the Rutherfurd children, by the fact that she represented for him another link to Lucy.

Bill Hassett had written in his diary early in 1942, "Despite persistent and continuous bad news from the Far East [FDR] remains calm and serene and never impatient or irritable. This man's imperturbability is based on supreme confidence in his plans and in the outcome of our contest which at present is going steadily against us. Never a note of despair, chin up, full of fight!" As the year progressed, FDR began to have solid reason for his unshatterable confidence. The naval victory at Midway in June 1942 had thrown Japan from the offensive onto the defensive. The first test of American arms against the German Wehrmacht in North Africa had been calamitous, but eventually the GIs played a role alongside the British in freeing the continent from the Afrika Korps. A jubilant FDR flew to Casablanca in January 1943 to meet Winston Churchill, stunning the prime minister with a surprise announcement at a press conference that the Allies would accept nothing short of "unconditional surrender." That summer Sicily fell to the Americans and British, followed soon by just such an unconditional surrender by Germany's halfhearted partner, Italy. On the Eastern front, Germany suffered a staggering defeat at Stalingrad, taking 237,000 casualties, including twenty-four captured generals, who were paraded through Moscow. After the victory in North Africa, Churchill had proclaimed, "This is not the end. It is not even the beginning of the end. But it is, perhaps, the end of the beginning." By the end of 1943, the Allies could convincingly claim that they had reached the beginning of the end.

Anna's growing usefulness to the president and his affection for his only daughter led him to include her in the official party that he would take to Tehran in the fall of 1943 for a meeting with Winston Churchill and, for the first time, with Joseph Stalin. The trip began on November 11 with an exhausting nine-day Atlantic crossing aboard the battleship *Iowa*, and ended with a long flight to a Soviet-run airfield in the shadow of the Elburz Mountains outside Iran's capital. During the conference, Anna watched her father attempt to work the Roosevelt charm on the Soviet dictator. FDR had told Bill Bullitt, his former ambassador to Moscow, "I think if I give him everything I possibly can and ask for nothing from him . . . noblesse oblige, he won't try to annex anything and will work with me for a world of democracy and peace." What alarmed Anna during the following five days of negotiations, interspersed with toast-tippling lunches and heavy dinners, was how bad her father looked. He picked at his food. His collar hung loosely around a scrawny neck, accentuating his declining weight. His hands shook as he smoked, scattering ashes over his clothes and official documents. His lips were grapecolored, purple half-moons darkened the pouches under his eyes, and his fingernails had a bluish tinge. Most disturbing, his breathing had become audible and the once sonorous voice was now reedy. At times, his mouth hung open as his thoughts trailed off unfinished.

Yet, after they returned to Washington, the president again displayed his astonishing resilience. His staff had become accustomed to seeing their chief slumped in fatigue in his wheelchair one minute and the next propelling himself into a press conference, grinning and effervescent, his cigarette holder clamped in his teeth, his chin thrust upward. His humor rarely dimmed. Asked by a reporter if he had read Kathleen Winsor's racy 1944 best-seller, *Forever Amber*, he answered, "Only the dirty parts."

Some observers of Roosevelt have painted him as sexually squeamish. The biographer Bernard Asbell concluded, "Everything we know about this man suggests conflict and consequently, repression of sexual drive." However, John Gunther, in *Roosevelt in Retrospect*, saw a different man: "FDR liked women, knew plenty about them, and had a healthy, salty attitude toward sex." Bill Hassett, in his diary, wrote, "The President never boasts about his lineage unless it be boastful to recall that his early Delano ancestor Philippe de la Noye was fined in the early days of the Massachusetts Bay colony 'for fornicating a wench in the bushes.' " Hassett responded to FDR, "We should be tolerant of Philippe's lapse since he was a surveyor and as such had to run his lines wherever the job took him." To which FDR replied, "The lines are fallen into line in pleasant places." On an occasion when the president summoned Hassett into the bathroom where he was shaving, he told him, "Have a seat on the can, and remember your pants are up." When his aide passed along a newspaper clipping that a Washington bishop was home with a sprained ankle, the president scribbled in the margin, "Did he fall or was he pushed?"

While FDR, the wartime leader, was riding high, Franklin, the private man, still sought out female companionship to ease the crushing weight of his burdens. Between her first recorded visit in July 1941 and the end of 1942, Lucy had come to the White House, as Mrs. Paul Johnson, eleven times, sometimes arriving twice in the same day. After FDR's return from Tehran in November, he presented her daughter, Barbara, with a hand-painted Persian tile. When Churchill came to Washington in May 1943 to address a joint session of Congress, FDR saved coveted tickets for choice seats for the Duke and Duchess of Windsor and Lieutenant and Mrs. John Rutherfurd. Yet, throughout 1943 recorded visits to the White House by Lucy cease. She may have been shifted to the unofficial longhand log the usher kept or he may have confined contact with her to their country drives. Most likely her life was consumed in attending the bedridden, declining Winty. However, she would eventually return to the White House, and more dramatically than before.

Of his five children, Anna, his only daughter, was clearly FDR's favorite. Memorably pretty from childhood, she grew up to be a striking woman, with blue eyes, tawny blond hair, arched brows, an aristocratically sculpted face, and a fashion model's slim, long-legged figure. Katharine Hepburn comes to mind. She was lightly educated—Miss Chapin's finishing school and an unlikely year at Cornell University taking an agricultural course—but she possessed a keen, curious mind and the direct manner of her mother. Though she had been Daddy's little girl as a youngster, upon learning of FDR's infidelity with Lucy, Anna had turned to Eleanor. By the 1930s, as the daughter of a towering world figure, she felt awestruck in the presence of her own father.

After she had married the newspaperman John Boettiger in 1935, the couple had gone off to Seattle, Washington, on something of a journalist's dream job. The newspaper mogul William Randolph Hearst hired Boettiger as publisher of the *Seattle Post-Intelligencer* while Anna became associate editor of the paper's women's pages. The war changed all that. Boettiger, though age forty in 1942, was nevertheless uneasy to still be a civilian. FDR had just come back from Casablanca and made a casual remark that stung his son-in-law to the quick. Excited by the president's well-told tale of his journey, the journalist said, "I'd give my eyeteeth to go along on such a trip." He could not, FDR responded. A puzzled Boettiger asked why? "You're not in uniform," the president answered. The next day, Boettiger wrote General Dwight D. Eisenhower, with whom he had a friendly connection, asking to be commissioned and sent to North Africa. Soon afterward Anna saw her husband off to war.

The White House had become a lonely place for the president. Lucy's presence was spasmodic. Missy had receded into the past. Princess Martha left the White House to live with her children in the Maryland countryside. FDR's one reliable housemate, the wise, ever available Harry Hopkins, had in 1942 married Louise Macy, a glamorous former Paris editor of *Harper's Bazaar*. At the president's urging, the newlyweds moved into the Lincoln Suite in the White House. FDR was instantly smitten by Louise. She, like every woman to whom he was attracted, was stylish, sociable, amusing, and shared his love of gossip. Eleanor was less taken with the arrival of yet another permanent White House guest. "Louise would arrange dinner parties and seat the table," Anna recalled. "My mother would be home and this would annoy the pants off her." Louise's presumptuousness had become an all too familiar pattern. An earlier offender had been Jimmy Roosevelt's first wife, the stunning Boston debutante Betsey Cushing, whom FDR came to adore. "Betsey never did anything for Father except always turn up for cocktails when he was alone, in those few minutes before the guests came in," Anna observed. "There was always Betsey, chic and lovely, full of light quips." "Betsey would come and say, 'Pa says he wants so-and-so after dinner.'" "Betsey thinks she owns him, you know," Eleanor complained. According to Anna, romantic rivalry had nothing to do with Eleanor's displeasure. "This would annoy Mother because she felt that Betsey was trying to usurp some sort of position with Father. This was her position." Eleanor was "a jealous person," Anna believed. "She was jealous even of me."

As Christmas of 1943 approached, the Hopkinses moved into their own home in Georgetown. The president was left more alone than ever. Eleanor was in perpetual motion, traveling from training camps to war zones to hospitals to endless speakers' podiums. At the cocktail hour the president found himself plaintively asking the usher to "see who's home and ask them to stop in." All too often he was told no one was available. FDR would eat off a tray by himself in his study and go to bed early.

Over the Christmas holiday the solitude was broken. Anna took a break from her job in Seattle and stayed for four weeks with her three lively children, Anna Eleanor, known as "Sistie," age seventeen, Curtis, called "Buzzie," age fourteen, and John Boettiger, age four. As Anna prepared to return to Seattle, Franklin began to find reasons for her to stay longer. Being close to him, after long separations, her intimidation began to fade as father and daughter rediscovered each other. They shared a taste for silly jokes, just as FDR and Missy had. Anna regaled him with tales of the sexual escapades of his two roguish sons, Franklin Jr. and Elliott. Young Franklin, she told a rapt FDR, had fallen for General Eisenhower's English driver, Kay Summersby. Roosevelt was delighted. He had picnicked with her and Ike during his Casablanca visit and found Summersby a charmer. He knew, he said, that his commander in Europe was sleeping with Kay. Anna and Franklin Jr. enjoyed swapping tales about their father's occasionally surprising caprices. Young Franklin while on leave told of suddenly popping into the president's study and finding a strange woman massaging FDR's wasted legs whom the president blithely introduced as "my old friend, Mrs. Winthrop Rutherfurd." "Father could relax more easily with Anna than with Mother," Elliott Roosevelt observed. "He could enjoy his drink without feeling guilty." Further, Anna proved smart and competent as she willingly took on Missy-like tasks, helping FDR serve at the cocktail hour, arranging the seating for dinners, dealing with callers for whom the president had no time. He began to see Anna creditably performing a role for which Eleanor had neither the time nor inclination. He had found in his daughter a soul mate.

## Chapter 31

# ANNA'S DILEMMA

· · · · · · ·

Early in March 1944, Missy LeHand, the woman who had painfully come to realize FDR's enduring attachment to Lucy, suffered another shattering setback. Hearing that Missy was growing stronger and getting about on a cane, the president and Grace Tully had hatched a plan to bring her to the White House for a visit in mid-March. On learning of this intention, Eleanor objected. She was scheduled to visit military bases and preferred to have Missy come after she returned. She wrote Missy canceling the March invitation and suggesting a date in April. Her motives were practical but misunderstood. The cancellation broke Missy's spirit. She saw herself rejected and viewed the later date as a pretext to put her off. Missy's sister wrote Eleanor, "We did everything we possibly could do to make her go to Washington this month but she simply wouldn't allow us to talk about it." March would have been a trying time for a visitor anyway. For days FDR was in and out of bed, feverish and fatigued. He longed to leave Washington and get home to Hyde Park, which he did, arriving on Saturday, March 25, 1944.

Shortly before, on March 19, Winthrop Rutherfurd had died. His body, long ravaged by strokes and grown frail from confinement to a wheelchair, could not shake off a stubborn bout of influenza. He expired a month past his eighty-second birthday at his winter home, Ridgely Hall, in Aiken. It had been a beautifully crafted life on the whole, spent doing what he chose to do—glittering society, polo, golf, his dogs, cattle, and farms, unspoiled by the necessity of earning a livelihood. Lucy, a month short of her fifty-third birthday, mourning black accentuating the whiteness of her skin, wisps of gray now streaking her still lustrous hair, accompanied the body back to Allamuchy in New Jersey for burial. Winthrop was laid to rest in the family plot under a large, flat gravestone

along with his father, a famed astronomer, his first wife, Alice, and son
Lewis. It defines Lucy to note that, unfailingly, selflessly, and lovingly,
she had devoted herself to the happiness of this man for twenty-four
years, while remaining romantically in thrall to another.

One week after Winthrop's burial, Lucy was on her way to Hyde Park,
her first visit to the place as rooted in Franklin as his genes. Again,
Eleanor would be away. Daisy Suckley noticed that the day before,
Franklin perked up. "He took things easy . . . had a good nap before
lunch and after lunch. . . . When he finally was up he berated himself,
joking that he had become 'Robert Louis Stevenson in the last stages of
consumption.'" Late Sunday morning, a government sedan arrived from
the Poughkeepsie station and deposited Lucy at Hyde Park. Franklin
had his Ford ready, sat her next to him, and prepared to show her his
world. They drove first to Top Cottage, Secret Service agents trailing behind. The press had taken to calling it FDR's "dream house," an expression he hated, but which fit his intentions when his presidency ended.

March in upstate New York could be a dour season, the sky leaden,
trees bare, patches of dingy snow persisting in sunless corners. But this
day, as they gazed across the Hudson to the Catskill Mountains, the sun
shone brilliantly as if for them alone. They left Top Cottage and wound
their way back down to the presidential library where Daisy, now the official archivist, sat engulfed by Franklin's papers, delighted to see Lucy
again. The library had become FDR's passion. He liked telling visitors
about an exchange of letters with the librarian of Congress, the poet
Archibald MacLeish, who had recently written him referring to the
"Franklin Delano Roosevelt Memorial Library." FDR wrote back, "Dear
Archie, You have been grossly deceived. I am still alive."

Daisy had become a willing accomplice in perpetuating the Franklin
and Lucy romance. The two women had met first during Daisy's long ago
visit to Aiken where she had reported on Franklin's struggle with polio.
In more recent encounters at the White House, they had become kindred souls. The ever class-conscious Daisy quickly recognized a great
lady, and began calling Lucy "my new cousin." What they had most in
common was unconditional devotion to Franklin. The current visit particularly pleased Daisy for its tonic effect on FDR since she had been
a witness to his recent malaise at the White House. At dinner one
evening, during that unhappy interlude, as soon as he could decently
leave his guests, FDR asked Daisy to follow him to his study. In a voice

heavy with fatigue he described his dilemma. "I'm either Exhibit A, or left completely alone," he told her. "I never heard a word of complaint before from him," Daisy wrote in her diary, "but it seemed to slip out, unintentionally, & spoke volumes." His meetings with Princess Martha, which he previously found refreshing, had begun to pall. As one observer put it, "With people like Martha, his performance always had to be on." He still loved playing up to beautiful women, but now it took effort. With Lucy, Daisy observed, Franklin felt no need to perform. He could be talkative or silent, animated or withdrawn, as the mood struck him.

At 6:30 on the Sunday evening of Lucy's Hyde Park visit, the idyll ended. She boarded the train from Poughkeepsie and headed home. She might well have reflected that the world she had just left and the man it had produced could have been, in different circumstances, her own. Daisy, back at her own home, eagerly awaited Franklin's report of what had happened with his visitor after she had left him and Lucy alone. He finally called her at 9:30 P.M., describing the pleasure Lucy had brought him. He sounded "stuffed up," however, and told her that he had gone to bed with a fever of 100 degrees. She was concerned but relieved knowing that once back in Washington he was scheduled for tests at Bethesda Naval Hospital.

Anna had worried about her father's health ever since moving into the White House, taking over the eclectic duties that Missy had once performed. She had made herself nearly as indispensable as her predecessor, though she had not dared to assume the role without asking her mother's permission. "I would love to have you," Eleanor had responded, "but I want no more difficult relationships like Louise [Hopkins], Betsey and Missy."

Arguably, no leader in history shackled with FDR's physical infirmities had ever borne heavier burdens with more grace. Taking over a country sunk in depression, he was now leading that nation in war. The challenges he faced, mobilizing America's manpower and industrial sinews for the conflict, preparing for the mightiest and possibly bloodiest invasion ever envisioned, overseeing development of an atomic bomb, all the while juggling the outsized egos of world leaders, would likely have broken a lesser, even if healthier, man. When cabinet officers, generals, and admirals complained of the weight of their responsibilities, Grace Tully remembered FDR saying, "All right, send it over to me. My shoulders are broad. I can carry the load." But Anna was not fooled by her father's exorbitantly purchased displays of vigor. During his down days that March, she had gone to Admiral McIntire, pleading with the president's physician to have his patient given a thorough examination. The admiral did not welcome a layman's intrusion into his domain, but he had agreed to set up the appointments at Bethesda. The ever protective McIntire fobbed off the coming tests to the press as merely the president's "annual checkup." After Franklin left Hyde Park, Daisy wrote in her diary of the upcoming examination, "I pray they do the right thing by him."

At Bethesda the president was examined by the hospital's leading cardiologist, Lieutenant Commander Howard Bruenn. After exhaustive testing, the youthful Bruenn went to the White House and met with Admiral McIntire in the privacy of the Map Room, the president's intelligence center. His diagnosis was grim. FDR was suffering from severe hypertension, his blood pressure a stratospheric 218 over 120. His arteries were hardening and the left ventricle of his heart failing. Over the years the heart had become enlarged by its effort to pump blood through ever narrowing passageways. The constricted vessels were delivering less nourishment to the brain, especially sugar, reducing the president's capacity to think, concentrate, or absorb information. FDR exhibited a classic case of arteriosclerosis. Roosevelt, Bruenn found, was a prematurely aged sixty-two-year-old and he estimated the patient's remaining life between months and at most two years. McIntire passed along the verdict to Anna and arranged to have Bruenn assigned to the White House full-time.

Astonishingly, during his examination at Bethesda, the president had not asked Bruenn a single question. Afterward he had simply shaken the cardiologist's hand and said, "Thanks, Doc." Nor did he subsequently inquire during Bruenn's daily thumpings and probings as to why he had been assigned a cardiologist in the first place. The politically aware McIntire understood the president's presumed lack of curiosity about the truth of his condition. The leader of a nation at war must project strength himself if his nation is to be seen as strong. Asked by *Life* magazine for an interview about his famous patient, McIntire perpetrated an audacious fiction. "His past physical examination is equally as good as the one made twelve years ago," the admiral claimed. Further, he warned the interviewer, "no mention was to be made of the number of cigarettes the President smokes in a day." No one on the White House staff, except for McIntire, Bruenn, and Anna, not even the first lady, knew how desperately ill Franklin Roosevelt was.

FDR improved marginally after coming under Bruenn's care. The digitalis prescribed was reducing the size of his heart. Yet he still felt bone-tired. He hoped to soak up the sun at the Navy base in Cuba's Guantánamo Bay, but his weakened condition and the risk of unnecessarily having him at sea during wartime scrubbed that plan. Instead, FDR got word to Lucy that in April he would be vacationing at Hobcaw, the South Carolina estate of the financier Bernard Baruch, and hoped to see her there. Hobcaw, Baruch's 23,000-acre plantation in South Carolina, was crowned by a red-brick mansion overlooking the Waccomaw River and embraced streams and forests teeming with deer and wild boar. Passing up a holiday with his family, FDR arrived at Hobcaw just before noon on Easter Sunday, April 19. "I want to sleep and sleep twelve hours a night," he said upon his arrival.

He found the egotistical Baruch a figure of compelling curiosity, particularly since, starting work at $3 a week in his native South Carolina, he had amassed millions as a shrewd market investor by the time he was thirty, a success in business that had eluded FDR. He was further impressed that Baruch was seen so often in the company of women, as Roosevelt put it, "the most beautiful ever." Daisy Suckley confirmed that the financier was "notorious for his succession of affairs with women, including the glamorous playwright and future congresswoman, Clare Boothe Luce." At one point, Baruch had temporarily lost the use of his legs from a circulatory complication after an operation. On one of Dorothy Schiff's visits to FDR she remembered that he "went into great detail about Mr. Baruch's illness." She was astonished to hear him say that the paralysis explained "Baruch's physical and mental failure in recent years." The observation struck her as odd, since "The President himself suffers from complete paralysis of his legs, but neither he nor anyone else . . . considers it a weakness in the President."

The Roosevelt entourage at Hobcaw included Admiral William Leahy, chief of staff to the commander in chief, Admiral McIntire, Dr. Bruenn, and General Watson. The traveling press was kept at arm's length eight miles away in the Prince George's Hotel. Commander Bruenn was encouraged by the almost instant improvement in his patient's behavior. FDR was eating better, consuming a carefully regulated diet of 1,800 calories per day, and had cut down on his smoking to six cig-

arettes daily. "His color was good . . . the lungs clear, the heart was unchanged," Bruenn recorded in his notes, though the president's blood
pressure was still a disturbing 226 over 118. Bruenn tracked the typical
routine for the vacationing president: "Awakened 9:30 am, breakfast
in bed, reading newspapers and going over correspondence." FDR
emerged from his bedroom in time for lunch, "then retired for a nap following which he went fishing in a Coast Guard patrol boat, CG-54005,
with the Secret Service in another boat aft." Blue skies and a bracing
breeze energized the president as he hauled plump catfish from the
Black River. By 9:30 P.M. he was in bed.

Eleanor, just back from visiting U.S. military bases in Latin America
and the Caribbean, flew down with Anna to Hobcaw for a day. She had
long since shed the anti-Semitism that had caused her, over twenty years
before, to shrink from "a Jew party" given for the Baruchs. By now, she was
a closer friend of the financier than FDR and once wrote, "Baruch is still
the most comforting person I know." She brought with her to Hobcaw
John Curtin, prime minister of Australia, and the Costa Rica president,
Teodoro Picado. The party stayed only for lunch and left with Eleanor satisfied that Hobcaw "was the very best move Franklin could have made."

On April 28, nine days into the vacation, guests detected a palpable
excitement in FDR. Lucy Mercer Rutherfurd was coming. She would be
arriving with her daughter-in-law, Mrs. Guy Rutherfurd, and her stepdaughter, Alice, and Alice's husband, Arturo Ramos. Baruch had reluctantly given up several priceless gas rationing coupons so that the visitors
could drive the 140 miles from Aiken. While waiting for his guests, the
president drew on a scrap of paper a luncheon seating arrangement for
twelve, with himself at the head, and "Mrs. R" to his right. On her arrival, Lucy met a man so thin that he resembled an older version of the
lean-faced cavalier she had known long ago rather than the barrel-
chested FDR she had become accustomed to in recent years.

Lunch was interrupted but not ended when an aide whispered into
the president's ear that the seventy-year-old Republican Frank Knox,
whom FDR had lured into his cabinet as secretary of the navy, had died
of a heart attack. The president's expression remained unchanged and
he went on with the lunch. While he appeared to take Knox's death
coolly, afterward he suffered stomach pains, nausea, and tremors, and
McIntire had to give him a codeine injection to get him through a press
conference during which he was to discuss his appointee's sudden pass-

ing. As the reporters gathered at Hobcaw, Merriman Smith, the United Press White House man, thought Roosevelt seemed to speak of Knox's death with little feeling. "I've been told people of superior breeding never let their emotions come to the surface publicly," Smith concluded. Eleanor, back in Washington, assumed that Franklin would return immediately for Knox's funeral. She had scheduled an out-of-town trip and numerous speaking engagements, which she canceled to be with Franklin at this time. Instead, he told the reporters that, on doctor's orders, he would have to stay another week in South Carolina. That day, Bruenn measured his blood pressure at a record 230 over 120.

The faithful Daisy Suckley also came to Hobcaw during this stay. After a lunch in which she watched FDR dab listlessly at a dish of minced chicken on toast, she wrote in her diary of another confidence he had shared with no one else: "I had a good talk with the P. about himself," she wrote. "He said he had discovered that the doctors had agreed together about what to tell him, so that he found out they were not telling him the whole truth and that he was evidently more sick than they said! It is foolish to attempt to put anything over on <u>him</u>."

While FDR had become increasingly unconcerned about masking his visits with Lucy, his daughter, Anna, remained circumspect. When, years after the president's death, Commander Bruenn asked Anna to approve an article he had written for the *Annals of Internal Medicine* that mentioned FDR's health during the Hobcaw visit, including who was present, she responded, "I added, as a suggestion, mother's name and mine because of the possible reaction of gossip mongers." She was concerned that if only the names of Lucy and her family appeared in Bruenn's article, someone "might decide to contact you as to what you know about Mrs. Rutherfurd."

By May 7, the president was back at his desk in Washington from which he wrote Missy LeHand a dutiful letter about Hobcaw. "I worked a little each day, fished, drove around the countryside, and slept the rest of the time," he said. He told her that Harry Hopkins was doing well after a stay at the Mayo Clinic. Franklin Jr. was about to get command of a destroyer and three of his grandchildren were living in the White House with their mother, Anna. "I do hope you will come down and see us soon," he wrote, and closed, "Much love, affectionately, FDR."

· · ·

On the evening of June 5, Grace Tully watched the president, outwardly calm, playing with Fala while his grandson Johnny Boettiger somersaulted on the sofa. She noticed, however, that FDR's hands shook uncontrollably and his skin had taken on the pallor of cement. At 11:05 P.M., he asked Eleanor and Daisy to join him in his study. Grim-faced, he sipped a glass of orange juice, and told them that within hours tens of thousands of young Americans would be storming the beaches of Normandy. History's mightiest armada, 6,500 vessels carrying over 137,000 American, British, and Canadian troops, was already breasting the English Channel. The long-awaited invasion of Europe was at hand, an operation that Winston Churchill told General Eisenhower aroused in him nightmarish visions of the Channel choked with Allied corpses. Worst-case casualty estimates ranged as high as seventy thousand men. Seeking to break the fearful silence his revelation caused, FDR switched to joking about what he intended to do with Hitler as soon as the führer was captured. The next night, when it appeared that the Allies had established a secure beachhead, Anna watched her father, in a radio broadcast, lead the nation in prayer. "Lord look after these soldiers of freedom, for they will need thy blessings," he said. "Their road will be long and hard. For the enemy is strong."

This overburdened leader was now about to confront his daughter with a near impossible personal request. On a day early in July with the temperature breaking still another record that summer, Anna was sitting beside her father in his sweltering study jotting down tasks he wanted her to handle. She uncomplainingly took on any chore that could lighten his burden whether, as she put it, "my job was helping plan the 1944 campaign, pouring tea for General de Gaulle, or filling Father's empty cigarette case." This day, out of the blue, he said, "Would it be all right if I asked an old friend to dinner." "I guessed who it was," she recalled of the moment, and then FDR confirmed that he had in mind "Mrs. Rutherfurd. It was a terrible decision to have to make in a hurry," Anna remembered. She recognized that this sick man, whom she watched, day after day, bearing titanic responsibility, was now largely reduced to the companionship of Daisy and another cousin, Laura "Polly" Delano. She knew, if she abetted her father's wish, that deceit was inevitable. Her mother would be away during the time FDR wanted Lucy to visit. He was asking Anna to become his accomplice in a maneuver to conceal from her mother a rendezvous with the woman who had been the source of Eleanor's heartbreak twenty-six years before. She had confessed the affair to the seventeen-year-old Anna and the emotional havoc it had cost her. Anna, however, made "a quick decision that the private lives of these people were not my business. After all, it was their business." Now age thirty-eight, she had witnessed enough of life's vagaries that she felt no right to judge others. She herself had stepped outside the bounds of convention to seize her own happiness when she had become involved in the affair with John Boettiger while both were married. As her son Curtis saw it, "She was trying to keep Pa going, trying to keep him alive, trying to ease what was obviously a terminal illness, whether for a year or two." Yes, she told her father, she would arrange a dinner. Soon afterward, Anna wrote her husband, saying she hoped she wouldn't be caught in a crossfire between her parents.

Besides dinner at the White House, the president hoped to take Lucy to Shangri-La, the name he had given to a former Civilian Conservation Corps summer camp tucked into Maryland's Catoctin Mountains seventy-five miles from Washington, today called Camp David. He had picked the name from James Hilton's novel *Lost Horizon*, set in the mythical paradise of Shangri-La. Far closer than Hyde Park, he could escape there within hours where he liked to sit in a small screened porch playing solitaire or just gazing out at the mountains, exercising what Merriman Smith called the "fetish of his for privacy during the war." It was to Shangri-La that he had once taken Prime Minister Churchill fishing, where he had received word of the execution of six Nazi saboteurs arrested in the United States, and where he had awaited word that American troops had made it ashore in North Africa. Shangri-La would be the perfect place for him to share treasured hours with Lucy.

But first he had to get through meetings with General Charles de Gaulle, who would be arriving at the White House Thursday afternoon, July 6. The visit was in part a sop to the proud French leader who had effectively been barred from involvement in the D-Day invasion of his own country. Along with placating de Gaulle, FDR intended to use the occasion to coordinate the Allied advance in France with guerrilla tactics by the French resistance. De Gaulle's ego, matching his six-foot-five-inch height, grated on both Roosevelt and Churchill. They were willing to accept the general as the leader of Free French soldiers fighting alongside them against Germany, but resented de Gaulle's presumption that, lacking any official sanction, he was the leader of all France. "We call him

Joan of Arc," Churchill remarked, "and we're looking for some bishops to burn him."

On his arrival at the White House, de Gaulle "stepped from the automobile with an air of arrogance bordering on downright insolence," Bill Hassett remembered, "his Cyrano de Bergerac nose high in the air." Upon their meeting, the president was charm itself and de Gaulle later wrote of "Roosevelt's glittering personality." The next evening the president gave a state dinner for de Gaulle, but rushed through it, since afterward he was expecting a visit from Lucy. At 8:45 P.M. the usher recorded for the first time in the White House log the arrival of "Mrs. Rutherfurd" instead of "Mrs. Paul Johnson." She stayed with Franklin late into the evening before returning to her sister, Violetta's, home.

The final meeting with de Gaulle ended on Saturday afternoon July 7. Afterward, FDR had himself driven to 2238 Q Street, where he picked up Lucy and brought her back to the White House for the dinner Anna had arranged. He also asked Anna's husband, Major John Boettiger, now posted to the Pentagon, to be present. Initially Anna felt plagued by guilt. She had set up the dinner knowing full well that her unsuspecting mother was at Hyde Park celebrating her part in the War Department's new policy ending racial segregation in buses on military bases. Anna had arranged for Lucy and her father to be brought in by the less-conspicuous driveway running between the White House and the State, War and Navy Building. She had further instructed the staff not to release the guest list, lest her mother see it.

Just before eight o'clock, the usher led a tall, striking woman into the president's study. Anna had a dim childhood memory revived of a personable secretary who had come to work for her mother at 1761 N Street thirty-one years before. As FDR prepared cocktails, Anna began to relax, sensing the easy rapport between her father and Lucy. As the butler, Alonzo Field, served dinner, she could not fail to note the contentment in her father's expression. Lucy's enduring appeal to him became all too understandable. She was not merely attractive, but poised, bright, well read, asked sensible questions, and bantered lightheartedly with her father. Anna had known other women who pleased him, but, as she observed, "I had the feeling with LM there was something meaningful . . . he had a meaningful relationship with this gal. I could remember watching her as Father talked and realized this woman had all the qualities of giving a man her undivided attention. She certainly had innate dignity."

That evening, as if by a prearranged signal, Anna and John said good night, leaving Franklin and Lucy alone. It was past midnight before she left.

On Sunday morning, the trip to Shangri-La began. Just after 11:00 A.M. the president's limousine pulled up outside 2238 Q Street. On their arrival at the retreat they passed by six oak cabins, the most commodious with four bedrooms reserved for the president. The day proved idyllic, the weather perfect, the setting majestic, just the two of them with the security team keeping at a nonintrusive distance. Late in the afternoon, they were driven back to Washington, quietly basking in the warmth of the day just spent.

On Sunday night, July 30, 1944, Missy LeHand went to the movies with her divorced sister, Ann, and a friend, Maydell Ramsey. They left the home at 101 Orchard Street in West Somerville that Missy owned and where Ann lived rent-free, and headed for Harvard Square. Along with the double feature, the program included a newsreel during which there suddenly appeared on the screen the image of the president, his face haggard, his cheeks sunken, dark circles under his eyes, and his voice weak. Missy began fidgeting and told Ann she wanted to go home. As soon as they were back at Orchard Street, she pulled out old photographs she kept in her bedroom. Her anxiety grew visibly as she gaped at pictures of her and Franklin smiling on a porch at Warm Springs, his chest broad and biceps bulging in the pool, a robust figure barely resembling the faded specter she had just seen in the theater. She finally surrendered the photos and went to bed. Just after midnight Ann rushed in to investigate loud groaning gasps coming from Missy's bedroom. Missy had suffered a cerebral embolism. She died just after nine that morning. She was forty-six years old.

At the moment of Missy's death, FDR was aboard the heavy cruiser USS *Baltimore*, having just met with General Douglas MacArthur and Admiral Chester Nimitz at Honolulu. After the successful island-hopping campaigns in the Pacific against Guadalcanal, Tarawa, and Saipan, they had discussed the next possible objectives, Iwo Jima, Okinawa, the Philippines, which MacArthur argued for, or Formosa, which Nimitz preferred. FDR then headed for Adak in the Aleutian Islands chain where he would seek to boost the morale of the troops and shipyard workers in that desolate outpost. En route he was handed a radiogram from Bill Hassett and Stephen Early, the president's press secretary. "Regret to inform you that Missy LeHand died in the Naval Hospital at Chelsea, Massachusetts at 9:05 today," it read. "Have notified Mrs. Roosevelt, Miss Tully. Await instructions. Will issue statement in the President's name." The statement they released was lifeless. "Memories of more than a score of years of devoted service enhance the sense of personal loss which Miss LeHand's passing brings," it read. "Hers was a quiet efficiency which made her a real genius in getting things done," and closed, "Her memory will be held in affectionate remembrance and appreciation."

It was not possible for the seaborne president to return in time for Missy's funeral, but Eleanor journeyed to St. John's Church in North Cambridge, Massachusetts, along with over 1,200 other mourners, including Missy's friend, former ambassador Joseph Kennedy. When FDR finally returned to the White House, he was met by a crestfallen Grace Tully, who said, "You and I lost a very dear friend." FDR "was about to cry," she recalled, "and so was I, and he said, 'Yes, poor Missy.' But he never liked to show any emotion. At least I never saw him show any." Joe Lash once observed "how different FDR was . . . from Lincoln, who displayed his anguish in his seamed face. Roosevelt in contrast, treats all problems impersonally as if they had no organic relation to him—people the same way. Otherwise he could not have stood three terms in office."

In October, Missy's will, showing her last residence as Hyde Park, was probated. She left the Orchard Street house to two brothers, rather than to Ann, of whom Grace Tully observed, she "couldn't care less about the sister who would go out and charge everything to Missy that she could lay her hands on." She left two favorite nieces her cottage at Warm Springs. She bequeathed her jewelry to Eleanor. Any item from her White House apartment she left to Franklin, Eleanor, Grace Tully, and family members, "as each of them may care to select." Franklin had continued to support her, but she possessed little money of her own. She made bequests of $500 each to her sister, an aunt, and Grace Tully. Eight months after her death a new cargo ship slid down the ways at the Ingalls Shipbuilding Corporation in Pascagoula, Mississippi, christened, at the direction of the president, the SS *Marguerite A. LeHand.* FDR sent a message to be read at the launching ceremony expressing his wish that this "craft which bears so honored a name will make a safe journey and always find a peaceful harbor." Years later at a Manhattan dinner party the subject of Franklin's romance with Lucy came up. Polly Delano announced flatly that "Missy was the only woman Franklin loved, everybody knows that." That he loved her in his fashion, but not exclusively, was true.

On August 23, some three weeks after Missy's death, Lucy was back visiting the White House. FDR had just received news that Paris was free. He was in high spirits, according to his secretary of war, Henry Stimson, "in better physical form than I expected." The president beamed at reports of tens of thousands of Parisians pouring into the boulevards throwing flowers and kisses at their American liberators. Eleanor, out of town, was not there to share the festive occasion. But Anna, along with Lucy, daughter Barbara, and stepson John Rutherfurd followed the president as he was wheeled onto the South Portico for a tea celebrating the Allied victory.

*Chapter 32*

# "MOTHER WAS NOT CAPABLE OF GIVING HIM THIS"

· · · · · · ·

FRANKLIN HAD TOLD DAISY at Hobcaw that he knew he was far sicker than his doctors had let on. That spring of 1944, over lunch at Hyde Park, he again shared his private thoughts with her as he faced the decision as to whether, in his condition, he should run for a fourth term. Politically, his time may have already passed, he said. "He remembered Woodrow Wilson telling him that the public is willing to be 'Liberal' about a third of the time, gets tired of new things and reverts to Conservatism the other two-thirds of the time," she wrote in her diary. "If the election were held tomorrow," he told her, "he would be beaten by almost any Republican." But the health issue remained paramount. "What will decide me will be the way I feel in a couple of months," he said. "If I know I'm not going to be able to carry on for another four years, it wouldn't be fair to the American people to run for another term." Like most who dealt with FDR, she had difficulty following the byzantine paths of his thinking. Was he fishing for encouragement to run again, or honestly assessing his political stock? The Brain Truster Rexford Tugwell believed that FDR made his decisions through heavenly guidance. "He felt, I judged, that he had a duty to do and that he was under a certain general direction to work it out through politics. . . . And always, when new undertakings were before him, he asked all his colleagues in it to accompany him if they would in asking for divine blessing on what they were about to do." That summer he evidently concluded that his duty was to run. "All that is within me cries out to go back to my home on the Hudson River," he told the press in announcing his decision, "but the future existence of the nation and the future existence of our chosen form of government are at stake." Upon being anointed again at the Democratic nominating convention in Chicago, he shed his ultra-liberal vice president, Henry Wallace, for Senator Harry Truman as his running mate and began preparing for his fourth presidential bid.

Before hitting the campaign trail he planned to squeeze in one last retreat to Hyde Park over the Labor Day weekend. The train pulled out of the president's secure siding in the basement of the Bureau of Engraving and Printing at 10:45 P.M. on August 31. The three traveling pool reporters were puzzled when they were told that they would arrive at Hyde Park at six the following evening, over nineteen hours to cover less than three hundred miles. Apparently, they assumed, the president had insisted on a slow pace since the jarring of the cars at high speeds pained his thinly fleshed buttocks.

That night they had turned in after whiling away the evening drinking and playing gin rummy when at 2:30 they were jolted awake by a sudden stop of the train. Peering out into the black night they saw no station, no buildings, few lights giving them any clue as to where they were. Ever since the war, the president's travel plans had been kept secret until his arrival at his destination and the newsmen concluded that this pause in the middle of nowhere had something to do with security or a mechanical breakdown.

The days preceding the president's trip had produced organized chaos at the Rutherfurd estate in Allamuchy township. Lucy kept her gardeners hard at work trimming shrubs and hedges, mowing acres of lawn, pruning trees, and cutting flowers while the maids waxed floors, vacuumed rugs, dusted furniture, and polished silver, making the mansion gleam. She oversaw the complete redecoration of a guest bedroom and had a private phone line installed in it. A weary maid sighed, "You'd think the President was coming." "He is," Lucy replied.

As daylight broke, the reporters descended from the train and found themselves at a siding rusty from disuse. A reporter asked a trainman if they were still on the Pennsylvania Railroad line. No, he was told, this was the Lehigh & Hudson. Where were they? the reporter asked. "Allamuchy," the trainman answered. "Where the hell is that?" the reporter said. They milled about until 8:30 when they saw the president, freshly shaved and smartly dressed, wheeled onto the tiny elevator jutting from the far end of his car. FDR's official massive, bullet- and bombproof Ford appeared as if from nowhere. Before being carried into it, the president informed the reporters that he was going to make a brief visit to "an old friend" whose husband had recently died. As the automobile whisked him and his Secret Service detail away, the reporters reboarded the train for breakfast and resumption of their gin game.

Franklin's arrival at Allamuchy was the emotional equivalent of Lucy's coming to Hyde Park, the first chance for her to show him the world she inhabited. On the way in, one of the New Jersey state troopers in the motorcycle escort, Joseph J. Skelly, remembered the president "looked very drawn." But upon seeing Lucy he lit up visibly. The meeting was hardly a lovers' tryst. Lucy had invited to Allamuchy stepchildren, step-grandchildren, and in-laws to meet the president. The youngsters romped over the grounds as they had through the years, playing softball within earshot of tinkling cow bells, listening to the yelping of their late grandfather's fox terriers, and hunting for Indian arrowheads. Daisy Suckley had come along with the president and spent most of the time chasing after Fala, who happily ran free through the woods that skirted the Rutherfurds' private lake.

FDR had barely greeted the guests when he offered to take the children for a spin in his car, top down and led again by the motorcycle escort, sirens shrieking. Guy Rutherfurd's son, Guy Jr., recalled the ride as "the fastest I'd ever traveled." FDR next offered to inspect the estate's farmlands and woodlands with Lucy's stepson the towering John Rutherfurd, home on leave from the Navy, and Edward Danks, the estate manager. He described his qualifications as "just an old tree farmer," and assured Rutherfurd and Danks that he knew how to make a property pay.

At one o'clock, Lucy summoned her guests to lunch. Daisy remembered the hostess, wearing a black figured dress, as "a lovely person, full of charm and with beauty of character shining in her face. No wonder the Pres. has cherished her friendship all these years." The Lucy she had first met twenty-two years before at Aiken had been a sad figure. But this day Lucy was radiant as she began seating her table for lunch. A Secret Service agent cautioned her that the president was always to be seated at the head of the table. Lucy hesitated at violating protocol until Franklin announced that he would sit wherever he pleased, which was at Lucy's right. Also at the table was the hostess's extended clan, stepson

John with his wife, stepdaughter Alice, "very tall, 5–11, slender & lovely looking," according to Daisy, and a "princess," once married to Winthrop Rutherfurd's late brother. Two black servants, wearing white gloves, served a jellied soup, squab, cut beans, and ice cream. Franklin begged off on the lobster course Lucy had arranged. He had dined on lobster the night before and Eleanor intended to serve it again at Val-Kill that evening. With lunch over, Lucy offered the redecorated bedroom to Franklin, should he want to nap. "But he wasn't going to miss any of his visit," Daisy recalled. He did, at one point, closet himself in the room where Lucy had installed the special phone line and the Army Signal Corps arranged for FDR to speak to Winston Churchill with only her present.

At 3:30 P.M. a staff aide reminded FDR that Mrs. Roosevelt would be waiting at the Highland station. He reluctantly allowed himself to be carried into the car. As the presidential party left the house they passed by a table in the hallway laden with trinkets, balloons, yo-yos, and marbles, small gifts that Lucy always left out for the visiting children, "anything that would tickle the fancy of a five or six year old," Guy Rutherfurd Jr. recalled. "Granny was just the most wonderful, thoughtful person. She really took great care with us."

Ten minutes later, FDR was back aboard the train. The day was "out of a book—a complete setting for a novel, with all the characters at the lunch table," Daisy remembered. Bill Hassett described the visit to Lucy in his diary and the boost Allamuchy had given to the president's spirits. But, years later, when the diary was to be published, Hassett tore out those pages.

As the train pulled away from the siding, FDR asked the Secret Service if the Lehigh & Hudson route could be used again to reach Hyde Park instead of the usual run up the New York Central tracks. One spot troubled the agents. The change meant passing over Hell Gate Bridge in New York. A laughing FDR answered that he didn't think the bridge would be blown up at this stage in the war. The new route deposited him at 6:45 P.M. at Highland station on the opposite bank of the Hudson River from Hyde Park. Eleanor was waiting, curious to know what had taken him so long. Franklin explained that the Secret Service believed this new route was safer. They drove across the bridge to Poughkeepsie and on up the five miles to Val-Kill, where Eleanor's lobster dinner was waiting.

• • •

For a time, Dorothy Schiff had been FDR's fair-haired girl, but her privileged position, she sensed, had continued to decline. In the summer of 1944, just before FDR had decided to run again for the presidency, she was again with him, this time at the White House. "During what I thought was his last term, I asked him whether he would write a column for the *Post* when he retired since Teddy Roosevelt had written for the *Atlantic*," Schiff recalled of the conversation. He turned her down and suggested she ask his interior secretary, Harold Ickes, whom FDR referred to as "the old curmudgeon." Despite what she knew was a flagging friendship, Schiff nevertheless found herself among the guests invited to dinner at Hyde Park over the Labor Day weekend, though why, unless FDR wanted to insure the backing of her *New York Post*, she was unsure. As soon as the holiday respite ended, the president would face an exhausting reelection schedule, and Schiff wondered if he was up to it. He looked terrible, she thought. She found his speech halting and he moved more slowly than she remembered. He ate only cooked cereal, which he explained was because he was having trouble with his teeth. She thought he might be exhibiting signs of a stroke.

FDR's altered attitude toward Schiff could be explained by an observation of his son Elliott. "Between his close companions and Father, there was always an implicit understanding," Elliott noted. "There must be loyalty on both sides. He was more brutal in cutting off any man or woman if he suspected he was being used by them, which was something he refused to tolerate." What standard Schiff had breached with FDR, she did not know, since a fall from grace usually went unexplained. Most likely she had run afoul of FDR's preference for women like Daisy, Polly Delano, Missy, and Lucy, who wanted nothing from him. Whatever the reason, she knew that the once warm, flirtatious bond had been broken. Upon leaving Hyde Park, she was never to see the president again.

FDR managed to draw upon hidden reservoirs of strength as he launched his fourth presidential campaign. He toured New York City in an open Packard during a steady rain, drenched to the skin. The next day several Secret Service men and reporters had come down with colds, but

FDR suffered not a sniffle. At one point, he campaigned in seven states in three days. The adulation of the crowds seemed to send an adrenaline surge through his sick body. On November 7 he defeated the Republican candidate, New York governor and former racket-busting prosecutor, Thomas E. Dewey, taking 53.5 percent of the popular vote. Dewey conceded his loss in the wee morning hours from a near empty ballroom in his campaign headquarters, gracelessly omitting any congratulatory message to the winner. The discourtesy prompted FDR to announce, as he was wheeled into his bedroom at Hyde Park, "I still think he's a son of a bitch."

The burst of campaign euphoria spent, the president craved the ease and sun of Warm Springs. He planned a full three weeks' stay at the Little White House to coincide with his customary belated Thanksgiving dinner with polio patients. Since Daisy Suckley and Polly Delano would join him, Eleanor decided, "I don't have to go." She preferred to spend the holiday with Joe and Trude Lash, who had married soon after Trude's divorce came through.

Unlike Daisy's hazy relationship, Polly was Franklin's first cousin, six years younger than him. She was no fool and read him shrewdly. She knew how to perform exactly as all women did whose company FDR welcomed. Polly shared Franklin's and Daisy's taste for gossip, though hers had a nastier edge, not unlike tart-tongued Alice Roosevelt Longworth. Polly's family estate sprawled over two hundred acres near Rhinebeck, ten miles north of Hyde Park. There, she indulged in what one acquaintance called "her whole life," raising dachshunds and Irish setters. Within her circle, the woman was considered an exotic. "Two more different women would be hard to imagine," Elliott Roosevelt observed of Aunt Polly and Daisy. "Polly looked like a Dresden doll; Daisy was homey as an old cardigan." Now in her early fifties, Polly was still attractive, high-spirited, and blithely unconventional. Her features were striking, high cheekbones, hair dyed a pale purple culminating in a widow's peak that she painted on every morning. She would appear at breakfast in brightly colored velvet pants, silk blouses, her fingers bejeweled with diamond rings and a half dozen bracelets jangling from her wrists. She powdered her cheeks white, reminiscent of a legend about her past. As a young woman, she was said to have fallen in love with a rich Japanese nobleman, Otohiko Matsukata, a classmate of Franklin's at Harvard and later first secretary at the embassy in Washington. The love match was deemed "totally unacceptable to the Delano family," which had made its fortune off Asians, Curtis Roosevelt remembered. "The pressure was too great. The affair ended and Polly never married," though the description "old maid" hardly fit this flirtatious coquette. She was comfortable enough with Franklin that she did not hesitate to phone him at the White House in the midst of a meeting to share her grief that one of her dogs had died. Polly could also be seen in Roosevelt motorcades with one of her Irish setters, sitting alongside Daisy, who held Fala. She possessed another prime qualification for Franklin's company. According to Curtis Roosevelt, Polly "never wanted anything from him except his approval. . . . Others, Betsey Cushing or Dorothy Schiff, may well have wanted recognition."

She readily joined the tight circle abetting Franklin and Lucy's secret life. "She believed that Mother had been the wrong choice as a wife for her cousin," Elliott Roosevelt recalled. "Our tiny bejeweled Aunt felt sure that Lucy Mercer and Father should never have given up each other. She saw no reason why they should not meet again." Jimmy Roosevelt wrote in his family memoir, "When I was having some sort of marital trouble, Cousin Polly said to me, 'You know, your father was just as much a rascal as you are.'" When he asked what she meant, she told an unwitting Jimmy of the Lucy Mercer affair. "She asked me if my Father had ever spoken of it and I said he had not." Aunt Polly closed the conversation with, "Well we better just forget it then." Her vanity was formidable and she once claimed that Franklin's love for her was great in his later years. Eleanor found Polly maddeningly superficial. After the first lady met Churchill, the only thing Polly wanted to know was whether he was sexy. Eleanor answered wearily, "I just don't know, Polly, I just don't know."

On November 27, the presidential party departed Washington for Warm Springs by train with Daisy and Polly; Admiral McIntire, the president's cardiologist; Lieutenant Commander Howard Bruenn; key staff members; and White House servants. On their arrival, the two cousins unpacked in one of three bedrooms in the main house. The weather was unseasonably cold and they fretted over Franklin's proneness to respiratory ills. The next day, they found him suffering from a toothache, which led McIntire to summon an Army dentist from Fort Benning. "The Pres. continued joking except at the actual moment of extraction," Daisy recalled and, afterward, his teeth clenching a bandage, "He managed to continue talking, however, without stopping." His undaunted spirit, Daisy believed, was explained in part by the guest he was expecting the next day. Lucy would be arriving from Aiken on Friday. Her coming meant that Daisy and Polly would have to vacate the Little White House and move into a guest cottage heated only by a fireplace, which Daisy admitted was "something of a nuisance." Yet their priority was to enable Franklin and Lucy to be together in the same cottage.

Awaiting Lucy's arrival, the president kept busy, signing appointments to federal offices, particularly major changes in the State Department. Franklin's choices had upset Eleanor. He had picked the undersecretary Edward Stettinius to replace the retiring Cordell Hull as secretary of State, and allowed Stettinius to select his two assistant secretaries. Eleanor found these men unacceptably conservative. She particularly objected to James Dunn, a rich, socially prominent diplomat, and told FDR, "the reason I feel we cannot trust [him] is that we know he backed Franco and his regime in Spain." She opposed the appointment of Will Clayton, because, she believed, the vastly wealthy cotton broker would be too sympathetic to German industrialists in the postwar world.

The president whiled away the rest of Friday afternoon, napping and sitting on the porch in the bright sun under his cape doing crossword puzzles until six o'clock when Lucy arrived with her daughter, Barbara. Daisy was again overcome. "Mrs. Rutherfurd is perfectly lovely, tall, stately, & with the sweetest expression," she wrote in her diary, and found the daughter, Barbara, "quite pretty, with dark arched eyebrows, tall, too thin. She is quiet and looks serious for her age." Daisy and Lucy quickly resumed their alliance. "She is much worried by the Pres. looks, finds him thin and tired looking. I don't dare acknowledge that I feel the same way about him."

Along with the Rutherfurds, an FDR favorite, the retiring Canadian ambassador, Leighton McCarthy, joined them for cocktails in the pine-paneled living room. Suddenly they were plunged into darkness. The day before an explosion had shaken the house that turned out only to be coal gas igniting in the furnace. "When anything like this happens," Daisy wrote of the power failure, "everyone wonders in the back of his mind if there is anything sinister in it!! All the [Secret Service] are alert, the Marines peer into the darkness of the woods." The president, however, merrily continued mixing his guests drinks by the light of a single candle. For a man once so physically active, anything smacking of adventure was a welcome relief from the hermetic existence he led. He prepared an old-fashioned for Lucy, which she insisted be weak. She said that she had never touched cocktails until she was fifty and exclaimed in mock horror that she couldn't get used to seeing her daughter drink. FDR pushed a second old-fashioned on Lucy. After a half hour a blown fuse was discovered and light restored. "There is no sabotage," Daisy gratefully noted in her diary that night. During dinner, she had watched Franklin closely to see how much he ate of the broiled chicken and lobster. After dinner, FDR shooed his other guests to their bedrooms while Lucy remained with him.

The next day dawned sunny and clear, but still frigid. A shivering Lucy got up and threw a fur coat over her nightgown. Daisy came to the president's room, put an extra sweater on him, and tucked a coat over his shoulders. Still, FDR insisted that they all board his touring car, the top down, for an outing to Dowdell's Knob. He patted the seat alongside him, signaling Lucy to sit there, while Daisy wedged herself into a corner and Polly rode the jump seat. Fala sat up front next to the driver. Lucy's daughter was left behind, down with a nasty cold. On the winding drive up to the Knob, they passed forlorn houses, their paint peeling and porches sagging from years of neglect during the Depression followed now by wartime shortages of labor and materials. The president assumed the tone of a genial professor of geology explaining to his students that they were mounting the southern slope of the Appalachian range, which, he said, declined from this point clear down to the Gulf of Mexico.

Months later, Lucy was to describe to the president's daughter, Anna, that morning on Dowdell's Knob. Franklin had taken her aside, she told Anna, and "I had the most fascinating hour I've ever had. He just sat there and told me some of what he regarded as the real problems facing the world now. I just couldn't get over thinking that I was really listening." He confided to her that he was trying to engineer another three-power summit with Churchill and Stalin, his aim being to draw the Soviet Union into the war against Japan. Lucy "didn't know she was telling me something that was very revealing to me," Anna recalled of the conversation. She now understood that no secrets were kept from this woman. As Lucy spoke of being entranced by the president's words, "I realized," Anna noted, that "Mother was not capable of giving him this—just listening."

After two nights at the Little White House, the guests prepared to return to Aiken. That Sunday morning, Daisy remembered, "I had a little chance to talk to Lucy Rutherfurd. We understand each other perfectly, I think, and feel the same about F.D.R. She has worried & does worry terribly, about him, & has felt for years that he has been terribly lonely. . . . We got to the point of literally weeping on each other's shoulder & we kissed each other, I think just because we each felt thankful that the other understood & wants to help Franklin."

The president whipped through his mail that morning during a hurried breakfast served by his current valet, Arthur Prettyman, under the watchful eye of a maid, Lizzie McDuffie. Daisy Suckley marveled at the elderly black woman's easy rapport with the nation's president. "She was just a 'friend' for 5 minutes," she noted in her diary, "told funny stories, laughed unrestrainedly, & gestured most amusingly & even poked him on the shoulder on one occasion to press home a point! She then resumed her position as maid." To Daisy, the interplay with a servant was "again an example of the Pres. humanity."

FDR ordered up an early lunch since he had a surprise for his guests. He was going to accompany them as far as the small town of Talbotton, twenty miles beyond Warm Springs. Bill Hassett took note of this trip in his diary, but years later, when he published the work, he blanked out Lucy's name. The party left at 2:00 P.M., the president again choosing the touring car and placing Lucy next to him while Daisy and Polly were relegated to the Rutherfurd auto. Both vehicles were flanked fore and aft by Secret Service sedans. The temperature during the night had plunged to 17 degrees and had only warmed up slightly by afternoon. Still, the president insisted on keeping the top down. The day was otherwise glorious, the air crisp, and the sun gilding the surrounding hillsides. FDR was clearly enjoying himself as the big car swerved around sharp curves, then dipped and rose through hilly country. All went well until a Secret Service car hit a pig. The motorcade stopped among weathered shacks planted in the parched earth, while an agent sought out the pig's owner, a black farmer who looked stunned when he was handed a $5 bill. "No one ever pays them anything when pigs, chickens etc. are run over by car," Daisy observed. FDR ordered the driver to continue at a leisurely pace and an hour passed before they completed the twenty miles to Talbotton. There, Lucy and Barbara bid FDR goodbye, moved into their own car, and drove off to Aiken while the president gestured Daisy and

Polly into his auto. "Franklin was 'let down' after the visitors had gone," Daisy noticed.

Five days later, Lucy wrote Daisy at Warm Springs. She was over-joyed, she said, to "see for myself what an angel you are. I knew it must be so as I had heard it from the Source I Do Not Question. As you know as well as anyone in the world the warmth of his praise and his love." She apologized for "evicting you, but you can imagine how very wonderful it was for me to feel myself under the same roof and within the sound of the voice we all love." She hinted at the confidences Franklin had shared with her on Dowdell's Knob, making a veiled reference to the time "when the great meeting takes place," which would turn out to be the gathering of FDR, Churchill, and Stalin at Yalta early in the coming year. As Daisy would one day tell Franklin's adviser on the Soviet Union, Charles E. Bohlen, regarding Lucy, "the President kept no wartime se-crets from her." Lucy closed her letter asking Daisy to come to see her or, seizing upon another link with Franklin, offering to help her to "work on your beloved papers."

FDR continued to unwind at Warm Springs, signing a few letters, working on his stamp collection, and playing Chinese checkers with a competitive ferocity that amazed Daisy. "He got really interested & not able to sleep!!" she remembered. Three days later, Lucy wrote Daisy again saying, "It is only a week ago that we left you but to me it seems months—or years—& I have been hoping for word from F. You who live within the arc lights do not know how hard it can be when one is beyond their rays." Referring to a conversation they had had at Warm Springs, she hinted at confidences between her and Daisy and added, "Yes, of course, everything is naturally 'off the record!' It never occurred to me that needed to be said." As for what the holiday had meant to her, Daisy confided to her diary, "To be in a position to see F.D.R. every day for three weeks, to wait on him, to be at hand when he wants anything, whether it's a cigarette or just someone to talk to, is the greatest privilege in the world, and an education in itself. I am a lucky person."

The president seized upon one last opportunity to wring from his va-cation another rendezvous with Lucy. The Roosevelt party was sched-uled to depart Warm Springs by rail on Sunday, December 17. FDR had Daisy call Lucy to tell her to meet the train in Atlanta and then ride with him to Washington. "It will be lovely to see her again," Daisy noted in her diary. When the train arrived in Atlanta a well-turned-out Lucy stood waiting on the platform. The president was in the parlor car with Daisy and Ambassador McCarthy, when a Secret Service agent ushered Lucy in. Daisy tactfully whispered to McCarthy that the president had something he needed to discuss with Mrs. Rutherfurd, at which point they "left her with the Pres. so they can have a little talk without an audience."

FDR returned to Washington much refreshed. Dr. Bruenn was pleased that his patient's complexion had resumed a healthy glow and that he appeared in fine fettle. Back at work, and with victory in Europe apparently at hand, the president's thoughts turned to the postwar world. His grand concept, which he said he wanted to live long enough to realize, was to establish a world government, a "United Nations." His organization must succeed where his idol, Woodrow Wilson, had failed with the League of Nations, to bring America into an international community. Soon, however, the president's good humor was jolted by dispatches pouring into the Map Room. For months scuttlebutt among GIs advancing along a front stretching from the English Channel to the Swiss border had been "Home by Christmas." But on December 16, German panzers exploded from the Ardennes forest in Belgium, launching Operation Wacht am Rhein, which history would record as the Battle of the Bulge. As casualties mounted, eventually to reach twenty thousand American dead, the president summoned his secretary of war, Henry Stimson, and General Leslie Groves, director of the Manhattan Project, the ultrasecret enterprise to build an atom bomb. The president wanted the bomb dropped on Germany. Groves, a beefy bulldog of a man, described by a fellow army engineer as "the biggest sonovabitch I've met in my life, but also one of the most capable individuals," told the president that the bomb could not even be tested for months.

By mid-January 1945, the Allies had beaten back the Ardennes offensive and FDR felt comfortable enough to concoct another opportunity to see Lucy. He wanted her to visit Hyde Park again. Becoming increasingly heedless about concealing their relationship, he invited her to leave with him on the presidential train from Washington. Of their arrival on Friday morning, January 12, Daisy Suckley recorded in her diary, "Lucy (my new cousin) came up on the train with him, so she had a nice long morning in which to talk to him." Evidently, the two had more than a morning in which to talk, since the White House log showed the president leaving Washington at 11:40 the night before. "She is such a lovely person and a very real 'old friend,'" Daisy added. "She and I have one very big thing in common, our unselfish devotion to F."

Daisy was waiting in the Roosevelt Library when Franklin and Lucy arrived. She wheeled FDR through the rooms while the president, like an enthusiastic tour guide, described each feature to Lucy. Next he took the two women in his Ford on a spin through roads as familiar as the back of his hand. They returned to Hyde Park for a lunch of an omelet, fried tomatoes, creamed potatoes, and a brown Betty dessert. Afterward Daisy tactfully took "myself off as soon as I had finished my coffee so they could talk." At 3:30 that afternoon Lucy was driven in a howling snowstorm to the Poughkeepsie station and headed home.

Within a half hour a self-invented therapist named Harry Lenny arrived at Hyde Park carrying with him FDR's latest hopes. Franklin, now almost sixty-three, a paraplegic for twenty-four years, still entertained dreams that he could be made to walk again. Lenny had won a following by persuading patients, including Daisy and Polly, that he could work wonders with a massage technique he had hit upon. In order not to offend or invite too many questions from FDR's regular therapist, Commander Fox, Lenny adopted the guise of a simple masseur. He asked Daisy to fix it up so that he could speak freely to the president without Fox present. She was also to tell FDR to eat "no sweets, no starches, no liquids, & no citrus fruit for the next 24 hours" as part of the cure. If he became thirsty "he can put a slice of lemon on his tongue." Lenny had assured her, "Everything is going well, & beginning to work as it should." That afternoon, he treated both Franklin and Polly Delano during a two-hour session. Afterward, Daisy wrote in her diary of an exultant Franklin, "F discovered that he could move his little toe & Lenny says this muscular gain is extending to the calf muscles, but that the total gain in the whole body will of course take a long time." The president further told Daisy that "his feet have not been cold for two weeks, or since the beginning of these treatments." Daisy happily began packing to return to Washington with the president on Monday morning in preparation for an event likely never to occur again in America, the inauguration of a president for a fourth term.

## Chapter 33

## "WE MUST SPEAK IN RIDDLES"

· · · · · · ·

Despite the president's hopes raised by the Harry Lenny treatments, his failing health was all too obvious to the man physically closest to him, his valet, Arthur Prettyman. It was January 20 and within hours FDR would be taking the oath of office. As Prettyman lifted Roosevelt from his bed into the bathtub, he noted the man's continuing weight loss. Even the once muscular chest and shoulders had shrunk. Prettyman helped the president soap himself and, watching FDR's trembling hands, knew that he would have to shave him, too. Franklin's son Jimmy, now a Marine Corps colonel, came in and helped dress his father in a dark single-breasted suit and striped tie, with the black shoes attached to the black braces. FDR had chosen to take the oath on the South Portico of the White House instead of the traditional swearing in at the Capitol. Referring to the millions now fighting abroad, he had said to the inauguration planners, "Who is there to parade?" The unspoken reason was to reduce the demands on his waning strength.

The invited guests, shivering in the cold just a degree above freezing, stood within the White House grounds, while thousands of spectators sought to catch a glimpse of the ceremony from behind the tall wrought iron fence rimming the Ellipse. Among those invited stood Lucy Mercer Rutherfurd clutching the "Order of Service" printed on heavy white stock with a handwritten inscription, "LMR from Franklin D. Roosevelt." In her purse she carried an inaugural coin with FDR in profile on one side and "January 20, 1945" on the other. How she had voted was never in doubt. As her daughter, Barbara, put it, "She was definitely a Roosevelt person."

At the bottom of the curved twin staircases leading from the portico to the frozen earth stood FDR's thirteen grandchildren, blue with cold.

Behind them sat fifty wounded servicemen in wheelchairs. As the pink-cheeked musicians of the Marine Corps band finished "Hail to the Chief," Jimmy helped his father take the few steps to the rostrum where Chief Justice Harlan Fiske Stone held the Roosevelt family Bible. With the oath administered, the president began to speak, his voice shaky at first, but growing in strength. "We Americans of today, together with our allies, are passing through a period of supreme test," he said. "It is a test of our courage, of our resolve, of our wisdom, our essential democracy. . . . As I stand here today, having taken the solemn oath of office in the presence of my fellow countrymen—in the presence of our God—I know that it is America's purpose that we shall not fail." In five minutes, the speech was over.

Entering the White House, Daisy and Polly joined two thousand other guests happily escaping the icy air for the warmth of the State Dining Room where plates of chicken salad, a roll, and a piece of cake were set out on a long table. Lucy had made the decision not to enter the White House, and Daisy, in her diary that night, reported, "stopping off for a little visit with Lucy Rutherfurd in Q Street to tell her all about the inside, which she could not see from the lawn."

The next day Daisy faced a dilemma. She had been invited for lunch with Lucy and Violetta's family. But on her way out, stopping by to check on Franklin, he asked her, "Do you want to save my life?" "I would always be glad to save the President's life," Daisy answered. Another formal luncheon was scheduled to take place downstairs, which FDR hoped to skip. "Stay and have lunch with me on a tray," he said. She agreed and raced off to squeeze in a short visit with Lucy at her sister's home before returning to Franklin. Lucy drove her back to the White House. During the ride, they discussed the president's poor appetite. His eating habits had led Daisy to begin feeding him small amounts of what she called "gruel," oatmeal, to stimulate his appetite. In her diary a few days later, noting again how little he had eaten at dinner, she went to his bedroom at 10:00 P.M., "and I took a coffee cup full of gruel. I knew that if I took even a coffee cup full, it would probably look too big & he wouldn't take any. So much for that. It worked!" She concluded later that this entry revealed too much of the president's sickness and crossed the words out.

Whatever his physical condition, Roosevelt's grand ventures always acted as a tonic to his spirits. Just three days after his inauguration, he boarded the heavy cruiser USS *Quincy*, at Newport News, Virginia, bound first for Malta, where he would meet with Prime Minister Churchill, and then fly to the Black Sea resort of Yalta in the Crimea to join Joseph Stalin and Churchill for their final three-power summit. Each leader would bring his own priority to Yalta. The British wanted to preserve their empire after the war, the Soviets wanted to solidify their conquests in Europe and regain lost territories in the Far East, and Roosevelt wanted to draw the Soviet Union into the conflict against Japan. At that point the Japanese were still proving tenacious. The atom bomb was only an experiment and could prove a $2 billion dud. Invasion of the Japanese homeland appeared inescapable and was set for November 1945. In the worst forecast American casualties were estimated at up to half a million. Churchill feared the Japanese war could drag on into 1948. Soviet entry could lighten this dark prospect.

Eleanor Roosevelt had hoped to accompany her husband on this journey. Instead he chose his daughter, Anna. "If you go," he told Eleanor, "they will all feel they have to make a great fuss, but if Anna goes, it will be simpler." Eleanor, he advised, should stay behind to represent him at several of the annual fund-raising balls held to benefit the March of Dimes campaign to fight polio. Anna subsequently attempted to explain that she had not supplanted her mother. "Mother never said anything to me about wanting to go," she said, but in the next breath she admitted, "I can remember asking Father, 'Do you suppose I can go to Yalta? I'm the only one who hasn't been to one of the big conferences,'" omitting her presence at Tehran the year before. Her case was clinched when FDR learned that Churchill's daughter Sarah and Kathy, the daughter of Averell Harriman, his ambassador to the Soviet Union, would be attending, but no wives.

At dusk, as the *Quincy* got underway, Anna found herself sitting on deck with her father watching the Virginia coast slip by. The president was in an erudite mood, surprising his daughter with his detailed knowledge of aquatic bird life along the shore. In the midst of his musings, he stopped suddenly and pointed toward the land, and said, "Over there is where Lucy's family used to live, that's where they had their plantation," referring to the property of Minna Mercer's father, John Tunis. On the seventh day out, his sixty-third birthday, FDR became as excited as a child when at breakfast he was presented with a box full of little gifts sent along by Lucy and Daisy, a windproof cigarette holder, a thermometer, a comb, and other trinkets. That evening Anna arranged a party at

which five cakes were served, four representing FDR's presidential victories, while the fifth, a small one decorated with a question mark,
hinted at a possible fifth term.

After nine days at sea the *Quincy* arrived at the Maltese port of Val-
letta where FDR and Churchill conferred before departing for the Soviet
Union, a seven-hour flight for FDR on the presidential plane, the *Sacred
Cow*, to a snow-encrusted airfield near Saki in the Crimea. There followed a seemingly endless jarring eighty-mile drive along a rutted dirt
road through steppes and mountains to Yalta. Of Stalin's choice for the
rendezvous, Churchill remarked, "If we had spent ten years on research,
we could not have found a worse place." He told his aide they would
only survive "by bringing an adequate supply of whiskey." After witness-
ing the president's infirmity the year before at Tehran, Stalin had said,
"the next time I will come to him." Instead, when the 1945 meeting was
being planned, he announced that he could not leave his country at so
sensitive a juncture in the war. Consequently, the man with the failing
heart whose life was measured in months traveled seven thousand miles
to accommodate a dictator who still had years to live. Both of FDR's
physicians went along on the trip, and Anna wrote to her husband, "Ross
[McIntire] and Bruenn are both worried because of the old 'ticker' trouble, which of course, no one knows about but those two and me. . . . It's
truly worrisome—and there's not a helva [sic] lot anyone can do about
it." She closed with a warning to Boettiger, "Better tear off and destroy
this paragraph." After laying a practiced eye on Roosevelt at Yalta,
Churchill's physician, Lord Moran, wrote, "He has all the symptoms of
hardening of the arteries of the brain in an advanced stage, so that I give
him only a few months to live."

By now, the pact between Lucy and Daisy had become cemented by
the secrets they shared. While FDR was at Yalta, Lucy wrote Daisy of
her emotional confusion. "There seems to be so much to be decided,"
she said, "what is right and what is wrong for so many people & I feel
myself incapable of judging anything." What needed to be decided was
left unsaid but hinted at a future for her and Franklin to which only
Daisy was privy. "Yes, it is difficult when we must speak in riddles but we
must," Lucy went on, "we have spoken to one another very frankly—and
it must end there. One cannot <u>discuss</u> something that is sacred." She
pleaded with Daisy to share "whatever news you have as you are in official touch & I am not." She added a postscript explaining that she had

found a candidate, a porter, to look after the president on his train travels, and added, "If you follow this up, would [you] <u>not</u> mention my name at all—at all." Finally the president got a message through to Daisy from Yalta, "I'm in the last stretch of the conference—& though the P.M. meetings are long and tiring I'm <u>really all right</u>, & it really has been a success. I either work or sleep!"

With Yalta ended, the *Quincy* returned to Newport News on February 27. Two days later, FDR reported to a joint session of Congress on the outcome of the conference. He entered the chamber in a wheelchair and when it came time for him to speak no attempt was made to brace himself standing at a lectern or supported on a son's arm. Instead he moved to an upholstered chair and began: "I hope you will pardon me for the unusual posture of sitting down during the presentation of what I want to say, but I know that you will realize that it makes it a lot easier for me in not having to carry about ten pounds of steel around on the bottom of my legs, and also because I have just completed a fourteen thousand mile trip." His labor secretary, Frances Perkins, recalled, "I remember choking up to realize that he was actually saying, 'You see, I'm a crippled man.' He had never said it before and it was one of the things that nobody ever said to him or ever mentioned in his presence. It wasn't done. It couldn't be done. He had to bring himself to full humility to say it before Congress."

Days later, Franklin and Eleanor were seated at dinner for a rare evening together when Eleanor began pressing her current agenda on him. Ordinarily, Anna recalled, FDR would put her off with an amusing remark, or say "I agree with you totally and I will talk to so and so tomorrow." In his more patient days he had kept in his desk drawer a parody that amused him of Edgar Allan Poe's "The Raven," evoking his hyperkinetic wife: "And despite her global milling / of the voice there is no stilling / With its platitudes galore / As it rushes on advising, criticizing, moralizing, patronizing, paralyzing ever more / advertising Eleanor." But this evening his face sagged with fatigue and Anna said, "Mummy, can't you see you're making Pa ill?" Instead of retreating, Anna noted, she "pressed more strongly and perhaps with less tact than in the past. The nerves of both of them were raw. Mother was not as tactful as she used to be, Father not as kidding as he used to be. . . . Although she knew the doctors had said he should have his half hour of relaxation—no business, just sitting around, maybe a drink, but she would come in more and more frequently with an enormous bundle of letters which she wished to discuss with him immediately and have a decision on. . . . I felt sorry for Mother, what she wanted was OK, but for him it was one more thing at the end of a tough day. . . . She could pester the hell out of him."

"It is very hard to live with someone who is almost a saint," Anna Rosenberg, FDR's labor adviser, observed as Eleanor, fighting against racial bigotry, women's inequality, slum housing, exploitation of the working class, laid all her lofty causes in the president's lap. "He had his tricks and evasions," Rosenberg had learned. "Sometimes he had to ridicule her in order not to be troubled by her." Eleanor's cajoling was magnified by the fact, perceived by the New Deal economist John Kenneth Galbraith, that to get to FDR, you went first to Eleanor. "She was considered the open point of access on all humane and liberal concerns," as many others besides Galbraith had discovered. Franklin Roosevelt's dilemma was essentially that he was married not simply to a wife, but to a stateswoman. He knew what she had grown into and respected and admired her for it. She might be a scold, and a nag, but he could never shut her out completely because, even as he bridled, he knew she brought him back to his true bearings. But her very stature, now outside his sphere of control, only sharpened his loneliness. A woman so furiously rushing about to right the world's wrongs, who would shout a warning, an opinion, a criticism over her shoulder while rushing from the White House to storm the next barricade, could not provide the solace for which FDR hungered. Jimmy Roosevelt accepted that his mother was not capable of giving his father "that touch of triviality he needed to lighten his burdens." But Anna well understood which woman could fulfill that role. "She was a wonderful listener," Anna said of Lucy Rutherfurd, "an intelligent listener in that she knew the right questions, while Mother would get in there and say 'I think you are wrong, Franklin.'" Anna's final judgment of her parents' marriage, however, was positive. "Through all those last years, and in the last year and a half, I was very close," she told an interviewer. "I saw that the two had preserved a mutual respect and their own type of affection and a tremendous feeling of duty toward each other."

Eleanor was soon back on the road, journeying to North Carolina to address the legislative assembly in Raleigh, then to a conference on "Education in the Mountains." The way was now clear for Lucy to return to the White House, which she did over three successive days. On March 12, Franklin arrived outside Violetta's home to pick her up for a drive through the countryside. They were back in time for dinner with Anna and John Boettiger in the president's study. The next night, a more formal occasion, FDR invited the Canadian prime minister, MacKenzie King, to dine with them. Anna served as hostess while FDR introduced King to Lucy Rutherfurd, whom the prime minister remembered as a "very lovely woman of great charm." The third day, she was back with just FDR and Anna for a small lunch in the sun parlor. She returned at 7:30 for dinner and spent the next three hours alone with the president. She would one day describe to Anna how she remembered these occasions: "his ringing laugh and one thinks of all the ridiculous things he used to say—and do—and enjoy. The picture of him sitting and waiting for you one night with the rabbi's cap on his extraordinarily beautiful head is still vivid." Anna saw nothing underhanded in Lucy's visits, rather that "they were occasions which I welcomed for my father because they were light-hearted and gay, affording a few hours of much needed relaxation for a loved father and world leader in a time of crisis." Even a president, she recognized, could not slay dragons every day. The secret machinations to bring Franklin and Lucy together continued essentially to spare Eleanor pain while another factor also intruded. All his life, from the days of his college boy code, FDR had enjoyed subterfuge for its own sake. The carefully calibrated comings and goings of his wife and Lucy added a dash of spice to the liaison. The writer John Gunther perceptively noted that FDR "went North by going South and loved it. He was tricky for fun." Rexford Tugwell observed of the president, "He deliberately concealed the processes of his mind." The day after Lucy's latest private dinner with Franklin, Eleanor returned from North Carolina in time to celebrate the Roosevelts' fortieth wedding anniversary at a small luncheon with the Morgenthaus, Harry Hooker, Franklin's old law partner, and Anna.

During his presidency, FDR, a man who could not take a step unaided, had traveled a half million miles, including over two hundred trips back to Hyde Park. The Saturday after the anniversary celebration, he and Eleanor boarded the train for still another journey home. There, he exhibited the sharp dichotomy between body and soul that had come to characterize his behavior. His secretary, Grace Tully, thought he looked terrible. Yet, he became practically febrile with plans for the future. He informed Eleanor that in late April he intended to go to San Francisco to witness the birth of the United Nations. He wanted her to come and hear him speak. Then, with victory in Europe assured, they would go to England, stay with the king and queen at Buckingham Palace, and visit the front, as he had done in 1918, in short, reap the plaudits due a conquering hero. Winston Churchill promised that the British people would give to Franklin Roosevelt "the greatest reception ever accorded to any human being since Lord Nelson made his triumphant return to England."

But on this trip to Hyde Park, the cold gray that shrouded the Hudson Valley began to dampen instead of revive his spirits. He slept poorly and finally told Eleanor, "It's no good, I must go to Warm Springs." He may have wanted his wife at his side for a triumphal procession through Europe, but having her with him during a desperately needed rest had far less appeal. He had someone else in mind. He put Eleanor off. She remembered Franklin telling her, "there were certain things he had to do, and I'd better wait and come down later. I would not bother him as I would by discussing questions of state; he would be allowed to get a real rest, and would have companionship—and that was what I felt he most needed." She was not concerned that he might be lonely, since "two people he enjoyed having with him, Margaret Suckley and Polly Delano," had been willingly conscripted for the trip. FDR wanted Anna to come too, but at the last minute, her youngest child, six-year-old Johnny, came down with a serious glandular condition and had to be taken to Bethesda Naval Hospital.

*Chapter 34*

# THE DEATH OF A PRESIDENT

· · · · · · ·

ON FRIDAY, MARCH 30, word spread quickly throughout Warm Springs, the president was coming. In the days before, telephone crews had been tearing up the streets and laying underground cables, always a signal of his impending arrival. Hazel Stephens, a physical therapist and the Warm Springs Foundation's recreation director, stood among the crowd waiting at the tiny train station. The electric atmosphere that FDR generated was heightened for Hazel, since in the past weeks she had been rehearsing a cast of polio patients to perform a blackface minstrel show for him.

At 1:30 P.M., the train pulled in and the presidential party started to descend, the Secret Service first, then faces now familiar, Grace Tully, Bill Hassett, Dr. Bruenn, Commander Fox, Daisy Suckley with Fala, and Polly Delano with a Scotch terrier she called Sister. Roosevelt's blue Ford, top down, with license plate FDR·1, drew up alongside the railroad car. The president, wearing this day a dark blue suit and his battered gray fedora, brim upturned, was lowered by the small elevator. Unnoticed by most onlookers, Mike Reilly, the president's brawny security chief, was having unaccustomed difficulty bundling FDR into the automobile's front seat. Ordinarily the president would be turned with his back facing the seat, place an arm on each side of the doorway, and propel himself inside. But this day Reilly found himself handling a deadweight.

Hazel Stephens did notice that, unlike his usual practice, the president chose not to drive himself. Instead, a Secret Service agent, Charles Fredericks, who went back to the Taft administration in 1909, drove. The presidential motorcade took a slow turn first around a circle in front of the Warm Springs Foundation's Georgia Hall, lined with waving, clap-

ping patients in wheelchairs and leaning on crutches. The president returned a listless wave and a wan smile. His weight loss since his previous visit was all too visible. He had admitted to Bill Hassett that he had
dropped twenty-five pounds. That evening, after FDR had been put to
bed, Hassett went to Commander Bruenn and, with his unadorned directness, leveled his judgment: "He is slipping away from us and no
earthly power can save him." Of course, the president's condition was
serious, Bruenn responded, but not hopeless. What he needed was more
rest. Bruenn's diagnosis was not coolly objective. The cardiologist had
come to the White House a staunch Republican, yet he had fallen under
the Roosevelt spell and now idolized his patient.

Two days after his arrival a Secret Service agent wheeled the president into the foundation's small chapel for the Easter Sunday service.
Every corner and niche was filled to overflowing with white lilies, carnations, and gladiolus. Hazel Stephens studied the thin, gray face of the
man in the wheelchair, staring blankly ahead, singing along weakly with
the choir. He dropped his hymnbook, then his glasses, which an agent
scurried to retrieve. Hazel thought little of his muddled behavior. The
president often arrived at Warm Springs in an exhausted state and then
his spirits would rally. Bill Hassett, however, wrote in his diary that night
that he had attended the service that morning "with an overpowering
sense of last things."

Over the following days, FDR did rally. One evening a gratified Daisy
Suckley watched him put away "a very rich mushroom soup, scrambled
eggs, bacon, peas, stewed peaches and cream." The old exuberance
resurfaced. "The Drs. love this little time with F," she wrote of the president being readied for bed. "We can hear the laughter from the living
room." She and Polly savored another bedtime routine. "I get the gruel &
Polly & I take it to him. I sit on the edge of the bed & he 'puts on an act':
he is too weak to raise his head, his hands are weak, he must be fed! So
I proceed to feed him with a teaspoon & he loves it! . . . On paper it
sounds too silly for words, and it is silly but he's very funny and laughs at
himself with us. Polly says all the men in her family are like that—and
those who have accomplished the most in the world can be the silliest &
funniest! It is wonderful to be able to be that way—a great safety valve
for a man to whom the whole world turns." Long afterward, she again
crossed out all references to feeding the president. One evening he
turned serious and began describing to Daisy the trip he intended to

take to San Francisco on April 25 for the inauguration of the United Nations. Then he dropped a bombshell on the closemouthed little spinster that reporters would have prized. "He says that he can probably resign some time next year when . . . the United Nations, is well started."

One morning a White House courier arrived with the official pouch. Among its contents was a column written by Walter Lippmann, the highly regarded political pundit. It was Lippmann who in 1932 had dismissed Roosevelt as an unprincipled lightweight. FDR's alarming appearance of late had apparently prompted Lippmann to a reappraisal, which the president delightedly read aloud to his staff. "His estimate of the vital interests of the United States has been accurate and far-sighted," Lippmann had written. "He has served these interests with audacity and patience, shrewdly and with calculation and he has led this country out of the greatest peril which it has ever been to the highest point of security, influence and respect which it has ever attained."

On Saturday evening, April 7, Franklin called his wife at Hyde Park. The conversation was brief, with Eleanor explaining that she was exhausted. She and Tommy Thompson had just arrived the day before and had been working nonstop to get Hyde Park ready for the summer. She compensated the next day, writing him a chatty account of their widely dispersed offspring. "Much love to you dear," she closed, "I'm so glad you are gaining. You sounded cheerful for the first time last night and I hope you'll weigh 170 lbs when you return."

Late in March, Madame Shoumatoff had again found herself in Aiken, this time to paint Lucy Mercer's stepgrandson. Lucy had recently returned from her latest visit to FDR and told the painter, "He seems very anxious to have his portrait done now." Shoumatoff had seen news stories of the president after Yalta and thought, "These last photos look ghastly." Lucy added somberly, "If this portrait is painted, it should not be postponed." Shoumatoff was puzzled, wondering whether she was hearing "Lucy's idea or did FDR really want it?" Her portrait of the boy completed, Shoumatoff returned to her home in Locust Valley, New York, but soon received a call from Lucy informing her that she should return to Aiken and that they would be going to Warm Springs together. She had heard from Franklin and everything was all set for painting the president. Ever since FDR's arrival, phone calls had indeed begun wing-ing between Aiken and the Little White House. The president's telephone log showed eight such calls from Lucy in the first ten days of his stay.

After lunch, on Monday, April 9, Shoumatoff drove her Cadillac convertible from Ridgely Hall with Lucy and Nicholas Robbins. Robbins was a photographer known for his fine photographic reproductions of paintings. Shoumatoff employed him to take photos that she could paint from when her subjects were not available for posing. With the artist driving, they pulled onto Highway 78 and began the 186-mile journey to Warm Springs. Robbins was a fussy little baldheaded man in his late fifties with thickly tufted eyebrows and an impenetrable Russian accent. He had been born Nicholas Kotzubensky, but when he became a naturalized American the judge suggested he shorten his name to Kobbins, which was mistakenly recorded as Robbins. Before fleeing the Revolution, the photographer had been a considerable landholder in the Crimea. Madame Shoumatoff found him ordinarily lovable and referred to Robbins as "Cuz," but he soon proved an exasperating back-seat driver. As they crossed the South Carolina border into Georgia, Robbins, surrounded by maps, kept second-guessing her about directions, speed, and passing. She found his guidance useless, since "he was gazing at Lucy more than he was watching the road." Robbins, a bachelor with an eye for the ladies, would later remark, "I have seen two smiles like that in my life. One was on Leonardo da Vinci's 'Mona Lisa,' and the other was Mrs. Rutherfurd's."

At the Little White House compound the guest cottage had been reserved for Lucy and the artist. Daisy and Polly filled it with flowers and had Lizzie, the maid, scrubbing away for two days. The photographer was to stay in a local hotel. Daisy was particularly eager for Lucy to see the changes wrought in Franklin. "He sits a little straighter in his chair, his voice is a little clearer and stronger, his face less drawn," she wrote in her diary on the eve of Lucy's arrival. "He is, normally, such a consistently cheerful, responsive person, that one hates to see him making an effort just to talk." The president too was impatient to see Lucy and, taking Daisy and Fala with him, decided to intercept the Shoumatoff car near Macon, Georgia. They had driven some eighty-five miles with the president staring intently into each oncoming auto, "imagining it was slowing up," Daisy recalled. Finally he gave up, and they turned around and headed back, stopping for a cold drink at a drugstore in Manchester just five miles from Warm Springs.

Lucy had become equally agitated as the Cadillac failed to encounter FDR's car. "Nobody loves us, nobody cares for us," she sighed in mock despair, though Shoumatoff believed "she was really disappointed." They were entering Manchester when they spotted a crowd gathered around a parked automobile. In the back seat sat the president of the United States wearing his Navy cape and sipping a Coca-Cola from the bottle. As FDR caught sight of Lucy, Shoumatoff noted, his face beamed. He invited them into his car while the artist directed Robbins to drive her Cadillac to Warm Springs.

FDR sent Daisy and Fala to sit up front alongside the driver while he motioned for Lucy to take the seat beside him. Madame Shoumatoff climbed in after her. The president and Lucy began chatting intimately leading the artist to fix her gaze out the window at the passing country-side. On their arrival at the Little White House, Shoumatoff turned her head away as a Secret Service agent lifted the president from the car. "There was something so pathetic about his disability," she remembered thinking at the time. Lucy and she were taken to the guest cottage, and each given a bedroom. The usually decorous Lucy flopped onto her bed, Shoumatoff noted, with evident relief.

After a rest, and freshening up, the two women joined Daisy, Polly, and FDR for cocktails in the combination living and dining room of his cottage. Shoumatoff's artist eye was impressed by Polly with her "bright blue hair, striking dinner pajamas and a profile as beautiful as a cameo." FDR, his face haggard, was nevertheless in high spirits, regaling the guests as he mixed drinks and told stories of what had gone on behind the scenes at Yalta. Stalin had given him a case of vodka and caviar, which, he said, he promised to serve the next night. The Soviet dictator "was quite a jolly fellow," he noted, "but I'm convinced he poisoned his wife!" He went on gossiping unguardedly with the assurance of one who knows that nothing he said would leave the room.

Ever since his arrival at Warm Springs, the president had called his daughter, Anna, nightly, concerned about the condition of his grandson Johnny at the Bethesda Naval Hospital. "But there was a funny little thing," Anna later noted. "He never once mentioned Lucy Mercer. . . . I didn't know Lucy was there. Had no idea."

Tuesday, April 10, dawned warm with the sky a cloudless blue. FDR flipped through three newspapers scanning the war news while having breakfast in bed. Allied troops had just entered the Krupp armament works in the Ruhr, Germany's industrial heartland. In the east, Königsberg, capital of East Prussia, had surrendered to the Red Army. The RAF had sunk the pocket battleship *Admiral Scheer*. The war in Europe could end any day, the president observed to his staff. "When the European war ends, Japan will collapse almost immediately," he added.

He was wheeled into the living room to sit for Madame Shoumatoff. She began studying photos taken earlier by Robbins, who had posed the president sitting outside on the porch for better light. But the backdrop looked dull. He had next photographed FDR inside with and without his cape. During the shooting, the president asked Robbins to take a picture of Lucy, which came out splendidly, her hands primly clasped in her lap, the eyebrows arched over blue eyes that appeared simultaneously intimate yet peering off into the distance while a faint smile crossed her lips, hinting at secret thoughts. But the photos of the president, the gray skin sagging, the neck corded, the trace of a smile unconvincing, looked dreadful. Robbins was later to claim to the FDR biographer Bernard Asbell that he had taken a photo of Franklin and Lucy together that day. If true, it would have been the only such picture extant. Robbins told Asbell that he would show him the photo at some point but would not permit him to use it. Robbins died, however, before the alleged picture ever surfaced and if such exists its whereabouts remain unknown.

Madame Shoumatoff decided that the president should wear his cape to give more substance to his diminished frame. She folded the cape around his shoulders and wondered what to do with his hands. FDR had been glancing at a program for the Jefferson Day speech he was to deliver four days hence on April 13. Shoumatoff asked if she might roll the program into a scroll for him to hold. The president brightened, saying it could stand for the United Nations Charter. The artist's manner grated on Bill Hassett. "She interfered constantly with the paperwork; measured the President's nose, made other facial measurements, asked the boss to turn this way and that; seemed to think nothing mattered but her whim of the moment. Through it all, the President looked so fatigued and weary," he wrote in his diary.

FDR still looked exhausted after a late afternoon nap, but at 5:00 P.M. insisted on driving Lucy, accompanied only by Fala, up to Dowdell's

Knob, with the security detail waiting in the nearby woods. The two watched the sun go down over the next hour, and Daisy, upon their return, was pleased to note that FDR's color had returned to a healthy pink.

Wednesday morning, the 11th, Lucy and Madame Shoumatoff had breakfast together in the guesthouse. Over coffee, Lucy shyly handed the artist a photograph the president had given her the day before of himself, smiling, standing tall, taken during their romance while he was assistant secretary of the navy. The artist sensed that Lucy wanted to unburden herself but was unsure how to proceed. "She had never talked to me about the time she first met Roosevelt," Shoumatoff recalled of the conversation, "and even now she was rather vague and reserved." Still, in her oblique way, Lucy came as close as she ever would to revealing to someone outside the family what had happened between her and Franklin.

As Madame Shoumatoff recalled Lucy's account of the affair, "From the very beginning, there was a strong feeling of mutual admiration and affection between them. Inexorably drawn to each other, this feeling became increasingly intense and in view of the fact that Franklin was married and had five children and Lucy herself was a strict Catholic, she knew that they must part since she could not consider a divorce. . . . Lucy married Winthrop Rutherfurd and dedicated her life to her new family." Lucy then, according to Shoumatoff, made the disingenuous claim to the artist that "Only once during the lifetime of Mr. Rutherfurd . . . did she officially appear at the White House. This was when FDR was desperately sick with, I believe, pneumonia. She did not mention that there were any other meetings before her husband died. This particular meeting was at the request of Franklin Roosevelt with the consent of Mrs. Roosevelt, and not only sanctioned, but urged by Mr. Rutherfurd himself."

Later that morning Daisy managed to have another of her prized chats alone with Lucy. She had something for Franklin, Lucy told her, taking a small container of a medicinal substance from her purse. Daisy decided that before giving the remedy to FDR, Dr. Bruenn should take a look at it. He was unimpressed. "It has little in it that sugar has not," he told her.

The president, whom Bill Hassett believed was "slipping away," nevertheless sat his assistant down and started to outline a punishing schedule that he wanted arranged. As recorded in Hassett's diary, "The boss has resisted every attempt to make him change his mind. He will go come hell or high water. He expected to leave for Washington within a week, give a dinner for the Regent of Iraq on the evening of April 19. And travel to Chicago the next day en route to San Francisco." He would make his speech to the United Nations on the 25th, he told Hassett, and then head for San Diego to visit Anne Roosevelt, his son John's wife, and his grandchildren. He next called in a secretary and began dictating a first draft of his United Nations speech. "A good speech, too," Hassett thought. "The work, my friends, is peace; more than an end of this war," it began, "an end to the beginning of all wars . . . toward the greatest contribution that any generation of human beings can make."

Daisy had spent much of the day crocheting and chatting with Lucy and Polly, a conversation that invariably came back to Franklin's health. At 4:30 P.M., the president announced that he was taking a ride. Daisy started to excuse herself so that Franklin and Lucy could go alone. No, he wanted Daisy along, and Fala too, he said. "I threw on my hat & my Sears Roebuck raincoat over my rather messy dress, jumped in & off we went for a two hour drive in warm, wonderful air." That night, before she went to bed, Daisy recorded what she had observed during the trip. "Lucy is so sweet with F— No wonder he loves to have her around— Toward the end of the drive, it began to be chilly and she put her sweater over his knees—I can imagine just how she took care of her husband— She would think of <u>little</u> things which make so much difference to a semi-invalid, or even a person who is just tired, like F." This passage too was subsequently crossed out in her diary.

Henry Morgenthau Jr., the secretary of the treasury, "Henry the Morgue" to FDR, arrived at Warm Springs at 7:30 P.M., taking an opportunity to see the president while en route from Washington to Florida to be with his wife, who had recently suffered a heart attack. He found FDR mixing cocktails at a card table, his withered legs propped on a footstool. "I was terribly shocked when I saw him, and I found that he had aged terrifically and looked very haggard," Morgenthau remembered. "His hands shook so that he started to knock the glasses over, and I had to hold each glass as he poured out the cocktail. I noticed that he took two cocktails and then seemed to feel a little bit better. I found his memory bad, and he was constantly confusing names. He hasn't weighed himself so he didn't know whether he had gained weight or not. I have never seen him have so much difficulty transferring himself from his wheelchair to a regular chair, and I was in agony watching him."

Yet Morgenthau was surprised to see the president put away a dinner of veal, noodles, and a waffle topped with ice cream and chocolate syrup. After dinner FDR amused his guests, poking good-natured fun at some of Eleanor's experiences as a furniture maker at Val-Kill. Morgenthau, with the war in Europe drawing to an end, raised his current obsession, the Morgenthau Plan, which essentially called for "removing all industry from Germany and simply reducing them to an agricultural population of small landowners." But this night, Franklin was more interested in lighthearted conversation. Morgenthau's sober counsel prompted him to tell a story about the German finance minister, Hjalmar Schacht, who had come to see him in the 1930s, "three or four times, saying that the Germans were going broke." He then added with feigned annoyance, "and they never did!" Even his vision of addressing the United Nations took on a playful note. "I am going there on my train," he said, "and at three o'clock in the afternoon I will appear on the stage in my wheelchair, and I will make the speech." He clasped his hands in mock prayer. "And then they will applaud me, and I will leave and go back on my train, go down to Los Angeles and dump my daughter-in-law, and I will be back in Hyde Park on May first." Morgenthau left early that evening for Florida, still shocked by the diminished leader he had seen.

FDR called his daughter, Anna, again. He wanted to know how little Johnny was progressing. He sounded chipper, telling her that tomorrow should be a grand day. Ruth Stevens, a Warm Springs neighbor, would be putting on her customary barbecue for him and all his friends at Mayor Frank Allcorn's place on top of Pine Mountain. Stevens was a favorite of his, a woman as direct as a punch in the nose with a poetic command of profanity. He was eager to try the Brunswick stew she made especially for him, he told Anna. He then ended the conversation with his favorite child. Later that night he and his guests sat around the fireplace while another gifted storyteller, Madame Shoumatoff, held them spellbound with tales of ghosts recalled from her Russian girlhood, the favorite about a black pearl necklace belonging to Catherine the Great. Dr. Bruenn came in and told FDR it was time to go to bed. "The President, like a little boy, asked to stay up longer," Shoumatoff remembered. But Bruenn was insistent. His cousins followed Franklin to his bedroom where Daisy fed him the soothing gruel. He was still in high spirits. "The trouble is that just as soon as he gets a little better he feels full of pep and proceeds to use it up all over again," Daisy observed. "It's next to impossible to stop him at just the right moment between his having a happy interesting time, and his getting overtired."

Eleanor Roosevelt, in Washington, awoke early on the morning of Thursday, April 12, summoning the faithful Tommy Thompson to go over with her the schedule for the day, a press conference, an afternoon charity benefit supporting the thrift shop at the Sulgrave Club, then departure to New York for a round of speaking engagements. At the press conference reporters asked about the upcoming opening of the United Nations at San Francisco. Would the president go? What would he say? Would she be going with him? She was happy to inform them that she would indeed accompany her husband to San Francisco. The planned trip to the United Nations mirrored what the Roosevelt marriage had become, barely intersecting on the personal level, but a true union of souls on issues that mattered to both of them.

That morning the president was awake at 8:30, reasonably well rested but complaining of a slight headache and a stiff neck. He could hear peals of laughter coming from the kitchen. When the maid, Lizzie McDuffie, came in to clean the bedroom, she noted that he had his cape draped over his shoulders though the day promised to be warm and humid. The president asked her what the laughing was about. "Reincarnation," Lizzie answered. "I don't know if I believe it or not," she said, "but if there is such a thing, I want to come back as a canary bird." She watched FDR slowly eye her from head to toe. "I weighed about two hundred pounds and he burst into laughter and said what he always said whenever anything amused him, 'Don't you love it? Don't you just love it?' "

After breakfast FDR was wheeled into the living room and parked behind the card table that also served as his desk. He whisked through day-old Atlanta newspapers. Lucy came in and handed him an editorial clipped from a Palm Beach paper about his address to Congress after Yalta, which she had been carrying in her purse since February. The editorial dealt with the rarity of honest language in politics. The writer quoted FDR's apology to Congress for sitting down while he spoke because of the weight of his braces and the marathon journey he had just completed. Whatever Roosevelt's political victories, the editorial noted, "he will leave an example of mental fortitude and capacity to rise above bodily affliction that will be an inspiration to the physically handicapped." As he looked up, Lucy remarked, "I suppose you get tired even of the nice articles." He responded dryly, "I do not get many nice ones."

He then set to work. He dictated a cable to Averell Harriman, his special envoy in Moscow. Stalin had recently sent offensive messages to the president questioning America's reliability as an ally. Harriman wanted to counterpunch with a tough reply. Not about to alienate Stalin with victory within their grasp, FDR instructed Harriman to go easy and tell the Soviet dictator that their misunderstandings were strictly minor. William J. Donovan, the president's intelligence chief as director of the OSS, had sent the president a warning out of Switzerland that the Germans were reportedly planning to retreat into the Bavarian and Austrian Alps to stage a last-ditch stand in a "National Redoubt" that could lengthen the war by years. Bill Hassett began feeding him a steady stream of bills to sign, prompting FDR to wave his pen and say triumphantly, "Here's where I make a law." With each signature, Hassett spread the documents over every chair, sofa and table, waiting for the ink to dry, which FDR referred to as hanging out the laundry. The president next turned to his stamp collection and put a call through to Washington to make sure he was sent the first stamp commemorating creation of the United Nations. He sifted through a batch that he particularly relished, Japanese occupation stamps captured in the recently liberated Philippine Islands. Madame Shoumatoff arrived near noon and, sensing how absorbed FDR was, offered to come back later. "Oh no," he said, "I'll be through in a few minutes and I will be ready for you." His appearance amazed her. He was wearing a gray double-breasted suit and a Harvard red tie. "I was struck by his exceptionally good color." She remembered "that gray look had disappeared."

For the president, the mood in the wood-paneled room could not have been more congenial. Through the open cottage doorway where Madame Shoumatoff had positioned her easel, the fragrance of azaleas outside wafted in as the day continued to warm. Green signs of spring could be glimpsed on the surrounding fields and hillsides. People who brought familiarity, comfort, and ease to his life surrounded him. Daisy was crocheting while chatting with Lucy about the afternoon barbecue and the minstrel show. Polly returned from watering the roses in her room, her Scotch terrier, Sister, trailing behind.

At twenty minutes to one, Arthur Prettyman, the valet, came in and set a cup of gruel, a pitcher of cream, and a glass with a green fluid beside the president. FDR grimaced and without lifting his eyes from his reading, downed the latter, a vile concoction that was supposed to increase his appetite. Daisy got up, poured cream into the gruel, and mixed it. Franklin absently took a few mouthfuls, still absorbed in his papers. Madame Shoumatoff at her easel disliked having anyone see her work in progress; but Daisy had discovered that by standing near the fireplace she could look into an oval mirror and see how the painting was progressing. She stole a peek, sat down, and resumed her crocheting. A Filipino steward, Joe Esperancilla, came in and began to set the table for lunch. FDR looked up and said, "We have got just about fifteen minutes more to work." Shoumatoff, already painting rapidly, quickened her pace and continued to complete the upper part of the face and FDR's hairline.

The room had gone silent when Daisy saw Franklin's head suddenly slump forward, his hands thrashing at his side. She sprang up and asked, "Have you dropped your cigarette?" He "looked at me with his forehead furrowed in pain and tried to smile. He put his left hand up to the back of his head & said, 'I have a terrific pain in the back of my head!' He spoke so faintly, she remembered, that "I don't think anyone else heard it." She grabbed the phone and told the operator, "Please get in touch with Dr. Bruenn and ask him to come at once to the President's cottage." Madame Shoumatoff shouted for Prettyman and Esperancilla to carry the president into his bedroom. They found the inert body unexpectedly heavy, and so Polly and Daisy took FDR's feet and the four managed to get the stricken man onto his bed. "I was cold as ice, in my heart, cold & precise in my voice," Daisy later recalled. "I opened his collar & tie. . . . I held his right hand. Polly was on his left, her hand on his heart, fanning him. Two or three times he rolled his head from side to side, opened his eyes. Polly thinks he looked at us all in turn. He may have. I could see no signs of real recognition in those eyes." Within minutes he fell unconscious. Lucy hurried in and began waving smelling salts under the president's nose, to no avail. Within a few minutes, Bruenn arrived.

Hazel Stephens had been pressured to get the minstrel show ready early. She had thought that she had until Friday the 13th to present it. But Grace Tully had informed her, "The Boss would like to have a request perfor-

mance of the minstrel on Thursday, April 12 at 5:30 P.M." Soldiers from the
Signal Corps had erected a two-level stage for her with five microphones.
The cast was nervously awaiting the opening curtain, all polio patients but
for two professional dancers brought in from Atlanta, and an FDR favorite,
Graham Jackson, a black pianist and accordionist. Jackson had obtained
leave to come in from Macon, where he was stationed as a recruiting chief
petty officer in the Coast Guard. He would be performing this day the
twenty-fourth time for the president. As soon as the barbecue ended,
Stephens could expect the presidential motorcade to pull up.

Eleanor Roosevelt arrived that afternoon at the Sulgrave Club where she
sat next to President Wilson's widow, Edith. The first lady was scheduled
to speak and so had dressed in a suit of a soft red fabric that she was told
became her. She would leave after hearing the pianist Evelyn Tyner perform, and then head for New York.

Recognizing the awkwardness of her presence in Warm Springs at this
moment, Lucy, eyes red and swollen, told Madame Shoumatoff, "We
must pack and go." They began throwing their belongings into their luggage, Shoumatoff taking extra pains in handling the unfinished presidential portrait. As they left the cottage, Nicholas Robbins appeared
driving the artist's convertible. Mike Reilly, the chief bodyguard, scurried around to find enough gas for the trip to Aiken. By 2:30 they were
underway with Shoumatoff taking the wheel. They had been on the road
for several hours when Lucy insisted they stop at a hotel. She had to
phone Warm Springs, she said. Repeated attempts to place a call from a
pay phone failed. Shoumatoff said that she would go to the hotel switchboard and ask the operator to put through an emergency call. She found
the operator in tears and returned to Lucy, waiting in the hotel lobby, to
tell her what the woman had just heard on the radio. "The President is
dead," Shoumatoff said. Lucy, she remembered, "sat motionless and remained utterly silent."

Dr. Bruenn's terse notes recorded the final moments. "3:31 Breathing
suddenly stopped and replaced by occasional gasps. Heart sounds not
audible. Artificial respiration began, caffein, sodium benzoate given.
Adrenalin administered into the heart muscle. 3:35 Pronounced dead."

The president had died of a massive cerebral hemorrhage. At his death he had served eighty-three days into his fourth term. "In the quiet beauty of the Georgia spring, like a thief in the night," Hassett wrote in his diary, "came the day of the Lord, the immortal spirit no longer supported the failing flesh and at 3:35 pm the President gave up the ghost." His next duty, Hassett realized, was to locate an undertaker.

Hazel Stephens had been applying makeup to her minstrel show cast when Graham Jackson came running across the stage calling out, "He's dead! The President's dead!" The performers, stunned, hung about the playhouse, weeping, their grief incongruous in their painted faces and clown costumes of pink shirts, green vests, white pants, huge orange cardboard neckties, and pie-sized buttons.

Evelyn Tyner, the pianist, was in the midst of her performance when a member of the Sulgrave Club tiptoed to Eleanor and whispered that she had just received an urgent telephone call. Excusing herself, she went to the phone and heard the agitated voice of the president's press secretary, Steve Early. He asked her to come back to the White House at once. She did not ask why. "I knew down in my heart that something dreadful had happened," she later recalled of the moment. She then returned to the head table and sat through the completion of the pianist's piece before getting up and announcing, "I'm called back to the White House and I want to apologize for leaving before this delightful concert is finished." She left to a standing ovation. On her return, Early and Admiral McIntire reported what they had just learned from Bruenn at Warm Springs. Her daughter, Anna, was with her son at Bethesda Naval Hospital when she was told of her father's death.

Vice President Harry Truman had just returned from presiding over the Senate and had gone to Room H-128, a high-ceilinged after-hours hide-away, to sip bourbon with the Speaker of the House, Sam Rayburn. At 5:15 P.M. he received the call from Mrs. Roosevelt telling him that the president was dead. He snatched his hat and ran from the room. Upon arriving at the White House, face taut, mouth set in a thin line, wearing a gray suit and a polka dot tie, he asked Eleanor, "What can I do?" She answered, "Is there anything we can do for you? You are the one in trouble now."

She sent off a message to her four sons in uniform, Marine Colonel James Roosevelt, Navy lieutenants Franklin Jr. and John, all in the Pacific, and Brigadier General Elliott Roosevelt in Europe. "Darlings," she wrote, "Pa slept away this afternoon. He did his job to the end as he would want you to do. Bless you. All our love, Mother." With the flag over the White House lowered to half-mast, Truman was sworn in as president at 7:00 P.M. by Chief Justice Harlan F. Stone, his hand on a Bible Truman had found on the table in the president's cabinet room. Six minutes later Eleanor was out of the White House with Early and McIntire and soon the three were airborne for Warm Springs. She told McIntire, "I am more sorry for the people of the country and the world than I am for us."

It fell to Bill Hassett to announce to reporters from the three national news services at Warm Springs the death of the president. He was asked who was with him at the end. He mentioned the doctor, the servants, and three women, Margaret Suckley, Polly Delano, and Grace Tully. He explained that at the moment he was stricken, FDR was being sketched by an artist named Nicholas Robbins. In the chaos of a president's sudden death, a staff member might be excused for getting his facts wrong. But William Hassett was no amateur observer. He was a Vermont Yankee Catholic of flinty integrity who had made his mark years before as a keen-eyed reporter. Hassett had made no honest mistake in substituting the name Nicholas Robbins for Elizabeth Shoumatoff. He had been only too aware of the irritating presence in the Little White House of the artist, whom he had described as "Amazon type, guttural voice, altogether too aggressive." Shoumatoff's being there, he feared, would expose Lucy Rutherfurd's presence, and this fact must be suppressed, as he was to attempt later by deleting all mention of her from his published diary. Thanks to Hassett's performance, no reporter at the time knew that the president's old love was with him on the day he died.

It was dark, nearly midnight, when a black Lincoln sedan deposited Eleanor before the Little White House where the lights were still blazing. Upon entering the living room, calm and composed, she embraced Daisy, then Polly, then Grace Tully. "Tully dear," she said, "I am so sorry for all of you." She sat down on a sofa and asked the women to tell her exactly what had happened. Tully described her actions in the final hour. Daisy said that she had been crocheting when she saw Franklin slump. Eleanor next turned to Polly.

The faintly outlandish woman spoke with smug directness. Franklin, she said, was being painted by the Russian artist Madame Shoumatoff when he collapsed, and that she had come to Warm Springs with Lucy Rutherfurd. The two women had been here for the past four days, she added. It was difficult to read in that disciplined demeanor what Eleanor felt at hearing Polly's words. Life had left her "well prepared," she would later write of her habit of suppressing hurt. "You build a facade for every-one to see and you live separately inside the facade." Still, she had just been battered by the truth that her old rival, about whom not a word had been exchanged for nearly thirty years, was with Franklin rather than herself as his life was ebbing. Of Polly Delano's motive for speaking out, the woman would later say that had she not told Eleanor, somebody else would. Nevertheless, she had chosen, without the shortest decent inter-val, to be first. A niece of Mrs. Roosevelt's, Eleanor Wotkyns, Hall Roo-sevelt's daughter, later said of Polly, "She was a small, petty woman, jealous all her life of Eleanor's great success. . . . She hadn't done a thing in life except raise red setters and let her chauffeur drive her to dog shows. This was an act of revenge."

Eleanor's anguish was not yet over. She had excused herself to go into the bedroom to be with her husband, closing the door behind her. She re-turned after five minutes still dry-eyed, sat down, and resumed question-ing Polly. Had the Rutherfurd woman been in Franklin's company before? she wanted to know. Yes, Polly said, several times at the White House. And who had been present on these occasions? Her daughter, Anna, Polly answered, who had arranged these visits. Eleanor's expression re-mained an unreadable mask, and she said nothing more at this point.

At the least opportune moment, Louise Hackmeister, the telephone operator, informed Eleanor that she had a call from Lorena Hickok. The month before, Hick, now suffering from diabetes, had left a stressful job at the Democratic National Committee and the White House and moved to Moriches, Long Island, living alone with her dog. She told Eleanor that she wanted to be with her at this time of need. "Hick, I don't want you to come," Eleanor answered. "You of all people must re-alize what a load I am carrying now. If you came at this time, you'd just be another worry." What someone else might have taken as a rebuff,

Hick managed to turn into a compliment. "I was never so honored in my life before!" she later wrote a friend. Eleanor had been so worried about her diabetes that she did not want the stress of a journey by Hick "added to the burden she was already carrying."

During the return to Aiken an overwrought Madame Shoumatoff became hopelessly lost. She finally gave up the wheel to Nicholas Robbins, who took them in the wrong direction, adding another eighty miles to the trip before they finally reached Lucy's home after midnight. Their quiet conversation in the last hours dealt wholly with the ill-starred directions taken, the small talk people engage in to distract themselves from terrible truths. "Lucy's daughter awaited us and was certainly in a state," Shoumatoff recalled of the young woman FDR regarded as his goddaughter. Lucy, torn between grief and concern that her presence at Warm Springs might be exposed, surprised Shoumatoff. "I was rather amazed at how naive Lucy was," she later said, "thinking that her name would not be mentioned at all."

Hazel Stephens rose early the next morning to find that generals, admirals, and over five thousand soldiers had flooded into Warm Springs during the night. She stood amid 130 wheelchair-bound patients, limping adults, and children in braces gathered in front of Georgia Hall. They watched the approach of a drummer beating out a mournful cadence followed by a dark green hearse, and behind it pallbearers representing each military service. The patients strained to glimpse Mrs. Roosevelt, clad in black, riding with Admiral McIntire in the black Lincoln. The hearse stopped in front of Georgia Hall where the only sound heard was Graham Jackson playing "Goin' Home" on the accordion, the man's lips trembling, tears rolling down his cheeks, his eyes shut, an image that would become the photographic icon of a nation's grief. The spectators sobbed quietly and dabbed at their eyes. A military band began a dirge as the procession moved ahead amid solemn-faced paratroopers and officer cadets spaced four feet apart lining the route all the way to the train station. As the flag-draped coffin disappeared into the car, "All of us felt that a personal friend had left us never to return," Hazel Stephens recalled thinking.

While the funeral train rolled slowly north, Eleanor remembered, "I lay in my berth all night with the window shade up, looking out at the countryside he had loved and watching the faces of the people at stations, and even at the crossroads, who came to pay their last tribute all through the night. The only recollection I clearly have is thinking about 'The Lonesome Train,' the musical poem about Lincoln's death. 'A lonesome train on a lonesome track / Seven coaches painted black / A slow train, a quiet train / Carrying Lincoln home again . . .' I had always liked it so well—and now this was so much like it."

She would later claim that she had "an almost impersonal feeling at her husband's death, partly because much further back I had to accept the fact that a man must be what he is and that all human beings have needs and temptations." She persuaded herself that whatever sorrow she now felt was as another bereaved American at the loss of "a symbol of strength and fortitude." Eleanor had told friends that after the Lucy Mercer affair, she no longer loved her husband. However, what she had experienced was not the death of love, but enduring unhappiness because Franklin's behavior had imposed on her the necessity to suppress her love for him if she were to survive emotionally. Revealingly, at the later funeral service in the White House's East Room, she wore only a single piece of jewelry, the gold pin with diamonds that Franklin had designed himself and given to her on their wedding day, reminiscent of a time when he had indeed loved her.

Quiet, observant, plainspoken Daisy Suckley perhaps best caught the nuances of the Roosevelt marriage when she wrote: "Poor E.R.—I believe she loved him more deeply than she knows herself, and his feeling for her was deep & lasting. That fact that they could not relax together, or play together, is the tragedy of their joint lives, for I believe, from everything that I have seen of them, that they had everything else in common. It was probably a matter of personalities, of a certain lack of humor on her part—I can not blame either of them. They are both remarkable people—sky high above the average."

Dealing with her father's request to help him see Lucy Rutherfurd had been a racking decision for Anna. She was now about to taste the bitter fruit of that act. After the funeral, Eleanor asked her daughter to come with her to her sitting room in the family quarters of the White House. Curtis Roosevelt once observed that his grandmother "without opening her mouth could drip disapproval." At this moment Anna faced not only the withering gaze but accusing words. How was it that Lucy Rutherfurd had come back into her husband's life? Eleanor demanded. Was Anna responsible? Anna tried to explain her emotional crosscurrents when her father had first asked her to invite Lucy to the White House. She had sought to balance loyalty to her mother while pleasing her beloved father whom the doctors had given as little as months to live. She explained that all the meetings had been aboveboard. "There were always people around." As Anna's brother Jimmy put it, "A child caught between two parents can only pursue as honorable a course as possible." And Anna could not be sure if she had. "Mother was so upset about everything," she remembered, "and now so upset with me."

Anna was outraged by what she considered the deliberate malice of Aunt Polly. As she later reflected, "I could never forgive her. She told mother I was present as hostess at the White House when Lucy had come to dinner. But she was there too, and Daisy." She wondered if the breach with her mother could ever be healed. However tense the moment, "after two or three days, that was all," Anna gratefully recalled. "We never spoke about it again."


The press, despite Bill Hassett's muddied trail, soon managed to learn that Madame Shoumatoff had been the artist at Warm Springs, not Nicholas Robbins. Reporters tracked her down at her daughter Zoric's home in Locust Valley four days after the president's death. They jammed into the living room, where the artist was pleased at the end that "I answered all the questions without revealing Lucy's name."


Franklin Roosevelt was never to know the triumphal journey to Britain of which he had dreamed. The wild reception that Churchill had predicted yielded instead to posthumous homage. Five days after FDR's death the prime minister stood before Parliament, benches full, galleries overflowing, ordinary Britons crowding the entranceways, as he pronounced Franklin Roosevelt the greatest of all Americans, perhaps above Washington and Lincoln, because his leadership had influenced not just America, but the entire world. "What an enviable death was his," the prime minister intoned. "He had brought his country through the worst of its perils and the heaviest of its toil. Victory had cast its sure and steady beam upon him. . . . He had raised the strength, might, and glory of the great Republic to a height never attained by any nation in history." Churchill, who had sat alongside the crippled president through gruel-ing journeys and exhausting negotiations abroad, understood better than most Americans, shielded from their leader's handicap, what FDR had overcome. "Not one man in ten millions . . . would have attempted to plunge into a life of physical and mental exertion," he said. "Not one in a generation would have succeeded . . . in becoming indisputable mas-ter of the scene." Churchill recalled his last moments with Roosevelt: "At Yalta, I noticed the President was ailing. His captivating smile, his gay and charming manner had not deserted him, but his face had a transparency, an air of purification, and often there was a faraway look in his eyes. . . . I must confess that I had an indefinable sense of fear."

To the American people, the sudden removal from their midst of their leader of the past twelve years struck like a thunderclap, leaving them numb and uncomprehending. The shock struck across the political spectrum from worshippers to detractors. "The President's death," said the arch-Republican Senator Robert Taft, "removed the greatest figure of our time at the very climax of his career." The commander-in-chief had fallen, Arthur Krock wrote in *The New York Times*, with his armies "at the gates of Berlin and the shores of Japan's home islands."

The day after his death, newspapers carried their regular feature, "Today's Army-Navy Casualty List" with name, next of kin, and address. The day's first entry read: Roosevelt, Franklin D. Commander-in-Chief. Wife Mrs. Anna Eleanor Roosevelt. The White House."

Back in Aiken, Lucy wrote about Franklin, then filed her thoughts away with other mementos of his that she was to keep for the rest of her life. Calling FDR "A supremely great American, & one of the towering figures of world history," she wrote, "It is difficult to adjust to a world without him. His bitterest enemies have been shocked into a realization or a half realization of his greatness. If ever in the history of mankind anyone gave his life to its service, Franklin Roosevelt did." She then added a postscript in French as if recalling the language they had shared in their most private moments: *"On aurait voulu de voir achever cette tâche de géant qu'il affrontait avec tant de souriante grandeur."* One would have wished to see this gigantic task finished which he met with such smiling greatness.

*Chapter 35*

# LETTERS LOST AND FOUND

· · · · · · ·

SHORTLY AFTER THE FUNERAL, Eleanor faced the task of sorting through Franklin's personal belongings before turning Hyde Park over to the government. Among them she found the small watercolor portrait of him that Madame Shoumatoff had painted in 1943. She may or may not have been aware of its existence but could not have failed to note that the artist was the same one who had been painting Franklin on the day of his death and who had entered his life through Lucy Rutherfurd. Whether she could not bear to keep the painting, given this connection, or out of magnanimity, she decided that Lucy should have it. Still, she could not bring herself to send it. She gave the painting to Daisy Suckley to do so.

On May 2, Lucy wrote back, the only correspondence she had sent to Eleanor since her days as social secretary. "Margaret Suckley has written to me that you gave her the little watercolor of Franklin by Mme. Shoumatoff," she said. "Thank you so very much. You must know that it will be treasured always." She dismissed her return into Franklin's life as a brief, coincidental encounter. "I had wanted to write you for a long time to tell you that I had seen Franklin and of his great kindness about my husband when he was desperately ill in Washington. . . . and that I hoped so I might see you." Four years, however, had passed since Winty's treatment in Washington and Franklin's helpful intercession. Lucy's frequent visits with FDR since then had been marked by evading his wife, not seeking her out. Lucy generously admitted envy of Eleanor, "whom I have always felt to be the most blessed and privileged of women. . . . The whole universe finds it difficult to adjust itself to a world without Franklin, and to you and to his family. The emptiness must be appalling." She closed, "I send you—as I find it impossible not to, my love and deep sympathy, as always, affectionately, Lucy Rutherfurd."

The painting that prompted this letter remains with Lucy's descendants. Her daughter, Barbara, once told Jonathan Daniels that her mother "had offered this portrait . . . to the Hyde Park library, but that Mrs. Roosevelt would not let them accept it." Asked if this response "was because of resentment of his friendship with her mother," she answered, "Yes." Madame Shoumatoff's Warm Springs portrait of FDR was never finished. For years she kept it in storage in a warehouse and was eventually persuaded to donate it to the Little White House museum where it remains on display.

After FDR's death the link between Lucy and Anna grew beyond mutual expediency. Soon after delivery of the painting to Lucy, Anna phoned her as if seizing upon another link in their common grief. Lucy responded with a letter dated May 9, 1945. "Anna dear," she wrote, "I did not know that it was in me just now to be so glad to hear the sound of any voice and to hear you laugh was beyond words wonderful. I know that you meant more to your father than anyone." She continued, "I love to think of his very great pride in you. He told me so often with such feeling of all that you meant of joy and comfort on the trip to Yalta. He said you had been so extraordinary & what a difference it made to have you. He told me of your charm & your tact & how everyone loved you. He told me how capable you were & how you forgot nothing. . . . I hope he told you these things, but sometimes one forgets." She reiterated the thoughts she had written to herself after Franklin's death, telling Anna, "the world has lost one of the greatest men that ever lived, to me the greatest. He towers above them all effortlessly." She closed, sending her love, "because you are his child and because you are yourself," and signed the letter, "I am very devotedly & with heartbroken sympathy, Lucy Rutherfurd."

Anna was to keep this letter in a locked desk drawer for the rest of her life, showing it only to family members and a few friends. After receiving it, she had sent Lucy a copy of a parable written by the Canadian poet and novelist Dorothy Dumbrille, entitled "The Traveler." It began:

The Traveler stood at the Gate, his face lined with fatigue, his shoulders drooped.

"I had hoped I would not have to come so soon," he said.

But the Angel answered him: "You are weary, My Son and your work on Earth is finished."

"Only a few months more," he pleaded, "then I would have laid down my work gladly.

"Your work will be carried on, My Son."

The parable closed with the Traveler saying,

"I would enter the Portal, Sir, but . . . I have been many years a cripple, unable to walk alone."

"Let fall your staff, My Son," said the Angel. "Come."

And the Traveler let his stick fall to the ground and stood upright, alone, and walked through the Portal.

The sentiment may have been overwrought, but the fact that Anna sent it and Lucy kept it all her life establishes that their shared love of Franklin Roosevelt had brought these two women beyond friendship to something approaching kinship.

On the same day that Lucy wrote Anna, she also wrote Daisy Suckley. "Dear Little Margaret, Thank you so much for the snapshots at 'Top Cottage.' I have looked at them long and with the magnifying glass—and they are good." She also thanked Daisy for copying and sending her a photograph of FDR "that I liked best of the 1917 era," taken at the height of their romance. Daisy next offered to send photos taken during the president's last days, which Lucy gratefully acknowledged in a response dated May 20. "I love having the one from Warm Springs," she wrote, "though they make the pain in one's heart even sharper." Daisy had also asked Lucy if she knew where the diary was that Franklin had kept during his 1918 trip to Europe during World War I. Lucy wrote back that she was not sure of its whereabouts but gave a detailed account of the journey confirming that Franklin had indeed seen her after his return and the discovery of their love. The precision of her recall also indicated how closely she had held these memories for nearly three decades. Of Franklin's schedule on June 29, 1918, she wrote Daisy, "He then called on King George V met Churchill spoke I think at a Gray's Inn dinner where there was much oratory." She went on to describe the battlefield itinerary Franklin had followed, who had accompanied him, and what he had witnessed.

The next month, Lucy was again drawn to Hyde Park, though not as unnoticed as she had hoped. After the visit, she wrote Daisy, "It distresses me that you were given so much trouble by my descent upon you. I had been led to believe that I could slide in and out without being a burden to anyone. But evidently this was not meant to be, & I am sorry that you were held up all down the line in your work and by the guards." Referring to Daisy as "You, who know all the facts," she closed, "I loved seeing you, however, and thank you for making it all as easy as possible." While there she had been issued a Department of the Interior pass, signed by the acting director, which she kept among her other mementos of FDR for life.

Lucy and Madame Shoumatoff had not seen each other since parting in Aiken after FDR's death. Two months later, in June, they met for lunch at the Hotel Pierre in New York. "I don't know how we got through that luncheon," the artist recalled. "So many things to talk over." Afterward they retreated to Lucy's suite where she stretched out on the bed, her eyes red from crying. Shoumatoff had just settled herself on a window seat when Lucy suddenly burst out, "I have burned all his letters." "Oh Lucy, you could not have done that!" Shoumatoff said. "But why? It does not concern anyone!" "It does, it will later," the artist insisted. "No, no!" Lucy responded. "Someday," Shoumatoff countered, "it is bound to come out and it might not be in the right way. You know, Lucy, I have it all written down, because in the years to come it should be known the way it was." "I don't mind what you have written because I trust you," Lucy replied, "but I do not wish anything to be brought out while I am alive!" Doubtless, she had burned the most intimate, revealing letters but not all, as evidenced by the fact that several from Franklin to her were discovered by her family long years after Lucy's death.

The relationship between Franklin's daughter, Anna, and the Rutherfurd family would continue as if the bond were familial rather than incidental. Anna sent Barbara Rutherfurd a pair of her father's cuff links, likely a gift from Lucy to FDR. Barbara responded, "I can't tell you how much I appreciate it and will love them always because they belonged to your father." In 1946, Barbara was to be married to Robert Knowles Jr., great-grandson of the poet Henry Wadsworth Longfellow. Anna was invited. She could not attend, but always kept the invitation, along with letters from Lucy, among her private papers.

The Roosevelt marriage may have settled into a partnership, a contract, a friendship, or just habit. When Joe Lash asked Eleanor's longtime friend Esther Lape if she thought Eleanor was in love with Franklin in her later years, Lape answered that Eleanor had told her she was not. "That is what she told me in very clear terms. That was her story. Maybe she even half believed it. But I didn't. I don't think she ever stopped loving him. . . . That was why he always had the ability to hurt her and did." Sometime after Franklin's death Eleanor invited Dorothy Schiff to lunch and her guest was amazed by the widow's rose-tinted memories. "She sounded as if they had never had anything but a happy marriage," Schiff recalled. Eleanor would say, "Do you remember, Dorothy, how he loved doing such and such? And how much he enjoyed this and that? It was all said without jealousy, venom or anything like that."

If her marriage to Franklin was flawed, no one, nevertheless, better understood the byzantine coils of his mind than his wife. In one of her autobiographies, *This I Remember*, she wrote, "Often people have told me they were misled by Franklin. I have sometimes felt that he left them, after an interview, with the idea that he was in entire agreement with them. I would know quite well, however, that he was not and that they would be very much surprised when later his actions were in complete contradiction to what they thought his attitude would be. . . . He nodded his head and frequently said, 'I see,' or something of the sort. This did not mean that he was convinced of the truth of the arguments, or even that he entirely understood them, but only that he appreciated the way in which they were presented."

In her later years Eleanor was to express surprising magnanimity over Franklin's transgression, even of Lucy's role. Of the woman's presence at Warm Springs, Eleanor told her son Elliott, "I have thought very hard about that. . . . I can only blame my own pigheadedness not Father. . . . It was my responsibility." But what of Lucy's complicity? Elliott asked. "She deserves forgiveness as much as anyone," his mother answered. She reflected for a moment, then turned to the long-ago affair and its enduring pain for her and said, "If only I had found the courage to talk to

Franklin." She should have said, she believed, "Let's bury this whole matter and begin over again together."

The years had given her a cleareyed vision of the differing hungers of men and women. "The act of being physically unfaithful seems much less important to the average man," she once said, and a man finds it "hard to understand why the woman he loves looks upon it as all important." "He might have been happier with a wife who was completely uncritical," she also admitted. "That, I was never able to be, and he had to find it in other people."

## Chapter 36

# "LUCY WAS FATHER'S EMOTION FOR LIFE"

· · · · · · ·

Lucy had made a practice of stopping at Chapel Hill in North Carolina on her way north from Aiken to Allamuchy to see her favorite cousin, Elizabeth Henderson Cotten. On one such visit in 1946, Elizabeth's son, Lyman, who as a youth had always been drawn to Lucy, took her for a ride to a nearby scenic vista, the Battle Bench. Cotten, who had become a college professor, remembered, "A student in one of my classes was at the bench and asked me if I had a match. Lucy laughed and said, 'That boy did not want a match, he just wanted an opportunity to speak to you.'" Cotten thought otherwise. "I was sure the boy wanted to look at Lucy Mercer . . . and it reflects the effect of Lucy's beauty and charm." Lucy, at the time, was fifty-five. The gift of indestructible attractiveness appears to have been passed down from mother to daughter. Minnie Mercer, while physically well preserved, however, had become a crotchety, demanding old woman, frightened of ending up in the poorhouse. Yet her daughters, one rich, the other well off, never left her in want. She spent much of her life in a succession of comfortable residential hotels. When she reached seventy-eight, her daughters decided that Minnie belonged in a nursing home, the Waverly Sanitarium in Rockville, Maryland, twelve miles outside Washington.

The relationship between mother and daughters was dutiful but the bond between Lucy and Violetta remained strong, loving, and supportive. But by 1947 a cloud had settled over the elder sister. Dr. Marbury had fallen in love with another woman and asked his wife for a divorce. Heartsick, Violetta sought solace with her sister, Lucy, now often alone, at Ridgely Hall in Aiken. Lucy was able in some measure to ease Violetta's misery. But on November 8, a shot rang out in the house. The death certificate read, "gunshot wound of the head." Violetta, at age fifty-eight, was a suicide.

In recent months, Lucy herself had begun to feel unwell, easily tired, with little appetite, and prone to frequent illnesses. Still grieving over Violetta, she had to deal with yet another loss. On Christmas Day, her mother died in the sanitarium at age eighty-four. Minnie was buried three days later in Arlington National Cemetery alongside the man who had been her husband in name only for the past forty-five years and her grandson whose burial Franklin had arranged during his first presidential term.

In little over three years, Lucy had suffered the loss of the husband she had served so lovingly, the man she had loved all her adult life, a beloved sister, and the difficult woman who was nevertheless her mother. "I think my Aunt must have lost her will to live, after these successive blows," Lucy Blundon believed. At the same time, the world Lucy had known was beginning to crumble. Her stepson Guy had come out to Allamuchy to visit her, and as he came down for dinner on the terrace that evening, Lucy said, "I'm sorry, Guy dear, but you forgot to dress." "Mother," he said, "I'm not dressing for dinner anymore." Lucy accepted his decision with wordless tolerance. Her lassitude deepened and late in the spring of 1948 she was flown from South Carolina to Memorial Hospital in New York. She was diagnosed with leukemia, which advanced quickly, her only remedy being morphine to ease the pain. She outlived Violetta by eight months and died on July 31, 1948, at age fifty-seven. Lucy was buried alongside Winthrop Rutherfurd in the family plot near the Allamuchy estate.

That Lucy as a young woman had fallen in love with the dashing Franklin was hardly surprising. Some members of the Rutherfurd family recalled that in her later years she kept his photograph in her bedroom. That the love survived long separations and his physical incapacity is testimony to the length and depth of their feeling for each other and his undiminished magnetism. It was a sad story in that two people so well matched, yet bending to obligations larger than themselves, had to settle for a relationship fitful, truncated, and thwarted, a marriage that could never be.

The columnist Murray Kempton imagined an FDR who might have chosen a life with Lucy. He saw them "growing old together, say near

Newburgh, he languidly farming and dimly drawing wills and litigating country quarrels and she stealing now and then into the dreary little church to grieve a while for the spiritual loss that had bought their happiness. The Depression is hard on him; but when he dies, he has managed to recoup by selling his remaining acres for a postwar housing development. His obituary is exactly the size the *Times* metes out for former assistant secretaries of the navy who had been nominated for vice president of the United States in a bad year for their party. She lives a long while afterward, is restored to the Church, and works in the library and always thinks of him tenderly."

Franklin and Lucy's life together might not have been as bleak as the picture Kempton painted. On a different trajectory, he would likely have escaped the scourge of polio, and he was a man of magnificent gifts, though, if divorced, employing his talents toward an ascent to the presidency would have been unthinkable in the moral climate of the times. The more salient point is how would history have been altered if Franklin had chosen love over ambition? No heroic rise from polio to the presidency, no irrepressible optimist to rally the nation through the throes of the Depression, no consummate captain in wartime to lead the country to victory over despotism, and no emergence of likely the premier figure of the twentieth century. If Lucy Mercer, as the historian Arthur Schlesinger Jr. put it, "in any way helped Franklin Roosevelt sustain the frightful burdens of leadership in the second world war, the nation has good reason to be grateful to her."

Undeniably, the affair involved deception, breaking society's rules, and inflicting pain. But, Schlesinger also concluded, "Eleanor Roosevelt, Franklin Roosevelt and Lucy Mercer all emerge from the story with honor."

"As far as emotions were concerned," daughter Anna believed, "Lucy was Father's emotion for life."

*Chapter 37*

# FIRST LADY OF THE WORLD

· · · · · · ·

Eleanor Roosevelt's friendship with Earl Miller was to have one last awkard chapter. An item in Ed Sullivan's "Little Old New York" column in the city's *Daily News* of January 13, 1947, reported that a Navy commander's wife's divorce action "will rock the country if she names the correspondent." Nothing more came of Sullivan's insinuation until the following year when a *New York Daily Mirror* headline shouted, "Suing Wife 'Feared' Bodyguard of F.D.R." The story went on to report that Simone Miller claimed she had been rushed into marriage on June 23, 1941, while Earl was in the Navy to "quell certain rumors about him and a woman of prominent reputation." The *Mirror* story had been triggered by a suit for separation and financial support that Simone had brought against her husband on August 16, 1948, in the New York State Supreme Court in Albany. She charged "That for several years last past the defendant has openly consorted with various female companions and in particular consorted openly and notoriously with one female friend by reason whereof the plaintiff has suffered humiliation and embarrassment and has been made mentally and physically ill." She also sought custody of her two children, six-year-old Earl Jr. and three-year-old Anna Eleanor, the girl named, Simone told a reporter, for "Mrs. Eleanor Roosevelt."

On October 27, 1948, the court handed down its decision in the case of *Miller v. Miller* finding the defendant "guilty of cruel and inhuman treatment of the plaintiff." Simone was granted custody of the children and $2,500 annually for her support. Earl later wrote to Joe Lash describing how he had beaten up a passerby whom he had overheard on an Albany street refer to him as "Mrs. Roosevelt's sweetheart." Lash, in his writing, erroneously reported that Eleanor, "shortly after the war . . . was named as a correspondent in a suit for divorce filed by the wife of Earl Miller." Actually, only the separation had been reached and the Miller marriage would not be terminated by divorce for another eleven years.

Over the next dozen years, Eleanor would continue traveling and lecturing. She would chair President John F. Kennedy's Commission on the Status of Women, and maintain "My Day," which became one of the longest running columns in American journalism. For all her undiminished pace, Lorena Hickok wrote Esther Lape in the early 1960s, "I began to notice a change in her three years ago. It seemed to me she was slowly drifting away from us. But when I mentioned it, people thought I was crazy. Before an audience, or TV or as a hostess, she appeared to be her old vigorous, alert interested self. She was, after all, what they call in show business, 'an old trouper.' . . . [Yet] she seemed to be going further and further away."

Hick by now had become to Eleanor rather like an old dress, once a favorite that she now took out infrequently. Hick's sight began to fail as diabetes continued to exact its toll, her finances continued shaky, and she became increasingly dependent on Eleanor's residual feelings of obligation. Eleanor brought her up from Long Island to share Val-Kill with her. The arrangement was not a success. Eleanor, long since fashion-conscious, became impatient with Hick running about in baggy men's pants and shapeless sweaters. While Eleanor was not one to stand on ceremony, she found it unseemly to have Hick possessively calling her "Darling" in front of guests. Eleanor next found Hick a small log cabin nearby, part of a motel, and after that failed to work out, moved her into an apartment at 19 Park Place in Hyde Park Village. "Poor Hick," Eleanor's latest secretary, Maureen Corr, commented. "I felt sorry for her. She was such a pathetic soul. She latched on to Mrs. Roosevelt and then gave up her own wonderful career, which is so dumb. Because of her devotion to Mrs. Roosevelt, she thought this was someone she could lean on for the rest of her life."

While Hick's standing had waned, Eleanor had long since found another emotional anchorage. She first met Dr. David Gurewitsch at a White House reception in 1939, when the tall, handsome thirty-seven-year-old was working as a rehabilitation physician at New York's Columbia Presbyterian Medical Center. Their paths did not cross again until

1945 when Eleanor visited Trude Lash, one of Gurewitsch's patients. Eleanor immediately engaged the Swiss-born Jewish Gurewitsch as her own physician. In 1947 she learned that Gurewitsch had been diagnosed with tuberculosis and that he intended to seek treatment in Davos, Switzerland. Eleanor arranged to be on the same plane with him on a flight to Geneva where she was to attend a meeting of the United Nations Commission on Human Rights. The flight was plagued with bad weather and mechanical breakdowns, which left the two together in Newfoundland and later in Shannon, Ireland. Of this period, Gurewitsch was to write, "We discovered that although we had each come from different parts of the world, from different backgrounds, and were of different ages, we had much in common. We had both grown up fatherless and during our impressionable years had been raised by grandparents. We each had experienced feelings of deprivation. . . . After these unusual four and a half days and by the time our plane landed in Geneva, what had essentially been a professional relationship changed into a friendship that grew with the years." At the time this friendship blossomed, Eleanor was sixty-three and Gurewitsch forty-five.

Gurewitsch began taking his vacations abroad with Eleanor, usually accompanied by Maureen Corr. He spoke Russian and in 1957 traveled with Eleanor to the Soviet Union where he helped translate when she interviewed Premier Nikita Khrushchev on the Cold War arms race for Dorothy Schiff's *New York Post*. The warmth of the friendship troubled an earlier intimate. "Joe Lash was in many ways a companion to my grandmother," Curtis Roosevelt observed. "David usurped Joe. I think he had withdrawal symptoms when he realized that David had taken his place. David fit in more with what my grandmother liked. David would tease my grandmother. Joe couldn't." Maureen Corr noticed that after Gurewitsch came upon the scene, Eleanor went on a diet and became even more conscious of how she dressed. Coincidentally, she had suffered an automobile accident that required removing her front teeth. After dentures were substituted, "the improvement in her appearance was striking," one witness noted.

Eleanor gave Gurewitsch a photograph of herself in her youth inscribed, "To David, from a girl he never knew." She wanted him to call her by her first name, just as she called him "David." But he could not. She remained "Mrs. Roosevelt." As Eleanor's lifelong friend Esther Lape once told Gurewitsch, "Eleanor loved you deeply, pervasively, continuously. You were dearer to her, as she not infrequently said, than anyone else in the world. Yes, she not only loved you, she was 'in love' with you. You loved her and were not in love with her."

As Gurewitsch became increasingly secure in his role, Maureen Corr saw him not quite so nobly as Lape did. "Mrs. Roosevelt loved him, but he would not have loved her," Corr observed. She knew this was so, "because of the way he treated her." He was always late for appointments. "We're always waiting for David, I would tell her, but she would never criticize him." She also knew of his involvements with other women. Then, in February 1958, Gurewitsch married Edna Perkel, an art historian and dealer. "I thought it must be a terrible blow to Mrs. Roosevelt, but she never expressed it," Corr remembered. Instead, her ingrained self-abnegation prevailed and Eleanor offered her New York City apartment for the wedding. Subsequently, she joined the Gurewitsches in buying a townhouse at 55 East 74th Street, with Eleanor occupying separate quarters. To Corr, the platonic ménage à trois demonstrated the lifelong outsider role to which Eleanor seemed fated. "She was the third person with Nan Cook and Marion Dickerman," Corr noted. "And then there was Joe Lash and Trude, and Mrs. Roosevelt was the third person in that relationship. Then there was David and Edna, and again she was the third person. Mrs. Roosevelt was always the loving outsider."

As for love of her children, Eleanor's judgment of herself was hard, recalling the fumbling, anxious, overwhelmed young mother she had been. Her relationship to her daughter, Anna, occasionally in competition over the role of White House hostess, tested almost to the breaking point by the Lucy Rutherfurd episode, was in the end strong and loving. Still, long afterward, Anna seemed to need reassurance that her role in bringing her father and Lucy together was defensible. Twenty-seven years after receiving the letter from Lucy lamenting FDR's death, she showed it to Bernard Asbell to persuade him that what had happened between her father and Mrs. Rutherfurd was innocent, simply "an important friendship to both of them." Jimmy Roosevelt judged his mother as inattentive, blaming her for his poor childhood health, even his premature baldness. Franklin Jr., who bore an astonishing resemblance to FDR, looked for a time to be Eleanor's brightest hope to don his father's mantle. He served three terms in Congress but was often absent and negligent, subsequently burning out in failed attempts at higher office. John, the youngest and perhaps steadiest, disappointed her by abandoning the party of his parents, and becoming a Republican. In the 1952 presidential campaign, he served as chairman of Citizens for Eisenhower opposing the Democratic candidate, Adlai Stevenson, to whom his mother was utterly devoted. Eleanor's most motherly concern was reserved for Elliott, perhaps because he bore the name of her beloved father, but more likely because of a troubling rootlessness as Elliott drifted from job to job, home to home, and marriage to marriage. She made him her business partner in Hyde Park land ventures, which she explained by saying, "I surmise Elliott has to be established and encouraged and become more secure." Her sons suggested the pampered rich in F. Scott Fitzgerald's *The Great Gatsby*: "They were careless people. . . . They smashed up things and creatures and then retreated back into their carelessness, or whatever it was that kept them together, and let other people clean up the mess they made." Eleanor, who had stuck out a forty-year marriage through thick and thin, saw her five offspring married a total of nineteen times. Doubtless, her greatest pride in her boys occurred during the war years in which all served honorably, even heroically.

Eleanor's health continued to fail. She became anemic and required iron shots, suffered an attack of phlebitis, and over the Labor Day weekend in 1961 experienced a troubling episode of internal bleeding. She began limiting her visits to the Hyde Park mansion, now open to the public, to escorting visiting dignitaries. "She really had no interest in that house," Maureen Corr observed. Eleanor had grown increasingly dependent on the near worshipful friendship of Ray Corry, the museum director, who found himself conducting the tours upstairs while a fatigued Eleanor sat on a bench in the downstairs hallway. Soon she declined even to get out of her car, while Corry led the visitors by himself.

Finally, her root condition was diagnosed. She was suffering from the resurgence of an apparently long dormant case of tuberculosis of the bone marrow along with the anemia. Tuberculosis was also the disease that had caused the curvature of her Aunty Bye's spine, and for a time young Eleanor had worn a brace to straighten out her backbone. She entered a New York hospital where Gurewitsch believed she could be saved. But, as the hopelessness of her condition became inescapable, Maureen Corr remembered, "I heard her say to David, 'I want to die, I want to die, I want to die.' I heard her from outside her room say it three times. Mrs. Roosevelt couldn't be Mrs. Roosevelt unless she was active. She knew she could only be an invalid, and that she could not accept." Dorothy

Schiff recalled Franklin Jr. telling her that "his mother had an agreement with Dr. Gurewitsch that he would not allow her to live under degrading circumstances. . . . He would not give her life-sustaining aid of any kind if she had a terminal illness. Franklin said his sister loused up the whole thing by coming to New York and sending for three specialists who overruled David and did the very thing Eleanor was trying to avoid. She lived for seven more weeks in indignity, catheter bottle under the bed, etc."

Eleanor Roosevelt died on November 7, 1962, at the age of seventy-eight. Her funeral three days later at St. James Episcopal Church in Hyde Park was attended by President John F. Kennedy and Vice President Lyndon Johnson, former presidents Truman and Eisenhower, along with Bess Truman, Jackie Kennedy, and Lady Bird Johnson. She was buried in the Hyde Park rose garden alongside her husband. When everyone was gone and night had fallen, a furtive Lorena Hickok, too distraught to attend the funeral, slipped onto the grounds and placed a wreath on Eleanor's grave. She subsequently learned that Eleanor had left her $1,000 in her will. She would outlive the woman she had so fiercely loved by six years.

At a United Nations memorial service for Eleanor, representatives of 110 countries stood for a minute of silent tribute. Adlai Stevenson, then the U.S. ambassador to the United Nations, declared in his eulogy, "She would rather light candles than curse the darkness, and her glow warmed the world." The next day ten thousand mourners crowded about the Cathedral Church of St. John the Divine in New York to attend another memorial service. Harry Truman called her the "First Lady of the World." *The New York Times* pronounced her "one of the great ladies in the history of the country." The black journalist Carl Rowan wrote, "Whether in praise or criticism, millions view Eleanor Roosevelt as one of the major reasons for the change in status of colored people, particularly American Negroes, during the last quarter century." "No woman of this generation, and few in the annals of history have so well understood and articulated the yearnings of men and women for social justice," commented the Indian prime minister, Jawaharlal Nehru. Historians might debate the ranking of the greatest presidents, but among eminent American women, Eleanor Roosevelt almost invariably ranks first.

The public adulation captured the iconic Eleanor but rarely penetrated the complex persona beneath. The emotional defenses of a lifetime were never completely lowered. Once, staying with Eleanor at a

London Hotel, Maureen Corr answered a phone call from an old acquaintance of her employer. Eleanor ducked the call, telling her secretary, "She wants something." "But Mrs. Roosevelt," Corr said, "don't you think people love you for yourself?" "No, dear," Eleanor answered. "I don't."

One who knew Eleanor well, Cynthia Lowry, an Associated Press writer, said of her, "She was a curious mixture of kindly, deep concern for people and impersonality. . . . Mrs. Roosevelt really became interested in individuals only when they had problems." Jim Bishop, who chronicled FDR's last year, found that to Eleanor physical "manifestations of love were easy to dispense with . . . and this was peculiar because this very proper wife found it easy to give all of her heart to suffering millions she never met." Anna said of her mother, "I've always thought it possible to have great compassion for the masses . . . that were poor or unemployed or whatever, but not much interest in the individual. I think that was true of her." Arthur Schlesinger Jr. told an interviewer, "I was very much chagrined when I got to years later and I came to know her cousin Alice Longworth. Although I wholly agreed with Mrs. Roosevelt's politics and wholly disagreed with Mrs. Longworth's politics, I found Mrs. Longworth far more fun to be with. Mrs. Roosevelt was rather serious, rather humorless. . . . She wasn't a hell of a lot of fun. But there are many more important things in life." In a penetrating testament, Cissy Patterson, once an outrageous figure in Washington society, now the serious publisher of *The Washington Times Herald*, concluded, "Mrs. Roosevelt has solved the problem of living better than anyone I know."

She would have her unregenerate detractors, however, to the end of her life and beyond. J. Edgar Hoover's file on Eleanor Roosevelt exceeded three thousand pages as if his agency had been tracking an enemy of the republic instead of a heroine to millions of Americans and to the world. Her cousin Alice continued playing the ageless enfant terrible, doing her caricature impersonation of Eleanor years after the woman's death. Yet, by the end, even Alice had come around, too intelligent and too honest with herself to deny Eleanor's worth. When an interviewer mentioned Aunt Pussie's comment that young Eleanor had been an "ugly duckling," Alice angrily countered, "Something much better than a swan." She told Joe Lash, "People think they can gratify me by saying [Eleanor] was unattractive. She wasn't at all. She had that great beauty of the eyes." She further told Lash, "She had great charm, always something lovable about her." One woman, Ginny Blair, who knew both cousins, concluded, "Eleanor Roosevelt was a great woman. I don't think that Alice could touch the hem of her gown."

Her life had been a victory of personal ascendance—from deep insecurity to quiet confidence; from the straitjacket of Victorian morality to a generous tolerance of human foibles; from an opponent of women's suffrage to a champion of equality between the sexes; from genteel bigotry to leading the struggle for racial and religious freedom; from a wifely role lived in the shadow of an illustrious husband to her own place in the sun. Yet, she remained withal, a woman subject to a woman's needs and vulnerabilities. To the end there stood on her dresser a memento of the happiest era of her life, a photograph of Mlle. Marie Souvestre recalling Eleanor's Allenswood years. And in a drawer she kept a yellowed, fading reminder of her most painful ordeal, the clipping of the poem "Psyche," which had given her heart to go on, and that ended:

> *The soul that had believed*
> *And was deceived*
> *Ends by believing more*
> *Than ever before.*

She had written across the top of the poem, "1918."

*Chapter 38*

# A JUDGMENT

. . . . . . .

T HE YEAR 1997 saw publication of a book, *Rating the Presidents*, a sophisticated calculation weighing five factors—leadership, accomplishments, political skill, appointments, and character—in judging the nation's forty-one chief executives through 1996. Ranked first was Abraham Lincoln. Second was Franklin D. Roosevelt, rated ahead of George Washington. Another survey of fifty eminent historians polled by Arthur M. Schlesinger Sr. of Harvard rated only Lincoln and Washington ahead of FDR. To attempt to understand this extraordinary figure without taking into account the women who influenced him would be to offer a history with critical pages torn out, rather like seeking to comprehend George Washington without his love for the unattainable Sally Fairfax, Jefferson without his involvement with a slave, Sally Hemings, or his relationship with Maria Cosway, James Madison without the pivotal role of his wife, Dolley, Lincoln without his tempestuous marriage to Mary Todd, Woodrow Wilson without the Mary Peck affair and his courtship of Edith Bolling Galt, and in more recent times, the self-destructive promiscuity of Presidents Kennedy and Bill Clinton.

In Franklin Roosevelt's life the female influences were immense and formative, beginning with the unconditional, near smothering love of his mother wedded to her limitless expectations for him, followed by the complex amalgam of love and badgering by his wife, who admitted, "I felt akin to a hair shirt," the heedless pursuit of his romance with Lucy Mercer Rutherfurd, his symbiotic, semi-married liaison with Missy LeHand, along with character-revealing associations with several other women. This man who could not walk, yet strode the world stage like a colossus, exhibited an intense, lifelong need to prove desirable to women, to win their uncritical admiration and approval, to trust in them, to be doted on, amused, and adored by them.

Clearly Lucy was the love of his life. Another of Franklin's many distant relatives, the columnist Joseph Alsop, went so far as to place their love affair nearly on a par with FDR's polio as a shaping experience. "To begin with," Alsop wrote, "it is a reasonable surmise that his wartime love affair, profoundly and forever resented by Eleanor Roosevelt, caused their relationship to be transformed for good from a normal marriage into the highly successful working partnership many people will still remember. Much more important, as my mother always believed, and so do I, his disappointment in a strong and strongly felt love [for Lucy] did much to banish the 'feather duster' side of Franklin Roosevelt, and to deepen, toughen and mature his character and personality even prior to his paralysis."

Thirty-eight years after FDR's death, the affair could still kindle controversy over the relationship between a leader's public and private morals. Charles Peters, writing in the *Washington Monthly,* drew a parallel between the scandal that led to the impeachment of President Clinton, and the uproar in 1966 when the Roosevelt-Mercer affair was revealed in Jonathan Daniels's book *The Time Between the Wars.* "The greatest President of the past century," Peters wrote, "may have had sexual relations of one kind or another not only with Lucy Mercer Rutherfurd, but also with his secretary, Marguerite LeHand, Princess Martha of Norway, his distant cousin, Daisy Suckley, and Dorothy Schiff, then publisher of the *New York Post.*" Peters's projection of FDR's possible involvements is exaggerated, but his conclusion is arresting. "Suppose that during the darkest days of the Depression or World War II, a reporter revealed one of those relationships, and Roosevelt lied about it for the same reasons that Clinton did," he asks, "can anyone imagine that the resulting damage to his authority would have been good for the country?" History not infrequently presents us with a trade-off between sexual spotlessness and the genius for leadership, the former influencing only the lives of a few, the latter affecting millions.

The still underappreciated triumph of Roosevelt's life is his living with the havoc of polio yet persevering and attaining the summit. No nation has ever chosen as its head of state a cripple—which Americans did not once but four times. Illustrative of how successfully he blurred his handicap is the fact that whether being praised by his admirers or pilloried by his enemies, it was always as a full man. Time and again he is portrayed in political cartoons running, jumping, even soaring, a figure in action. Madame Shoumatoff was invited to speak at Warm Springs in 1970 on the twenty-fifth anniversary of FDR's death and noted aptly, "you can not disable ability and you can not discourage courage . . . and that is the greatest heritage he left to us all."

The belief has been advanced, principally by his wife, that polio was the trial by fire that steeled FDR's character. Yet, it is difficult to accept that a man of his gifts would otherwise have been a mediocrity. His promise emerged early, in his twenties, by an upset election to the state legislature and in his early thirties by his appointment as second in command of the Navy Department. At thirty-eight he ran for vice president of the United States. He was like a runner favored to win the cup but who collapses into the cinders, seriously injured, yet manages to lift himself up and still crosses the finish line first. His son James refused to "accept the theory that Father would not have been a great man and a great public figure had he not gone through his personal Gethsemane." He concluded, "I believe it was not polio that forged Father's character, but that it was Father's character that enabled him to rise above the affliction." His unflappability in almost any situation was captured by Geoffrey Ward after hearing rare tapes of FDR recorded in the Oval Office in 1940. "There he sits imprisoned in his chair, locked in combat with Wendell Willkie, the most formidable opponent ever sent against him, facing the worst war in history—and he couldn't be having a better time. Nothing seems to faze him. He is amused and amusing, apparently unafraid of anything, and somehow serene in the conviction that whatever happens, everything will turn out fine, provided he's in charge."

He had been ill-treated by fate in becoming paralyzed by polio. Otherwise, he had come into this world under a lucky star. He was born rich with all the freedom of choice and action that a fortune confers. He retained a boyish enthusiasm throughout life that fueled his boundless curiosity and mental energy. He was brave-hearted, as John Gunther noted, after "he rolled in the gutter with death." His ego leaped over boundaries that constrain conventional thinkers, leading him to surprise with bold, instinctive initiatives that altered history. He had an irrepressible sense of humor, which leavens any day. He had a quick intelligence and was gifted with a retentive memory. A book he read, a lecture he heard, a conversation he held, stuck with him seemingly forever so that he could adorn his speech with relevant history, humor, and apt anec-dote. It was a quality that gave a sheen of brilliance, perhaps running ahead of his actual intellect. On the day of Pearl Harbor, he harked back to the Russo-Japanese War, spontaneously instructing leaders gathered in the White House on how the sneak attack was "equaled only by the Japanese episode of 1904, when two squadrons, cruisers . . . without any warning—I think on a Sunday morning, by the way—Japanese cruisers sank all of the Russian vessels." His era was also fortunate. The author Allida Black has observed, "while other presidents before and after have been weakened by charges ranging from sleeping with a slave to bigamy, to fathering an illegitimate child, to adultery, to entertaining dangerously unbridled appetites, FDR escapes widespread condemnation." His ex-culpation is largely explained by the fact that revelations about his pri-vate life surfaced only after his legacy in history had been securely established. Further, the press largely left his personal affairs alone.

Late in her life even Alice Roosevelt Longworth came around. In 1940 she had said, "I'd rather vote for Hitler than vote for Franklin for a third term." Interviewed at age eighty-five on television's 60 *Minutes,* she de-scribed how among her set they charged that "Franklin . . . should never have been elected, should have been impeached as it were . . . not quite seriously, but we were pretty bad about it." In the end, she conceded, "It's high time someone realized how idiotically we all carried on."

In a rare burst of modesty, FDR told Sam Rosenman during his third term that the only memorial he wanted was "a block about this size (putting his hands on his desk). I don't care what it is made of, whether limestone or granite or what not, but I want it to be plain, without any ornamentation, with the simple carving, 'In memory of . . .' " Given his ego and acute sense of history, he may have been surprised when he was taken at his word, initially memorialized in the capital with only a mod-est block of white Vermont marble unveiled exactly twenty years after his death in front of the National Archives building on Pennsylvania Av-enue. Finally, in 1997, fifty-two years after his death, a memorial on a Rooseveltian scale rose on the banks of the Potomac River, four mean-dering stone spaces each representing one of FDR's terms spread over seven and a half acres, graced by shade trees, waterfalls, alcoves, statu-ary, and inscriptions, the largest of all presidential memorials.

His character was far from perfect. The poll that ranked FDR second among presidents rated him fifteenth for "character and integrity." Even a staunch admirer of his, the historian Allan Nevins, concluded, "Roosevelt at times was indefensibly evasive even with intimates . . . and lacked straightforwardness." "You won't talk frankly even with people who are loyal to you," Harold Ickes, his secretary of the interior, charged in a moment of exasperation. He could be vindictive and nurse a grudge. Banishment from his circle usually meant a life sentence. His intellect was not the equal of Winston Churchill's. But Nevins has perhaps best caught the synergy of FDR's mind and spirit. "A leader who puts second-rate qualities of intellect and character into first-rate application to the needs of his time may be a greater man than the leader who puts first-rate qualities into second-rate application. Roosevelt signally illustrates this observation." In a rare admission of the sinuosity of his thinking, FDR once answered his son Jimmy's question about "the dishonesty of his stand on war," after promising the American people that their boys were not going to be sent into any foreign wars. "I knew we were going to war," he explained to his son. "But I couldn't come out and say a war was coming, because the people would have panicked and turned from me. . . . So you play the game the way it has been played over the years, and you play to win." The reasoning was pure, undiluted FDR.

Curtis Roosevelt has said of his grandfather's impenetrability, "I think the price to be paid for exercising his discipline is a closing off of your emotional life. You have limited intimacy. You don't let anyone in." Yet, it was this very insulating quality, the detachment, the manipulativeness, the tendency to leave behind those who were flagging, the almost superhuman self-control, that allowed him to play the chess master looking down from above, coolly moving pieces to take the nation where he wanted it to go. He was entirely willing to employ devious means toward desirable ends. And these ends were earth-shaking. His bold confrontation of the Depression at a time when America was losing faith in itself saved democracy and the entrepreneurial spark of capitalism. He led the nation to victory in a war that posed the fiercest crisis of the twentieth century. "In Franklin Roosevelt," Churchill said, there died "the greatest champion of freedom who has ever brought help and comfort from the New World to the Old." What invites ceaseless speculation but in the end resists explanation is how this initially rather shallow- and effete-appearing young man was transformed to arguably the transcendent figure of the twentieth century.

Franklin Roosevelt may have distilled his estimation of the women in his life in what he once told Frances Perkins: "I am willing to take more chances. I've got more nerve about women and their status in the world." The women in his life cluster around him like protective handmaidens, shaping, spurring, caring, diverting, bringing happiness and a spiritual wholeness to this physically abbreviated man. They were as the poet William Wordsworth described a good woman:

> The reason firm, the temperate will,
> Endurance, foresight, strength, and skill,
> A perfect woman, nobly planned,
> To warn, to comfort, and command.

In such women, Franklin Roosevelt would be blessed throughout his life, again and again.

# ACKNOWLEDGMENTS

· · · · · · ·

The book came into being initially through the support of two people who believed early in its merit, my distinguished editor, Robert Loomis, and my inexhaustible literary agent, Esther Newberg. I was dependent throughout the project on the staff of the Franklin D. Roosevelt Library in Hyde Park, New York, under the able leadership of director Cynthia Koch. Robert Clark, the library's supervising archivist, unfailingly helped with my endless inquiries. Among his archivists I particularly want to thank Karen Anson, Virginia Lewick, Robert Parks, and Alycia Vivona, as well as Mark Renovich for his expert guidance on photographs. Lynn Bassanese went beyond her current duties to help me, and Francesca Urbin proved an informed Hyde Park guide. A rich repository of Roosevelt material is located at Wilderstein Preservation, Inc., where Duane Watson and his wife, Linda, made available to me the papers of FDR's confidante, Margaret Daisy Suckley.

I am fortunate to have the New York State Library near at hand, where I could count on the knowledge and assistance of Mary Woodward and Mary Redmond. At the State University of New York at Albany I benefited from the research skills of William Young, formerly with the university's library. I am deeply indebted to my neighborhood Guilderland, New York, library under the direction of Barbara Nichols Randall. I rank Mary Alingh, Thomas Barnes, Maria Buhl, Rosemary Engelhardt, Margaret Garrett, Gillian Leonard, Ann Wemple, and Eileen Williams high among any reference librarians with whom I have ever dealt. Numerous other archivists and librarians aided me at the Library of Congress, the Columbia Oral History Program, the New York Public Library, the Houghton Library at Harvard University, and the University of North Carolina Archives. Several people deeply informed about Franklin D. Roosevelt were unstinting in the time they gave me to discuss my subject, including William J. vanden Heuvel, Christopher Breiseth, Geoffrey Ward, Allida Black, and Ellen Feldman.

Several people with personal knowledge of my story agreed to talk to me, including Curtis Roosevelt, Leith Rutherfurd Talamo, Guy Rutherfurd Sr., Guy Rutherfurd Jr., Mary Michele Rutherfurd, Mr. and Mrs. Montague Blundon, Barbara Knowles, Lucy Knowles, Alice Knowles, Maureen Corr, Alex Shoumatoff, Nicholas Shoumatoff, and Tonia Shoumatoff Foster. Several highly knowledgeable persons were kind enough to read my manuscript and provide their insight, including my longtime colleague Tanya Melich, and Verne Newton, former director of the Roosevelt Library. Along with all the Roosevelt researchers, I am particularly grateful to Verne for successfully carrying forward the Pare Lorentz project to make the president's detailed daily schedule available at the presidential library through FDR: Day by Day.

Writers of nonfiction inevitably stand on the shoulders of those who have written before them. While I have read widely in the literature of FDR, among earlier authors to whom I feel especially indebted are Blanche Wiesen Cook, the late Jonathan Daniels, Hugh Gallagher, Doris Kearns Goodwin, the late Joseph P. Lash, and the aforementioned Geoffrey Ward.

Others played varied roles in this project and I want to recognize their contributions. Thomas Clingan, clerk of the Albany County Court, guided me through court documents. Frank Lasch advised me on legal points. I particularly appreciate the research done for me by Derek and Monique Blackburn regarding contacts in Canada, and Emily T. Shaw for help with key photos. Henry Jurenka, Roger Hind, Wolfgang Neumann, Dr. Michael Mattioli, and John Foley all helped me in ways they will recognize and they have my deep gratitude.

Finally, two critical participants in the project were my wife, Sylvia, and my daughter, Vanya Perez, both of whom researched, advised on, and produced the final manuscript.

# NOTES

· · · · · · ·

Source notes are keyed to the page number and a quotation or phrase occurring on that page. Citations from books, periodicals, and other attributed sources begin with the author's name followed by the title and page numbers. The sources are fully identified in the bibliography. Where more than one work by the same author is cited, a distinguishing word from the appropriate title appears after the author's name. Frequently cited sources and names are abbreviated as follows:

| | |
|---|---|
| AER | *Autobiography of Eleanor Roosevelt* |
| ARH | Anna Roosevelt Halsted |
| ARHP | Anna Roosevelt Halsted Papers, Franklin D. Roosevelt Library |
| ARL | Alice Roosevelt Longworth |
| COH | Oral History Project, Columbia University |
| DSP | Papers of Dorothy Schiff, New York Public Library |
| ER | Eleanor Roosevelt |
| FBP | FDRL, Roosevelt Family, Business, and Personal Papers |
| FDR | Franklin Delano Roosevelt |
| FDRL | Franklin D. Roosevelt Library |
| FDRPL | Elliott Roosevelt: *F.D.R.: His Personal Letters* |
| HH | Houghton Library, Harvard University |
| JDP | Jonathan Daniels Papers, University of North Carolina |
| JLP | FDRL, Papers of Joseph Lash |
| LH | Lorena Hickok |
| LMR | Lucy Mercer Rutherfurd |
| LOC | Library of Congress |
| MLH | Marguerite LeHand |
| MS | Margaret Suckley |
| MSP | Margaret Suckley Papers, Wilderstein Preservation, Inc.; Rhinebeck, New York |
| NYT | *New York Times* |
| PASN | FDRL, FDR Papers as Assistant Secretary of the Navy, 1913–1920 |
| PPF | FDRL, President's Personal Files |
| PSF | FDRL, President's Secretary's Files |

RFP   FDRL, Roosevelt Family Papers Donated by the Children
SDR   Sara Delano Roosevelt
*TIMS*   Eleanor Roosevelt, *This Is My Story*
*TIR*   Eleanor Roosevelt, *This I Remember*

## INTRODUCTION

xii  "Historians have . . .": Arthur Schlesinger Jr., "FDR's Secret Romance," p. 71.

## CHAPTER 1 · · SCARLET LETTERS

3  "You must get . . .": Geoffrey C. Ward, *A First-Class Temperament*, p. 346.

4  "Theodore left . . .": Ibid., pp. 346–47.

4  "The papers say . . .": SDR to FDR, FBP.

4  "I was charmed . . .": James MacGregor Burns and Susan Dunn, *The Three Roosevelts*, p. 152.

4  "I really think . . .": Ibid.

4  "I don't understand . . .": Peter Collier and David Horowitz, *The Roosevelts*, p. 193.

4  "Oh, did you . . .": Ibid., p. 193.

4  "I should be ashamed . . .": Ward, *Temperament*, p. 346.

4  "Neither you nor I . . .": Ibid.

5  "Franklin Roosevelt should . . .": Kenneth S. Davis, *FDR: The Beckoning of Destiny*, p. 461.

5  "to look into . . .": Josephus Daniels to FDR, PASN.

5  "such other purposes . . .": Ward, *Temperament*, p. 390.

5  "give up war work . . .": Ibid., p. 385.

5  "Don't tell . . .": Collier and Horowitz, p. 235.

6  "The good old ocean . . .": FDR, Diary, Box 33, PASN.

6  "a wonderful sight . . .": FDR, Diary, Box 33, PASN.

6  "is just like . . .": FDR, Diary, Box 33, PASN.

6  "His one regret . . .": FDR, Diary, Box 33, PASN.

6  "I was in the presence . . .": FDR, Diary, Box 33, PASN.

6  "He almost ran . . .": Ward, *Temperament*, p. 397.

6  "trying to bite . . .": Ward, *Temperament*, p. 398.

7  "plans called for . . .": FDR, Diary, Box 33, PASN.

7  "the long whining . . .": FDR, Diary, Box 33, PASN.

8  "I will never know . . .": FDR, Diary, Box 33, PASN.

8  "discarded overcoats . . .": Ward, *Temperament*, pp. 399–400.

8  "my Marines": FDR, Diary, Box 33, PASN.

8  "our sensitive . . .": Ward, *Temperament*, p. 400.

8  "How's the job . . .": Robert Dunn, *World Alive*, p. 276.

8 "will at no . . .": Joseph E. Persico, *Eleventh Month, Eleventh Day, Eleventh Hour*, p. 258.

8 "the boy in him . . .": Hermann Hagedorn, *The Roosevelt Family of Sagamore Hill*, pp. 412–14.

9 "frightfully busy . . .": FDR, Diary, Box 33, PASN.

9 "it didn't seem to . . .": Capt. Edward McCauley Jr., Memoirs, PASN.

9 "Everybody got drunk . . .": Livy, Diary, PASN.

10 "I saw service . . .": Frank Freidel, *Franklin D. Roosevelt: The Apprenticeship*, p. 337.

10 "Saw F.D. . . .": Livy, Diary, PASN.

11 "The bottom dropped . . .": *FDRPL*, p. 95.

## CHAPTER 2 · · MASTER FRANKLIN

12 "I do not pretend . . .": Geoffrey C. Ward, *Before the Trumpet*, p. 71.

14 "Stanford White was . . .": Ibid., p. 104.

14 "In this way . . .": Ibid., p. 16.

15 "Why, he never . . .": Ibid., p. 60.

16 "Our society was . . .": Burns and Dunn, p. 17.

16 "picturesque custom . . .": Jonathan Daniels, *The End of Innocence*, p. 131.

17 Sara "has a . . .": Davis, *Beckoning*, p. 52.

17 "I knew my obligations . . .": Conrad Black, *Franklin Delano Roosevelt*, p. 43.

18 "of his little . . .": Mrs. James Roosevelt, *My Boy Franklin*, p. 31.

18 "Franklin began going . . .": SDR, Diary, RBP.

18 "otherwise he would . . .": Interview, Mr. and Mrs. Sheffield Cowles Jr., December 28, 1954, HH.

18 "Mommie, if I . . .": Hugh Gregory Gallagher, *FDR's Splendid Deception*, p. 5.

18 "Don't you think . . .": Rita Halle Kleeman, "Biography of Sara Delano Roosevelt," Undated manuscript, p. 1, FDRL.

19 "I miss our river . . .": Binder 20, MSP.

20 "Help the helpless! . . .": Blanche Wiesen Cook, *Eleanor Roosevelt*, Vol. 1, p. 145.

20 "My little man . . .": Rita Halle Kleeman, *Gracious Lady*, p. 146.

## CHAPTER 3 · · POOR LITTLE RICH GIRL

22 "Eleanor, I hardly . . .": Joseph Alsop, *FDR: A Centenary Remembrance*, p. 41.

22 "She is such . . .": *TIMS*, pp. 17–18.

22 "You have no looks . . .": Burns and Dunn, p. 85.

22 "Poor little soul . . .": Collier and Horowitz, p. 20.

22 "I often felt . . .": Abram L. Sachar, *An Affectionate Portrait,* p. 2.

23 "grateful to be allowed . . .": *TIMS,* p. 13.

23 "I had a bad rush . . .": Joseph P. Lash, *Eleanor and Franklin,* p. 7.

23 "has seen the baby . . .": Joseph P. Lash, *Love, Eleanor,* p. 10.

24 "a maniac morally . . .": Ward, *Trumpet,* p. 279.

24 "little short of criminal . . .": Edmund Morris, *The Rise of Theodore Roosevelt,* p. 431.

24 "Elliott Roosevelt Demented": Burns and Dunn, p. 86.

24 "Wrecked by Liquor . . .": Ibid.

24 "So ends the final . . .": Ward, *Trumpet,* p. 279.

24 "The life of every party": Lash, *Love, Eleanor,* p. 13.

24 "reading stark naked . . .": Ibid.

24 "I declined . . .": Ibid.

25 "dominated my life . . .": *TIMS,* p. 6.

25 "I can remember . . .": Ibid., p. 19.

25 "Ellie is going to . . .": Joseph P. Lash, *Life Was Meant to Be Lived: Centenary,* p. 95.

25 "From that time on . . .": *TIMS,* p. 34.

25 "It wasn't drink . . .": Eleanor Roosevelt Oral History Project, June 20, 1979, FDRL.

26 "My mother would ask . . .": Lash interview, Box 44, ARHP.

26 "wholly at the mercy . . .": Rexford G. Tugwell, *The Democratic Roosevelt,* p. 6.

26 "She could have had . . .": Corinne Alsop interview, December 28, 1954, HH.

26 "a person somewhat . . .": Ibid.

27 "was dressed by her . . .": Ibid.

27 "It may seem strange . . .": Lash, *Love, Eleanor,* p. 26.

## CHAPTER 4 · · FROM RICHES TO RAGS

28 "Remember Carroll's . . .": Jonathan Daniels, *Washington Quadrille,* p. 101.

28 "a fraction of an inch . . .": Minna Mercer deposition, Mercer Family Papers, Misc. Documents, November 10, 1919, FDRL.

29 "easily the most . . .": Bernard Asbell, partial manuscript, *When F.D.R. Died,* pp. viii–6, FDRL.

29 "2d Lieutenant . . .": *U.S. Marine Corps Military History,* Carroll Mercer, March 20, 1919.

29 "This is my birthday . . .": Resa Willis, *FDR and Lucy,* p. 13.

30 "Cousin Minnie became . . .": Elizabeth Cotten to Jonathan Daniels, January 29, 1967, JDP.

31 "Rubbish . . .": Daniels, *Quadrille,* p. 34.

31 "descended to obscurity . . .": Ibid., p. 68.

31 "inside decorator . . .": Ward, *Temperament,* p. 360.

31 "by finding rich . . .": Ted Morgan, *FDR: A Biography,* p. 201.

## CHAPTER 5 · · A HARVARD MAN

32 "I hope he will . . .": SDR to Warren Delano, May 17, 1900, RFP.

33 "I am very glad . . .": Davis, *Beckoning,* p. 110.

33 "When he approaches . . .": Tugwell, *Democratic Roosevelt,* p. 33.

34 "I wish you would . . .": Freidel, *Apprenticeship,* p. 49.

34 "Make me a . . .": Davis, *Beckoning,* p. 107.

34 "of more than . . .": Frank D. Ashburn, *Peabody of Groton,* p. 341.

34 "a magnificent . . .": Francis Biddle, *In Brief Authority,* preface, p. 41.

34 "firm jawed . . .": Frank Freidel, *Apprenticeship,* p. 69.

35 "I want to be . . .": SDR to Warren Delano, December 14, 1902, RFP.

35 "I know that Taddy . . .": Lash, *Love, Eleanor,* p. 43.

36 "The disgusting business . . .": FDR to SDR, October 23, 1900, FBP.

37 "Life was full . . .": Ward, *Temperament,* p. 247.

37 "so funny at times . . .": Betty Boyd Caroli, *The Roosevelt Women,* p. 264.

37 "He was a quite . . .": Sheffield Cowles interview, November 22, 1954, HH.

37 "This is to certify . . .": Box 19, Harvard College memorabilia, FBP.

37 "Last night . . .": Freidel, *Apprenticeship,* p. 56.

38 "I don't believe . . .": Ibid., p. 69.

38 "I am trying . . .": SDR to Warren Delano, November 30, 1901, RFP.

38 "Everything was glorious . . .": FDR, Diary, 1901–3, Box 39, RFP.

38 "On top of them . . .": Corinne Alsop interview, December 28, 1954.

38 "a good little . . .": Collier and Horowitz, p. 22.

39 "Miss Nancy . . .": Ibid.

39 "Franklin was great fun . . .": Sachar, p. 33.

39 "of all the debutantes . . .": Ward, *Trumpet,* p. 253.

40 "Who else . . .": Ibid.

40 "all dined . . .": FDR Diary, Box 39, FDRL.

41 "By now she was . . .": Author telephone notes with Emily Shaw, July 18, 2005.

41 "In a day and age . . .": Ward, *Trumpet,* p. 253.

41 "Once upon . . .": Ibid., p. 255.

41 "so careless . . .": Ibid.

42 "As I knew . . .": James Roosevelt and Sidney Shalett, *Affectionately, FDR,* pp. 22–23.

42 "Monsieur . . .": Joseph E. Persico, *Roosevelt's Secret War,* p. 255.

42 "Franklin is trying . . .": SDR to Warren Delano, May 21, 1901, FBP.

43 "I telephoned . . .": Kleeman, "Biography of Sara Delano Roosevelt," pp. 9–10, FDRL.

43 "Terrible shock . . .": Box 39, FBP.

43 "My brother Ted . . .": Sachar, p. 30.

43 "President's Cousin, Elected . . .": Kleeman, "Biography of Sara Delano Roosevelt," pp. 9–10, FDRL.

44 "a flabby . . .": Davis, *Beckoning*, p. 146.

44 "I came to ask . . .": Ibid.

44 "In some way . . .": Freidel, *Apprenticeship*, p. 56.

45 "I was a lieutenant . . .": W. Sheffield Cowles interview, December 28, 1954, HH.

## CHAPTER 6 · · COURTSHIP

47 "She was not . . .": Corinne Alsop interview, December 28, 1954, HH.

48 "penetrated . . .": Davis, *Beckoning*, p. 185.

48 "I was always . . .": *AER*, p. 12.

48 "the warmest heart . . .": Maurine H. Beasley, Holly Shulman, and Henry R. Beasley, eds., *The Eleanor Roosevelt Encyclopedia*, p. 490.

48 "I think that day . . .": Davis, *Beckoning*, p. 85.

48 "When I arrived . . .": Corinne Robinson Alsop interview, Box 44, JLP.

48 "This was the . . .": *AER*, p. 24.

48 "habit of lying . . .": Davis, *Beckoning*, p. 85.

49 "Mlle. Souvestre . . .": *TIMS*, p. 71.

49 "Never again . . .": *AER*, p. 31.

49 "started me on . . .": Doris Kearns Goodwin, *No Ordinary Time*, p. 96.

49 "the happiest . . .": Lash, *Eleanor and Franklin*, p. 87.

49 "My grandmother was . . .": ER Oral History Project, interview by Justine Wise Polier, FDRL.

49 "Eleanor came . . .": Lash, *Centenary*, p. 10.

49 "You're too plain . . .": Elliott Roosevelt and James Brough, *An Untold Story*, p. 109.

50 "utter agony . . .": *TIMS*, pp. 100–101.

50 "I went to . . .": ER Oral History Project interview by Justine Wise Polier, FDRL.

50 "You couldn't find . . .": Beasley, et al., p. 323.

51 "Mary N & Eleanor Roos . . .": FDR Diary, November 22, 1902, Box 39, FBP.

51 "At 11 with . . .": FDR Diary, January 1, 1903, Box 39, FBP.

51 "E is an angel . . .": FDR Diary, July 7, 1903, Box 39, FBP.

51 "young people . . .": Ward, *Trumpet*, p. 308.

52 "I think he is . . .": Corinne Alsop Diary, HH.

52 "both undertook . . .": Joseph Lash, interviews of ER, Box 44, JLP.

52 "dreadful silences": Linda Donn, *The Roosevelt Cousins*, p. 81.

52 "My God . . .": Eleanor Roosevelt and Helen Ferris, *Your Teens and Mine*, p. 181.

52 "She possessed . . .": Donn, p. 104.

53 "a charming man . . .": *TIMS*, p. 110.

53 "He must have . . .": Elliott Roosevelt, *Untold Story*, p. 33.

55 "Franklin gave me . . .": Kleeman, "Biography of Sara Delano Roosevelt," p. 11, FDRL.

55 "To Groton at 9 . . .": National Archives quarterly *Prologue,* Spring 1972.

55 "I have only . . .": Allen Churchill, *The Roosevelts,* p. 226.

56 "I am so happy . . .": Cook, Vol. 1, p. 139.

56 "Dearest Mama . . .": FDR to SDR, December 4, 1903, RFP.

56 "Dearest Cousin . . .": ER to SDR, December 2, 1903, RFP.

56 "This morning I . . .": SDR to FDR, December 4, 1903, RFP.

57 "I am so . . .": SDR to FDR, December 6, 1903, RFP.

57 "it is a quiet . . .": SDR to FDR, December 4, 1903, RFP.

57 "Of course . . .": Cook, Vol. 1, p. 142.

58 "canoe trip . . .": FDR Diary, Box 39, FDRL.

58 "more claim . . .": Ward, *Trumpet,* p. 336.

58 "You are mighty . . .": *TIMS,* p. 110.

59 "One young . . .": Ward, *Trumpet,* p. 25.

59 "I am sure . . .": SDR to Warren Delano, November 23, 1904, RFP.

CHAPTER 7 · · MR. AND MRS. FRANKLIN D. ROOSEVELT

60 "I shall never . . .": Collier and Horowitz, p. 20.

60 "I shall look . . .": Ward, *Temperament,* p. 18.

60 "We three . . .": Cook, Vol. 1, p. 159.

60 "I've never seen . . .": Caroli, p. 260.

61 "never quite forgave . . .": Daniels, *Quadrille,* p. 203.

61 "It is not . . .": *TIMS,* pp. 126–27.

61 "It frightened me . . .": Ward, *Temperament,* p. 16.

61 "You knew a man . . .": Bernard Asbell, *The F.D.R. Memoirs,* p. 217.

61 "To have signed . . .": Ibid.

61 "Flowers, books . . .": Carol Felsenthal, *Alice Roosevelt Longworth,* p. 68.

61 "Gentle ladies . . .": William Hassett Diary, Box 21, FDRL.

62 "Miss Alice . . .": Box 4, ARHP.

62 "I smoked . . .": Box 1, ARHP.

62 "With whom I should . . .": Donn, p. 68.

62 "crazier than ever . . .": Felsenthal, p. 68.

62 "While I always . . .": Lash, *Love, Eleanor,* p. 60.

62 "suddenly leapt . . .": Ward, *Temperament,* p. 16.

62 "To perform a duty . . .": Lash, *Love, Eleanor,* p. 42.

63 "Only some . . .": Burns and Dunn, *Three Roosevelts,* p. 79.

63 "My father and . . .": Ibid., p. 78.

64 "Hooray for Teddy . . .": Allen Churchill, p. 229.

64 "Well Franklin . . .": Cook, Vol. 1, p. 67.

64 "Father always . . .": *TIMS,* pp. 124–26.

65 "Dear you were . . .": Morgan, p. 103.

65 "Eleanor has been . . .": *FDRPL*, Vol. 2, pp. 46–47.

65 "Franklin has been . . .": Ibid.


### CHAPTER 8 · · "DEAREST MUMMY"

67 "I pray that . . .": SDR to ER, October 11, 1905, RFP.

67 "It became part . . .": ER letters, RFP.

67 "I think one . . .": Asbell, *Memoirs*, p. 225.

67 "If there is anything . . .": Donn, p. 104.

68 "My grandmother . . .": Author interview of Curtis Roosevelt, November 15–16, 2005.

68 "Thank you so much . . .": Ward, *Temperament*, p. 12.

68 "Eleanor went to . . .": Author interview of Curtis Roosevelt.

68 "When Eleanor became . . .": Joseph Lash interview of Laura Delano, Boxes 44–45, JLP.

69 "A modern mother . . .": Steinberg, p. 47.

69 "I beg to call . . .": Richard Harrity and Ralph Martin, *The Human Side of FDR*, p. 76.

70 "saying with engaging frankness . . .": Asbell, *Memoirs*, pp. 227–28.

70 "Granny quickly managed . . .": Interview of ARH, COH.

71 "A Christmas present . . .": SDR to FDR and ER, FBP.

71 Inside the house . . .: Elliott Roosevelt interview, Eleanor Roosevelt Oral History Project, June 20, 1979, FDRL.

72 "I even felt . . .": Elliott Roosevelt, *Untold Story*, p. 48.

72 "When Sis was a young . . .": Ibid.


### CHAPTER 9 · · PATRICIAN POLITICIAN

73 "won't like to hear . . .": Morgan, p. 112.

74 "a little shaver . . .": Burns and Dunn, p. 116.

74 "Roosevelt is tall . . .": Allen Churchill, p. 244.

74 "my boy sitting . . .": SDR to FDR, January 5, 1911, FBP.

74 "Beloved and Revered . . .": Cook, Vol. 1, p. 199.

76 "very disapproving . . .": *TIMS*, p. 193.

76 "I took my cue . . .": ARH, COH.

77 "I thought he was . . .": Ward, *Temperament*, p. 183.

77 "How would you like . . .": Ibid., p. 200.

77 "I'd like it . . .": Cook, Vol. 1, p. 200.

77 "please me better . . .": John Gunther, *Roosevelt in Retrospect*, p. 208.

77 "My own dear . . .": FDR to ER, March 17, 1913, RFP.

78 "I am baptized . . .": FDR to SDR, *FDRPL*, Vol. 1, pp. 199–200.

78 "a *very* big . . .": Cook, Vol. 1, p. 201.

78 "His distinguished . . .": Ward, *Temperament*, p. 200.

## CHAPTER 10 · · THE SOCIAL SECRETARY

79 "If Auntie Bye . . .": Lash, *Centenary,* p. 9.
79 "Will you tell . . .": *TIMS,* pp. 208–9.
80 "We all used to . . .": ARL, COH.
80 "I've made 60 . . .": Lash, *Centenary,* p. 28.
80 "I'm trying to . . .": *TIMS,* pp. 208–9.
80 "Nearly all the . . .": *AER,* p. 75.
80 "quite frankly . . .": Ibid.
81 "I was appalled . . .": Ibid.
81 "tedious afternoon . . .": Bernard Asbell, *Mother and Daughter,* p. 24.
81 "Mrs. Mercer has . . .": Daniels, *Quadrille,* p. 70.
81 "stood between . . .": Ibid., p. 101.
82 "My aunt was not . . .": Author interview of Lucy Marbury, July 20, 2005.
82 "I tried at first . . .": Asbell, *Mother and Daughter,* p. 24.
83 "the young Roosevelts . . .": Daniels, *Quadrille,* p. 67.
83 "air the dog . . .": Ibid., p. 71.
83 "When I was . . .": Interview, Box 70, ARHP.
83 "I think she was . . .": Willis, p. 20.
83 "The face was . . .": Conrad Black, p. 85.
84 "the most attractive . . .": Elliott Roosevelt, *Untold Story,* p. 22.
84 "Ah, the lovely Lucy . . .": Goodwin, p. 20.
84 "Mr. Roosevelt is . . .": Ward, *Temperament,* p. 216.
85 "As Mr. Roosevelt made . . .": Persico, *Secret War,* p. 120.
85 "the funniest looking . . .": Ward, *Temperament,* p. 217.
86 "Lieber Ludwig . . .": Louis Howe Papers, Box 21, FDRL.
86 "I don't know where . . .": Daniels, *Innocence,* p. 81.

## CHAPTER 11 · · EVERY MAN WHO KNEW HER FELL IN LOVE

87 "one of those . . .": Michael Teague, *Mrs. L,* p. 57.
88 "Arrived safely . . .": James R. Kearney, *Anna Eleanor Roosevelt,* p. 24.
88 "the greatest catastrophe . . .": Robert K. Massie, *Dreadnought,* pp. 883, 887.
88 "A complete smash up . . .": *FDRPL,* Vol. 1, pp. 245–46.
88 "I am running . . .": Ibid.
88 "To understand . . .": Ibid.
88 "the greatest war . . .": Ward, *Temperament,* p. 244.
88 "To my astonishment . . .": Ibid.
89 "There is such a . . .": Persico, *Secret War,* p. 91.
90 "Mother had . . .": Elliott Roosevelt, *Untold Story,* p. 81; Lash, *Love, Eleanor,* p. 71.
90 "that was the end . . .": Ward, *Temperament,* p. 313.
90 "engaging picture . . .": Reporter quoted, PASN.

90 "My debonair . . .": Correspondence between FDR and Admiral and Mrs. W. Sheffield Cowles, RFP.

90 "the girls will . . .": Ibid.

90 "I had no idea . . .": Gunther, p. 214.

90 "Men and women . . .": Elliott Roosevelt, *Untold Story*, p. 6.

90 "Nothing is more . . .": James Roosevelt with Bill Libby, *My Parents*, p. 17.

90 "Something set . . .": Hassett, Diary, March 29, 1942, p. 65, Box 21, FDRL.

91 "I have been . . .": FDR to ER, undated, FBP.

91 "I knew him . . .": Lash, *Centenary*, p. 29.

91 "the saloon . . .": Daniels, *Innocence*, p. 228.

91 "I have my doubts . . .": Jonathan Daniels letter to Frank Freidel, September 5, 1967, Box 64, Folder 2126, JDP.

91 "with the usual . . .": Ward, *Temperament*, p. 316.

92 "I think our nice . . .": Ibid.

92 "Isn't it horrid . . .": Ibid.

92 "something of a . . .": Elliott Roosevelt, *Untold Story*, p. 73.

92 "She tried . . .": Asbell, *Mother and Daughter*, p. 19.

92 "It did not come . . .": Ibid.

92 "Miss Mercer . . .": Morgan, p. 202.

93 "Every man who . . .": Asbell, *Mother and Daughter*, p. 24.

93 "I hate to feel . . .": Caroli, p. 266.

93 "very much in love": Daniels, *Quadrille*, p. 145.

## CHAPTER 12 · · THE EXTRA WOMAN

94 "The flies have . . .": ER to FDR, July 12, 1916, RFP.

94 "I have had . . .": Morgan, p. 203.

94 "In those days . . .": ARL, *60 Minutes*, CBS, April 22, 1969.

95 "I went back . . .": Elliott Roosevelt, *Untold Story*, p. 83.

95 "What's wrong, dear?": Ibid., p. 84.

95 "the bearded lady . . .": Conrad Black, p. 75.

95 "virile-minded . . .": Elliott Roosevelt, *Untold Story*, p. 82.

96 "I'm so fond . . .": Kleeman, "Biography of Sara Delano Roosevelt," "An End," p. 10, FDRL.

97 "a man I loved . . .": Willis, p. 26.

97 "You will be able . . .": Ruth Stevens, *Hi-Ya Neighbor*, p. 54.

99 "Dearest Babs . . .": FDR to ER, July 16, 1917, RFP.

99 "It seems years . . .": FDR to ER, July 17, 1917, RFP.

99 "Mrs. Roosevelt does . . .": Ward, *Temperament*, pp. 363–64.

99 "All I can say . . .": Ibid., p. 365.

100 "I do think . . .": Ibid.

100 "Why did you . . .": ER to FDR, July 23, 1917, RFP.

101 "but it worked out . . .": Elliott Roosevelt, *Untold Story*, pp. 87–88.

101 "Dearest Honey . . .": Morgan, p. 205.

101 "I wish you would . . .": Ibid.

101 "I know she will . . .": Elliott Roosevelt, *Untold Story,* p. 89.

101 "I do miss you . . .": Morgan, p. 205.

101 "You certainly . . .": Ward, *Temperament,* p. 369.

102 "There was no . . .": Elliott Roosevelt, *Untold Story,* p. 89.

102 "Walked over the . . .": FDR to ER, undated, RFP.

102 "in every way . . .": Ward, *Temperament,* p. 379.

103 "Dallied around . . .": Ibid., p. 380.

103 "lazy, selfish . . .": Morgan, p. 203.

103 "The Ladies of . . .": Ward, *Temperament,* p. 680.

104 "I found myself . . .": *TIMS,* pp. 250–63.

104 "There was no . . .": Ibid.

104 "executive ability . . .": Davis, *Beckoning,* p. 495.

104 "It is a pity . . .": Ward, *Temperament,* p. 372.

104 "All I was . . .": Felsenthal, p. 139.

105 "We did hear . . .": Ibid.

105 "No one would know . . .": Collier and Horowitz, p. 123.

105 "In the Civil War . . .": *TIMS,* p. 251.

106 "I knew she had . . .": Morgan, p. 205.

106 "You are entirely . . .": Ibid.

107 "Don't telegraph . . .": Elliott Roosevelt, *Untold Story,* p. 85.

107 "often, I used . . .": Willis, p. 31.

107 "I saw you . . .": ARL, *60 Minutes,* CBS, April 22, 1969.

107 "Franklin deserved . . .": ARL, *60 Minutes,* CBS, April 22, 1969.

107 "The Roosevelt voice . . .": Ibid.

107 "They would have . . .": Willis, p. 130.

108 "flushed with wine . . .": Sachar, p. 33.

108 "a string bean . . .": Ibid.

108 "I knew you were . . .": Alsop, p. 67.

108 "have blamed Franklin . . .": Ibid.

108 "She inquired . . .": Felsenthal, p. 138.

109 "I want you to . . .": Ibid., pp. 104–7.

109 "He'd rather be . . .": Willis, p. 30.

109 "I believe these . . .": Ralph G. Martin, *The Extraordinary Life of Eleanor Medill Patterson,* p. 189.

109 "she lacked . . .": Lash, *Love, Eleanor,* p. 62.

CHAPTER 13 · · INHIBITIONS SNAP LIKE COBWEBS

110 "FDR did not seem . . .": Gallagher, p. 144.

110 "In the face of . . .": Lash, *Eleanor and Franklin,* p. 383.

111 "Oh, no . . .": Mrs. Sheffield Cowles Jr. interview, November 22, 1954, HH.

112 "a rather well-kept . . .": James Roosevelt, *My Parents,* p. 101.

112 "He needed . . .": Verne Newton, former director, FDRL, to author, June 22, 2005.

112 "Lucy began to ask . . .": Morgan, p. 207.

113 "A Terrible Tale . . .": *Buffalo Telegraph,* July 21, 1884.

113 "Above all . . .": Rexford G. Tugwell, *Grover Cleveland,* p. 190.

113 "no seduction . . .": Ibid., pp. 92–93.

113 "I am nothing . . .": Edwin A. Weinstein, *Woodrow Wilson,* p. 78.

114 "Wilson fell . . .": Ibid., p. 188.

114 "Best beloved . . .": Ibid., p. 191.

114 "see my dear . . .": Ibid., p. 192.

114 "I have known nine . . .": Alistair Cooke, "Letter from America," October 12, 1998, BBC News.

114 "I have known men . . .": Elizabeth Cady Stanton, essay, *Women's Penny Paper,* December 6, 1890, p. 3.

115 "having only monks . . .": Cooke, "Letter from America," October 12, 1998.

115 "profound effect . . .": Lash, *Love, Eleanor,* p. 70; Collier and Horowitz, p. 221.

115 "There are secrets . . .": Feodor Dostoyevsky, *Notes from Underground,* www.kiosek.com/dostoevsky/library/underground.txt.

## CHAPTER 14 · · THE HOMECOMING

117 "chronic nephritis . . .": Record of Death, District of Columbia, July 18, 1919.

117 "one of the most . . .": Daniels, *Quadrille,* p. 124.

117 "Poor Carroll Mercer . . .": Ibid.

117 "a drunkard . . .": Asbell, *Mother and Daughter,* p. 24.

117 "in all probability . . .": Daniels, *Quadrille,* p. 8.

118 "supporting Lucy . . .": Elliott Roosevelt, *Untold Story,* p. 111.

119 "One can be . . .": SDR to FDR and ER, October 14, 1917, RFP.

119 "I miss you . . .": Ward, *Temperament,* p. 381.

120 "As I have . . .": Ibid.

120 "No place could . . .": *AER,* p. 95.

120 "Mrs. Wilson now . . .": ER to SDR, July 17, 1918, RFP.

120 "with a unit . . .": ER to FDR, July 20, 1918, Box 15, FBP.

120 "I had not acquired . . .": Elliott Roosevelt, *Untold Story,* p. 94.

121 "A leg lay . . .": Alice Roosevelt Longworth, *Crowded Hours,* p. 282.

121 "I hate not being . . .": Lash, *Love, Eleanor,* p. 71.

121 "When you don't . . .": Ibid.

121 "Eleanor is the willing . . .": SDR to FDR, July 21, 1918, RFP.

## CHAPTER 15 · · THE STORM

122 "He's too . . .": Collier and Horowitz, p. 20.

123 "But to love Ellen . . .": Edith Wharton, *The Age of Innocence,* p. 306.

124 "She told me . . .": Box 70, ARHP.

124 "There are good . . .": Corinne Alsop interview, December 28, 1954, HH.

124 "it is criminal . . .": Lash, *Love, Eleanor,* p. 55.

124 "I beg you . . .": Lash, *Centenary,* p. 34.

124 "Sometimes even . . .": Gunther, pp. 196–97.

125 "I don't think one . . .": Willis, p. 33.

125 "all very well . . .": Alsop, p. 70.

125 "You have saved . . .": FDR to SDR, March 28, 1918, RFP.

126 "It wasn't just . . .": Morgan, p. 208.

127 "clear, concise . . .": Secretary of the Navy Annual Report, 1919, PASN.

127 "L.M. hinted . . .": Joseph Lash interview of ARH, October 29, 1968, Box 44, JLP.

127 "FDR may have . . .": Ibid.

127 "She loved . . .": Donn, p. 160.

128 "I know that . . .": Elizabeth Cotten to Jonathan Daniels, June 20, 1958, Box 64, JDP.

128 "But she realized . . .": Elizabeth Cotten to Jonathan Daniels, January 29, 1967, Box 64, JDP.

128 "Nothing is easier . . .": Elizabeth Cotten to Jonathan Daniels, June 20, 1958, Box 64, Folder 2139, JDP.

128 "You are quite . . .": Morgan, p. 200.

129 "he had made . . .": Box 44, JLP.

129 "It may not be . . .": Freidel, *Apprenticeship,* p. 317.

129 "an armed truce . . .": Lash, *Love, Eleanor,* p. 71.

130 "I have the memory . . .": Ibid., p. 70.

## CHAPTER 16 · · THE ADVANTAGE OF ADVERSITY

131 "As I looked . . .": Lorena A. Hickok, *Reluctant First Lady,* pp. 91–92.

131 "I might as well . . .": Lash, *Eleanor and Franklin,* p. 244.

132 "Just wait . . .": Elliott Roosevelt, *Untold Story,* p. 107.

132 "We have nothing . . .": Ibid.

132 "The scandals going . . .": Ibid.

132 "I hate . . .": ER, Diary, Box 4, p. 105, FDRL.

132 "I do not think . . .": ER, Diary, Box 4, p. 107, FDRL.

132 "Dined alone . . .": Ibid.; Lash, *Eleanor and Franklin,* p. 28.

132 "she did not . . .": James Roosevelt, *My Parents,* p. 98.

132 "No word . . .": Elliott Roosevelt, *Untold Story,* p. 108.

133 "I am worried . . .": Ibid.

133 "My grandmother's . . .": *TIR,* p. 300.

133 "any work . . .": Lash, *Eleanor and Franklin,* p. 238.

134 "I feel as though . . .": ER to FDR, July 23, 1919, RFP.

134 "Mama and I . . .": ER, Diary, Box 4, p. 115, FDRL.

134 "my darkies . . .": Elliott Roosevelt, *Untold Story,* p. 107.

134 "artistic temperament . . .": Davis, *Beckoning,* p. 594.

134 "could not make . . .": Ibid.

134 "It is a curious . . .": Elliott Roosevelt, *Untold Story,* p. 109.

135 The soul that . . .: "Psyche," by Virginia Moore, quoted in Goodwin, pp. 377–78.

135 "I think I learned . . .": *TIMS,* p. 260.

CHAPTER 17 · · A BRILLIANT MARRIAGE

136 "she is now . . .": Mercer Family, Misc. Documents, FDRL.

136 "to my children . . .": Daniels, *Quadrille,* p. 154.

136 "There is no possibility . . .": Mercer Family, Misc. Documents, FDRL.

136 "who was absent . . .": Ibid.

137 "Cousin Minnie . . .": Box 64, Folder 2125, JDP.

137 "she was very different . . .": Lyman Cotten Jr. to Jonathan Daniels, January 29, 1967, Box 64, Folder 2125, JDP.

137 "the handsomest . . .": Elliott Roosevelt, *Untold Story,* p. 110.

137 "the most beautiful . . .": w2.suite101.com/article.cfm_british_social_history.

138 "Winty was outclassed . . .": Daniels, *Quadrille,* p. 32.

138 "the prototype . . .": Willis, p. 49.

139 "Don't think . . .": Elizabeth Cotten to Jonathan Daniels, February 3, 1967, Box 64, Folder 2125, JDP.

139 "started like . . .": Alsop, pp. 71–72.

139 "old and ugly . . .": Daniels, *Quadrille,* p. 190.

139 "was a dull . . .": Box 62, Folder 2105, JDP.

140 "She was never . . .": Author interview of Guy Rutherfurd Jr., May 23, 2005.

140 "married Mr. Rutherfurd . . .": Daniels, *Quadrille,* p. 191.

140 "Did you know . . .": Elliott Roosevelt, *Untold Story,* p. 109.

141 "more a man . . .": James Roosevelt, *My Parents,* p. 118.

141 "It was the most . . .": Donn, p. 167.

141 "Young Roosevelt . . .": Conrad Black, p. 123.

142 "He told me . . .": Rexford Tugwell, COH.

142 "No one . . .": Sachar, p. 33.

142 "is first of all . . .": Lash, *Eleanor and Franklin,* p. 252.

142 "At the Roosevelt library . . .": Jonathan Daniels to Frank Freidel, August 27, 1967, Box 64, Folder 2126, JDP.

143 "Lay Navy Scandal . . .": *NYT,* July 23, 1920; Cook, Vol. 1, p. 306.

143 "a premeditated . . .": Cook, Vol. 1, p. 307.

143 "I am honestly . . .": Elliott Roosevelt, *Untold Story,* p. 111.

143 "the question was not . . .": FDR to SDR, February 11 (no year), RFP.

144 "the lovely throaty . . .": Asbell, *Memoirs,* p. 236.

144 "rather large features . . .": Ibid.

145 "Even as a . . .": Ibid., p. 247.

145 "no background . . .": Ward, *Temperament*, p. 678.

145 "Oh, that's all right . . .": Ibid., p. 568.

145 "Franklin gave . . .": Ibid., p. 562.

## CHAPTER 18 · · THE DIAGNOSIS

146 "Franklin D. Roosevelt . . .": Elliott Roosevelt, *Untold Story*, p. 131.

146 "perfectly grand": Ward, *Temperament*, p. 679.

147 "Mr. Roosevelt had a . . .": ER to MLH, August 17, 1921, Box 4, FBP.

147 "I'd never felt . . .": Gallagher, p. 2.

147 "We brought it . . .": Ibid., pp. 1–2.

148 "I didn't get . . .": Ibid.

148 "he began to complain . . .": Cook, Vol. 1, p. 308.

148 "You will certainly . . .": Elliott Roosevelt, *Untold Story*, p. 144.

148 "One night he was . . .": Kearney, p. 14.

149 "the most trying . . .": Lash, *Love, Eleanor*, p. 81.

150 "I never would have . . .": MLH to FDR, August 22, 1921, FBP.

150 "It is perfectly . . .": Annie Delano Hitch to ER, Box 18, RFP.

150 "The extent of recovery . . .": Gallagher, p. 27.

151 "The atmosphere . . .": Lash, *Love, Eleanor*, pp. 270–71.

151 "I am sure . . .": *TIMS*, p. 334.

151 "when we sit . . .": Elliott Roosevelt, *Untold Story*, p. 165.

151 "Dear Old Rosy . . .": Ward, *Temperament*, p. 680.

152 "knock you out . . .": Frank Freidel, *Franklin D. Roosevelt: The Ordeal*, p. 103.

152 "I couldn't help . . .": John R. Boettiger, *A Love in Shadow*, p. 89.

153 "He apparently . . .": Ibid.

153 "A man is a God . . .": Gunther, p. 219.

153 "Everyone is much . . .": Elliott Roosevelt, *Untold Story*, p. 150.

153 "Do you mind . . .": Ibid., pp. 86–87.

154 "Now please don't . . .": Correspondence between FDR and Charles Haskell, February 10 and 14, 1923, FBP.

154 "Every day . . .": Gallagher, p. 24.

154 "was entirely . . .": Daniels, *Quadrille*, p. 207.

154 "two years which . . .": Box 70, ARHP.

154 "Father had had . . .": Ibid.

154 "I couldn't talk . . .": Bernard Asbell interview of ARH, ARHP.

155 "was an adolescent . . .": Boettiger, p. 87.

155 "Out of the blue . . .": Box 70, draft article, ARHP.

155 "I have always had . . .": Boettiger, p. 87.

155 "I remember my first . . .": Box 70, ARHP.

155 "because I was a woman . . .": Bernard Asbell interview of ARH, ARHP.

155 "I had been accepted . . .": Box 84, ARHP.

156 "I remember her . . .": Binder 18, MSP.

## CHAPTER 19 · · MISSY

157 "I had never . . .": Asbell, *Memoirs,* p. 237.

157 "I remember going . . .": Joseph Lash interview of ARH, October 29, 1968, Box 44, JLP.

158 "an attractive woman . . .": *TIMS,* p. 32.

159 "to get the hell . . .": Author interview of Curtis Roosevelt, November 15–16, 2005.

160 "There were days . . .": Gallagher, p. 137.

160 "L.D. went to . . .": Asbell, *Memoirs,* p. 240.

160 "Hell to pay . . .": Ibid.

161 "great lady . . .": Box 63, Folder 2121, JDP.

161 "Because you're a bowery . . .": Karenna Gore Schiff, *Lighting the Way,* p. 155.

162 "the happy warrior . . .": Conrad Black, p. 165.

162 "It was a . . .": Sachar, p. 33.

163 "in awful condition . . .": Franklin D. Roosevelt Jr., and Donald Day, *Franklin D. Roosevelt's Own Story,* p. 82.

163 "walk around in . . .": Freidel, *Ordeal,* p. 193.

163 "every organization . . .": William Warren Rogers, Jr., "The Death of a President," pp. 1–2.

163 "if anyone were to . . .": Lash, *Centenary,* p. 49.

164 "she and I both . . .": Ward, *Temperament,* p. 708.

164 "so gay and so . . .": Corinne Alsop interview, November 22, 1954, HH.

165 "Absolutely not . . .": Goodwin, p. 154.

165 "I'm going to be . . .": Ward, *Temperament,* pp. 709–10.

165 "Anna and I often . . .": James Roosevelt, *My Parents,* p. 104.

165 "filled a need . . .": Ibid.

165 "Who could tell?": Joseph Lash interview of ARH, October 29, 1968, Box 44, JLP.

165 "no symptoms of . . .": Gallagher, pp. 130–32.

165 "Is the President potent?": May 12, 1971, Box 64, DSP.

166 "He lived his life . . .": Gallagher, p. 132.

166 "He learned that . . .": Asbell, *Memoirs,* p. 241.

## CHAPTER 20 · · SAFE HARBOR

167 "Few people dropped . . .": Marion Dickerman, March 1973, COH.

168 "I am a dyed-in-the-wool . . .": *NYT,* April 13, 1945.

168 "There I was . . .": Conrad Black, p. 721.

168 "I'll walk without . . .": Gallagher, p. 63.

169 "You needn't worry . . .": Asbell, *Memoirs,* p. 243.

169 "There was a big . . .": Bernard Asbell, "Missy: The Tragic Story of the Secretary Who Loved President Roosevelt," pp. 72–73.

170 "is rather low . . .": Asbell, *Memoirs,* p. 252.

170 "She, of course . . .": Bernard LeHand to FDR, July 10, 1927, Box 21, RFP.

170 "It was a . . .": Asbell, "Tragic Story," p. 73.

170 "crack-up": Asbell, *Memoirs,* p. 252.

170 "I can't find any . . .": Bernard Asbell interview of ARH.

171 "Between now and the 16th . . ." et al.: FDR to LMR, May 22, 1926; September 15, 1927, postmarked December 22, 1927, May 18, 1928, Rutherfurd Family Collection, Aiken, South Carolina.

171 "Dear Franklin . . .": LMR to FDR, April 16, 1927, FBP.

172 "a traveling circus . . .": LMR to FDR, July 2, 1927, FBP.


CHAPTER 21 · · ELEANOR AND FRIENDS


173 "was my husband's home . . .": Ward, *Temperament,* p. 275.

173 "If you just . . .": Ibid.

173 "Before us why . . .": Mr. and Mrs. Sheffield Cowles Jr. interview, December 28, 1954, HH.

173 "They all in their . . .": Lash, *Love, Eleanor,* p. 74.

173 "I have known . . .": Cook, Vol. 1, p. 443.

174 "and she could be . . .": Bernard Asbell interview of ARH, Box 44.

174 "the source . . .": Gunther, p. 164.

174 "By the time . . .": ARH, COH.

174 "who persuaded me not . . .": Ibid.

174 "What she wanted . . .": Lash, *Centenary,* p. 30.

174 "If mother had . . .": Bernard Asbell interview of ARH, Box 44.

174 "Franklin could banter . . .": Joseph Lash interview of ARH, October 29, 1968, Box 44, JLP.

174 "From the polio time . . .": Ibid.

174 "I wanted to get out . . .": Ibid.

174 "I am so angry . . .": Lash, *Eleanor and Franklin,* p. 301.

175 "I did not think . . .": Ibid.

175 "We kidded mother . . .": Elliott Roosevelt, *Untold Story,* p. 258.

175 "build a shack . . .": Lash, *Centenary,* p. 47.

176 "I gave courses . . .": Beasley et al., pp. 516–17.

176 "She got involved . . .": Joseph Lash interview of James Roosevelt, December 19, 1966, Boxes 44–45, JLP.

176 "I'd rather be . . .": Beasley et al., p. 281.

176 "a certain gentleman . . .": Marion Dickerman, March 1973, COH.

177 "I'd feel I'd like . . .": ER to Marion Dickerman, August 27, 1925, Dickerman Papers, Box 4, FDRL.

177 "she-males": Elliott Roosevelt, *Untold Story,* p. 130.

177 "female impersonators . . .": Collier and Horowitz, p. 271.

178 "No sort of love . . .": Cook, Vol. 1, p. 318.

178 "She was absolutely . . .": Joseph Lash, interview of Esther Lape, February 24, 1970, Boxes 44–45, JLP.

178 "Her whole background . . .": Marion Dickerman, March 1973, COH.

## CHAPTER 22 · · GOVERNOR ROOSEVELT

180 "Oh Jim . . .": Author interview of Lucy Blundon, July 20, 2005.

180 "Mr. Danks would come . . .": Ibid.

181 "the epitome of . . .": Ibid.

181 "He worshipped . . .": Ibid.

181 "He was desperately . . .": Willis, p. 76.

181 "Why, you're almost . . .": Author interview of Lucy Blundon, July 20, 2005.

182 "I am temperamentally . . .": Freidel, *Ordeal,* p. 216.

182 "the quality of soul . . .": FDR Public Papers, speech nominating Al Smith, June 27, 1928, Democratic National Convention, Houston.

183 "If they are looking . . .": Davis, *Beckoning,* p. 849.

183 "You're still not . . .": Goodwin, p. 118.

183 "Don't hand me that . . .": Ward, *Temperament,* p. 793.

183 "Frank, I told you . . .": Ibid.

183 "Don't you dare . . .": Ward, *Temperament,* p. 794.

184 "There is something . . .": Gallagher, p. 71.

184 "We do not elect . . .": *NYT,* October 3, 1928.

184 "The governor did not . . .": Bernard Bellush, *Franklin D. Roosevelt as Governor of New York,* pp. 12–13.

184 "said the beads . . .": Conrad Black, p. 185.

184 "Governor Smith's election . . .": Ibid.

184 "If the rest . . .": Lash, *Centenary,* p. 47.

184 "as if to . . .": Ibid., p. 49.

185 "now that Franklin . . .": Elliott Roosevelt, *Untold Story,* p. 258.

185 "Elliott makes a lot . . .": James Roosevelt, *My Parents,* p. 105.

185 "Can you walk . . .": Elliott Roosevelt, *Untold Story,* p. 264.

186 "I don't like . . .": Ibid., p. 265.

186 "wholehearted loyalty . . .": Marion Dickerman, March 1973, COH.

186 "Dear F.D. . . .": Asbell, "Tragic Story," p. 76.

187 "gave him strength . . .": *TIMS,* p. 342.

187 "Do you think . . .": Bernard Asbell, *Memoirs,* p. 343.

187 "Franklin Roosevelt . . .": Daniels, *Quadrille,* p. 206.

187 "I think polio . . .": Author interview of Curtis Roosevelt, November 15–16, 2005.

187 "The only thing that . . .": FDRPL Vol. 2, p. xviii.

187 "The man was a . . .": Gallagher, p. xi.

188 "I guess that will . . .": ARH, COH.

188 "No movies . . .": Gallagher, p. 94.

CHAPTER 23 · · ELEANOR AND THE STATE TROOPER

189 "I was without . . .": Earl Miller to Miriam Abelow, August 22, 1966, Miriam Abelow Papers, Box 1, FDRL.

189 "I had to go on . . .": Lash, *Love, Eleanor*, p. 119.

190 "To while away . . .": Elliott Roosevelt, *Untold Story*, p. 274.

190 "I never again . . .": Ibid., p. 275.

190 "I did all the . . .": Lash, *Love, Eleanor*, p. 119.

190 "He used to be . . .": Marion Dickerman, March 1973, COH.

191 "They must have . . .": Lash, *Love, Eleanor*, p. 120.

191 "The trouble with . . .": Beasley et al., p. 340.

191 "Her expression . . .": Lash, *Love, Eleanor*, p. 119.

191 "My dear, if you haven't . . .": Hickok, p. 86.

191 "Now, listen . . .": Cook, Vol. 1, p. 117.

191 "She credits me . . .": Lash, *Love, Eleanor*, p. 117.

191 "When they saw . . .": Ibid.

191 "I wish someone . . .": Ibid., p. 119.

191 "concerned about . . .": Marion Dickerman, March 1973, COH.

192 "The fact that . . .": Author interview of Curtis Roosevelt, November 15–16, 2005.

192 "He used to annoy . . .": Lash, *Centenary*, p. 52.

192 "Oh, I was expecting . . .": Beasley et al., p. 341.

192 "Earl gave Eleanor . . .": Marion Dickerman, March 1973, COH.

192 "gave her . . .": Asbell, *Mother and Daughter*, p. 72.

193 "Mother was . . .": Ibid.

193 "I believe there may . . .": Ibid.

193 "to protect her . . .": Ibid., p. 73.

193 "he did not seem . . .": Ibid., p. 72.

193 "It is obvious . . .": Cook, Vol. 1, p. 442.

193 "He interested her . . .": Lash, *Love, Eleanor*, p. 123.

194 "Wouldn't Mrs. R. . . .": Ibid., p. 122.

194 "the affair between . . .": Ibid., p. 118.

194 "When Mrs. R. told me . . .": Ibid., p. 122.

194 "Missy had me . . .": Ibid., p. 118.

195 "smoked less . . .": Asbell, "Tragic Story," p. 74.

195 "simply made passes . . .": Elliott Roosevelt, *Untold Story*, p. 275.

195 "I was never . . .": Lash, *Love, Eleanor*, p. 119.

195 "That's why . . .": Ibid.

195 "As a present . . .": Cook, Vol. 1, p. 464.

195 "As I sat . . .": Lash, *Love, Eleanor*, p. 118.

195 "after you get to . . .": Ibid.

196 "I think she . . .": Ibid., p. 121.

196 "They were my . . .": Earl Miller to Miriam Abelow, December 11, 1962, Miriam Abelow Papers, Box 1, FDRL.

196 "Livy's death . . .": Goodwin, p. 89.

197 "If Thomas Jefferson . . .": FDR, Jefferson Day address, April 26, 1930, New York City, FDRL.

197 "Much love . . .": Asbell, "Tragic Story," pp. 50–51.

197 "I hate so to see . . .": Kearney, p. 255.

197 "Father's letter . . .": Asbell, *Mother and Daughter*, pp. 50–51.

198 "I had him atop . . .": Earl Miller to Miriam Abelow, Miriam Abelow Papers, Box 1, FDRL.

198 "We have today . . .": Gunther, p. 267.

198 "We believe . . .": Gallagher, pp. 130–32.

199 "There's a star . . .": MLH to Rexford Tugwell, COH.

199 "a prisoner . . .": Kenneth S. Davis, *FDR: The New York Years*, p. 331.

199 "You are not . . .": Kenneth S. Davis, *Invincible Summer*, pp. 107–8.

199 "From a personal . . .": *TIR*, p. 69.

## CHAPTER 24 · · ELEANOR AND HICK

200 "mostly respectable-looking . . .": Alsop, p. 143.

200 "All my life . . .": Gallagher, p. 87.

201 "a slippery . . .": Conrad Black, p. 220.

201 "A second class . . .": Beasley et al., p. xiii.

202 "I am certain . . .": FDR, 1933 Inaugural Address, FDR Public Papers, FDRL.

202 "fine shadings . . .": Samuel I. Rosenman, *Working with Roosevelt*, p. 249.

202 "So, first of all . . .": FDR, 1933 Inaugural Address, FDR Public Papers, FDRL.

202 "it is even possible . . .": Esther Lape to Samuel Rosenman, October 31, 1949, Rosenman Papers, FDRL.

202 "I was happy . . .": Gallagher, p. 87.

203 "After a long . . .": Hickok, p. 92.

203 "Your ring is . . .": Doris Faber, *The Life of Lorena Hickok*, pp. 53–54, 110.

203 "I do remember . . .": *TIR*, p. 78.

203 "It was hardly . . .": Lillian Rogers Parks with Francis Spatz Leighton, *The Roosevelts*, p. 5.

204 "at least for . . .": Doris Faber, "Biography of Lorena Hickok," undated manuscript, p. 4, FDRL.

204 "Hick my dearest . . .": Ibid., p. 2.

204 "My pictures . . .": Ibid., p. 3.

204 "I miss you so much . . .": Ibid., p. 168.

204 "I couldn't bear . . .": Ibid.

204 "I couldn't say . . .": Rodger Streitmatter, *Empty Without You*, p. xx.

205 "I remember your . . .": Faber, *Life*, p. 152.

205 "The first contact . . .": Faber, "Biography," p. 19.

205 "kept wondering . . .": Ibid., p. 18.

205 "bitter hatred": Ibid., p. 20.

205 "an agonizing routine . . .": LH, unpublished manuscript, Papers of LH, Box 14, FDRL.

206 "Hick had a . . .": Faber, "Biography," p. 9a.

207 "The new mistress . . .": Ibid., p. 106.

207 "Nobody can ever . . .": Faber, *Life*, p. 110.

208 "Money was not . . .": LH, unpublished manuscript, Papers of LH, Box 1, FDRL.

208 "a reporter should . . .": Lash, *Love, Eleanor*, p. 133.

208 "let herself slip . . .": Goodwin, p. 223.

208 "When the Roosevelts . . .": Parks, p. 206.

209 "Put a seam . . .": Ibid., p. 17.

209 "wasn't a bad . . .": Ibid., p. 212.

209 "when I hear . . .": Ibid., p. 204.

209 "in a compromising . . .": Ibid., pp. 205–6, 214.

209 "used to try . . .": Hickok, p. 118.

209 "I had an understanding . . .": LH, unpublished manuscript, Papers of LH, Box 14, FDRL.

210 "There were perhaps . . .": Ward, *Trumpet*, p. 301.

210 "casually accepted . . .": Louise Tutelian, "Eleanor Roosevelt's Place Apart," p. 1.

210 "Girls routinely . . .": Lash, *Love, Eleanor*, p. xiii.

210 "Assure me . . .": Tutelian, p. 3.

210 "I'm going to . . .": Ibid., p. 7.

210 "Contacts between . . .": Ibid., p. 9.

211 "Every woman wants . . .": Willis, p. 117.

211 "You've made me . . .": Ibid.

211 "My grandmother . . .": Author interview of Curtis Roosevelt, November 15–16, 2005.

211 "I love you beyond . . .": Faber, "Biography," p. 99.

211 "It hardly seems likely . . .": Ibid., p. 96.

211 "The fact is . . .": Cook, Vol. 1, p. 479.

211 "shared a relationship . . .": Streitmatter, p. xiv.

212 "used expressions . . .": Lash, draft speech, 1979, Box 64, DSP.

212 "had so many . . .": Goodwin, p. 221.

212 "Sometimes people . . .": Joseph Lash interview of ARH, October 29, 1968, Box 44, JLP.

212 "Her sensibilities . . .": Collier and Horowitz, p. 269.

212 "calm and reassuring . . .": Faber, "Biography," p. 179.

212 "abetted this . . .": Ibid.

212 "We'll have years . . .": Streitmatter, p. xxi.

212 "It is sad . . .": Ibid.

213 "One corner cupboard . . .": Ibid.

213 "I know I've . . .": Lash, *Love, Eleanor,* p. 222.

213 "My dear, if . . .": Streitmatter, p. 22.

213 "I think one . . .": Ibid., p. 44.

213 "Dearest, it was . . .": Ibid., p. 68.

213 "though I was . . .": Lash, *Centenary,* p. 12.

213 "In her . . .": Beasley et al., p. 59.

213 "clear implications . . .": Streitmatter, pp. xiv–xv.

214 "Hick brought . . .": Joseph Lash interview of Esther Lape, February 24, 1970, Boxes 44–45, JLP.

## CHAPTER 25 · · "CLOSE TO BEING A WIFE"

215 "People edged . . .": John Dos Passos, "The Radio Voice."

215 "When Father . . .": ER Oral History Project, FDRL.

216 "I still lived . . .": *AER,* p. 66.

217 "It was pretty . . .": ER Oral History Project, FDRL.

217 "Mother always . . .": Asbell, *Memoirs,* p. 410.

217 "The boss . . .": Parks, p. 211.

217 "would leave things . . .": Joseph Lash interview of James Roosevelt, December 19, 1966, Boxes 44–45, JLP.

217 "Eleanor basket": Goodwin, p. 15.

217 "Dearest Honey": Parks, p. 177.

218 "It is common sense . . .": Ward, *Trumpet,* p. 6.

218 "he would forcefully . . .": Joseph Lash interview of James Roosevelt, December 19, 1966, Boxes 44–45, JLP.

218 "It was he . . .": Beasley et al., p. xx.

219 "Even if . . .": Parks, p. 177.

219 "she would recoil . . .": Ibid., p. 211.

219 "one can be . . .": Lash, *Love, Eleanor,* p. 240.

219 "Watch them . . .": Florence Kerr, July 29, 1974, COH.

219 "I accepted . . .": James Roosevelt, *My Parents,* p. 98.

219 "just did . . .": Ibid., p. 109.

219 "never saw . . .": J. B. West with Mary Lynn Kotz, *Upstairs at the White House,* p. 23.

219 "She smiled . . .": Ibid., p. 13

219 "I was sitting . . .": Ibid., p. 30.

220 "was sunshine . . .": Parks, photo caption.

220 "when Missy gave . . .": Ibid., p. 177.

220 "Without making . . .": Goodwin, p. 119.

220 "What goes?": Parks, p. 5.

221 "Missy was somehow . . .": Ibid., p. 180.

221 "A man has no . . .": Ibid., pp. 195–96.

221 "he just didn't . . .": Ibid., p. 183.

221 "there was no . . .": Asbell, "Tragic Story," p. 121.

221 "She knows . . .": *Newsweek,* August 12, 1933.

221 "No invitation . . .": Asbell, "Tragic Story," p. 121.

222 "Then he served . . .": Gallagher, p. 135.

222 "She knew when to escort . . .": Goodwin, p. 119.

222 "I noticed . . .": Marion Dickerman, March 1973, COH.

222 "Can I dine . . .": PPF, File 3739.

223 "I have seen . . .": Grace Tully, *F.D.R.: My Boss,* p. 113.

223 "for Franklin Junior's . . .": James Roosevelt, *Affectionately,* p. 234.

223 "There was never . . .": Gallagher, p. 134.

223 "That's his . . .": Asbell, *Memoirs,* p. 246.

223 "Christmas is . . .": MLH to ER, undated, Box 21, RFP.

223 "I am a dictator": William F. Leuchtenberg, *Franklin D. Roosevelt and the New Deal,* p. 209.

223 "Dear Effdee . . .": MLH to FDR, December 16, 1936, Box 21, RFP.

224 "I know she . . .": James Roosevelt, *My Parents,* p. 109.

224 "I think she did . . .": Bernard Asbell interview of ARH.

224 "I think you have . . .": Ibid., p. 6.

224 "Dearest Eleanor . . .": MLH to ER, undated, Box 21, RFP.

224 "Are you always . . .": Lash, Diary, June 4, 1940, JLP.

224 "the ten best . . .": Hickok, p. 86.

224 "Missy made sure . . .": Parks, p. 184.

225 "he certainly was . . .": Florence Kerr, July 29, 1974, COH.

225 "so severely handicapped . . .": Ibid.

225 "frankest of the . . .": Asbell, *Memoirs,* p. 263.

225 "You must also . . .": Ibid.

225 "She was, all in all . . .": Samuel Rosenman, COH.

225 "There is no . . .": Raymond Moley, *The First New Deal,* pp. 273–75.

225 "If I should . . .": Streitmatter, p. 183.

225 "might have been . . .": Donn, p. 198.

226 "Franklin loved Missy . . .": Ibid.


## CHAPTER 26 · · FOUR MORE YEARS

227 "'Go look . . .'": Author interview of Lucy Blundon, July 20, 2005.

227 "wearing glasses . . .": Willis, p. 91.

228 "constantly preoccupied . . .": Elizabeth Shoumatoff, *FDR's Unfinished Portrait,* p. 77.

228 "She stayed in . . .": Author interview of Lucy Blundon, July 20, 2005.

228 "My mother did . . .": Ibid.

228 "No provision . . .": Charles W. Griffith to Minna Mercer, December 20, 1933, Mercer Family, Misc. Documents, FDRL.

229 "tired, fed up . . .": Daniels, *Quadrille,* pp. 261–62.

229 "it might be construed . . .": Daniels, *Quadrille,* p. 262.

230 "I can't tell you . . .": Beasley et al., p. 299; Daniels, *Quadrille*, p. 263.

230 "Tommy never . . .": Bernard Asbell interview of ARH.

230 "She was not . . .": Lash, *Eleanor and Friends*, p. 344.

230 "I realize . . .": Lash, *Love, Eleanor*, p. 242.

230 "Everyone's cocksure . . .": Ibid.

231 "To hell . . .": Walter Trohan, *Political Animals*, pp. 82–83.

231 "the world cannot . . .": FDR, speech, March 8, 1936, Democratic National Convention, Philadelphia, FDR Public Papers, FDRL.

231 "I have seen war . . .": Rosenman, *Public Papers*, Vol. 5, p. 289.

232 "A rather . . .": Asbell, *Mother and Daughter*, p. 70.

232 "you went in . . .": Corinne Alsop interview, HH.

232 "Smart Aleck Administration . . .": Alice Roosevelt Longworth Papers, Library of Congress.

232 "Franklin is on . . .": Conrad Black, p. 376.

233 "Here was mother . . .": Joseph Lash interview of ARH, October 29, 1968, Box 44, JLP.

233 "if you want . . .": Lash, *Centenary*, p. 54.

233 "He was like a piteous . . .": Streitmatter, p. 183.

233 "I had a feeling . . .": Joseph Lash interview of ARH, October 29, 1968, Box 44, JLP.

233 "Devoted friend . . .": Lela Stiles, *The Man Behind Roosevelt*, p. 300.

234 "A pencil drops . . .": Author interview of Curtis Roosevelt, November 15–16, 2005.

234 "Mr. President we'll . . .": Gunther, p. 236.

234 "As I stood . . .": Olive Ewing Clapper, *Washington Tapestry*, pp. 22–23.

235 "I can remember . . .": ER, COH.

235 "You sit in your . . .": Persico, *Secret War*, pp. 26–27.

235 "I see millions . . .": FDR, 1937 Inaugural Address, FDR Public Papers, FDRL.

235 "a traitor . . .": Box 62, Folder 2105, JDP; Daniels, *Quadrille*, p. 263.

## CHAPTER 27 · · EXIT HICKOK: ENTER SCHIFF

236 "Of course . . .": Lash, *Love, Eleanor*, p. 218.

236 "Dear one . . .": Ibid.

236 "You told me . . .": Streitmatter, p. 14.

237 "You barely . . .": Ibid., p. 148.

237 "Oh I'm bad . . .": Faber, *Life*, p. 174.

237 "Hick darling . . .": Streitmatter, p. 207.

237 "I think you will . . .": Geoffrey Ward, "Outing Mrs. Roosevelt," *New York Review of Books*, September 24, 1992.

237 "Over the years . . .": Lash, *Love, Eleanor*, p. 235.

238 "I went to sleep . . .": Ibid., p. 223.

238 "I am now . . .": Streitmatter, p. 199.

238 "I was considered . . .": *NYT,* May 28, 1976.

238 "said I had . . .": Jeffrey Potter, *Men, Money and Magic,* p. 10.

239 "I heard that . . .": Ibid., p. 134.

239 "This is . . .": Notes, November 23, 1981, DSP.

239 "Dorothy, I'm so . . .": Potter, p. 135.

239 "Something happened . . .": Ibid.

239 "Sit next . . .": Ibid.

239 "I was still . . .": Box 258, DSP.

240 "Granny sat at one . . .": Potter, p. 141.

240 "She was aware . . .": Ibid.

240 "Franklin, why . . .": Ibid., p. 150.

240 "as often . . .": Ibid., p. 136.

240 "He loved . . .": Ibid., p. 143.

240 "whenever I would be slid . . .": Box 64, DSP.

241 "George was overwhelmed . . .": *NYT,* May 28, 1996.

241 "He would ask . . .": Potter, p. 155.

241 "ability to ask . . .": Ibid., p. 151.

241 "Not a word . . .": Box 258, DSP.

241 "I hate that . . .": Box 64, DSP.

242 "I can't say . . .": Ibid.

242 "I remember when . . .": Box 258, DSP.

242 "has got under . . .": *NYT,* May 2, 1982.

243 "I didn't say . . .": Box 64, DSP.

243 "Why, you would . . .": Potter, p. 154.

243 "If you would . . .": Ibid., p. 167.

243 "Well Sam . . .": Box 64, DSP.

243 "In his spoiled . . .": Potter, p. 168.

244 "I didn't really . . .": Ibid., p. 155.

244 "It threw . . .": Ibid., p. 156.

244 "We got there . . .": Box 258, DSP.

244 "what the President . . .": Potter, p. 159.

244 "A lot of my . . .": Ibid., p. 169.

245 "Why darling . . .": Box 258, DSP.

245 "confirming her claim . . .": Potter, p. 169.

245 "Franklin the First . . .": Ibid., p. 171.

245 "Oh dear . . .": *NYT,* June 12, 1939.

245 "goosed her . . .": Boxes 44–45, JLP.

246 "he probably . . .": *NYT,* May 28, 1976.

246 "At first I . . .": Box 258, DSP.

246 "Of course not. I'm better . . .": Ibid.

246 "Before long . . .": Potter, p. 169.

246 "The book was . . .": Box 64, DSP.

246 "She did not . . .": *NYT,* May 28, 1976.

246 "was fairly bold . . .": Ibid.

CHAPTER 28 · · 1941: YEAR OF GAIN, YEAR OF LOSS

247 "Jerry, after . . .": Gunther, p. 34.

248 "the most . . .": Persico, *Secret War,* p. 41.

248 "never had . . .": *NYT,* July 17, 1940.

248 "We want Roosevelt!": Conrad Black, p. 531.

248 "Any old-time . . .": Persico, *Secret War,* p. 47.

248 "I have said . . .": Ibid., p. 48.

249 "Who is that . . .": Author interview of Lucy Blundon, July 20, 2005.

249 "There seems . . .": West, p. 26.

249 "I see it's . . .": Ibid.

250 "charming and . . .": Box 64, Folder 2124, JDP.

250 "He used to . . .": Goodwin, p. 155.

251 "Bullitt used her . . .": Ibid.

251 "wanted to marry . . .": Ibid.

251 "feeling I think . . .": Ibid.

251 "I don't think . . .": Elliott Roosevelt, *Untold Story,* p. 259.

251 "a good looking . . .": James Roosevelt, *My Parents,* p. 17.

252 "exactly as . . .": Willis, p. 98.

252 "She never forgot . . .": Marion Dickerman, March 1973, COH.

252 "putting on . . .": Parks, p. 200.

252 "It looks like . . .": Ibid.

252 "He loved her . . .": Bernard Asbell interview of ARH.

252 "Father and Mother . . .": Joseph Lash interview of ARH, October 29, 1968, Box 44, JLP.

252 "lovely ladies . . .": Gunther, p. 72.

252 "There was always . . .": Willis, p. 99.

253 "My grandmother . . .": Author interview of Curtis Roosevelt, November 15–16, 2005.

253 "nightmares of . . .": Box 258, DSP.

253 "Near the end . . .": Tully, p. 246.

253 "when I arrived . . .": Parks, p. 186.

254 "11:30 am . . .": Willis, p. 97.

254 "Returned from office . . .": Ibid.

254 "17:40 . . .": Ibid.

255 "I think it's . . .": Author interview of Curtis Roosevelt, November 15–16, 2005.

255 "we shall no longer . . .": Persico, *Secret War,* p. 83.

256 "extremely reserved": Author interview of Rosamund Durban McDuffie.

256 "The littlest Babs": FDR to LMR, October 29, 1941, Knowles Family Collection, Aiken, South Carolina.

257 "happy visits . . .": Box 62, Folder 2105, JDP.

257 "I could not see . . .": Daniels, letter to Frank Freidel, September 5, 1967, JDP.

257 "goddaughter . . .": Ibid.

258 "I know I am . . .": Elliott Roosevelt, *Untold Story*, p. 304.

258 "Mrs. Roosevelt, what is . . .": Roland Redmond Oral History, FDRL.

258 "considerably more . . .": Christine M. Totten, "Remembering Sara Delano Roosevelt on Her 150th Anniversary."

258 "She never heard . . .": Davis, *Beckoning*, p. 207.

258 "She wrote my mother . . .": Author interview of Curtis Roosevelt, November 15–16, 2005.

259 "I will be . . .": Goodwin, p. 271.

259 "Father came across . . .": Elliott Roosevelt, *Untold Story*, p. 304.

259 "with all the lines . . .": Ward, *Temperament*, p. 7; "My Day," September 8, 1941.

259 "I couldn't feel . . .": Collier and Horowitz, p. 401.

260 "it's always . . .": Marion Dickerman, March 1973, COH.

260 "This was the little . . .": Lash, *Centenary*, p. 86.

260 "She showed him . . .": Frank Freidel, *Franklin D. Roosevelt: A Rendezvous with Destiny*, p. 509.

261 "Many human . . .": "My Day," April 14, 1942.

261 "What vitality . . .": Totten, "Remembering Sara Delano Roosevelt."

261 "she kept a . . .": Ibid.

262 "things are . . .": Persico, *Secret War*, p. 141.

262 "The President was able . . .": Ibid., p. 87.

262 "Although crippled . . .": Robert E. Sherwood, *Roosevelt and Hopkins*, p. 882.

263 "Oh my . . .": Parks, p. 195.

263 "ladylike . . .": Jim Bishop, *FDR's Last Year*, p. 560.

263 "This kind of letter . . .": LMR to FDR, undated, Box 70, ARHP.

264 "I have heard . . .": Daniels, *Quadrille*, p. 152.

264 "did not share . . .": Goodwin, p. 520.

265 "although she loved . . .": Alsop, p. 68.

265 "You had to have . . .": Asbell, "Tragic Story," p. 123.

CHAPTER 29 · · MISSY PROTECTED,
LUCY INDULGED, ELEANOR OUTRAGED

266 "the worst cook . . .": Persico, *Secret War*, p. xxiv.

267 "Mr. President . . .": Ibid.

267 "His reaction . . .": Ibid.

267 "It looks . . .": Ibid., p. 235.

267 "were caught . . .": Ibid., p. 134.

267 "Missy telephoned . . .": PPF, 3737.

267 "She was still shocked": Author interview of Curtis Roosevelt, November 15–16, 2005.

267 "She started crying . . .": Ann Rochon to FDR, December 31, 1942, PPF, 3737.

268 "I don't know . . .": Asbell, *Memoirs,* p. 402.

268 "See ya . . .": Asbell, "Tragic Story," p. 123.

268 "He didn't like . . .": Author interview of Curtis Roosevelt, November 15–16, 2005.

268 "I wanted her to feel . . .": Asbell, "Tragic Story," p. 123.

268 "The letters told . . .": Asbell, *Memoirs,* p. 403.

268 "It seemed only . . .": Goodwin, p. 245.

269 "I felt a clear . . .": Harold Ickes, Diary, July 12, 1941, LOC.

269 "Some may try . . .": James Roosevelt, *My Parents,* p. 108.

270 "There was nothing . . .": Asbell, *Memoirs,* p. 403.

270 "to be his wife . . .": Goodwin, p. 371.

270 "Upper class . . .": Louis Adamic, *Dinner at the White House,* p. 193.

271 "Dear Mr. President . . .": Guy Rutherfurd to FDR, June 25, 1942, PSF.

271 "My Johnny is . . .": FDR to John Rutherfurd, July 30, 1942, PSF.

271 "It is today . . .": Rutherfurd file, June 14, 1943, PSF.

271 "I want you to . . .": Author interview of Barbara Knowles, September 9, 2005.

272 "will be 15 . . .": LMR to FDR, March 18, 1942, PSF.

272 "I was very close . . .": Persico, *Secret War,* p. 36.

272 "Italian-appearing . . .": Ibid., p. 207.

273 "No contact . . .": Ibid.

273 "The ushers call her . . .": Joseph Lash, *A World of Love,* p. xxi.

274 "I'd never have . . .": Streitmatter, p. xviii.

274 "Let a good cause . . .": James Roosevelt, *Affectionately,* p. 23.

275 "Why do you . . .": *NYT,* October 31, 1942, p. 8.

275 "No, but she will . . .": Freidel, *Rendezvous,* p. 509.

275 "I'd rather have . . .": Lash, *World of Love,* p. 68.

275 "First it was . . .": West, p. 31.

275 "the only girl . . .": Joseph Lash Interview of Earl Miller, Boxes 44–45, JLP.

275 "stage mother . . .": Earl Miller to Lash, Boxes 44–45, JLP.

276 "a very fine . . .": Earl Miller to Miriam Abelow, August 22, 1966, FDRL.

277 "FDR just sat . . .": Murray Kempton, "The Kindly Stranger," *New York Review of Books,* April 15, 1982.

277 "What deep needs . . .": Beasley et al., p. 306.

277 "At times . . .": Lash, Diary, April 22, 1940, JLP.

277 "Tall, absolutely . . .": Howard Fast, *Being Red,* p. 95.

277 "In repose . . .": Kearney, p. 250.

277 "Put a hand . . .": Joseph Lash interview of ARH, October 29, 1968, Box 44, JLP.

278 "what I went through . . .": Freidel, *Rendezvous,* p. 509.

278 "indicated quite clearly . . .": Persico, *Secret War,* p. 229.

278 "I'm so happy . . .": Ibid.

278 "Subject and Mrs. Pratt . . .": Ibid., p. 230.

279 "This type . . .": Ibid.

279 "Oh gosh . . .": Ibid.
279 "the inability . . .": Lash, *World of Love,* pp. 340, 347–48.


CHAPTER 30 · · A DISTANT COUSIN, A CHERISHED DAUGHTER

280 "He wanted the house . . .": Potter, p. 173.
280 "He explained . . .": Box 258, DSP.
280 "Mr. President . . .": Ibid.
281 "kidding him . . .": Potter, p. 173.
281 "He didn't want me . . .": Box 258, DSP.
281 "my part . . .": Goodwin, p. 135.
281 "Perhaps it is . . .": FDR to MS, March 7, 1935, FDRL.
281 "We Suckleys . . .": Binder 4, MSP.
282 "your affectionate cousin . . .": Binder 21, MSP.
282 "why he is able . . .": Suckley, Diary, March 11, 1943, MSP.
282 "Windsor is . . .": Binder 20, MSP.
283 "We have all . . .": Ibid.
283 "He is a . . .": Ibid.
283 "The P. had . . .": Binder 16, MSP.
284 "These Republican leaders . . .": FDR Public Papers and Addresses 1944, FDRL.
284 "very thick walls . . .": *NYT,* September 7, 2007.
284 "Franklin D. Roosevelt is . . .": www.fdrlibrary.marist.edu.
284 "Dear Miss Suckley . . .": Binder 5, MSP.
285 "His wife is a . . .": Binder 15, MSP.
285 "chaste, but . . .": Beasley et al., p. 508.
285 "There is no reason . . .": *NYT,* September 7, 2007.
285 "The President is . . .": Suckley, Diary, September 30, 1933, MSP.
286 "You should really . . .": Shoumatoff, p. 80.
286 "an extremely tall . . .": Ibid., p. 74.
286 "in spite of . . .": Ibid.
286 "She impressed . . .": Ibid.
287 "had been . . .": Ibid.
287 "I did not think . . .": Ibid., pp. 80–81.
287 "led me . . .": Ibid., p. 81.
287 "to stretch . . .": Ibid., p. 82.
288 "Some people think . . .": Ibid., p. 81.
288 "was all praise . . .": Ibid., p. 90.
288 "While it was . . .": Ibid.
288 "Despite persistent . . .": Hassett, Diary, Box 2, FDRL.
289 "This is not . . .": Lord Mayor's luncheon, Mansion House, London, 1942, www.quotationspage.com/quotes/24921.
289 "I think if . . .": Persico, *Secret War,* p. 273.

290 "Only the dirty . . .": Ibid., p. 123.

290 "Everything we know . . .": Asbell, "Tragic Story," p. 123.

290 "FDR liked women . . .": Gunther, pp. 71–73.

290 "The President never . . .": Hassett, Diary, Box 21, FDRL.

290 "Have a seat . . .": Ibid.

290 "Did he fall . . .": Ibid.

291 "I'd give my . . .": Boettiger, p. 238.

292 "Louise would arrange . . .": Asbell, "Tragic Story," p. 123.

292 "Betsey never did . . .": Joseph Lash interview of ARH, October 29, 1968, Box 44, JLP.

292 "This would annoy . . .": Bernard Asbell interview of ARH.

292 "She was jealous . . .": Dr. James Halstead, ER Oral History Project, FDRL.

292 "see who's home . . .": Willis, p. 122.

293 "my old friend . . .": Ward, *Temperament*, p. 777.

293 "Father could . . .": Willis, p. 122.

## CHAPTER 31 · · ANNA'S DILEMMA

294 "We did everything . . .": Ann Rochon to ER, undated, Box 1731, ER Papers, FDRL.

295 "He took things . . .": Geoffrey C. Ward, *Companions*, p. 287.

295 "Franklin Delano Roosevelt . . .": Bishop, pp. 70–71.

295 "my new cousin . . .": Ward, *Companions*, p. 380.

296 "I'm either . . .": Jonathan Meacham, *Franklin and Winston*, p. 274.

296 "I never heard . . .": Ibid.

296 "With people like . . .": Goodwin, p. 502.

296 "I would love . . .": Joseph Lash interview of ARH, October 29, 1968, Box 44, JLP.

296 "All right . . .": Gallagher, p. 187.

297 "I pray . . .": Ward, *Companions*, p. 287.

297 "Thanks, Doc": Persico, *Secret War*, p. 312.

297 "His past . . .": Bishop, p. 73.

298 "I want to sleep . . .": Goodwin, p. 497.

298 "the most beautiful . . .": Box 258, DSP.

298 "notorious for . . .": Goodwin, p. 125.

298 "went into . . .": Box 64, DSP.

298 "Baruch's physical and . . .": Ibid.

299 "His color was . . .": Dr. Howard Bruenn, article draft, April 1970, Howard G. Bruenn Papers, FDRL.

299 "Awakened 9:30 . . .": Ibid.

299 "Baruch is still . . .": Beasley et al., p. 46.

299 "was the very . . .": Daniels, *Quadrille*, p. 297.

300 "I've been told . . .": A. Merriman Smith, *Thank You Mr. President*, pp. 140–41.

300 "I had a good talk . . .": Persico, *Secret War,* p. 313.

300 "I added . . .": ARH to Dr. Howard Bruenn, July 15, 1969, Bruenn Papers, FDRL.

300 "I worked a little . . .": FDR to MLH, May 10, 1944, Box 21, RFP.

301 "Lord look after . . .": Persico, *Secret War,* p. 315.

301 "my job was . . .": Daniels, *Quadrille,* p. 298.

301 "Would it be . . .": Bishop, p. 559.

301 "I guessed who . . .": ARH, COH.

302 "a quick decision . . .": Ibid.

302 "She was trying . . .": Author interview of Curtis Roosevelt, November 15–16, 2005.

302 "fetish of his . . .": Persico, *Secret War,* p. 449.

302 "We call him . . .": Ibid., p. 304.

303 "stepped from . . .": William D. Hassett, *Off the Record with F.D.R.,* p. 259.

303 "Roosevelt's glittering . . .": Conrad Black, p. 957.

303 "I had the feeling . . .": Joseph Lash interview of ARH, October 29, 1968, Box 44, JLP.

305 "Regret to . . .": Asbell, "Tragic Story," pp. 125–26.

305 "Memories of . . .": PPF, 3737.

305 "You and I lost . . .": Asbell, "Tragic Story," p. 126.

305 "how different . . .": Lash, Diary, March 30, 1942, Box 31, JLP.

305 "couldn't care less . . .": Asbell, "Tragic Story," p. 126.

305 "as each of them . . .": MLH, will, PPF, 3737.

305 "craft which . . .": Asbell, "Tragic Story," p. 126.

306 "Missy was the only . . .": Ward, *Temperament,* p. 710.

306 "in better physical . . .": Diary, Henry Stimson, August 23, 1944, Yale University.

CHAPTER 32 · · "MOTHER WAS NOT CAPABLE OF GIVING HIM THIS"

307 "He remembered . . .": Persico, *Secret War,* p. 344.

307 "What will decide . . .": Ibid.

307 "He felt . . .": Tugwell, *Democratic,* p. 32.

307 "All that is . . .": *U.S. News,* July 21, 1944, p. 27.

308 "You'd think . . .": Goodwin, p. 542.

309 "an old friend . . .": Bishop, p. 135.

309 "the fastest . . .": Author interview of Guy Rutherfurd Jr., May 23, 2005.

309 "just an old . . .": Willis, p. 132.

309 "a lovely person . . .": Binder 18, MSP.

310 "very tall . . .": Ibid.

310 "But he wasn't . . .": Ibid.

310 "anything that would . . .": Author interview of Guy Rutherfurd Jr., May 23, 2005.

310 "out of a book . . .": Binder 18, MSP.

311 "During what I . . .": Box 64, DSP.

311 "Between his close . . .": Elliott Roosevelt, *Untold Story,* p. 280.

312 "I still think . . .": Persico, *Secret War,* p. 352.

312 "I don't have . . .": Lash, *World of Love,* p. 151.

312 "her whole life": Author interview of Curtis Roosevelt, November 15–16, 2005.

312 "Two more different . . .": Elliott Roosevelt, *Untold Story,* p. 281.

313 "totally unacceptable . . .": Goodwin, p. 361.

313 "never wanted . . .": Author interview of Curtis Roosevelt, November 15–16, 2005.

313 "She believed . . .": Elliott Roosevelt, *Untold Story,* p. 281.

313 "When I was having . . .": James Roosevelt, *My Parents,* p. 99.

313 "I just don't . . .": Goodwin, p. 362.

313 "The Pres. . . .": Ward, *Companions,* p. 349.

314 "something of . . .": Ibid., p. 350.

314 "the reason . . .": Goodwin, p. 562.

314 "Mrs. Rutherfurd is . . .": Ward, *Companions,* p. 351.

314 "When anything . . .": Binder 18, MSP.

315 "There is no . . .": Ibid.

315 "I had the most . . .": Bernard Asbell interview of ARH.

315 "didn't know . . .": Ibid.

316 "I had a little . . .": Binder 18, MSP.

316 "She was just . . .": Ibid.

316 "No one ever . . .": Ibid.

317 "Franklin was . . .": Ibid.

317 "see for myself . . .": Ward, *Companions,* p. 358.

317 "the President kept . . .": Willis, p. 131.

317 "work on your . . .": Ward, *Companions,* pp. 358–59.

317 "He got really . . .": Binder 18, MSP.

317 "It is only . . .": LMR to Suckley, December 11, 1944, MSP.

317 "To be in a . . .": Binder 18, MSP.

317 "It will be lovely . . .": Ibid.

318 "left her . . .": Ibid.

318 "the biggest . . .": Persico, *Secret War,* p. 362.

318 "Lucy (my new cousin) . . .": Binder 18, MSP.

319 "myself off . . .": Ibid.

319 "no sweets . . .": Ibid.

319 "F discovered . . .": Ibid.


CHAPTER 33 · · "WE MUST SPEAK IN RIDDLES"

320 "Who is there . . .": Rosenman, *Working with Roosevelt,* p. 516.

320 "She was definitely . . .": Author interview of Barbara Knowles, September 9, 2005.

321 "We Americans . . .": FDR, 1944 inaugural address, FDR Public Papers, FDRL.

321 "stopping off . . .": Binder 19, MSP.

321 "Do you want . . .": Ibid.

321 "and I took a coffee cup . . .": Ibid.

322 "If you go . . .": *TIR*, p. 339.

322 "Mother never said . . .": ARH, COH.

322 "Over there . . .": Bernard Asbell interview of ARH, p. 20.

323 "If we had . . .": Persico, *Secret War*, p. 390.

323 "the next time . . .": Ibid., p. 389.

323 "Ross [McIntire] . . .": Ibid., p. 391.

323 "He has all . . .": Ibid.

323 "There seems to be . . .": LMR to Suckley, February 9, 1945, MSP.

324 "I'm in the . . .": Binder 19, MSP.

324 "I hope you will . . .": FDR to Joint Session of Congress, February 29, 1945, FDR Public Papers, FDRL.

324 "I remember choking . . .": Frances Perkins, COH.

324 "And despite her . . .": Morgan, p. 676.

324 "Mummy, can't you . . .": Author interview of Curtis Roosevelt, November 15–16, 2005.

324 "pressed more strongly . . .": Joseph Lash interview of ARH, October 29, 1968, Box 44, JLP.

325 "It is very hard . . .": Beasley et al., p. 323.

325 "She was considered . . .": Meacham, p. 24.

325 "that touch of . . .": Daniels, *Quadrille*, p. 291.

325 "She was a . . .": Joseph Lash interview of ARH, October 29, 1968, Box 44, JLP.

325 "Through all those . . .": Ibid.

326 "very lovely woman . . .": Irwin F. Gellman, *Secret Affairs*, p. 373.

326 "his ringing laugh . . .": Box 70, ARHP.

326 "they were occasions . . .": Ibid.

326 "went North . . .": Persico, *Secret War*, p. 97.

326 "He deliberately . . .": Gunther, p. 53.

327 "the greatest reception . . .": Rosenman, *Working with Roosevelt*, p. 546.

327 "It's no good . . .": Bishop, p. 520.

327 "there were certain . . .": "The Lucy Mercer Story," Box 62, Folder 2105, JDP.

327 "two people . . .": Goodwin, p. 598.

## CHAPTER 34 · · THE DEATH OF A PRESIDENT

329 "He is slipping . . .": Ward, *Companions*, p. 402.

329 "with an overpowering . . .": Hassett, Diary, Box 22, FDRL.

329 "a very rich . . .": Binder 19, MSP.

329 "I get the gruel . . .": Ibid.

330 "He says that . . .": Ibid.

330 "His estimate . . .": Conrad Black, p. 1108.

330 "Much love to you . . .": Lash, *World of Love,* pp. 181–82.

330 "He seems very . . .": Shoumatoff, p. 98.

331 "he was gazing . . .": Ibid., p. 101.

331 "I have seen . . .": Bernard Asbell, draft ms. "When FDR Died," FDRL.

331 "He sits a little . . .": Binder 19, MSP.

331 "imagining it was . . .": Ibid.

332 "Nobody loves us . . .": Shoumatoff, p. 101.

332 "There was something . . .": Ibid., p. 102.

332 "bright blue hair . . .": Ibid., p. 101.

332 "was quite a jolly . . .": Ibid., p. 103.

332 "But there was . . .": ARH Oral History, FDRL.

333 "When the . . .": Shoumatoff, p. 107.

333 "She interfered . . .": Hassett, Diary, Box 22, FDRL.

334 "She had never . . .": Shoumatoff, p. 109.

334 "From the very . . .": Ibid.

334 "It has little . . .": Binder 19, MSP.

334 "The boss has resisted . . .": Hassett, Diary, Box 22, FDRL.

335 "The work, my friends . . .": FDR, U.N. speech, San Francisco Conference, April 25, 1945, nationsencyclopedia.com.

335 "I threw on my hat . . .": Binder 19, MSP.

335 "Lucy is so sweet . . .": Ibid.

335 "I was terribly . . .": John Morton Blum, *The Morgenthau Diaries,* p. 416.

336 "removing all . . .": Persico, *Secret War,* p. 433.

336 "three or four . . .": Ibid.

336 "I am going there . . .": Ibid.

336 "The President, like . . .": Shoumatoff, p. 114.

336 "The trouble is . . .": Binder 19, MSP.

337 "Reincarnation . . .": Bernard Asbell interview of Lizzie McDuffie, May 13, 1960, FDRL.

338 "he will leave . . .": Palm Beach editorial, Knowles Family Collection, Aiken, South Carolina.

338 "I suppose . . .": Ibid.

338 "Here's where . . .": *NYT,* April 13, 1945.

338 "Oh no . . .": Shoumatoff, p. 115.

338 "I was struck . . .": Ibid., p. 116

339 "We have got . . .": Gunther, p. 369.

339 "Have you dropped . . .": Binder 19, MSP.

339 "I was cold . . .": Ibid.

339 "The Boss . . .": Rogers, p. 4.

340 "We must pack . . .": Shoumatoff, p. 119.

340 "The President is dead": Ibid., p. 120.

340 "3:31 Breathing . . .": Bruenn, Clinical Notes on Illness and Death of Franklin Delano Roosevelt, Bruenn Papers, FDRL.

341 "In the quiet . . .": Hassett, Diary, Box 22, FDRL.

341 "He's dead! . . .": www.cviog.uga.edu.

341 "I knew down . . .": *TIR,* p. 344.

341 "I'm called back . . .": Asbell, *When F.D.R. Died,* p. 51.

341 "What can I do?": David McCullough, *Truman,* p. 342.

342 "Darlings . . .": Map Room Files, Box 14, FDRL.

342 "I am more sorry . . .": *NYT,* April 13, 1945.

342 "Amazon type . . .": Hassett, Diary, Box 22, FDRL.

342 "Tully dear . . .": Lash, *Eleanor and Franklin,* p. 722.

343 "You build . . .": Asbell, *When F.D.R. Died,* p. 155.

343 "She was a . . .": Goodwin, p. 611.

343 "Hick, I don't . . .": LH letter to Molly Dawson, May 3, 1945, Box 13, LH Papers, FDRL.

344 "Lucy's daughter . . .": Shoumatoff, p. 121.

344 "I was rather . . .": Ibid., p. 126.

344 "All of us . . .": www.cviog.uga.edu.

344 "I lay in my . . .": Lash, *Eleanor and Franklin,* p. 723.

345 "an almost . . .": Ibid., p. 722.

345 "a symbol of . . .": Ibid., pp. 722–23.

345 "Poor E.R. . . .": Binder 19, MSP.

345 "without opening . . .": Author interview of Curtis Roosevelt, November 15–16, 2005.

346 "There were always people . . .": Goodwin, p. 614.

346 "A child caught . . .": Asbell, *Mother and Daughter,* p. 186.

346 "Mother was so . . .": Joseph Lash interview of ARH, October 29, 1968, Box 44, JLP.

346 "after two or three . . .": Ibid.

346 "I answered all . . .": Shoumatoff, p. 126.

346 "What an enviable death . . .": Conrad Black, pp. 1119–20.

347 "The President's death . . .": Asbell, *When F.D.R. Died,* p. 117.

347 "at the gates . . .": *NYT,* April 13, 1945.

347 "Roosevelt, Franklin D. . . .": Burns, *Roosevelt: Soldier of Freedom,* p. 602.

347 "A supremely great . . .": Knowles Family Collection, Aiken, South Carolina.

## CHAPTER 35 · · LETTERS LOST AND FOUND

348 "Margaret Suckley has . . .": LMR to Margaret Suckley. May 2, 1945, Unusual Letter File, FDRL.

349 "had offered . . .": Jonathan Daniels interview of Barbara Knowles, February 17, 1952, Box 64, Folder 2139, JDP.

349 "Anna dear . . .": LMR to ARH, May 9, 1945, ARHP.

349 "The Traveler . . .": Dorothy Dumbrille, *Stairway to the Stars,* no page.

350 "Dear Little Margaret . . .": LMR to MS, May 9, 1945, MSP.

350 "I love having . . .": LMR to DS, May 20, 1945, MSP.

350 "It distresses me . . .": LMR to MS, June 1945, MSP.

351 "I don't know how . . .": Shoumatoff, pp. 72–73.

351 "I can't tell . . .": Barbara Rutherfurd to ARH, ARHP.

352 "That is what . . .": Joseph Lash interview of Esther Lape, February 24, 1970, Boxes 44–45, JLP.

352 "She sounded . . .": Potter, p. 169.

352 "Often people . . .": *TIR,* pp. 2–3.

352 "I have thought . . .": Donn, p. 197.

352 "The act of being . . .": Ibid., p. 162.

353 "He might have . . .": Ward, *Companions,* p. xvi.

## CHAPTER 36 · · "LUCY WAS FATHER'S EMOTION FOR LIFE"

354 "A student . . .": Box 64, Folder 2125, JDP.

355 "gunshot wound . . .": Daniels, *Quadrille,* p. 321.

355 "I think my Aunt . . .": Author interview of Lucy Blundon, July 20, 2005.

355 "I'm sorry, Guy . . .": Ibid.

355 "growing old . . .": *New York Review of Books,* April 15, 1982.

356 "in any way . . .": Schlesinger, p. 71.

356 "Eleanor Roosevelt . . .": Ibid.

356 "As far as . . .": Joseph Lash interview of ARH, October 29, 1968, Box 44, JLP.

## CHAPTER 37 · · FIRST LADY OF THE WORLD

357 "will rock the country . . .": New York *Daily News,* January 13, 1947.

357 "Suing Wife 'Feared' . . .": *New York Daily Mirror,* August 18, 1948.

357 "guilty of cruel . . .": *Miller v. Miller,* New York State Supreme Court, October 27, 1948.

357 "Mrs. Roosevelt's sweetheart": Miller to Lash, undated, JLP.

357 "shortly after the war . . .": Lash, *Centenary,* p. 151.

358 "I began to notice . . .": LH to Esther Lape, November 21, 1962, Esther Lape Papers, Box 2, FDRL.

358 "Poor Hick . . .": Author interview of Maureen Corr, July 30, 2005.

359 "We discovered . . .": Beasley et al., pp. 219–20.

359 "Joe Lash was . . .": Author interview of Curtis Roosevelt, November 15–16, 2005.

359 "the improvement . . .": Tugwell, *Democratic,* p. 250.

359 "To David . . .": Beasley et al., p. 221.

359 "Eleanor loved you . . .": Edna P. Gurewitsch, *Kindred Souls,* p. 5.

360 "Mrs. Roosevelt loved . . .": Author interview of Maureen Corr, July 30, 2005.

360 "an important friendship . . .": Asbell, *Mother and Daughter,* p. 187.

361 "I surmise . . .": Beasley et al., p. 450.

361 "They were careless . . .": Quoted in Black, *Champion,* p. 906.

361 "She really had no . . .": Author interview of Maureen Corr, July 30, 2005.

361 "I heard her say . . .": Ibid.

362 "his mother had . . .": Box 65, DSP.

362 "She would rather . . .": Beasley et al., p. 122.

362 "First Lady . . .": Lash, *Centenary,* p. 131.

362 "one of the great . . .": *NYT,* November 8, 1962.

362 "Whether in praise . . .": Beasley et al., p. 124.

362 "No woman . . .": Ibid., p. 122.

363 "She wants something . . .": Author interview of Maureen Corr, July 30, 2005.

363 "She was a curious . . .": *Los Angeles Herald-Examiner,* November 9, 1962.

363 "manifestations of love . . .": Bishop, p. 557.

363 "I've always thought . . .": ARH interview, May 17, 1979, ER Oral History Project, FDRL.

363 "I was very much . . .": Arthur Schlesinger Jr. interview, September 25, 1979, ER Oral History Project, FDRL.

363 "Mrs. Roosevelt has . . .": Lash, *Love, Eleanor,* p. 152.

363 "Something much better . . .": Donn, p. 199.

363 "People think they . . .": Joseph Lash interview of ARL, August 5, 1966, Boxes 44–45, JLP.

363 "She had great charm . . .": Ibid., February 6, 1967, Boxes 44–45.

364 "Eleanor Roosevelt was . . .": Felsenthal, p. 180.

364 The soul that had believed . . .: Goodwin, pp. 377–78.

## CHAPTER 38 · · A JUDGMENT

365 "I felt akin . . .": Allan Nevins, "Roosevelt in History," p. 101.

366 "To begin with . . .": Alsop, p. 73.

366 "The greatest President . . .": Charles Peters, *Washington Monthly,* July–August 2004.

367 "you can not disable . . .": Shoumatoff, p. 133.

367 "accept the theory . . .": Daniels, *Quadrille,* p. 206.

367 "There he sits . . .": Ward, *Trumpet,* p. 1.

367 "he rolled in the gutter . . .": Gunther, p. 147.

368 "equaled only . . .": Persico, *Secret War,* p. 135.

368 "while other presidents . . .": Allida Black, "For FDR an Enduring Relationship."

368 "I'd rather vote for . . .": Felsenthal, p. 194.

368 "Franklin . . . should never . . .": ARL, *60 Minutes,* CBS, April 22, 1969.

368 "a block about this size . . .": journals.uchicago.edu.

368 "character and integrity . . .": William J. Ridings and Stuart B. McIver, *Rating the Presidents,* p. xi.

369 "Roosevelt at times . . .": Nevins, "Roosevelt in History," p. 101.

369 "You won't talk . . .": Persico, *Secret War*, p. 96.

369 "A leader who puts . . .": Nevins, "Roosevelt in History," p. 101.

369 "the dishonesty of . . .": Persico, *Secret War*, p. 45.

369 "I think the price . . .": Author interview of Curtis Roosevelt, November 15–16, 2005.

369 "In Franklin Roosevelt . . .": Winston Churchill, *Triumph and Tragedy*, p. 417.

370 "I am willing to take . . .": Karenna Gore Schiff, *Lighting the Way*, p. 160.

370 The reason firm . . .: "She Was a Phantom of Delight" by William Wordsworth, in Francis T. Palgrave, ed., *The Golden Treasury of the Best Songs and Lyrical Poems in the English Language*. London: Macmillan, 1875.

# BIBLIOGRAPHY

· · · · · · ·

Adamic, Louis. *Dinner at the White House*. New York: Harper & Brothers, 1946.

Alsop, Joseph. *FDR: A Centenary Remembrance*. New York: Viking, 1982.

Asbell, Bernard. *The F.D.R. Memoirs*. Garden City, NY: Doubleday, 1973.

———. "Missy: The Tragic Story of the Secretary Who Loved President Roosevelt." *Ladies' Home Journal,* June 1973.

———. *When F.D.R. Died*. New York: Holt, Rinehart & Winston, 1961.

Asbell, Bernard, ed. *Mother and Daughter: The Letters of Eleanor and Anna Roosevelt*. New York: Coward, McCann & Geoghegan, 1982.

Ashburn, Frank D. *Peabody of Groton*. New York: Coward McCann, 1944.

Beasley, Maurine H., Holly Shulman, and Henry R. Beasley, eds. *The Eleanor Roosevelt Encyclopedia*. Westport, CT: Greenwood, 2001.

Bellush, Bernard. *Franklin D Roosevelt as Governor of New York*. New York: Columbia University Press, 1968.

Biddle, Francis. *In Brief Authority*. Garden City, NY: Doubleday, 1962.

Bishop, Jim. *FDR's Last Year: April 1944–April 1945*. New York: William Morrow, 1974.

Black, Allida M. "For FDR an Enduring Relationship." *Washington Post Outlook,* March 1, 1998.

Black, Conrad. *Franklin Delano Roosevelt: Champion of Freedom*. New York: PublicAffairs, 2003.

Blum, John Morton. *The Morgenthau Diaries*. Boston: Houghton Mifflin, 1967.

Boettiger, John R. *A Love in Shadow*. New York: W. W. Norton, 1978.

Burns, James MacGregor. *Roosevelt: The Soldier of Freedom*. New York: Harcourt Brace Jovanovich, 1970.

Burns, James MacGregor, and Susan Dunn. *The Three Roosevelts: Patrician Leaders Who Transformed America*. New York: Atlantic Monthly Press, 2001.

Carmichael, Donald Scott. *FDR Columnist*. Chicago: Pellegrini & Cudahy, 1947.

Caroli, Betty Boyd. *The Roosevelt Women*. New York: Basic Books, 1998.

Churchill, Allen. *The Roosevelts: American Aristocrats*. New York: Harper & Row, 1965.

Churchill, Winston. *Triumph and Tragedy*. Boston: Houghton Mifflin, 1985.

Clapper, Olive Ewing. *Washington Tapestry.* New York: McGraw Hill, 1946.

Collier, Peter, and David Horowitz. *The Roosevelts: An American Saga.* New York: Simon & Schuster, 1994.

Cook, Blanche Wiesen. *Eleanor Roosevelt: Volume 1, 1884–1933.* New York: Viking, 1992.

———. *Eleanor Roosevelt: Volume 2, The Defining Years, 1933–1938.* New York: Viking, 1999.

Daniels, Jonathan. *The End of Innocence.* New York: J. B. Lippincott, 1954.

———. *The Time Between the Wars: Armistice to Pearl Harbor.* Garden City, NY: Doubleday, 1966.

———. *Washington Quadrille: The Dance Beside the Documents.* Garden City, NY: Doubleday, 1968.

———. *White House Witness: 1942–1945.* Garden City, NY: Doubleday, 1975.

Davis, Kenneth S. *FDR: The Beckoning of Destiny.* New York: G. P. Putnam's Sons, 1971.

———. *FDR: The New York Years: 1928–1933.* New York: Random House, 1985.

———. *Invincible Summer: An Intimate Portrait of the Roosevelts.* New York: Atheneum, 1974.

Donn, Linda. *The Roosevelt Cousins: Growing Up Together, 1882–1924.* New York: Alfred A. Knopf, 2001.

Dos Passos, John. "The Radio Voice." *Common Sense,* February 1934.

Dumbrille, Dorothy. *Stairway to the Stars.* Toronto: Thomas Alden, 1946.

Dunn, Robert. *World Alive: A Personal Story.* New York: Crown, 1952.

Faber, Doris. "Biography of Lorena Hickok." Undated manuscript. Papers of Doris Faber regarding *The Life of Lorena Hickok,* FDRL.

———. *The Life of Lorena Hickok: E.R.'s Friend.* New York: William Morrow, 1980.

Fast, Howard. *Being Red.* New York: Houghton Mifflin, 1990.

Felsenthal, Carol. *Alice Roosevelt Longworth.* New York: G. P. Putnam's Sons, 1988.

Freidel, Frank. *Franklin D. Roosevelt: The Apprenticeship.* Boston: Little, Brown, 1952.

———. *Franklin D. Roosevelt: Launching the New Deal.* Boston: Little, Brown, 1978.

———. *Franklin D. Roosevelt: The Ordeal.* Boston: Little, Brown, 1954.

———. *Franklin D. Roosevelt: A Rendezvous with Destiny.* Boston: Little, Brown, 1990.

Gallagher, Hugh Gregory. *FDR's Splendid Deception.* Arlington, VA: Vandamere, 1994.

Gardner, Joseph. *Departing Glory: Theodore Roosevelt as Ex-President.* New York: Charles Scribner's Sons, 1973.

Gellman, Irwin F. *Secret Affairs: Franklin Roosevelt, Cordell Hull, and Sumner Welles.* Baltimore: Johns Hopkins University Press, 1995.

Goodwin, Doris Kearns. *No Ordinary Time: Franklin and Eleanor Roosevelt: The Home Front in World War II.* New York: Simon & Schuster, 1994.

Gunther, John. *Roosevelt in Retrospect: A Profile in History.* New York: Harper Brothers, 1950.

Gurewitsch, Edna P. *Kindred Souls: The Friendship of Eleanor Roosevelt and David Gurewitsch.* New York: St. Martin's, 2002.

Hagedorn, Hermann. *The Roosevelt Family of Sagamore Hill.* New York: Macmillan, 1954.

Harrity, Richard, and Ralph Martin. *The Human Side of FDR.* New York: Duell, Sloane & Pearce, 1960.

Hassett, William D. *Off the Record with F.D.R.: 1942–1945.* New Brunswick: Rutgers University Press, 1958.

Hickok, Lorena A. *Reluctant First Lady.* New York: Dodd, Mead, 1962.

Kearney, James R. *Anna Eleanor Roosevelt: The Evolution of a Reformer.* Boston: Houghton Mifflin, 1968.

Kimball, Warren. *The Juggler: Franklin Roosevelt as Wartime Statesman.* Princeton: Princeton University Press, 1991.

Kleeman, Rita Halle. "Biography of Sara Delano Roosevelt." Undated manuscript. Correspondence and Notes for *Gracious Lady,* FDRL.

———. *Gracious Lady: The Life of Sara Delano Roosevelt.* New York: Appleton-Century, 1935.

Lash, Joseph P. *Eleanor: The Years Alone.* New York: W. W. Norton, 1972.

———. *Eleanor and Franklin: The Story of Their Relationship Based on Eleanor Roosevelt's Private Papers.* New York: W. W. Norton, 1971.

———. *Life Was Meant to Be Lived: A Centenary Portrait of Eleanor Roosevelt.* New York: W. W. Norton, 1984.

———. *Love, Eleanor: Eleanor Roosevelt and Her Friends.* Garden City, NY: Doubleday, 1982.

———. *A World of Love: Eleanor Roosevelt and Her Friends, 1943–1962.* Garden City, NY: Doubleday, 1984.

Leuchtenberg, William F. *Franklin D. Roosevelt and the New Deal, 1932–1940.* Ithaca: Cornell University Press, 1983.

Longworth, Alice Roosevelt. *Crowded Hours.* New York: Charles Scribner's Sons, 1933.

Martin, Ralph G. *The Extraordinary Life of Eleanor Medill Patterson.* New York: Simon & Schuster, 1979.

Massie, Robert K. *Dreadnought.* New York: Random House, 1991.

McCullough, David. *Truman.* New York: Simon & Schuster, 1992.

Meacham, Jonathan. *Franklin and Winston: An Intimate Portrait of an Epic Friendship.* New York: Random House, 2003.

Miller, Nathan. *The Roosevelt Chronicles.* Garden City, NY: Doubleday, 1979.

Moley, Raymond. *The First New Deal.* New York: Harcourt, Brace & World, 1966.

Morgan, Ted. *FDR: A Biography.* New York: Simon & Schuster, 1985.

Morris, Edmund. *The Rise of Theodore Roosevelt.* New York: Coward, McCann & Geoghegan, 1979.

Nevins, Allan. *Grover Cleveland: A Study in Courage.* New York: Dodd, Mead, 1966.

———. "Roosevelt in History." *American Heritage,* June 1966.

Palmer, Charles F. *Adventures of a Slum Fighter.* Atlanta: Tupper & Love, 1955.

Parks, Lillian Rogers, with Frances Spatz Leighton. *The Roosevelts: A Family in Turmoil.* Englewood Cliffs, NJ: Prentice Hall, 1981.

Persico, Joseph E. *Eleventh Month, Eleventh Day, Eleventh Hour: Armistice Day, 1918.* New York: Random House, 2004.

———. *Roosevelt's Secret War: FDR and World War II Espionage.* New York: Random House, 2001.

Potter, Jeffrey. *Men, Money and Magic: The Story of Dorothy Schiff.* New York: Coward, McCann & Geoghegan, 1976.

Ridings, William J., Jr., and Stuart B. McIver. *Rating the Presidents.* Secaucus, NJ: Citadel, 1997.

Rogers, William Warren, Jr. "The Death of a President, April 12, 1945: An Account from Warm Springs." *Georgia Historical Quarterly,* Vol. 75, No. 1 (Summer 1991).

Roosevelt, Eleanor. *The Autobiography of Eleanor Roosevelt.* New York: Harper & Brothers, 1961.

———. "I Remember Hyde Park." *McCall's,* February 1963.

———. "Ten Rules for Success in Marriage." *Pictorial Review,* December 1931.

———. *This I Remember.* New York: Harper & Brothers, 1949.

———. *This Is My Story.* New York: Harper & Brothers, 1937.

Roosevelt, Eleanor, and Helen Ferris. *Your Teens and Mine.* Garden City, NY: Doubleday, 1961.

Roosevelt, Elliott, and James Brough. *An Untold Story: The Roosevelts of Hyde Park.* New York: G. P. Putnam's Sons, 1973.

Roosevelt, Elliott, and James N. Rosenau, eds. *F.D.R.: His Personal Letters.* New York: Duell, Sloane & Pearce, 1948.

Roosevelt, Franklin D., Jr., and Donald Day. *Franklin D. Roosevelt's Own Story.* Boston: Little, Brown, 1951.

Roosevelt, James, with Bill Libby. *My Parents: A Differing View.* Chicago: Playboy Press, 1976.

Roosevelt, James, and Sidney Shalett. *Affectionately, FDR: A Son's Story of a Lonely Man.* New York: Harcourt, Brace, 1959.

Roosevelt, Mrs. James. *My Boy Franklin.* New York: Ray Long & Richard R. Smith, 1933.

Rosenman, Samuel I. *The Public Papers and Addresses of Franklin D. Roosevelt.* 13 Vols. New York: Random House, 1938–1950.

———. *Working with Roosevelt.* New York: Harper, 1952.

Sachar, Abram L. *An Affectionate Portrait.* Waltham, MA: Brandeis University Press, 1963.

Schiff, Karenna Gore. *Lighting the Way: Nine Women Who Changed Modern America.* New York: Miramax, 2005.

Schlesinger, Arthur, Jr. "FDR's Secret Romance." *Ladies' Home Journal,* November 1966.

Seixas, Judith S., and Geraldine Youcha. *Children of Alcoholism: A Survivor's Manual*. New York: Crown, 1984.

Sherwood, Robert E. *Roosevelt and Hopkins: An Intimate History*. New York: Harper & Brothers, 1950.

Shoumatoff, Elizabeth. *FDR's Unfinished Portrait*. Pittsburgh: University of Pittsburgh Press, 1990.

Smith, A. Merriman. *Thank You Mr. President: A White House Notebook*. New York: Harper, 1946.

Smith-Rosenberg, Carroll. "The Female World of Love and Ritual: Relations Between Women in Nineteenth Century America." *Signs: Journal of Women in Culture and Society*, Vol. 1, No. 1 (Autumn 1975).

Steinberg, Alfred. *Eleanor Roosevelt*. New York: G. P. Putnam's Sons, 1959.

Stevens, Ruth. *Hi-Ya Neighbor*. Atlanta: Tupper & Love, 1947.

Stiles, Lela. *The Man Behind Roosevelt: The Story of Louis McHenry Howe*. Cleveland: World, 1954.

Streitmatter, Rodger. *Empty Without You: The Intimate Letters of Eleanor Roosevelt and Lorena Hickok*. New York: Free Press, 1998.

Teague, Michael. *Mrs. L.: Conversations with Alice Roosevelt Longworth*. Garden City, NY: Doubleday, 1961.

Totten, Christine M. "Remembering Sara Delano Roosevelt on Her 150th Anniversary." *Rendezvous: News and Notes from the Franklin D. Roosevelt Library and Institute*, Winter 2005.

Trohan, Walter. *Political Animals*. Garden City, NY: Doubleday, 1975.

Tugwell, Rexford G. *The Democratic Roosevelt*. Garden City, NY: Doubleday, 1957.

———. *Grover Cleveland*. New York: Macmillan, 1968.

Tully, Grace. *F.D.R.: My Boss*. New York: Charles Scribner's Sons, 1949.

Tutelian, Louise. "Eleanor Roosevelt's Place Apart." *New York Times*, December 17, 2004.

vanden Heuvel, Jean. "The Sharpest Wit in Washington." *Saturday Evening Post*, December 4, 1965.

Ward, Geoffrey C. *Before the Trumpet*. New York: Harper & Row, 1985.

———. *A First-Class Temperament: The Emergence of Franklin Roosevelt*. New York: Harper & Row, 1989.

Ward, Geoffrey C., ed. *Closest Companions: The Unknown Story of the Intimate Friendship Between Franklin Roosevelt and Margaret Suckley*. Boston: Houghton Mifflin, 1995.

Weinstein, Edwin A. *Woodrow Wilson: A Medical and Psychological Biography*. Princeton: Princeton University Press, 1981.

West, J. B., with Mary Lynn Kotz. *Upstairs at the White House: My Life with the First Ladies*. New York: Coward, McCann & Geoghegan, 1973.

Wharton, Edith. *The Age of Innocence*. New York: Collier, 1987.

———. *A Backward Glance*. New York: D. Appleton-Century, 1934.

Willis, Resa. *FDR and Lucy: Lovers and Friends*. New York: Routledge, 2004.

# INDEX

· · · · · · ·

"Abraham's Treatment," 154
Abram, Morris, 246
Actii family, 12
Adamic, Louis, 270–71
Adams, Henry, 131
Adams, Marian "Clover," 131
*Admiral Scheer,* 333
African Americans, 163, 176
   ER and, 134, 173, 325, 362
   military service of, 132, 141
Afrika Korps, 289
*Age of Innocence, The* (Wharton), 123
Agricultural Adjustment Act (AAA),
   232, 242
Aiken, S.C., 112–13, 156, 171, 180, 181,
   201, 216, 228, 256, 265, 286, 287,
   294, 330–31, 340, 344, 354–55
Albert I, King of Belgium, 9
Alden, John, 12
Alden, Priscilla Mullin, 12, 39
"Alexander's Ragtime Band" (Berlin),
   100, 262
Algonac, 13, 18, 118
*Algonquin,* 96
Algonquin Round Table, 239
Allamuchy, 171, 179–81, 235, 271,
   294–95, 308–10, 355
Allcorn, Frank, 336
Allenswood School, 47–49, 64, 103,
   210, 364

Alsop, Joseph, 200, 366
Alumni Memorial War Foundation, 179
American Expeditionary Forces, 3, 7
*American Legion,* 252
American Revolution, 28
American Student Union, 277
American Youth Congress, 277
*Anatomy Lesson, The* (Rembrandt), 241
*Annals of Internal Medicine,* 300
anti-Catholicism, 184
anti-Semitism, 176, 231, 240, 281, 299
Arlington National Cemetery, 117, 216,
   355
Army, U.S., 8, 104–5, 128, 136
   Commissary Corps of, 31
   Counter Intelligence Corps (CIC)
      of, 276, 278–79
   First Division of, 121
   postal service of, 7
   Signal Corps of, 310, 340
Army Air Corps, 271
*Army and Navy Journal,* 29
Asbell, Bernard, 170, 257, 290, 360
Associated Press, 199, 205, 207, 238,
   363
Astor, Ava, 138
Astor, Caroline Webster
   Schermerhorn, 16–17, 36
Astor, John Jacob, 138
Astor family, 13, 16–17, 64

Astrid, Princess of Norway, 251
*Atlantic,* 311
*Atlantic Journal,* 198
Atlantic Middleweight Boxing
    Championship, 189
Atlantic Ocean, 6, 15, 96, 103, 252,
    255, 283
atom bomb project, *see* Manhattan
    Project
*Augusta,* 283
Austen, Jane, 138

*Babies, Just Babies,* 229
Backer, George, 239, 241, 243,
    244, 246
Baker, Newton, 4
*Baltimore,* USS, 304–5
*Baltimore Sun,* 144
Barkley, Alben, 248
Baruch, Bernard, 104–5, 176,
    298–99
*Battle Creek Journal,* 205
Bear Mountain, 146–47, 150
Beekman family, 156, 281
*Belgenland,* SS, 172
Belgium, 88, 132, 247, 318
Belleau Woods, Battle of, 8
Belmont, Alva Vanderbilt, 137–38
Belmont family, 64
Bennett, Eben, 87, 148
Bennett, Richard, 250
Berlin, Irving, 262
Bethesda Naval Hospital, 232–33,
    296–98, 327, 332, 341
Bethlehem Steel, 263
Bethune, Mary McLeod, 134
Biddle, Francis, 34
Biddle, Nicholas, 53, 58
Bishop, Jim, 363
Black, Allida, 368
Black, Van Lear, 144, 147
Black Sox Scandal, 143

Blair, Ginny, 364
Blenheim Palace, 138
Bloomsbury group, 47
Blundon, Lucy Marbury, 180, 181, 227,
    249, 355
Blundon, Montague, 249
Boer War, 47–48
Boettiger, Anna Eleanor
    "Sistie," 292
Boettiger, Anna Roosevelt Dall, 195,
    239, 242, 268, 341
    childhood and adolescence of, 69,
        76, 83, 92, 130, 145, 147–48,
        152–53, 154–55, 157–58, 174,
        291, 302
    education of, 291
    on ER, 50, 70, 72, 90, 92, 154–55,
        174, 178, 192, 212, 217, 230, 233,
        252, 258–59, 277, 292, 322,
        324–25
    ER's relationship with, 66, 124, 127,
        154–55, 157–58, 174, 175, 197–98,
        212, 292, 296, 301–2, 345–46,
        360, 362
    on FDR, 152–53, 165, 174, 188, 233,
        252, 332
    FDR's relationship with, 153, 165,
        174, 289, 291, 292–93, 296–98,
        300, 301–4, 306, 322–27, 336, 343,
        349–50
    on LMR, 83, 127, 315, 354
    LMR and, 127, 300, 301–3, 325–26,
        343, 345–46, 349–50, 351, 360
    marriages of, 174–75, 212, 291
    motherhood of, 171, 292
    physical appearance of, 155, 291
Boettiger, John, 212, 291, 302–3,
    323, 326
Boettiger, John, Jr., 292, 327, 332,
    336, 341
Bohlen, Charles E., 317
Bolshevik Revolution, 286, 331
Bonus Marchers, 215

Borah, William E., 109

Boston, Mass., 32, 35, 37–38, 39, 41, 57, 63

*Bostonians, The* (James), 210–11

"Boston marriage," 210–11

Boy Scout Foundation of Greater New York, 146–47, 150, 239

Bradley, Charles, 42, 58, 282

Bradshaw, Tom, 167

Brain Trust, 33, 197, 207, 225, 307

Brearley School, 239

British Parliament, 346–47

Brown, Elliot, 10, 103

Brown, Lathrop, 3, 35, 57

Browning, Elizabeth Barrett, 56

Browning, Robert, 22

Bruenn, Howard, 297–300, 313, 318, 323, 328–29, 334, 336, 339, 340

Bryan, William Jennings, 44, 89

*Buffalo Telegraph,* 113

Bulge, Battle of the, 318

Bullitt, William, 250–51, 289

Bull Moose Party, 76, 86

Bundles for Britain, 275

Burton, George, 279

Byrd, Richard E., 132

Calvinism, 113

Cambridge University, 91

Camp, Walter, 3, 84

Camp David, 302

Campobello Island, 19, 20–21, 54, 71–72, 85, 87, 88, 92–94, 96–102, 105–6, 120, 122, 132, 146–51

capitalism, 240, 276, 277

Carey, Maggie, 124–25

Carter, Ledyard and Milburn, 69, 70, 73

Cary, Howard, 53, 58

Casablanca summit (1943), 289, 291, 292

Catherine the Great, Empress of Russia, 336

Catskill Mountains, 119, 245, 295

Cermak, Anton, 207

Chaney, Mayris "Tiny," 193

Charlotte, Grand Duchess of Luxembourg, 287

Chesapeake Bay, 84–85, 97–98

*Chicago Post,* 95

Chicago World's Fair, 124

China, 12–13, 54

Cholmley, Aline, 65

Cholmley, Sir Hugh, 58, 65

Churchill, Clementine, 274–75

Churchill, Sarah, 322

Churchill, Winston, 165, 255, 290, 301, 313, 369

FDR and, 283, 289, 302–3, 310, 315, 317, 322, 323, 327, 346–47, 350

Church of England, 29, 128

Civilian Conservation Corps (CCC), 218, 302

Civil War, U.S., 9, 63–64, 74, 105

Clapper, Olive, 234–35

Clark, Grenville, 70

Clayton, Will, 314

Clemenceau, Georges, 6–7

Cleveland, Grover, 20, 113, 114

Clinton, William Jefferson, 114, 115, 365

impeachment of, 366

*Closest Companion: The Unknown Story of the Intimate Friendship Between Franklin Roosevelt and Margaret Suckley* (Ward), 156

Coast Guard, U.S., 299, 340

Cold War, 359

Collier, Baron, 145

Collier, Mrs. Pierce, 55

Columbia Presbyterian Medical Center, 358

Columbia University, 139, 199, 276

Law School of, 58, 65, 68, 69

Commission on the Status of
  Women, 358
communism, 277, 286
Congress, U.S., 89, 96, 109, 207, 231,
  290, 324, 337
  FDR's initiatives passed by, 248,
    255–56
  see also House of Representatives,
    U.S.; Senate, U.S.
Connally, Tom, 267
Connor, Robert D. W., 284
Constant Nymph, The (Kennedy), 178
Consumer's League, 50
contraception, 72, 87, 126, 175
Cook, Blanche Wiesen, 193, 211
Cook, Nancy, 240, 245, 360
  ER and, 158–59, 162, 175–78, 190,
    192–94, 199, 230
Cooke, Alistair, 115
Copernicus, Nicolaus, 282
Copley, Charles Townsend, 52
Corcoran, Thomas, 219
Cornell University, 207, 291
Corr, Maureen, 358–60, 361, 363
Corry, Raymond, 257, 361
Cosway, Maria, xii, 365
Cotten, Elizabeth Henderson (LMR's
  cousin), 30, 31, 93, 127–28, 137,
    140, 354
Cotten, Lyman, Jr., 137, 139, 354
Cotten, Lyman A., 137
Coué, Emile, 154
Court of St. James, 242
Courtship of Miles Standish, The
  (Longfellow), 12
Cowles, Alice "Bye" Roosevelt, 14–15,
  24, 26, 47, 51, 53, 107, 124, 164,
    177, 361
  ER and, 79–80, 82
  on FDR, 90, 93
  marriage of, 45, 79
Cowles, William Sheffield, 45, 79

Cowles, William Sheffield, Jr., 79,
  144, 173
  on FDR, 45, 107, 129
Cox, James, 141–42
Creek Indians, 167
Crim, Howell G., 219
Cuba, 3, 102, 298
Curtin, John, 299
Curtis, Barbara, 220, 223, 250–51
Curtis, Egbert, 223, 265

Dall, Curtis, 174–75, 212
Dana, Frances, 39
Dana, Richard Henry, 39
Daniels, Jonathan, 91, 139, 161, 170,
  257, 349, 366
Daniels, Josephus, 80
  FDR and, 8, 77, 78, 84, 85, 88–89,
    95, 96, 98, 103, 126–27, 152
  as Secretary of the Navy, 3–5, 8, 77,
    84, 88–89, 95, 96, 98, 103, 118,
    126–27, 132, 137
Danks, Edward, 180, 309
Dan's New York Social Blue Book, 31
Davies, Joseph, 89
Davis, Alice Gardiner, 103
Davis, Henry E., 136
Davis, John, 162
Davis, Kenneth S., 194
Davis, Livingston "Livy," 146
  ER's dislike of, 9, 103
  FDR's relationship with, 9, 10, 102–3,
    122, 124, 132, 151–52, 155, 160, 196
  lifestyle of, 9, 103, 123
  LMR and, 155, 156, 172, 196
  suicide of, 196
Declaration of Independence, 28
de Gaulle, Charles, 301, 302–3
de Lannoy, Charles, 12
Delano, Franklin, 17
Delano, Fred, 148–49, 151

Delano, Jennie, 68–69

Delano, Kassie, 121

Delano, Laura, 18, 152

Delano, Laura "Polly," 68–69, 301, 306,
    311–17, 319, 321, 327, 328–29,
    331–32, 338, 342–43, 346

Delano, Lyman, 53

Delano, Warren (FDR's nephew), 17

Delano, Warren (FDR's uncle), 15,
    32–33, 35, 38, 42, 54, 58, 59

Delano, Warren, II, 12–13, 15, 18, 19, 85

Delano family, 12–13, 54, 58, 118, 261,
    290, 313

de la Noye, Philippe, 12, 39, 54, 290

democracy, 231, 321

Democratic National Committee,
    206, 343
  Women's Division of, 208, 273

Democratic National Convention:
  of 1912, 76–77
  of 1920, 141
  of 1924, 161–62
  of 1928, 171, 182
  of 1932, 199
  of 1936, 231, 239
  of 1940, 248
  of 1944, 307–8

Democratic Party, 20, 73–74, 76–77,
    86, 152
  FDR's activism in, 43, 63, 73–74, 90,
    95, 141–42, 144, 145, 150, 161–62,
    182–84
  reform wing of, 73

Denmark, 247

Depression, Great, 188, 196–97,
    198–200, 220, 230, 248, 276, 315,
    356, 366
  FDR's relief initiatives in, 197, 207,
    208, 215, 218, 231–32, 296, 369
  poverty and hunger in, 197, 198,
    200, 235
  unemployment in, 197, 200, 215, 231

DeRoode, Albert W., 44

Dewey, John, 202

Dewey, Thomas E., 312

Dickens, Charles, 25, 76

Dickerman, Marion, 159, 230, 245,
    252, 360
  on ER, 184, 190, 191, 192, 194
  ER and, 162, 167, 175–78, 194, 199
  on FDR, 167, 186, 222

diphtheria, 21, 25, 121

Disney, Walt, 262

Dominican Republic, 102

Donovan, William J., 338

Dos Passos, John, 215

Dostoyevsky, Fyodor, 115

Dot (horse), 190

Dow Jones Industrial Average, 196, 200

Draper, George H., 10, 151

Dreyfus, Alfred, 48

*Dumbo*, 262

Dumbrille, Dorothy, 349–50

Dunn, James, 314

Dunn, Mary, 106

Dunn, Robert, 8

*Dyer*, USS, 5–6, 8, 120, 220


Early, Stephen, 229, 305, 341, 342

economic panics:
  of 1857, 12
  of 1893, 30–31
  of 1929, 196, 200

Edward VIII, King of England,
    260, 282

Eisenhower, Dwight D., 291, 292–93,
    301, 361, 362

*Eleanor Roosevelt Encyclopedia,
    The*, 285

elections, U.S.:
  of 1900, 37–38, 43, 44
  of 1904, 63
  of 1908, 76

elections, U.S. (cont'd):
of 1912, 4, 76–77
of 1914, 86
of 1916, 95
of 1920, 141–42, 144, 162, 183
of 1924, 161–62, 164, 182
of 1928, 182–84, 196
of 1930, 196, 197
of 1932, 142, 183, 198–200, 207, 232
of 1936, 183, 230–34, 236
of 1940, 233, 247–49
of 1944, 307–8, 311–12
of 1952, 361
Eliot, Charles William, 44
Elizabeth, Queen Consort of George
VI, 245, 327
Ellerslie, 106, 138
Ely, Albert H., 87
Emerson, Ralph Waldo, 153
Emerson, William, 204
Emmet, Granville T., 143
Emmet, Marvin and Roosevelt,
143–44, 145, 146, 147
Empty Without You (Streitmatter), 211
England, 41, 47–49, 50, 56, 58, 65, 102,
172, 251
Episcopal Church, 30, 87, 128
Equal Rights Amendment, 176
Esperancilla, Joe, 339
Esterhazy, Countess of, 117, 136
Eton, 91
Eustis, Edith Morton, 106, 122, 137,
138–39, 250
Eustis, William, 106, 122, 137

Faber, Doris, 204, 207, 211, 212
Fairfax, Sally, 365
Fairhaven, Mass., 54–55, 58, 132–33
Fala (dog), 249, 284, 285, 309, 315, 328,
331, 332, 335
Fast, Howard, 277
Faux-Monnayeurs, Les (Gide), 178

Federal Bureau of Investigation (FBI),
272–73, 279
Federal Emergency Relief
Administration (FERA), 208,
215, 219
"Female World of Love and Ritual,
The: Relations Between Women
in Nineteenth-Century America"
(Smith-Rosenberg), 210
feminism, 114, 176
Ferndon, Nona, 40
Fidelity & Deposit Company, 171, 185
FDR as vice president of, 144, 145,
146, 147, 153, 181
Field, Alonzo, 303
Fish family, 16
Fitzgerald, F. Scott, 361
Fleeson, Doris, 221
Florida, 157, 159–61, 164, 168, 178,
247, 282
Flusser, USS, 85
Foch, Ferdinand, 7
Forbes, Dora Delano, 13
Forbes, Will, 13
Ford, Edsel, 240
Forever Amber (Winsor), 290
Fortune, 12
Fox, Eddie, 193
Fox, George, 253, 319, 328
France, 48, 65, 132, 250
Allied invasion of, 301, 302
in World War I, 3, 6–9, 88, 102, 121,
136–37
World War II fall of, 247, 251
Franco, Francisco, 314
Franco-Prussian War, 47
Frank, Jerome, 247
Frankfurter, Felix, 282
Franklin D. Roosevelt Presidential
Library, 40, 112, 123, 142, 171, 204,
211, 257, 284, 285, 295, 319, 349
Franz Ferdinand, Archduke of
Austria, 88

Fredericks, Charles, 328
Free French resistance, 302
Freidel, Frank, 142–43, 257
French army, 48
Fry, Henry D., 28, 30
Furman, Bess, 252

Galbraith, John Kenneth, 325
Gallagher, Hugh Gregory, 110, 150,
    187–88
Gandy, Kitty, 66
Gardiner, Emory, 164
Garibaldi, Giuseppe, 16
Gennerich, Gus, 203–4, 223
George V, King of England, 6, 350
George VI, King of England, 245, 327
George Washington, USS, 132
Gerard, James W., 86
German-American Bund, 272–73
German navy, 10, 129
    U-boats of, 6, 89, 96, 103, 104,
        261, 283
German Wehrmacht, in North
    Africa, 289
Germany, Imperial, 13, 86, 88–89
    militarism of, 88–89, 96
    in World War I, 6, 7–8, 9, 10, 88–89,
        95–96
Germany, Nazi:
    declaration of war against U.S.
        by, 269
    in World War II, 231, 247, 251, 289,
        318, 338
Gestapo, 279
Gide, André, 178
Gilded Age, 13–14, 137
Gladstone, William, 114
Gloster (horse), 19
Goelet, Robert "Bobby," 62
"Goin' Home," 344
Golden, Henry, 91–92
Golden, John, 275

Gone with the Wind (Mitchell),
    108, 218
Good Humored Ladies, The, 9
Good Neighbor Policy, 223
Goodwin, Doris Kearns, 264, 285
Grace, Eugene, 263
Grant, Nellie, 108
Grant, Ulysses S., 108
Grayson, Cary, 100, 102
Great Britain, 88, 242, 346–47
    U.S. Lend-Lease program for, 255–56
    in World War II, 255–56, 262,
        274–75, 283, 289
    see also England; London
Greatest Story Ever Told, The
    (Oursler), 222
Great Gatsby, The (Fitzgerald), 361
Great Northern, 10
Green, Gilbert, 277
Greer, USS, 261
Grey, Sir Edward, 88
Gridiron Dinner, 233
Grief (Peace of God) (Saint-Gaudens),
    131, 203
Groton School, 45, 55, 164, 258, 272
    FDR's education at, 9–10, 32–34,
        35, 64
Groves, Leslie, 318
Gunther, John, 290, 326, 367
Gurewitsch, David, 358–60, 361–62
Gurewitsch, Edna Perkel, 360

Haakon VII, King of Norway, 251, 281
Hackmeister, Louise, 343
Hagedorn, Hermann, 8
Haig, Douglas, 7
Haiti, 102
Half Moon, 19, 40, 51–52, 87, 125
Hall, Edith "Pussie," see Morgan,
    Edith "Pussie" Hall
Hall, Edward, 26, 47, 49
Hall, Mary, 26, 27, 47–49, 61, 133

Hall, Richard B. W., 239

Hall, Valentine, 26, 47, 49, 189–90

Halpin, Maria, 113

Halsey, William F., 85

Hamilton, Alexander, xii

Harding, Warren, 114, 141–42

Harold, Prince of Norway
(Harold V), 251

*Harper's Bazaar*, 291

Harriman, Averell, 50, 322, 338

Harriman, E. H., 50

Harriman, Kathy, 322

Harriman, Mary, 50

Harrison, Benjamin, 106

Harron, Marion Janet, 274

Harvard Club, 70

*Harvard Crimson*, 42–44
    FDR as editor of, 43–44, 46, 52

Harvard Republican Club, 37

Harvard University, 52, 69, 100, 102,
    109, 145, 260, 365
    FDR's education at, 3, 8, 34–38, 40,
        42–46, 52, 54, 61, 90, 121, 144, 268
    "Gold Coast" of, 35, 103, 123
    Medical School of, 148–49
    Porcellian Club rejection of FDR
        at, 45
    social clubs and fraternities at, 35,
        44–45, 109
    tercentenary celebration of, 185

Haskell, Charles, 154

Hassett, William, 90, 288, 290, 305,
    310, 316, 328–29, 333–35, 338,
    341–42

Haughey, Louis, 167–68

Hearst, William Randolph, 291

Hemings, Sally, 365

Henderson, Mary, 127

Henderson family, 30, 31, 93, 127–28,
    137, 139

Hennessy, Michael E., 44

Hickok, Alice Lorena "Hick," 202–14

character and personality of, 206,
    208–9, 237

correspondence of ER and, 203,
    204–5, 207, 209, 211, 212–13, 214,
    230, 233, 236–37, 238, 274, 278

early life and education of, 205, 237

ER's relationship with, 199, 202–5,
    207–14, 218, 219, 221, 230, 236–38,
    273–74, 275, 343–44, 358, 362

journalism career of, 205–7, 208,
    209, 237, 238, 358

physical appearance of, 206, 209

sexual orientation of, 206, 211,
    236, 237

White House residency of, 208–9,
    219, 221, 273–74, 343

Hilton, James, 302

Hindenburg, Paul von, 95–96

Hitch, Annie Delano, 150

Hitler, Adolf, 231, 247, 301, 368

Hobcaw, 298–300, 307

Holmes, Oliver Wendell, 201

homosexuality, 143, 178, 211, 212, 236
    *see also* lesbianism

Hooker, Harry, 3, 127, 326

Hoover, Herbert, 183, 200
    presidency of, 184, 198–99, 215

Hoover, J. Edgar, 272–73, 279, 363

Hooverville shantytowns, 198

Hopkins, Harry, xi, 270, 279, 300
    FDR's relationship with, 219, 247,
        257, 269, 291
    White House residency of, 257, 266,
        291–92

Hopkins, Louise Macy, 291–93, 296

Horsey sisters, 102

*Housatonic*, 96

House, Edward M., 4

House of Representatives, U.S., 109
    Un-American Activities Committee
        (HUAC) of, 277

Howe, Grace Hartley, 75, 86

Howe, Louis, xi, 74–76, 89, 177, 199
ER and, 126, 142, 157–58, 194, 233
FDR advised against divorce by, 126
FDR's relationship with, 76, 85–86,
115, 126, 147–49, 150, 151–52, 155,
157, 179, 232, 233, 269
as FDR's special assistant, 85–86,
91, 95, 102, 126, 128, 141–42, 147,
150, 158, 161, 183
health problems and smoking of, 75,
86, 157
illness and death of, 232–33, 269
journalism career of, 75, 208
marriage and family of, 75, 86
physical appearance and persona of,
75–76, 85–86, 126, 157
political genius of, 76, 233
Roosevelt family disapproval of, 76,
86, 157, 174, 233
White House residency of, 208,
232, 238
Hubbard, LeRoy, 170
Hudson River, 13–15, 18–20, 23, 26, 54,
57, 73, 145, 147, 156, 173, 186, 243,
245, 281, 295, 307, 310
Hudson Valley, 16, 19, 73, 138, 175,
243–45, 327
gentry of, 23, 26, 138, 156, 281, 282
Hughes, Charles Evans, 95, 202, 249
Hugo, Victor, 19
Hull, Cordell, 314
Hunter College, 261
Hu Shih, 266
Hyde Park, 13–19, 28, 34, 35, 51, 53, 65,
70–71, 73, 74, 80, 87, 88, 93, 96,
106, 111, 118–20, 123, 125, 145, 146,
151–52, 156, 158, 176, 195, 223,
239–41, 244, 251–52, 258–60
costly maintenance of, 119
LMR's visits to, 295–96, 309, 318–19
"snuggery" in, 119, 280
wing added to, 87

Hyde Park, N.Y., 20, 112, 126, 308,
358, 361

Ickes, Harold, 269, 311, 369
Illinois, 96
Indianapolis, 223
infantile paralysis, see poliomyelitis
influenza pandemic (1918–19), 10
Ingalls Shipbuilding Corporation, 305
Inspector, The, 190
Interior Department, U.S., 351
Irwin, C. E. "Ed," 268
Irwin, Mabel, 268
isolationism, 248
Italy, 7, 16, 48, 65–66, 289

Jackson, Andrew, 254
Jackson, Graham, 340, 341, 344
Jackson, R. H., 7
James, Henry, 47, 210–11
James, William, 47, 110–11
Janeway, Eliot, 268–69
Japan, 261–62, 265
Pearl Harbor attacked by, 267, 269,
271, 368
U.S. war against, 288–89, 315,
322, 333
Jay family, 64
Jefferson, Thomas, xii, 197, 245, 365
Jews, 176, 238, 277, 281
"Our Crowd" type of, 240
see also anti-Semitism
Johnson, Claudia "Lady Bird," 362
Johnson, Lyndon B., 362
Jonay, Roberta, 275–76
Joseph, Louis, 163
Joseph Gawler's Sons funeral
parlor, 117
Junior League, 50
Jusser, Jules, 89

Keen, W. W., 148
Kempton, Murray, 355–56
Kennedy, Jacqueline, 362
Kennedy, John F., 114, 250, 358,
    362, 365
Kennedy, Joseph P., 242, 250, 305
Kennedy, Margaret, 178
Kent, Samuel Nash, 143
Kerensky, Alexander, 286
Kerr, Florence, 225
Khrushchev, Nikita, 359
Kidnapping the First Lady, 193
King, MacKenzie, 326
Knickerbocker Club, 23, 70
Knowles, Alice, 171
Knowles, Barbara Rutherfurd, 155, 227,
    262, 306, 314, 316, 320, 369
    FDR and, 256–57, 271, 290
    marriage of, 351–52
Knowles, Robert, Jr., 351
Knox, Frank, 266–67, 299–300
Krock, Arthur, 347
Krupp armament works, 333
Kuhn, Mrs. Hartman, 71–72


Ladenburg, May, 104–5
Ladenburg, Thalmann and
    Company, 104
Ladies' Home Journal, 229–30
La Guardia, Fiorello, 244, 283
Lamartine, Alphonse de, 19
Landon, Alfred, 232, 233
Lape, Esther, 158, 178, 190, 192, 194,
    199, 214, 273–74, 352, 358, 359–60
La Rochefoucauld, François de, 124
Larooco, 159–61, 164–66, 169, 181,
    196, 255
Lash, Joseph P., 127, 193–95, 211, 212,
    230, 252, 275, 276–79, 305, 352,
    357–58, 359, 360, 363–64
Lash, Trude Pratt, 212, 277–79, 312,
    359, 360

Law, Nigel, 84, 91, 102, 140
    FDR's affair facilitated by, 97, 98,
    100, 101, 122
Lawrence, John S., 159, 166
Lawrence College, 205
League of Nations, 141, 318
League of Women Voters, 158, 165
Leahy, William, 298
Ledyard, Lewis C., 69
Lee, Robert E., 97
LeHand, Ann, 304
LeHand, Bernard, 170
LeHand, Marguerite "Missy," 144–45,
    194–95, 199
    background and education of,
    144–45, 166, 222, 282
    bequests of, 305
    character and personality of, 145,
    146, 160, 166, 170, 220–22,
    224, 270
    death of, 304–6
    ER and, 186, 195, 220, 221, 224,
    225–26, 294
    FDR's bequest to, 269–70
    FDR's relationship with, xi, 145, 146,
    159–60, 163–66, 169–70, 172, 176,
    182–84, 185–86, 194, 217, 220–26,
    246, 247, 250, 251, 253, 254–55,
    265, 267–70, 280, 292, 294, 300,
    304, 306, 365, 366
    as FDR's secretary, 144, 145, 146,
    147, 149–50, 153, 160, 165, 220,
    222–23, 269–70, 296
    nervous breakdowns of, 170, 172,
    184, 195, 253–55
    personal social life of, 221, 222,
    250–51
    physical appearance of, 144, 160,
    222, 224, 280
    strokes of, 254–55, 265, 269, 284
    suicide attempts of, 268, 270
Lehigh & Hudson Railroad, 308, 310
Lehman, Herbert, 235

Lehman, Mrs. Herbert, 240
Lenin, Vladimir Ilych, 286
Lenny, Harry, 319, 320
Leonardo da Vinci, 331
lesbianism, 48, 158–59, 175, 177–78, 192, 210–14
*Letter to the World: Seven Women Who Shaped the American Century* (Ware), 213
*Leviathan*, 10, 123, 274
Library of Congress, 40, 295
*Life*, 297
Lincoln, Abraham, 266, 305, 345, 346, 365
Lincoln, Mary Todd, 365
Lindbergh, Charles, 205
Lippincott, Camilla, 272
Lippmann, Walter, 201, 330
Livingston family, 16, 64
Lloyd George, David, 6
London, 36–37, 128, 136
    bombing of, 275, 282
    Buckingham Palace in, 6, 327
"Lonesome Train, The" (Lampell and Robinson), 345
Longfellow, Henry Wadsworth, 12, 39, 351
Longworth, Alice Roosevelt, 3, 4, 43, 63, 79, 94–96, 107–9, 118, 121, 125, 177, 312, 363
    on ER, 107–8, 162, 211, 363–64
    ER's relationship with, 61–62, 64, 104–5, 107–8
    espionage caper of, 104–5
    on FDR, 38–39, 59, 64, 232, 368
    FDR and, 104–5, 107–8, 109, 122, 142, 232
    unconventional behavior of, 62, 80–81, 87, 104–5, 107, 109, 111, 363
    White House wedding of, 108–9
Longworth, Nicholas, 80, 96, 108–9, 111, 125
*Los Angeles Times*, 213

*Lost Horizon* (Hilton), 302
Lovett, Robert W., 148–49, 151
Lowry, Cynthia, 363
Luce, Clare Boothe, 298
Ludlow, Mrs. E. Livingston, 64
*Lusitania*, 89, 91
Lynch, Thomas J., 142


McAdoo, William G., 154
MacArthur, Douglas, 304
McCall, Samuel, 44
McCarthy, Charles, 128, 144
McCarthy, Leighton, 314, 318
McCauley, Edward, 9
McDonald, William, 164
McDuffie, Irvin, 234
McDuffie, Lizzie, 316, 331, 337
McDuffie, Rosamund Durban, 256
McEachern, Elspeth, 65
McIlhenny, John, 97
McIntire, Ross, 233, 253–54, 271, 297–98, 299–300, 313, 323, 341, 343, 344
McKinley, William, 31, 37, 43, 44
MacLeish, Archibald, 295
Madison, Dolley, 365
Madison, James, 365
Mahoney, Helena, 168
Maine, 19, 33, 52, 71, 85, 94, 148
Manhattan Project, 296, 318, 322
Mann, Elliott Roosevelt, 23
Mann, Katy, 23
Marbury, Lucy, *see* Blundon, Lucy Marbury
Marbury, Violetta C. Mercer, 30, 31, 65, 137, 139, 216, 303, 326
    LMR and, 180, 181, 201, 202, 227, 256, 321, 354–55
    nursing career of, 81, 121, 136–37
    suicide of, 355
Marbury, William B., 137, 201, 354
Marbury, William "Billy," 216

March of Dimes, 322
*Marguerite A. LeHand,* SS, 305
Marine Corps, U.S., 8, 28–30, 45, 102,
    104, 136, 271, 320, 321
Markham, Edwin, 231
Marlborough, Consuelo Vanderbilt,
    Duchess of, 137–38
Marlborough, ninth Duke of, 138
Marshall, George C., 279
Martenszen, Claes, *see* Roosevelt,
    Claes
Martha, Princess of Norway, 251–52,
    261–62, 270, 281, 287, 291,
    294, 366
Marvin, Langdon D., 3, 143, 145
Marwood, 250
Maryland, 28, 128, 251, 291, 302
"Maryland, My Maryland," 28
Massachusetts, 138, 160, 164, 170, 290
Massachusetts Institute of Technology
    (MIT), 37
Matsukata, Otohiko, 313
Max, Prince of Baden, 128
*Mayflower,* 12
Mayo Clinic, 300
Mead, George, 263–64
Mead Corporation, 263
Mercer, Carroll, 28–31, 111, 128,
    216, 355
    death of, 117, 118
    financial ruin of, 30–31, 81, 82, 106,
        117, 136, 140
    military service of, 28–30, 31,
        117, 136
Mercer, Lucy Page, *see* Rutherfurd,
    Lucy Page Mercer
Mercer, Minna "Minnie" Tunis
    Norcorp, 28–31, 93, 98, 117, 121,
        139, 322
    death of, 355
    financial problems of, 30–31, 98,
        136–37, 140, 228
    interior decorating of, 31, 65, 81

LMR and, 137, 179, 181, 228, 354
marriages and divorce of, 28, 29, 30,
    100–101, 111, 128
Roman Catholic conversion of,
    30, 128
social position of, 29, 30, 31, 81, 106,
    136, 228
Mercer, Violetta, *see* Marbury, Violetta
    C. Mercer
Midway, Battle of, 288–89
Miller, Adolph, 108
Miller, Anna Eleanor, 257
Miller, Earl, 189–96, 198, 203–4, 212
    early life of, 189, 190, 191, 192
    ER's relationship with, 189–94, 196,
        199, 203, 204, 236–37, 274–75,
        357–58
    marriages of, 195, 236, 275, 276,
        357–58
    Navy career of, 189, 275, 357
    as reputed ladies' man, 191, 194–95,
        212, 236–37, 275–76, 357
Miller, Earl, Jr., 257
Miller, Ruth Bellinger, 195, 236
Miller, Simone von Haven, 276,
    357–58
*Miller v. Miller,* 357–58
Milton Academy, 179
*Minneapolis Tribune,* 206
Miss Chapin's School, 291
Moley, Raymond, 225
Monticello, 245
Moore, Virginia, 135
Moran, Lord, 323
Morgan, Edith "Pussie" Hall, 26, 49,
    134, 139, 152, 363
Morgan, Forbes, 49, 134
Morgan, J. P., 240
Morgan, Ted, 112–13
Morgenthau, Henry, Jr., xi, 219, 279,
    326, 335–36
Morgenthau, Henry, III, 251
Morris, Charles, 159, 160

Morse, Ella "Ellie," 206
Mortimer family, 64
Morton, Levi P., 106, 138
Moscow, 251, 289, 338
Muller, Barbara, 169
Munn, Charles, 100
*My Boy Franklin* (S. Roosevelt), 18
"My Day" (Eleanor Roosevelt), 211,
    229–30, 242, 245, 259, 358
*My Parents* (J. Roosevelt), 39, 112


National Archives, 40, 204,
    284–85, 368
National Recovery Administration
    (NRA), 232, 242
Navy, U.S., 5, 9, 10, 89, 128–29, 189,
    261, 271, 275, 283, 357
  General Board of, 137
  Great White Fleet of, 84
  investigation of homosexuality
    in, 143
  in World War I, 91, 96
  in World War II, 267, 288
Navy Department, U.S., 161
  "Eyes for the Navy" program of, 102
  FDR as assistant secretary of, xii,
    3–10, 77–80, 83–86, 88–89,
    94–100, 112, 126–30, 137, 143, 144,
    189, 250, 254, 334, 356, 367
  TR as assistant secretary of, 3–4, 70,
    77, 84
Navy League, 104, 105
Navy Red Cross, 104
Navy Relief Society, 104
Nazi-Soviet pact of 1939, 277
Nehru, Jawaharlal, 362
Nelson, Horatio, Lord, 327
Nesbit, Evelyn, 14
Nesbitt, Henrietta, 266
Nevins, Allan, 369
New Amsterdam, 15
Newbold, Mary, 58, 59

New Deal, 41, 207, 219, 225, 239, 248,
    268, 325
  agencies created in, 208, 215, 218,
    232, 242
  First 100 Days of, 215, 216
  legislation of, 207, 215, 232, 242
New Jersey, 138, 179, 272–73
*New Moon*, 19
*Newsweek*, 213, 221
Newton, Verne, 112
New York:
  FDR as governor of, 4, 5, 44,
    182–86, 188–89, 191–92, 196–99,
    203, 205–7, 215, 276
  politics in, 73–74, 77, 86, 141, 150,
    158, 162, 182–84
  TR as governor of, 4, 24, 37, 44,
    70, 162
New York, N.Y., 15, 26, 35, 200
  FDR's townhouse in, 10, 144, 152,
    157–58, 173, 177, 207, 261
  Greenwich Village in, 158, 190, 275
  Harlem in, 276
  Madison Square Garden, 14, 51
  Memorial Hospital in, 355
  poverty and disease in, 50, 200
  society and social clubs of, 16–17,
    23, 31, 49–50, 64, 69–70, 125, 134,
    137–38
  St. Patrick's Day in, 63–64
  tenderloin district of, 36
New York Assembly Ball, 49–50, 134
New York Central Railroad, 74, 310
*New York Daily Mirror*, 357
New York *Daily News*, 357
*New York Herald*, 24, 75
*New York Post*, 165, 184, 246, 280, 311,
    359, 366
New York State Assembly, 70
New York State Bar, 69
New York State Democratic
    Committee, 150
  Women's Division of, 158

New York State Democratic
  Conventions, 182, 184
New York State Department of
  Corrections, 203
New York State Senate:
  Agriculture Committee of, 77
  FDR's service in 26th District of, 4,
    73–74, 76–77, 126, 176, 367
  TR's service in, 4, 70
New York State Supreme Court,
  357–58
*New York Telegraph,* 43–44
*New York Times,* 99–100, 143, 204, 213,
  347, 362
New York Yacht Club, 69
Nimitz, Chester, 304
*No Ordinary Time* (Goodwin), 264
Norcorp, Percy, 28, 29
Nordlund Bund camp, 272–73
Norris, George, 235
Norway, 103, 165, 247, 251


Oames, Edwards and Jones, 136
Oatlands, 106
Obolensky, Serge, 238
*Oceanic,* 65
O'Connor, Basil, 168, 269
Office of Strategic Services (OSS), 338
Olav, Prince of Norway (Olav V), 251
Oldgate, 177
Operation Wacht am Rhein (Battle of
  the Bulge), 318
Orlando, Vittorio, 7
Oursler, Fulton, 144, 222, 228–29
*Oxford Book of Verse, The,* 114


Palmer, A. Mitchell, 108, 121
Panama, 29, 285
Pan American Union, 262
Panic of 1857, 12
Panic of 1893, 30–31

Paris, 8, 13, 23–24, 42, 132, 136, 138
  liberation of, 306
Parish, Henry, Jr., 49, 58, 64
Parish, Susan "Suzie" (ER's cousin),
  25, 154–55
Parker, Edwin H., 17
Parks, Lillian, 203, 208–9, 217, 219,
  220, 221, 224, 252, 253–54,
  263, 278
Patriotic Economy League, 99
Patten sisters, 107, 118
Patterson, Cissy, 109, 363
Peabody, Endicott, 32, 34, 64
Peabody, George Foster, 162–63
Pearl Harbor, 263, 283
  Japanese attack on, 267, 269,
    271, 368
Peck, Mary, 113–14, 365
Pennsylvania Railroad, 308
Pension Office, U.S., 136, 228
Perkins, Ed, 73
Perkins, Frances, 141, 160, 187,
  324, 370
Perona, John, 273
Pershing, John "Black Jack," 7
Peters, Charles, 366
Phillips, William, 89, 91, 93
Picado, Teodoro, 299
Pine Mountain, 167, 182, 244, 315, 317,
  334, 336
Poe, Edgar Allan, 324
Poincairé, Raymond, 6
poliomyelitis:
  causes of death associated with, 149
  lack of proven therapies for, 149
  1916 epidemic of, 94
  private and public treatment of, 149,
    163–66, 182
  *see also* Roosevelt, Franklin Delano,
    as polio patient
Polk, Frank, 139
Polk, Lilly, 139
Pook's Hill, 252

Potomac River, 91, 100, 368
Potter, Jeffrey, 246
*Poughkeepsie Eagle News,* 142
"President's Mystery Story, The," 229
Prettyman, Arthur, 316, 320, 339
*Pride and Prejudice* (Austen), 138
*Prince of Wales,* 283
Princeton University, 113–14, 228, 271
Princip, Gavrilo, 88
*Prinzessin Victoria Luise,* 57–58
Prohibition, 169, 185, 197, 215
"Psyche" (Moore), 135, 364

Quincy, Dorothy, 38
*Quincy,* USS, 321–24
*Quinnebaug,* USS, 29

racism, 132–33, 134, 141, 163
Ragnhild, Princess of Norway, 251
railroads, 15
    campaign trains on, 142, 145,
        157, 234
    FDR's funeral train on, 344–45
    FDR's private cars on, 202, 280, 308,
        310, 318
*Raleigh News and Observer,* 77, 126
Ramos, Alice Rutherfurd, 138, 227,
    299, 310
Ramos, Arthur, 299
Ramsey, Maydell, 304
Raset, Zena, 260
*Rating the Presidents,* 365
"Raven, The" (Poe), 324
Rayburn, Sam, 341
Read, Elizabeth, 158, 190, 194, 199
Red Army, 333
Red Cross, 3, 4, 271
Reed, John, 250
Reed, Louise Bryant, 250
Reilly, Mike, 249–50, 328, 340
Rembrandt van Rijn, 241

Republican National Convention of
    1940, 247–48
Republican Party, 37–38, 39, 41, 43, 63,
    73, 141–42, 196–97, 202, 232,
    238–39, 247–48, 361
*Richmond,* USS, 28
Ridgely Hall, 180, 201, 235, 294, 331,
    354–55
Roaring Twenties, 232
Robbins, Irene, 108
Robbins, Nicholas, 331–33, 340, 342,
    344, 346
Robbins, Warren Delano, 108
Robinson, Corinne, 22, 47, 49, 60–63,
    109, 232
    on ER, 26, 27, 48, 52
    on FDR, 38, 39, 52, 60–61, 115,
        124, 164
Robinson, Corinne Roosevelt, 49,
    52, 53
Robinson, Teddy, 53
Rochon, Ann, 270
Rogers, Archibald, 18, 21
Rogers, Edmund, 18, 21
Roman Catholic Church, 39, 161
    conversion to, 30, 128, 138
    divorce and annulment in, 128
Roosevelt, Alice "Bye," *see* Cowles,
    Alice "Bye" Roosevelt
Roosevelt, Anna, *see* Boettiger, Anna
    Roosevelt Dall
Roosevelt, Anna Eleanor, *see*
    Roosevelt, Eleanor
Roosevelt, Anna Hall, 49
    Elliott Roosevelt and, 18, 23,
        24, 25
    ER's relationship with, 22–23, 122
    illness and death of, 24–25, 62
Roosevelt, Anne, 335
Roosevelt, Archibald, 3, 8
Roosevelt, Betsey Cushing, 112–13,
    265, 292, 296, 313
Roosevelt, Claes, 15

Roosevelt, Curtis, 159, 255, 292, 313
  birth of, 171
  on ER, 68, 175, 192, 211, 253, 258–59,
    267, 315, 345–36, 359
  on FDR, 187, 234, 253, 268,
    302, 369
Roosevelt, Edith Carow, 22, 51, 63,
    107, 109
Roosevelt, Eleanor:
  acquired self-confidence and
    independence of, 48–49, 50,
    122–23, 134, 157–59, 163–64, 173,
    176–77, 184, 192, 197, 202–3, 211,
    238, 270, 364
  athleticism of, 48, 177, 190, 198
  autobiographies of, 129–30, 148, 229,
    274, 352
  biographies of, 127, 193–94, 204, 211,
    264, 276
  birth of, 22, 23, 270
  campaigning of, 142, 162, 164,
    184, 206
  childhood and adolescence of,
    18–19, 22–27, 31, 47–59, 92, 155,
    210, 274
  civil rights advocacy of, 134, 325,
    362, 364
  correspondence of FDR and, xii, 7,
    9, 52, 56, 62, 77–78, 88, 91, 92, 94,
    99–100, 101, 102, 106, 121, 134–35,
    165, 173, 195, 197, 198, 217, 330
  courtship and marriage of FDR and,
    xii, 22, 50–65, 74, 108, 129
  criticism of, 278, 279, 360, 363
  death of, 107, 361–62
  debate on sexual orientation of, 178,
    210–14
  deficient clothes sense of, 92, 173,
    191, 206, 224, 241
  diary of, 132, 134, 178
  domestic and parenting instincts
    lacked by, 69, 72, 92, 173–74, 360

  driving of, 177, 189, 202
  education of, 47–49, 103, 154,
    210, 364
  emotional neediness of, 173, 211,
    213, 238, 277
  energy and stamina of, 219, 230, 270,
    275, 324, 325
  European trips of, 22, 47–49, 65–66,
    132, 136, 274–75
  FDR's bequest to, 269
  FDR's relationship with, xi, xii, 5,
    10–12, 18–19, 22, 27, 46, 50–66,
    67–68, 69, 71, 72, 77–78, 93, 95,
    97, 98–102, 108, 110, 122–30,
    132–33, 134–35, 149, 151–52, 154,
    157–58, 159, 163–64, 172, 175–76,
    178, 197–98, 213, 216–22, 224–26,
    230, 244–45, 260, 270, 278, 300,
    324–25, 327, 345, 352–53
  as first lady, 199, 202–5, 207–10,
    216–22, 224–26, 229–30, 232–33
  high-pitched voice of, 72, 92,
    158, 275
  household staff of, 79–80, 88, 99,
    134, 173
  illnesses of, 66, 97, 164, 177, 361
  independent income of, 54,
    66, 125
  insecurity and fear of, 22–23, 26–27,
    48, 49–50, 57, 60, 61, 65, 68, 69,
    79, 92, 122, 124, 131–32, 177, 190,
    192, 193, 364
  international renown of, 238,
    362, 363
  jealousy and suspicion of, 65, 66,
    92, 95, 98, 105–6, 108, 115, 129,
    133, 292
  knitting of, 107–8, 162
  leadership and organizing skills of,
    103–4, 120, 133
  mouth and teeth of, 22, 26, 53, 92,
    131, 191, 206, 219, 359

nagging of FDR by, xi, 52, 93, 102,
  105, 132–33, 159, 216–18, 225,
  324–25
nicknames of, 54, 56, 69, 77, 99
photographs of, 131, 191
plainness of, xii, 22, 26, 49, 52, 53,
  55, 92, 134, 191, 206, 277, 363
political and social activism of,
  157–58, 165, 212, 219, 277, 278,
  322, 325, 337, 358
political partnership of FDR and,
  142, 164, 191, 218, 230, 262,
  274–75, 314, 322, 325, 337, 366
pregnancies and childbirths of, 66,
  69, 70, 72, 87, 89–90, 91, 93, 101,
  108–9, 127, 133
press coverage of, 58, 99–100,
  142, 213
private cottage of, 175–78, 192, 195,
  239, 240, 243, 245, 358
radio broadcasts of, 229, 230, 236–37
response to FDR's death by, 341–49
sexual attitudes and experience of,
  55, 61, 62, 66, 72, 87, 90, 123, 127,
  133, 166, 175, 212–14
social and moral conscience of, 134,
  212, 216–18, 364
social debut of, 49–50, 134
social responsibilities of, 79, 80–81,
  82, 83, 86, 95, 96–97, 133, 139
speeches of, 158, 165, 187, 191, 195,
  229, 232, 233, 278, 300, 325,
  337, 358
spiritual renewal of, 135, 203
stature of, 26, 49, 83, 92, 201, 206,
  225, 277
teaching of, 176, 184, 193, 197, 224
Victorian values of, 61, 68, 132, 176,
  178, 193, 210, 364
volunteer work of, 50, 52, 56, 103–4,
  107, 120, 121, 123, 129, 133, 135,
  165, 176

war work of, 103–4, 107, 120, 121,
  123, 129, 135
water and the sea distasteful to, 97,
  100, 157, 159, 177, 190
women friends of, xii, 158–59, 162,
  167, 175–78, 190, 191, 192–93, 199,
  202–5, 207–14, 217
writing of, 129–30, 148, 163–64, 173,
  211, 229–30, 242, 245, 259, 274,
  352, 356
Roosevelt, Elizabeth Riley, 36–37, 111
Roosevelt, Elliott (ER's father), 18,
  22–25, 50, 138
  death of, 25–26, 60, 122, 133, 274
  education of, 23
  ER's relationship with, 23, 24–25,
    26–27, 54, 122, 274
  good looks and charm of, 22, 23, 24
  illegitimate son of, 23, 111
  illnesses and alcoholism of, 23, 24,
    25, 26, 70, 122, 274
  TR and, 23, 24, 53, 124
Roosevelt, Elliott (FDR's son), 25, 39,
  89–90, 185, 190, 251, 312–13
  birth of, 72, 87
  childhood and adolescence of, 89,
    147–48, 182
  on ER and FDR, 53–54, 72, 90, 92,
    102, 118, 175, 190, 212, 215–16, 259,
    293, 311, 313, 352
  family memoir of, 39, 102, 118
  military service of, 271, 292, 342, 361
Roosevelt, Elliott, Jr. (ER's brother),
  23, 25
Roosevelt, Ethel, 60, 122
Roosevelt, Franklin, Jr. (FDR's son),
  217, 362
  birth of, 87, 89
  childhood and adolescence of, 221,
    258
  military service of, 271, 292–93, 300,
    342, 361

Roosevelt, Franklin, Jr. (FDR's son)
(cont'd):
political career of, 360
Roosevelt, Franklin, Jr. (FDR's son,
first by this name), 72
Roosevelt, Franklin Delano:
admiration and approval sought by,
xi, 92, 103, 186, 216, 252, 261,
365–66
appeal of royalty to, 6, 64, 251,
260, 287
arteriosclerosis and hypertension
diagnosed in, 297, 299, 300
attempted assassination of, 207
"bank holiday" declared by, 207, 215
biographies of, 142–43, 257, 264, 290
birth of, 12, 17, 123, 261
boastfulness and exaggeration of,
43–44, 129, 202
campaigning of, 74, 141–42, 182–84,
207, 230–33, 234, 248, 284,
311–12
childhood and adolescence of,
18–22, 27, 28, 32–37, 65, 94, 106,
139, 155
classic good looks and charm of, xii,
27, 34, 40, 52, 53, 60, 74, 77,
83–84, 90, 92, 93, 121, 227, 258
daily routine of, 220
death of, xi, xii, 112, 129, 188, 276,
300, 340–46, 351, 352
diary of, 5–6, 7, 38, 39–40, 51, 55, 58,
63, 127
distinctive laughter and grin of, 162,
223, 239, 258, 277, 326
early political career of, xii, 3–10,
73–74, 76–80, 83–86, 88–89,
94–100, 112, 126–27
early Republican affiliation of,
37–38
earned income of, 86, 125, 143, 144,
185, 229
egalitarianism of, 119

egotism and noblesse oblige in, 20,
129, 241, 246, 289, 367
European trips of, 5–10, 20, 32, 42,
58, 65–66, 120, 121, 127, 129,
132, 196
failed Senate race of, 86
failing health of, 289, 296–98, 299,
300, 302, 304, 307, 311, 320, 323,
326–27, 328–40, 347
family background of, 12–17
"fear itself" phrase of, 202, 239
feelings repressed by, 20–21, 33,
67–68, 110, 290, 300, 305, 369
fireside chats of, 197, 207, 215,
260–61
first presidential campaign and
election of, 198–200, 207, 232
fishing and hunting of, 132, 157, 159,
160, 181, 299, 302
golfing of, 3, 33, 91, 97, 102, 103, 126,
132, 150, 187, 196
gubernatorial campaign and
administration of, 4, 5, 44,
182–86, 188–89, 191–92, 196–99,
203, 205–7, 215, 276
handling of crises by, 33, 242, 267
handwriting of, 33, 256
heroes of, 241
historical interest and perspective
of, 34, 46, 368
honors of, 185, 368
humor and imagination of, 74, 76,
99–100, 111, 146, 152, 160, 164,
169, 185, 223, 242, 252, 282, 284,
287, 290, 292, 301, 326, 337
illnesses of, 9–11, 18, 32–33, 58, 76,
98–99, 101, 121, 123, 125, 129, 144,
149, 274, 294
inaugurations of, 201–3, 204, 207,
227, 235, 239, 243, 249, 259,
319–21
indifferent academic record of,
34–35, 42, 45–46, 66

influence of women on, xi, 18–20, 21, 115, 365–66, 370

inheritance of, 35, 66, 125–26, 130, 169

inscrutability of, xi, xii, 128, 186, 288, 326, 369

intelligence and curiosity of, 19, 34, 43, 52, 367, 369

irritability and impatience of, 119, 120, 132, 217, 235, 267

large family desired by, 41, 69, 72, 90

legal education and career of, 58, 65, 68, 69, 70, 73, 126, 143–44, 145, 146, 147, 153, 168, 181

mutual attraction of women and, 90, 92, 132, 150, 224, 246, 251–53, 288, 290, 292, 296, 369–70

myopia of, 84

ornithological interest of, 19, 65, 181, 322

parental indulgence of, 18, 19, 21, 22, 32, 123

patrician speaking voice of, 32, 45, 141, 202, 240

peacetime draft initiated by, 248

photographs and films of, 121, 142, 188, 198, 220, 264, 285, 304, 333, 334, 350, 355

physique and stature of, 32–33, 34, 35, 53, 74, 77, 90

political ambition of, 3–4, 34, 40, 70, 73–74, 77, 86, 89, 95, 113, 115, 126, 128, 141–42, 172, 182, 184, 187, 199

political criticism of, 201, 235, 242, 277, 330, 368, 369

portraits of, 287–88, 348–49

presidency of, 18, 19, 33, 34, 61, 170, 201, 207–8, 215–36, 239–42, 247–57, 260–346, 355, 365–60

presidential ranking of, 365, 368

press coverage of, 143, 150, 184, 188, 198, 297, 307, 337–38, 346, 347

private and prep school education of, 9–10, 32–34, 35, 64

reading speed and retention of, 19, 218, 367–68

respite from burdens sought by, xi, 102–3, 159–61, 217, 261, 262, 290, 356

sailing pastime of, 19, 33, 38, 40, 51–52, 84–85, 87, 97–98, 100–101, 146–47, 243

self-confidence of, 21, 27, 44, 53, 70, 90, 129, 230, 240, 244, 248, 288, 367

sexuality and virility of, 55, 63, 84, 90, 91, 95, 110–12, 123, 133, 165–66, 198, 252–53, 264–65, 285, 290, 366

shifting of allegiances by, 21, 233, 268–69

smoking of, 220, 277, 287, 289, 290, 297, 298–99

social consciousness of, 20, 52, 146–47

social life and hard play of, 9, 66, 68, 69–70, 91, 97–98, 100–103, 129, 132, 138, 144, 196

speculative investments of, 168–69

speeches of, 74, 95, 127, 141, 142, 161–62, 179, 182, 183, 197, 202, 231, 233, 235, 242, 248, 262, 284, 321, 324, 337

stamp collecting of, 181, 218, 221, 241, 266, 317, 338

subterfuge enjoyed by, 40, 326

undergraduate education of, 3, 8, 34–38, 40, 42–46, 52, 54, 61, 90, 121, 144, 268

vice presidential campaign of, 141–43, 144, 145, 146, 150, 157, 161, 162, 356, 367

visionary leadership and initiatives of, 18, 103, 129, 197, 255–56, 296–97, 330, 346–47, 367

Roosevelt, Franklin Delano (cont'd):
  vitality and effervescence of, 3, 19,
    39, 53, 90, 106, 141, 143, 149, 150,
    166, 182, 261, 272, 297
  World War I European mission of,
    5–10, 120, 121, 127, 129, 196, 220,
    231, 274, 350
  writing projects of, 56, 67–68, 103,
    151–52, 160, 179, 228–29
  youthful romances and flirtations of,
    33–34, 38–43, 55, 58–59, 63,
    65–66, 124, 268, 282
Roosevelt, Franklin Delano, as polio
    patient, 147–54, 174, 257, 356
  braces and wheelchairs of, 153, 161,
    231, 234, 241, 252, 259, 266,
    268, 285
  character-shaping experience of,
    187–88, 356, 366–67
  cures and treatments sought by,
    153–54, 163–64, 168, 171, 261,
    319, 320
  depressions of, 160, 165
  diagnosis of, 148–49
  early symptoms of, 147–48
  ER's care and encouragement of,
    149, 151–52, 154, 157, 159
  grim prognosis of, 150, 151
  impairment concealed by, 150, 155,
    182, 188, 198, 347, 366–67
  Louis Howe's care of, 147–49, 150,
    151–52, 155, 233
  manually controlled Ford driven by,
    167, 221, 239, 240–41, 244,
    319, 328
  optimism and courage displayed by,
    150, 151, 152, 153–54, 159, 164, 165,
    168, 183, 200–201, 235, 367
  paralysis and pain of, 147, 148,
    149–50, 151, 152–53, 154, 165–66,
    168, 187–88, 198, 200–201, 225,
    231, 234–35, 250, 261, 298,
    366–67

physical dependency of, 149,
    150–51, 162, 182, 186, 200, 202,
    231, 234, 328
  self-locomotion of, 152–53, 161–62,
    181, 188, 234
  swimming and exercise of, 154, 157,
    160, 161, 163, 166, 168, 186,
    201–2, 244
  upper body strength of, 152, 182,
    198, 201–2, 304, 320
Roosevelt, Franklin Delano—Lucy
    Mercer Rutherfurd relationship:
  accomplices in, 97, 98, 100, 101, 106,
    107, 109, 122, 137, 138, 250,
    262–63, 295, 301–2, 303–4, 326,
    343, 345–46, 360
  career risks of, 113, 115, 123, 126–27,
    130, 140, 268
  central love affair of, xi–xii, 5, 7,
    10–12, 93, 97–98, 100–102, 105–13,
    115–18, 121–30, 137, 140, 154–55,
    166, 170–71, 175, 178, 189, 203,
    225, 245, 256–57, 264–65, 287,
    291, 306, 313, 334, 345, 355–56,
    365, 366
  consideration of divorce and
    remarriage in, 116, 124–26,
    127–28, 130, 201, 245
  correspondence in, xii, 7, 10, 11–12,
    121, 122, 123, 127, 131, 155, 171–72,
    178, 256–57, 261, 263–64,
    272, 351
  ER's reaction to, 11–12, 92, 95, 98,
    105–6, 108, 115–16, 118–25,
    127–29, 131–32, 155, 172, 178,
    203, 245, 261, 274, 278, 302,
    352–53, 366
  FDR's original termination of,
    127–28, 129, 268
  ongoing contact in, xii, 139, 155–56,
    170–72, 179, 201, 202, 215, 216,
    227, 235, 246, 249–51, 254–57,
    262–65, 271–73, 286–88, 290–91,

293, 295–96, 298–300, 301–4,
308–10, 314–21, 325–26, 330–35,
337–40, 342, 348
sexual component of, 110–13, 166,
264–65
Roosevelt, Hall, 23, 343
alcoholism of, 111, 260
childhood of, 25–26, 55, 260
death of, 260
ER and, 55, 111, 260
military service of, 3, 105
Roosevelt, Helen, 53, 177
Roosevelt, Helen Schermerhorn Astor,
16–17, 36
Roosevelt, H. L., 97
Roosevelt, James (FDR's father),
13–17, 79, 113
family background of, 15
FDR's relationship with, 19–21,
35, 52
first marriage of, 14, 15
Harvard education of, 34, 45
illness and death of, 20, 32, 35, 36,
38, 40, 51, 151
Sara Roosevelt's relationship with,
15–17, 20, 140
wealth and property of, 15–16,
19, 74
youth and travel of, 16
Roosevelt, James "Jimmy" (FDR's
son), 70, 205
childhood of, 143, 147–48, 165,
176, 360
on ER, 129, 132, 176, 192, 193, 217,
218, 219, 260, 325, 346, 360
on FDR, 39, 61, 112, 129, 132, 165,
166, 185, 200, 218, 219, 251, 260,
269, 270, 367
FDR and, 162, 165, 200, 202, 231,
320, 321, 369
marriages of, 112, 265, 292
memoir of, 39, 112, 129, 185, 193
military service of, 271, 320, 342, 361

Roosevelt, James Roosevelt "Rosy," 14,
16–17, 35–37, 51
death of, 169
Harvard education of, 34
marriages and family of, 16–17,
36–37, 53, 111
Roosevelt, James "Taddy" (FDR's half-
nephew), 17, 34, 35–36, 42, 45
death of, 37
marriage of, 36, 37, 111
Roosevelt, John, 89–90, 93, 271, 335,
342, 360–61
Roosevelt, Kermit, 3, 8
Roosevelt, Mittie, 14, 15
Roosevelt, Quentin, 3, 8
Roosevelt, Rebecca Howland, 14, 15
Roosevelt, Sadie Messinger "Dutch
Sadie," 36, 37
Roosevelt, Sara Delano, 10–15, 37,
50–51, 76, 96
courtship and marriage of, 15, 16,
17, 140
diary of, 18, 55
dominating and intrusive nature of,
xi, 19, 20, 21, 33, 40, 60, 68, 70–71,
119–20, 125–26, 133–34, 144,
173–74, 258–59, 261
early life and education of, 13–15, 19
ER's correspondence with, 56, 60,
65, 67, 68, 118, 119–20, 132,
140, 175
ER's relationship with, 51, 54–55,
56–57, 59, 60–61, 67, 68–69,
70–72, 92, 101, 105, 119–20, 121,
131, 133–34, 144, 151–52, 173–75,
258–59
family background of, 12–13, 15
FDR's correspondence with, 4, 7,
32, 33, 34, 35–36, 38, 41–42,
56–57, 65, 67, 68, 78, 101, 121, 125,
163, 164, 169, 170
FDR's inheritance controlled by, 35,
66, 125–26, 130, 174, 185, 245, 258

Roosevelt, Sara Delano (cont'd):
   FDR's relationship with, xi, 5, 10–11,
      18–20, 21, 32–33, 35, 38, 40, 46,
      54–55, 56–59, 60–61, 66, 70–71,
      73, 74, 125–26, 130, 143, 151, 152,
      153, 156, 161, 172, 174, 181, 201,
      215–16, 240, 258, 259, 285
   as a grandmother, 174–75, 258, 261
   illness and death of, 259–60, 261
   moral and social code of, 21, 111,
      119–20, 166
   physical appearance of, 13, 14, 51,
      83, 257–58
   pregnancy and childbirth of, 17–18
Roosevelt, Theodore, 15, 26, 70, 95,
      107, 125, 138, 148, 241, 281, 311
   as assistant secretary of Navy
      Department, 3–4, 70, 77, 84
   death of, 142
   Elliott Roosevelt and, 23, 24,
      53, 124
   ER's relationship with, 53, 61, 62,
      63–64
   failed third-party candidacy of, 4,
      76, 86
   family values of, 3, 4, 8, 40, 61,
      63–64, 87, 90
   FDR's relationship with, 3–4, 37, 43,
      64, 89, 96, 142
   as Federal Public Service
      commissioner, 24
   Harvard education of, 45
   military service of, 3–4, 37, 49
   as New York governor, 4, 24, 37, 44,
      70, 162
   presidency of, 3, 4, 14, 22, 43, 50, 51,
      53, 58, 62, 63–64, 76, 77, 78, 80,
      97, 141, 206
   progressive agenda of, 76
   vice presidency of, 43, 141
   visual and aural problems of, 3,
      4, 84
Roosevelt, Theodore, Jr., 3, 8, 43, 162

Roosevelt and O'Connor, 168
Roosevelt family:
   Hyde Park branch of, 13–18, 53, 162
   intermarriage in, 14, 38, 51, 53, 64
   mutual pride and competition in,
      39, 142, 162, 232
   Oyster Bay branch of, 14–15, 18–19,
      23, 38–39, 40, 53, 61, 125, 142,
      193, 232
Roosevelt in Retrospect (Gunther), 290
Roosevelts, The: A Family in Turmoil
      (Parks), 203
Roosevelt's Secret War (Persico), xi
Root, Elihu, 31
Rosenberg, Anna, 325
Rosenman, Sam, xi, 186, 202, 225, 234,
      243, 248, 262, 368
Rough Riders, 3–4, 31, 49, 64
Rowan, Carl, 362
Royal Air Force (RAF), 333
Royal Navy, 9, 272, 283
"Rules for Success in Marriage"
      (Eleanor Roosevelt), 173
Russia, 88, 200, 250–51, 286, 287
Russo-Japanese War, 368
Rutherfurd, Alice Morton, 106,
      138, 295
Rutherfurd, Barbara, see Knowles,
      Barbara Rutherfurd
Rutherfurd, Guy, 140, 264, 271,
      309, 355
Rutherfurd, Guy, Jr., 309, 310
Rutherfurd, Hugo, 271
Rutherfurd, John, 228, 271, 290, 306,
      309–10
Rutherfurd, Lewis, 139, 295
Rutherfurd, Lucy Page Mercer, 81–84,
      136, 276, 347, 348
   birth of, 28, 30
   character and personality of, 83,
      128, 140, 265, 286, 325
   childhood and adolescence of, 30,
      31, 65, 140

death of, 121, 179, 249, 351, 355
education of, 81
ER's dismissal of, 98, 100, 105, 118
family background of, 28–29, 82, 322
graciousness and poise of, 82, 83,
    89, 92, 139, 263
hero-worship of FDR by, 93,
    111, 112
"Livy" Davis and, 155, 156, 172, 196
marriage of, 139–40, 324
as mother and stepmother, 140, 155,
    172, 179, 227–28, 263, 271,
    309–10
Navy "yeomanette" service of, 98,
    117–18, 137, 254
physical appearance of, xii, 31, 82,
    83, 86, 89, 92, 98, 100, 101, 124,
    137, 139, 140, 156, 249, 250, 256,
    286, 309, 333
pseudonym of, 216, 250, 254, 256,
    262, 290, 303
regal stature and posture of, 83, 92,
    98, 137, 156, 201
resilience of, 129, 140
Roman Catholic faith of, 30, 110,
    111, 115, 128, 180, 334
Roosevelt social circle and, 89,
    96–98, 122
as social secretary to ER, xii, 11,
    82–84, 86–88, 89, 93, 100–101,
    105–6, 122, 348
speaking voice of, 92, 181
see also Roosevelt, Franklin
    Delano—Lucy Mercer
    Rutherfurd relationship
Rutherfurd, Winthrop, Jr., 255, 271
Rutherfurd, Winthrop "Winty," 106–7,
    137–40, 202
character and personality of, 180–81,
    249, 294
children of, 106, 138–39, 140,
    227–28, 271
dog and cattle breeding of, 180, 294

failing health and death of, 228, 249,
    273, 291, 294–95, 355
first wife of, 106, 138, 180, 295
LMR's relationship with, 139–40,
    172, 181, 228, 235, 249, 286–87,
    291, 295, 355
Republican affiliation of, 202,
    235, 271
Roman Catholic faith of, 138, 180
social position and wealth of,
    137–38, 140, 179–81
Rutherfurd family, 178, 351–52


Sabalo, 147
Sacred Cow (presidential plane), 323
Saint Elizabeths Hospital, 104
Saint-Gaudens, Augustus, 131, 203
Salley, Eulalie, 181
Salvation Army, 37
Sanger, Margaret, 175
Saratoga Springs Sun, 75
Sargent, John Singer, 288
Saturday Evening Post, 221
Schacht, Hjalmar, 336
Schermerhorn family, 16
Schiff, Dorothy, 165–66, 238–46, 259,
    313, 352, 359, 361–62
    FDR and, 165, 238, 239–46, 280–81,
        298, 311, 366
    marriages of, 239, 246
    New York Post published by, 165,
        280, 311, 359, 366
Schiff, Jacob Henry, 239
Schlesinger, Arthur M., Jr., xii,
    356, 363
Schlesinger, Arthur M., Sr., 265
Schley, Grant Barney, 31
Schumann-Heink, Ernestine, 203
Schuyler family, 16
Scientific American, 19
Scotland, 9, 103
Seagraves, Eleanor, 208

*Seattle Post-Intelligencer,* 291
Second Continental Congress, 28
Secret Service, 216, 227, 241, 244, 249,
 262, 263, 283, 295, 299, 309, 310,
 311, 314, 316, 318, 328–29, 332
Securities and Exchange Commission
 (SEC), 232, 247
Senate, U.S., 182, 143, 182, 341
 FDR's failed bid for, 86
 Foreign Relations Committee
 of, 267
*Sequoia,* 243
Serbia, 88
settlement houses, 50, 52, 56, 70,
 103, 176
Shakespeare, William, 111, 115
Sherman, Florence, 24
Sherwood, Robert, 248, 262
Shoreham Hotel, 276
Shoumatoff, Elizabeth, 228, 286–88,
 330–34, 336, 338–40, 342–43, 344,
 346, 348–49, 351, 367
Shoumatoff, Leo, 286
Shoumatoff, Nicholas, 286
Sister (dog), 328, 338
*60 Minutes,* 368
Skelly, Joseph J., 309
Smith, Alfred E., 161, 189
 FDR's nominations of, 161–62, 182
 as New York governor, 182–84, 186
 presidential campaigns of, 161,
 182–84, 206
Smith, George, 180
Smith, Merriman, 300, 302
Smith-Rosenberg, Carroll, 210
Snow, C. P., 240
Social Register, 31
Social Security Act, 232
Society for the Prevention of Cruelty
 to Children, 69
Sohier, Alice, 39–42, 43, 50, 51, 58, 63
Sohier, William D., 39, 126
Somerville, Harry, 253

Souvestre, Marie, 47–49, 50, 123, 154,
 210, 364
Soviet Union, 89, 200, 250, 359
 1939 Nazi pact with, 277
 U.S. alliance with, 289, 315, 317,
 322, 338
Spain, 3, 314
Spanish-American War, 3, 31, 136
Stalin, Joseph, 289, 315, 317, 322, 323,
 332, 338
Stalingrad, Battle of, 289
Stanton, Elizabeth Cady, 114–15
State Department, U.S., 266, 314
Stephens, Hazel, 328–29, 339–40,
 341, 344
Stettinius, Edward, 314
Stevens, Ruth, 336
Stevenson, Adlai, 361, 362
Stevenson, Robert Louis, 295
Stimson, Henry, 265, 306, 318
St. James Episcopal Church, 20, 362
St. John's Episcopal Church, 30,
 117, 266
St. John the Divine Cathedral, 362
St. Matthew's Cathedral, 30
stock market crash of 1893, 31
stock market crash of 1929, 196, 200
Stone, Harlan Fiske, 321, 342
St. Paul's school, 23
Strachey, Dorothy, 47
Strachey, Lytton, 47
Streitmatter, Rodger, 211
Stuyvesant, Peter, 137–38
Stuyvesant family, 16
Suckley, Margaret "Daisy," 345, 348
 character and personality of, 281,
 282, 285
 diary of, 282, 283, 284, 296, 297, 314,
 315, 317, 318–19, 321
 FDR's relationship with, xi, 19,
 155–56, 281–85, 295–96, 300, 301,
 307, 309–19, 321, 322, 327, 328–39,
 346, 366

LMR and, 156, 295–96, 309–10,
    314–15, 316–19, 321, 322, 323–24,
    334, 338, 350–51, 352
Sullivan, Ed, 257
Summersby, Kay, 292–93
Supreme Court, U.S., 249
    FDR's attempted expansion of, 242
Switzerland, 177, 338, 359
Sylph, 91, 97–98, 100–101

Taft, Robert, 347
Taft, William Howard, 76, 107, 328
Tammany Hall, 73, 74, 77, 86, 141
Tax Court, U.S., 274
Teamsters Union, 284
Teapot Dome scandal, 162
Tehran summit (1943), 289, 322, 323
Temporary Emergency Relief
    Administration (TERA), 197, 215
Tennessee Valley Authority
    (TVA), 232
Thackeray, Theodore, 246
Thaw, Harry K., 14
"There's a Long, Long Trail
    A-Winding," 215
This I Remember (Eleanor
    Roosevelt), 352
This Is My Story (Eleanor Roosevelt),
    129–30, 229, 274
Thompson, Dorothy, 261
Thompson, Malvina "Tommy,"
    273–74, 279
    as ER's secretary, 192–93, 206, 230,
    278, 330, 337
Time Between the Wars, The
    (Daniels), 366
Tivoli, 26, 49, 50, 74, 189–90
Todhunter School, 159, 177, 199
    ER's teaching at, 176, 184, 193,
    197, 224
Tojo, Hideki, 261
Toombs, Henry, 175, 243, 244

Top Cottage, 243–45, 247, 281, 284,
    285, 295, 350
Town Topics, 49, 58, 81, 97, 117
"Traveler, The" (Dumbrille), 349–50
Trinidad, 58, 63
Truman, Bess, 362
Truman, Harry, 308, 341, 362
Tugwell, Rexford, 33–34, 199, 307, 326
Tully, Grace, 186, 265, 342–43
    as FDR's secretary, 280–81, 288, 294,
    296, 326–27, 339–40
    on Missy LeHand, 144, 170, 223,
    267, 268, 305
Tunis, John, 29, 322
Tunney, Gene, 275
Tuscaloosa, USS, 282
Twining, Kingsley, 113
Two Years Before the Mast (Dana), 39
Tyner, Evelyn, 340, 341

unemployment benefits, 232
United Features, 229–30
United Nations, 318, 327, 330, 333,
    335, 337, 338, 362
    Commission on Human Rights
    of, 359
United Press, 300
Untold Story, The (Elliot
    Roosevelt), 118

Val-Kill (Stone Cottage), 175–78, 190,
    192, 195, 239, 240, 243, 245,
    310, 358
Val-Kill Industries, 176–77, 184, 199,
    213, 230, 336
Vanderbilt, Consuelo, see
    Marlborough, Consuelo
    Vanderbilt, Duchess of
Vanderbilt, Cornelius, 137
Vanderbilt family, 13, 64, 137–38
Vanderlip, Narcissa, 158

Van Rensselaer family, 16, 64
Vargas, Getulio, 223
Vasser College, 150, 177
Verdun, Battle of, 7
Versailles peace talks, 45, 132, 136
Versailles Treaty (1919), 231
*Vigilancia*, 96
*Vireo*, 147
Virginia, 97–98, 249–50
Virginia, University of, 264, 271

Wagner, Robert, 182, 183
Wallace, Henry, 308
Wallingford, Nan, 87
Walsh, Thomas J., 162
Walter Reed Hospital, 249
Warburg, Mrs. Paul, 240
Ward, Geoffrey, 39, 156, 367
Ware, Susan, 213
War Industries Board, 104
Warm Springs, Ga., 176, 213, 223,
    234, 255
  ER at, 213, 342–44
  FDR's investments in, 168–69, 171
  FDR's life at, xi, xii, 163–64, 165–71,
    181–83, 197–98, 244, 265, 304,
    312–18, 327
  "Little White House" at, 169, 244,
    312, 314, 316, 331, 332, 342, 349
  LMR's visits to, 314–18, 330–35,
    337–40, 342–43, 344, 352
  Meriwether Inn at, 163, 168–69, 183
  rehabilitation center at, 170, 244
Warm Springs Foundation, 182, 229,
    240, 269, 328–29
Washington, D.C., 28–31, 63, 79–84,
    91, 93–99
  capitol in, 201, 235, 249, 320
  Georgetown in, 201, 292
  gossip mill in, 30, 81, 96–97, 106,
    107, 112, 114, 117, 118, 208–9
  1919 race riots in, 132–33, 141

Rock Creek Cemetery in, 131, 203
  society and social clubs of, 28, 29,
    30, 79, 80–81, 82, 89, 91, 106, 108,
    112, 117, 125, 136, 228, 363
  summer and "summer wives" in,
    94–95, 152
  Union Station in, 104
Washington, George, 97, 160, 346, 365
*Washington Monthly*, 366
*Washington Post*, 117, 213
*Washington Times Herald*, 363
Watson, Edwin "Pa," 234, 273, 279, 298
Webster, Mabel, 209
Weinstein, Edwin H., 114
Welles, Sumner, 251
*Weona II*, 157, 159
West, J. B., 219, 249, 275
*Westboro* campaign train, 142, 145
Wharton, Edith, 16, 123, 138
White, Stanford, 13–14, 15
White House, 20, 51, 77, 80, 86,
    141, 184
  Lincoln Suite at, 266, 291–92
  LMR's visits to, 250, 251, 254, 255,
    256, 262–64, 272, 273, 290–91,
    293, 301–4, 306, 325–26, 334,
    343, 346
  Map Room in, 297, 318
  marriages in, 108–9
  Oval Office in, 216, 220
  South Portico of, 306, 320–21
  staff of, 203, 208–9, 217, 218–21, 222,
    224, 225, 251–54, 262–63, 266,
    273–74, 303
white supremacy, 163
*Whither Bound?* (F. Roosevelt), 179
Wilderstein, 156, 285
Wilhelm II, Kaiser, 6, 117, 128
Wilhelmina, Queen of Holland, 287
William I "the Conqueror," King of
    England, 12
Willkie, Wendell, 247–49, 367
Wilson, Downs L., 98

Wilson, Edith Bolling Galt, 114, 120, 340, 365
Wilson, Ellen Axson, 89, 113, 114
Wilson, Woodrow, xii, 241, 318, 365
  debilitating stroke of, 141, 253
  declaration of war against Germany by, 96, 141
  FDR and, 4–5, 45, 89, 95, 96, 103, 128, 132, 141, 307
  pacifism of, 89, 95, 96, 141
  passionate character of, 113–14
  presidency of, 4–5, 45, 76–77, 84, 86, 89, 95, 96, 100, 114, 120, 127, 140–41, 143, 253
Windsor, Duchess of, 260, 282–83, 290
Windsor, Duke of, 260, 282–83, 290
Winsor, Kathleen, 290
Winthrop, John, 138
Woman's Home Companion, 229
"Woman's Shortcomings, A" (Browning), 56
women's suffrage, 176, 181, 364
Women's Trade Union League, 165
Wood, Leonard, 5
Wordsworth, William, 370
Works Progress Administration (WPA), 232
World Series of 1919, 143
World's Fair of 1939, 251
World War I, xii, 3–10, 95, 154, 177
  Allied forces in, 6–9, 88, 96
  early U.S. neutrality in, 88–89, 95, 96
  events leading to, 88

FDR's desire to enlist in, 4–5, 8, 96, 128–29
U.S. entry into, 96, 97, 248
U.S. ships sunk in, 89, 91, 96
veterans of, 132, 141, 189
World War II, 85, 188, 366, 369
  Allies in, 283, 289, 301, 302–3, 306, 322, 333
  capture and execution of Nazi saboteurs in, 186, 302
  D-Day invasion in, 301, 302
  early U.S. defeats in, 269, 288, 289
  fall of France in, 247
  German aggression in, 231, 247, 289
  in the Pacific, 255, 267, 269, 271, 288–89, 304–5, 315, 322, 333
  U.S. casualties in, 318
  U.S. entry into, 269
Wotkyns, Eleanor, 343

Yale News, 43
Yale University, 63, 75, 84
Yalta summit (1945), 317, 322–24, 332, 347, 349
York River, 100
Yosemite National Park, 237
Young Communist League (YCL), 277

Zangara, Giuseppe, 207
Zimmerman, Arthur, 96
Zita, Empress of Austria-Hungary, 275

## ABOUT THE AUTHOR

· · · · · · ·

JOSEPH E. PERSICO is the author of *Roosevelt's Secret War: FDR and World War II Espionage; Eleventh Month, Eleventh Day, Eleventh Hour: Armistice Day, 1918—World War I and Its Violent Climax; Piercing the Reich;* and *Nuremberg: Infamy on Trial,* which was made into a television docudrama. He also collaborated with Colin Powell on his autobiography, *My American Journey.* He lives in Guilderland, New York.

## ABOUT THE TYPE

. . . . . . .

This book was set in Fairfield, the first typeface from the hand of the distinguished American artist and engraver Rudolph Ruzicka (1883–1978). In its structure Fairfield displays the sober and sane qualities of the master craftsman whose talent has long been dedicated to clarity. It is this trait that accounts for the trim grace and vigor, the spirited design and sensitive balance, of this original typeface.